Paying for Care

4th edition

Pauline Thompson
Helen Winfield
David Simmons
Jo Linney

Child Poverty Action Group

Published by CPAG
94 White Lion Street, London N1 9PF

A CIP record for this book is available from the British Library.

ISBN 1 901698 52 1
Design by Devious Designs 0114 275 5634
Typeset and printed by Clowes, Beccles, Suffolk

The authors

Pauline Thompson is the policy officer for community care finance at Age Concern England. She has many years experience both as a social worker and as a local authority welfare rights adviser, and writes on community care issues in the *Disability Rights Handbook*.

Helen Winfield is a welfare rights adviser and trainer for Wolverhampton Social Services and is a member of the management committee of the Birmingham Tribunal Unit.

David Simmons is a welfare rights worker at CPAG.

Jo Linney is a freelance consultant who has worked extensively on the implementation of the Supporting People programme. She was Chair of the Board of Trustees of CPAG for four years until November 2001.

Acknowledgements

The authors would like to thank Geoff Tait, Margaret Richards, Mike Ellison and Jane Hayball for their contributions to the checking of this *Handbook*.

Special thanks are due to Andrew Sim and Angela Toal for checking the law and practice relating to Scotland and Sandra Burton for checking the content applying to Wales.

Thanks are also due to Nicola Johnston for editing and managing the production of the book, and to Alison Moore, Paula McDiarmid and Tracey Stevenson for their input into the production process.

We would also like to thank staff at the Department for Work and Pensions, Inland Revenue, Department of Health, Welsh Assembly and Scottish Executive for their co-operation.

Finally, thanks go to all the authors' families who endured many lost weekends during the writing of this *Handbook*.

The authors have made their best endeavours to try to ensure that the law covered in this *Handbook* was correct as at 31 July 2003.

Contents

How to use this *Handbook*

This *Handbook* aims to provide all the information you will need about claiming practical and financial assistance in meeting your care needs from social services, health authorities and the Department of Social Security. It aims to give practical help in the areas where disputes are likely to arise between those who need assistance and those who are responsible for administering and providing it. If you are not satisfied with the help you are being offered, the *Handbook* aims to guide you in challenging decisions made about you.

The organisation of the **contents** is explained in the introduction (Chapter 1). The main subjects in each chapter are also summarised in the contents page at the front of the *Handbook*. The main subject heads and page numbers are repeated at the beginning of each chapter.

It is often helpful to refer to the sources from which the information in the text is drawn, which is the relevant law and official guidance, as well as caselaw which often clarifies what the law and guidance should mean in practice. **References** to these are given in the notes at the end of each chapter and are numbered in the order in which they appear in the text. The references are usually to Acts or Regulations, but sometimes they are to formal guidance issued by government departments (or the Scottish Executive or National Assembly for Wales), and sometimes to caselaw. The notes are in abbreviated form and the abbreviations used are explained in Appendix 6.

Abbreviations are often also used in the text to save space, but an abbreviation is always given in full the first time it is used in a chapter or section (followed by the abbreviation in brackets).

The **index**, like the contents, will also help you to find the information you are looking for. Entries in bold type direct you to the general information on the subject, or where the subject is covered more fully. Sub-entries under the bold headings are listed alphabetically and direct you to specific aspects of the subject.

There are many **cross-references** in the text which are also designed to assist you in finding other relevant information about a particular topic. They give either the chapter or page number(s), as appropriate.

Whereas many of the sources of information about social security benefits will be familiar to readers of other CPAG Handbooks, the main **sources** of legislative powers and duties of social services departments (social work departments in Scotland) may be less familiar, and for ease of reference these are set out in full in Appendix 1 (followed by a list of key guidance circulars in Appendix 2).

The *Handbook* covers the law and practice which applies in England and Wales (and includes references to some differences in sources of guidance and terminology). The different provisions which apply to Scotland, but which more often than not are of similar effect, have also been covered. Although much of the law relating to social security is similar in effect in Northern Ireland, the very different arrangements for health and social welfare generally (although also sometimes similar in effect) are such that it has not been possible to cover them in this *Handbook*.

Because the areas of policy, practice, law, caselaw and guidance covered in this *Handbook* are notoriously the subject of constant change, readers are urged to use the *Handbook* in conjunction with other sources which may provide regular updates or may provide more extensive detail on particular aspects which are beyond the scope of this *Handbook* (such as those sources referred to in Appendix 5). It is, however intended that this *Handbook* will be revised annually so that each new edition will aim to provide a guide which will be up-to-date at the time of publication and which will highlight particular areas which will be likely to change in the near future.

Although the authors have made their best efforts to ensure that the information contained in this *Handbook* is correct or at least represents a reasonable interpretation, the authors readily acknowledge that, in view of the pace of change in an emerging and contentious area of law and the complexities and uncertainty of some of the issues analysed, some errors or omissions may be inventible, or else will become apparent over the course of time. Any comments from any readers which may be considered to improve the text or the structure of the *Handbook* in future editions would be gratefully received (and should be sent c/o CPAG).

Abbreviations used in the text

AA	Attendance allowance
BL	Budgeting loan
CA	Carer's allowance
CAB	Citizens Advice Bureau
CCG	Community care grant
CL	Crisis loan
COSLA	Convention of Scottish Local Authorities
CTB	Council tax benefit
CTC	Child tax credit
DLA mobility	Disability living allowance – mobility component
DLA care	Disability living allowance – care component
DWP	Department for Work and Pensions
EC	European Community
ECJ	European Court of Justice
EEC	European Economic Community
EMO	Examining medical officer
EU	European Union
GP	General practitioner
HB	Housing benefit
IB	Incapacity benefit
IS	Income support
MP	Member of Parliament
MSP	Member of Scottish Parliament
PEA	Personal expenses allowance
PAYE	Pay-As-You-Earn
PC	Pension credit
SDA	Severe disablement allowance
SERPS	State Earnings-Related Pension Scheme
SSP	Statutory sick pay
WTC	Working tax credit

Benefit rates

Income support (and income-based jobseeker's allowance)

		April 2003 to April 2004
Personal allowances		£
Single		
Under 18 years (usual rate)		32.90
Under 18 years (higher rate)		43.25
18 to 24 years		43.25
25 years and over		54.65
Lone parent		
Under 18 years (usual rate)		32.90
Under 18 years (higher rate)		43.25
18 or over		54.65
Couple		
Both under 18 years (higher rate)		65.30
Both over 18 years		85.75
Children		
Under 19 years		38.50
Premiums		
Family	Ordinary rate	15.75
	Lone parent rate*	15.90
Disability	Single	23.30
	Couple	33.25
Enhanced disability	Single	11.40
	Disabled child rate	16.60
	Couple	16.45
Pensioner (60 to 74 years)	Single	47.45
	Couple	70.05
Enhanced pensioner (75 to 79)	Single	47.45
	Couple	70.05
Higher Pensioner	Single	47.45
	Couple	70.05
Severe disability	per qualifying person	42.95
Disabled child	each child	41.30
Carers		25.10

Bereavement		22.80
**only paid on claims beginning before 6 April 1998*		

Care home

Personal expenses allowance		17.50
Local authority care home 'part III' rate		77.45
Residential allowance (independent care home)		
	Greater London	72.85
	Elsewhere	65.50

Hospital (after 52 weeks)

Single person/reduction for couples	15.50

Social fund payments

Maternity grant		500.00
Cold weather payment		8.50
Winter fuel payment:	Basic rate	200.00
	Lower rate	100.00
	Aged 80 and over	300.00

Housing and council tax benefit

Personal allowances

Single		
16 to 24 years		43.25
25 years and over		54.65
Lone parent		
Under 18 years		43.25
18 years and over		54.65
Couple		
Both under 18 years		65.30
One or both over 18 years		85.75
Children As for income support		
Premiums As for Income support except:		
Family premium	Lone parent rate*	22.20
	Baby addition	10.45

**only paid on claims beginning before 6 April 1998*

Capital limits

IS/JSA (IB)	Under 60 years	Lower	3,000
		Higher	8,000
	60 years plus	Lower	6,000
		Higher	12,000
	Care home	Lower	10,000
		Higher	16,000

PC	Care home	Lower	10,000
		Higher	no limit
	Other	Lower	6,000
		Higher	no limit
HB/CTB	Under 60 years	Lower	3,000
		Higher	16,000
	60 years plus	Lower	6,000
		Higher	16,000
	Care home (HB only)	Lower	10,000
		Higher	16,000
		Pension credit guarantee*	no limit

**from October 2003*

Earnings disregards (for IS/JSA/PC/HB/CTB)

Single person		5.00
Couple		10.00
Disability or carer premium		20.00
Lone parents (IS/JSA only)		20.00
Lone parents (HB/CTB only)		25.00
Childcare costs (HB/CTB only)	1 child	94.50
	2 or more children	140.00
30 hours element in WTC (HB/CTB only)		11.90

Other disregards (for IS/JSA/PC/HB/CTB)

Maintenance	(HB/CTB)	15.00
	(IS/JSA)	10.00
War pension	(for IS/JSA/PC)	10.00
Widowed parent's allowance	(PC only)	10.00
Charitable or voluntary payments		20.00

(No disregard for PC unless discretionary trustees payment (from October 2003))

Non-dependant deductions

From HB and IS/JSA housing costs:

Under 25 years on IS/JSA		NIL
Over 18 years not in remunerative work		7.40
Over 25 years on IS/JSA/PC		7.40
Over 18 in remunerative work		
gross income	under £92.00	7.40
	£92.00 to £136.99	17.00
	£137.00 to £176.99	23.35
	£177.00 to £234.99	38.20
	£235.00 to £292.99	43.50
	£293.00 or more	47.75

From CTB

On IS/JSA (any age)		NIL
Over 18 years in remunerative work (or on PC)		
gross income	under £137.00	2.30
	£137.00 to £234.99	4.60
	£235.00 to £292.99	5.80
	£293.00 or more	6.95
Other, over 18 years		2.30
On PC* and not in remunerative work		NIL

**from October 2003*

Second Adult Rebates

(Alternative maximum council tax benefit)

Second adult(s) on IS/JSA	25%
Second adult(s) income less than £137.00	15%
Income £137.00 to £176.99	7.5%

Attendance allowance

Lower rate	38.30
Higher rate	57.20

Bereavement benefits

Bereavement payment (lump sum)	2,000
Widowed parent's allowance	77.45
Bereavement allowance	77.45
Dependant child	11.35

Carer's allowance (previously invalid care allowance)

Claimant	43.15
Spouse/Adult dependent	25.80
Dependant child	11.35
Earnings limit for claimant	77.00

Child benefit

First, only or eldest child:	Ordinary rate	16.05
	Lone parent rate†	17.55
Each subsequent child		10.75
Guardian's allowance		11.55

†Only paid on claims beginning before 1 June 1998

Disability living allowance

Care component	Higher	57.20
	Middle	38.20
	Lower	15.15
Mobility component	Higher	39.95
	Lower	15.15

Incapacity benefit		
Claimant		
Long term		72.15
Short term under pension age	Lower	54.40
	Higher	64.35
Short term over pension age	Lower	69.20
Short term over pension age	Higher	72.15
Spouse/Adult dependant		
Long term		43.15
Short term lower/higher		33.65
Short term over pension age		41.50
Dependant child		
All rates		11.35
Age addition (long term)		
Incapacity before age 35 years	Higher	15.15
Incapacity age 35 to 44 years	Lower	7.60
Alternative transitional age addition		
Incapacity before age 40 years	Higher	15.15
Incapacity age 40 to 49 years	Lower	9.70
Incapacity age 50 to 59 years – men (lower)		4.85
Incapacity aged 50 to 54 years – women (lower)		4.85
Permitted work earnings limit		67.50
Industrial death benefit		
Widow's pension:	Higher permanent rate	77.45
	Lower permanent rate	23.24
Widower's pension		77.45
Industrial disablement benefit		
Maximum 100%		116.80
Minimum 14%		23.36
Reduced earnings allowance+ maximum		46.72
Retirement allowance+ maximum		11.68
+For disablement before October 1990 only		
Jobseeker's allowance (contribution-based)		
Aged 18 to 24 years		43.25
Aged 25 years and over		54.65
Maternity allowance		
Standard rate		100.00
Adult dependant		33.65
Retirement pension		
Single person (basic)		77.45
Spouse/adult dependant		46.35

Dependant child		11.35
Non-contributory (over 80 years)		46.35
Age addition for over 80 years		0.25
Severe disablement allowance (pre-April 2001 claims only)		
Claimant		43.60
Adult dependant		29.90
Dependant child		11.35
Age related additions		
Under 40 years	Higher rate	15.15
40 to 49 years	Middle rate	9.70
50 to 59 years	Lower rate	4.85
Statutory adoption pay		100.00
Statutory maternity pay		
Lower rate		100.00
Higher rate		90% of earnings
Statutory paternity pay		100.00
Statutory sick pay		
Standard rate		64.35
Earnings threshold		77.00

Child dependency increases reduced by £1.80 for first child and no longer payable with claims made since April 2003

Proposed changes to charging with the introduction of pension credit

In late July 2003 the Department of Health in England, the Welsh Assembly Government and the Scottish Executive Health Department sought consultation on proposed changes to residential care charges and, in England and Wales only, on home care charges, with the introduction of pension credit from 6 October 2003.[1]

Chapters 4 (Paying for services at home), 10 (Financial assessments and charges in care homes), 11 (Income – financial assessments) and 15 (Liable relatives – social services) should be read with the following proposals for changes in mind.

1. Residential care charge

Savings disregard

The introduction of a new savings disregard in the financial assessment is the proposal in response to the introduction of pension credit (PC) in general and the savings credit element of PC in particular. This disregard would apply to residents aged 65 or over (the same age group able to claim the savings credit part of PC).

For single residents with income (before any PC award) of between £77.45 (basic state retirement pension) and £102.10 (the standard minimum guarantee – see 177) (April 2003 rates) the savings disregard would be £4.50 or an amount equal to the actual savings credit in payment whichever is less.

For single residents with income (before any PC award) in excess of £102.10 (the standard minimum guarantee) the savings disregard would be £4.50.

This is proposed in England and Wales. In Scotland, the Scottish Executive also seeks views on any alternative, more complicated allowance with increases in proportion with the resident's income.

For couples in residential care or couples where one member is temporarily in residential care and the other member is at home (where one member of a couple is permanently in a care home they are treated as single people and therefore the previous paragraphs would apply) with income (before any PC award) of between £123.80 (basic state retirement pension plus adult dependant addition) and

£155.80 (standard minimum guarantee for couples – see p177) the savings disregard would be £6.75 or an amount equal to the actual savings credit in payment whichever is less.

For couples with income (before any PC award) in excess of £155.80 (standard minimum guarantee for couple) the savings disregard would be £6.75.

The savings disregard would not be affected by whether or not the resident qualifies for the severely disabled or carer's additional amounts of guarantee credit (see p177) and it is proposed that any DLA care component/AA in payment for the first four weeks of a person's stay would **not** be included in identifying those residents whose income exceeds the lower threshold for the savings disregard.

Note: the savings disregard for couples is part of the consultation in England and Wales whereas in Scotland it forms part of the intended changes but has not been included in the consultation.

Other proposed changes due to the introduction of PC

In England and Wales it is stated in the consultation papers that it is desirable to have equivalent charging regimes for older and younger residents in care and therefore many of the changes in the social security legislation that make PC differ from income support (IS) (eg, the different capital limits and tariff income) are not proposed as changes to the charging rules.

However, there are three areas where changes in PC rules (as compared to IS) may lead to changes in the existing charging rules:

- **liable relatives** – for PC purposes there are no liable relative rules. In England and Wales it is stated that they are considering the position. The Scottish Executive states that it is 'interested in views on the possibility of removing the liable relative rule';
- **couples where one is temporarily in care** – for PC purposes the calculation will be based on the couple rate of the appropriate amount rather than two single persons' rates added together as in IS (see Chapter 15). This means that it will no longer be a simple exercise of taking one of the single person's amounts in respect of the resident into account in the financial assessment thus leaving the partner at home with a full single person's entitlement. However, it is stated in the consultation that the guidance will be strengthened in respect of residents aged 60 or over so that the individual at home can effectively maintain the household in the partner's absence;
- **cash in lieu of concessionary coal** – for PC purposes this will be ignored. For charging purposes it is currently taken into account as income. This will not change for permanent residents but it is proposed to fully disregard such payments for temporary residents of any age.

Note: the couples guidance and the 'cash in lieu of concessionary coal' change is part of the consultation in England and Wales whereas in Scotland it forms part of the intended changes but has not been included in the consultation.

Backdating of PC

Claims for PC made before October 2004 will be backdated to the date of entitlement. After October 2004 claims will be backdated for up to three months where entitlement exists. In England the Department of Health guidance will remind local authorities that financial assessments should take 'due regard' of backdated payments of PC.

Other changes

The guidance in England and Wales will also remind local authorities of the hospital downrating changes, the abolition of the residential allowance and the Part III rate of IS. In addition it is proposed that the definition of 'less dependant' residents in the guidance is updated to refer to the Care Standards Act 2000.

2. Home Care Charges (England and Wales only)

It is stated that from 6 October 2003 service users net income as a minimum should be protected at the appropriate guaranteed level plus 25 per cent. It is proposed that in addition to this the savings credit element of PC should be disregarded in calculating service user's incomes.

Notes

1. *Proposed changes to Residential Care Charges and Home Care Charges from 6 October 2003*, Department of Health Consultation, 30 July 2003; *Proposed changes to the Residential Care Charging Rules from 6 October 2003 – A Consultation Paper*, Welsh Assembly Government, 31 July 2003; *Pension Credit: Proposals for Changing the Residential Care Financial Assessment*, Scottish Executive Health Department, 23 July 2003.

Part 1

Introduction

Chapter 1

Introduction

This chapter covers:

1. The purpose and scope of this *Handbook*

Since the community care reforms came into force in 1993, there has been a revolution in social services law and practice applying to older people, people with physical disabilities, learning difficulties, long-term illnesses, mental health problems or addictions, and to their carers. The current social security scheme is also the result of many changes, and remains massive in scope. Nearly all individuals at some time in their lives will come into contact with the social security and/or care system. Often it is at a stressful time, and many people find it difficult to know what help could be provided, and where to go to get help.

This *Handbook* aims to draw together the effects of the laws relating to social security and community care and consider how they work in practice and how they could work better within the existing limitations. It aims to provide a guide for adults in need of care and support, their carers and relatives, and professionals involved in administering or advising on the effects of each scheme.

Some people are fortunate not to require any financial assistance from social services or the NHS or the Department for Work and Pensions (DWP) even if they have significant personal care needs due to old age, health problems or disabilities. More commonly, however, many will need at least some assistance, whether by way of care, or by cash, or in kind. This applies whether they live at home in the community, or in a care home. The introduction of 'free' nursing care in care homes providing nursing in England and Wales in 2001, and of 'free' personal care for people aged 65 and over both at home and in care homes in Scotland in July 2002, means more people are entitled to some help from the state towards the costs of their care.

This *Handbook* explains what services and help people can expect from the state, both to remain in their own home or if they need any form of residential care. It covers the benefits you can receive from social security, the help you can get from the NHS (which is largely free) and the help you can get from local authorities' housing and social services departments (which is normally charged for). An understanding in some detail of both what the state *has to* or just *may* provide, can help you to know whether you are likely to have to arrange your own care or meet some or all of the cost yourself.

Part 1 sets out an overview of the community care and social security schemes, and covers the background, history and policy intentions behind them. It also explains the different responsibilities and roles of central government departments, local authorities and health bodies in providing for the care and support needs of adults in their areas, and looks forward to developments that have been proposed over the next few years. It then covers briefly how you might wish to fund your own care.

Part 2 covers the range of services and assistance available to adults living at home in the community. It explains the range of community care services and about the assessment for these services (Chapter 2); supported housing that is available (Chapter 3); paying for care and support at home (Chapter 4); sources of financial assistance for a range of services needed because of disability, including payments for care services, grants to ensure your housing meets your needs, help with health charges and concessions on transport (Chapter 5); and social security benefits (Chapters 6, 7 and 8).

Part 3 deals with the general provisions which apply to social services departments and health authorities when a person needs care in a care home. It covers the duties of social services and health authorities in arranging for accommodation in care homes and whether care is free or paid for (Chapter 9); the financial assessment and the way it is administered and how the type of stay affects this (Chapter 10); the amounts of any personal expenses allowance which most people will be left with to meet items not provided in the home (Chapter 13); the responsibilities of any liable relatives (Chapter 15); and how you can meet the care home charges if the home you have chosen is more expensive than the local authority thinks you need (Chapter 14). It also deals with how social services departments may recover any charges owing to them (Chapter 16); and it gives full details about how income (Chapter 11), and capital and property (Chapter 12) is treated, what social security benefits you can get in a care home (Chapter 17), calculations (Chapter 18) and common problems (Chapter 19).

For reasons of space, there are a number of areas which are beyond the scope of this *Handbook*. In particular, it does not attempt to cover in any significant detail the very different responsibilities of welfare agencies which may apply in respect of young people (under the age of 18) and children in need. Nor does it cover the different private financial or insurance arrangements which individuals may have the opportunity to make so that they do not require state assistance for their care needs (although some of these are briefly referred to at the end of this chapter). Where appropriate, however, references are made in the text to other sources of information on particular aspects which may be of interest but which are not covered in this *Handbook*.

2. What is community care

Although community care (or care in the community) is a term which has a common usage, it can mean different things to different people. Some think of it as excluding care in a care home, although many care home owners go to considerable lengths to ensure that their care home is part of the local community and that residents can make use of local facilities. Equally, staying long term in hospital does not necessarily mean you are no longer part of the community. The hospital itself may be a vital part of the community, employing local people and utilising local services.

Others take the view that community care encompasses *anything* which helps older or disabled people remain in their homes for as long as possible. In addition to the services described in this *Handbook* they include all the informal care that goes on as part of everyday life. Community care could, therefore, encompass help from friends, relatives and neighbours. It would include the role of local facilities such as pubs and hairdressers in welcoming older or disabled people. It could also include ways that the local environment supports all people, such as paths being in a good state of repair, accessible transport and buildings, and actions which ensure people feel safe to go out – eg, adequate policing and lighting.

The working definition

The previous government in its 1989 White Paper gave the following definition of community care:

> Community care means providing the right level of intervention and support to enable people to achieve maximum independence and control over their own lives. For this aim to become a reality, the development of a wide range of services provided in a variety of settings is essential. These services form part of a spectrum of care, ranging from domiciliary support provided to people in their own homes, strengthened by the availability of respite care and day care for those with more intensive care needs, through sheltered housing, group homes and hostels where increasing levels of care are available, to residential care and nursing homes and long-stay hospital care for those for whom other forms of care are no longer enough.[1]

The White Paper went on to recognise that in reality most care is not provided by statutory bodies but by family, friends and neighbours, so the right level of support for them at the right time is vital. It also confirmed the important role of health care, and the role of the benefits system in providing financial support.

It would be fair to say that the aims of community care remain the same under the present government. However, the previous government's introduction of direct payments added a new dimension where, in addition to having services provided for them, people were given the ability to purchase their own services. In its 1998 White Paper, the current government outlined planned changes aiming to lead to the following improvements:

- 'people will be offered a service that is designed not just to keep them going, but to improve their capabilities and allow them maximum possible independence;
- when people need social services help, that help will be arranged in a way that lets them do as much as possible for themselves and allows them wherever possible to live in their own homes;
- many more people will be able to have real control over their care support through direct payment schemes;
- health and social services will target support especially for people who are at risk of losing their independence (for instance elderly people living alone during the winter; people who have just left hospital, or who have a visual impairment, and are finding it hard to cope at home), to make sure that special efforts are made to avoid such people having to be admitted to hospital or a care home;
- carers who look after family members, neighbours or friends will be given greater support by social services and other agencies, to allow them to continue to care where that is what they and the person they are caring for want.'[2]

These ambitions are also expressed in equivalent White Papers for Wales and Scotland.[3]

Since 1998 there have been numerous initiatives, frameworks, strategies and targets set to try to achieve these aims. How far the practice of community care lives up to these aims is a source of debate. There is no doubt that some individuals receive excellent services which provide them with the care they need when they need it. Equally, the measures that authorities have adopted due to resource constraints (described in Chapters 2 and 9) and the extent to which the social security system supports people in need, can leave individuals and their families in a state of high anxiety about whether they will get the services they need, and whether they will be able to afford them. There has been much debate about whether the funding for community care is sufficient to achieve the policy objectives.

3. **Community care changes in 1993**

Although the 1993 changes to the legislation are of paramount importance to the way community care is now delivered, there appear to be two major misconceptions. These are that:

- community care was new in 1993; *and*
- it is only from that date that people have been charged for the services they receive, or for care in a care home.

Note: The term **'care home'** has from 2002 replaced the terms 'residential home' and 'nursing home' which were used until this date. This is because the legislation which came into effect in 2002 uses the term 'care home' to describe homes which have to be registered and which provide personal care, and also those which provide nursing care in addition to personal care. The old terms are used where the text refers to the past.

Community care before 1993

The movement to close long-stay hospitals, in particular for those with a learning disability or a mental health problem, had actually started as far back as the 1970s, as a result of a concern about costs and various high profile cases of abuse, as well as pressure from campaigning groups and staff for these clients to lead more normal lives than could ever be achieved in hospital settings.[4]

Measures to enable people to remain in their own homes date back to the National Assistance Act 1948, and statements remarkably similar to the current exhortations on community care can be found periodically since then. The Ministry of Health stated in its 1953 Annual Report that there was 'universal recognition of the urgency of the task of enabling old people to go on living in their own homes as long as possible'.[5]

The services listed in the NHS and Community Care Act 1990 as community care services were not new but arose from legislation enacted between 1948 and 1983. These services are explained in detail in Chapter 2.

Charges for care

Many people are surprised to find that since 1948 charges for care in care homes have been mandatory, and discretionary for domiciliary care.

There were relatively few changes made in 1993 to the charging regime for care in residential settings as there were already provisions for charging residents who lived in local authority accommodation. Residents in independent care homes received help though social security benefits, but only got means-tested help if they had less than the capital limits that prevailed at the time. Residents who had their own property were expected to sell it in order to pay for the cost of their care.

A number of social services departments charged for domiciliary services before 1993 under the discretionary charging rules. The main change since 1993 is that this number has greatly increased. Fewer social services departments charge a low 'flat rate' but instead have charging regimes which reflect the number of hours of care received and are also based on the means of the person receiving the care (so are means-tested). Also, more services, in particular day care and equipment have become subject to charging. However, from 9 June 2003 in England, there should no longer be charges for equipment (see p37).

The main changes

In 1993 local authorities took on the responsibility for funding care in independent care homes as well as their own local authority homes. Residents could only access help with funding if they were assessed as needing care in a care home, whereas previously the DSS had not assessed whether the person actually *needed* care in a care home. Because of this there had been a huge expansion of care homes during the 1980s and there was concern about the rapidly growing costs to the social security budget. Instead of entitlement to benefits to help meet the cost of residential or nursing homes, social services now had liability for the fees if they decided such care was needed. The aim was that this would free up more money to be spent on developing home care to help people remain in their own homes as long as possible.

The DSS transferred the funding for the payments it had previously made for people in care homes, to the Department of Health. In turn this funding was passed on to local authorities in order that they could use it to pay for care either in the person's own home or for care in a care home. Charges for care in a care home were then made according to national rules very similar (but not quite the same) as the rules for income support (IS). They have gradually drifted apart again over the last ten years. These rules are explained in detail in Part 3. Charges for domiciliary care remained discretionary, and these are explained in detail in Chapter 4.

In essence, the 1993 changes gave social services the lead in providing access to services. 'This 'gate keeping' role would be done through assessment and care management, which' were seen as the cornerstones of high-quality care and formalised the process of decision making and the management of cases once services were provided or arranged.

From 1993, in order to have services provided or arranged by social services, you first had to be assessed as needing them. It was not envisaged that social services would necessarily provide the services, but would promote the development of a flourishing independent sector alongside good-quality public services. Care management would thus involve budgeting for an individual's care and buying in services from the public and the independent sectors. Many social services departments were divided into separate units: purchasers who commissioned services, and providers who provided the services.

If social services considered that you needed residential care, they would either provide it themselves in one of their own homes or buy it from the independent sector.

It was hoped that in the long term fewer people would need residential or nursing home care as more received the help they needed in their own homes. The aim was that there should not be any incentive in favour of residential care, as there had been under social security.[6]

Social services had previously been allowed to arrange for residential care in the independent sector, but the new provisions also allowed them to buy care in nursing homes.[7] This was because social security had previously paid benefits to people in nursing homes. It was, therefore, seen as part of the transfer from social security rather than any major shift from NHS responsibilities. This has come under the spotlight in a case held in the Court of Appeal and the judgment gives an interesting history of the relationship between nursing care as a health or social service.[8] It continues to be an area of confusion and concern, and there has recently been yet another special report by the Health Services Ombudsman about whether the NHS has used overly restrictive criteria when deciding if a person is the responsibility of the NHS (see p54).

The 1993 community care changes did not affect social security benefits for those living at home. If you are in a care home you also receive the social security benefits to which you are entitled, although there are some special rules for some benefits in care homes which are explained in Chapter 17.

The legislative changes

The 1993 changes were the result of the NHS and Community Care Act 1990. They cover:

- the powers of local authorities to purchase residential accommodation from independent residential and nursing homes;
- the exclusion of this power where people were already in a care home at 31 March 1993 (but note this exclusion was removed in 2002);
- the setting of a standard charge for those in independent sector homes and the recovery of the charge from the resident based on the ability to pay;
- the requirement to have a community care plan (now replaced in England by the local delivery plan);
- the assessment of needs for community care services;
- the inspection of residential premises (but note that this has been superseded by new rules for independent inspection by the national regulatory bodies – see p17);
- the setting up of a complaints procedure;
- the default powers of the Secretary of State;
- grants to local authorities for services to the mentally ill.[9]

The Act did not consolidate previous legislation but merely made alterations to it, most notably to the National Assistance Act 1948. Regulations and policy and practice guidance (see p30) provided the details of how the changes were to be implemented. The legislation made no changes to either health or housing functions, but concentrated entirely on the duties and functions of social services as the lead agency. Since then other enactments have made changes either to the way services are delivered (eg, the Health Act 1999 and the Health and Social Care Act 2001 which assist joint working), allowing for direct payments rather than the provision of services (the Community Care Direct Payments Act 1996 and sections 57 and 58 Health and Social Care Act 2001) and extending carers' rights to assessment and services (Carers and Disabled Children Act 2000). See Appendix 1 for the key legislation.

In Scotland the National Assistance Act 1948 provides the legal basis for charging for care in a care home. Part IV of the NHS and Community Care Act 1990 amends the Social Work (Scotland) Act 1968 and outlines local authority responsibilities for community care as listed above. The new Community Care and Health (Scotland) Act 2002 gives a definition of the personal and social care for which no charges should be made for people aged 65 or over (see Appendix 1), and also contains provision to assist joint working and amends the Social Work Scotland Act 1968 in relation to direct payments and to give carers greater rights.

4. **Systems to deliver services and benefits**

If you need help in the form of services or benefits you should normally first contact your local social services or housing department or social security office, depending on the nature of your need. If you have a health need you should see your district nurse or GP.

This section briefly describes the role of central government departments in providing services, and the structure of local services. Chapter 2 describes in more detail the individual responsibilities of health, housing and social services and where those responsibilities overlap.

Please note that the terms 'social services' or 'social services department' have been used throughout this *Handbook*. Different names are used in different areas, such as Adult Care Services or Community Care Services. However, they are normally still part of the local authority and undertake social services functions. In a few areas care trusts have developed (see p30). The use of the term 'NHS body' covers the many different names that are currently being evolved in each of the three countries for the providers or commissioners of health care at a local level.

Health services

Responsibility for the overall policy for health services lies with the Department of Health (England), the National Assembly for Wales and Scottish Executive

Health Department. They set the framework of policy objectives and resources for the delivery and administration of health services. They issue directions, and circulars to the appropriate NHS bodies and independent contractors such as GPs and dentists. In relation to community care, the same guidance is often issued to social services.

Local NHS bodies set policies at a local level for the resident population and are responsible for commissioning an appropriate range of health services to meet local needs. These include hospitals and community nursing and pharmaceutical services, GPs, dentists and opticians. Although not democratically elected, health bodies are accountable locally and are required to consult their local community. In England 'patient forums' will largely take over the scrutiny role of community health councils, which are to be abolished in December 2003. There are also 'overview and scrutiny committees' made up of local councillors who should be consulted on changes planned for local NHS services. Community health councils will remain in Wales. The National Health Service Reform (Scotland) Bill, introduced in June 2003, will abolish local health councils and replace them with a Scottish Health Council. This will support health boards in ensuring they fulfill their duty to give the public more say in the running of the NHS (see below).

An area might have both NHS hospital trusts (called acute hospital trusts in Scotland), which provide hospital services, and primary care trusts which co-ordinate the provision of community health services. In Wales there are local health groups, and local health care co-operatives in Scotland. Together with nurses, a representative from social services and a local lay representative, these groups identify the health needs of the local population and some have developed to commission community-based health services.

In England, the primary care trusts (PCTs) commission all health services locally. So, for instance, the PCT would commission your care if you needed to go into hospital, and also ensure that there are enough local GPs, opticians, dentists, patient transport, etc. Some PCTs can also take on the status of 'care trusts', which can also commission social care services (see p30). There are also 28 Strategic Health Authorities which are responsible for developing strategies for local health services, and for ensuring high-quality performance. They also act as a bridge between local trusts and the Department of Health.

In Wales, the National Assembly abolished the five health authorities in April 2003 and distributed their functions between newly established local health boards, which match the local authority area. These boards will have increased control over commissioning and delivering health care and some, in turn, have joined together in 10 or 12 local partnerships. There are three regional directorates to ensure co-ordinated provision at a regional level. A new Wales Centre for Health is being established, made up of National Assembly members.[10]

In Scotland, 15 Health Boards (and 7 Special NHS Boards) ensure local NHS organisations work together and that strategic direction can be implemented. Currently in Scotland, the NHS is subject to reorganisation under the National

Health Service Reform (Scotland) Bill. Proposals include giving more powers to health boards and to establish 'community health partnerships' centred on GP practices.

Local authority services (social services and housing)

Two different government departments in England and Scotland are responsible for policy making in the areas of social services and housing: the Department of Health for social services (the Department of Health and Community Care in Scotland) and the Office of the Deputy Prime Minister for housing (the Development Department in Scotland). In Wales, the National Assembly is responsible for policy development and implementation. These departments issue guidance, circulars and letters to inform or, in some cases instruct, local authorities. Legislation sometimes states that the Secretary of State for Health, the National Assembly for Wales or the Scottish Health and Community Care Minister can issue mandatory directions to social services. Guidance can also have considerable force if it is issued under section 7 of the Local Authority Social Services Act 1970 in England and Wales or section 5 Social Work (Scotland) Act 1968 (see Appendix 1). The housing department can also be issued with directions (such as the Code of Guidance on Homelessness).[11]

Central government funding for all services provided by local authorities, comes from the Revenue Support Grant and other grants such as Supporting People (see Chapter 3) and the Mental Illness Specific Grant. The amount each local authority receives is calculated using the formula grant system, which considers demographic factors in the area and is used to calculate the formula spending share (FSS) for each area. The FSS for social services includes factors such as the number of older people in receipt of income support and attendance allowance. It is advantageous to local authorities to encourage the take up of these benefits, as it can mean they receive a greater proportion of the Revenue Support Grant. However, the total amount remains the decision of government.

The local authority can decide how it will divide the money it receives from government between all its departments (although some amounts are ring fenced – eg, the grant for mental health). Some spend less on social services than would be expected from the FSS, others spend considerably more.

In addition to government money, local authorities top up their funding through locally raised council tax, rents for housing and charges for services.

Local authority officers are responsible for the day-to-day running of services, but it is elected council members who are responsible for the policies and quality of the services provided. This is why it is sometimes useful to bring your case to the attention of a councillor (see p58).

Different types of local authority

Not all local authorities have both housing and social services functions, although the majority now do. There are four types of local authority:

- county authorities based on fairly large geographical areas, often reflecting historical shires (eg, Lancashire). There are social services departments in county authorities and they normally have a number of offices so that you do not have to travel too far to the nearest social services office;
- district or borough authorities within a county area. They do not have any social services functions but provide housing services;
- metropolitan district authorities and London borough councils are based in urban areas and have responsibility for both housing and social services;
- unitary authorities were created out of some county and district/borough authorities. They are responsible for both social services and housing. Some still retain the title district or borough in their name. All authorities in Wales and Scotland are unitary.

Some authorities which are responsible for both housing and social services have combined their committees and have just one director responsible for both social services and housing.

Social security

The DWP is responsible for policy in relation to benefits, including housing benefit and council tax benefit administered by local authorities. Most benefits, however, are administered by the two new executive arms of the DWP which, from 2002, are gradually replacing the Benefits Agency. These are the Pension Service for older people and Jobcentre Plus for people of working age. There is a third service to cover disability benefits called the Disability and Carer's Service, which will continue to be largely based on the current structure for administering such benefits. Some benefits are now paid in the form of tax credits (see p192), which are administered by the Inland Revenue.

The Pension Service is still developing and over time will be regionally based, with telephone claims becoming the norm. However, there should be locally based services provided in a number of different venues to suit the needs of the local population. These could be in social services offices, post offices or in the offices of a local voluntary organisation. You will be told locally where you can see an official of the DWP if you need to discuss your claim face to face.

For people of working age, the new Jobcentre Plus will become operational around the country to replace the current JobCentres. It should be able to offer advice on a wider range of benefits for people of working age than is currently available.

The DWP sets the framework and resources for the delivery and administration of benefits. The accuracy of decisions and clearance times for claims is monitored nationally. The payment of benefit, other than the discretionary social fund, is not limited to budgets. If you are entitled to a benefit, it will be paid.

Claims for some benefits (eg, attendance allowance or disability living allowance) are processed at central offices. The claim form will tell you which office to send it to. Information should be passed between local and central offices, but this does not always happen. If you are claiming benefits from more than one office it may help to speed things up if you inform both offices.

DWP staff are responsible for making decisions on claims for benefits and are issued with guidance on the interpretation and application of the law. This is called *The Decision Makers Guide*. Although this guidance is usually strictly adhered to, it is not binding on DWP staff, and certainly not binding on higher authorities such as tribunals.

Working together

In order to achieve good community care services it is essential that all these key players work together. At governmental level, moves have been made to get departments to work more closely together. At Westminster there is an Inter-Ministerial Group for Older People chaired by a Minister for Older People. Its purpose is to ensure that government strategy and policy is effectively co-ordinated, avoids duplication and takes account of the needs of older people. The *Strategy for Older People in Wales* proposes a similar cabinet subcommittee to develop a holistic approach to planning for older people.

Provisions under the Health Act 1999 in England and Wales and under the Community Care and Health (Scotland) Act 2002 enable health and local authority departments to pool budgets and jointly commission services. This means that health and social services can pass funding between themselves more easily. However, because there are different boundaries for different organisations an NHS body may have to reach agreement with a number of local authorities in its area. Or a social services department (especially in shire authorities) can have several NHS bodies and housing departments within its area and may need to negotiate different ways of working with each. Housing departments in a district or borough council may not always have the same agenda as a social services department based in a county authority, and each will have its own culture and way of working.

An underrated aspect of community care is the importance of prompt and accurate payment of benefit, both for the claimant and social services. This is especially true in the case of residents in care homes, where the amount social services charges reflects the amount of benefit paid. There was a national service level agreement between the Benefits Agency and social services, which will need to be renegotiated with the new services as they roll out.[12]

In addition to working together, statutory agencies need to work with all the other key players who provide or use care services. As the main purchasers of care, social services are in a strong position when setting the price they are prepared to pay for domiciliary care or care in a care home. There has been disquiet expressed by providers of both domiciliary care and residential care that the prices fixed by social services are too low for the tasks expected. Various initiatives which tend to push prices up, such as the minimum wage, the European working time directive and the constraints within local authority budgets, can create underlying tensions within joint working. The tensions are such that recently there have been some court cases where care homes have used the courts to try to establish the price that should be paid.[13] In Scotland, a price has now been agreed after protracted negotiations between a consortium of care home owners and the Confederation of Scottish Local Authorities (COSLA).

5. Future trends in services, benefits and charges

There are currently changes in the pipeline which are likely, directly or indirectly, to affect the services you receive, the benefits you get and the charges you pay. Some of the service changes are specific to community care services, but others are changes to the way all public services are delivered, and as such will inevitably affect community care services over time.

Changes affecting services

Devolution and regionalisation

From July 1999 the Scottish Parliament and Welsh Assembly started to develop their own policies in relation to community care. Social security has not been devolved but remains the responsibility of central government. Although, as can be seen from this *Handbook*, there have always been some differences between Scottish and English law, this is increasingly applying to Wales. Each country produces its own plans for the future of local government and the NHS, and it is the Parliament and Assembly respectively who make their own decisions. This edition of the *Handbook* shows how the three countries differ in relation to what you have to pay when you need care. Although many of the overall aims are the same in all three countries, greater differences in the detail of how these aims are achieved are emerging.

A development which will affect services in London is the Greater London Assembly established in July 2000. The Mayor has been given specific responsibility for the promotion of health in the Greater London area.

Across the rest of England, new regional development agencies were introduced from April 1999 to co-ordinate economic, social and physical regeneration in the regions, with a duty to consult new voluntary regional chambers. These are likely to increase the scope for more regional co-ordination and action in relation to many aspects of local government, including community care. A White Paper introduced the opportunity for English regions to take a greater responsibility, giving people in the regions the chance to choose whether to establish an elected assembly for their region.[14] There is currently a Bill in Parliament to enable this to happen.[15]

In England and Wales there is also a Local Government Bill currently before Parliament giving local authorities more freedom to respond to the needs of their local communities. This will include deregulation and shifting control over local authority borrowing to the local level, allowing local authorities to charge for discretionary services, allow local referendums, and provide greater autonomy and less monitoring for high performing authorities.[16]

Trends towards consistency

At the same time as the moves to greater local decision-making through the reforms mentioned above, and the establishment of locally based health groups (see p10), there are clear messages from government about the need for greater consistency across the country both in standards and access to services. The following are some of the initiatives in England that could alter your chances of getting the care you need. Although these might not be happening in quite the same way in Wales[17] and Scotland,[18] many initiatives will broadly follow the same principles.

National objectives and priorities

The NHS White Paper *The New NHS Modern, Dependable* (1997) and the Social Services White Paper *Modernising Social Services* (1998) introduced the setting of national objectives and priorities. They include cutting health inequalities; improving mental health services; promoting independence; and tackling the causes of cancer and heart disease. National objectives for social services have been issued fitting into the priorities guidance[19] which stress promoting independence, in particular the capacity to remain in or take up work; working with others to avoid unnecessary admission to hospital; supporting carers; and ensuring resources are planned and provided at levels which represent best value for money. Recently there have been concerns to improve hospital discharge and avoid delays, leading to the Community Care (Delayed Discharges etc) Act 2003. In England from January 2004 local authorities will bear the cost where they are responsible for delaying discharge from hospital. NHS hospitals will be responsible for the costs of emergency re-admissions to ensure that patients are not discharged prematurely.[20] A number of plans have been published and targets have been set in each of the three countries of the UK to improve services.[21] Scotland has recently produced a White Paper outlining key strategies for health improvement, national quality standards and inspection and empowering staff.[22]

National service frameworks

There are plans for a complete series of national service frameworks (NSFs) within the NHS. In England ten frameworks have been published, including those for mental health services, coronary heart disease, diabetes, long-term health conditions, renal conditions and older people. The NSF for older people has as its first standard that 'NHS services will be provided, regardless of age, on the basis of clinical need alone. Social care services will not use age in their eligibility criteria or policies to restrict access to available services.'[23] The aim of the frameworks is to reduce unacceptable variations in care and standards of treatment and to put in place programmes to support implementation and establish performance measures. The frameworks have milestones to be achieved over the next few years, and new milestones will be developed. In Wales there are NSFs for diabetes, coronary heart disease and mental health services. An NSF for older people is soon to be consulted upon. The top three priorities for NHS Scotland are heart disease, cancer and mental health.

In addition, there are the Commission for Health Improvement and the National Institute of Clinical Excellence (Scottish Health Technology Centre in Scotland) which oversee standards.

Fair access to care

Alongside NSFs, a new *Fair access to care* initiative is being developed in England and Wales to introduce greater consistency in the system for deciding who qualifies for services on the assessment of risk (see p49).[24] Guidance sets out the principles that local authorities should follow when devising or applying eligibility criteria (see p49) using clear objectives based on the need to promote independence. Regular reviews of people receiving services will ensure that the services continue to meet objectives. In England, by December 2004 local authorities should start assessments of older people within 48 hours after first contact and complete the assessment within one month. Services will be in place within one month following an assessment.[25] No such initiative currently exists in Scotland.

National regulatory standards

The new regulatory standards that care homes and domiciliary care providers have to meet are in effect from various dates starting in 2002.[26] It is not intended that supported housing is included within the care home regulatory framework, which is aimed at homes that are required to be registered. Extra care housing is likely to come under the domiciliary care standards. The domiciliary standards are in effect in England and will come into effect in Wales from July 2003 (with plans to regulate day centres from the end of 2004). In Scotland *Care at home* standards are expected to come into effect in late autumn 2003 and housing support services will also be regulated. There is a National Care Standards Commission, a Care Standards Inspectorate in Wales, and Scottish Commission for the Regulation of Care (known as The Care Commission) to oversee these standards. In addition, there are the General Social Care Council, the Care Council for Wales, and the Scottish Social Services Council responsible for promoting high standards of practice, conduct and training among social care workers and for maintaining a register of social workers.[27] These bodies will gradually build up changes in the way care is provided and the standards of that care over the next few years. In England, the National Care Standards Commission will merge with the Social Services Inspectorate and be known as the Commission for Social Care Inspection working closely with the equivalent health inspection body, the Commission for Health Audit and Inspection.[28]

Performance indicators and the performance assessment framework

Performance indicators have been set for England, Wales and Scotland. The performance assessment framework uses the indicators to identify where authorities need to improve. There is no PAF for Scottish local authorities but there is a health PAF. It allows authorities to compare their performance on a consistent basis. There is a similar framework for the NHS. Good practice in local authorities and NHS bodies will be rewarded by 'beacon status' (not in Scotland). In England there are more freedoms given to local authorities which are performing well, and there is currently a Bill before Parliament to introduce 'foundation trusts' which, although still part of the NHS, will not be subject to direction by the Secretary of State and will have more freedoms in how they manage their budget and provide services.

People with mental health problems

There is a new strategy for mental health which aims to balance independence with the safety of individuals and the wider community and make services more responsive to people's needs. Extra money has been given for more mental health staff in primary care, and early intervention teams to provide active support to reduce the period of untreated psychosis. By 2004 breaks for carers who are supporting people with mental health problems will have increased.

The Mental Health Act 1983 is currently being reviewed and a draft Mental Health Bill has been published in England. A draft Mental Incapacity Bill has recently been published in England and Wales giving proposals for decision making when someone lacks capacity. It includes proposals for changing an enduring power of attorney (see p286) so that as well as managing the person's financial affairs the attorney could make decisions about the health and welfare of the person. The proposed changes to the mental incapacity legislation are waiting for Parliamentary time.

In Scotland, the Adults with Incapacity (Scotland) Act 2000 is now in force. There is also a new Mental Health (Care and Treatment) Act 2003 which will start coming into force over the next months and years.

Changes to benefits and taxes

Many of the major changes are mentioned within this *Handbook* as they come into effect in 2003/04. Some further changes which affect people with disabilities or their carers are:

Housing benefit

It is intended to simplify the administration of housing benefit (HB). Many of these reforms aim to help people get back into work without disrupting their benefit. From April 2004 it is proposed that:

- claimants will only have to tell the local authority that they have started work and do not need to submit new claims. HB will be paid at the previous out of work rate until the new benefit level is recalculated even if this is beyond the four-week run on period;
- claimants will no longer be required to reclaim HB periodically;
- claimants on incapacity benefit or severe disablement allowance will also be able to benefit from the four-week run on period;
- there will be a disregard of £11.90 on earnings for all those entitled to working tax credit.

It is also proposed to pilot a major reform of housing benefit which will introduce 'standard housing allowances' based upon the area in which a claimant lives and the number of people occupying their property.

Help back to work

A series of measures will be piloted from October 2003 to provide new recipients of incapacity-related benefits with greater support earlier in their claims. A Green Paper *Pathways to Work* sets out a package to help people on incapacity benefit get back to work. It includes early support from skilled advisers; new rehabilitation services run jointly by Jobcentre Plus and the NHS; a return to work credit of £40 a week for 52 weeks for those finding a job paying less than £15,000 a year and a fund of up to £300 to help find a job.[29] Three areas have been chosen as pilots.

Council Tax

In England bills for council tax based on new property values will be issued in 2007 and legislation will be put into place to require ten-yearly revaluation of properties. A consultation is planned on council tax discounts and exemptions, and legislation is proposed to enable additional bands to be created without primary legislation.[30] The Local Government Bill currently before Parliament contains provisions to allow councils to both reduce the council tax discount or to allow extra discount or exemption if it would cause hardship.

Pensions

A scheme for inherited SERPS protects those who are over state pension age by 5 October 2002, by exempting them from the changes. For those within ten years of the state pension age in October 2000 there will be a phased introduction of the changes.[31]

The age at which you may qualify for a state retirement pension is currently 65 for men and 60 for women. The change to equalise the ages will be phased in over a ten-year period from 2010 to 2020. In practice this will mean that:

- women born before 6 April 1950 will not be affected and will receive their state pension at 60;
- women born between 6 April 1950 and 5 April 1955 will have a state pension age of between 60 and 65 depending on their date of birth;
- women born after 5 April 1955 will not be entitled to a state pension until they are 65.

A Green Paper on pensions includes proposals to: simplify the pensions tax regime; improve information in pension forecasts; simplify the structure of contracted out benefits; consolidate pensions legislation; and implement, by December 2006, age legislation which makes compulsory retirement ages unlawful. From 2010 people will gain at least 10 per cent for each year they delay drawing their pension. They could also be offered the choice of either an increased regular state pension or taking the extra as a taxable lump sum.

Administration and payment of benefits

As outlined in Chapters 1 and 6, there are changes to the way benefits are administered in a rolling programme over time.

The government has started to introduce arrangements so that all benefits will be directly paid by automated credit transfer into claimants' bank accounts or through a post office account (instead of by order book or girocheque).[32] It is still possible to get your benefits using an order book until the end of 2004. This is important as issues about third party collection have not yet been resolved and so people who have care workers collecting their benefits may find it difficult to access their benefit when their normal care worker is on holiday or off sick. At the time of writing, the DWP is working on ways of accessing benefits for people who need third parties to collect them.

Changes to charges

A few further changes may take place in the future, and there may be some changes from October 2003 as a result of the introduction of pension credit (PC). Now that there are significant differences between income support and PC and tax credits, it is likely that the system of charges for care in a care home will develop separately and no longer follow social security rules so closely.

Although Wales has so far followed the English charging system, the Assembly has stated that it will continue to explore opportunities for alleviating the burden of paying for personal care. So, for instance, the capital limits may increasingly diverge, and there are differences planned from April 2004 about how to deal with disability-related costs for domiciliary charges. Further, there has been a commitment in the Labour Party manifesto that it will abolish home care charges for older people with disabilities.

Paying for care in a care home

One possible change in charges for care in a care home may in future be the introduction of a mandatory disregard where a carer remains in the former home belonging to a resident in a care home. There has been a commitment to keep this 'under review and should resources become available, consider further whether to amend the regulations'.[33]

What next?

Although the proposals described above give some indication of possible changes, it is inevitable that the system will continue to evolve. Decisions made in the courts could also influence future trends.

The one certainty about paying for care and receiving benefits is that the system is constantly evolving and up-to-date information is essential.

6. Arrangements to fund care yourself

Many people pay for their own care. This means buying your own help or paying the fees for care in a care home directly to the home. You may have too much money to qualify for social services help in a care home, or you may not come within social services eligibility criteria for needing help (see p49), or the sort of help you want is not provided – eg, gardening or housework. This section looks briefly at ways of using your money to pay for your care. *However, it is always wise to check whether or not you should get state help before arranging to pay for your own care. In addition, it is helpful to get an assessment of your needs by social services or the NHS in order to be sure of the type of help you do need and to talk through the various options you may have.*

Using your money to pay for care

If you only need small amounts of care you may be able to pay for it without too much difficulty. This *Handbook* describes the various benefits to which you might be entitled and also the powers and duties of the various statutory agencies. Before you arrange to pay for your own care you should check whether it should be provided for you, if this is what you would prefer. Local authorities cannot refuse to arrange your care at home just because you have resources of your own.[34] In addition, Scottish guidance makes it clear that because of recent caselaw in Scotland local authorities must arrange your care in a care home regardless of your ability to pay,[35] although they can take your resources into account at the earlier stage of deciding how best to meet the need.

The care you need can sometimes be very expensive, especially if you want to remain at home but need a lot of care. Care homes can also be very expensive.

Therefore, if you have capital which you want to preserve you might want to think of ways to make it last longer and you should get independent advice about how best to invest it.

There are two main ways of using your capital to pay for care: equity release and long-term care insurance.

Equity release

The most common form of equity release scheme is a 'home reversion scheme' which involves selling your home or part of your home to a 'reversion company'. In return you receive a cash sum (with which you could buy long-term care insurance) or a monthly annuity income. You can remain in the house rent-free or for a nominal rent for the rest of your life. When the property is sold, the reversion company receives a share of the proceeds. For instance, if you sold a 50 per cent share then the reversion company will receive 50 per cent of the proceeds. However, when you sell your home (or a share of it) to the reversion company you will not receive the full open market value because you retain the right to live there for the rest of your life. The value you receive depends on your age and sex. Older people will get more than younger people and men get more than women.

There are also 'home income plans' where you take out a mortgage loan against your home, usually up to a specified amount, and the money is used to buy an annuity which pays you a regular income for life. The interest payments on the loan are deducted from this monthly income.

Long-term care insurance

Some insurance companies offer schemes to help pay for long-term care, either in your own home or in a care home. You can pay:

- regular premiums or a lump sum to pay for your care in the future (a pre-funded policy); *or*
- a lump sum to purchase care immediately (an immediate needs plan).

The costs of the policy depend on your age, sex and state of health when you buy long-term care insurance. The premiums are lower the younger you are. Immediate needs policies have the advantage that you know you need the care you are paying for.

An immediate needs policy will start straightaway. With a pre-funded scheme, payment will start when you can no longer perform an agreed number of 'activities of daily living'. Your policy will give a precise definition and number. The activities typically include: getting around, bathing, dressing, feeding yourself etc. Mental conditions such as Alzheimer's disease are also covered. Some conditions are not covered – eg, depression, schizophrenia, alcohol/drug abuse, and HIV/AIDS. There is often a waiting period before your claim will be paid if you have a pre-funded scheme. Usually this is about 13 weeks but can be adjusted to shorter or longer periods, which will affect your premium.

Getting advice

It is very important to get independent advice when thinking about any scheme which involves your capital. You should get advice on the way payments from either equity release or long-term care insurance might affect your entitlement to benefits or care services from either social services or from the NHS. Financial advisers should be aware of the benefits you could claim or when the NHS or local authority will fund services, but there is no guarantee they will be aware of all the benefits and services described in this *Handbook*.

The schemes described above are not yet all subject to financial regulation. Some companies have signed up to a voluntary code of practice (eg, Safe Home Income Plans) and the Association of British Insurers encourages its members to belong to the Insurance Ombudsman, the Personal Insurance Arbitration Service or the Personal Investment Authority Ombudsman Bureau. The government has agreed to the regulation of long-term care insurance and will be consulting on the detail, with the introduction planned for 2004. There is also a commitment to regulate equity release schemes.

You should always be clear about what you hope to achieve through equity release or long-term care insurance. Then check if those requirements will be met by a particular product.

Notes

2. **What is community care**
   1 *Caring for People: Community Care in the Next Decade and Beyond, 1989,* HMSO (now The Stationery Office), para 2.2
   2 *Modernising Social Services, Promoting Independence, Improving Protection, Raising Standards,* 1998, DoH, p21
   3 *Social Services: Building for the Future, A White Paper for Wales,* National Assembly for Wales 1999. *Modernising Community Care: An Action Plan,* the Scottish Office 1998

3. **Community care changes in 1993**
   4 *See* the White Papers *Better Services for the Mentally Handicapped* (1971) and *Better Services for the Mentally Ill* (1975), DHSS
   5 Ministry of Health 1954(b), quoted in Means and Smith, *From Poor Law to Community Care*
   6 *Caring For People,* 1989, Key Objectives para 1.11
   7 s26(1A) NAA 1948 and s13A SW(S)A 1968 as amended by the NHSCCA 1990
   8 *R v N and E Devon ex parte Coughlan* (CA) (CCLR) September 1999
   9 ss42-58 NHSCCA 1990

4. **Systems to deliver services and benefits**
   10 Health (Wales) Act 2003
   11 s71 HA 1985
   12 Joint IS/JSA Bulletin 10/00
   13 *Bettercare Group Ltd, The Registered Homes Confederation of N. Ireland and Bedfordshire Care Group v The Director General of Fair Trading* CCLR, March 2003; *R on the application of Birmingham Care Consortium v Enfield LBC* CCLR, December 2002

5. **Future trends in services: benefits and charges**

14 *Your Region, Your Choice – Revitalising the English Region,* Cabinet Office and DTLR 2002
15 Regional Assemblies (Preparations) Bill
16 The White Paper for this Bill is *Strong Local Leadership – Quality Public Services,* DTLR 2001
17 The key documents for Wales are *A Healthier Future for Wales,* July 2000 and *The Strategy for Older People in Wales,* 2003
18 The key document for Scotland is *Our National Health, a plan for action a plan for change,* 2000
19 *A New Approach to Social Services Performance,* DoH 1999
20 DoH Press Release 2002/0992, 18 April 2002
21 These are the *NHS Plan* (England) DH 2000, *Our National Health* (Scotland) 2000, *A plan for the NHS in Wales* 2001
22 *Partnership for Care: Scotland's Health White Paper,* Scottish Executive 2003
23 *NHS Plan,* DH 2000 and the *NSF for Older People,* DH 2001
24 In Wales called a *Unified and fair system for assessing and managing care*
25 DH press release 23 July 2002
26 CSA 2000 and Regulation of Care (Scotland) Act 2001
27 CSA 2000 and Regulation of Care (Scotland) Act 2001
28 *Delivering the NHS Plan,* DH April 2002
29 DWP press release 26 March 2003
30 *Strong Local Leadership – Quality Public Services,* DTLR 2001
31 DSS Press Release 00/376
32 DSS Press Release 00/229
33 House of Lords, *Hansard* HL 26 April 2001, col 1528

6. **Arrangements to fund care yourself**

34 *Fair Access to Care Practice Guidance 2003 Q 8.5*
35 HLD (2003)7 Annex D

Part 2

People living at home

Chapter 2

Community care services at home

This chapter covers:

1. What are community care services

Although all services helping you remain in the community could be described as 'community care services' they are defined in legislation. The services covered in this *Handbook,* however, are not limited strictly to these services, because other services, such as those you can get from the NHS and housing, are equally vital in helping you remain at home.

The legislation

England and Wales

The services defined in the National Health Service and Community Care Act 1990[1] as 'community care' services are those which local authorities may provide or arrange under any of the following enactments:

- Part III of the National Assistance Act 1948 (ss21 and 29);
- section 45 of the Health Services and Public Health Act 1968;
- section 21 and Schedule 8 to the National Health Service Act 1977;
- section 117 of the Mental Health Act 1983.

Scotland

The National Health Service and Community Care Act 1990 defines community care services as those provided by local authorities under Part II of the Social Work (Scotland) Act 1968[2] or sections 7, 8 or 11 of the Mental Health (Scotland) Act 1984. The National

Assistance Act 1948 mainly applies to England but it provides the legal basis for charging for residential care (see p31). The Community Care and Health (Scotland) Act 2002 introduces free personal care and also enhances individual rights to direct payments and carers' assessments.

The legislation is explained in more detail on p30 where it relates to services which are provided in non-residential settings and in Chapter 9 where it relates to residential services.

Note that although we do not cover the legislation relating to residential services in this chapter, as this is covered in Chapter 9, sections 3, 4 and 5 of this chapter apply equally to care at home and care in a residential setting.

The non-residential provision which counts as community care services within the legislation spans a wide variety of services, including: practical assistance in the home (home helps); respite care to give you or your carer a break; equipment to help your daily living; adaptations to your home; telephones, televisions, radios; help with travel; facilities for rehabilitation; meals-on-wheels, day centres, recreational activities, outings and wardens in sheltered housing. It also includes social services advice, support and information.

In some cases social services has the *power* to provide services and in others it has a *duty* to provide services. Sometimes this duty is a *general duty* to ensure that services are available for the local population, and sometimes it is a *specific duty* to you as an individual to provide services you have been assessed as needing.

Sometimes a service is provided by the NHS (eg, a laundry service or incontinence pads), but in the event of it not providing the service or only providing it inadequately, you may find that social services makes these provisions. The social fund (see p201) has made a payment for incontinence pads when an applicant failed to meet the health authority's stringent criteria.[3] With the NHS and social services increasingly using 'pooled budgets' it is often difficult to know which organisation has the responsibility.

There might be confusion over who is responsible for adaptations to your home. Assistance in carrying out works of adaptation is listed as a community care service and as such could be the responsibility of the social services department. Grants for facilities to improve housing for disabled people (see p100) are normally the responsibility of the housing department, but social services has a duty to assist where the local housing authority refuses or is unable to approve the application even if the housing department has established that you need the adaptations.[4] Under the new Community Care (Delayed Discharges etc) Act in England, from 9 June 2003 community equipment and minor adaptations of £1,000 or less are free.[5] Similar provisions are likely in Wales.

If you need services you will probably not care which department supplies them. However, there are some vital issues in relation to:

- charging. You will probably be charged for a service if it is supplied by social services rather than by the NHS;
- your rights. It is important to know when there is a duty to provide you with a service, and how far you can choose the way that service is provided;
- knowing which department to go to or where to complain. It is sometimes not clear which department has responsibility for a service and it is not uncommon to have to complain to more than one department.

In England there is a joint charter for social services, health and housing which may help you through the community care maze.[6] There are national guidelines for local charters which should indicate how long you may be expected to wait for an assessment or a service and how to complain to each of the departments. There is a similar charter in Wales called the *Health and Social Care Guide.*

2. The responsibilities of social services, health and housing

Social services, health and housing authorities each work to different statutes and their respective responsibilities have been the subject of an increasing amount of caselaw in the courts. Appendix 5 lists books and texts that are essential to any adviser in this area or for individual research on the legislation. The responsibilities of social services, health and housing departments are constantly evolving, with changes being driven by government and caselaw. Not all the changes need legislation and departments are often informed by circulars about changes in the interpretation of the law or about conditions attached to the money they are allocated. Increasingly in England it is 'performance indicators' that set the scene for how services will be delivered. For instance, from December 2004 it will be a performance indicator that assessments start within 48 hours of referral and finish within a month and that services are in place within the following month. The performance indicators affect the 'star rating' of the authority which in turn affects the amount of freedom an authority has to manage its own services without conditions from government.

In addition to the responsibilities to people with disabilities listed in this chapter there is a general power for local authorities in England and Wales to take any action they consider will promote or improve the economic, social or environmental well-being of their area.[7] This can include action to help individuals. A recent case held that this power was broad enough to enable local authorities to provide financial assistance to secure accommodation. If the only way to avoid a breach of the European Convention was to invoke this power, then the authority was bound to invoke it.[8]

Responsibilities of social services

The prime responsibility for ensuring that community care services are provided rests with social services departments. In England, some social services functions may increasingly be taken on by 'care trusts', which are NHS bodies. A number of pilots started from April 2002. Even though the services might be provided by an NHS body, you can be charged for the service if it is a social care service. Local authority councillors are still ultimately responsible for the service. Care trusts are responsible for providing services under the legislation listed in this chapter as if they were social services departments.

They decide, through the assessment process (see p44), who will receive care services. The assessment is part of what is known as 'care management'. A decision that you need services leads on to the design and setting up of a 'care package' to meet your identified needs. This may include a range of services provided by social services, health or housing departments, independent providers or family and friends. The care package should be monitored and reviewed to ensure it continues to meet your needs, and changed if necessary.[9]

Social services and care trusts work to acts, regulations and directions (which have the force of law) and to guidance from the Secretary of State for Health, or from the National Assembly for Wales, or the Scottish Ministers in Scotland. Guidance can be:

- formal (often called policy guidance);[10] *or*
- general (often called practice guidance).

Formal guidance should be followed and deviation from it without good reason would be unlawful.[11] Practice guidance is not issued under the legislation, but even this should not be disregarded by local authorities on a regular basis.[12]

In addition the Social Services Inspectorate (Social Work Services Inspectorate in Scotland) issues advice notes or letters to local authorities.

Increasingly in England the Department of Health and the Office of the Deputy Prime Minister use their websites to disseminate information in the form of notes rather than guidance. Advisers should be aware of this and if possible check the website frequently. Each Thursday there is a *Chief Executive's Bulletin* placed on the Department of Health website which summarises recent information. There is a similar weekly bulletin in Scotland on the Scottish Executive website (see Appendix 3).

Community care services provided or arranged by social services

Community care services have a specific legal meaning and have been provided under various Acts of Parliament since 1948 (see p27). The terms in regulations are therefore often outdated and can be offensive to modern thinking.

This section looks at the legislation under which domiciliary services are provided. Appendix 1 gives the legislation in full. The brief summary here outlines the powers and duties to provide particular services to particular groups.

Help if you are disabled: Part III National Assistance Act 1948, section 29 (England and Wales)

Section 29 underpins the provision of non-residential care if you are disabled. Although s2 of the Chronically Sick and Disabled Persons Act 1970 (see p32) gives you stronger rights, it is linked to s29 of the National Assistance Act.[13] Section 29 gives social services duties in relation to people who are:

- ordinarily resident in the local authority's area (see p264);[14]
- are 18 or over, 'blind deaf or dumb, or suffer from a mental disorder' or are 'substantially and permanently handicapped by illness, injury or congenital deformity or such other disabilities that may be prescribed'. This includes partial sight and hearing.[15]

The *general duties* (which are only powers if you do not ordinarily live in the social services area) are to:

- compile and maintain registers of disabled people (you do not have to be on the register to get a service);
- provide a social work service and such advice and support as are needed for people at home or elsewhere (this can include benefits advice);[16]
- provide, at centres or elsewhere, facilities for social rehabilitation and to help you adjust to disability including assistance in overcoming limitations of mobility or communication;
- provide, at centres or elsewhere, facilities for occupational, social, cultural or recreational activities and, if appropriate, payment for work you have done.

These are not individual duties arising from your assessed needs, but just general duties towards the local population.

In addition there are *powers* to provide holiday homes, travel (free or subsidised if you do not get other travel concessions), help in finding accommodation, contributions to the costs of wardens, information about services available under s29, instruction in overcoming your disability, workshops or work you can do at home.[17] These powers cover you whether or not you are ordinarily resident in the social services area.

Social services may not make cash payments (other than for work you have done) under s29. But see p88 for direct payments.

Help if you are disabled: Social Work (Scotland) Act 1968

In Scotland, the Social Work (Scotland) Act gives local authorities the duty to 'promote social welfare by making available advice, guidance and assistance on such a scale as may be appropriate for their area'. These duties relate to people who are:

- ordinarily resident in the local authority area (see p264);[18]

- 'persons in need',[19] which include the elderly, physically or mentally disabled or those suffering from a limiting illness (disabled is not defined in the legislation).

The social work department has a general duty to promote social welfare by providing:

- advice, guidance and assistance to help promote social welfare;
- services in the home to enable a person to maintain as independent an existence as is practicable.

The social work department can give help in the form of practical assistance or cash (see also p88 for direct payments). Under s12 of the Social Work (Scotland) Act, cash can only be given in circumstances which amount to an emergency. Practical help can be given in circumstances which do not amount to an emergency – eg, paying a bill. Section 12 payments are used widely, as the only criterion set down by the Act is that the giving of assistance in either form would avoid the local authority being caused greater expense in the future.[20]

Help if you are disabled: Chronically Sick and Disabled Persons Act 1970 (England, Wales and Scotland), section 2

Although not listed as a community care service, s2 of the Chronically Sick and Disabled Persons Act 1970 links to s29 of the National Assistance Act (and s12 of the Social Work (Scotland) Act). The Act places a duty on social services to make arrangements for specific services for individuals. It has been the subject of important community care legal cases, in particular in relation to whether social services can take its own resources into account when deciding whether you need services, whether it will provide services to you, and if so what services[21] (see p49).

You can get any or all of the services listed in s2 if:

- you are defined as disabled by social services (see p31) or as a person in need in Scotland (see p31). But note s2 does not specify you have to be over 18;
- you are ordinarily resident within the social services area[22] (see p264); *and*
- social services is satisfied that it needs to make arrangements for you to meet your needs.

There is a specific duty on social services to establish the number of people who are disabled within its area, to publish what services it provides for them and to give to existing service users information about other services.[23]

The services listed in s2 are wide ranging and must be provided if you have been assessed as needing them. They include:

- practical assistance in the home – this can range from housework, to pension collection, to personal care tasks. Many social services departments have concentrated on personal care tasks in recent years and moved away from basic household tasks;

- provision of or assistance in obtaining radio, television, library or similar recreational facilities;
- lectures, games, outings or other recreational facilities outside the home or assistance for you to take advantage of educational facilities;[24]
- facilities for or assistance with travel to and from services;
- assistance in carrying out adaptations to your home or the provision of any additional facility designed for your safety, comfort and convenience. This is a separate duty from that of the housing department to provide grants for facilities to improve housing for disabled people. The guidance makes it clear that social services has the lead role and that the duty to act remains regardless of the housing department's actions. Additional facilities include fittings such as handrails, alarm systems and hoists;[25]
- help for you to take a holiday. Caselaw has established that social services cannot restrict themselves to only providing holidays they have arranged themselves. It has also been found that to assist only with the extra costs caused by disability, not with the ordinary hotel and travel costs, had fettered the authority's discretion and was not consistent with the Act;[26]
- meals either at home or elsewhere;
- provision of, or help in getting, a telephone or any special equipment to use the phone.[27] Since the Act came into force, technology has changed so it may be possible to consider items such as modems and fax machines.

Help if you are an older person: Health Services and Public Health Act 1968, section 45 (England and Wales)

If you are an older person who does not fit into the definition of disabled (see p31) but still need services because of frailty due to old age then you may be able to make use of the general provision which s45 gives to 'promote the welfare of old people'. Directions by the Secretary of State explain that its purpose is to promote the welfare of older people and as far as possible prevent or postpone personal deterioration or breakdown.[28] The directions merely *empower* social services to provide the following services, some of which are *duties* under s2 of the Chronically Sick and Disabled Persons Act. If you are an older person who is also disabled, your services should be provided under s2 and so you will have some additional rights. The services listed for older people are:

- meals and recreation in the home and elsewhere;
- information on services for the elderly;
- assistance with travel to s45 services;
- assistance in finding boarding accommodation;
- social work support and advice;
- home help and home adaptations – including laundry services;
- wardens.

If social services want to provide services outside of the directions, they can do so provided they get the specific approval of the Secretary of State.

Help from social services – National Health Service Act 1977, section 21 (England and Wales)

Most of this Act relates to services provided by the NHS, but there are specific responsibilities for social services to make arrangements for:

- expectant mothers;
- the prevention of illness and the care and aftercare of adults suffering from illness; *and*
- the provision of adequate home help services in the area for households with a person who is suffering from illness, is pregnant or a lying-in mother, is aged, or disabled by illness or congenital deformity. It is linked to laundry services which can include the provision of washing machines.[29] As there is no age limit it could apply to children.

As with most community care legislation, it is subject to the Secretary of State's directions. However, the provision of adequate home help and laundry services is not subject to direction and therefore is a *duty*, although it is only a *general duty* to provide for the area.

Social services has *powers* to provide services for expectant and nursing mothers of any age; centres or other facilities with a view to preventing illness or for aftercare; meals at such centres or at home; social work services, advice and support; night sitter services; recuperative holidays, social and recreational facilities; and services specifically for those dependent on alcohol or drugs.[30]

Social services has a *general duty* to those who are, or who have been, suffering from a mental illness to make arrangements:

- for centres for training and occupation;
- for sufficient approved social workers to act under the Mental Health Act 1983;
- to exercise the functions of the authority for those received into guardianship;
- for the provision of social work services to help in the identification, diagnosis, assessment and social treatment of mental disorder and to provide social work support at home and elsewhere.

Help from social services in Scotland

In Scotland there is no equivalent to either s45 (see p33) or to social services provision in the National Health Service Act 1977 (see p34). Local authorities in Scotland have a duty to provide a home help service to 'persons in need' and expectant or lying-in mothers; and a laundry service to people receiving this service. This is a general duty to provide for the area.[31] Under the Mental Health (Scotland) Act 1984 social work or local authorities have a duty to provide aftercare for people who have or have had a mental illness or a learning disability. They must also provide 'suitable training and occupation for people with learning disabilities' and ensure that there is adequate transport to take people to day care or training centres.[32]

Aftercare if you have previously been detained in hospital: Mental Health Act 1983, section 117 (England and Wales)

Health and social services and health both have a responsibility to provide aftercare services if you have been detained in hospital for treatment.[33] This is an individual duty and remains until both health and social services are satisfied that you no longer need such aftercare services.[34] Some people are subject to aftercare under supervision which may impose conditions on where you live, your attendance at a set time and place for medical treatment, and that the person supervising your care has access to your home.[35]

Aftercare services are not defined in the Act. They would normally include social work support and help with employment, accommodation or family relationship problems, the provision of domiciliary services and the use of day centre and residential facilities.[36]

Social services has no power to charge you for these services (see p77). Seek advice if you are told you will be charged, or if you have been charged in the past for these services. The House of Lords in 2002 confirmed earlier judgments that s117 services cannot be charged for.[37]

Aftercare in Scotland: Mental Health (Scotland) Act 1984, section 8

Currently the Mental Health (Scotland) Act 1984 places a legal duty on social work departments to provide aftercare for people who are, or have been, suffering from a mental disorder. This means a mental illness or learning disability[38] and would include someone with dementia. In providing aftercare services the local authority must co-operate with the relevant health board. The powers apply regardless of whether the person is, or has been, in hospital. Aftercare is not defined in the Act but could include similar services to examples given for England and Wales (see above). Unlike in England, social work departments in Scotland currently have a general power to charge for aftercare services. However, the introduction of free personal care for people aged 65 or over means that some of the services provided as aftercare will no longer be charged for. The situation in Scotland may change when new Mental Health legislation comes into force (likely to be in 2004).

Services if you are a carer: Carers and Disabled Children Act 2000 (England and Wales)

Carers *may* have services in their own right if:

- they are 16 or over;
- they are providing or intending to provide a substantial amount of care on a regular basis to someone aged 18 or over; *and*

- an assessment leads to the decision that the carer has needs in relation to the care which s/he provides or intends to provide.[39]

There is no restriction on the services that social services can provide, but they must, in the local authority's view, help the carer to care for the person cared for. The service to the carer could take the form of a service delivered to the person cared for, as long as they both agree and it is a community care service (see p27). However, it may not, except in prescribed circumstances, include anything of an intimate nature.[40] This is so that services which should really be provided to the cared for person are still given directly to her/him.

Carers can receive direct payments for the services for the carer (see p88).[41] A voucher scheme has been introduced in England to help carers access short-term breaks.[42] Vouchers are being piloted in three areas in Wales, with a view to the scheme being introduced in summer 2004.

Parents of a disabled child may also ask for an assessment for services to help them provide care for their child.[43] This could also be in the form of direct payments or vouchers.

In England, policy and practice guidance for carers has been issued. It is available on the carers website (www.carers.gov.uk). There is similar guidance in Wales (www.wales.gov.uk/subisocialcarers).

Services if you are a carer: Community Care and Health (Scotland) Act 2002

From October 2002 it is the duty of local authorities and NHS boards to inform carers (including carers under 16) that they have a right to be assessed independently and there will be a duty to take into account carers' views when constructing a care plan for the person who is cared for. There are, however, no plans to provide direct services to carers as they are regarded as key partners in providing care, not service users themselves. However, carers may have the right to a community care assessment if they are a person in need themselves. Parents of disabled children are able to receive direct payments to purchase services for their child (see p89).[44]

Equipment that you can get from social services

Equipment can often be just as vital as services in helping you stay independent and remain at home. The legislation described above gives social services the duty (see p34) or the power (see p34) to provide equipment. Social services can provide an extensive range of equipment that includes help with:

- getting off the toilet – eg, a raised seat or rails;
- getting in and out of the bath – eg, bath boards, rails or hoists;
- getting in and out of a chair – eg, high-backed chairs or riser chairs;
- dressing – eg, stocking aids and long-handled shoe horns;
- cooking and eating – eg, safety pans, cooker guards, special cutlery;
- reading – eg, magnifiers and page turners.

There are many other ways in which equipment can help. You could be provided with ordinary equipment such as a microwave, washing machine, or TV remote control, although in practice this is fairly uncommon.

New and improved equipment for people with disabilities is always being developed. It is important, therefore, to ask someone who is knowledgeable if there is a new gadget available which will exactly meet your needs. There are various books on the subject of equipment (see Appendix 5).

There are about 40 Disabled Living Centres in the UK (see Appendix 3) which display and demonstrate a wide range of equipment and give advice. They are open to the public and to professionals and may give advice by phone or letter if you cannot visit. If you are buying equipment it is very important to make sure you get the item that suits your needs.

Social services has a duty to provide general information about the services they provide under the Chronically Sick and Disabled Persons Act. If you are receiving services under this Act, social services also must also inform you of other services you might need (see p32). This includes providing information about equipment provided by social services, the NHS, housing or voluntary organisations.

Generally, equipment from social services is arranged by occupational therapists (OTs), although it may be arranged by physiotherapists, rehabilitation workers for people with sight problems and social workers for people with hearing problems.

In order to get equipment you often need to be assessed (see p44) by qualified staff such as OTs. Social services should have adequate staff to enable them to carry out that function,[45] but the shortage of OTs has been a common problem. If the problem has been acknowledged but not been tackled, contact the Local Government Ombudsman who may find maladministration (see p58).[46] In England, once it has been decided that you need equipment social services should aim to get it delivered within three weeks if it is less than £1,000.[47] From 2004 all equipment needed should be in place within a week.[48]

In England, from 9 June 2003 there should be no charge for community equipment or for 'minor' adaptations of £1,000 or less which you have been assessed as needing.[49] In Scotland, equipment that is defined as coming within 'free personal care' such as personal reminder systems for taking medicines, or sound/movement alarms are free. Also any equipment that is installed within four weeks of you coming out of hospital is free. Guidance issued to local authorities by COSLA recommends that local authorities should not charge for equipment and if they do, they should only do so for small items up to £20.[50]

In England, there is funding for social services and health departments to provide an integrated community equipment service under the intermediate care initiatives (see p43) and the National Service Framework for Older People.[51] There are proposals in Scotland for an integrated community equipment service. In Scotland, from June 2003, direct payments can be used to buy equipment or adaptions directly from a local authority (where the equipment or adaptions are deemed to come under community (social work) care legislation).

Social services responsibilities for planning and providing information

As most people only approach social services for help at a time of great need and they do not know what to expect, information is vital. This was recognised when community care was reformed and various duties were placed on social services departments to plan services and inform people about them.

Planning

Each local authority must prepare and publish a plan outlining community care services to be provided[52] and this must be updated each year.[53] In England this does not have to be a stand alone document, but can be part of the overall plans produced jointly with health bodies for the area.[54] In drawing up plans, social services must consult with health, housing and voluntary organisations which represent groups likely to need services. If a provider organisation writes to ask to be consulted then it must be.[55] Guidance tells social services to identify the following:

- assessment – the care needs of the local population, how those care needs will be assessed, and how identified needs will be incorporated into the planning process;
- services – how priorities for arranging services are made, how they intend to offer practical help and how they intend to develop domiciliary services;
- quality – how they monitor service quality, the role of the inspection unit, and the role of complaints procedures;
- choice – how they intend to increase consumer choice and develop a mixed economy of care;
- resources – the resource implications of planned and future developments and how they intend to improve cost effectiveness;
- consultation – how they intend to consult;
- publishing information – how they intend to inform service users and their carers about services, and how and when they will publish their plan for the following year.[56]

The duty to inform

Apart from having to publish its plan and complaints procedures (see p55) the only other duties to inform people of the services they can get are set out in the legislation described on p34. Policy guidance states that local authorities must have published information accessible to all potential service users and carers, in formats suitable for those with communication difficulties or differences in language or culture. The information should set out the types of community care services available, the criteria for the provision of services, the assessment procedures and the standards by which care management will be measured.[57]

Local authorities in England and Wales are also required to produce charters based on a national framework.[58] These should give an indication of the services people can expect to receive, and how quickly they will be provided. Charters do not have any legal effect, but it is possible to complain if standards in a charter are not met. In one case the Local Government Ombudsman found maladministration when a community care charter gave misleading timescales for assessment.[59] In England, community care charters are now replaced by joint local long-term care charters covering health, social care and housing called *Better Care, Higher Standards*. There is a similar charter in Wales, *The Health and Social Care Guide*.

Responsibilities of the NHS

Health services, which are an essential element of community care, are not classified as community care services and are provided under different legislation which was largely unchanged by the community care legislation. Unlike social services, there are no specific duties to individuals who need health care services. If when assessing you (see p45), social services think you have a health care need, then in England and Wales it must notify the appropriate health body and invite it to assist in the assessment. The health body has no duty to respond or co-operate. In Scotland, the social work department must notify the health board and ask what services it is likely to provide and then take this into account in the completed assessments.[60]

In England there will be a new duty (starting in October 2003) on NHS bodies to inform the local authority of a hospital inpatient's possible need for community care services when s/he is discharged.[61] Although the same provisions cover Wales it is not known whether they will be introduced there.

Health bodies have only a broad duty to provide services to the extent the Secretary of State (in Scotland the Scottish Ministers, in Wales the National Assembly Health and Social Services Secretary) considers necessary to meet all reasonable requirements. Such services include:

- medical, dental, nursing and ambulance services;
- hospital and other accommodation for services provided by the NHS; *and*
- facilities for the prevention of illness, care of those suffering an illness and aftercare for those who have suffered an illness which are appropriate for a health service to provide.[62]

Health bodies, therefore, have wide discretion in deciding what meets 'all reasonable requirements', even to the extent of deciding that a particular service will not be provided at all. As long as a decision about the level (or non-provision) of a service is justifiable on the grounds of local priorities and resources, then it would be difficult to challenge.[63]

There is guidance about NHS responsibility for continuing health care needs. In England this guidance has been updated in the light of *R v N and E Devon ex parte Coughlan*. (Wales has similar updated guidance in draft form.) Scotland is not intending to change its guidance.[64] It covers NHS care in homes providing nursing care (see p259) and NHS care that should be offered at home. The English and Welsh guidance may be altered in response to a recent special report of the Health Service Ombudsman who found that in some areas the guidance was being interpreted in too restrictive a manner, and that the national guidance was not clear (see p54 for more details).[65] In England the 28 Strategic Health Authorities should have produced guidance by 28 March 2003, although at the time of writing some is still in draft form. This guidance must be agreed by all the NHS and local authority partners in the area that the Strategic Health Authority covers.

The current national guidance in each country allows health bodies to decide (in agreement with social services) what health services will be provided. Local policies must be published. The following services must be available in each area:

- specialist medical and nursing care;
- rehabilitation and recovery services. Local policies should prevent premature discharge and should agree with local authorities any additional social or educational support required as part of an agreed package of rehabilitation;
- palliative health care including support for people in their own homes;[66]
- continuing inpatient care in hospital or a home providing nursing care (see p259);
- respite health care;
- specialist health care support for people in care homes or in the community. This could include specialist palliative care, incontinence advice, stoma care, diabetic advice, physiotherapy, speech and language therapy, or chiropody. It should also include specialist equipment;
- community health services (such as district nurses) for people in care homes (see p275);
- primary health care (ie, health care from GP surgeries, district nurses, dentists and opticians);
- specialist transport services to and from hospital or other health care facilities, and where emergency admission to a care home is necessary.

Given that there are wide differences between areas, it is important to find out what is available under the local criteria, and to challenge it if you consider it to be too restrictive (see p51). The long-term care charter *Better Care, Higher Standards* should provide information about health services in each area in England.[67]

Hospital discharge

The guidance issued on continuing health care in Scotland and Wales also covers the question of hospital discharge. In England, the new guidance no longer covers hospital discharge, but there are plans to update the guidance following the implementation of the Community Care (Delayed Discharges etc) Act. In the meantime, the view is that the previous guidance on hospital discharge should continue to be followed in spite of the fact that it has been cancelled. *Discharge from Hospital: pathway, process and practice,* a new workbook produced in January 2003 covers points of good practice in hospital discharge.

It is very important that any stay in hospital has a planned discharge so that you do not go home without the services you need. The consultant will normally decide (but should do so in consultation with others) whether or not you continue to need acute care. If your needs are such that you may need intensive support there should be a multi-disciplinary assessment.[68] You, your family and your carer should be kept fully informed so that you can make decisions, and you should be provided with written details of the likely cost of any option you are considering. If the NHS is arranging services you should receive information in writing saying what aspects of your care the NHS is funding.[69] This is particularly important if you need care in a home providing nursing care, which can in some cases be fully funded by the NHS if you meet the local criteria. There is a right of review of discharge decisions (see p53).

In England, the *Better Care, Higher Standards* charter states that:

- you can expect local housing, health and social services to work with you, and if you agree, your carer, to make the necessary arrangements;
- a written care plan should be agreed so that you know what will happen after you leave hospital.

If you consider that the hospital has not involved you enough, has not ensured that the services you need are in place, or has failed to follow the guidance, you should complain (see p51).

Legislation in England and Wales allows that where a local authority is responsible for delaying a patient's discharge from hospital, then it should be fined for each day you have to remain in hospital because it has not put services in place for you. It is not planned to introduce this in Wales. In England it will be partially introduced in October 2003, so that the NHS will have to inform social services that a patient might need community care services, but the implementation of fining local authorities for each day they delay will not be introduced until January 2004. Social services will have very strict time limits in which to assess your needs and arrange the package of care you need. It will be even more important to complain if you think the services you have been offered are not enough or will mean that you have to go into a care home not of your choice.[70] For more details of the way the Act will work see www.doh.gov.uk/reimbursement.

Equipment you can get from the NHS

As well as providing services, the NHS is responsible for providing certain equipment. In England, this may be through the integrated community equipment service. You should talk to your doctor, district nurse or health visitor first about any equipment you might need.

The sort of equipment you may be able to get includes:

- wheelchairs;
- commodes (normally for short-term use);
- bathing equipment including hoists (if your need is for a medical bath);
- eating and drinking equipment if there is a medical need. This can include food preparation equipment such as a liquidiser;
- bed equipment such as a cradle to keep the bed clothes off you, a back rest, raising blocks, bed rails if your need is defined as a health need rather than a social need. It may include the bed itself if you need a special bed;
- environmental control equipment (on loan);
- walking aids;
- artificial limbs;
- hearing aids;
- low vision aids;
- TENS machines for pain relief;
- special footwear;
- incontinence pads and other equipment.

As with all services provided through the NHS it will depend on the resources available as to whether particular equipment will be supplied in your area. If your local area does not supply the item you need, you should complain (see p51).

Equipment issued on prescription

GPs can provide a range of appliances as well as drugs on prescription. These include incontinence devices (this includes pads in Scotland), stoma care appliances, oxygen cylinders, diabetes equipment and elastic stockings.[71]

Home care equipment

Your GP may be able to help you get orthopaedic footwear, breast prostheses, cervical collars, communication equipment, nebulisers, supports for limbs or trunk, hoists, special beds and mattresses, and walking aids.

Help with incontinence

Some equipment for incontinence is issued under prescription including catheter bags, catheters, male urinals, and night drainage bags. Incontinence pads can be supplied by the NHS and usually are, but sometimes their supply can be limited. Guidance has been issued to say that if any changes to incontinence aids are proposed, an assured alternative should be put in place before action is taken.[72]

Pad disposal services are often jointly run by the NHS and social services. Laundry services are usually run by social services but the NHS may have a local laundry service. Some areas will have neither a disposal service nor a laundry service.

Incontinence advisers are now available in many areas and it is important to seek advice about incontinence, which is only a symptom of a variety of physical or mental conditions. In England, the Department of Health has published a good practice guide on continence services.[73]

Wheelchairs

In addition to a range of ordinary wheelchairs, the NHS now provides outdoor/indoor electric wheelchairs[74] if you are assessed as needing one because you are unable to walk or propel an ordinary wheelchair. Each health authority has its own criteria within the national guidelines, but if you move to another area your wheelchair should not be taken from you without good clinical reason. In Scotland, the criteria are set nationally and if you move to a different area then you can take your wheelchair with you. The Scottish Seating and Wheelchair Group has issued guidelines for the provision of wheelchairs through the NHS in Scotland.

In England there is a voucher scheme which allows you to put extra cash towards a more expensive wheelchair than the NHS will provide.[75]

Intermediate care services (England and Wales)

As part of the National Service Framework for older people and the National Plan for the NHS, intermediate care services have been introduced in England and Wales. The responsibility is shared between the NHS and social services and the services are aimed at enabling people to leave hospital earlier than they otherwise would, or preventing hospital admission. In order to count as an intermediate care service it must involve cross-professional working, provide active therapy, treatment or opportunities for recovery and be short term lasting normally not more than six weeks and often one to two weeks. Where such services are being provided as intermediate care they should be free. They can be in a step downward of a hospital, in a care home or in your own home.[76] In Wales there is also guidance on free home care for up to six weeks following a hospital stay (see p75).[77]

Responsibility of housing departments

Housing is a vital part of community care, but like health services it is not listed as a community care service within the legislation. If, when assessing you, social services find that you need housing services, they can invite the housing department to assist, but there is no duty for housing to respond.[78] In Scotland, the social work department can notify the housing authority and request information from them as to what services are likely to be made available.[79] However, the housing department may be under a duty to make enquiries if you are homeless and in apparent priority need.[80] Priority need is defined as being vulnerable due to old age, mental illness or handicap or physical disability or other reason such as pregnancy or where there are children. It will then have a specific duty towards you as long as you are not intentionally homeless.

Guidance stresses the important role of housing departments and suggests they should be involved in:

- community care planning;
- community care assessments;
- local housing strategies involving co-operation with housing associations and considering special needs housing;
- provisions for homeless people;
- home adaptations.[81]

Different types of housing

Housing departments may assist you in getting accommodation with a housing association or provide the following:

- housing designed to give you access at all times to all principal rooms if you need a wheelchair to get about;
- sheltered housing. This is mainly intended for older people and there is usually a minimum age (often 60). There is almost always an alarm system linked to a 24-hour control service. Some schemes have a resident warden; others have a mobile warden who visits the scheme regularly. A service charge may be included in the rent. These services now come under Supporting People services (see p67);
- extra care sheltered housing. These offer extra care facilities such as help with bathing or dressing, and they will often have a dining room where meals are available. They can be run jointly with social services;
- lifetime homes. A few councils and housing associations build homes which are adaptable to changing needs, including level access and downstairs toilet facilities, a wide front door, a living room that can take a bed, kitchens designed for easy use and safety.

Chapter 3 explains in more detail about supported housing and Supporting People services and Chapter 4 about the charges for these services.

Houses in England and Wales built after October 1999 must have basic accessibility features such as a level threshold and downstairs toilet.[82] In Scotland, Scottish Homes, the national housing agency, requires all housing funded by them to incorporate barrier free standards. Unfortunately most older homes do not have these features so you may need adaptations or assistance with repairs. The financial assistance you can get to help make your home easier for you to live in is described in Chapter 5.

3. Getting the services you need

If you are having difficulties managing everyday tasks, or are in hospital and think that you will need some help when you leave, you will need to ask social services for a care assessment. Someone else can refer you, although it should always be with your permission unless you are unable to give it because of your mental condition. In England and Wales the NHS will have a new duty to notify your local social services department if you are an inpatient and likely to need community care services when you leave hospital. They must consult you (or your carer) before they notify social services.[83] The care assessment is important as it is the first stage of getting support from social services.

Once you have come to the notice of social services they have a duty to assess and make a decision about whether or not you are entitled to services. If you are, then a care plan will be drawn up, with your agreement, put into place and reviewed on a regular basis to make sure it continues to meet your needs. The care plan could include care in a care home, or a wide range of services to help you stay at home.

The assessment of your needs

Social services must assess you if:

- you appear to them to be in need of a community care service – ie, those listed on p27;[84]
- you are disabled;[85]
- you help look after someone else.[86]

Assessment is a service in its own right.[87]

Most social services operate a screening process to decide who is eligible for an assessment, how quickly it will be provided and the type of assessment you will get. In England, your local long-term care charter, *Better Care, Higher Standards,* should give you an indication of how the assessment will be done and how long you should expect to wait. If your need is urgent, social services can provide the services first and assess you as soon as possible afterwards.[88] A new single assessment process is currently being introduced for older people (in Scotland called the single shared assessment, and in Wales the unified assessment). It aims to minimise the need for you to repeat the same information to a number of different professionals, and should mean that you get the right level of assessment depending on the complexity of your needs.[89] It applies to both the NHS and local authorities.

Screening for assessment

The practice of screening referred to in policy guidance[90] has been questioned, in particular when it screens people out of an assessment. Local authorities have been told to set a low threshold for assessment.[91] Even if social services think there is no prospect of providing a service because of lack of resources (see p49) they should still assess you.[92]

Sometimes screening takes place over the phone, and you may have been deemed to have had an assessment without ever seeing anyone or even realising that the phone call was the assessment. You should complain if you feel that you have not been given a proper opportunity to be assessed.

How quickly will the assessment be carried out?

There are no national rules about how quickly an assessment should be carried out. Many local authorities set their own timescales. You should be told in your local *Better Care, Higher Standards* charter the maximum time you will have to wait for an assessment. An Ombudsman has found maladministration in a case where the local charter set unrealistic timescales.[93]

From December 2004 in England all assessments of older people should start within 48 hours of referral and finish within 28 days. Once the Community Care (Delayed Discharges etc) Act comes into effect in England, if you are a hospital patient your assessment for your discharge plan should start before you go into hospital in the case of elective treatment and very quickly after you enter hospital if you do so as an emergency. Strict time limits have been placed on the time local authorities have to do the assessments and get services in place. Once a patient is ready for discharge, social services can be fined if they have caused any delay.

Waiting lists for assessments have been the subject of numerous investigations by the Local Government Ombudsman especially in relation to assessments for equipment, which require the intervention of an occupational therapist. Due to the large number of complaints in relation to disabled facilities grants, the Local Government Ombudsman has suggested what s/he considers to be 'reasonable times' for awaiting an assessment – ie, two months for urgent cases, four months for serious cases and six months for non-urgent cases.[94] However, two months may be too long if your need is very urgent.

If you are in need of drug and alcohol services, there has been guidance on assessment and 'fast track' assessment.[95]

The fact that social services are permitted to prioritise the waiting time for your assessment presupposes they have enough information to make a judgement on how long you should wait. It is therefore important when you first contact social services that you make clear the exact nature of your needs and whether your situation is urgent.

The nature of the assessment

The type of assessment you get depends on the nature of your needs. Assessments vary from 'simple assessments' – for items like bus passes and disabled car badges which will often be done by reception staff – to 'comprehensive assessments' if you have needs which cut across departments and which are likely to lead to intensive support. For older people, under the new single assessment process there are four types of assessment:

- a contact assessment which takes basic details, explores whether you have wider health and social care problems, and deals with simple requests;

- an overview assessment, where your needs are such that various aspects of care need to be explored;
- a specialist assessment to explore specific problems by an appropriate member of staff such as OTs, geriatricians or old age psychiatrists;
- a comprehensive assessment, if your needs are such that you are likely to be offered intensive or complex support which may involve a range of different professionals.

You should be encouraged to contribute fully to your assessment. There is similar guidance about assessment in England, Wales and Scotland.[96] In England it is proposed to issue directions regarding assessment.

If, during the assessment, a need for health or housing services becomes apparent, social services has a duty to notify the relevant department and invite it to assist in the assessment.[97] There is no duty on either of those services to respond, although in practice it is rare for them to refuse.

The assessment could take place in your own home or in hospital. You should be fully involved in your assessment, which should look at all of your needs as a whole.[98] This should include your social and psychological needs.[99]

Carers' assessments

A carer is defined as someone who provides or is about to provide a substantial amount of care on a regular basis.[100] It is left to social services to decide what constitutes a substantial amount of care. If your carer is not thought to provide substantial amounts of care, s/he should still have a role in your assessment.[101] Paid carers and volunteers cannot have a carer's assessment.

There is a duty to assess your carer if s/he requests it, at the same time as your assessment.[102] This is not a freestanding assessment but is done in conjunction with your own assessment. A carer's assessment takes place normally only on request, but guidance to social services says they should ensure it is routine practice to inform carers of their right to an assessment.[103]

In addition in England and Wales, carers aged 16 years or over are entitled to be assessed in their own right independent of the cared for person if that person is someone for whom social services may provide or arrange community care services.[104] Similar provisions will be introduced in Scotland from July 2003 and will also cover the rights of children who are carers to have an assessment.[105]

The result of your carer's assessment must be taken into account when making a decision about services. The object of the assessment is to identify your carer's ability to provide and continue to provide care. Practice guidance has made it clear that in assessing your carer's ability to care, social services should not assume her/his willingness to continue caring or to continue to care at the same level.

Recording the assessment

You should be told the outcome of your assessment and the decision on service provision.[106] Guidance suggests you should get a written record of your assessment which will normally be combined with your care plan. In England the long-term care charter, *Better Care, Higher Standards,* states that you should be given a decision in writing.

If you have difficulty in getting a copy of your assessment (or care plan), you can request a copy of your file under the Data Protection Act 1998.

Your care plan

If, having assessed your needs, social services decides that you need services, they should give you a care plan, which should give details of:

- overall objectives;
- specific objectives;
- the services that will be provided and by whom;
- the cost to you;
- other options considered;
- any point of difference between you and the care assessor;
- any unmet needs;
- who will be responsible for monitoring and reviewing; *and*
- the date of the first planned review.

This should have been discussed with you and have your agreement. There is no statutory duty for social services to provide a written care plan, and you may find that you are not offered one. However, the new single assessment guidance for older people makes it clear that you should get a written copy of your care plan. If you are a younger person and want to see your care plan then you could ask for access to your file (see above).

Your care plan can include a wide range of services, with a mix of social services help and care from the NHS and your carers. Services can be provided directly by social services or from an independent provider. You could, as an alternative, receive a payment from social services to arrange your own care (see p88).

How soon should services be provided?

The law is silent on how soon services should be provided (except in the case of disabled facilities grants in England and Wales, where it can be up to 12 months). Whether or not the delay is excessive will depend on your particular circumstances. Some social services appear to use delays as a way of keeping within their resources (see p49). From December 2004 it will be a performance indicator that services should be provided within four weeks of the assessment being completed. From January 2004 if you are in an acute ward in hospital it is likely that you will get services put in place quickly, in order that the local authority avoids being fined (see p41).[107] If you feel that you have been kept waiting too long for your services you should complain (see p51).

Monitoring and reviewing your services

Although there is nothing in the legislation about monitoring and reviewing services, there is guidance. This states that there should be regular reviews to ensure that the objectives of the care plan are being met and to establish whether any changes are required because of changing needs or service delivery policies. In the case of older people under the single assessment guidance it is made clear that a review should be held within three months and from then on at least every 12 months. This is also specified in the long-term care charter *Better Care, Higher Standards*.

The review should also monitor the quality of the services provided, taking account of your views and the views of your carer.[108] If you have concerns about the quality of your care (eg, the manner, the reliability, and trustworthiness of the carer provided via the local authority) you should raise this without waiting for a review.

4. How far the authority's resources can be taken into account

For housing and social services, there are specific duties that arise and there have been various legal challenges to establish whether the local authority's resources can be taken into account.

This section looks at how local authorities try to manage their resources. It also looks at eligibility criteria, when resources can be taken into account in an assessment, and ceilings on home care services. Local authorities often use waiting lists to manage finite resources. Another way local authorities can increase resources is through discretionary charges (see p95).

Eligibility criteria

After you have been assessed, social services must make a decision about whether your needs are eligible for services.[109] To determine who should get services, social services use 'eligibility criteria'. This process has been described as a 'system of banding which assigns individuals to particular categories, depending on the extent of the difficulties they encounter in carrying out everyday tasks and relating the level of response to the degree of such difficulties. Any 'banding' should not, however, be rigidly applied, as account needs to be taken of individuals' circumstances'.[110] A banding system is normally a series of priority groups, and those in low priority may not have their needs met. More recent guidance states that councils should 'assess an individual's presenting needs, and prioritise their eligible needs, according to the risks to their independence in both the short- and longer-term were help not to be provided.'[111]

Different local authorities will have different criteria, so you could get a service in one area, but if you move to another, you would not be eligible. Where resources are scarce, the eligibility criteria may be tightened so that people who may have been receiving a service are now defined as no longer needing that service.

Your local authority's plan should give a description of its eligibility criteria. The criteria might also be described in leaflets about community care in your area.

In England and Wales, there is guidance (*Fair Access to Care* – England; *Creating a Unified and Fair System for Assessing and Managing Care* – Wales) which sets out the principles which authorities should follow when devising and applying eligibility criteria.[112] In Scotland a 'resource use measure' is being implemented which is intended to ensure fairer access to services.[113]

When resources can be taken into account in your assessment

Social services cannot take its resources into account when deciding whether you are entitled to an assessment.[114]

When assessing your needs, and deciding whether it is necessary to provide services, resources are taken into account in so far as the local eligibility criteria have been influenced by the local authority's resources. If a local authority tightens its eligibility criteria because of lack of resources, it must assess you against these new eligibility criteria before withdrawing any services you already receive.[115]

Once social services has decided that you need services, resources can no longer be taken into account. There is a duty to provide such services.[116] It is likely that the same principles would apply in a community care assessment under s12 of the Social Work (Scotland) Act 1968. This is equally true of education services[117] and housing services for disabled facilities grants.[118]

Resources can play a part when deciding between various options which would equally meet your assessed need – eg, they could choose the cheaper option of residential care.[119]

Practice guidance for *Fair Access to Care* makes it clear that just because you have your own resources you should not be denied services. Local authorities should arrange services at home irrespective of your resources or capacity, if that is what you want them to do.[120] Complain if you are told to arrange your own care because you have enough money to pay for it.

Ceilings on home care services

It is quite common, particularly for older people, to find there is a financial ceiling on the amount of home care which will be provided. Sometimes this is expressed in hours. For example, you may find that the maximum social services will provide is 10-15 hours service, as any more home care would make care in a care home a cheaper option. The ceiling may be equivalent to the net or gross cost to social services of providing residential care.

The ceilings imposed are particularly noticeable for older people, with many authorities imposing no ceilings (or setting very much higher ones) on support packages for younger people. The effects of the National Service Framework for Older People and the guidance in *Fair Access to Care* may mean that such age discriminatory policies can be challenged, as both these documents, which are statutory guidance, state that decisions about eligibility criteria should be made without reference to age, and not stick rigidly to predetermined cost ceilings.

If you are told that you need services beyond those that social services are prepared to pay for, you should seek advice. It may also be possible to use the European Convention on Human Rights (see p61).

5. How to complain

Social services and the NHS each have standard complaints procedures. Housing has no specific procedures other than the normal local authority complaints procedure, which may be similar in practice to that of social services, certainly in the initial stages. There is, however, a national appeals process regarding homelessness and guidance on this, which housing departments have to follow.

This section looks at how to complain to social services and to NHS bodies. It then looks at what other steps you can take if you are not satisfied.

Note that the Health and Social Care (Community Care and Standards) Bill 2003 is likely to introduce changes to the way complaints are made within the NHS and social services from April 2004. It is proposed that if a complaint cannot be resolved at the local stage then you can take your complaint to either the Commission for Health Audit and Inspection or the Commission for Social Care Inspection. If your complaint involves both social and health care there will be closer co-operation between the bodies in dealing with such complaints.

The following reflects the current position.

Complaining about health services

The current NHS complaints procedure was introduced in 1996, as there were many concerns about how difficult it was to know who to complain to about something that had happened within the NHS. The legislation was brought in to unify all the various channels for complaints about both clinical (eg, complaint about medical treatment) and non-clinical (eg, failure of an ambulance to arrive promptly) issues.[121] It does not cover disciplinary matters or criminal offences. If your complaint is about negligence then the complaints procedure can be used unless you have explicitly indicated an intention to take legal action. As well as directions, guidance was issued setting out the procedures which are explained below.[122] This complaints procedure itself has been criticised and is currently under review.[123] A new NHS Charter has replaced the Patients Charter.[124]

Each sector within the NHS must produce a written complaints procedure which must be published. You can complain if you are a user or former user of the NHS. Other people may complain on your behalf if they have your consent, and there are specific considerations if the patient lacks mental capacity or has died.

The complaint should be made as soon as possible after the event, and in any case within six months. There is discretion to extend the time limit where it would be unreasonable in the circumstances not to, and where it is still possible to investigate the facts of the case.

From April 2003 every NHS trust and primary care trust (PCT) in England should have established a Patient Advice and Liaison Service (PALS) to provide on-the-spot help, support and information to patients, their families and carers. They can offer information about how to complain. If you are considering making a complaint you may also find it helpful to speak to your local community health council (health council in Scotland). In England (but not in Scotland or Wales) community health councils are likely to be abolished by December 2003 and will be replaced by patients' forums. There will also be Independent Complaints Advocacy Services which will focus on helping individuals to pursue complaints with and about a particular NHS service.

The first stage – local resolution

You should try to resolve the complaint locally on an informal basis. NHS bodies should have details about how to complain in leaflets and some now have such details on their websites. There should be a complaints manager who is responsible for ensuring complaints are responded to and that this first stage is properly carried out. There are differences between trusts and GPs. In the case of trusts, written complaints must receive a response in writing from the chief executive. GPs have to comply with minimum standards in their practices. They must publicise the complaints procedure and ensure that patients know where to log a complaint. An initial response should be made within two working days, and the person nominated to investigate complaints should make all necessary enquires and respond within two weeks.

The whole of this first stage can be conducted orally, but it may be best to put your complaint in writing so that you have a record of when you made it and the points that you raised in your complaint. If you want to take it further, guidance suggests that you should be sent a letter which also indicates your right to seek an independent review panel.

The second stage – the independent review panel

If you are still dissatisfied you can ask for an independent review panel to be set up. Any request for an independent review panel must be passed to the panel's convenor within 28 days. It is not automatic that your case will be heard at a panel. A decision will be made by the convenor based on a signed statement by you. The convenor will:

- decide whether all opportunities to resolve the complaint have been explored at the first stage;
- consult with an independent lay chair to get an external independent view; *and*
- take appropriate clinical advice.

A decision will be given within 20 working days from the date the convenor received the request. If you are refused a review you can ask the convenor to reconsider, and as a last resort you can complain to the Health Service Ombudsman if you are refused (see p60).

The independent review panel normally comprises three people:

- an independent chair who must not be a past or present employee of the NHS, nor a member of the clinical profession, nor have had formal links with the trust or health authority;
- the convenor; *and*
- either a representative of the purchaser (in the case of an NHS trust), or an independent person.

If the complaint is about clinical matters there will also be two independent clinical assessors.

The panel should be convened within four weeks of the decision to convene it and should complete its work within 12 weeks. It should be an informal process, and although you cannot have legal representation, a person of your choice can accompany you.

A draft of the panel's report will be sent to the relevant parties 14 days before it is formally issued, in order to check its accuracy. Following the final report, the chief executive must inform you in writing of what action will be taken as a result of the panel's deliberations and of your right to take your case to the Ombudsman.

Requesting a review of a discharge from hospital decision (England and Wales)

There is a separate procedure[125] if you think you should not leave hospital, or your care in a care home providing nursing should continue to be fully funded by the NHS (see p263).

You, your family or any carer has the right to ask for a review of the decision that you no longer need inpatient care. This can give some breathing space as during the review you should remain as an inpatient, although the request should be dealt with urgently and you should have an answer within two weeks. This can be extended if there are exceptional circumstances which make the timescale impossible.[126]

In reaching a decision the NHS body should seek advice from an independent panel which will consider your case and make a recommendation. The NHS body has the right not to convene a panel if your need falls well outside its eligibility criteria for continuing inpatient care. If it is decided not to convene the panel you should be given the reasons in writing. The Ombudsman has criticised a health body which refused to hold a panel hearing on the grounds that the patient did not meet the eligibility criteria. She interprets the guidance as meaning that only where there is no doubt whatsoever that the eligibility criteria would not be met should the possibility of not convening a panel be considered.[127]

This review procedure cannot be used to challenge the content of a local NHS body's eligibility criteria. You can only challenge the way the criteria have been applied to you. Neither can it be used to review the type of inpatient care and where it is offered, the content of any alternative care package or any other aspect of your treatment in hospital. It cannot be used for resolving funding disputes between the NHS body and local authority. In all these cases you can use the complaints procedure, and there is nothing to stop you using both procedures at the same time.

The review procedure can only be used to:

- check that the procedures have been followed correctly in reaching the decision; *and/or*
- ensure that the eligibility criteria have been properly and consistently applied.

The NHS body is required to appoint a designated officer to check that all the informal channels have been used and collect information for the panel, including interviewing you and any family or relevant carers.

The panel consists of an independent chair and representatives from health bodies and local authorities. It has access to an independent clinical adviser to advise the panel on the original clinical judgement and how it relates to the eligibility criteria.

The role of the panel is advisory but the expectation is that its recommendations will be accepted in all but the most exceptional circumstances. You must be given reasons in writing if its recommendations are rejected.

The panel must produce a report each year on the number of cases it has considered and the outcomes.

This review procedure has been extended to cover decisions about the level of payment for nursing care you get in a care home (see p55).

Appealing against a discharge decision (Scotland)

If you are in hospital in Scotland you have the right to appeal against the clinical decision to discharge you from continuing NHS care.[128]

Information on this procedure and any advocacy services must be available from hospital staff on request. The appeal is in two stages. Once the consultant has decided that you can be discharged, you or your carer/advocate have ten days to request a review of the decision by the Director of Public Health. This should be completed within two weeks. If it is decided that you should be discharged, you have the right to request a second opinion from an independent consultant from another health board area.

You cannot be discharged during the appeal process. The aim of this appeal process is to ensure that the criteria set out in the guidance have been correctly applied. It cannot be used to complain about the content of the criteria. The appeal procedure is separate from the NHS complaints procedure and there is nothing to stop you using both procedures at the same time.

Reviews against other decisions about the need for NHS services and NHS funding of nursing care (England and Wales)

In England and Wales the type of review explained on p140 for hospital discharge has been extended. Review panels can now cover decisions about the need for continuing NHS health care or continuing NHS services contributing to a health and social care package (see p39).[129] It can also be used for any complaints about the NHS funding of registered nursing care in a home providing nursing (see p39).

The procedure is the same as that described on p51. Any existing care package, whether hospital care or community health services should not be withdrawn in any circumstances until the outcome of the review is known.

Complaining about social services

Social services must have a complaints procedure in place, and information about it must be published.[130] As well as Directions, there is the policy and good practice guidance, *The Right to Complain* (*A Right to Complain* in Scotland). To have the right to complain you must be a 'qualifying individual'– ie, social services has a power or duty to provide you with services and your needs or possible needs for a service have come to the attention of social services. Social services can use their discretion to deal with your complaint even if you are not a qualifying individual (for instance the person who used to get the services about which there is a complaint has died, or lacks the mental capacity to complain themselves).[131]

Each authority must have a designated complaints officer.[132]

The stages of your complaint

Stage 1 – the informal stage

If you have a complaint, social services must attempt to resolve it informally. Your complaint does not need to be in writing. The good practice guide states that just because a complaint is informal it does not mean it is casual. There does not need to be a written record, as this stage is one of negotiation and conciliation. There is no timescale, which can cause problems if a complaint drags on without resolution. If at this stage your problem has not been resolved within what you think is a reasonable time (which may well depend on the gravity of your situation), you should insist that you are allowed to go on to the next stage of the complaints procedure, and you may wish to take the delay up with the Ombudsman (see p58).

Stage 2 – the formal stage

At this stage you need to formally register your complaint in writing. Social services must offer you assistance (or let you know where you can get assistance – eg, advocacy) on the use of the complaints procedure. They could help you make sure you have covered all the points you want to make in your formal complaint.

Once it has received your complaint, social services must investigate it and respond to you within 28 days. In England and Wales, if the investigation will take longer, you must be told why (before the 28 days is up) and how long it is likely to take. However, the response must be within three months.[133]

These response times are often not met, especially in complex cases where a number of people need to be interviewed. If you think the authority is being slow you should point out the time limits and ask for reasons why they are not being met.

Social services must notify you in writing of the outcome of your complaint. They should also notify any other person who has sufficient interest. They do not need to give reasons for the decision.

Stage 3 – the review stage

If you are still unhappy with the outcome of your complaint you can, within 28 days of receiving the decision, ask for your complaint to be referred to a review panel.[134] This panel should hear your complaint within 28 days of your request, and you should be told 10 days beforehand of the time and place the panel will meet. In Scotland, the review committee has to make its recommendation within 56 days of your request.

The panel should be made up of three people. The chair must be an 'independent person' who is not a member of, or employed by, social services, or the spouse of such a person. The other two members can be any individuals whom the authority considers suitable. Often social services appoint a councillor as one member and an officer as the other. This can bring into question the independence of the panel. The guidance just says that at least one member has to be independent, so there is nothing to stop you asking for all the members to be independent of the authority.

The panel should be as informal as possible. It can be helpful to take someone along with you for support or to help present your case but it must not be a barrister or solicitor acting in her/his official capacity. There may be social services officers present in addition to the three panel members (you should be told in advance who they will be) and it may feel intimidating if, like most people, you are not used to such hearings. You may put your complaint in writing or talk to the panel. If you plan to give an oral submission it is worth making notes to make sure you keep to a structure and include all the points you want to make.

The panel should look at all the facts and re-examine the previous decision. It must reach its decision within 24 hours and give its recommendations and reasons to you, the local authority and to anyone else who is considered to have sufficient interest. If the decision is split between the three panel members this also must be recorded.

The panel should not take into consideration irrelevant factors. In one case the Ombudsman found against an authority where the panel came to the decision that, although the person had lost over £4,200 in benefit due to misleading advice, only a small amount of compensation should be offered as the panel thought it was not appropriate to reimburse lost benefit. This was considered to be an irrelevant factor.[135]

The social services department has 28 days (42 in Scotland) to decide what action to take, to notify you and all those who received the panel's recommendations, and to give reasons for its decision. It must have very good reasons for departing from the panel's recommendations.[136]

Complaints about the standard of care provided

If you have a complaint about the care that is provided by a regulated provider under the Care Standards Act 2000 in England and Wales and the Regulation of Care Act 2000 in Scotland, then you should complain to the provider under the complaints procedures that it must have in place as part of being regulated. It is part of the regulatory process that you should have details of the complaints procedure and how complaints are dealt with. You should also be made aware that if you are dissatisfied with the outcome of the complaint you can take up the matter with the National Care Standards Commission (England), the Scottish Commission for the Regulation of Care (which will be known as the Care Commission) or the Care Standards Inspectorate for Wales.

This does not debar you from also using the NHS or social services complaints procedures if your care was commissioned by either of these bodies. As a commissioner of services for your care, each has a responsibility to ensure the services are adequate.

Other remedies

At the same time as, or instead of, a complaint to health, housing or social services you may want to think of other action you can take. Sometimes it is difficult to decide which course of action will have the best outcome. It is useful to talk this over with someone experienced in community care issues. Most national organisations for older or disabled people have helplines and they may be able to suggest the options you could consider to remedy your situation (see Appendix 3).

Local action

There are other actions which could be pursued at the same time as a formal complaint or as a way of attempting to resolve your situation without recourse to the complaints procedure.

Local advice groups, your councillor or MP/MSP/National Assembly Member

Sometimes you can get help in resolving your problem with the authority by contacting a local advice group, your councillor or MP/MSP. In Wales, you can also write to your National Assembly Member (AM). Some gentle querying of a decision by a knowledgeable adviser may get to the root of the problem far faster than the complaints procedure. Councillors and MPs will often take up your case. Sometimes your MP/MSP/AM will pass your complaint to the minister responsible for health. This can sometimes lead to resolution, as officials will look at the complaint and, where necessary, take it up with the local authority or health service, although this is only likely to happen where the authority is clearly outside the law.

Local (or national) newspapers

Although you may want to think twice about going to the papers, sometimes in an urgent or very difficult situation it can resolve your problems. It has proved quite an effective remedy against waiting in hospital for funding for a care home, or against withdrawal of services.

Contacting the local authority monitoring officer

This is one of the lesser-known remedies which can at times be very speedy and effective. Each local authority is required to have an officer (often the chief executive) to ensure that the authority's policies and decisions are within the law.[137] If you think that a decision has been made which does not follow the law then a letter to the monitoring officer will ensure that the legal department looks at it. It may be worth making sure you are right before taking this action, but in an emergency it can produce a very swift response.

Using the Ombudsman

There is a Health Services Ombudsman for matters relating to the NHS and a Local Government Ombudsman covering all areas dealt with by local authorities. They can investigate cases of maladministration, which can be quite widely defined. The Local Government Ombudsman has issued 42 principles of good administration. These include:

- staff understanding the law and local policies;
- establishing the relevant facts;
- communication of policies and consistent application of policies;
- giving reasons for decisions;
- adequate record keeping;

- avoiding misleading statements;
- ensuring that decisions and actions are taken within a reasonable time.

You should make your complaint to either the Health Services or Local Government Ombudsman within 12 months of the action which you are complaining about. This time limit can be extended if it is reasonable to do so.[138] An investigator will examine your case, look at the relevant papers, interview you if necessary and interview the officers. Sometimes the investigations are discontinued either because it becomes apparent there was no maladministration or because the authority settles the dispute.

Some cases are reported. If that is to be done, you and the local authority or health authority will have an opportunity to comment on the report for factual correctness before it is finalised. If the case is reported, the authority will be named, but your name will be changed and the officers identified by a letter of the alphabet. Although Ombudsman decisions do not have the force of law, some can be very influential and become well known throughout local authorities and health services. They can occasionally lead to changes in law or to guidance. Sometimes they can influence practice not only in your area but others.

Complaints to the Ombudsman have the advantage of being free, so can be very useful if you cannot get legal aid to pursue your complaint through the courts. Their great disadvantage is that they can take a very long time: 18 months to two years is not uncommon.

If you have a complaint about your services which you have taken to the regulatory body in your country (see p17) and you are still dissatisfied, or feel that your complaint has not been properly dealt with you can take your complaint to the Parliamentary Ombudsman.

The Local Government Ombudsman

The Local Government Ombudsman can look into maladministration in any department of the local authority. S/he will look at the way a decision has been made, and if maladministration is found, may suggest financial compensation. In some cases this can be a considerable sum.

Many decisions have covered delays by housing (in particular disabled facilities grants and housing benefit) and social services – eg, waiting times for assessment or services. Sometimes decisions cover issues such as fettering of discretion, which could also be pursued through the courts.

You cannot complain to the Ombudsman without first having given the local authority the opportunity to answer your complaint.[139] Usually this will mean going through the complaints procedure. However, the Ombudsman will intervene earlier than this if the complaint is taking a long time, in which case this delay itself may be taken up as part of your complaint to the Ombudsman. Councils have eight weeks to respond to a complaint, after which the Ombudsman can be approached if you are not content with the response. You do not have to exhaust all stages of the council's complaints procedure. The eight-week time scale does not include complaints against social services though.[140] If you think social services is taking an excessively long time to respond to your complaint, you might still wish to write to the Ombudsman after eight weeks. The local authority is not obliged to follow the recommendations of the Ombudsman, but if it refuses it can be compelled to publish an agreed statement in a local newspaper.[141]

The Health Services Ombudsman (Health Service Commissioner)

The Health Services Ombudsman is known as the Health Service Commissioner. S/he can investigate complaints about the failure of a service, the failure to provide a service where there is a duty, clinical matters and maladministration. You must have already given the health service an opportunity to investigate your complaint.[142]

You can also use the Commissioner to complain against GPs, dentists, opticians who provide NHS services, and chemists.

The Commissioner can make suggestions for remedies if s/he upholds your complaint. You could get a decision changed or repayment of costs incurred. Sometimes the Commissioner recommends changes to procedures so that other people will not be similarly affected.

Secretary of State's default powers

If either social services or the NHS fail to carry out their duties the Secretary of State can declare them to be in default of their duty[143] and direct them to do so. In Wales these powers have devolved to the First Secretary of the National Assembly. In Scotland these powers have now transferred to the First Minister. In practice that step has never been taken, but if you write to the Secretary of State asking her/him to use her/his default powers, an investigation by officers of the relevant department may informally resolve your problem if the facts show that the authority is clearly in breach of the law.

Judicial review

The main legal remedy in cases which involve public bodies such as local authorities and the NHS is judicial review. Until recently rarely used, there is now an increasing body of caselaw and there have been some very important test cases addressing some of the most contentious community care issues.

The most common grounds for judicial review are:

- the decision is illegal (*ultra vires*);
- the authority has misunderstood the relevant law;
- the decision is unreasonable given the facts;
- the decision shows an improper exercise of discretionary power – eg, that the authority has fettered its discretion;
- the authority has taken into account an irrelevant consideration.

To take your complaint to judicial review you will need to seek legal advice and in particular discuss the costs, as it can be very expensive if you are not eligible for legal aid.[144] Judicial review can be a lengthy process, but at times, when your situation is very urgent, action can be taken within days and sometimes on the same day.

There are strict time limits and you must start your case within three months of the decision relating to your complaint. Normally your solicitor will write a 'letter before action' which tells the authority the grounds of the complaint and indicates that unless it is resolved, an application will be made to the courts to grant leave for a hearing.

Sometimes this letter itself will resolve the problem (often because the authority's legal department sees the case for the first time and realises there are flaws in the decision, or because a decision is made not to get involved in litigation). Courts are increasingly keen that disputes get settled by local resolution wherever possible.

If this does not happen you must seek leave from the High Court for a full hearing. Sometimes your case will still get settled before the full hearing. The Court can:

- overturn the decision and order the authority to take the decision again (*certiorari*). This can sometimes mean the authority could still make the same decision, but this time may make it correctly;
- forbid the authority to do something (*injunction*). This is often used as an interim way of making sure services are put back in place while waiting for the hearing by forbidding them to be withdrawn;
- oblige the authority to take positive action (*mandamus*);
- forbid the authority from doing something inconsistent with its legal power (*prohibition*);
- make a statement about your rights and the general legal position (*declaration*).

Your case may go on to the Court of Appeal either on the grounds that there is a realistic prospect of success on a point of law or that the case is of public interest and so merits a hearing in a higher court. Eventually your case could go to the House of Lords.

In Scotland, a similar process for judicial review exists through raising action in the Court of Session in Edinburgh. There are other (seldom used) remedies under Scottish law: consult an adviser or a lawyer for details.

European Court of Human Rights and Human Rights Act 1998

The European Court of Human Rights and Human Rights Act 1998 are beginning to have a direct effect on decisions made in community care. The Human Rights Act means that the same basic set of rights which you used to need to take to Europe under the European Convention on Human Rights are considered in UK courts. Even prior to the Act coming into force there was evidence that the courts were taking it into consideration in their decisions.[145] There have been a number of cases since the Act came into force, including cases on home closures and the independence of complaints panels.

The articles in the European Convention on Human Rights that are of significance in community care are:

- the right to life (Article 2);
- the right not to be subject to torture or degrading treatment or punishment (Article 3);
- the right to liberty and security of the person (Article 5);
- the right to a fair hearing by an independent and impartial tribunal (Article 6);
- the right to respect for family life, home and correspondence (Article 8).

The Convention includes the right to an effective remedy if a violation of any right has been committed by a public body. It also requires that your rights and freedoms are secured without discrimination.

Local authorities and health services should scrutinise decisions on the basis of whether they impinge on any of these rights.

This is a remedy which is likely to become increasingly common over the next few years and the extent of these rights will be tested in the courts.

Notes

1. **What are community care services**

1 s46(3) NHSCCA 1990
2 s5A(4) SW(S)A 1968
3 *R v Social Fund Inspector ex parte Connick*, 8 June 1993
4 DoE Guidance 17/96
5 CC(DD)(QS)(E) Regs
6 *Better Care, Higher Standards* DH/ DETR

2. **The responsibilities of social services: health and housing**

7 s2 Local Government Act 2000
8 *R on the application of J v Enfield LBC* CCLR, September 2002
9 *Community Care in the Next Decade and Beyond* – Policy Guidance – 1990. Assessment and care management SWSG11/1991
10 s7(1) LASSA 1970; s5(1) SW(S)A 1968
11 *R v North Yorkshire County Council ex parte Hargreaves* CCLR, December 1997 and *R v Islington LBC ex parte Rixon* CCLR, March 1998
12 *R v Islington ex parte Rixon* CCLR, March 1998
13 *R v Powys CC ex parte Hambidge* Court of Appeal CCLR, September 1998
14 LAC (93)7; WOC 41/93
15 LAC (93)10; WOC 35/93 Appendix 4
16 There have been a number of Ombudsman Reports on the extent of advice and the accuracy of such advice. LGORS 91/C/1246, 94/B/2128 and 93/A/3738
17 LAC (93)10; WOC 35/93 Appendix 2
18 SWSA 1968; SWSG 11/96
19 s94 SW(S)A 1968
20 s12(2) SW(S)A 1968
21 *R v Gloucestershire CC ex parte Barry* CCLR, December 1997
22 LAC (93)7; WOC 41/93

23 s1 CSDPA 1970
24 *R v Haringey ex parte Norton* CCLR, March 1998. Because these words are in the Act social services has to assess you for them if you are a disabled person.
25 Guidance is given in LAC (90)7; SDD40/1985
26 *R v Ealing LBC ex parte Leaman* (TLR), 10 February 1984 and *R v N Yorkshire ex parte Hargreaves* (No.2) CCLR, June 1998
27 The AMA/ACC issued a joint circular in 1971 but there has been no government guidance.
28 DHSS Circular 19/71 is the only and still current circular.
29 s21 and Sch 8 NHSA 1977
30 LAC (93)10; WOC 35/93 Appendix 3
31 s14 SW(S)A 1968
32 ss8 and 11 MH(S)A 1984
33 Under ss3, 37, 47, or 48 MHA 1983
34 s117(2) MHA 1983 and *R v Ealing District Health Authority ex parte Fox* 1993, All ER 170 QBD
35 LAC (96)8/HSG (96)11, WHC (95)6
36 *Clunis v Camden and Islington Health Authority*, CCLR, March 1998
37 *R v Manchester CC ex parte Stennett* HL, CCLR, September 2002
38 s1(2) MH(S)A 1984
39 s1 CDCA 2000
40 s2(3) CDCA 2000
41 s5 CDCA 2000
42 Carers and Disabled Children (Vouchers)(England) Regs 2003 SI 2003 No.1216
43 s6 CDCA 2000. Local authorities must take the assessment into account when deciding what, if any, services to provide under s17 CA 1989.
44 Draft CCD 10/2002
45 s6 LASSA 1970; s3 SW(S)A 1968
46 LGOR 92/A/4108
47 *Better Care, Higher Standards* DH/DETR
48 Speech by Secretary of State 23 July 2002
49 CC(DD)(QS)(E) Regs
50 *Guidance on charging policies for non-residential services that enable older people to remain in their own home. COSLA 2002*
51 LAC (2001)13; HSC 2001/008
52 s46 NHSCCA 1990; s5(A) SW(S)A 1968
53 LAC (91)16; SW1/91
54 Community Care Plans (England) Directions 2003
55 LAC (93)4; WOC 16/93/SW4/93
56 *Community Care and the Next Decade and Beyond – Policy Guidance* 1990 para 2.25; SWSG 11/1 para 7
57 *Policy Guidance* 1990 para 3.56 SWSG 11/91
58 LAC (94)24; WDC/6/92
59 LGOR 97/A/4069
60 s47(3) NHSCCA 1990; s12A(3) SW(S)A 1968
61 CC(DD)A 2003
62 s3 NHSA 1977 and Part III NHS(S)A 1978
63 See *R v N and E Devon ex parte Coughlan*, (CA) CCLR, September 1999 which discusses the duties of the Secretary of State to provide nursing.
64 HSC 2001/015; LAC (2001)18, WHC (95)7, WOC 16/95, NHS MEL(1996) 22 para 10
65 *NHS Funding of Long term care*, Health Service Ombudsman, February 2003
66 Further guidance on palliative care is found in EL (93)14 and EL (94)14; MEL (94)104
67 *Better Care, Higher Standards* DH and DETR
68 HSG (95)8 and LAC (95)5 (although note this guidance has been cancelled in England); WHC (95)7/WOC 16/95; NHS MEL (1996)22 para 17
69 *ibid* para 25
70 CC(DD)A 2003
71 NHS (GPS) Reg 1992
72 EL (91)28 Management Executive *Continence Services and the Supply of Incontinence Aids*
73 *Good practice in continence services*, DH 2000
74 HSG (96)34; MEL 92/67
75 HSG (96)53 and HSC 1998/004
76 LAC (2001)1; HSC 2001/001; NAFWC 43/02; WHC (2002)128
77 NAfWC 05/02
78 s47(3) NHSCCA 1990
79 s12A(3) SW(S)A 1968
80 Part VII HA 1996; Part II H(S)A 1987
81 DoE Guidance 10/92 SWSG 7/94
82 Part M Building Regs 1991 – Access and facilities for disabled people. Approved document 17 1999.

3. **Getting the services you need**

83 CC(DD)A 2003
84 s47(1) NHSCCA 1990; s12(A) SW(S)A 1968
85 s47(2) NHSCCA; s12(A) SW(S)A 1968; s4 DPSCRA 1986

86 ss4 and 8 DPSCRA 1986 and s1 CRSA 1995, s2 of this Act added a new s3A into the SW(S)A 1968
87 *Community Care in the Next Decade and Beyond* – Policy Guidance 1990, para 3.15
88 s47(5) NHSCCA 1990; s12(5) SW(S)A 1968
89 LAC (2002)1; CCD8/2001; NAfWC 09/02
90 *Community Care into the Next Decade and Beyond* –Policy Guidance 1990 para 3.20; *Assessment and Care Management* (SW11/1991) para 5.2.
91 LAC (2002)1; CCD8/2001; NAFWC 09/02
92 *R v Bristol ex parte Penfold* CCLR, September 1998
93 LGOR 97/A/4069
94 LGOR 94/C/1165 and 94/C/0805
95 LAC (93)2 SWSG 14/93
96 LAC (2002)1; NAfWC 09/02; CCD8/2001
97 s47(3) NHS and CCA 1990; s12A(3) SWSA 1968
98 *Community Care into the Next Decade and Beyond* – Policy Guidance 1990 para 3.9; Assessment Care Management (SW11/1991) para 5.
99 *R v Haringey ex parte Norton* CCLR, March 1998 and *R v Avon CC ex parte M* CCLR, June 1999
100 s1(1)V CRSA 1995 and s1 CDCA 2000
101 *Policy Guidance* 1990 para 3.27-3.29
102 s1(1)A CRSA 1995
103 LAC (96)7; WOC 16/96 para 20; SWSG 11/96
104 s1 CDCA 2000
105 CCH(S)A 2002
106 *Policy Guidance* 1990 para 3.56 EW.S; SW11/1991 para 5.9
107 CC(DD)A 2003
108 *Policy Guidance* 1990 para 3.52; SW11/1991 para 19.2

4. **How far the authority's resources can be taken into account**

109 s41(1)(b) NHSCCA 1990; s12A(b) SW(S)A 1968
110 CI (92)34 known as the Laming letter. Although cancelled in 1994 this letter is still used and quoted in legal judgments.
111 LAC (2002)13; *Fair Access to Care Guidance*
112 LAC (2002)13; NAfWC 09/02; WHC(2002)32
113 CCD 9/2002
114 *R v Bristol ex parte Penfold* CCLR, September 1998
115 *R v Gloucestershire ex parte Barry* CCLR, December 1997
116 *R v Gloucestershire ex parte Barry* CCLR, December 1997
117 *R v Sussex ex parte Tandy* CCLR, June 1998
118 *R v Birmingham ex parte Mohammed* CCLR, September 1998
119 *R v Lancashire ex parte Ingham (R v Gloucestershire ex parte Barry* (CA)) CCLR, December 1997
120 Q and A 8.5 *Fair Access to Car Practice Guidance*

5. **How to complain**

121 Directions were made under the NHSA 1977; NHS(S)A 1978 and HCPA 1995
122 EL (95)121, EL(96)19, and EL (96)58 (in Scotland, *Listening, acting, improving* Guidance on the implementation of the NHS complaints procedure 1996)
123 *NHS Complaints Reform – making things right*
124 *Your Guide to the NHS* DH 2001
125 LAC (2001)18; HSC 2001/015; WOC 16/95; WHC (95)7
126 LAC (2001)18: HSC 2001/015; WHC (95)7
127 Case E1626/01-02 Annex E of the Special Report *NHS funding of long-term care.* Health Services Ombudsman 2003
128 NHS MEL (96)22
129 LAC (2001)18; HSC 2001/015; LAC (2001)26; HSC 2001/17
130 s7B LASSA 1970 and *Complaints Procedure Directions* 1990; s5B SW(S)A 1968 and SW(RP)(S)D 1996
131 *Policy Guidance* 1990 para 6.5
132 Direction 4(1) England and Wales; Direction 3A Scotland
133 Direction 6(1) England and Wales
134 Direction 7(2) England and Wales; Direction 8(3) Scotland
135 LGOR 93/A/3738
136 *R v Islington ex parte Rixon* CCLR, March 1998 and *R v Avon CC ex parte M* CCLR, June 1999
137 s5 LGHA 1989
138 s26 LGA 1974; s9 HSCA 1993; s25 LG(S)A 1975
139 s26 LGA 1974; s25 LG(S)A 1975
140 Annual Report of the Local Government Ombudsman 2000
141 s31 LGA 1974
142 HSCA 1993

143 s7D LASSA 1970; s85 NHSA 1977; s211 LG(S)A 1975
144 Now called legal help (green form) and legal representation.
145 *R v N and E Devon ex parte Coughlan* CCLR, September 1999

Chapter 3

Supported housing and Supporting People

This chapter covers:

Even though you may encounter difficulties in trying to live independently in your own home, your personal care needs may not be so great that residential or nursing care would be a desirable, appropriate or available option. There are many different types of supported accommodation schemes which aim to meet different needs. Some offer accommodation which has been specially adapted or designed to suit particular physical needs. Others offer services with the support of wardens or other care staff and additional facilities, which may sometimes be supplemented by community care services arranged by social services (see Chapter 2).

Some supported housing schemes offer so much care and support that it can be difficult to distinguish them from care homes. The different terms used in this chapter to describe different types of supported housing do not necessarily have any particular significance in themselves for social security (or community care) purposes. The effect of a stay in supported housing on your entitlement to certain social security benefits will depend less on how your accommodation is described by your landlord or the provider of the accommodation than on any combination of the following factors:

- whether it is registered as a care home;
- whether the accommodation is owned or managed by a local authority;
- the extent to which social services or NHS powers and duties have been applied in accommodating you, or in assisting you with the costs of your accommodation;
- how long you have been living in your accommodation and any previous arrangements that may have been made to accommodate you.

These factors will determine whether or not your accommodation will be classed as a care home for the purposes of determining your entitlement to housing benefit, council tax benefit, attendance allowance or disability living allowance (see Chapter 7).

For further details of how your benefit may be affected by a stay in accommodation classed as a registered care home, and for definitions of registered care homes, see Chapter 17.

The accommodation discussed in this chapter is not treated as registered accommodation. If you are resident in such a supported accommodation scheme you may usually therefore claim social security benefits in much the same way as if you were living in ordinary accommodation. There will often be no need for social services to be involved in making any arrangements for you to live there. This means there will be no question of social services being seen as having responsibility for, or recovering any contribution towards, the cost of the accommodation. In other cases, although social services may be involved in arranging the accommodation, special arrangements sometimes apply.

Registration requirements are applied by the National Care Standards Commission (or Scottish Commission for the Regulation of Care or, in Wales, the Care Standards Inspectorate). These specify that establishments must be registered if they provide accommodation together with nursing or personal care (which includes assistance with bodily functions such as feeding, bathing and toileting, if required) for people who are or have been ill, disabled, infirm, mentally disordered or dependent on drugs or alcohol.[1] Establishments are no longer exempted from the registration requirements just because they do not also provide board.

The registration status of the accommodation you live in or are considering moving into will affect which benefits you can claim or which charges you may have to pay. If you are unsure, you should check with the accommodation provider, or with your local social services, or the Care Standards Commission (or, in Wales, Inspectorate, or the Scottish Commission for the Regulation of Care), or seek independent advice (see Appendix 4).

1. Supporting People

'Supporting People' is a new government programme which was implemented from April 2003. The aim of the programme is to ensure that supported housing services are funded from one single budget, are monitored for quality, and take into account local need. The programme requires the administrators of the Supporting People programme to consult with service users, providers and others involved in supported accommodation when developing their local Supporting People Strategy.[2]

The Supporting People programme is administered locally by the 'administering authority' on behalf of all the Supporting People partners. The administering authority is the local authority (for the different types of local authority see p12). 'Partners' include health trusts, probation services, social services and local housing departments.

All administering authorities have had to submit their local Supporting People Strategies to the government (the Office of The Deputy Prime Minister in England; the Scottish Executive in Scotland; and the Welsh Assembly in Wales). All housing support services will be reviewed during the first three years of the Supporting People programme to ensure that they are providing a good quality service that is needed locally in line with the local Supporting People strategy. The reviews will be carried out by the local Supporting People team and will take into account service users' opinions.

The Supporting People programme funds only housing support services, aimed at facilitating and enabling independent living. It does not aim to provide assistance with personal care needs, which remain the responsibility of social services (see Chapter 2). Housing support services include advice to enable you to maintain your accommodation and advice in using domestic appliances safely, or checking and advising on general health and safety problems. The services that administering authorities can provide under Supporting People and any exclusion (eg, personal care services) are laid down in Supporting People Grant Conditions and Directions (the definitions for each country vary).[3]

Until April 2003 most housing support services were charged through the rent system. Since April 2000 where users were eligible for housing benefit these charges were paid through the transitional housing benefit scheme.[4] In England the rules for charging and subsidizing for housing support services has changed and while many tenants will continue to be charged for services through their rents, in some areas the charges may be levied directly by the local authority. In Scotland, most authorities charge for support and the payment is collected by the local authority after the financial assessment (see Chapter 4 for further details on charging and assistance with paying support charges).

Information on Supporting People is available from your local authority and on the websites of the Office of The Deputy Prime Minister (www.spkweb.org.uk), the Scottish Executive (www.scotland.gov.uk/housing/supportingpeople) and the National Assembly for Wales (www.wales.gov.uk/subihousing).

2. **Sheltered and very sheltered housing**

The term sheltered housing (or very sheltered housing, depending on the level of support provided) is commonly used to refer to groups of flats usually supported by a warden and mainly intended for occupation by older people in an establishment which does not have to be registered as a care home. Sheltered housing schemes are commonly provided by local authority housing departments or housing associations, although many are also provided by profit-making bodies.

Sheltered housing schemes vary from services where an emergency alarm is provided and linked to a mobile on-call warden, to services termed as 'extra care' where higher level housing support is provided with a personal care package.

If you live in sheltered or very sheltered housing you will be able to claim social security benefits in the same way as if you were living in ordinary accommodation or your own home. For example, you could claim all appropriate income support personal allowances and premiums (or pension credit from October 2003), attendance allowance or any care/mobility component of disability living allowance for your own needs, as well as housing benefit to meet eligible housing costs (for the accommodation and for certain services which may include those provided by the warden) and council tax benefit to meet any council tax liabilities. Exemptions or relief (following a financial assessment) from Supporting People service charges may also apply. If you have personal care needs which the housing scheme cannot provide, additional community care services may be provided by social services, although you may be charged for them (see Chapter 4).

A sheltered housing scheme will, therefore, usually be more financially attractive both to you and to social services than a care home. You will also have greater security of tenure in a sheltered scheme (where you will usually be a tenant) than in a care home (where you will usually only have a licence to occupy). Until April 2003 most sheltered housing was not covered by the registration requirements for care homes, and therefore not subject to the same standards of inspection and monitoring, but the introduction of Supporting People has required service providers to be subject to quality monitoring and review as a condition of receiving Supporting People grants.

The level of support in some very sheltered (or 'extra care') housing schemes may be as great as, if not greater than, that provided in some registered care homes. The distinction in treatment for social security purposes will depend on whether the accommodation needs to be registered as a care home.

If you are considering sheltered housing you should check with the landlord or seek independent advice to see what arrangements will apply.

3. Hostels and other supported accommodation

Support services are provided in a range of designated 'supported accommodation' providing a wide range of services from single units to multi-occupancy with the tenants having entitlement to the full range of benefits. Some schemes which may be described as care homes or hostels do not have to be registered as care homes because they do not provide the necessary degree of personal care.

A wide variety of hostels offer support for those with a broad range of different needs (eg, for those with mental health difficulties or drug/alcohol dependencies) and the extent of the support available varies widely from hostel to hostel. Residents of hostels are normally licensees rather than tenants, but group homes are normally covered by tenancy agreements.

Some accommodation in certain parts of some registered care homes may be exempt from the registration requirements – eg, because no (or insufficient) personal care is provided. This may be because certain units of accommodation attached to the home are sometimes used for less dependent residents (or for staff). Sometimes these are self-contained units or bungalows in the grounds of the core home and are often referred to as 'cluster' homes. Similarly, some self-contained units may be clustered around the grounds of a core local authority care home or even in the grounds of a hospital. Units are often used to accommodate a number of residents together for mutual support and to encourage independent living.

If you are resident in a hostel or other supported accommodation hostel or similar accommodation, you can claim benefits in the same way as if you were living your own home (see Chapter 7), including income support (or pension credit from October 2003) and attendance allowance or disability living allowance. You can also claim council tax benefit to meet any council tax liabilities and housing benefit to meet eligible housing costs. Exemptions or relief (following a financial assessment) from Supporting People service charges may also apply. Additional community care services may be provided to meet personal care needs not provided in your accommodation – eg, help with getting up in the morning or provision of a day centre although you may be charged for them (see Chapter 4).

4. Adult placement schemes

Adult placement schemes are arrangements where (usually) social services find suitable carers to look after adults with personal care needs in the carers' own home. The National Association of Adult Placement Services defines the arrangements as:

> the provision of accommodation for vulnerable adults in the homes of specially recruited people living in the community who are approved for this purpose by an official agency. The carers undertake to integrate such service users into their household and provide appropriate help, for an

agreed fee, whilst the agency continues to ensure that both the carer and the service user placed receive support and assistance.[5]

Placements may be arranged on a long-term basis, or for short-term breaks, or for regular (sometimes even non-residential) befriending purposes. Such accommodation arrangements have the advantage of offering a home environment in the community and a greater degree of individual care and attention, which will have been considered more appropriate for a person's needs than a registered care home. Such arrangements are most commonly used to accommodate adults under pensionable age with severe physical or learning disabilities, but older and less dependent adults sometimes also opt for, or are placed in, such schemes.

Since April 1992 most adult placements in England and Wales have fallen within the scope of the registration requirements for small care homes. Some adult placements have escaped the registration requirements because they do not provide the required degree of personal care. In Scotland, it has been much less common for adult placements to be registered. These placements may therefore be covered by the Supporting People programme.

The term 'adult placement' has no particular significance for social security (or community care) purposes. The extent to which social security benefits may be relied on by those in adult placement schemes depends instead on whether the accommodation is registered as a care home or not, and how long the arrangement has lasted. It may also depend on the extent to which social services has been involved in the arrangements for the placement – eg, sometimes social services formally place adults with carers because they have a statutory duty to do so yet sometimes they merely introduce the adult and the carer who then make their own independent arrangements.

New placements in registered or unregistered adult placements from 8 April 2002 should be treated in the same way as for registered or unregistered care homes. If you first moved into an adult placement scheme before April 2002, your entitlement to benefits will have depended on your own particular circumstances (for further details, see the 2nd edition of this *Handbook*). If you have been entitled to a transitional payment of housing benefit as well as income support and attendance allowance (AA)/disability living allowance (DLA), these should continue in payment until you leave.

If social services is not making any payment towards the cost of your accommodation (even if they are paying towards the cost of any care you need) or if the accommodation is not registered (or if you were entitled before it was registered), you may also be entitled to AA/DLA (see p370). You may also be provided with community care services in respect of personal care needs which are not met by your carer(s), although you may be charged for them (see Chapters 2 and 4).

5. Abbeyfield Homes

Special arrangements apply to residents of homes provided by the Abbeyfield Society. Most Abbeyfield Homes are not required to be registered as care homes. Some of the services they provide are likely to be covered by the Supporting People programme (see p67). However, a small number are registered and some provide nursing care.

Residents of Abbeyfield Homes usually have their own room, although they may share communal facilities and meals, and are generally more independent than those who need residential care (residents are often moved into care homes when they become more dependent). All Abbeyfield residents are treated in the same way, as if they were in sheltered accommodation (see p68), except that residents in Abbeyfield Homes are treated as licensees rather than tenants.[6] They may therefore claim social security benefits as if they were in ordinary accommodation or in their own homes (see Chapter 7), which may include income support (or pension credit from October 2003), attendance allowance, disability living allowance, council tax benefit and housing benefit for any eligible housing costs. Residents may also be provided with community care services but may be charged for them.

6. Temporary stays in supported housing

Although social security rules have been designed to allow for your housing costs on your normal home to be met (by income support (IS) or housing benefit (HB)) during periods of temporary absences, and also provide that IS may be paid towards the costs of any temporary stays in a care home (see Chapter 17), the rules create difficulties if you need help with your housing costs on your own home *and* you need to pay for a temporary stay in supported housing (eg, for a period of respite for you and/or your carer, or as part of a programme of rehabilitation for alcohol/drug dependency).

If you depend on IS or HB for help with the mortgage or rent you pay for the home you normally live in, the housing costs on your own home will normally only continue to paid be for up to 52 weeks if you are temporarily absent because you are in a care home or hospital or you need medically approved care, or 13 weeks in other circumstances, for each period of temporary absence from your own home.

If you are away from your home for more than 52 (or 13) weeks, not only will your ongoing housing costs not continue to be met by IS or HB, but you will also permanently lose any entitlement you have to transitional HB for your normal home, and (unless you or your partner are aged 60 or over) there may be a waiting period before you can start to be paid housing costs with your IS when you return (see p172).

While you are receiving IS or HB for the costs of the home you normally live in, you are not usually entitled to receive IS/HB for the costs of any temporary stay in other (eg, supported) accommodation (other than a care home). You may, however, be paid IS/HB for two homes (for up to four weeks only) if you have moved into a new home and cannot reasonably avoid having to pay for the other one as well. HB guidance, which states that this only applies if you have permanently moved into a new home, may be wrong.[7] You may therefore be able to argue that if you need a temporary stay in supported housing, you should be able to claim HB for your temporary home as well as IS/HB for your normal home (but this may only apply for the first four weeks of any stay).

If you are unable to pay for the costs of temporary accommodation, social services *may* arrange to pay for it if they consider that you need it (see Chapter 9). Although they may then make a financial assessment to see whether you should contribute towards the costs, they may *make allowances* for any costs you still have to make to maintain your own home. In practice, because (unlike for temporary stays in a care home) you will not usually be able to claim any benefits towards the costs of your temporary accommodation, this may be a more expensive option for social services than a temporary stay in a care home, and they may be reluctant to consider meeting your needs in this way. However, they will not be able to *pay* for any costs on your own home even if you do not have sufficient income of your own to pay for them (eg, because you do not qualify for IS housing costs or HB because your temporary absence from it is for more than 13/52 weeks).

It may, therefore, be impossible to pay for the costs of prolonged temporary stays in supported housing without accruing debts on your own home. The only alternatives would be to arrange for a series of temporary stays (even if you only return to your own home for one weekend or day every 13/52 weeks), or for community care services to meet your needs as far as possible in your own home, or to give up your own home and move into supported housing or a care home on a permanent basis.

7. Housing support in your own home ('floating support')

Over the last few years there has been an increase in housing support services that are delivered into individuals' own homes to help them remain independent. This may be as a result of a crisis – eg, returning home after a stay in hospital. These services are often referred to as 'floating support' and do not include help with personal care but are aimed at providing low-level support to enable you to return or remain home. These services can be delivered to people living in owner-occupier accommodation.

Notes

1 s3 and s121(9) CSA 2000

1. Supporting People

2 Annex B Supporting People Programme Grant (England); s8 Supporting People Strategic and Interim Guidance (Scottish Executive); s3 Arrangement for the Implementation of Supporting People in Wales

3 Supporting People Programme Grant (England) Conditions 2003; Housing (Scotland) Act 2001; Guidance to Local Authorities on the Implementation and Administration of Supporting People in Wales

4 Sch 1b Housing Benefit (General) Regulations 1987; HB Circulars A47/99 and A10/2000

3. Adult placement schemes

5 *Information on the funding of adult placements*, National Association of Adult Placement Services, 1997

4. Abbeyfield Homes

6 *Abbeyfield (Harpenden) Society Ltd v Woods* [1968] 1 All ER 352, CA

7 Temporary stays in supported housing

8 Reg 5(5)(d) HB Regs; para 3.55.4 GM

Chapter 4

Paying for services at home

This chapter covers:

1. Charges for care services at home

Not many care services you receive either at home or in day centres will be free. Services provided as NHS health services are free. Local authorities though have the discretion to charge for most care services to help you remain in your own home, and most do charge.[1] Although personal care is free in Scotland for those 65 or over, it is likely that local authorities will still charge for other aspects of your care such as shopping and housework. Charges for housing support services are based on both national directions and local discretion. There are national rules to calculate charges for housing grants for people with disabilities (see p100) and national charges for health items covered by health benefits (see p95).

This section looks at what cannot be charged for by social services and the scope of the discretion to charge.

Services for which charges cannot be made (England and Wales)

- You cannot be charged for aftercare services provided under s117 of the Mental Health Act 1983 (see p35).
- If you have any form of CJD and use domiciliary care services you should be treated as automatically exempt from charges.[2]
- In England, if your care is under 'intermediate care' which is care aimed at helping you leave hospital earlier, or to avoid the need for you to go into hospital, then, since 9 June 2003, it will be free.[3] Such care is normally only expected to last for up to six weeks and will often be for a shorter time. It can be at home or in residential settings.
- In Wales, from January 2002 there is a similar scheme for home care aiming to help vulnerable people to have the care they need either on return from

hospital or to prevent inappropriate admission. It is normally for six weeks, although it may be more. There are also proposals to introduce intermediate care which will be free.[4]

- In England, if you have been assessed as needing community equipment it will be free. Minor adaptations of £1000 or less are also free.[5]

Services for which charges cannot be made (Scotland)

- You can get four weeks free care (including tasks such as shopping and housework) following a stay in hospital either overnight or for surgery as a day patient.[6]
- No charges can be made for day centres or travelling to day centres for people with learning disabilities.[7]
- Local authorities should not charge for services if you have a mental health condition and are subject to a community care or supervision order.[8]
- Personal care is free for those who are 65 or over. See Appendix 1 for the definitions of personal care, support and social care that should be free under the Community Care and Health (Scotland) Act 2002.[9]
- Guidance for people aged 65 and over recommends that local authorities should consider not charging for day care, aids and adaptations.[10]

How charges are decided (England and Wales)

It is up to each local authority to decide for what, if anything, it considers reasonable to charge.[11] If you can show social services that it is not reasonable to expect you to pay that charge then it can be waived or reduced to what is considered reasonable for you to pay.[12]

Guidance has been issued in England and Wales, commonly called *Fairer Charging,* to give a framework for local authorities to follow when deciding what is reasonable for you to pay.[13] All authorities in England must have policies in place which meet the requirements of the guidance by April 2003. In Wales, authorities must be working towards implementing the guidance from April 2003, with full implementation in April 2004. However, it was a manifesto pledge in Wales that home care would be free for older people with disabilities.

The question of reasonableness has been raised in the courts. In one case the 'overriding criterion of reasonableness' enabled social services to make charges long after the person had finished receiving services (in this case when compensation came through).[14] In another case the judge found that it was not necessary to consult about raising charges or when formulating a charging policy as difficulties in paying charges can be taken up individually.[15] However, a more recent High Court judgment concluded that when a local authority, which had consulted when first introducing its charging policy, had made some fundamental changes to this policy, 'fairness required that there should be proper consultation before they were introduced'.[16] *Fairer Charging* guidance makes it clear that consultation about charges and any increases or changes in charges is routinely expected. There is a requirement in the guidance that local authorities should specifically consult users on whether to take disability expenditure into account for users not in receipt of disability related benefits, whether to set an overriding maximum charge, and on their policies in relation to savings.

Which services are charged for?

Most authorities charge for home care, and nearly all charge for meals on wheels and meals in day centres. An increasing number charge for day care, and some charge for the transport to day care.

Who should be charged?

The legislation implies that only the service user should be charged. The *Fairer Charging* guidance confirms this by saying that the legislation envisages that councils will have regard only to a service user's means in assessing the ability to pay a charge. Family members should not be required to pay unless they are acting on your behalf and are responsible for your finances because you are unable to manage them, and so paying out of your money (see p284). However, there may be times when you could have a beneficial interest in the value of an asset – eg, a bank account, even though it is not in your name.[17] It is for the council to decide in the light of its own legal advice whether a request might reasonably be made for the partner to disclose such resources. Practice has varied considerably around the country regarding spouses/partners who may be asked for information about their finances, and their income and capital may be included in the calculation of how much you have to pay. If your spouse/partner's resources are being taken into account, or if you are charged the full cost if your spouse/partner refuses to give information about his or her resources, you should seek advice. This question has been the subject of an Ombudsman investigation, and it was found that the council's inclusion of a spouse's invalid care allowance (now called carer's allowance) and carer's premium in the initial assessment was wrong. However, it could take into account a spouse's means in deciding whether to reduce the charge because of hardship.[18]

Taking account of benefits

One of the most controversial aspects of social services charging is in relation to charging people who are on income support (IS), income-based jobseeker's allowance (JSA) or receiving attendance allowance (AA) or the care component of disability living allowance (DLA).

The *Fairer Charging* guidance offers a framework for local authorities to use for people in receipt of benefits such as IS, AA, or incapacity benefit. Your income should not be reduced below 'basic' levels of IS/JSA (this does not have to include the severe disability premium so might be less than you get in IS) plus a buffer of not less than 25 per cent above the basic IS level. Local authorities should exempt from charges anyone whose overall income does not exceed the defined basic levels.

Social services cannot charge against the mobility component of DLA or the war pensioner's mobility supplement.[19] However, the guidance allows charges to be made against what are known as the disability related benefits: the severe disability premium of IS; AA; DLA; constant attendance allowance and the exceptionally severe disablement allowance. It is open to local authorities to decide whether to take these benefits into account subject to the overriding principles that charges do not reduce a user's net income below basic levels of IS plus a 25 per cent buffer and they do not result in the user being left without the means to pay for any other necessary care or support or other costs arising from disability. Where disability benefits are taken into account, local authorities should assess your disability related expenditure (see below). In Wales, the treatment of disability related benefits has not yet been decided and is due to be implemented in April 2004.[20]

Fairer Charging guidance also refers to a case[21] where it was found wrong for an authority to charge more for daytime services because the person received the higher rate AA/DLA which included an amount for night time care. The guidance states that if the council purchases no element of night care, then the night care element (ie, the difference between the middle and higher rate) should not be taken into account as income in the assessment.

Taking account of your extra disability related costs

Most local authorities take disability benefits into account and so also have to allow for your extra costs of disability. Even if you do not get a disability benefit (eg, because you are in the six month waiting period for AA), there is nothing to stop you asking for your disability related costs to be taken into account. It is worth thinking about all the costs that you have that you would not have if you were fit and well. Some authorities list the typical items on their financial assessment forms, but you should mention other costs that you have. This could include a gardener, taxis, extra heating, special diet, hairdressing if you cannot wash your hair or the cost of maintaining equipment. If you need to buy extra care because some services are no longer offered by social services, or because a ceiling has been imposed (see p50), you should ask that this be taken into account when assessing your charge. You may well have significant extra costs in these circumstances.

The guidance lists examples of typical extra costs of disability, and there is also practice guidance to help local authorities decide in individual cases. If you think that not all your extra costs are being considered you should ask to see both the policy guidance and practice guidance.[22]

Some local authorities have chosen to allow a standard amount for disability related costs in order to avoid intrusive questioning. The amount allowed varies between authorities, but in all cases if your costs are more than the standard allowance, you should be given an individual assessment of your costs.

In Wales, it is proposed that there will be a set amount allowed for disability related costs but the figure has yet to be announced. In the meantime those authorities working towards following the guidance from April 2003 should take account of your disability related costs. Once the set amount comes into effect in April 2004 you can still ask for a full assessment if you think your costs are higher.

You should complain if social services refuse to take your extra costs into account (see p51).

Taking account of other income and capital

Other income you receive such as pensions (either state or private), incapacity benefits or private income can be taken into account. However, earnings must be disregarded. This is to avoid a disincentive to work. On the same principle, tax credits should also be disregarded, although at the time of writing there has been no guidance on this.

Most local authorities take your capital and savings into account. The *Fairer Charging* guidance stipulates that those that do should not set limits lower than those used for charges for residential accommodation when deciding if you should pay the full cost for your services or working out tariff income from your savings. For 2003/04 this is £19,500 upper limit and £12,000 for the lower limit (£20,000 and £12,250 in Wales). Local authorities can set higher limits if they wish.

Local authorities should have consulted specifically on their policies in relation to savings, including when service users may have a particular need for savings. They should also review cases regularly where savings are being used up by charges.

How charges are decided (Scotland)

Scotland has issued guidance on charges for non-personal care services for older people produced by the Convention of Scottish Local Authorities (COSLA).[23] The guidance on free personal care states that local authorities must ensure that until at least 31 March 2003 no individual should have paid more than s/he was previously paying, unless a reassessment of her/his care needs results in an increase of the level of non-personal services provided.[24] See p76 and the list in Appendix1 for the services that should not be charged for. However note there is some concern about the preparation of food as the Scottish Executive appears to have limited it to specialised meals (ie, pureed food). Seek advice if you are charged for help with meal preparation.

As yet there is no new guidance in Scotland for charging people under 65 for care which also includes personal care. Guidance which was issued in 1997 therefore should still be followed for people under 65.[25] However, the COSLA guidance states that some of the principles and practice of its guidance may be equally applicable to charging for other care services and other user groups. If you are a younger service user and think your charges are unfair it may be worth checking the COSLA guidance. The Scottish Executive intends to review the guidance produced by COSLA before deciding whether to use the powers to regulate charging for domiciliary care. This is not expected to happen until after October 2003.

The COSLA guidance for charging for non-personal services provides a framework that aims to maintain local accountability and discretion while encouraging best practice. The guidance recommends the following:

- charges should not take single older people and couples below the IS personal allowance and IS pensioner premium and a buffer of 12.5 per cent – ie, £115 for a single person and £175 for a couple;
- if income is above this level, charges should be based on a percentage taper, but charges should not exceed the cost of providing the service. The guidance gives a range of examples of different tapers;
- there should be a common approach to the treatment of income which would take into account net earnings, all social security benefits (with the exception of the mobility component of DLA) and be net of housing and council tax costs. Authorities should exercise discretion to disregard some forms of income – eg, war pensions and industrial disablement benefits. The guidance goes on to say that authorities may wish to include other disregards such as household insurance and water costs, or disability related costs. It reminds authorities of the caselaw about night time attendance allowance/DLA (see p140);
- in the case of couples both partners' income should be taken into account 'as both partners would benefit from domestic services provided to them';
- where the service user has dependant child(ren) there is a recommended fixed disregard of £50 for each child;
- local authorities should adopt capital limits similar to that applied in respect of IS but without an upper limit beyond which people would be refused service. Tariff income could start at £6,000 based on £1 for £250 or part thereof;
- that day care and aids and adaptations should be free, although a suggested midway position is that a charge for small items up to £20 could be made.

Information you should receive (England, Wales and Scotland)

You should receive information about your authority's charging policy. You will normally be asked to fill in a financial assessment. This should be done after your needs assessment (see p45) although in practice the two are often done at the same time. Under the new guidance you should also receive benefits advice at the time of your financial assessment, either by the person who is working out your charge or, if you prefer, from an independent source. In Scotland, it just states that local authorities should be proactive in benefit maximisation and that there should be dedicated staff.

Once your charge has been worked out, you should get a written statement explaining how much you need to pay and how to pay it. It should also explain how you can ask for your charge to be waived or lowered. Charges should not be made for any period before an assessment has been communicated to you. You should also not have any increase in charges before you have received notification of the increase.

Social services should offer you a choice of how to pay your charge.[26] If social services are not providing the service themselves but are using an independent provider, they may ask that you pay the charge directly to the provider. You should not be required to do this as, depending on the way your authority's charging system works, the provider could obtain knowledge of your finances, which raises issues of confidentiality.

If you have not received a service for any reason you should not be expected to pay for it unless you have received clear information about notifications of changes that will affect your charge – eg, you should know how much notice of cancellation you need to give in order not to pay if you are on holiday. You should not have to pay if your carer does not turn up. Some computer systems have difficulty in dealing with all the changes that can occur in a care plan. Complain if you think you have been charged for services you have not received.

If you cannot afford your charge

You should ask social services to look at your situation again and give them as much detail as possible to support your case – eg, extra costs you have because of disability, or whether capital is earmarked for a purpose.

Some people withdraw from the service because of the cost. Before you do this you should make sure the local authority will not waive the charge. Failing that, ask for a reassessment of your needs to establish that you will not be left at severe risk if you no longer receive, or have fewer, services. In a recent Ombudsman investigation a service user withdrew from services because of the cost. The officers were ignorant of the fact that care should not be withdrawn where someone refuses to pay, and the Ombudsman took the view that had they been aware of the relevant provisions the care would have been continued while the financial situation was sorted out.[27]

Social services cannot withdraw your service if you are unable, or refuse, to pay the charge. As social services has a duty to provide the service you need, this cannot be overruled by the power to charge. Both the new guidance and the previous advice note make it clear that services should not be withdrawn.

Social services can, however, recover the charge as a civil debt through the Magistrates' Courts (or Sheriff Court in Scotland).[28]

2. **Charges for housing support services**

Housing support services that used to be funded from a variety of sources are now integrated into a locally administered fund. It is known as Supporting People and the new system started in April 2003. The changes and a list of the types of services you get under Supporting People are explained on p67. You should continue to receive your housing support services but the way you are charged has changed. This is particularly the case if you used to get you support services met through housing benefit (HB) or income support (IS). You still get HB and IS for other housing costs that do not come under Supporting People services. This section explains how you will be charged for your housing support services.[29] In most cases you will still need to pay your charge directly to the provider of the housing support services, so you will not see any difference in the arrangements for collection. You should also not see too much difference in the amount you are expected to pay, as the aim has been to try to keep a 'steady state'. If you are a tenant, the local Supporting People team will pay a subsidy to your provider to cover the difference between what you are assessed has having to pay and the cost of the service. If you receive both home care and Supporting People services for which you are charged then it will depend on local arrangements whether you pay via your landlord or directly to the local authority.

People who do not have to pay for Supporting People services

You will not have to pay for your Supporting People service (or get full help towards the cost) if you:

- get HB;
- get IS/jobseeker's allowance (JSA) and used to have an amount paid in your IS/JSA for services that are now included in Supporting People services, or if you are a new owner occupier getting IS/JSA and are receiving housing support services and this receipt is included in the title deeds. As you are an owner occupier you will have an agreement to meet the charges for these services, and so you will be paid an amount to cover your supporting charge by your local Supporting People team, rather than receive it through your IS/JSA. If you were living in such accommodation prior to April 2003 and getting IS/JSA, you should have received a letter from the DWP explaining this and advising you to go to your local Supporting People team.[30] In England you will be paid in a lump sum for the year, and in Scotland and Wales paid on a monthly basis;
- are in a short term scheme aimed at bringing about or increasing the capacity for independent living in less than two years (note in Wales such schemes are funded directly by the Assembly rather than locally under Supporting People Revenue Grant Services and cannot be charged);
- your support services are part of your package of care under section117 of the Mental Health Act 1983;

- in Scotland, up to and including 31 March 2003, your housing support services were funded in full or in part by the special needs allowance package;
- in Scotland you are a 'protected tenant' (or the successor of a protected tenant) and you have been occupying and receiving housing support services for at least one month prior to 1 April 2003 (this just applies to services which were part of the rent pool for tenants in local authority housing or tenancies where the landlords used rent pooling). This protection lasts as long as you are a tenant in the same service. If you need to increase your Supporting People services then you will have to pay for the extra (but see p83 for getting help with these charges).

People who get transitional protection

If you were already getting help with your support costs you will get transitional protection if:

- you no longer qualify for HB just because the housing support services are no longer reckoned as part of your housing costs for these benefits. You should not be charged any more than you were for your support costs than you were while you were getting these benefits (allowing for inflation). This protection will continue until the service is reviewed. The review date should be agreed between the provider and the local authority but should normally take place within three years of April 2003;
- you no longer get IS/JSA because your housing support charges have been taken out of the calculation. You will receive an equivalent amount to what you would have received from the DWP. You will also continue to be passported on to council tax benefit.[31] There is no end date to this transitional protection while you remain in that accommodation;
- in England and Wales, you were already in a tenancy by 1 April 2003 where the support costs were pooled, you should be transitionally protected by getting services of the same level, quality, nature and cost until a service review has taken place (within three years of April 2003). After this review councils can still offer some form of protection against steep increases in your costs. New tenants can also be protected from the full charge until the first service review.

Getting help from the local means test

If you do not get HB or IS/JSA you can apply for help under the *Fairer Charging* guidance (see p76) or in Scotland the guidance issued in 1997 and if you are 65 or over the new COSLA guidance (see p79). Even if you get some transitional protection you can ask for extra help, it will depend on the local authority whether their local policies are more generous. Authorities have been told they must try to avoid a 'cliff edge' whereby someone who is only just above HB thresholds would be liable to pay the full support charge without any taper. There is though no requirement for authorities to reassess everybody who does not get full help or is not transitionally protected immediately. Your housing support provider should tell you about your right to apply for help. If you think you need help towards paying the costs of your support services you could ask to be assessed using the local authority means test. You should complain if you are refused an assessment to see if you can get help with your Supporting People charges.

If you get home care services as well as Supporting People services then you should be assessed under the local authority means test (although if you get HB your Supporting People charge will still be nil as you are exempt from charges for your housing support). The guidance in England and Wales states that *Fairer Charging* financial assessments should be used to determine charges for all new tenants who are not covered by transitional protection arrangements, although you will need to request an assessment. Local authorities in England have been told they should work towards full integration of Supporting People and *Fairer Charging* at the earliest date possible, thereby providing a uniform financial assessment approach to support and home care. If you live in an authority which does not charge for home care services, the authority could still decide to charge for Supporting People services and in this case it should use the *Fairer Charging* or COSLA guidance.

The system is very new and it remains to be seen how easily the framework for Supporting People matches that of *Fairer Charging*. In some authorities you might find that you are better off having a *Fairer Charging* calculation than you would be receiving transitional protection. It remains to be seen how local authorities deal with couples. The regulations in England state the authority may impose a charge for provision of a welfare service to 'any person' where a service is provided to that person.[32] It has yet to be established where the provision is to a couple of whom only one may need the service, whether the partners resources should be taken into account. The English guidance is silent on couples but the Welsh guidance suggests that it is relevant to consider the income of the whole household where the service is considered to be delivered to a household. No party who cannot be considered to be a recipient of a support service should have their income considered as part of the assessment. This might be an area which only gets decided through caselaw.

If you think your Supporting People charge is wrong you can complain to your Supporting People team. You should get details of how to complain. If your support charge has been worked out by using *Fairer Charging* then you use the complaints process that has been set up to deal with these complaints.

3. **Buying your own care**

If you are unable to get help with your care from the state you will need to consider other ways of obtaining help. You may have relatives and friends who will undertake caring tasks or do some gardening for you. However, you may need to pay someone to do these jobs. Sometimes you need to buy in extra care over and above that supplied by social services. The points to take into account if you pay for your own fees in a care home are described on p88.

This section looks at some of the practical issues of buying your own care. It applies equally whether you receive direct payments (see p88) or money from the Independent Living Funds (p91), or whether you are buying care yourself with your own money. See p21 for a brief description of ways in which you might raise money to pay for care. This *Handbook* describes the various benefits to which you may be entitled and the powers and duties of the various statutory agencies. Before you arrange your own care it is useful to check whether it should be provided for you if this is what you would prefer.

Note that social services cannot refuse to provide you with the services you need just because you are able to afford to pay for your care. If you are assessed as needing a service, it must be provided if this is what you wish.[33]

Finding a carer

If you have been assessed by social services but found not to need the type of care they offer, they may be able to give you information about local schemes which offer the service you need. Voluntary organisations sometimes provide domestic care, or have gardening or handy-person schemes, so may be a good place to start. Social services may also be able to give you a list of private and voluntary agencies in the area which provide care. Agencies which provide personal care are subject to regulation from April 2003 in England and July 2003 in Wales so you may prefer to use them rather than find your own worker. As well as the safeguard of having an organisation to complain to if things go wrong, you should be assured of getting the service even if the person who normally comes to you is unable to do so. If possible, try to use an agency which has been personally recommended. No date has been set for regulation of agencies in Scotland but it is expected to be late in 2003.

You may need to advertise for your own carer. You can do this in a Jobcentre Plus even if you only want someone a few hours a week or in local papers, or on a noticeboard. If you advertise you may want to consider how prospective applicants contact you. If you live alone and feel that you could be vulnerable you may want to think about using a PO box number, or asking a relative or friend if you could use their address or phone number.

Points to consider when paying for your own care

There are national and local organisations which help people who buy their own care using direct payments from social services (see p88) or the Independent Living Fund (see p91). There is also published information to help, particularly about employing your own staff. The National Centre for Independent Living may be able to give you details of this literature (see Appendix 3).

The following are a few considerations to take into account if you are paying for your own care:

- if you are employing your own carer it can be useful to have someone with you when you are interviewing applicants;
- you should always take up written references on someone you plan to employ;
- if you are using an agency or employing someone yourself, you should be very clear exactly what you expect, the number of hours to be worked, and how much you will be paying;
- if you are employing your own staff and do not know how much to pay, the local Jobcentre Plus will be able to tell you how much is usually paid for such work;
- if you have not employed people before, it is important to seek advice about your responsibilities as an employer and to check carefully what insurance cover you might need;
- it is useful to put everything in writing before the person starts working for you so you are both clear about the conditions;
- if you use an agency you should ask for a contract (although most agencies will offer you one and those agencies providing personal care will have to provide you with a clear statement of what you are getting and the fees that you will be paying as part of their registration requirements).

Notes

1. **Charges for care services at home**

1 s17 HASSASSAA 1983
2 *Fairer Charging Policies for Home Care and other non-residential Social Services*, DH 2001
3 LAC 2001(1) and CC(DD)(QS)(E) Regs
4 NAfWC 05/02 and NAWC 43/02
5 CC(DD)(QS)(E) Regs
6 CCD 2/2001
7 s11 MH(S)A 1984
8 s8 MH(S)A 1984 and SWSG 1/97
9 *See also* CCD/04/02 which gives guidance on the implementation of free personal care
10 Guidance on charging policies for non-residential services that enable older people to remain in their own home; COSLA 2002
11 s17(1) HASSASSAA 1983; s87(1A)(6) SW(S)A 1968, this was inserted by s18 HASSASSAA 1983
12 s17(3) HASSASSAA 1983; s87 SW(S)A 1968
13 *Fairer Charging Policies for Home Care and other non-residential Social Services*, DH 2001 LAC (2001) 32; NAfWC 28/02; NAfWC 17//03
14 *Avon CC v Hooper* (CCLR), September 1998
15 *R v Powys CC ex parte Hambidge (2)* (CCLR), September 1999
16 *R v Coventry City Council ex parte Carton and Others*, QBD(Admin), CCLR, March 2001
17 para 59 *Fairer Charging Policies for home care and other non-residential Social Services*, DH 2001
18 LGOR 99/C/1983 Durham City Council

19 para 25 *Fairer Charging Policies for home care and other non-residential social services*, DH 2001
20 NAfWC 17/03
21 *R v Coventry City Council ex parte Carton and Others*, QBD(Admin), CCLR, March 2001
22 Para 41 *Fairer Charging Policies for home care and other non-residential social services* and see also practice guidance issued in 2002. Both are available on the DH web site.
23 Guidance on charging policies for non-residential services that enable older people to remain in their own home; COSLA 2002
24 CCD 04/2002
25 SWSG 1/97
26 The Local Government Association has produced a Good Practice Guide for Discretionary Charges
27 LGOR 99/C/1983 Durham City Council
28 s17(4) HASSASSAA 1983; s87 SW(S)A 1968

2. **Charges for housing support services**
29 The information in this section is taken from Supporting People Guidance ODPM 31 March 2003 available at www.spkweb.org.uk; *Charging and Financial Assessment*, January 2003, Scottish Executive available at www.scotland.gov.uk; *Supporting People in Wales Charging* and *Financial Assessments for Recipients of Supporting People Services*, Welsh Assembly, March 2003 available at www.housing wales.gov.uk
30 IS/JSA Bulletin 10/03
31 IS/JSA Bulletin10/03
32 Local Authorities (Charges for Specified Welfare Services) (England) Regs 2003 SI 2003 907
33 Q85 *Fair Access to Care Practice Guidance*

5

Chapter 5

Financial assistance for services at home

This chapter covers:

1. Direct payments from social services

Instead of having the services you need provided or arranged by social services, you can choose to have a 'direct payment'. This means that social services pay you an amount of money equivalent to the amount it would have cost them to provide the service, so that you can choose how best to meet your needs. It is also possible to have some services provided by social services and some which you buy using your direct payment.[1]

Who can get a direct payment?

Once you have been assessed as needing community care services, you can get a direct payment if you are:

- 16 or over;
- a 'disabled person' (see p31) or a 'person in need in Scotland' (see p31)[2] (although from April 2004 in Scotland this is being extended to 'any person' who requires community care services);
- a carer (which includes parents of a disabled child) for whom the local authority has decided to provide services.[3] The ability to make direct payments to carers only applies in England and Wales. In Scotland, carers do not receive services in their own right (as they are considered to be partners in care rather

than service users), therefore they will not normally receive direct payments. However, from June 2003, it becomes a duty for local authorities to offer direct payments to be made to parents of disabled children to purchase services their children require;

- an attorney or guardian (see p284) in Scotland (only) to set up, alter and receive direct payments on someone's behalf from 1 June 2003;[4]
- willing to manage your direct payment;
- able to manage your direct payment either by yourself or with assistance[5] (although note above the different provisions recently introduced in Scotland).

In England, there are plans to consult on 'indirect payments' which could be paid to third parties to be spent on behalf of a person who is not able to manage a direct payment. However, the High Court has already decided that it is lawful to pay an independent trust that has been set up for the service user. In this case a user independent trust had been set up comprising of trustees who are the parents of the disabled person, and representatives of a disability organisation and the local authority. The Court held that this fell within the meaning of a 'voluntary organisation' within the terms of the legislation and so it was lawful for the local authority to pay the trust to provide the services needed.[6]

The regulations specify that some people, whose liberty to arrange their care is restricted by certain mental health or criminal justice legislation, cannot receive direct payments. This will apply if you are:

- on leave of absence from hospital under mental health legislation;
- conditionally discharged but subject to restrictions under criminal justice legislation;
- subject to guardianship or supervised discharge under mental health legislation;
- receiving any form of aftercare under a compulsory court order;
- under a probation order or you have been conditionally released on licence with a requirement to undergo treatment for a mental health condition, or for drug or alcohol dependency.

Policy and practice guidance stresses that social services should consider what assistance would enable a prospective direct payment user to manage, rather than assuming the person cannot manage. This is particularly important if the person has a learning disability, and may be able to manage with some help. It suggests that someone with a fluctuating condition may be able to manage if there is greater assistance during the time when the condition has worsened. It also suggests that if you receive a direct payment and have expressed a preference for this to continue when setting up an enduring power of attorney then it can continue.[7] In England, new guidance is expected during summer 2003 so information may alter.

From 8 April in England, as long as you will be able to manage a direct payment, it must be offered, and made to you if you decide you want a direct payment. This provision will come into effect in Scotland on 1 June 2003,[8] and is likely to be introduced in Wales sometime during summer 2003. Until now some social services departments have offered direct payments only to very small numbers of people or restricted them to particular client groups.

There is guidance and regulations covering direct payments paid to carers under the Carers and Disabled Children Act 2000.[9] Carers in England also receive vouchers for short-term breaks.[10] Vouchers are being piloted in three areas in Wales and the pilots will run for about six months to the end of 2003 and it is planned to launch the vouchers scheme in summer 2004.

What a direct payment cannot be used for

Direct payments cannot be used to pay:

- your spouse or partner living in the same house;
- a close relative, or her/his spouse, if s/he lives in the same house as you (close relative has the same meaning as for benefit purposes – see p169).[11]
  In England new regulations specify that if the authority is satisfied that securing the services from a spouse or close relative regardless of where they live is necessary to meet your need, or in the case of a child in need to promote the child's welfare, then the above restrictions do not apply.[12] It is expected the new guidance will reflect this;
- for residential accommodation for any period of more than four weeks in a 12-month period. Within this time, periods of less than four weeks separated by periods of more than four weeks will not be added together.[13] In England for a child it is 120 days in any 12-month period;[14]
- for purchasing services from social services. However, in Scotland from 1 June 2003 you can purchase services from the local authority.[15]

The level of your direct payment

The direct payment should not normally be more than it would have cost social services to provide (or arrange) the service themselves. It should be enough for you to cover all the legal costs of being an employer – ie, national insurance contributions, annual leave, sick pay, employers' liability insurance. If circumstances warrant it, social services should be prepared to go above the cost they would normally incur in providing the same services.

If you manage to buy services more cheaply than expected, your direct payment may be reduced to that level rather than allowing you to use what is left over to buy in other services that are not specified in your care plan.

Any charges you would have had to pay if you had been receiving services from the authority will normally be deducted from direct payments (see p95 for a description of domiciliary charges). It is possible, however, for the payment to be made in full and for you to pay any required charges back.

Monitoring and support

Social services has to monitor the direct payment to make sure you do not misuse it and that your needs are being adequately met. They can recover money if it has not been used for the services for which it was paid, or if you have not kept to conditions that may have been imposed.[16] Social services has been told honest mistakes should not be penalised.

When setting up direct payment schemes, social services should ensure there is a support group to provide appropriate information, advice, training and peer support. Such groups often produce leaflets about recruiting someone to care for you (often known as personal assistants), dealing with the administration of the direct payment, being a good employer, and dealing with emergencies. Ask social services or the National Centre for Independent Living (see Appendix 3) to put you in touch with a local support group.

2. The Independent Living Funds

There are two Independent Living Funds which may make cash payments to you so you can employ carers to help you live independently in your own home. These are government funded, independent and discretionary trust funds managed by a Board of Trustees. A legally binding trust deed sets out the scope of the schemes. Awards are discretionary, but the trustees must follow basic eligibility criteria and guidelines.[17]

The Independent Living (Extension) Fund took over from the original Fund which was set up in 1988 as an interim measure until the implementation of community care legislation and a review of social security benefits for people with disabilities. It was wound up in 1993 and no new applications are accepted. You can only get help if you were being assisted under the original arrangements. These were relatively generous, and often enabled people to buy care without any involvement from social services before the new community care arrangements were introduced. The maximum payment is £665 a week.

The Independent Living (1993) Fund applies to all new applications for assistance and works in partnership with social services to devise 'joint care packages' combining services and/or direct payments from social services (see p88) with cash payments from the Fund. Applications to the 1993 Fund can only be made through social services. The Fund will then arrange for one of its own social workers to discuss your care needs with you and negotiate an appropriate joint care package (and provide advice and assistance with meeting the duties you will have as an employer of your carers).

The maximum payment from the Fund is £395 a week.

To be eligible for help from the Independent Living (1993) Fund you must:

- be so severely disabled that you need help with personal care or household duties to maintain an independent life in the community; *and*
- be living alone or with people who are unable to fully meet your care needs. No payments will be made in respect of paying a partner or close relative who lives with you but payment may be made to those who do not. In such cases, the carer may also be able to claim carer's allowance for looking after you, although this means that your contribution may be reduced if you are no longer entitled to the severe disability premium; *and*
- be at least 16 and under 66 years old. But if you apply before you are 66 you carry on getting payments from the fund; *and*
- be receiving the higher rate care component of disability living allowance (DLA – see p140); *and*
- be receiving income support (IS) or jobseeker's allowance (JSA) (or have an income at or about that level after you have contributed to your own care costs but note earnings of yourself and your partner are disregarded – see below);[18] *and*
- have less than £18,500 in savings including the savings of your partner; *and*
- be receiving direct payments or services costing at least £200 a week (after any charge you pay for them) from social services. The cost to social services for providing home care, day centre care, supervision, regular respite care and meals on wheels, for example, *less* any charge you pay to them for such services, will count towards the £200, but capital or running costs of any equipment, social work salaries, services provided by the NHS, and childcare costs, for example, do not count. The costs of any services provided under the Supporting People programme (see p67) also do not count;[19] *and*
- it is expected that the cost, to the ILF and social services together, of meeting your support needs for the first six months will be less than £665 a week; *and*
- have care needs that are generally stable and will be met by the joint care package for the following six months.

This last condition means that some terminally ill people may not qualify. The requirement that you must be in receipt of DLA may cause practical problems if there is any delay in processing your claim as no retrospective awards are ever paid and social services may be reluctant to arrange care packages costing over £200. It may also cause practical problems if your award is terminated or reduced. Although the Fund will continue to make payments provided you are seeking a review of or appealing against the decision to stop or reduce your benefit until any appeal has run its course, you will still be expected to pay your contribution to the care package based on the award of DLA you will no longer have (see below).

There are special rules about funding costs above £575 a week. If the cost is between £575 and £625 a week, the maximum payment from the Fund will remain at £375 a week, with social services putting in the balance. If the initial cost falls between £625 and £665, the amount above £625 must be divided equally between social services and the Fund. The ceiling of £665 a week can be reviewed after six months, although any extra requires social services to top up the maximum paid by the Fund.[20]

Contributions toward your Independent Living Funds payments

If you meet the eligibility criteria, you will usually be expected to make a contribution to the Fund towards the cost of your care. This applies to both funds. It will be half of your DLA care component plus all of your severe disability premium if it is payable with any IS/JSA you receive (see p169). If you do not get IS/JSA you will be expected to contribute any income in excess of the amount you would get if you did qualify. However, earnings of either you or your partner are disregarded. If you do have other excess income, the calculations are based on IS rates, except that most housing costs (including all mortgage payments and endowments or rent, and council tax and water rates liabilities) and child support maintenance payments are usually allowed. Tariff income is assumed on capital above £11,500. The Independent Living Fund will also usually refuse to become involved if a substantial sum is held in a trust fund for you. However, there is discretion to ignore capital which is intended for imminent major purchases, and in line with IS/JSA capital from lump sum payments for vaccine damage, former Far Eastern prisoners of war and victims of CJD are disregarded (see p226).

If you are paying charges to social services for the care they are providing, this may also be taken into account. For a new application, this means that if social services expects you to contribute all or part of your award of DLA and/or severe disability premium, the Fund may offset this from any contribution it would otherwise expect from you. In practice this means that you are expected to pay, in total, the higher of the amount that either the Fund or social services require you to pay. The Fund will not, however, reduce its charge if social services increase their charges.

If your needs change

If there is a significant change in your circumstances the Fund will reassess, and may increase, your award if appropriate and if there are sufficient funds in its budget. The Fund will not, however, increase its own contribution if the change is due to any reduction in care provided by social services or to a new or increased charge payable to them for their services. If your award is under the Extension Fund, it may contact social services about any extra services you now need which they should provide. If the Fund agrees to pay any extra, this will be subject to a total limit of £665.

If your award is under the 1993 Fund it will always attempt to renegotiate a care package with social services to see who should take on responsibility for meeting any of your additional needs. Provided you have been receiving assistance for a reasonable period (usually six months), the 1993 Fund's contribution will not be discontinued (and there appears to be no limit to how much it may be increased by, budgets permitting) even if social services consider it necessary to increase their contribution to the extent that the total cost of the care package then exceeds £665.

For either of the funds, any services provided by social services in respect of your increased needs are subject to a charge, the Fund may offset this charge from any contribution you would otherwise be expected to make.

Awards will be suspended if you go into hospital or a care home. However, if you privately employ a carer, you can apply for an appropriate retainer to be paid for up to four weeks to avoid potential disruption of care. Payments are reinstated if you return home within 26 weeks.

Two further changes have been announced which are planned to come into effect at some stage. These are:

- payments to privately employed personal assistants for up to eight weeks following the death of a client; *and*
- allowing the maximum sum to be exceeded in any week if the annualised average weekly payment does not exceed this maximum payment. This is to enable unexpected costs to be met, such as replacement care where a regular carer is sick.

Complaints or appeals may be made to the Director of the Funds and may be considered by a subcommittee of the Board of Trustees. For details contact your local social services department or the Independent Living Fund (see Appendix 3).

3. Special funds for sick and disabled people

The Macfarlane and Eileen Trusts

The Macfarlane Trust, the Macfarlane (Special Payments) Trust, and the Macfarlane (Special Payments) (No.2) Trust make payments to haemophiliacs who contract HIV through blood transfusions or tissue transplants.

The Macfarlane Trust also administers the Eileen Trust which helps people infected with HIV through NHS blood transfusions or transplants.

For further information, contact the Macfarlane Trust, PO Box 627, London SW1H OQG (tel: 020 7233 0342).

The Family Fund

The Family Fund gives grants and other help to families with children who have severe disabilities. It commonly helps with holidays, furniture, equipment and transport needs.

For information, contact the Family Fund, PO Box 50, York YO1 1UY (tel: 01904 621115).

4. Health benefits[21]

This section deals with the following areas of provision under the NHS:

- prescriptions;
- dental treatment and dentures;
- sight tests;
- glasses;
- wigs and fabric supports;
- fares to hospital.

Although the NHS generally provides free health care, there are charges for the items listed above. You will be exempt from these charges, however, if:

- you, or a member of your family, are receiving income support (IS – see p210) or income-based jobseeker's allowance (JSA – see p175); *or*
- you, or a member of your family, have an annual income of £14,200 or less (for tax credit purposes) and get:
  - both working tax credit (WTC) and child tax credit; *or*
  - WTC with a disability element paid in it; *or*
  - child tax credit but are not eligible for WTC as you work less than 16 hours;
- you have an NHS tax credit exemption certificate; *or*
- you are a permanent resident in a care home and social services are assisting you with the costs of your accommodation (if you are not receiving social services funding, you may qualify for help under the low income scheme – see p98); *or*
- you are under 16; *or*
- you are under 19 and in full-time education; *or*
- you are a war disablement pensioner and you need the item or service because of your war disability; *or*
- you are an asylum seeker (or the dependant of one) who is receiving support from the National Asylum Support Service or a local authority; *or*
- you are aged 16 or 17 and being financially maintained by a local authority after being in local authority care; *or*
- your income is low enough (see p98).

You may also be exempt from some charges because of your age or health condition. If you are not exempt on any of the above grounds, you may be entitled to remission of charges under the low income scheme (see p98).

Prescriptions

You qualify for free prescriptions if:

- you are in one of the exempt groups listed on p95; *or*
- you are aged 60 or over; *or*
- in Wales only, you are aged under 25; *or*
- you are pregnant or have a child under the age of one; *or*
- you suffer from one or more of the following conditions:
  - a continuing physical disability which prevents you leaving your home except with the help of another person;
  - epilepsy, requiring continuous anti-convulsive therapy;
  - a permanent fistula, including a caecostomy, ileostomy, laryngostomy or colostomy, needing continuous surgical dressing or an appliance;
  - diabetes mellitus (except where treatment is by diet alone);
  - diabetes insipidus and other forms of hypopituitarism;
  - myxoedema, hypoparathyroidism or myasthenia gravis;
  - forms of hypoadrenalism (including Addison's disease) for which specific substitution therapy is required.

If you are diagnosed with one of these conditions you need to get a form FP92(A) or EC92(A) in Scotland, from your GP or hospital to get your exemption certificate.

If you need a lot of prescriptions but do not qualify for free prescriptions, you can save money by buying a pre-payment certificate for four months or a year (apply on form FP95, or EC95 in Scotland, available from DWP or post offices). You can now pay by credit or debit card by phoning 0845 850 0030.

Dental treatment and dentures

You qualify for free NHS dental treatment (including check-ups) and appliances (including dentures) if:

- you are in one of the exempt groups listed on p95; *or*
- you are aged under 18 (in Wales, for an examination only, you are aged under 25 or over 60); *or*
- you are pregnant or have a child under the age of one.

Sight tests

You qualify for a free NHS sight test if:

- you are in one of the exempt groups listed on p95; *or*
- you are aged 60 or over; *or*
- you are registered blind or partially sighted; *or*

- you have been prescribed complex lenses; *or*
- you suffer from diabetes or glaucoma; *or*
- you are aged 40 or over and are the parent, brother, sister or child of someone suffering from glaucoma; *or*
- you are a patient of the Hospital Eye Service.

If you cannot get to the opticians for a sight test you may be able to arrange for an optician to visit you at home. If you are entitled to a free NHS sight test, you will not have to pay for the visit.

Glasses

You qualify for a voucher which you can use to buy or repair glasses or contact lenses if:
- you are in one of the exempt groups listed on p95; *or*
- you are a Hospital Eye Service patient needing frequent changes of glasses or lenses; *or*
- you have been prescribed complex lenses.

You must:
- need glasses or contact lenses for the first time or because your old glasses have worn out; *or*
- have a different prescription than previously; *or*
- have lost or damaged your glasses or lenses because you are ill and you need complex lenses, or you are getting a qualifying benefit (see p95) or qualify for help under the low income scheme (see p98).

Wigs and fabric supports

You qualify for free wigs and fabric supports if:
- you are in one of the exempt groups listed on p95; *or*
- you are a hospital in patient when the wig or fabric support is supplied.

Fares to hospital

You qualify for help with your fares to hospital if:
- you are in one of the groups exempt from charges under the rules set out on p95; *or*
- you are a patient at a genito-urinary clinic more than 15 miles from your home (more than five miles if you need to attend on a weekly basis).

You are entitled to payment for the cost of travelling by the cheapest means of transport available. This usually means standard class public transport. If you have to go by car or taxi, you should be paid your petrol costs or taxi fare, and car parking charges where they are unavoidable. The travel expenses of a companion can also be met if you need to be accompanied for a medical reason.[22]

If you are travelling abroad to receive NHS treatment, you are entitled to payment for the cost of travel to and from the airport, ferry port or international train station if you are in one of the above groups. You are also entitled to payment or repayment of onward travelling expenses to the treatment centre, whether or not you fall within one of the above groups (the amount and mode of transport is determined prior to travel by the health authority).

If you are receiving IS or JSA you may also be eligible for help from the social fund with the costs of visiting a close relative or partner (see Chapter 7).

The low income scheme

You may be entitled to full or partial remission of NHS charges on the grounds of low income if you are not already exempt on other grounds. To qualify for help under the low income scheme you must have less than £8,000 capital (£12,000 if you or your partner are aged 60 or over). If you are not receiving social services funding in a care home (and so entitled to full help) you may be entitled to help under the low income scheme based on the capital limits in the country in which you live (see p315). See Chapter 12 for details of how your capital is calculated. A calculation is then carried out to compare your 'income' with your 'requirements' (see below). If your income is less than your requirements, you are exempt from health charges. If your income exceeds your requirements, the amount of your excess income determines how much help you get with health charges.

Income

Your income is calculated in the same way as for IS (see Chapter 8) except that:

- your income is normally only taken into account in the week in which it is paid;
- regular maintenance payments count as weekly income and irregular payments are averaged over the 13 weeks prior to your claim;
- insurance policy payments for housing costs not met by IS count as income but payments for unsecured loans for repairs and improvements (including premiums) are ignored;
- the capital limit for tariff income (see p233) is based on the lower capital limit of the country where you live (see p315) if you are permanently in a care home;
- student loans are divided by 52, unless you are in your final year or doing a one-year course, in which case the loan is divided by the number of weeks you are studying (a £10 disregard from loans applies if you are eligible for a premium or you receive an allowance for deafness).

Requirements

Your requirements are the same as your IS applicable amount would be (see p169) except that:

- you are entitled to normal allowances, whatever your immigration status is;
- the disability premium (see p170) is included after 28 (instead of 52) weeks of incapacity;
- your housing costs include interest and capital payments on all loans secured on your home, any loans to adapt your home for the needs of a disabled person, any council tax liabilities (less council tax benefit), and any rent (less housing benefit). Deductions are made in respect of any non-dependants (see p186).

Excess income

Your excess income is the difference between your income and your requirements.

- The amount of help you can claim for hospital fares is reduced by the amount of your excess income.
- The cost of a sight test is reduced to the amount of your excess income if lower, plus the amount by which the cost exceeds the NHS sight test fee.
- The value of a voucher for glasses or lenses is reduced by twice your excess income.
- Charges for dental treatment and for wigs and fabric supports which are higher than three times your excess income are remitted.
- You cannot get partial remission of charges for prescriptions.

Applications for help with health care costs

- If you are exempt because of age or receipt of a qualifying benefit or tax credit, you need to complete the declaration on the back of the prescription form, or complete a form provided by your dentist, optician or hospital receptionist before you receive treatment.
- To claim free prescriptions because you have a prescribed condition, you should apply for an exemption certificate on form FP92A (EC92A in Scotland), obtainable from your doctor, hospital or pharmacist.
- If you are pregnant, or have a child under one, you should apply for an exemption certificate on form FW8, obtainable from your doctor, midwife or health visitor.
- For free treatment for war pensioners contact the Veterans Agency (previously called the War Pensions Agency) for details (tel: 0800 169 2277).
- To apply for remission of charges on the grounds of low income, you need to complete form HC1. If you are supported by the local authority and are either in a care home, or are 16 or 17 and recently left care, you should use HC1(SC). Both these forms should be available from your doctor, dentist, optician, hospital or DWP office. They are also available from the Health Literature Line (0870 155 5455). If you qualify for free services you will be sent a certificate HC2. If you qualify for partial remission you will be sent certificate HC3. Another person can apply on your behalf if you are unable to act for yourself.

Certificates are normally valid for six months, or 12 months if you are 60 or over or entitled to a disability premium or living permanently in a care home.

- You will normally be asked to provide proof that you are entitled to full or partial remission of charges, although you should not be denied an item or service if you are unable to provide the required evidence. If you receive help to which you were not entitled, you can be issued with a penalty notice requiring you to pay the charge you should have paid plus a penalty of five times that charge (up to a maximum of £100).
- If you pay a charge for an item or service which you could have obtained free or at reduced cost, you can obtain a refund by applying within three months (or longer if you have good reasons) on form HC5 (FP57 or EC57 for prescriptions but you have to get it when you get your prescription) available from your chemist, optician, dentist, hospital or DWP office.

Health care equipment

Health care equipment such as special footwear, leg appliances, wigs, surgical supports, wheelchairs, incontinence pads, hearing aids and low vision aids can be provided by health authorities, hospitals and GPs, either free of charge or on prescription.

5. Housing grants in England and Wales

This section briefly covers the availability of housing grants in England and Wales. A similar system exists in Northern Ireland. See p103 for grants in Scotland.

In July 2002 the Government introduced new regulations governing how local authorities assist with housing repairs, adaptations and improvements.[23] These were legislated through the Regulatory Reform (Housing Assistance) Order 2002. The Order repeals the detailed legislation provisions with respect to housing grants, home repair assistance and other such grants. Instead, it gives each local authority the flexibility to determine policies and procedures which best meet local housing priorities with locally developed solutions. Assistance can be given in the form of a grant, loan, materials, labour or advice (or any combination of these). In order to provide assistance under the Order a local authority must adopt and publish a local policy. You should contact your local housing department to find out what is available in your area.

Disabled facilities grants

While the Order repealed legislation on other housing grants, it maintains the disabled facilities grant (DFG) as the only mandatory grant which local authorities have a duty to make available.

DFGs are means-tested and are available for the provision of facilities for a disabled person, in a dwelling (including some mobile homes and houseboats) or a common part of a building (eg, a staircase) containing one or more flats.

You can apply for a DFG if you are a:

- home-owner;
- private tenant;
- landlord with a disabled tenant; *or*
- housing association tenant.

You are treated as disabled if:

- your sight, hearing or speech is substantially impaired; *or*
- you have a mental disorder or impairment; *or*
- you are physically substantially disabled by illness, injury, or impairment present since birth, or otherwise; *or*
- you are registered (or could be registered) as disabled with social services. If you are not registered disabled an occupational therapist or disablement assessment officer will usually assess your needs.

Mandatory grants (up to a maximum of £25,000 (£30,000 in Wales)) can be awarded for:

- facilitating disabled access to and from a dwelling or a room;
- provision of a bedroom, toilet, bathroom, shower or wash basins;
- making a dwelling safe;
- facilitating a disabled occupant's use of a source of power, light or heat, or food preparation facilities;
- improving or providing a suitable heating system; *or*
- facilitating access and movement around the home to enable the disabled occupant to care for someone dependent on them who also lives there.

The means test is similar to that which applies to housing benefit (HB – see p180) except that:

- there are no non-dependant deductions;
- the applicable amount is increased by £51.60 (£67.08 for disabled children);
- if you are on income support (IS)/income-based jobseeker's allowance (JSA), the applicable amount is automatically £1 and your income and capital are disregarded, giving a zero contribution;
- there is no maximum capital limit and the first £6,000 is disregarded (with tariff income applying on capital above this);
- if you are disabled or a carer, the earnings disregard is £15;
- there is a system of stepped tapers on excess income which is used to calculate how much you would be able to repay on a notional loan to pay for the work

over a period of 10 years for owner-occupiers and five years for tenants. The national means-test does not apply to applications from landlords.

Applications should be made to your local housing department, which must then consult with social services. In practice, people are commonly referred first to social services who then arrange for an occupational therapy assessment. Applications should be determined within six months and if approved, the work should normally be carried out within one year. Housing departments have a discretion to approve a grant but stipulate that it will not be paid for up to a year after the application was made, and may revise their decision if your circumstances change before the works are completed.

If you do not get a decision within six months of applying, contact the housing department to determine why and request that a decision be made. Seek advice if you still do not get a decision (see Appendix 4).

Warm Front grants in England

The 'Warm Front' scheme offers grants for improvements in insulation and heating systems to owner occupiers and tenants in England.[24]

You can qualify for a 'Warm Front' grant of up to £1,500 if:

- you have a child under 16 or are at least 26 weeks pregnant (you must have a maternity certificate MAT B1) and are receiving any of the following benefits:
  - IS;
  - HB;
  - council tax benefit (CTB);
  - income-based JSA; *or*
- you own or privately rent your home and receive one or more of the following benefits:
  - working tax credit (WTC) (with a household income less than £14,200 a year);
  - child tax credit (CTC) (with a household income less than £14,200 a year);
  - disability living allowance (DLA);
  - attendance allowance (AA);
  - IS (which must include a disability premium);
  - HB (which must include a disability premium);
  - CTB (which must include a disability premium);
  - war disablement pension (which must include the mobility supplement or constant attendance allowance);
  - industrial injuries disablement benefit (which must include constant attendance allowance).

To qualify for a 'Warm Front Plus' grant of up to £2,500, you must be aged 60 or over and getting IS, income-based JSA, WTC, HB or CTB. You may also be entitled to help with security costs (including locks) if you live in a specified 'high crime area'.

For more details call freephone 0800 952 1555.

Home Energy Efficiency Grants in Wales

The Home Energy Efficiency Scheme (HEES) offers grants for improvements in insulation and heating systems to owner occupiers and tenants in Wales.[25]

To qualify for a grant of up to £1,500 you must be getting:

- WTC (with a household income less than £14,200 a year); *or*
- have a child under 16 and be in receipt of one or more of the following benefits:
  - HB (plus child benefit for a child under 16); *or*
  - CTB (plus child benefit for a child under 16); *or*
  - CTC (with a household income less than £14,200 a year).

You can qualify for an 'HEES Plus' grant of up to £2,700, if you are:

- 60 or over and receiving:
  - minimum income guarantee or pension credit (from October 2003); *or*
  - CTB; *or*
  - HB;
- a lone parent with a child under 16 who is getting:
  - HB; *or*
  - CTB; *or*
  - WTC (with a household income less than £14,200 a year);
- a householder with a child under 16 and receiving:
  - HB (which must include a disability premium); *or*
  - CTB (which must include a disability premium); *or*
  - WTC (with a household income less than £14,200 a year); *or*
  - AA; *or*
  - DLA; *or*
  - war disablement pension (which must include the mobility supplement or constant attendance allowance); *or*
  - industrial injuries disablement benefit (which must include constant attendance allowance).

For more details call freephone 0800 316 2815.

6. **Housing grants in Scotland**

Improvement and repair grants

In Scotland, grants are available to owners and tenants to help meet the cost of improvement and repair work to houses in the private sector. Almost all grants are awarded at the discretion of the local councils. As a general rule, grants are automatically available only when a council has served a statutory notice, such as a repairs notice or an improvement order, or if your house is in an area which has been declared a Housing Action Area for Improvement.

Local authorities also decide the total amount of money which will be available for grant assistance. Their budgets are limited and they can only give grants up to the budget they have set for the purpose. The level of grant and the maximum amount which can be paid are set by law.

Grants are mandatory when standard amenities are required (eg, bath, shower, basins, sinks, toilet) and there are prescribed limits for each amenity. Standard amenity grants are awarded at 50 per cent of whatever costs are approved by the council.

Discretionary grants can be awarded for work to both the internal and external fabric of a house which is necessary to maintain the useful life of the property – eg, repairs to the roof or replacing rotten window frames. These grants are awarded at up to 75 per cent of a maximum approved expense limit of £12,600. In exceptional circumstances, the local authority can apply to the Scottish Executive for an increase in the grant limit.

The Scottish Executive intends to reform the present system to target grants on houses in the worst condition, and on those people in greatest financial need. Some local authorities already take an applicant's resources into consideration when making a decision about awarding a grant. For further information, contact your local housing department.

Improvement grants for people with disabilities

If you are registered disabled, or could be registered disabled, you have a right to an assessment of your needs by the social work department, including your needs for 'adaptations to your home, or equipment for your use for your greater safety, comfort or convenience'.[26] Following assessment, the social work department should either provide what is needed or provide assistance, including financial assistance to help with the cost of the adaptation. The housing department may offer a discretionary improvement grant towards the costs of the works.[27] The grant may cover:

- alteration or enlargement; *or*
- making the house suitable for your accommodation, welfare or employment.

The housing department can pay up to 75 per cent of the approved costs of works, within prescribed limits. Mandatory grants are available to all households for the provision of standard amenities. Even if the house already has one of these amenities, a disabled person may still be entitled to a grant for another if this is essential to her/his needs – eg, a further toilet on the ground floor.

Financial assistance from the social work department is separate from and can be paid in addition to any improvement grant for adaptation – eg, to meet the 25 per cent (or more) of the cost not met by the grant.[28]

For further details contact your local council housing and social work departments.

The Warm Deal

The 'Warm Deal' scheme offers grants of up to £500 to owner occupiers and tenants in Scotland towards:

- cavity wall insulation;
- loft, tank and pipe insulation;
- draught proofing;
- four energy-efficient light bulbs;
- energy advice.

To qualify you (or your partner) must be getting one or more of the following benefits or tax credits:

- income support;
- income based jobseeker's allowance;
- housing benefit;
- council tax benefit;
- child tax credit;
- working tax credit;
- disability living allowance;
- attendance allowance;
- disablement benefit (with constant attendance allowance); *or*
- war disablement pension (with mobility supplement or constant attendance allowance).

You may qualify for a reduced grant if you are not in receipt of one of the above benefits but you are aged 60 or over. For more information, call freephone 0800 072 0150.

Other housing grants

In Scotland, discretionary grants can also be available for replacing lead plumbing or reducing exposure to radon gas, or for mutual repairs to common parts of a building. Mandatory grants may be available in certain circumstances to provide fire escapes in houses in multiple occupation. Contact your local housing department for further information.

7. Transport concessions for disabled people

In addition to any help with travel costs which you may be entitled to from social services (see Chapter 2) or from the social fund (see Chapter 8) or from the NHS (see p97), you may also be entitled to:

- help under the Motability scheme;
- road tax exemption;
- blue badge parking concessions;
- disabled person's railcard concessions.

Motability

Motability is a registered charity incorporated by Royal Charter to assist people with disabilities with the hire purchase or hire and running costs of a car.

You are only entitled to assistance from Motability if you receive the higher rate mobility component of disability living allowance (DLA) or war pensioner's mobility supplement (see p141). Motability can only assist you if your benefit award will run for at least another two years (to buy a used car), or three years (to hire a car), or four years (to buy a new car). Although you can now have a hire purchase agreement on a used car for up to five years as long as your benefit award covers that period. Motability can arrange for the Disability Benefits Unit (DBU) to pay all or part of your DLA direct to them so that they can arrange for concessionary rates for the hire or hire purchase, adaptation, insurance and service costs (as appropriate) of a suitable vehicle for your use (or for use by another person for your benefit). You may be expected to make a down payment on the cost of an unusually expensive car, and higher contributions may be necessary if you drive more than 15,000 miles a year. Motability may also be able to help with the costs of driving lessons.

For information, advice and assistance, contact: Motability, Goodman House, Station Approach, Harlow, Essex CM20 2ET (tel: 01279 635666).

Road tax exemption

If you get the higher rate mobility component of DLA (or war pensioner's mobility supplement) you are also entitled to exemption from road tax (vehicle excise duty) for one car if it is being used solely by you or for your benefit. Applications for exemption certificates (which can then be used for applying for a tax exempt disc from the Vehicle Licensing Agency) are available from the DBU or War Pensions Agency responsible for paying your benefit. Road tax exemption cannot be backdated even if there is a delay in processing your claim for benefit.

Road tax exemption is also still available for cars used by passengers who have been getting attendance allowance (AA) or the care component of DLA since before 12 April 1993, provided they had already been granted exemption by that date.

Blue badge parking concessions

The blue (previously orange) badge scheme[29] provides parking concessions to allow people with severe walking difficulties and people who are blind (or people who are driving them) to park (either in specially reserved parking bays or in other restricted parking areas) near shops, public buildings and other places, usually for extended periods and without charge. The scheme applies throughout England, Wales and Scotland except in four London areas (the City of London, Westminster, Kensington and Chelsea, and parts of Camden).

You are entitled to a blue badge if you are over two years old and you:

- receive the higher rate mobility component of DLA (or war pensioner's mobility supplement); *or*
- are registered blind; *or*
- have a 'permanent and substantial disability which causes inability to walk or very considerable difficulty in walking'; *or*
- drive regularly and have a severe disability in both arms so that you cannot turn a steering wheel by hand (even if the wheel is fitted with a turning knob).

Blue badges are normally administered by social services departments in local authorities (who have a discretion to charge up to £2 to issue a badge).

Disabled person's railcard concessions

You are entitled to a disabled person's railcard if you:

- receive AA; *or*
- receive the middle or higher rate care component or higher rate mobility component of DLA (or war pensioner's mobility supplement); *or*
- receive severe disablement allowance; *or*
- receive 80 per cent or more war pension; *or*
- are registered as visually impaired or are deaf; *or*
- have recurrent attacks of epilepsy.

The railcard entitles you to one-third off the cost of most train journeys. You can also take a companion with you at a reduced rate. For details, contact your local station which may also provide details of other fare concessions offered by train operators and about assistance with access and travel arrangements. See also www.railcard.co.uk.

Other travel concessions

As well as the above concessions there are a number of other concessions for rail and bus travel in particular for older people. Senior railcards available to anyone aged 60 or over provide fare reductions outside of rush hour to holders. All local authorities must offer free or reduced bus fares to people over 60. In Scotland, since October 2002 all pensioners are entitled to free off-peak travel within the bounds of the local authority, although reciprocal arrangements mean cross boundary travel is possible. From April 2003 it is available to all people over 60. In Wales anyone over 60 is entitled to free bus travel within their own local authority. Many coach firms offer discounts off their standard fares for people over certain ages. Different operators have different age limits.

If you are disabled and cannot use public transport there are a number of door-to-door transport schemes. They are operated locally. In most London boroughs there are taxicard schemes. Contact you local council for more details.

If you are disabled and a holder of a blue badge you can get 100 per cent discount on the congestion charges in London. You have to apply for registration with a one-off payment of £10, and you can register up to two vehicles which you normally use when travelling in central London. You can change the vehicle by phone if necessary, or nominate it for particular days or on the day you travel. Your registration is valid for one year or until your blue badge expires and you will be invited to renew your registration 30 days before it expires. If you are clinically assessed as being too ill to travel to an appointment on public transport you may be eligible to claim a reimbursement of the congestion charge from your treating hospital.[30]

8. Charities

There are hundreds of local and national charities that provide a wide range of help to people in need. Your local social services may know of appropriate charities which may be able to assist you, or you can consult publications such as the *Guide to Grants for Individuals in Need* or the *Charities Digest* in your local library.

Notes

1. **Direct payments from social services**
   1 CCDPA 1996, s57 HSCA 2001 and s7 CCH(S)A 2002
   2 As defined under s29 NAA 1948 or under s94 SW(S)A 1968
   3 s5 CDCA 2000
   4 s7 CCH(S)A 2002
   5 Reg 2 CCSCCSDO(E) Regs
   6 *R (And B, X and Y) v East Sussex CC*, CCLR, June 2003
   7 *Direct Payments – Policy and Practice Guidance*, DoH 1999
   8 CCD 4/2003
   9 *Policy and Practice Guidance*, CDCA 2000; *Direct Payments for Young People*, DH; 2000 NAfW 2000 (available only on www.carers.gov.uk in England and www.wales.gov.uk/subisocialcarers); The Community Care, Services for Carers and Children's Services (Direct Payments (England) Regs 2003 SI 2003/762
   10 The Carers and Disabled Children(Vouchers) (England) Regs SI2003/1216

11 Reg 3 CCDP Regs
12 Reg 2 CCSCCSDP(E) Regs
13 Reg 4 CCDP Regs and reg 7 CCSCCSDP(E) Regs
14 Reg 7 CCSCCSDP(E) Regs
15 CCD 4/2003
16 s2 CCDPA 1996 and in England reg 9 CCSCCSDP(E) Regs

2. **The Independent Living Funds**

17 Independent Living (Extension) Fund Guidance Notes and Independent Living (1993) Fund Guidance Notes
18 This is one of a number of changes recommended and accepted by the Government as part of the ILF Quinquennial Review published December 2001, available on the DWP website.
19 ILF Newsletter January 2003
20 ILF Newsletter April 2002

4. **Health benefits**

21 NHS(TERC) Regs; NHS(TERC)(S) Regs; NHS(CDA) Regs; NHS(CDA)(S) Regs; NHS(CDA)(W) Regs; NHS(DC) Regs; NHS(DC)(S Regs; NHS(GOS) Regs; NHS(OCP) Regs; NHS(OCP)(S) Regs; NHSA 1977
22 Hospital Travel Costs Guidance Document, DH 2001

5. **Housing grants in England and Wales**

23 The Regulatory Reform (Housing Assistance)(England and Wales) Order 2002
24 HEES(E) Regs
25 HEES(W) Regs

6. **Housing grants in Scotland**

26 s2 CSDPA 1970
27 H(S)A 1987 Part XIII
28 Scottish Office Circular SDD 40/1985

7. **Transport concessions for disabled people**

29 DP(BMV) Regs 1982
30 www.cclondon.com

Chapter 6

Claiming social security benefits and tax credits

This chapter covers:

This chapter only gives an outline of the benefits and tax credits systems. For more details, see CPAG's *Welfare Benefits and Tax Credits Handbook*.

Chapter 7 covers the rules for the individual benefits and tax credits you can claim.

Chapter 17 covers the special rules which apply if you are living in a care home.

1. Administration of benefits and tax credits

The administration of the social security system is undergoing fundamental change and the new structure will not be fully in place until 2006. Most social security benefits are administered and paid by the Department for Work and Pensions (DWP). This will be done via three services:

- **Jobcentre Plus** will deal with most benefits for people under the age of 60 through a network of local offices. The service will be heavily 'work focussed', in that most claimants will be required to attend regular interviews aimed at helping them find work as a condition of claiming benefit. The service will also act as an employment agency, linking claimants with job vacancies. Disabled claimants will be able to access specialised help to find work through disability employment advisers and job brokers (as part of the 'New Deal' for disabled people).
- **The Pension Service** will deal with most benefits for claimants aged 60 and over, including state retirement pension, pension credit and winter fuel

payments, through 26 regional offices (accessed by post and telephone) and a network of local personal access points.
- **The Disability and Carer's Service** will deal with disability living allowance, attendance allowance, carer's allowance and vaccine damage payments through regional and central offices (see Appendix 3 for contact details).

Jobcentre Plus offices and The Pension Service are gradually replacing local JobCentres and Benefit Agency offices (also known as social security offices), which were previously run by the now defunct Department of Social Security (DSS) and Department for Education and Employment. You should be able to get claim forms and information about benefits from any of these local DWP offices (which may be listed in the telephone directory under social security, Benefits Agency or JobCentres).

Tax credits, which are paid to people who have children and to people in low paid work, are administered by the **Inland Revenue.** They are similar in character to other social security benefits and should not be confused with income tax allowances. The Inland Revenue also deals with child benefit.

Other authorities which deal with specific areas of social security include:
- **local authorities (councils)**, which administer and pay housing benefit and council tax benefit (sometimes via private companies to whom some of this function may be contracted out);
- **The Veterans Agency** (part of the Ministry of Defence), which deals with war pensions;
- **The Appeals Service** (see p126), which is responsible for appeals against benefit and tax credit decisions.

2. Claims and decisions

Who can claim

Chapter 7 sets out who is eligible to claim each benefit and tax credit.

If you are claiming a means-tested benefit (see Chapter 7) and you have a partner (see p226):
- you must make a claim for both of you;
- in some cases, both of you will be eligible to be the claimant and you may be better off if one partner is the claimant rather than the other (eg, where this entitles you to a disability premium – see p170 – note that you can normally 'swap' claimants at any time);
- you and your partner must make a 'joint claim' for tax credits and, in some cases, for jobseeker's allowance (JSA) (if you do not have children and depending on your age).

Appointees

If you are 'unable for the time being to act' for yourself (eg, because of ill health or disability), someone else can be authorised by the benefit authorities to act as your 'appointee' and deal with your benefit claims on your behalf (unless someone has already been appointed by a Court to look after your affairs).[1] The benefit authorities sometimes take the view that you are only 'unable to act' if you are mentally incapacitated. The law, however, does not state this and you should complain (see p129) if an appointment is refused because, for example, your inability to act is solely due to a physical disability.

Anyone aged 18 or over can be an appointee, including a partner, friend, relative, carer, or in some cases an officer of your local social services department. DWP guidance advises that owners or managers of care homes should only be made appointees as a last resort, if nobody else can be appointed (eg, a social services officer).[2] An appointee takes on all your rights and responsibilities as a claimant. S/he can claim benefits and receive payments on your behalf, must provide any evidence or information required in support of your claim, report any relevant changes in your circumstances, and may have to repay any benefit or tax credit which has been overpaid (see p131). Normally this will only apply from the date your appointment has been agreed, but if someone acts on your behalf before officially becoming your appointee, her/his actions can be retrospectively validated by the appointment.[3] Complying with the responsibilities of acting as an appointee can sometimes cause problems because the appointee has no rights to obtain information from bank accounts and occupational schemes which may be needed as evidence in connection with benefit claims. An appointeeship does not give authority to spend the claimant's benefit income or capital, which, if it accumulates, may affect entitlement to means-tested benefits over a period of time.

In the past, it was common practice for a separate appointment to be required for each benefit administered by the DWP, but common rules now apply to all appointments and it is arguable that one appointment should cover all benefits. Local practice varies, however, and you should always clarify the scope of an appointment with the DWP. In some cases, you may only want an appointee to deal with some of your benefits and will need to negotiate clear and suitable arrangements with the DWP. A separate appointment is technically necessary for housing benefit (HB)/council tax benefit (CTB), but in practice the local authority will usually simply confirm an existing DWP appointment. If you are claiming tax credits, you will need to arrange a separate appointment with the Inland Revenue.

Applications to become an appointee must be made in writing to the appropriate benefit authority (ie, the DWP, Inland Revenue or local authority). The DWP will often arrange to visit both the claimant and the prospective appointee before deciding whether an appointment is appropriate, but some local offices are prepared to accept the opinion of social services (eg, in a community care assessment) that a claimant is 'unable to act'.

An appointee is expected to give a month's written notice if s/he no longer wishes to act as appointee. An appointment can, however, be terminated at any time by the benefit authorities where, for example, they consider that it is no longer necessary, or no longer in the claimant's best interests, and someone else should be appointed instead (eg, a social services officer).

If you are an appointee for a claimant who dies, you must re-apply to be an appointee in order to settle any outstanding benefit matters.[4] An executor under a will can also pursue an outstanding claim or appeal on behalf of a deceased claimant even if any decision on the claim in question was made before the formal grant of probate (confirmation in Scotland).[5]

Note that an appointee is different to an 'agent', who is merely a person you authorise to cash or collect any payment of benefit for you.

For further information on the different options available to people who cannot manage their financial affairs, see p346.

How to claim

In order to qualify for a benefit or tax credit, you must make a claim[6] for it in writing, usually on an appropriate form. You can claim pension credit by telephone, but you will still have to sign and return a pre-completed form, which will be sent to you in the post.[7] Except for income support (IS) and JSA, any letter or other written communication may be accepted as a valid claim,[8] but in practice it is best to use the proper form if possible. Separate claims are normally required for each benefit. In a few cases, a claim for one benefit (eg, IS) can be treated as a claim for another benefit (eg, carer's allowance)[9] – see CPAG's *Welfare Benefits and Tax Credits Handbook* for the full list.

Most claim forms are available from your local DWP office (see p110). Some are also available in larger post offices. Claim forms for HB and CTB are available from your local authority. There are also various helplines you can telephone to get forms. Details of how to get the appropriate form and submit a claim for each benefit or tax credit are given in Chapter 7. You can also download many of the claim forms from the DWP website (www.dwp.gov.uk) and claim tax credits and child benefit online (www.inlandrevenue.gov.uk).

If you request a claim form by telephone, the claim may be registered from the date of the request, and provided you then complete and return the form within a specified time (one month for most benefits, or six weeks for attendance allowance (AA) and disability living allowance (DLA)) the claim will be treated as if it had been made on the date you first requested the form. If your claim is incomplete, you will usually be given a month to complete it properly. See p114 for the circumstances in which your claim can be backdated.

If you are claiming JSA, you will normally be required to attend an interview and regularly 'sign on' at the local JobCentre. In some areas covered by the new

Jobcentre Plus service (see p110), you may be required to attend a 'work focused interview' if you are under 60 and claiming certain other benefits.

Providing information and evidence to support your claim

For all benefits and tax credits, you are expected to provide information and evidence to support your claim.[10] The type of information and evidence you need is explained on the claim form or accompanying notes. You will usually be given a month to provide any missing information without it affecting the date of your claim. You (and your partner if s/he is included in your claim) will also need to provide your national insurance number or sufficient information for a number to be traced or allocated.[11] If you do not have a number, you will have to apply for one by attending an interview at a DWP office and providing evidence of your identity.

If you are claiming IS or JSA, your claim is not valid and you are not entitled to any benefit if you do not provide the information and evidence required on the claim form, unless:

- you could not complete the form or get the evidence required because of a physical, mental, learning or communication difficulty and it was not reasonably practicable for you to get help (you do not have to show that it was not reasonably practicable for another person to take the initiative to help you[12]); *or*
- the information or evidence does not exist, or you could not get it without serious risk of physical or mental harm, or you can only get it from a third party and it is not reasonably practicable to do so.[13]

You should inform the DWP as soon as possible if you think one of the above exemptions applies to you.

Backdating your claim

There are strict time limits for claiming some benefits (see Chapter 7 for details). You can claim some benefits in advance if you know you will shortly become entitled but you will not receive any payment until your entitlement begins.

You are not usually entitled to any benefit or tax credit for any day before your claim is received by the relevant benefit authority. In some cases, however, your claim can be backdated, normally for a maximum of three months – see below for details. You should note, however, that claims for AA and DLA cannot be backdated in any circumstances (but you will be given six weeks to complete the claim forms without losing any money).

Benefits which can be backdated without condition

Claims for the following benefits can be backdated for up to three months without condition (ie, regardless of the reasons you did not claim earlier):[14]

- incapacity benefit;

- industrial injuries benefits;
- retirement pension;
- pension credit;
- bereavement benefits;
- carer's allowance;
- child tax credit;
- working tax credit;
- child benefit and guardian's allowance;
- maternity allowance;
- additional amounts of non-means-tested benefits for adult dependants.

Note, however, that backdating is only possible if you ask for it and if you would have been entitled to the benefit for the relevant period had you claimed it.

Backdating claims for income support and jobseeker's allowance

Claims for IS and JSA can be backdated for up to **one month** if you could not reasonably have been expected to claim earlier because:[15]

- the office where you are supposed to claim was closed (eg, due to a strike) and there were no other arrangements for claims to be made; *or*
- you could not get to the office due to difficulties with the type of transport you normally use and there was no reasonable alternative; *or*
- there were adverse postal conditions – eg, bad weather or a postal strike; *or*
- you or your partner stopped getting another benefit but were not informed before your entitlement ceased; *or*
- you claimed IS or JSA in your own right within one month of separating from your partner; *or*
- a close relative (ie, your partner, parent, son, daughter, brother or sister) died in the month before your claim.

Alternatively, your claim can be backdated for up to **three months** if you can show that it was not reasonable to expect you to claim before you did for one or more of the following reasons:[16]

- you have learning, language or literacy difficulties, or are deaf or blind, or were sick or disabled (unless you are claiming JSA), or were caring for someone who is sick or disabled, or were dealing with a domestic emergency which affected you ***and,*** in each case, it was not 'reasonably practicable' for you to get help from another person to make your claim. The DWP should not assume that you cannot satisfy this provision if you have support available to you (eg, from family or social services), as the test is whether it is reasonably practicable for you to seek help, rather than whether another person could take the initiative to offer help;[17]
- you were given information by an officer from the DWP or Inland Revenue which led you to believe that you were not entitled to benefit. This may

include misleading information about your entitlement to benefit, a previous decision refusing the same or a different benefit which led you to believe you were not entitled, or where you are given the wrong claim form;[18]
- you were given advice in writing by a Citizens Advice Bureau or other advice worker, a solicitor or other professional adviser (eg, an accountant), a doctor or a local authority which led you to believe that you were entitled to benefit (this could include oral advice which is subsequently confirmed in writing[19]);
- you or your partner were given written information about your income or capital by your employer or a bank or building society and as a result you thought you were not entitled to benefit;
- you could not get to your local DWP office because of bad weather.

Note that backdating under the above rules is only possible if you ask for it and if you would have been entitled to IS or JSA for the relevant period had you claimed it.

If a person is acting as your appointee, then s/he, rather than you, must satisfy the above rules.[20] If someone is acting on your behalf on an informal basis, then you will have to satisfy the rules, unless you can show that it was reasonable for you to delegate responsibility for your claim and that you took care to ensure that the person helping you did it properly.[21]

Backdating claims following the award of a qualifying benefit

Special rules[22] apply on backdating claims if your entitlement to one benefit (other than HB or CTB) depends on the outcome of a claim for another benefit. This commonly occurs where you can only gain entitlement to IS if you are awarded DLA (which will entitle you to a disability or severe disability premium or addition), or you cannot get carer's allowance (CA) until the person you are looking after is awarded AA or DLA. The rules are designed to ensure that you do not lose entitlement to one benefit because of delays in getting a final decision about another benefit. The delays may occur in processing a claim, or because benefit is only awarded after a revision or an appeal (see p122).

The rules apply where:
- your claim for a benefit is refused because you (or in the case of a claim for CA, the person you are looking after) have not been awarded a qualifying benefit; *and*
- a claim for the qualifying benefit was made before, or not later than 10 working days after, your claim for the original benefit (or, for IS/JSA only, after the termination of an award); *and*
- the qualifying benefit is then awarded (on the initial claim, or on revision or appeal by a tribunal, social security commissioner or a court); *and*
- you reclaim the original benefit within three months of the decision to award the qualifying benefit.

Your claim for the original benefit is then backdated to the date you originally claimed it, or the first date of the period for which the qualifying benefit is payable (if later).

A similar rule applies if you are refused working tax credit because you are waiting for a decision on a claim for a qualifying benefit.[23]

At the time of writing, the rules do not apply to pension credit (PC), but this may have changed by the time PC takes effect in October 2003.

The above rules mean that you should not delay making a claim for any benefit until you receive a decision on a claim for a qualifying benefit. You should instead claim both benefits together and reclaim the original benefit when the qualifying benefit is awarded. For more details about backdating after the award of a qualifying benefit, see CPAG's *Welfare Benefits and Tax Credits Handbook.*

There is no equivalent provision which allows for the backdating of HB/CTB claims on the basis of a subsequent award of a qualifying benefit but you may be able to argue that delays in dealing with a qualifying benefit constitute good cause for backdating a claim for HB/CTB for up to 52 weeks (see below). If you are entitled to an increased amount of a benefit you are already getting following the award of a qualifying benefit, you should request a revision or supersession (see p124).

Backdating claims for housing benefit and council tax benefit

Your entitlement to HB/CTB normally starts from the first Monday following the week in which your claim is received by the local authority, unless:[24]

- you have just become liable to pay rent or council tax on your home because, for example, you have just moved in, in which case your entitlement will start from the beginning of the week in which you make your claim; *or*
- you claim HB/CTB within four weeks of claiming IS, PC or JSA, in which case your HB/CTB claim is treated as made on the same day as your IS/PC/JSA claim; *or*
- you are receiving IS/PC/JSA when you become liable to pay rent, in which case you will be allowed four weeks to make your claim for HB/CTB without losing benefit; *or*
- there is a delay in your local authority fixing its council tax rate, in which case your claim for CTB can be backdated to when you first became entitled as long as you claim within four weeks of being notified of the rate.[25]

Claims for HB/CTB may also be renewed from the expiry date of a previous award if the renewal claim is made within four weeks of that date.[26]

A claim for HB/CTB can also be backdated for up to 52 weeks if you can show you have continuous good cause for failing to claim earlier. There is no definition of 'good cause' in the regulations but it has been held to mean 'some fact which having regard to all the circumstances (including the claimant's state of health and the information which he received and that which he might have obtained), would probably have caused a reasonable person of his age and experience to act (or fail to act) as the claimant did'.[27] This could cover situations where you failed to make a claim because of ill health, disability, language problems and misleading advice or information.

Note that the 52 weeks runs from the date you request backdating, rather than from the date of the original claim, so you should ask for your claim to be backdated as soon as possible, or you may lose out.

Decisions

Decisions about benefits and tax credits are made by 'decision makers' of the relevant benefit authority – ie, the DWP, Inland Revenue or local authority. Decisions are sometimes based on medical evidence provided by doctors acting on behalf of the DWP. You should note, however, that doctors have no decision-making powers relating to benefit clams.

You are entitled to written notification of all decisions, which must include notification of your right to appeal against the decision where appropriate.[28] In most cases, you are entitled to request a written statement of reasons for the decision within a month, which must be provided to you within 14 days (this does not apply to incapacity benefit decisions, however, which, according to the DWP, already include a statement of reasons, or to tax credit decisions).

Decisions should be made and notified within a reasonable timescale. If there are long delays, you should make a complaint (see p129).

Changes in your circumstances

Once you are awarded a benefit or tax credit, payment will continue until you are no longer entitled (DLA and AA are normally awarded for a fixed period. Your award can only be terminated or changed if the benefit authority carries out a revision or supersession (see p122).

In the case of most benefits, you must report changes of circumstances which may affect your entitlement to the office handling your claim.[29] If you do not promptly report such changes, any resulting overpayment of benefit may be recoverable from you (see p121) and if you are considered to have acted dishonestly, you may also be guilty of an offence. In the case of PC (see p176), you may not be required to report increases in certain types of income for a fixed period (see p180). In the case of tax credits, you can choose to wait until the end of the tax year to report some changes of circumstances (see p197).

If you are entitled to an increased award of benefit because of a change in your circumstances, you should request a supersession. In the case of tax credits, see p197. If you are refused benefit and your circumstances change, you should make a fresh claim. You should do this even if you have appealed against the refusal of benefit, because a tribunal cannot take into account any change of circumstances that occurs after the decision you are appealing about was made.

3. Payments

Method of payment

The Government is implementing a large scale programme over the next three years to change the normal method of paying benefits and tax credits (apart from housing benefit (HB) and council tax benefit (CTB) – see below). Payment by giro and order book through the post office will be phased out and replaced by direct payment into your account by credit transfer.

You will be given the choice of having your entitlement paid into:

- an ordinary bank or building society account;
- a 'basic bank account', which can be opened at most High Street banks and which will allow cash to be withdrawn at post office counters;
- a post office 'card account', which can only be used for receiving benefits and tax credits and making withdrawals using a plastic card and personal identification number (PIN).

Payment by order book or giro can continue to be made in exceptional circumstances and until the new system is fully in place (existing claimants will be contacted in a phased programme about changing to the new method of payment). The DWP are still consulting on an 'exceptions' service for those who cannot get to a post office and need someone else to collect their benefit. Payment into an account will be a condition of entitlement to child tax credit and the childcare element of working tax credit and failure to notify an account within eight weeks can result in the cessation of entitlement.[30] HB will be paid by giro or credit transfer if you are a private tenant.

If you are a local authority tenant, your HB is paid by reducing your rent. CTB is paid by reducing your council tax bill.

Most benefits are weekly benefits and are awarded and paid in respect of your entitlement for a whole week. Some benefits, such as incapacity benefit (IB), are daily benefits and may be awarded and paid for periods of less than a week. Certain weekly benefits, such as attendance allowance (AA), disability living allowance (DLA) and income support (IS), can be paid at a daily rate if you spend part of a week in hospital or in a care home.[31]

Most benefits are usually paid so that they can be cashed every week, but some benefits are paid fortnightly (eg, jobseeker's allowance (JSA) and IB), and some are paid four-weekly (eg, AA/DLA unless they are paid together with a weekly benefit such as IS). Some benefits are paid in advance, some in arrears, and some partly in advance and arrears.[32] Payments of benefit and tax credits into an account will be paid either weekly or four-weekly in arrears.

Payments to other people

Payments may sometimes be made to someone else on your behalf, for example:
- your 'appointee' (see p347);
- for HB, your landlord if you are a private tenant;
- for IS housing costs, your mortgage lender;
- for DLA mobility component, the Motability scheme (see p106).

Some of your IS (or income-based JSA) may be deducted and paid direct to:[33]
- certain creditors (eg, for court fines, or if you are in debt for fuel charges, water rates or council tax or rent arrears);
- a care home, or to a local authority as your contribution towards the costs of the care home, *if* it is decided that you have failed to budget for the costs and it is in your interests for the payments to be made in this way, *or* you are in a home run by a voluntary organisation for people with alcohol or drug dependancy;
- certain hostels, where HB is payable but does not cover all of your charges (eg, for meals, fuel, water charges and other services).

Some, or all, of any of your benefit(s) may also be paid to another person if this is considered to be necessary to protect your interests (or those of any member of your family)[34] – eg, if your partner is failing to support you, all or part of her/his benefit(s) may be paid to you.

You can authorise an 'agent' to cash and collect your benefit or tax credits on your behalf, by signing the back of your order book or giro. An agent can be given an additional card to collect payments from a post office card account on your behalf, although the DWP is still consulting about those who only need irregular collection from the post office. S/he may need a signed mandate or power of attorney, however, to cash payments from other types of accounts. Note that an agent does not have the legal duties of an 'appointee' (see p111).

Interim payments

An interim payment of benefit can be made to you if it seems that you may be entitled to benefit but it is not possible for your claim (or revision, supersession or appeal) to be dealt with immediately.[35] Local authorities **must** make an interim payment of HB to you if you are a private tenant and your HB claim cannot be dealt with within 14 days, unless it is clear that you will not be entitled to HB or you have failed, without good cause, to provide any necessary information or evidence in support of your claim.[36] Any overpayment of benefit resulting from an interim payment is recoverable from you. There is no right of appeal against the refusal of an interim payment (you will have to complain and if necessary, threaten judicial review – see p129).

Suspension of payment[37]

Even if a benefit has been awarded to you, payment may be suspended if:

- a question has arisen about your entitlement while information is being gathered; *or*
- your award may be superseded (p123) or revised (see p122); *or*
- it appears that you may be being overpaid (see below); *or*
- you are not living at the address you notified; *or*
- you have failed to provide information or evidence (or failed to submit to a medical examination); *or*
- the DWP or local authority is considering appealing against a decision made by a tribunal, commissioner or court to award benefit to you, or even to award benefit to someone else if the issue in the appeal could affect your claim (eg, in a 'test case').

You cannot appeal to a tribunal against a decision to suspend your benefit but you can make representations that the suspension should be lifted because, for example, you will otherwise suffer hardship. You could also threaten judicial review (see p129) if you believe that there are no grounds to suspend your benefit or that your individual circumstances have not been properly considered.

Overpayments

If you receive an overpayment of benefit or tax credit, you may have to repay it. The rules about overpayments are extremely complex and vary according to the benefit concerned and you should always seek advice (see Appendix 4) if you receive a decision stating that an overpayment is recoverable from you. You can appeal against most decisions about whether and how much you have been overpaid and whether the overpayment is recoverable. For further details about the rules on overpayments, see CPAG's *Welfare Benefits and Tax Credits Handbook*.

Most overpayments can only be recovered if they resulted from a misrepresentation or failure to disclose a material fact.[38] All overpayments of HB and CTB are recoverable, however, unless they resulted solely from an official error made by a local authority or DWP officer.[39] Overpayments of tax credits are always recoverable.[40] Overpayments can be recovered by weekly deductions from most benefits. Even if an overpayment is recoverable from you, you can argue that it should not be recovered because, for example, this will cause you exceptional hardship. You can also negotiate how you will repay an overpayment. If you are an appointee (see p112), you may be liable to repay an overpayment if you misrepresented a material fact without using due care and diligence.[41]

4. Challenging decisions

Most decisions can be challenged by **revision, supersession, or appeal** (supersession does not, however, apply to tax credits). Decisions about community care grants (see p200), budgeting loans (see p202) and crisis loans (see p203) can be challenged by requesting an **internal review** within 28 days. If you are dissatisfied with the outcome, you can request a **further review** within 28 days by an independent Social Fund Inspector. You should always consider challenging a decision if you think that it is wrong. You should always get advice (see Appendix 4) about the merits of your appeal particularly if you are seeking an increase of a benefit you are receiving. This is because a decision maker or tribunal can decrease or remove your entitlement altogether when dealing with a revision, supersession or appeal, so you could end up worse off than before.

Revisions

Revisions are designed to be a quick and easy way of getting an incorrect decision changed. You can ask a decision maker to reconsider a decision by requesting a revision. A decision maker can also undertake a revision on her/his own initiative. Alternatively, you can appeal against most decisions to an independent tribunal (see p127). It is sometimes simpler and quicker to get a decision changed by revision, however, particularly if you have new evidence to support your case. Further, if your application for revision is unsuccessful, you get a fresh decision against which you can usually appeal.

There are two types of revision:

- A revision can be requested on **any grounds** (apart from a change of circumstances – see p123) within a 'dispute period' of one month from the date the decision was issued.[42] The time limit can be extended up to 13 months if your application was late because of 'special circumstances' (eg, illness or wrong advice).[43] If you requested a statement of reasons for a decision, the dispute period for requesting a revision of most benefits is extended by a further 14 days.[44] In the case of housing benefit (HB) and council tax benefit (CTB), days between your request for a statement and its provision are ignored when calculating the time limit.
- A revision can also be requested at **any time** if:
  - there has been an official error[45] (ie, a mistake or omission by an official working for the benefit authorities, such as a failure to act on information s/he had about your claim) which you or somebody acting on your behalf did not cause or contribute to; *or*
  - you have misrepresented or failed to disclose facts and as a result, the decision is more favourable to you than it would otherwise have been;[46] *or*
  - the decision is about tax credits; *or*

- a decision would have been made differently had the result of an appeal you made about a different decision been known; *or*
- you have been awarded benefit, but are now entitled to it at a higher rate from the first day of the award because you, or a member of your family, have now been awarded another benefit (see p124).[47]

Decisions (apart from those relating to tax credits) can only be revised on the basis of your circumstances at the time the decision took effect.[48] If your circumstances have changed, you should ask for a supersession (see below) of any award you are getting, or make a fresh claim if you not receiving the benefit concerned.

Except for HB/CTB,[49] you do not have to apply for a revision in writing but it is always best to do so (and to keep a copy), to ensure that there is a written record of your application. Any issues not raised by your application for a revision do not have to be taken into account.[50] You should therefore ensure that you provide as much detail as possible in your application to ensure that anything that may be relevant is taken into account.

You will be issued a new decision following a revision, which either confirms or changes the original decision. You can generally appeal against the new decision, but there is no right of appeal if a decision maker decides there are no grounds for an 'any time' revision (unless the revision is about an HB or CTB decision).[51]

A revised decision normally takes effect from the date on which the original decision took effect.[52] This means that you can normally get arrears of benefit going back to that date. In the case of tax credits, you are only entitled to up to three months' arrears from the date you notify a change in your maximum entitlement (see p197).[53]

Supersessions

Supersessions are a way of getting a decision (apart from a tax credit decision) changed at any time on prescribed grounds, the most common of which is a change of circumstances. If, for example, you are getting attendance allowance (AA) or disability living allowance (DLA) and your care or mobility needs increase, you can request a supersession to get onto a higher rate of benefit. A decision can be superseded on application, or on the own initiative of a decision maker if:[54]

- there has been, or it is anticipated that there will be, a relevant change of circumstances since the decision took effect (**note:** a decision to refuse benefit cannot be superseded on this ground – you will have to make a fresh claim for benefit if your circumstances change); *or*
- the decision was made in ignorance of relevant facts or there was a mistake about the facts of your claim; *or*
- the decision was made by a decision maker and was legally wrong; *or*
- you have attended a medical examination relating to the personal capability assessment (see p159); *or*

- you have been awarded benefit, but are now entitled to it at a higher rate because you, or a member of your family, have now been awarded another benefit (see below).

Except for HB/CTB,[55] you do not have to apply for a supersession in writing but it is always best to do so (and to keep a copy), to ensure that there is a written record of your application. You will usually be required to complete a new application form when seeking a supersession of a DLA or AA award. Any issues not raised by your application for a supersession do not have to be taken into account.[56] You should therefore ensure that you provide as much detail as possible in your application to ensure that anything that may be relevant is taken into account. An application for a revision or a notification of a change of circumstances can be treated as an application for supersession.[57]

You should be issued a new decision following a supersession which either confirms or changes the new decision (unless your application for supersession was completely hopeless, in which case the decision maker may refuse to consider it). You can generally appeal against the new decision.[58]

A supersession generally takes effect from the date you applied for it, or the date it was undertaken on the initiative of a decision maker.[59] This means that no arrears are generally payable on supersession. If, however, you report a change of circumstances within a month, you can get up to one month's arrears of benefit. The time limit can be extended up to 13 months if there are special circumstances.[60] In the case of AA and DLA, the time limit runs from the date you qualify for a higher rate of benefit. The 13-month rule means that considerable arrears could be payable where, for example, you were unable to notify a change in your circumstances earlier because of illness or disability. If you are entitled to less benefit following a change of circumstances, a supersession will generally take effect from the date of the change.[61]

Revisions and supersessions following awards of another qualifying benefit

The rules on supersessions and revisions described above allow for any award of benefit to be increased from the start date of any subsequent decision to award a qualifying benefit on which your entitlement depends. If, for example, you are awarded income support (IS), and you are later awarded DLA or carer's allowance (CA), your IS award can be revised or superseded to include a disability, severe disability or carer's premium from the start date of your award of DLA or CA. The rules for HB/CTB are not the same as for other benefits, but guidance indicates that they should have the same effect.[62] A similar rule in relation to working tax credit, allows the disability and severe disability elements to be backdated on the award of a qualifying benefit.[63]

If your claim for a benefit is refused because you have not yet been awarded a qualifying benefit, see p116.

Appeals to a tribunal

Right of appeal

You have the right of appeal to an independent tribunal against most decisions relating to benefits and tax credits made by decision makers (including revision and supersession decisions – see above).[64] Decisions about statutory sick pay, statutory maternity pay, statutory paternity pay and statutory adoption pay and some decisions about your national insurance contributions, however, can only be appealed to the Tax Appeal Commissioners. There is also no right of appeal against certain types of decisions including:[65]

- the suspension of benefit;
- whether a claim for one benefit should be treated as a claim for another benefit;
- whether to make an interim payment;
- whether to appoint someone as an appointee (see p111);
- whether to accept a late appeal (see below);
- decisions about community care grants, budgeting loans and crisis loans (but you can request a review and further review by a social fund inspector).

Time limits

An appeal against a decision must be received by the office that issued the decision within one calendar month of the date the decision was issued.[66] The time limit is extended by 14 days if you have requested a statement of reasons for most benefits.[67] In the case of HB and CTB, days between your request for a statement and its provision are ignored when calculating the time limit.[68] The time limit for appealing against a tax credit decision is 30 days.[69]

If you miss the time limit for appealing, a late appeal can be accepted within 13 months of the notification of a decision if there are reasonable prospects of your appeal being successful, or you were unable to appeal in time because:[70]

- you, your partner or a dependant has died or suffered serious illness; *or*
- you are not resident in the UK; *or*
- normal postal services were disrupted; *or*
- there are other special circumstances which are 'wholly exceptional'.

There is no right of appeal against a refusal to admit a late appeal although you can ask for such a decision to be reconsidered, or you may be able to apply for a judicial review (see p129) if the decision is clearly unreasonable.

How to appeal[71]

You must appeal in writing, preferably using the appropriate appeal form and submit the appeal to the office that issued the decision you are appealing against.

The appeal must be signed by you, or by a properly authorised representative, and must include enough information to enable the decision in question to be identified and must state the grounds for your appeal. If the appellant dies, some other person may apply to be their appointee to proceed with the appeal on their behalf.

You (or your representative) may withdraw your appeal at any time before it is decided by giving notice in writing.[72]

What happens after you appeal

On receipt of your appeal, the relevant office prepares a set of appeal papers, which includes a submission by a decision maker explaining why the relevant decision was made and copies of all the evidence. This will be sent to you (and your named representative if you have one), together with an 'enquiry form' asking whether you want an oral or 'paper' hearing of your case (see below). You should always opt for an oral hearing because your chances of success are much greater. You must complete and return the form to The Appeals Service within 14 days, or your appeal will be 'struck out' (see below).

Appeals are administered and heard by The Appeals Service (TAS), which comprises:

- an executive agency of the DWP, which administers and arranges appeal hearings; *and*
- independent tribunals made up of panels of members, under the jurisdiction of a President and the Lord Chancellor.

Hearings are arranged at local venues. If you opt for an oral hearing, you are entitled to attend to present your case in person. Paper hearings are decided on the basis of the appeal papers only.

An appeal may not proceed for one of the following reasons:

- The appeal is 'struck out'.[73] This can happen if you have failed to complete the enquiry form within 14 days, or if the tribunal does not have jurisdiction to hear the appeal (eg, because there is no right of appeal or your appeal is outside the time limits), or if the appeal is 'misconceived' (eg, it cannot succeed because you are already getting all the benefit you are entitled to). A struck out appeal can be reinstated if you apply within a month (or later if it is in the interests of justice).
- The decision under appeal is revised in your favour before the appeal is heard. If this happens, the appeal lapses.[74] Note, however, that the appeal will lapse even if the decision is only partially revised in your favour. If you are still dissatisfied with the new decision, you will have to appeal again (eg, if you appeal against the refusal of AA and you are then awarded the lower rate on

revision, your appeal will lapse and if you believe you are entitled to the higher rate, you will have to appeal again). In the case of tax credits, your appeal will lapse if you come to an agreement with the Inland Revenue about the issues involved before the appeal is heard.
- If the outcome of your appeal could be affected by a test case pending before the Courts, the appeal can be postponed until the test case is decided.[75]

Tribunal hearings

Tribunals consist of up to three members drawn from a panel of people with a range of different experience.[76]

- Three-member tribunals (a lawyer, a doctor and a person with experience of disability) will hear appeals about DLA/AA, and entitlement to the disability elements of tax credits.[77]
- Two-member tribunals (a lawyer and a doctor) will hear appeals about whether:[78]
  - you are incapable of work; *or*
  - the extent of your disability for industrial injuries benefit.
- Two-member tribunals (a lawyer and a financial expert such as an accountant) will hear complex appeals about relevant financial issues – eg, the accounts of trust funds and profit and loss accounts.[79]
- One-member tribunals (a lawyer) will hear all other appeals.[80]

Tribunals may also invite another panel member to assist them as an 'expert'. The expert can attend, give evidence or provide a report, but may not take part in making the decision.[81]

The tribunal service will convene 'paper hearings' in the absence of appellants.

Hearings take place at a range of local venues, which should all be accessible for people with disabilities (if they are not, you should complain to TAS). You can apply for an oral hearing to be postponed if you cannot attend on the date arranged. A hearing can also be adjourned at the discretion of the tribunal.[82] If it is impossible for you to get to an appeal venue (eg, because you are housebound), you can request the appeal to be heard in your home (a domiciliary hearing). You will need to provide medical evidence of your inability to travel to a hearing.

The procedure at oral hearings is up to the Chair but it must be fair and impartial. You must be given the opportunity to state your case, give evidence, call witnesses and ask questions. You are also entitled to be represented by anyone you choose.[83] A Presenting Officer from the authority that made the decision may be present to explain and argue their case. Tribunals cannot carry out physical examinations (unless the appeal relates to the assessment of disablement for severe disablement allowance or industrial injuries benefits) and therefore have to rely on the written and oral evidence available to them in reaching their decision.[84]

Determination of appeals

Tribunals must determine a case completely afresh and arrive at a new decision which replaces the original decision. They must look at all the evidence and reach a decision on the 'balance of probabilities'. They are not obliged to consider issues that are 'not raised by' your appeal and in the case of tax credits, can ignore any wilful or unreasonable omissions from the notice of appeal.[85] They can also only look at the circumstances which existed at the time the decision in question was made, and not any subsequent changes (such as a deterioration in your health), which may have occurred by the date of your hearing.[86] You should, therefore, ensure that the evidence you are relying on relates to the period preceding the decision and that you make a fresh claim for benefit (or seek a supersession of an existing award), if your circumstances change while you are waiting for an appeal.

Tribunal decisions

The tribunal must issue you with a written notice of decision after a hearing. This is sometimes given to you in person at the end of an oral hearing. You can request a full statement of the tribunal's decision and the reasons for it, within one month of the date of the decision notice. This time limit may be extended, but only in the same very limited circumstances in which late appeals may be allowed (see p125), and there is an absolute limit of three months.[87]

You may apply for any tribunal decision to be set aside within a month (13 months in special circumstances). Decisions may be set aside if the tribunal considers that it is just to do so and there has been some procedural defect – eg, a hearing proceeded in your absence even though you wanted to attend, but you were not given notice of the hearing, or relevant documents were not received by the tribunal.[88]

Appealing against tribunal decisions

You can appeal against a tribunal decision to a Social Security Commissioner on the grounds that it is erroneous in law. You will need specialist advice and assistance to do this (see Appendix 4). There are strict time limits for pursuing an appeal. You must firstly obtain a full statement of the tribunal's decision and reasons (see above). You must then apply to TAS for leave to appeal within one month of being sent the statement (the time limit can be extended to 13 months for 'special reasons').

Preparing for appeals

You should bear the following points in mind when appealing against a decision.

- You should always seek advice about appealing. The law and procedures are complex and your appeal will be much more likely to succeed if you have expert help and advice. In particular, you should get advice about the strength of your appeal, as the tribunal will decide your case completely afresh and you could end up losing rather than gaining benefit.

- Preparing for an appeal involves carefully reading all the appeal papers, studying the relevant law and caselaw and deciding how you will argue and present your case. You should always opt for an oral hearing, as this will allow you to explain your case in person and greatly increase the chances of a successful outcome. If possible, you should also arrange for an expert representative to attend the hearing with you.
- The key to a successful outcome is evidence which shows that you satisfy the relevant legal conditions. Your own oral evidence to the tribunal will be important but independent written evidence which supports your case is also crucial. This particularly applies in appeals about AA, DLA or incapacity for work, where your appeal is unlikely to succeed without supporting medical evidence from your GP, consultant or other specialist.

Judicial review

Where there is no right of appeal against a decision (see p125), or in certain circumstances where a benefit authority is refusing to make a decision, or to exercise its discretion properly, you may be able to threaten and pursue judicial review proceedings in the High Court (Court of Session in Scotland). You will need to consult a solicitor or law centre about this. There is a three-month time limit for making an application (in Scotland, an application must be made as soon as possible).

5. Common problems

This section alerts you to some of the problems you may encounter when claiming social security benefits and tax credits. Many of the issues are complex and you should always seek advice and further information if you are unsure about anything (see Appendix 4).

Delays and maladministration

Unfortunately, delays and maladministration are prominent features of the benefit, tax credit and appeals systems. Inadequate resources, poor training, heavy reliance on computerised systems and constant changes in legislation can result in long delays in processing claims, payments and appeals and poor standards of service (eg, failures to respond to telephone and written enquiries). This frequently results in hardship and frustration for claimants, particularly as there is no right of appeal until a decision is issued.

There are, however, a number of remedies open to you, depending on the nature of the problem (often the threat of action results in the problem being resolved).

- All DWP, tax credit and Appeals Service offices should have a customer services manager or section to whom you can complain if a problem is not resolved by staff dealing with your case. Although there is no statutory duty on the DWP to process claims within a set time, it sets targets and will pay compensation if it is responsible for long delays.[89] You could also ask your MP (or Member of the Scottish Parliament or Welsh Assembly) to intervene on your behalf and/ or refer your case to the Parliamentary Ombudsman, who can investigate complaints of maladministration and award compensation where appropriate.

- If your complaint is about the administration of housing benefit (HB) or council tax benefit (CTB), you should use the local authority's formal complaints procedure. Local authorities have a statutory duty to pay you any HB or CTB you are entitled to within 14 days of receiving your claim, or as soon as reasonably practicable thereafter.[90] You can also complain to a local councillor and/or to the councillor who chairs the committee responsible for administering HB/CTB. If your problem is not resolved, you can make a complaint of maladministration to the Local Government Ombudsman, or to the council's Monitoring Officer.
- If there is a delay in payment following a decision to award you benefit (eg, by a tribunal), you may be able to take recovery proceedings in the county court (sheriff's court in Scotland). You should seek further advice about this (see Appendix 4).
- In certain circumstances, if a benefit authority is refusing to deal with a claim, you may be able to threaten and pursue judicial review proceedings (see p129). This tactic has been used successfully to deal with delays and refusals to issue a national insurance number to claimants.

Negligent advice

If you are given wrong or misleading advice by the benefit authorities, you can complain, refer the matter to the Ombudsman or make a claim for compensation (you may need legal advice to do this). If you are given wrong advice by an advice agency or solicitor, you may be able to claim compensation from them.

Underclaiming and underpayments

Many people do not claim all the benefits and tax credits to which they are entitled. There are a variety of reasons for this including the complexity of the system (particularly relating to means-tested benefits), a lack of available reliable information and sources of advice, dissatisfaction with previous experiences of claiming, and a reluctance among certain eligible claimants (particularly older people) to subject themselves to what is perceived as the stigmatising and intrusive effect of means testing.

Even if people do claim all the benefits to which they are entitled, it is not uncommon for them to 'underclaim'– ie, to claim a rate of benefit that is lower than that which should be payable to them. For example, they may claim attendance allowance (AA) but not declare all of their personal care needs so that only the lower rate instead of the higher rate is awarded to them. There are very restrictive rules on the backdating of claims for all benefits (see p114) so you may lose money if you do not claim at the earliest opportunity. You should always check that you are receiving all the benefits you are entitled to (most advice centres will undertake a benefit check for you).

Another common cause of underclaiming is the failure to appreciate that the award of one benefit ('qualifying benefit') can entitle you to another benefit (or an increased amount of another benefit). If you claim AA, for example, you may be able to claim the severe disability addition with your pension credit. A person caring for you may be able to claim carer's allowance (CA) and the carer's premium/addition and you may be able to keep your severe disability addition if s/he also claims a benefit which 'overlaps' with CA (eg, incapacity benefit – see p150). If an award of a qualifying benefit stops, this conversely could also result in the loss of other benefits and services (eg, the loss of your DLA could result in the loss of premiums, CA, assistance from the Independent Living Fund and access to the Motability scheme), making it extremely important to challenge the decision.

Special rules allow a claim for a benefit to be backdated when you are awarded another qualifying benefit (see p116). You must, however, ensure that you claim both benefits within the prescribed time limits. If, for example, the person you are looking after has claimed AA, you should claim CA straight away and not wait until the AA is awarded. Similarly, although special rules allow the amount of a benefit to be increased on the award of another qualifying benefit, you must ensure that notification of the award of the qualifying benefit (eg, AA) is notified to (and acted on by) the office dealing with the other benefit (eg, HB or income support (IS)), so that the award can be superseded and increased.

Even if you claim all the benefits to which you are entitled, your claim may not be correctly decided. The standard of decision making is often poor because of inadequate training, the complexity of the rules and confusing claim forms (claimants may be unclear as to what information is required from them, or decision makers may misunderstand the information provided to them). The assessment of your care and mobility needs for DLA, and your incapacity for work for incapacity benefits, are often based on an inadequate medical examination and/or a judgemental assessment of your answers on the claim form. You should always consider appealing if you think a decision is wrong.

Overclaiming and overpayments

Although it is normally best to claim all the benefits to which you may be entitled, there are occasions where this could make you, or another person, worse off. The following examples illustrate the point.

- Claiming CA can sometimes adversely affect the benefit entitlement of others, you may lose more than you gain (see p150).

- If you are living with somebody as a non-dependant (see p171) and claim working tax credit, the increase in your income may be less than the loss in HB suffered by the person with whom you are living because of an increase in the non-dependant deduction.
- If you try to claim extra benefit (eg, a higher rate of AA of DLA) by requesting a supersession or appeal, you could end up worse off if a decision maker or tribunal decides that you are not entitled to any benefit at all.

Overpayments of benefit and tax credits are very common and may arise because of innocent or deliberate failures by claimants, or errors and inefficiencies by the benefit authorities. The rules on the recoverability of overpayments are extremely complex and you should always get advice if you are told that an overpayment is recoverable from you. If you deliberately mislead the benefit authorities or fail to notify a change in your circumstances in order to qualify for more benefit or tax credits, you are committing fraud and may be prosecuted, or asked to pay a penalty, as well as repaying any overpayment. You should always seek specialist advice, preferably from a solicitor, if you are being investigated for possible fraud.

Poverty traps

Poverty traps are one of the characteristics of means-tested benefits. They occur when an increase in your income results in a loss of benefits, which may leave you not much better off, or in some cases worse off.

When you move onto the long-term rate of incapacity benefit (IB), for example, you may lose your entitlement to IS and your HB and CTB may be reduced. You may only be slightly better off and will lose access to community care grants and budgeting loans. Any maintenance you receive from a liable relative may also reduce or even eliminate your IS and HB/CTB (the amount of maintenance your liable relative pays may also increase if s/he claims additional benefits).

Poverty traps are most evident when you take up low-paid work. You may lose entitlement to benefits such as IS, IB and CA, as well as passported benefits such as access to social fund payments, health benefits (eg, free prescriptions and dental treatment), free school meals and maximum HB and CTB (you could lose up to 85 pence of every extra pound you earn after disregards, in reduced HB and CTB). You are also likely to have extra expenses such as fares to work and work clothes. You may, of course, still be considerably better off working and having a job may be important for your future health and prospects. You should always, however, fully explore the financial consequences of taking up work, or increasing your earnings. Most advice agencies should be able to carry out a 'better off' calculation for you (see Appendix 4).

Notes

2. **Claims and decisions**
1 Reg 33 SS(C&P) Regs; reg 71 HB Regs; reg 61 CTB Regs; reg18 TC(CN) Regs
2 paras 57 and 58, *Agents, Appointees and Receivers Guide,* April 1998
3 R(SB) 5/90
4 CIS/642/1992
5 CIS/379/1992
6 s1 SSAA 1992; s3(1) TCA 2002
7 Reg 4D SS(C&P) Regs
8 Reg 4 SS(C&P) Regs; reg 72(1) HB Regs; Reg 62(1) HB regs; reg 5(2) TC(C&N) Regs
9 Reg 9(1) and sch 1 SS(C&P) Regs
10 Reg 7(1) SS(C&P) Regs; reg 73 HB Regs; reg 63 CTB Regs; reg 5(3) TC(C&N) Regs
11 s1 SSAA 1992; Reg 5(4) TC(C&N) Regs
12 CIS/2057/1998
13 Reg 4(1A) and (1B) SS(C&P) Regs
14 Reg 19(2) and (3) and Sch 4 SS(C&P) Regs; reg 7 TC(CN) Regs
15 Reg 19(6) and (7) SS(C&P) Regs
16 Reg 19(4) and (5) SS(C&P) Regs
17 CIS/2057/1998
18 CIS/1721/1998; CIS/3749/1998; CSIS/256/1999; CIS/610/1998; CJSA/4066/1998; CIS/4354/1999; CIS/4490/1999; CIS/3994/1998
19 CIS/5430/1999; CJSA/1136/1998
20 R(SB) 17/83; R(IS) 5/91; CIS/812/1992
21 R(P) 2/85
22 Reg 6(11)-(30) and 19(6)-(7) SS(C&P) Regs; memo DMG vol1 04/02
23 Reg 8 TC(CN) Regs
24 Regs 65 and 72(5) HB Regs; regs 56 and 62(5) CTB Regs
25 Reg 62(11) CTB Regs
26 Regs 72 and 96A HB Regs; regs 62 and 81A CTB Regs
27 CS/371/1949; para A2.23 and Part A2 Annex A GM
28 Reg 28 SS&CS(DA) Regs; reg 10 HB&CTB(DA) Regs
29 Reg 32(1) SS(C&P) Regs; reg 75(HB) Regs; reg 65(CTB) Regs

3. **Payments**
30 Regs 9, 13 and 14 TC(PB) Regs
31 Reg 25 SS(C&P) Regs; s124(5) and (6) and reg 73 IS Regs
32 Regs 22-26A SS(C&P) Regs
33 Sch 9 SS(C&P) Regs
34 Reg 34 SS(C&P) Regs
35 Reg 2 SS(PAOR) Regs
36 Reg 91 HB Regs
37 Regs 16, 17 and 19 SS&CS(DA) Regs; regs 11 and 13 HB&CTB(DA) Regs
38 S71 SSAA 1992
39 Reg 99 HB Regs; reg 84 CTB Regs
40 S28 TCA 2002
41 CIS/2178/2001

4. **Challenging decisions**
42 s9 SSA 1998; reg 3(1) SS&CS(DA) Regs; Sch 7 para 3 CSPSSA 2000; reg 4 HB&CTB(DA) Regs
43 Reg 4 SS&CS(DA) Regs; reg 5 HB&CTB(DA) Regs
44 Reg 31 SS&CS(DA) Regs; reg 4(4) HB&CTB(DA) Regs
45 Regs 1(3) and 3(5)(a) SS&CS(DA) Regs; regs 1(2) and 4(2)(a) HB&CTB(DA) Regs
46 Reg 3(5)(b) SS&CS(DA) Regs; reg 4(2)(b) HB&CTB(DA) Regs
47 Reg 3(7) SS&CS(DA) Regs
48 Reg 3(9) SS&CS(DA) Regs; reg 4(10) HB&CTB(DA) Regs
49 Regs 4(8) and 7(7) HB&CTB(DA) Regs
50 s9(2) SSA 1998; Sch 7 para 3(s) CSPSSA 2000
51 Reg 31(2)(a) SS&CS(DA) Regs; reg 18(3)(b) HB&CTB(DA) Regs
52 s9(3) SSA 1998; Sch 7 para 3(3) CSPSSA 2000
53 Reg 25 TC(CN) Regs
54 Reg 6(2) SS&CS(DA) Regs; reg 7(2) HB&CTB(DA) Regs
55 Regs 4(8) and 7(7) HB&CTB(DA) Regs
56 s10(2) SSA 1998; Sch 7 para 4(3) CSPSSA 2000
57 Reg 6(5) SS&CS(DA) Regs; reg 7(6) HB&CTB(DA) Regs
58 *Wood v Secretary of State for Work and Pensions* [2003] EWCA Civ 53
59 s10(5) SSA 1998; Sch 7 para 4(5) CSPSSA 2000
60 Regs 7 and 8 SS&CS(DA) Regs; regs 8 and 9 HB&CTB(DA) Regs
61 Reg 7(2)(c) SS&CS(DA) Regs; reg 8(2) HB&CTB(DA) Regs
62 HB/CTB A38/2001 paras 10-12 on reg 68(7) HB Regs and reg 8(3) HB&CTB(DA) Regs

63 Reg 26 TC(C&N) Regs
64 s12 and Schs 2 and 3 SSA 1998; Sch 7 para 6 CSPSSA 2000; s38 TCA 2002
65 Sch 2 SSA 1998; reg 27 and Sch 2 SS&CS(DA) Regs; Sch 7 para 6(2); reg 16 and Sch HB&CTB(DA) Regs
66 Reg 31(1)(a) SS&CS(DA) Regs; reg 18(1) HB&CTB(DA) Regs
67 Reg 31(1)(b) SS&CS(DA) Regs
68 Reg 18(2) HB&CTB(DA) Regs
69 S39(1) TCA 2002
70 Reg 32 SS&CS(DA) Regs; reg 19 HB&CTB(DA) Regs; Reg 5 TC(A)(No. 2) Regs
71 Regs 33 and 34 SS&CS(DA) Regs; regs 20 and 21 HB&CTB(DA) Regs; TC(NA) Regs; reg 8 TC(A)(No.2) Regs
72 Regs 33(10) and 40 SS&CS(DA) Regs; regs 20(9) and 23 HB&CTB(DA) Regs
73 Regs 46-48 SS&CS(DA) Regs; reg 23 HB&CTB(DA) Regs; regs 16-17 TC(A)(No.2) Regs
74 S9(6) SSA 1998; reg 30 SS&CS(DA) Regs; Sch 7 para 3(3) and (6) CSPSSA 2000; reg 17 HB&CTB(DA) Regs; reg 3 TC(A) Regs
75 s26 SSA 1998; Sch 7 para 17 CSPSSA 2000
76 ss6(2) and 7(2) SSA 1998
77 Reg 36(6) SS&CS(DA) Regs; reg 9(2) TC(A)(No.2) Regs
78 Reg 36(2) SS&CS(DA) Regs
79 Reg 36(3) SS&CS(DA) Regs; reg 22(1) HB&CTB(DA) Regs; reg 9(3) TC(A)(No.2) Regs
80 Reg 36(1) and (9) SS&CS(DA) Regs; reg 22(1)(b) HB&CTB(DA) Regs; reg 9(1) TC(A)(No.2) Regs
81 Reg 50 SS&CS(DA) Regs; reg 23 HB&CTB(DA) Regs; reg 19 TC(A)(No.2) Regs
82 Reg 51 SS&CS(DA) Regs; reg 23 HB&CTB(DA) Regs; reg 20 TC(A)(No.2) Regs
83 Reg 49 SS&CS(DA) Regs; reg 23 HB&CTB(DA) Regs; reg18 TC(A)(No.2) Regs
84 s20(3) SSA 1998; reg 52 SS&CS(DA) Regs
85 s12(8)(a) SSA 1998; Sch 7 para 6(9)(a) CSPSSA 2000; s39(5) TCA 2002
86 S12(8)(b) SSA 1998; Sch 7 para 6(9)(b) CSPSSA 2000; reg 4 TC(A) Regs
87 Regs 53 and 54 SS&CS(DA) Regs; reg 23 HB&CTB(DA) Regs; regs 21 and 22 TC(A)(No.2) Regs
88 Reg 57 SS&CS(DA) Regs; reg 23 HB&CTB(DA) Regs; reg 25 TC(A)(No.2) Regs

5. **Common problems**

89 *Financial Redress for Maladministration Guide*
90 Regs 76(3), 77(1)(a) and 88(3) HB Regs; regs 66(3), 67(1)(a) and 77(3) CTB Regs

Chapter 7

Which benefits and tax credits you can claim

This chapter covers:

The following benefits are covered:

Disability benefits:

- disability living allowance (p139);
- attendance allowance (p144);
- industrial injuries benefits (p145);
- war pensions (p148);
- vaccine damage payments (p148).

Other non-means-tested benefits:

- carer's allowance (p148);
- state retirement pension (p152);
- bereavement benefits (p155);
- widows' benefits (p157);
- incapacity benefit (and statutory sick pay) (p158);
- severe disablement allowance (p163);
- contribution-based jobseeker's allowance (p163);
- maternity, paternity and adoption benefits (p163);
- child benefit and guardian's allowance (p164).

Means-tested benefits and tax credits:

- income support (p164);
- income-based jobseeker's allowance (p175);
- pension credit (p176);
- housing benefit (p180);

- council tax benefit (p188);
- tax credits (child tax credit and working tax credit)(p192);
- social fund payments (p197).

All the rates of benefit given apply from April 2003 to April 2004.

This chapter outlines the rules of entitlement to the main benefits and tax credits which you may be able to claim if you, or a member of your family, are sick or disabled, or a carer. The rules are complex and only an overview of the main conditions can be set out here. If you need further details, consult CPAG's *Welfare Benefits and Tax Credits Handbook* (see Appendix 5). If you are unsure whether you are receiving your correct entitlement, or you are refused benefit, you should seek advice (see Appendix 4). Some typical examples of how claimants can maximise their income from benefits and tax credits are given on p208.

Note that:

- general information about the administration of benefits and tax credits, claims, payments, appeals and common problems you may encounter is covered in Chapter 6;
- the assessment of income and capital for means-tested benefits is covered in Chapter 8;
- the special rules that apply if you are resident in a care home are covered in Chapter 17;
- special rules apply to people in prison or affected by a trade dispute (see CPAG's *Welfare Benefits and Tax Credits Handbook* for details).

1. Types and combinations of benefits and tax credits

Types of benefits

There are two main types of benefits and tax credits, **means-tested** and **non-means-tested.**

Means-tested

Means-tested benefits and tax credits are payable to people whose financial resources are below set levels. The amount you are entitled to depends on your financial and other circumstances.

The main means-tested benefits are:

- income support (IS);
- income-based jobseeker's allowance (JSA);
- pension credit (PC);
- housing benefit (HB);
- council tax benefit (CTB);

- tax credits (child tax credit and working tax credit);
- social fund payments.

Means-tested benefits and tax credits are covered from p164.

Non-means-tested

Non-means-tested benefits are payable to people who are sick, disabled, unemployed, pregnant or bereaved, or who are carers, pensioners, or have dependent children. They are generally paid regardless of your financial circumstances but some benefits are affected by earnings and occupational pensions.

The main non-means-tested benefits are listed below in terms of whether they are contributory or non-contributory. **Contributory benefits** are only payable to people who have made sufficient national insurance contributions. **Non-contributory benefits** are paid regardless of your national insurance contribution record.

Contributory benefits	*Non-contributory benefits*
state retirement pension	attendance allowance
bereavement and widow's benefits	disability living allowance
incapacity benefit (unless paid in youth – see p159)	carer's allowance
maternity benefits	industrial injuries benefits
contribution-based jobseeker's allowance	child benefit
	guardian's allowance

Non-means-tested benefits which are paid on the basis of disability are covered from p139. Other non-means-tested benefits are covered from p148.

Combinations of benefits

You can generally claim any combination of benefits and tax credits to which you are entitled but you should note the following points.

- If you are entitled to more than one of the following **non-means-tested 'earnings replacement benefits'**, you can only be paid the highest amount for which you qualify:[1]
  - retirement pension;
  - bereavement allowance or widow's pension;
  - widowed parent's allowance or widowed mother's allowance;
  - incapacity benefit (IB);
  - severe disablement allowance (SDA);
  - carer's allowance (CA);
  - maternity allowance;
  - contribution-based JSA.

- **Other non-means-tested benefits** can be paid in addition to any other benefits and tax credits you are entitled to. Attendance allowance (AA), which is paid to people aged 65 and over and disability living allowance (DLA), which is paid to people under 65, are particularly valuable benefits because they do not count as income when calculating your entitlement to means-tested benefits and tax credits (see below). They can also entitle you to additional amounts of means-tested benefits and tax credits.
- **Means-tested benefits and tax credits** can also be paid with any other benefits and tax credits you are entitled to, but the amount you get depends on your assessed income, including income from some other benefits and tax credits. Most non-means-tested benefits count as income (but not AA or DLA) but some act as qualifying benefits to additional amounts of means-tested benefits and tax credits. Income support (IS) and pension credit (PC) are commonly paid to 'top up' earnings replacement benefits such as incapacity benefit and retirement pension. If you are entitled to IS or the guarantee credit of PC, you are automatically eligible to maximum housing benefit and council tax benefit as well as social fund payments and health benefits (see Chapter 5), although you will still have to make separate claims for them. Child tax credit is payable to most families with children, in addition to child benefit.

The following table shows some typical combinations of benefits commonly claimed by the claimant groups listed in the first column. Child benefit and child tax credit would be payable if the claimant has dependent children. Housing benefit and council tax benefit would be payable if the claimant is liable to pay rent and council tax.

Claimant group	*Disability benefits*	*Other non-means-tested benefits*	*Means-tested benefits*	*Benefits for children*
Disabled pensioner	attendance allowance	retirement pension	pension credit, housing benefit, council tax benefit	
Younger disabled person	disability living allowance	incapacity benefit	income support, housing benefit, council tax benefit	child benefit, child tax credit
Disabled worker	disability living allowance		working tax credit, housing benefit, council tax benefit	child benefit, child tax credit
Carer		carer's allowance	income support, housing benefit, council tax benefit	child benefit, child tax credit

2. Disability benefits

Disability living allowance

Disability living allowance (DLA) is a weekly allowance paid to people who need help with personal care or who have difficulty getting around. Claimants must be under the age of 65 when they claim DLA, but once an award is in payment it can continue after the age of 65. There are no national insurance contribution conditions and DLA is not taxable. DLA is a particularly valuable benefit because it can be paid in addition to any other benefit, does not count as income for means-tested benefits and tax credits, and can entitle a claimant to extra amounts of means-tested benefits and tax credits.

Who can claim

You qualify for DLA if:[2]

- you are under the age of 65 when you first claim (if you have been awarded DLA you can continue to receive it after the age of 65); *and*
- you are present and ordinarily resident in Great Britain and have been present for at least 26 weeks in the past year (disregarding temporary absences of up to 26 weeks); *and*
- you are not subject to immigration control (see below); *and*
- you satisfy one of the care and/or mobility conditions (see p140), have done so throughout the three months prior to your claim and are likely to continue to do so for at least another six months (unless you are 'terminally ill' – see p142).

DLA consists of a 'care component' paid at three different rates and a 'mobility component' paid at two different rates. You can qualify for one or both components but only for one rate of each component. You can be given an award for a fixed or indefinite period.[3] If your needs change and you have satisfied the conditions for a higher rate or another component for at least three months, you should request a supersession (see p123). If you are terminally ill, see p142.

Subject to immigration control

You are subject to immigration control if you do not have leave to enter or remain in the UK, or if your leave is subject to the condition that you do not have recourse to public funds, or is subject to a formal sponsorship undertaking. You are not subject to immigration control for benefit purposes if you are a British citizen, a national of a country which is part of the European Economic Area (EEA – see p168), a refugee, or a person with 'exceptional leave to remain' in the UK.

There are also other exceptions and the rules are complex. For further information, see CPAG's *Welfare Benefits and Tax Credits Handbook*. You should always seek advice before claiming benefit, as this can sometimes affect your right to remain in the UK.

The care component[4]

- Higher rate care component – you qualify for the higher rate care component if you are so severely physically or mentally disabled that you require:
  - frequent attention throughout the day in connection with your bodily functions, or continual supervision throughout the day to avoid substantial danger to yourself or others; *and*
  - prolonged or repeated attention at night in connection with your bodily functions, or another person to be awake at night for a prolonged period or at frequent intervals to watch over you.

  If you are terminally ill (see p142), you are treated as satisfying the above conditions.
- Middle rate care component – you qualify for the middle rate care component if you satisfy either the 'day' or 'night' condition described above. You may also qualify automatically if you undergo regular renal dialysis.
- Lower rate care component – you qualify for the lower rate care component if:
  - you are aged 16 or over and so severely physically or mentally disabled that you cannot prepare a cooked main meal for yourself if you have the ingredients; *or*
  - you are so severely physically or mentally disabled that you require attention in connection with your bodily functions for a significant portion of the day, whether during a single period or a number of periods.

Additional rule for children

Children under 16 only qualify for the care component if they have attention or supervision requirements which are 'substantially in excess' of the normal requirements of children of the same age, or which children of the same age in normal health do not have.[5]

Meaning of terms

'Attention' means service of a close and intimate nature from another person, involving personal contact.[6] Attention is not confined to physical help but it must involve the physical presence of another person.[7]

'Frequent attention throughout the day' means help which is needed several times (not once or twice) at intervals spread throughout the day (not, for example, just in the early morning or evening).[8]

'A significant portion of the day' means about an hour.[9]

'Prolonged' attention at night means about 20 minutes.

'Repeated' simply means more than once.[10] You may, therefore, qualify if you need help to go to the toilet once in the night, which takes 20 minutes, or twice which only takes five minutes.

'Bodily functions' include breathing, hearing, seeing, eating, drinking, walking, sitting, sleeping, getting in and out of bed, dressing, undressing, using the toilet and moving around. They do not generally include domestic tasks such as cooking, shopping, cleaning or laundry.[11]

'Supervision' and **'watching over'** involves keeping an eye on somebody to prevent substantial danger. It can be precautionary, without resulting in actual intervention.[12]

'Continual supervision' means frequent or regular, rather than continuous, supervision.[13]

'Prolonged' watching over at night is probably about 20 minutes.

'Requires' means 'reasonably requires' and not 'medically requires'.[14] Attention which you need in order to live as normal a life as possible (including having a social life) should count.[15] The test is whether you *need* attention or supervision, rather than whether you actually *receive* it. If you can only manage to carry out a 'bodily function' with great difficulty, you can argue that you 'reasonably require' attention in connection with it.

The **'cooking test'** for the lower rate is an abstract test of whether your disabilities would prevent you from preparing a labour-intensive main meal for one, freshly cooked on a traditional cooker (it is irrelevant whether you actually cook or know how to cook).[16] You should qualify if you are unable to peel and chop vegetables, or cope with hot pans, or turn taps, or read labels and instructions, or tell whether food is clean or cooked, or if you lack the motivation or concentration to plan and cook a main meal.

The mobility component

There are two rates of the mobility component. Note that you cannot qualify for either rate if it is impossible for you to go out or be taken out (eg, you are in a coma or cannot be moved).[17] If you are awarded the higher rate mobility component, you will also be entitled to certain transport concessions (see p106).

Higher rate mobility component

You qualify for the higher rate mobility component if:[18]

- you are unable to walk or 'virtually unable to walk' (see below) because of a physical disability; *or*
- you are unable to walk out of doors without help because you are both blind and deaf; *or*
- you have no feet; *or*
- you are severely mentally impaired, have severe behavioural problems and qualify for the higher rate care component.

You are only treated as being **'virtually unable to walk'** if:[19]

- your ability to walk out of doors is so limited, as regards the distance, speed, length of time, or manner in which you can walk without severe discomfort, that you are virtually unable to walk; *or*
- the exertion required to walk would constitute a danger to your life or would be likely to lead to a serious deterioration in your health.

Note that you must be unable or virtually unable to walk for a physical, rather than a purely psychological reason, although many behavioural and mental problems have an organic or physical cause.[20] The test is applied as if you were using any artificial aid (eg, a stick) which would be suitable for you (unless you have no feet).[21] The test is whether you can walk out of doors, taking into account uneven surfaces and other obstacles and weather conditions.[22] There is no specific distance below which you qualify as 'virtually unable to walk'. Your stamina, speed, manner of walking and recovery time should be taken into account. Any walking you can only do with 'severe discomfort' must be ignored.[23] Severe discomfort can include pain, breathlessness and tiredness.[24]

Lower rate mobility component

You qualify for the lower rate mobility component if you are able to walk but are unable to take advantage of your walking ability outdoors, apart from on familiar routes, without guidance or supervision from another person for most of the time.

Any walking you can do on familiar routes is ignored. **'Guidance'** can include being physically led or directed, being helped to avoid obstacles and being persuaded or reassured. **'Supervision'** can include being monitored and encouraged. You may qualify for the lower rate if you have learning disabilities or are blind or deaf, or suffer from panic attacks, agoraphobia or epilepsy.[25]

You cannot qualify, however, on the basis of fear or anxiety, unless they are symptoms of a mental disability and are severe enough to prevent you from going out to unfamiliar places without guidance or supervision.[26]

Additional rules for children

Children can qualify for the higher rate mobility component from the age of three and the lower rate from the age of five. The three months before the relevant birthday can count towards the three-month qualifying period.[27]

Children under 16 can only qualify for the lower rate mobility component if they need substantially more guidance or supervision than children of the same age in normal health, or guidance or supervision which such other children would not need.[28]

Terminal illness

You are regarded as 'terminally ill' if you are suffering from a progressive disease and can reasonably be expected to die within six months as a result of that disease.[29] Claims for DLA on the basis of terminal illness are dealt with under 'special rules'. You automatically qualify for the higher rate care component if you are terminally ill without having to satisfy the three-month qualifying period, and you do not have to satisfy the three- and six-month qualifying conditions in respect of the mobility component (see p139).[30] You also do not have to have been in Great Britain for 26 weeks in the last year to qualify for DLA.[31] You do not have to complete the sections of the claim form relating to care needs but you do need to submit a special form called a DS1500, which has to be completed by your doctor, giving details of your medical condition. Somebody can claim DLA for you without your knowledge or authority if you are terminally ill.[32]

DLA and other benefits

DLA is a particularly valuable benefit because it can be paid on top of any other benefit and does not count as income for means-tested benefits and tax credits. It can also entitle you to extra amounts of means-tested benefits and tax credits (in the form of disability and severe disability additions) and access to the Independent Living Fund (see p91).

If you get the higher rate mobility component, you can also qualify for parking concessions under the blue badge scheme, exemption from road tax and help from the Motability scheme to lease or buy a car (see p106 for details).

Amount[33]

	£pw
Higher rate care component	57.20
Middle rate care component	38.30
Lower rate care component	15.15
Higher rate mobility component	39.95
Lower rate mobility component	15.15

How to claim

You can only claim DLA in respect of your own care and mobility needs. If your partner also qualifies, s/he should make a separate claim. A claim for a child under 16 must be made by an appointee (normally a parent). A claim can be made on your behalf by an appointee if you are unable to manage your own affairs (see p111).

Claims are initially dealt with by a regional DWP Disability Benefits Centre. A claim must be made on form DLA1. There is one claim pack for adults and one for children under 16. You can get a claim pack by contacting your local Disability Benefits Centre, or by using the tear-off slip on leaflet DS704 (available from your local DWP office), or by ringing 0800 882 200 (textphone 0800 243 355). The pack should be date stamped and you can be awarded benefit from the date on the form, provided the Disability Benefits Centre receives your completed application within six weeks.[34] Once your award is in payment, your claim is dealt with the Disability Benefits Unit in Blackpool.

The forms are long and difficult to complete and the information you give will largely determine the outcome of the application. You should always consider getting advice, therefore, if you are unsure about how to complete the forms. You should give as much information as possible about your difficulties. The questions on the forms are designed to test whether you satisfy the legal criteria for the care and mobility components. When answering the questions about your care needs you should bear in mind that the test concerns the help you need, and you can legitimately say you need help regardless of whether you actually receive it. When answering the questions about your mobility problems, remember to state how far you can walk *without severe discomfort* (see p141). When completing the claim pack for children, you need to give as many examples as possible of the extra attention, supervision and guidance they need compared with a healthy child of the same age.

You may be required to undergo a medical examination by a visiting doctor on behalf of the DWP if further information is needed to decide your claim.[35] It can be several weeks before you receive a decision but claims on the basis of terminal illness (see p142) should be dealt with more quickly (normally within 10 days).

Attendance allowance

Attendance allowance (AA) is paid to people aged 65 or over who need help with personal care (whether or not they have a carer). There are no national insurance contribution conditions and AA is not taxable. AA is a particularly valuable benefit to claim because it can be paid in addition to any other benefit, does not count as income for means-tested benefits and can entitle a claimant to disability additions paid with means-tested benefits (see p169).

Who can claim

You qualify for AA if:[36]

- you are aged 65 or over; *and*
- you are present and ordinarily resident in Great Britain and have been present for at least 26 weeks in the past year (disregarding temporary absences of up to 26 weeks); *and*
- you are not subject to immigration control (see p139); *and*
- you satisfy one of the care conditions (see below) and have done so throughout the six months prior to your claim, or you are terminally ill (see p145).

The care conditions

You can qualify for either a higher or lower rate of AA. The conditions for the higher rate of AA are the same as those for the higher rate care component of DLA (see p140). The conditions for the lower rate of AA are the same as those for the middle rate care component of DLA (see p140).[37] See the section on DLA for guidance on the rules. There is no equivalent in AA of the lower rate of care component of DLA, or the mobility component. If you are receiving the lower rate of AA and your care needs increase, you can request a supersession (see p123) after you have satisfied the conditions for the higher rate for six months.

Terminal illness

You are regarded as terminally ill for AA as for DLA (see p142). If you are terminally ill, you automatically qualify for the higher rate of AA without having to satisfy the six-month qualifying period.[38] You also do not have to have been in Great Britain for 26 weeks in the past year to qualify for AA.[39] The same rules relating to claims apply to AA as for DLA (see p142).

Amount[40]

	£pw
Higher rate	57.20
Lower rate	38.30

How to claim

You can only claim AA in respect of your own care needs. If your partner also qualifies, s/he should make a separate claim. A claim can be made on your behalf if you are unable to manage your own affairs (see p111), or if you are terminally ill (see p142).

Claims for AA are dealt with initially by a regional DWP Disability Benefits Centre. A claim must be made on form DS2. You can get a claim pack by contacting your local Disability Benefits Centre, by using the tear-off slip on leaflet DS702 (available from your local DWP office), or by ringing 0800 882 200 (textphone: 0800 243 355). The pack should be date-stamped and benefit is payable from the date stamped, provided the Disability Benefits Centre receives your completed application within six weeks.[41]

The forms are long and difficult to complete and the information you give will largely determine the outcome of the application. You should always consider getting advice, therefore, if you are unsure about how to complete the forms. You should give as much information as possible about your difficulties. The questions on the forms are designed to test whether you satisfy the legal criteria. When answering the questions about your care and supervision needs you should bear in mind that the test concerns the help you *need* rather than *receive* and you can legitimately say you need help even though you may not always get it.

You may be required to undergo a medical examination by a visiting doctor on behalf of the DWP if further information is needed to decide your claim.[42] It can be several weeks before you receive a decision but claims on the basis of terminal illness should be dealt with more quickly (normally within 10 days).

Industrial injuries benefits

Industrial injuries benefits are paid to people who are disabled as a result of an accident at work or a prescribed industrial disease. There are no national insurance contribution conditions and industrial injuries benefits are not taxable. There are actually three industrial injury benefits. The main benefit is called **disablement benefit**, which pays a weekly allowance depending on the extent of your disablement. You can claim it even if you are still working. The other two benefits, **reduced earnings allowance** and **retirement allowance**, are meant to compensate for loss of earnings. They are gradually being phased out, however, as they are only paid to people who became disabled prior to 1 October 1990.

Who can claim

You qualify for industrial injuries benefits if:[43]

- you suffer a 'personal injury' caused by an 'accident' which arose 'out of and in the course of' your employment as an 'employed earner'; *or*
- you are suffering from a 'prescribed disease' as a result of working in a 'prescribed occupation' (see below); *and*
- as a result, you have suffered a 'loss of faculty' which has caused 'disablement' (see p147).

In addition, you must satisfy the following rules to qualify for the different types of industrial injury benefit.

- To qualify for **disablement benefit**, your disablement must normally be assessed as at least 14 per cent (see p147) and 90 days (excluding Sundays) must normally have elapsed since the accident or onset of the disease.[44] To qualify for **reduced earnings allowance**, you must have had an accident or contracted a prescribed disease before 1 October 1990 and be assessed as at least 1 per cent disabled. You must also be incapable of following your regular or equivalent employment because of the accident or disease. The rules are complex and you should seek advice if you think you may qualify.[45]
- To qualify for **retirement allowance**, you must be over pensionable age and getting reduced earnings allowance when you gave up regular employment.[46]

Meaning of terms

'Personal injury' encompasses both physical and psychological damage.[47]

An **'accident'** is an 'unlooked for occurrence' or 'mishap'.[48] There can be difficulties if you become injured over a long period. The DWP may decide this is a 'process' rather than an 'accident'. Seek advice if this happens.

The accident must arise **'out of and in the course of'** your employment. This means it must have had some connection with your work and happened at a time and place you could reasonably be expected to be working.[49] You should be covered during normal breaks on your employer's property.[50] You are not generally covered while you are travelling to and from work, unless this can be seen as part of your job.[51]

'Employed earner' covers most employees but excludes most self-employed people (although agency workers, office cleaners and taxi drivers should be covered).[52]

A **'prescribed disease'** means a disease listed in regulations, which is known to have a link with a particular **'prescribed occupation'**, which is also so listed. You must show that you are suffering from the disease as a result of working in a relevant prescribed occupation.[53]

A **'loss of faculty'** means damage or impairment to the body or mind.

'Disablement' is any resulting inability to carry out a function.[54] The extent of your disablement is expressed in terms of a percentage figure. Some disabilities have prescribed percentages, set out in regulations but others are left to the discretion of a DWP decision maker. Decision makers are not doctors but their decisions are usually based on a medical report following a DWP medical examination.[55] If your disablement is only partly due to an accident or prescribed disease there may be an 'offset' or addition to your percentage disablement. The rules on this and if you have suffered two or more accidents or diseases are complex and you should seek advice if this applies to you.[56] The decision maker also decides the period of your assessment, which can be fixed or for life.[57] If your condition deteriorates, you should request a re-assessment.

Amount

Disablement benefit

The amount you get depends on the extent of your disablement.[58]

% disablement	£pw
14-24	23.36
25-34	35.04
35-44	46.72
45-54	58.40
55-64	70.08
65-74	81.76
75-84	93.44
85-94	105.12
95-100	116.80

Note: The amounts payable are less if you are under the age of 18.

You may also qualify for two increases of disablement benefit:

- **constant attendance allowance** of up to £93.60 a week is payable if you are assessed as 100 per cent disabled and need constant attendance;[59]
- **exceptionally severe disablement allowance** of £46.80 a week is payable if you are entitled to at least £46.80 constant attendance allowance and are likely to permanently require constant attendance.[60]

Reduced earnings allowance

You are entitled to the difference between the earnings you would have received in your previous regular occupation and the earnings you currently receive, or could receive in a job you could do. The calculation is complex and open to argument and you should seek advice if you are unhappy with your assessment. The maximum you can receive, however, is £46.72 a week and the total amount of your disablement benefit and reduced earnings allowance cannot exceed £163.52 a week.[61]

Retirement allowance

You are entitled to £11.68 a week, or 25 per cent of the reduced earnings allowance you were getting, whichever is the lower.[62]

How to claim

You should ask for the appropriate claim form at your local DWP office. Leaflet NI6 has details about claiming disablement benefit. You can apply for a declaration that you have had an accident on form BI95, in readiness for a subsequent claim for disablement benefit. You will normally be asked to attend a medical examination in connection with your claim (see p143).

War pensions

Various levels of war pensions and additions can be paid to forces personnel disabled by war service, civilians disabled by war injury and war widows. For further details, contact the Veterans Agency, Norcross, Blackpool FY5 3TA; telephone 0800 169 2277. War pensions are not taxable.

Vaccine damage payments

A tax-free lump sum payment of £100,000 is payable to anyone who is severely disabled as a result of specified vaccinations. If you received a lower payment in the past, you may be entitled to a top-up payment. For claim forms and further details contact the Vaccine Damage Payments Unit, Palatine House, Lancaster Road, Preston PR1 1HB.

3. Other non-means-tested benefits

Carer's allowance

Carer's allowance (CA) is paid to people who are caring for a severely disabled person. There are no national insurance contribution conditions but CA is taxable (apart from increases for children).

Who can claim

You qualify for CA if:[63]

- you are 'regularly and substantially' caring for a 'severely disabled person' (see p149); *and*

- you are present and ordinarily resident in Great Britain and have been present for at least 26 weeks in the past year (disregarding temporary absences of up to four weeks, or longer if you have gone abroad with the disabled person to look after her/him); *and*
- you are not subject to immigration control (p139); *and*
- you satisfy the rules about your age (see below); *and*
- your net earnings from any employment do not exceed £77 a week (see p150); *and*
- you are not attending a course of education for more than 20 hours a week, excluding time spent on 'unsupervised study' (note that private study involving course work may still count as 'supervised'[64]).

Regularly and substantially caring for a severely disabled person

To qualify for CA for any week, you must spend at least 35 hours in that week caring for a person who is receiving AA or the middle or higher rate care component of DLA (see pp140 and 144).[65] Care is not restricted to help with bodily functions and could include providing assistance (of any sort), supervision and even just company, as well as time spent preparing and clearing up after meals. You can have temporary breaks from caring without losing your CA, as long as they do not add up to more than four weeks in any six months (or 12 weeks if you or the disabled person has spent at least eight of those weeks in hospital).[66] Entitlement to CA also continues for up to eight weeks following the death of the person you are caring for.[67] You should also note the following rules:

- you cannot qualify for CA during any week in which you are caring for somebody for less than 35 hours a week (subject to the above rules about temporary breaks), even if you spend more than 35 hours on average looking after her/him;[68]
- you cannot satisfy the 35-hour rule by adding together the hours you spend looking after more than one disabled person;[69]
- if you are looking after two or more people for more than 35 hours a week each, you can only qualify for one award of CA. If you and another person each spend more than 35 hours a week looking after the same person, only one of you can receive CA (this rule may contravene the Human Rights Act but you will need specialist legal advice to challenge it).[70] If you both claim, the DWP will decide who to pay. One of you may be better off claiming CA than another.

Rules about your age

You must be aged 16 or over to claim CA.[71] If you were aged 65 or over and getting CA before 28 October 2002, you can continue to get it even if you are no longer caring for a disabled person, or you are earning more than £77 a week.[72]

Net earnings from employment[73]

Your net earnings are your gross earnings from paid work, less tax, national insurance contributions and half of any contributions you make towards a pension scheme. If you have to pay someone, other than a close relative, to look after the person you are caring for while you are working, the amount you pay can be deducted from your earnings up to a maximum of 50 per cent of your net earnings. 'Close relative' means a parent, son, daughter, brother, sister, or partner of yours or of the person you are caring for. Certain childcare costs can also be deducted from your earnings.

Carer's allowance and other benefits

The relationship between CA and other benefits can be complex and claiming CA is not always in the best interests of yourself and others. You should particularly bear in mind the following points. If you are unsure whether you should claim CA, you should always seek further advice (see Appendix 4).

- CA counts as income for means-tested benefits (see p231) but can entitle you to a carer's premium or addition with your income support (IS) or pension credit (PC) (see pp169 and 176).
- CA cannot be paid at the same time as another 'earnings replacement benefit' (see p137). It can still be worth claiming, however, because you are entitled to a carer's premium/addition with your IS, PC, housing benefit (HB) and council tax benefit (CTB) if you are entitled to CA, even though you are not actually receiving it because you are getting another 'earnings replacement benefit' (see p137). The carer's premium may also reduce your liability for home care charges by increasing the amount of the income you must be left with after paying charges.
- If you are receiving CA, the person you are caring for is not entitled to a severe disability premium or addition with her/his IS, PC, HB and CTB (see p169). In some circumstances, it may be better for the disabled person to get the severe disability/addition rather than you getting CA. Where, for example, you are receiving a means-tested benefit, your CA will be fully taken into account as income and you will only gain financially from the carer's premium/addition, which may be worth considerably less than the severe disability premium/addition. If, however, you have claimed CA but are not receiving it because you are getting another 'earnings replacement benefit' (see p137), the person you are caring for remains entitled to the severe disability premium/addition and you can also get the carer's premium/addition (see pp171 and 177). Backdated payments of CA do not affect payments of severe disability premium or addition which have already been made, so if, for example, you delay claiming CA and can get your claim backdated for three months, the person you are caring for can keep the severe disability premium or addition for that three months, whereas s/he would have lost it straight away had you claimed earlier.

- If you and somebody else are looking after the same person and are both eligible for CA, the above considerations may mean that it is financially better for one of you to claim it rather than the other.
- If you give up or fail to claim your entitlement to CA in order to qualify for, or get more, means-tested benefit, the DWP can treat you as if you were receiving it and deduct it from your means-tested benefit entitlement. This rule should not apply, however, if you give up CA so that the person you are caring for can get a severe disability premium/addition, as long as s/he is not a member of your family for benefit purposes.

Amount[74]

Basic allowance

The basic allowance is £43.15 a week.

Additional amounts

- You are entitled to an additional weekly increase of £25.80 for your spouse or an adult who is looking after your child, if s/he is residing with you. You still count as residing with her/him during the temporary absences or while either of you is in hospital. You are not entitled to an increase however, if s/he is getting another 'earnings replacement benefit' (see p137), or has weekly net earnings and/or a private or occupational pension exceeding £25.80. For details of how earnings are calculated for this purpose (including childcare allowances), see CPAG's *Welfare Benefits and Tax Credits Handbook*. Note that the earnings rules are different to those described in Chapter 8 for means-tested benefits.
- You may also qualify for a weekly increase of £9.55 for your eldest child and £11.35 for other children if you were entitled to such an increase on 5 April 2003. You may qualify for a weekly increase of Category A or B pension of £9.55 for your eldest child and £11.35 for other children, but only if you were entitled to such an increase on 5 April 2003.

How to claim

You should claim on form DS700 which you can get from your local DWP office. You must make a separate claim for any increases for dependants as they are not paid automatically.

If the person you are caring for has claimed AA or DLA, you should not wait until her/his claim is decided before you claim CA. Although your claim for CA will be refused, if you reclaim it within three months of her/him being awarded AA or the middle/higher DLA care component, your claim for ICA can be backdated to the date of your original claim, or the date from which AA/DLA is awarded (whichever is the later date).[75]

State retirement pension

State retirement pension is paid to people over pensionable age, which is currently 60 for women and 65 for men.[76] For most types of pensions, eligibility and the amount payable are dependent on your national insurance contribution record (see p153). State retirement pension is taxable (apart from increases for children).

Who can claim

There are three main categories of the basic state retirement pension (A, B and D). There is also an additional state pension scheme. Despite the name 'retirement pension', you do not actually have to retire to claim a pension (but you must be over pensionable age) and if you continue to work your earnings will not reduce your pension.

Category A pension

You qualify for a Category A pension if:[77]

- you satisfy the national insurance contribution conditions (see p153); *and*
- you are over pensionable age (see above).

Category B pension

You qualify for a Category B pension if you are a married woman and:[78]

- your husband satisfies the national insurance contribution conditions (see p153); *and*
- you and your husband are both over pensionable age (see above); *and*
- your husband is entitled to a Category A pension (see above).

You qualify for a Category B pension if you are a widow and:[79]

- your husband satisfied the national insurance contribution conditions (see p153) or died from an industrial injury or disease (see p145); *and*
- you were aged 60 or over when he died or you are aged 60 or over and entitled to a widow's pension; *or*
- your husband died on or after 9 April 2001 and you were entitled to bereavement allowance before you were 60, or widowed parent's allowance after you were 45.

You qualify for a Category B pension if you are a widower and:[80]

- your wife satisfied the national insurance contribution conditions (see p153); *and*
- you became 65 after 5 April 1979; *and*
- your wife died when you were both over pensionable age; *or*
- your wife died on or after 9 April 2001 and you were entitled to bereavement allowance before you were 65, or widowed parent's allowance after you were 45.

Category D pension

You qualify for a Category D pension if:[81]

- you are aged 80 or over; *and*
- you have been resident in Great Britain for at least 10 of the 20 years which include the day before your 80th birthday; *and*
- you are not entitled to a higher category pension.

Additional state pension

You may be entitled to additional state pension under the State Earnings-Related Pension Scheme (SERPS), depending on your (or your spouse's) earnings and national insurance contributions as an employee from 1978 to 2002.[82] SERPS was replaced by a new state second pension in April 2002 (SERPS entitlement already earned is protected).[83] You can accrue entitlement under the new scheme through your earnings as an employee. If you are receiving CA or long-term IB, or you are caring for a disabled adult or child, you may also be able to build up entitlement to state second pension while you are not working (if you are a carer but are not receiving CA, you may need to inform the Inland Revenue on form CF411, which you can get by calling 0845 915 8225 or textphone 0845 915 8435.

National insurance contribution conditions[84]

National insurance contributions are payable on earnings above a certain limit. You can also be credited with contributions during periods of unemployment, incapacity for work, or while you are receiving CA (see p151).

To qualify for a full Category A or B retirement pension, sufficient contributions must have been paid or credited for all the years of your 'working life' (less an allowance of up to five years). A minimum number of contributions must have been paid during at least one tax year. Your working life normally runs from the age of 16 up to pensionable age or the year of death (if earlier) but does not include years spent out of the labour market while bringing up a child or caring for a disabled person (note that if you are not getting CA, you should notify the Inland Revenue that you are a carer – see above). If you meet the national insurance conditions for a proportion of your working life, a reduced-rate pension may be payable. It may be possible to enhance your contribution record by paying Class 3 voluntary contributions at a later date (you should always get advice before doing this). Widows, widowers and divorcees may be able to use the contribution record of their late or former spouse to help them qualify for a Category A pension.

Amount

Full basic pension[85]

	£pw
Category A/Category B (widow/widower)	77.45
Category B (married woman)/Category D	46.35

Adult dependants[86]

You are entitled to a weekly increase of Category A retirement pension of up to £46.35 for a spouse (depending on your national insurance record) if s/he is 'residing with' you, or you are contributing to her/his maintenance at a weekly rate of at least the amount of the increase. You still count as 'residing with' your spouse during temporary absences or while either of you is in hospital. You are only entitled to an increase for your husband if you were previously getting an increase in incapacity benefit for him (see p156). You are not entitled to an increase for a spouse, however, if s/he is receiving another 'earnings replacement benefit' (see p136), or if s/he has weekly net earnings and/or a private or occupational pension exceeding £54.65 (or exceeding the amount of the increase if s/he is not residing with you). For full details of how earnings are calculated for this purpose (including childcare allowances), see CPAG's *Welfare Benefits and Tax Credits Handbook*. Note that the earnings rules are different to those described in Chapter 8 for means-tested benefits.[87]

If you are not receiving an increase for a spouse, you can claim an increase for another adult who is looking after a child for whom you are responsible. The rules are the same as for a spouse but you can also qualify for an increase for an adult you are employing if you are paying her/him at least £46.35 a week (in which case the 'earnings rule' only applies if s/he is living with you, and the amount you are paying her/him is ignored).

Other additions

There are a number of other additions which may be payable with the basic pension.

- You may qualify for a weekly increase of Category A or B pension of £9.55 for your eldest child and £11.35 for other children, but only if you were entitled to such an increase on 5 April 2003. The rules are the same as for CA (see p151).
- You may be entitled to graduated retirement benefit based on your national insurance contributions from 1961 to 1975.
- You can qualify for extra pension by not claiming (deferring) your entitlement for up to five years, or 'de-retiring'.[88] You should always take advice before doing this, as it may not always be in your best interest.

How to claim

The DWP's Pension Service should send you form BR1 about four months before you reach pensionable age. You can either complete and submit the claim form, or give your details over the telephone by calling the national teleclaim service on 0845 300 1084 (textphone 0845 300 2086). You must make a separate claim for increases for any dependants as they are not paid automatically. You can get a pension forecast of your likely entitlement by completing form BR19. You should claim a Category D pension on form BR2488.

Bereavement benefits

Bereavement benefits, which are payable to widows and widowers, replaced widows' benefits (see p157) from April 2001. You can claim bereavement benefits in respect of a spouse who died on or after 9 April 2001 (you can also claim widowed parent's allowance in respect of a wife who died before 9 April 2001, if you satisfied the qualifying conditions on 9 April 2001).

If your husband died before 9 April 2001, you are eligible for widows' benefits instead of bereavement benefits (see p157). If your wife died before 9 April 2001, the non-availability of equivalent widowers' benefits may breach the non-discrimination principle in the European Convention on Human Rights and you should seek advice.

Who can claim

There are three types of bereavement benefits (see below). You can get a bereavement payment and either widowed parent's allowance or bereavement allowance. Entitlement is not affected by any earnings or savings you have. Bereavement payment is not taxable. Bereavement allowance and widowed parent's allowance are taxable (apart from any increases for children).

To claim bereavement benefits, you must generally have been legally married to your late spouse when s/he died. The law is complex, however, and you should seek advice if:

- you lived with your late partner as 'husband and wife' for a long time but were never married; *or*
- your marriage was polygamous; *or*
- the DWP decides your marriage was not valid under UK law or does not accept that your spouse is dead.

You are not entitled to bereavement benefits if you remarry, or while you are living with another person as if you are 'husband and wife'.[89]

Bereavement payment

You qualify for a one-off lump sum bereavement payment of £2,000 if:[90]

- your spouse died on or after 9 April 2001; *and*

- s/he paid a minimum number of national insurance contributions in any one tax year, or died from an industrial injury or disease (see p145); *and*
- when s/he died, you were either under pensionable age (see p152), or s/he was not entitled to a Category A retirement pension (see p152).

Widowed parent's allowance

You qualify for a weekly widowed parent's allowance if:[91]

- you are under pensionable age (see p152); *and*
- your spouse died on or after 9 April 2001, or your wife died before 9 April 2001 and you were under 65 on that date and have not re-married; *and*
- your late spouse satisfied the national insurance contribution conditions (the conditions are as for retirement pensions – see p152), or died from an industrial injury or disease (see p145); *and*
- you are pregnant by your late husband (or by artificial means if you were residing with your husband when he died), or you are entitled to child benefit for a 'qualifying child' (ie, a child of yours and your late spouse, or a child for whom either of you were getting child benefit when your spouse died).

Bereavement allowance

You qualify for a weekly bereavement allowance for up to 52 weeks if:[92]

- you are under pensionable age (see p152); *and*
- your spouse died on or after 9 April 2001; *and*
- your spouse satisfied the national insurance contribution conditions (the conditions are as for retirement pensions, see p152), or died from an industrial injury or disease (see p145); *and*
- when s/he died you were aged over 45 but under pensionable age.

If you are entitled to widowed parent's allowance, you cannot qualify for bereavement allowance until your entitlement to widowed parent's allowance ceases. You may be entitled to claim IS, including a 'bereavement premium', after your entitlement to bereavement allowance ends, if you were aged 55-60 on 9 April 2001.

Amount[93]

Basic amounts

Bereavement payment	£2000 (lump sum)
Widowed parent's allowance	£77.45 pw
Bereavement allowance	£77.45 pw

Additional amounts

You may qualify for a weekly increase of £9.55 for your eldest child and £11.35 for other children, but only if you were entitled to such an increase on 5 April 2003.

The rules are the same for CA (see p151). Note that you can claim child tax credit if you have a dependent child (see p192). You may be entitled to additional widowed parent's allowance based on your late spouse's earnings and national insurance contributions under SERPS or the state second pension (see p153).

Reductions

Your widowed parent's allowance or bereavement allowance may be paid at a reduced rate if your spouse's national insurance record was incomplete (see p158 – but note that you may be able to increase your entitlement by paying Class 3 contributions).

Your bereavement allowance is reduced by seven per cent for each year or part year by which you were under 55 when your spouse died.[94]

How to claim

You should claim on form BB1 which you can get from your local DWP office. You must claim a bereavement payment within three months of your spouse's death, and your claim for widowed parent's allowance or a bereavement allowance can only be backdated for up to three months.[95] The time limits may be increased if you were unaware of your husband's death. You should seek advice if this applies to you.[96]

Widows' benefits[97]

Widows' benefits were replaced by bereavement benefits on 9 April 2001 and are only available to widows whose husbands died before that date.

Who can claim[98]

There are three types of widows' benefits.

- **Widow's payment** is a lump sum payment of £1,000. The rules are the same as for bereavement payment (see p155), except that for 'spouse' read 'husband'. You can only now qualify for a widow's payment if you have only recently become aware of your husband's death.
- **Widowed mother's allowance** is a weekly benefit for widows with dependent children. The rules are the same as for widowed parent's allowance (see p156), except that for 'spouse' read 'husband' and there is no upper age limit.
- **Widow's pension** is payable under the same rules as bereavement allowance (see p156), except that for 'spouse' read 'husband'. In addition, widow's pension is payable for an indefinite period up to the age of 65.

Amount[99]

The amounts payable (basic amounts, additional amounts and reductions) are the same as for the equivalent bereavement benefits (see p156) except that the widow's payment is £1,000 and SERPS additions (see p156) are payable with widow's pension.

How to claim[100]

Claim forms BW1 are available from your local DWP office. The time limits are the same as for bereavement benefits (see p155).

Incapacity benefit

Incapacity benefit (IB) is paid to people who are incapable of work and have made sufficient national insurance contributions or became incapable of work in youth. IB is taxable, apart from the short-term lower rate (see p162).

Who can claim

You qualify for IB if:[101]

- you are 'incapable of work' (see p159); *and*
- you satisfy the national insurance contribution conditions (see below), or became incapable of work in youth (see p159); *and*
- you are under pensionable age (see p152) if you are claiming long-term IB (see p162) or not more than five years over pensionable age if you are claiming short-term IB (see p162).

You should also note the following points:

- If you are an employee aged under 65, and your gross earnings are at least £77 a week, you will normally be entitled to statutory sick pay (SSP) of £64.35 a week from your employer for up to 28 weeks while you are off sick. For full details of the SSP rules, see CPAG's *Welfare Benefits and Tax Credits Handbook*. You may also be entitled to sick pay under your contract of employment. You cannot be paid IB while you are entitled to SSP.[102]
- You must be incapable of work for at least four consecutive days (a 'period of incapacity for work') to qualify for IB. Periods of incapacity which are separated by eight weeks or less are treated as a single period. In some circumstances, the linking period can be extended to up to two years if you have been working or training. The linking rules mean you may be able to automatically re-qualify for IB at the rate you were previously getting. The rules are complex, however, and you should seek advice (see Appendix 4) if you think using them may assist you.[103] IB is not payable for the first three days of a period of incapacity ('waiting days') but you do not have to wait a further three days if you become sick again in the same 'period of incapacity'.[104]
- You may be entitled to IB without satisfying the normal national insurance contribution conditions if you are a widow, widower or pensioner (see p162 if you are a pensioner). The rules are complex and you should seek further information or advice.

National insurance contribution conditions

There are two contribution conditions. Firstly, you must have paid a minimum number of national insurance contributions in one of the three tax years before the start of the calendar year in which you claim (if you were getting IB or invalid care allowance in the tax year before you claim, or disabled person's tax credit in the two years before you claim, the contributions can have been paid in *any* tax year). Secondly, you must have paid or been credited with a minimum number of contributions during each of the last two tax years before the start of the calendar year in which your period of incapacity for work began.[105] Tax years run from April to April.

Incapable of work in youth

You can qualify for IB without satisfying the national insurance contribution conditions if:[106]

- you are aged 16 or over when your entitlement begins; *and*
- you have been incapable of work for at least 28 consecutive weeks in your current period of incapacity for work (see above), which began before your 20th birthday (25th birthday if you were on a course of education or training which began at least three months before your 20th birthday and ended in the last two tax years before the calendar year in which you claim IB); *and*
- you are not aged under 19 and attending a course of education for 21 hours or more a week, excluding special tuition for people with disabilities; *and*
- you are present and ordinarily resident in the UK and have been here for at least 26 weeks in the last year; *and*
- you are not subject to immigration control (see p139).

If you previously qualified for IB on the basis of incapacity in youth, you may be able to re-qualify even if you are now over 20 (or 25). The rules are complex and you should seek advice if this may apply to you.

Incapable of work

Two tests are used to decide whether you are incapable of work:

- The **own-occupation test** applies for the first 28 weeks of incapacity if you have been working for at least 16 hours a week for more than eight weeks in the 21 weeks before your claim. You satisfy the test if you are incapable of carrying out your last job because of illness or disablement (physical or mental). All that is normally required is a medical certificate (Med 3) from your doctor.[107]
- The **personal capability assessment** applies when the own occupation test does not, or ceases to, apply.[108] Details of the assessment are set out below.

The **personal capability assessment** measures your ability to perform a range of physical and mental activities which are laid down in regulations.[109] These include walking, using stairs, sitting, standing, bending, reaching, lifting, speaking, hearing, seeing, controlling your bladder and bowels, coping with pressure and everyday tasks and interacting with people. Each activity is subdivided into a series of 'descriptors' which measure the varying degrees of difficulty a person may have in relation to that activity – eg, unable to walk a few steps/50 metres/200 metres/400 metres, without stopping or severe discomfort. Each descriptor is allocated a fixed number of points. To be incapable of work for benefit purposes, you must score at least 15 points for the physical descriptors, or 10 points for the mental descriptors or 15 points if you are combining scores for both physical and mental descriptors.[110] For a full list of the descriptors and details of their application, see CPAG's *Welfare Benefits and Tax Credits Handbook*.

The assessment is normally carried out in two stages:[111]

- *firstly,* you are sent a questionnaire (form IB50) which you must complete. You should normally submit a Med 4 certificate from your doctor with your questionnaire;
- *secondly,* you may be required to attend a DWP medical examination by a Medical Service doctor.

You may be re-assessed at any time and you should not assume that you will be found incapable of work because you have previously been assessed as incapable of work.[112]

You are treated as incapable of work without having to satisfy the personal capability assessment in the following circumstances.

- You are waiting to be assessed. It can take some time before you are sent a questionnaire and required to attend a DWP medical. You are treated as incapable of work in the meantime as long as you continue to submit medical certificates and you have not been found capable of work in the previous six months (unless you are suffering from a different or worsened condition).[113]
- You are receiving the highest rate care component of disability living allowance (see p140), or are registered blind, or terminally ill, or 80 per cent disabled for the purposes of severe disablement allowance (see p163) or disablement benefit (see p147).[114]
- You are suffering from certain severe conditions including tetraplegia, paraplegia, dementia, persistent vegetative state, a severe learning disability, a severe mental illness or a neurological or muscle wasting disease; inflammatory polyarthritis, severe cardio-respiratory impairment, dense paralysis on one side, severe damage to the brain or nervous system, severe immune deficiency, or a certified contagious or infectious disease.[115]
- You have been assessed as being capable of work but you are suffering from a severe, life threatening condition, or you are likely to undergo major surgery or therapy within three months of a Medical Service examination.[116]
- You are in hospital, or are having renal dialysis, total parenteral nutrition, plasmapheresis, chemotherapy or radiotherapy.[117]
- You have been receiving benefit on the basis of incapacity since 12 April 1995 (you must be aged 58 or over and satisfy other conditions, or receiving severe disablement allowance – see p163).[118]

- You were previously assessed as incapable of work and have since worked or been on a training course and become incapable of work again. The rules and conditions are complex and you should seek advice if this may apply to you.[119]

You are treated as capable of work (and are not, therefore, entitled to IB) for any week in which you actually do any work other than the following permitted work:[120]

- voluntary work, domestic work in your home, or caring for a relative;
- work for which you earn up to £20 a week;
- work paying up to £67.50 a week, which is part of a hospital treatment programme, or supervised by someone employed by a public or local authority, or voluntary organisation to find work for people with disabilities (this could include work done in a sheltered workshop);
- work of less than 16 hours a week paying up to £67.50 a week for a maximum of 26 weeks. This can be extended for a further 26 weeks if there is evidence (eg, from a JobCentre adviser) that this would be likely to improve your capacity to undertake full-time work. You should be sent a letter by the DWP explaining about the possible extension and other options after you have been working for 20 weeks. You can start a new period of work once you have been off benefit for at least eight weeks, or after 52 weeks has elapsed since you last worked.

Your earnings for the purposes of the above rules are your net earnings, after tax, national insurance contributions and in certain circumstances, childcare costs. For more details, see CPAG's *Welfare Benefits and Tax Credits Handbook*. Note that the earnings rules are different to those described in Chapter 8 for means-tested benefits.[121]

Note that you must inform the DWP in writing that you are undertaking, or about to undertake, paid work and in the case of the last bullet point, this must be done within 42 days of starting work.

All the above rules and procedures for deciding whether you are incapable of work also apply to severe disablement allowance (see p163), income support (IS – see p210) and the payment of the disability premium (see p169) with IS, housing benefit (see p180) and council tax benefit (see p188). A decision that you are incapable of work for the purposes of one benefit is conclusive for the purposes of subsequent claims for other benefits, so you do not have to be re-assessed separately for each benefit claim.[122]

You can appeal against any decision that you are capable of work (see p125) and you may be able to claim IS until your appeal is decided (see p166).

Amount

Basic amount

There are three rates of IB.[123]

- The lower rate of short-term IB is £54.40 a week. It is paid for the first 28 weeks of entitlement.
- The higher rate of short-term IB is £64.35 a week. It is paid after you have been receiving the lower rate of IB or SSP (see p158) for 28 weeks.
- The long-term rate of IB is £72.15 a week. It is paid after you have been receiving the higher rate of short-term IB for 28 weeks (ie, after a year of incapacity).

If you are terminally ill or entitled to the highest rate care component of disability living allowance, you are entitled to the long-term rate of IB after six months, rather than a year, of incapacity.[124] Previous periods of incapacity may link to your current period to entitle you to a higher rate of IB (see p158).

Additional amounts

- If you are over pensionable age (see p152), short-term IB is paid at an enhanced rate of £69.20 (lower rate) or £72.15 (higher rate). You only qualify if you are less than five years over pensionable age, your period of incapacity (see p159) began before you reached pensionable age and you have deferred entitlement to a Category A or B retirement pension, or 'de-retired' (see p152).[125] You do not need to have satisfied the normal national insurance conditions for IB (see p158) but you need to have satisfied the conditions for a Category A or B retirement pension (see p152).
- You are entitled to a weekly age addition of £15.15 with long-term IB if you were under 35, or £7.60 if you were under 45, when your period of incapacity began (see p159).[126]
- You may qualify for an extra £33.65 a week short-term IB (£41.50 if you are over pensionable age), or £43.15 long-term IB, for a spouse aged 60 or over, or for an adult who is looking after your child. The rules are the same as for Category A retirement pension (see p152) except that your spouse must be aged 60 or over, or you must be residing with her/him and responsible for a child, and the earnings/private or occupational pension limit is £33.65 a week for short-term IB (£41.50 if you are over pensionable age) and £54.65 a week for long-term IB (£43.15 if you are maintaining an adult dependant who does not live with you).[127]
- You may qualify for a weekly increase of short-term higher rate IB (and lower rate if you are over pensionable age) and long-term IB of £9.55 for your eldest child and £11.35 for other children but only if you were entitled to such an increase on 5 April 2003. The rules are the same for CA (see p151).[128] Note that you can claim child tax credit if you have a dependent child (see p192).

- If you were receiving invalidity benefit on 12 April 1995 and have remained incapable of work, you may be entitled to 'transitionally protected' higher amounts of IB.[129]

Reductions for private and occupational pensions

If your entitlement to IB began on or after 6 April 2001, your IB is reduced by 50 per cent of the weekly amount above £85 of any personal and occupational pensions you are receiving.[130] This does not apply, however, if you are getting the highest rate care component of disability living allowance.[131]

How to claim

You should claim on form SC1 which you can get from your local DWP office. If you are an employee and are not, or no longer, entitled to SSP (see p158), your employer should give you a form SSP1, which includes the SC1 claim form. You will normally be required to submit a Med 3 certificate from your doctor with your claim. You must make a separate claim for any increases for dependants as they are not paid automatically.

Severe disablement allowance[132]

Severe disablement allowance (SDA) was abolished for new claimants from 6 April 2001. This means that you can only qualify for SDA if you were already entitled to it before that date and remain incapable of work. You may be able to re-qualify for SDA in certain circumstances if your entitlement has stopped. The rules are complex and you should seek advice about this.

SDA is paid to severely disabled people over the age of 20 who have been incapable of work (see p159) for at least 28 weeks but cannot qualify for IB because they have not made sufficient national insurance contributions.

The basic rate of SDA is £43.60 a week. Age and dependants' additions are also payable.

Contribution-based jobseeker's allowance

Contribution-based jobseeker's allowance (JSA) is paid for up to six months to people who are not in full-time work or subject to immigration control (see p139). You must have made sufficient national insurance contributions to qualify and must be capable of work, available for work and actively seeking work (the 'labour market conditions'). If you do not satisfy the national insurance conditions, you may qualify for income-based JSA (see p175). If you do not satisfy the labour market conditions, you may qualify for income support (see p210). For more details about JSA, see CPAG's *Welfare Benefits and Tax Credits Handbook*.

Maternity, paternity and adoption benefits

There are two types of maternity benefits (plus the 'Sure Start maternity grant' – see p199).

- **Statutory maternity pay**[133] (SMP) is paid by employers to women who have ceased work because of pregnancy. You must have been working for an employer for at least 26 weeks and earning an average of more than £77 a week to qualify. SMP is paid for up to 26 weeks, at the rate of 90 per cent of your average earnings for 6 weeks and £100 a week for a further 20 weeks (or 90 per cent of your average earnings if this is less).
- **Maternity allowance**[134] is paid by the DWP to pregnant women who are not entitled to SMP. You must have been working as an employee or self-employed person for at least 26 of the 66 weeks before you have your baby. It is paid for 26 weeks at the same rate as SMP.

In addition, from 6 April 2003, you can qualify for:[135]
- **statutory adoption pay**, if you have adopted a child (the rules are similar to SMP and amount is the same);
- **statutory paternity pay**, if you are the partner of a new mother or adoptive parent and are taking leave from work to look after her or him or the new child (the rules are similar to SMP and the amount is the same but is only paid for up to two weeks).

Child benefit and guardian's allowance

Child benefit of £16.05 a week for the eldest or only child (£17.55 for certain lone parents) and £10.75 for other children, can be claimed by anyone who is responsible for a child who is under 16, or aged 16-18 and in (or recently left) full-time non-advanced education. Guardian's allowance (£11.55 a child) can be claimed by anyone bringing up a child whose parents are dead (or one is dead and the other is missing, or in prison for at least two years or detained in hospital 'under section'). Neither benefit is taxable and there are no national insurance contribution conditions. Both benefits are administered and paid by the Inland Revenue and you can get claim forms from local Inland Revenue and DWP offices.

4. Means-tested benefits and tax credits

Income support

Income support (IS) is a tax-free weekly benefit paid to specified categories of people who are not required to be available for work and whose income and capital are below set levels. People on IS are eligible for maximum housing and council tax benefit (see p180), social fund payments (see p197) and other sources of financial assistance (see Chapter 5). People who are not eligible for IS may be able to claim income-based jobseeker's allowance (JSA) instead, if they are available for and actively seeking work (see p175).

IS for people aged 60 or over is also referred to as the 'minimum income guarantee' (MIG) on claim forms and in leaflets. The MIG is still a payment of IS and is subject to the rules of entitlement set out below. From 6 October 2003, MIG is being replaced by pension credit (PC – see p176). Existing recipients of MIG will automatically be transferred onto PC (see p176).

From 6 April 2003, anyone responsible for a child can claim child tax credit (CTC – see p192). See p174 for how this will affect your IS.

If you are separated from your husband or wife (eg, because s/he is in a care home) and you are claiming IS as a single claimant (see below), you may be required to pay maintenance for her/him (see p174).

Who can claim

You qualify for IS if:[136]

- you are aged 16 or over; *and*
- you fall into one of the categories of people who are eligible to claim (see below); *and*
- neither you nor your partner (see p168) are working 'full time' (see p167 for details and the exceptions to this rule); *and*
- you are not studying full time (but see p167 for exceptions); *and*
- you are present and habitually resident in the UK and not subject to immigration control (see p167 for details); *and*
- you are not receiving income-based or contribution-based JSA (see p163) and your partner is not receiving income-based JSA (see p175); *and*
- your (and your partner's) income is less than your applicable amount (see p169); *and*
- you (and your partner) do not have savings and other capital worth more than £8,000, or £12,000 if you or your partner are aged 60 or over, or £16,000 if you live permanently in a care home (see p362). See Chapter 8 for details of how your capital is calculated.

If you are aged 16 or 17 and you are in full-time education, or you are a care leaver who is being maintained by a local authority, you are only eligible for IS in specified circumstances.[137]

If you are a 'person without accommodation', you are not entitled to any premiums for yourself or your family, nor any personal allowances for dependent children. 'Accommodation' should include any effective shelter suitable for continuous occupation, including caravans and tents (but excluding cardboard boxes, cars and bus shelters). If you are only temporarily absent from your normal accommodation, you should still be treated as having accommodation. If you are homeless, you may be required to collect your benefit from a local office.

If you qualify for IS, you can claim for yourself, your partner and your children (see p168). If you do not qualify but your partner does, s/he could be the claimant for your family. You can also 'swap' claimants if this would be advantageous (see p174). Where there is a choice of claiming IS or income-based JSA, you may be better off if you or your partner claims IS, as you may be entitled to more benefit (eg, the disability premium) and you will not have to be 'available for work' and 'actively seeking work'. From October 2003, if you have a partner and one of you is aged under 60 and the other is aged 60 or over, you will be able to choose whether to claim IS or PC. It will generally be better to claim PC because it has more generous capital rules (see Chapter 8), and some increases in income are ignored for a fixed period (see p216).

Categories of people eligible to claim IS

You are eligible to claim IS if:[138]

- you are aged 60 or over (in which case IS is referred to as the MIG) but this only applies until 5 October 2003, after which you will have to claim PC (see p176); *or*
- you are a single person aged 55-59 inclusive on 9 April 2001, whose spouse died on or after that date; *or*
- you are 'incapable of work', or treated as incapable of work, under the same rules and assessment procedures that apply to incapacity benefit (p158), or you are entitled to statutory sick pay (SSP); *or*
- you are appealing against a decision that you are capable of work in accordance with the 'own occupation test' or the personal capability assessment (see p159) (your IS personal allowance is reduced by 20 per cent while you are appealing against a personal capability assessment); *or*
- you are a 'disabled worker', or are working while living in a residential or nursing care home (see p167); *or*
- you are registered blind; *or*
- you are a carer and you are receiving carer's allowance (see p148), or you are looking after somebody who is receiving attendance allowance (see p144) or the middle or higher rate care component of disability living allowance (see p140), or you are looking after somebody who has claimed these benefits in the last 26 weeks and is waiting for a decision (you can also continue to claim IS for eight weeks after these conditions cease to apply); *or*
- you are a single parent who is responsible for a child under 16; *or*
- you are looking after your partner or child because they are temporarily ill, or you are looking after a child whose parent is ill or temporarily away, or you are fostering a child and do not have a partner, or you are on unpaid parental leave and were previously entitled to tax credits or housing/council tax benefit; *or*
- you are expecting a baby in the next 11 weeks or had a baby in the last 15 weeks; *or*
- you are a disabled student who can claim IS (see p167); *or*
- you are a person subject to immigration control (p139) who is entitled to urgent cases payments of IS (see p210).

There are other less common categories of eligible claimants. For a full list and details, see CPAG's *Welfare Benefits and Tax Credits Handbook.*

People working full time

You are not generally entitled to IS if you are working (for payment) 16 hours or more a week, or if your partner is working 24 or more hours a week.[139] If both of you work less than this, you can claim IS but most of your earnings will be taken into account. Even if you or your partner are working more than the prescribed hours, you are not excluded from IS under the full-time work rule if:[140]

- you are a 'disabled worker' – ie, you are mentally or physically disabled and as a result your earnings or hours of work are 75 per cent or less of what a person without your disability would expect from the same or comparable employment; *or*
- you are a carer who is eligible to claim IS (see p166); *or*
- you are working at home as a childminder, or you are being paid by social services or a health authority or voluntary organisation to foster a child or care for a person in your home; *or*
- you are living in a care home.

If you are a lone parent, you can continue to get IS for the first two weeks you are in full-time work, if you were receiving IS or income-based JSA for the previous 26 weeks.[141]

People studying full time

You are not generally entitled to IS if you are studying full time but there are exceptions. The rules are complex and for further details you should consult CPAG's *Welfare Benefits and Tax Credits Handbook*. You are not excluded from IS under the full-time student rule if:[142]

- you are under 19, in non-advanced education and so severely disabled that you are unlikely to get a job in the next 12 months; *or*
- you are 19 or over or in advanced education and you qualify for a disability or severe disability premium (see p169); *or*
- you have been incapable of work for 28 weeks; *or*
- you qualify for a disabled student's allowance because you are deaf; *or*
- you are a lone parent or over pensionable age.

Residence and immigration conditions

You must be present in the UK to get IS (or PC – see p176) but entitlement can continue during temporary absences of up to four weeks (eight weeks if you are taking a child abroad for medical treatment).[143]

You are not entitled to IS, PC, income-based JSA, housing benefit or council tax benefit unless you are **'habitually resident'** in the UK. This applies to all claimants including British citizens. Certain people are automatically treated as being habitually resident including refugees, people with exceptional or indefinite leave to remain in the UK and people classed as EEA (see below) 'workers' and their dependants. Other claimants can establish habitual residence if they have a settled intention to live in the UK and have been resident here for a period of time. For more details about the habitual residence test, see CPAG's *Welfare Benefits and Tax Credits Handbook.*

You are also not generally entitled to IS or the other means-tested benefits described in this chapter if you are **'subject to immigration control'**. You are 'subject to immigration control' if you do not have leave to enter or remain in the UK, or if your leave is subject to a sponsorship undertaking or a condition that you do not have recourse to public funds. Some people remain entitled to benefit, however, even though they are subject to immigration control. These include:

- nationals of EEA States (ie, the EU States plus Iceland, Norway and Liechtenstein) and nationals of Turkey, Cyprus, Hungary, Malta, Poland, Slovakia and the Czech Republic who are lawfully present in the UK;
- sponsored immigrants who have been here for five years or more, or whose sponsor has died;
- certain asylum seekers who claimed asylum on entering the UK before 2 April 2000 or who have been receiving benefit since 5 February 1996 (IS is payable at a reduced 'urgent cases' rate). Newly arrived asylum seekers must approach the National Asylum Support Service for support.

For more details about the effects of immigration status on benefit entitlement, see CPAG's *Welfare Benefits and Tax Credits Handbook*. You should always seek advice before claiming benefit, as this can sometimes affect your right to remain in the UK.

Claiming for others

When you claim IS, your claim is assessed for the whole of your 'family' who share your 'household'.

Meaning of terms

Your **'family'** means yourself, your 'partner' (if you have one) and any 'dependent children'.

'Partner' means someone of the opposite sex to whom you are married or with whom you are living as if you were married.

'Dependent children' (not necessarily your own) usually means any child or young person for whom you are responsible, who is under the age of 16, or aged 16-19 and in full-time non-advanced education.[144] Note, however, that IS allowances for children are being phased out from April 2004 (see p174).

'Household' is not defined in the law but involves people living together in a domestic establishment that has some degree of independence and self-sufficiency. If you separate permanently from your partner, you no longer count as members of the same household and you can only claim IS as single claimants. If you are temporarily separated from your partner, you continue to count as members of the same household, unless you have no intention of living together again, or you are likely to be apart for more than 52 weeks (this period can be extended if you or your partner are in hospital, or in a care home, provided the period of your separation is not likely to be 'substantially' longer than 52 weeks).[145] If you remain married but no longer count as members of the same household, you may be required to pay maintenance if your husband or wife is getting IS (see p174).

Amount

IS is a means-tested benefit and the amount you are entitled to depends on your financial and family circumstances. There are three steps involved in working out your IS. An example is given on p172.

Step one: Calculate your applicable amount. This represents the minimum weekly income the government decides you need to live on. It is made up of fixed amounts, depending on your age, the size of your family and other circumstances. Details of how to calculate your applicable amount are set out below.

Step two: Calculate your weekly income. Details of how to calculate your income are set out in Chapter 8. Note that not all your income counts when working out your IS. Any AA and DLA (see pp144 and 139) you receive, for example, are ignored but incapacity benefit and carer's allowance (see pp158 and 148) count in full. Some of your earnings are disregarded. If you have capital over fixed limits, you are treated as having a 'tariff income' (see p233 for details).

Step three: Deduct your income from your applicable amount. The resulting amount is your IS.[146] If your income exceeds your applicable amount, you are not entitled to IS.

Applicable amount

Your applicable amount is made up of three elements:

- personal allowances for you and your family;
- premiums in specific circumstances;
- housing costs, primarily for mortgage interest payments (rent payments are covered by the housing benefit scheme – see p180).

Personal allowances[147]

These are set amounts for single people, lone parents, couples (ie, people with partners – see p168) and dependent children. There are different rates for people of different ages. The rates are set out on pxiii.

Premiums

Premiums are set allowances intended to help with extra expenses associated with age, disability or children. You can qualify for one or more premiums but you can only receive one of the disability premiums, the pensioner premium, the higher pensioner premium and the bereavement premium (the highest you qualify for).[148] You also cannot get the enhanced disability premium with the pensioner or higher pensioner premium. The amounts payable are set out on pxiii. You may be able to claim arrears of a premium if you are entitled to it for a past period. Note that the family premium, the disabled child premium and the enhanced disability premium paid for a child will be phased out from April 2004 (see p174).

You are entitled to a:

- **family premium** if your family includes a child under 16, or under 19 and in full-time, non-advanced education.[149] Only one premium is payable, regardless of the number of children you have. The lone parent rate is only payable if you have been entitled to IS as a lone parent since 5 April 1998;
- **pensioner premium** if you or your partner are aged 60-79 inclusive. The couple rate is paid even if only one partner fulfils the conditions.[150] Note that from 6 October 2003, you can only qualify for a pensioner premium if your partner is aged 60-79 and is not claiming pension credit (PC – see p176);
- **higher pensioner premium** if:[151]
  - you or your partner are aged 80 or over; *or*
  - you were getting the disability premium (see below) when you became 60 (or in the eight weeks before) and have been getting IS since; *or*
  - you or your partner are aged 60-79 inclusive and either of you is registered blind or receiving a 'qualifying benefit' – ie, AA (see p144), DLA (see p139), severe disablement allowance (see p163), the disability or severe disability element of working tax credit (see p195), long-term incapacity benefit (IB – see p158) or retirement pension (if this replaced your long-term IB and you have been getting IS since).

  The couple rate is paid even if only one partner fulfils the conditions.[152] Note that from 6 October 2003, you can only qualify for a higher pensioner premium if your partner satisfies the above conditions and is not claiming pension credit (see p176);
- **disability premium** if:[153]
  - you are aged under 60 and are registered blind, or receiving a qualifying benefit (see above), or have been incapable of work (see p158 and below) for a continuous period of 52 weeks (or 28 weeks if you are terminally ill); *or*
  - your partner is aged under 60 and is registered blind or receiving a qualifying benefit.

  The couple rate is paid if you have a partner and if either condition is satisfied. Note that only the claimant's (not partner's) incapacity for work can qualify a couple for the premium (this is particularly relevant where there is a choice of claimant – see p174). Note also that you can only satisfy the incapable of work condition, if you have claimed IB (whether you are entitled to it or not) or if you are entitled to SSP (see p158). You may be able to establish that you have been incapable of work for a past period by submitting a backdated medical certificate from your GP;

- **enhanced disability premium** if you or a member of your family (see p168) are receiving the highest rate care component of DLA (see p140) and are aged less than 60;[154]
- **severe disability premium** if:[155]
  - you are receiving AA (see p144) or the middle or higher rate care component of DLA (see p139); *and*
  - you have no non-dependant, aged 18 or over, normally residing with you (see below); *and*
  - no one is being paid carer's allowance (CA) for looking after you (see p148). Note that a person is not treated as receiving CA if s/he is not getting it because of the overlapping benefit rules (see p137).

  If you have a partner you must both satisfy the above rules. If you do, the couple rate is paid. If your partner does not satisfy the first condition but is registered blind, or if only one of you has a carer receiving CA, you are entitled to the single person's rate.

  A 'non-dependant' is anybody aged 18 or over who normally lives with you (whether in their house or yours) and with whom you share accommodation, apart from a bathroom, toilet, or common access area, or a communal room in sheltered accommodation.[156] This could include your grown-up son or daughter, or your parent. It does not include anyone who is getting AA or the middle or higher rate care component of DLA. See p186 for who else does not count as a non-dependant.

  If a non-dependant comes to live with you for the first time to care for you or your partner, you can keep your entitlement to the severe disability premium for 12 weeks. After that, you will lose the premium and the carer should consider claiming CA. In other situations, however, you should be aware that if somebody is receiving CA for looking after you, you will lose your entitlement to the severe disability premium and this may leave you considerably worse off (see p150);
- **disabled child premium** for each child in your family who gets DLA or who is registered blind, as long as the child has less than £3,000 capital;[157]
- **carer's premium** if you or your partner are getting CA (see p148), or would get it but for the overlapping benefit rules (see p137). You remain entitled to the premium for eight weeks after you stop getting CA, or the person you are looking after stops getting AA or the care component of DLA. If both you and your partner satisfy the conditions for a carer's premium, you are entitled to double the normal rate;[158]
- **bereavement premium** if you are a single claimant and you were aged 55-59 on 9 April 2001 and you claim IS within eight weeks of ceasing to get a bereavement allowance (see p156). If you subsequently stop getting IS for less than eight weeks, you can requalify for the premium.[159]

Housing costs

The final element of your applicable amount is housing costs.[160] These are paid to home-owners to help meet the costs of:

- mortgage interest payments;
- interest payments on loans for specified home repairs and improvements (including adapting a dwelling for the special needs of a disabled person[161]);
- service charges, other than for specified repairs and improvements.

Housing costs for mortgage interest payments are usually paid directly to the lender.

The rules and conditions relating to IS housing costs are complex (see CPAG's *Welfare Benefits and Tax Credits Handbook* for more details). Note, particularly, the following restrictions.

- You may not be entitled to help with interest payments on a mortgage taken out while you were getting IS or income-based JSA but this rule does not apply if the loan was taken out to buy a more suitable home for the needs of a disabled person – ie, somebody who could satisfy the conditions for a disability, disabled child, pensioner or higher pensioner premium.
- Your housing costs may be restricted if excessive (but the needs of disabled members of your family must be considered). There is also an absolute ceiling of £100,000 on eligible loans.
- If you or your partner are aged 60 or over you will be paid all your housing costs straightaway. Most other claimants who took out a loan after 1 October 1995 are not entitled to housing costs until they have been receiving IS for 39 weeks. If, however, you took out your loan before 2 October 1995, or you are receiving CA, or are caring for somebody who is getting or has claimed AA or DLA middle or higher rate care components, you are not entitled to any housing costs for the first eight weeks of your IS claim. After this period you can get 50 per cent of your housing costs for the next 18 weeks and then full housing costs after 26 weeks. If you have not been able to qualify for IS because you have been receiving IB or SSP, periods spent on these benefits can count towards the waiting periods.
- Deductions may be made from your housing costs if you have a non-dependant living with you (see p169). The amounts deducted are the same as apply to HB (see p186 for details). Note that, as for HB, no deductions are made for non-dependants if you or your partner receive AA or DLA or are registered blind.
- You can only get help with interest payments, not capital repayments and insurance premiums, on eligible loans. Unless your rate of interest is less than 5 per cent, your standard rate of interest is used, which may be less than the rate you are actually paying.

Housing costs are payable in respect of the dwelling you normally occupy as your home.[162] If you are temporarily away from home, you can normally continue to get housing costs for 13 weeks, as long as your absence is unlikely to exceed 13 weeks.[163] This also applies if you are in a care home for a trial period.[164] If you are in a care home for short-term or respite care, you can continue to get housing costs on your normal home for up to 52 weeks.[165] The 52-week rule also applies if you are in hospital, or receiving medical treatment or convalescence, or providing medically approved care to another person. The 52-week period may, however, be extended if the reason for your temporary absence is that essential repairs are being carried out on your home.[166] In either case, once you return home, even if this is only for a weekend or even a day, you may claim housing costs for a new 13 or 52-week period of temporary absence.[167]

You may be paid housing costs for two homes for up to four weeks in certain circumstances (the rules are the same as for HB – see p181).[168] You may also be paid housing costs for up to four weeks before you move into a new home if your move is delayed because it is being adapted for a disabled person or because you are waiting for a social fund payment, and you are entitled to a disability or pensioner premium.[169]

You can continue to get housing costs for the first four weeks you or your partner are in full-time work if you have been receiving IS or income-based JSA for the previous 26 weeks.[170]

Example of an IS calculation

Mr and Mrs Earnshaw, both aged 35, have two children aged 8 and 12. They live in rented accommodation. Mr Earnshaw has a severe mental illness and Mrs Earnshaw spends a lot of time looking after and supervising him. Mr Earnshaw receives the middle rate care component of DLA. Mrs Earnshaw receives carer's allowance and child benefit. The family have no other income and no savings. Mrs Earnshaw claims IS as a carer.

Step one: Applicable amount	
Personal allowance for a couple	£85.75
Personal allowance for first child	£38.50
Personal allowance for second child	£38.50
Family premium	£15.75
Disability premium	£33.25
Carer's premium	£25.10
Total applicable amount	£236.85
Step two: Income (note DLA is ignored as income)	
CA (including increase for Mr Earnshaw)	£68.95
Child benefit for first child	£16.05
Child benefit for second child	£10.75
Total income	£95.75
Step three: Deduct income from applicable amount	
Applicable amount	£236.85
less income	£95.75
= IS	**£141.10**

Mrs Earnshaw is entitled IS of £141.10 a week

How to claim

You should claim IS on form A1, or form MIG1 if you are aged 60 or over (this only applies prior to 5 October 2003), which you can get from your local DWP office. If you are aged 60 or over, you can also claim IS prior to 6 October 2003 by giving your details over the telephone to the MIG claim line on 0800 028 1111 (textphone: 0800 028 3593). You must fully complete the claim form and supply any documentation required (eg, proof of savings and payslips) for your claim to be valid. If you are claiming because you are incapable of work you must also submit an SC1 form. If you have a mortgage you should ask your lender to complete form MI12, which comes with the claim pack.

You claim IS for yourself and your family (see p168). If you and your partner are both eligible to claim, you can choose who should be the claimant (see p111).

Income support and child tax credit

The IS (and income-based JSA – see p175) personal allowances for children and the family premium, disabled child premium and enhanced disability premium payable for a child, will be abolished for new claimants from 6 April 2004, who will be able to claim child tax credit (CTC) instead (see p192). Claimants already getting IS on 6 April 2004 will continue to have child and family elements included in their applicable amount until they are 'migrated' onto CTC between April and October 2004. Claimants aged 60 or over will no longer be able to claim IS from 6 October 2003 but can claim PC instead (see p176). Those responsible for a child will be able to claim CTC.

Until the above changes take effect, you can choose to claim both IS, including child and family elements, and CTC, which will count as income when calculating your IS. In some cases, you will be better off on CTC than you would be on IS, particularly if you have other income (apart from child benefit) which exceeds your IS adult personal allowances, premiums and housing costs. If you come off IS, however, you will no longer be eligible to claim a social fund community care grant, any direct payments from your IS (eg, for housing costs) will cease and you will have to re-claim HB and CTB. You should always, therefore, get independent advice about whether it is better for you to claim CTC, or to claim or stay on IS. Your local DWP office should be able to do a 'better-off' calculation for you.

Income support and the liability to maintain

If you are separated (but not divorced) from your husband or wife (eg, because s/he is in a care home) and you are claiming IS as a single claimant, you are liable to maintain her/him.[171] Most maintenance payments made to you count as income for IS (see p230 for details).

If you fail to maintain your spouse, the DWP may contact you about the payment of maintenance, or suggest that s/he takes legal proceedings to obtain maintenance (in which case the maintenance can sometimes be paid directly to the DWP, without it affecting your IS[172]). The DWP also has the power to take proceedings itself if it believes that you have sufficient resources to maintain your spouse but are refusing to do so.[173] As a last resort, you can be prosecuted for persistent failure to maintain (the maximum penalty is three months' imprisonment and/or a fine of £2,500.[174] In practice, the enforcement of maintenance orders is rare, and prosecutions are even rarer, particularly in the case of older or disabled couples who are separated because one is receiving care. If maintenance does become an issue, however, you should seek legal advice.

The rules about maintenance for children and the child support scheme are beyond the scope of this Handbook. For details, you should consult CPAG's *Welfare Benefits and Tax Credits Handbook* and CPAG's *Child Support Handbook* (see Appendix 5).

Income-based jobseeker's allowance[175]

Income-based JSA is paid to people under pensionable age (see p152) whose income and capital are below set limits. You cannot get income-based JSA and IS at the same time.

Who can claim

The rules are the same as for IS (see p165), except that you do not have to be in one of the categories of people eligible to claim IS but you do have to be available for work and actively seeking work (the labour market conditions). You must normally be willing and able to take up work of at least 40 hours a week but you may be permitted to restrict your availability if you have a disability or caring responsibilities. For full details, see CPAG's *Welfare Benefits and Tax Credits Handbook*. Special rules apply if you are aged 16 or 17.

People who have paid sufficient national insurance contributions may be able to claim contribution-based JSA (see p163) instead of, or in addition to, income-based JSA. People who are eligible to claim IS (see p166) may be better off doing so, to avoid having to satisfy the labour market conditions. Men aged 60-65 will be able to claim income-based JSA or pension credit (see p176) from 6 October 2003. They may be better off on PC because of its more generous capital and work rules and because they will not have to satisfy the labour market conditions. People responsible for a child will be able to choose to claim CTC from 6 April 2003 and the same 'better-off' issues may arise as for IS (see p174).

Amount

Income-based JSA is calculated in the same way as IS, taking into account the applicable amount and resources of your family (see p168). The rules about the liability to maintain that apply to IS also apply to income-based JSA (see p174).

How to claim

You must claim through your local Jobcentre Plus office (see p110). You will normally be required to attend a new jobseeker's interview and enter into a written jobseeker's agreement when you claim. You may have to regularly 'sign on' at the Jobcentre Plus and attend further interviews during your claim to establish that you satisfy the labour market conditions.

Pension credit

PC is a tax-free weekly benefit, which will be available from 6 October 2003. It will be paid to people aged 60 or over, whose income is below set levels and will replace the 'minimum income guarantee' of IS (see p210). Unlike IS, there is no capital limit for claiming PC (although an assumed 'tariff income' from capital will be taken into account – see p233), no full-time work rule (although earnings from work will be taken into account) and certain increases in income are ignored for a fixed period (see p221). People aged 60 or over who are on IS/MIG on 5 October 2003 will automatically be transferred onto PC.

PC consists of two different elements:

- **guarantee credit**, which is designed to bring your income up to a minimum level; *and*
- **savings credit**, which is designed to reward you if you have made some provision for your retirement over and above the basic state retirement pension.

You can qualify for either or both credits. People getting the guarantee credit are eligible for maximum housing (see p183) and council tax benefit (see p190), social fund payments (see p197) and other sources of financial assistance (see Chapter 5). PC does not include any amounts for children and if you are responsible for a child, you will have to claim child tax credit (see p192).

Who can claim

You qualify for PC if:[176]

- you are aged 60 or over, and in the case of savings credit, you or your partner (see p226) are aged 65 or over; *and*
- you are present and habitually resident in the UK and not subject to immigration control (the rules are similar to those that apply to IS – see p167); *and*
- your income is below set levels (see p216).

If you qualify for PC, you claim for yourself and your partner (if you have one) if you are both sharing a household. 'Partner' and 'household' are defined as for IS (see p226).[177]

Amount

PC is a means-tested benefit and the amount you are entitled to depends on your income and whether you have a partner, disabilities, caring responsibilities and eligible housing costs. Examples of calculations are given on p179.

Guarantee credit

There are three steps involved in calculating your entitlement to guarantee credit:[178]

Step one: Calculate your appropriate minimum guarantee. This represents the minimum weekly income the Government decides you need to live on. It is made up of fixed amounts, depending on your personal circumstances. Details of how to calculate your appropriate minimum guarantee are set out below.

Step two: Calculate your weekly income. This is the amount you have coming in each week from your pension and other sources. Not all your income counts (AA and DLA, for example, are ignored) and some income is subject to disregards. If you have capital of more than £6,000 (£10,000 if you live in a care home), you are treated as having income of £1 for every £500 of capital over that amount. Some capital, however, is disregarded. Full details of how to calculate your income and capital are set out in Chapter 8.

Step three: Deduct your income from your appropriate minimum guarantee. The resulting amount is your guarantee credit. If your income exceeds your appropriate minimum guarantee, you are not entitled to guarantee credit.

Appropriate minimum guarantee

Your appropriate minimum guarantee is made up of the following elements:[179]

- a standard minimum guarantee of £102.10 if you are a single claimant, or £155.80 if you have a partner;
- a severe disability addition of £42.95, if you satisfy the conditions that apply for the IS severe disability premium (see p171). If you have a partner you must both satisfy the conditions. If you do, you are entitled to an addition of £85.90. Otherwise you can get the single person's addition under the same rules as apply to IS;
- a carer's addition of £25.10, if you satisfy the same conditions that apply for the IS carer's premium. If you and your partner both satisfy the conditions, you are entitled to an addition of £50.20;
- eligible housing costs if you are a homeowner, in respect of mortgage interest payments, interest payments on loans for specified home repairs and improvements, and certain service charges. The rules are very similar to those that apply to IS housing costs (see p172);

- a transitional addition if you are receiving IS or income-based JSA when you first become entitled to PC, and your appropriate minimum guarantee is less than your IS/JSA applicable amount (see p169) (less any personal allowances or premiums for children and any residential allowance you are getting). You get the difference in the form of a transitional addition, to ensure you are not worse off on PC than you were on IS.

Savings credit

The maximum amount of savings credit you are entitled to is £14.79 a week if you are a single claimant and £19.20 a week if you have a partner. You or your partner must be aged 65 or over to qualify for savings credit.

The following steps are involved in calculating your entitlement to savings credit:[180]

Step one: Compare your qualifying income with the savings credit threshold. Your qualifying income is your total weekly income as calculated for guarantee credit (see p177) less any maintenance payments you are getting for yourself from your spouse or former spouse, and the following benefits: working tax credit, incapacity benefit, severe disablement allowance, contribution-based JSA and maternity allowance. The savings credit threshold is £77.45 if you are a single claimant and £123.80 if you have a partner. If your qualifying income is below the threshold, you will not qualify for any savings credit. If it is above the threshold, proceed to step two.

Step two: Calculate 60 per cent of your qualifying income between the savings credit threshold and the standard minimum guarantee (see p177). In other words, calculate the amount of qualifying income you have between £77.45 and £102.10 if you are a single claimant, or £123.80 and £155.80 if you have a partner, and multiply it by 60 per cent.

Step three: Compare your total weekly income with your appropriate minimum guarantee. Your total weekly income and appropriate minimum guarantee are calculated as for guarantee credit (see p177). If your income is less than your appropriate minimum guarantee, your savings credit is the amount calculated in step two (the maximum payable is £14.79 if you are a single claimant and £19.20 if you have a partner). If your income is more than your appropriate minimum guarantee, proceed to step four.

Step four: Calculate 40 per cent of your total weekly income above your appropriate minimum guarantee and deduct it from the amount of savings credit calculated in step three. The result is your savings credit. If the deduction is more than the savings credit calculated in step three, you are not entitled to any savings credit.

Examples of PC calculations

Mrs Andrews is aged 70 and lives alone in a house she owns, on which there is no mortgage. Her weekly income is £68 state retirement pension and £38.30 attendance allowance.

Her guarantee credit is calculated as follows:

Step one: Her appropriate minimum guarantee is £102.10 standard minimum guarantee *plus* £42.95 severe disability addition = £145.05

Step two: Her total weekly income is £68 (her AA is ignored as income).

Step three: Guarantee credit is £145.05 (appropriate minimum guarantee) *less* £68 (income) = £77.05

She is not entitled to savings credit because:

Step one: Her qualifying income of £68 is less than the savings credit threshold of £77.45

If Mrs Andrews also had a weekly occupational pension of £30, her guarantee credit would be calculated as follows:

Step one: Her appropriate minimum guarantee is £145.05

Step two: Her total weekly income is £98 (state pension and occupational pension).

Step three: Guarantee credit is £145.05 *less* £98 = £47.05

Her savings credit would be calculated as follows:

Step one: Her qualifying income of £98 is more than the savings credit threshold of £77.45, so she is eligible for savings credit.

Step two: The amount of her qualifying income (£98) between £77.45 and £102.10 is £98 *less* £77.45 = £20.55 x 60% = £12.33

Step three: Her total weekly income of £98 is less than her appropriate minimum guarantee of £145.05, so her savings credit is £12.33.

If Mrs Andrews also had savings of £31,000, her guarantee credit would be calculated as follows:

Step one: Her appropriate minimum guarantee is £145.05.

Step two: Her total weekly income is £98 (state pension and occupational pension) *plus* £50 deemed income from savings (£1 for every £500 in excess of £6,000) = £148.

Step three: As her income of £148 exceeds her appropriate minimum guarantee of £145.05, she is not entitled to guarantee credit.

Her savings credit would be calculated as follows:

Step one: Her qualifying income of £148 is more than the savings credit threshold of £77.45, so she is eligible for savings credit.

Step two: The amount of her qualifying income (£148) between £77.45 and £102.10 is £102.10 *less* £77.45 = £24.65 x 60% = £14.79.

Step three: Her total weekly income of £148 is more than her appropriate minimum guarantee of £145.05.

Step four: Her total weekly income of £148 exceeds her appropriate minimum guarantee of £145.05 by £2.95 x 40% = £1.18. Savings credit is £14.79 – £1.18 = £13.61

Change of circumstances

You are generally under a duty to notify the DWP of any changes of circumstances, including increases in your income, which may affect the amount of PC you are entitled to.

If, however, you or your partner are aged 65 or over and neither of you is under 60, you may be given an 'assessed income period' of up to five years (or seven years if you are transferring from IS to PC in October 2003), during which time any increases in the following types of income will not affect your PC and will not have to be notified:

- retirement pensions other than the state retirement pension (eg, private and occupational pensions);
- income from annuities;
- income from capital.

Increases in the above types of income will instead only take affect from the end of the assessed income period. The amount of increase taken into account will be the amount your pensions and annuities were due to increase (if at all) during the assessed income period in accordance with their terms. Increases or decreases in income from capital will be assessed using the formula of £1 for every £500 over £6,000 (£10,000 if you live in a care home). You can and should report any decreases in your income from the above sources during the assessed income period as this can lead to an immediate adjustment of your PC.

Your assessed income period will end if:

- you start or cease to live with a partner; *or*
- you or your partner become 65; *or*
- you are single and enter a care home permanently; *or*
- payment of any of your pensions or annuities stops temporarily or is less than the amount due.[181]

How to claim[182]

If you are getting IS on 5 October 2003, you will automatically be transferred onto PC. Everybody else must make a claim for PC. You can get the appropriate form from your local DWP office. You can also claim on the telephone, in which case you will be sent a pre-completed form to sign and return. You can claim up to four months before you qualify (eg, your 60th birthday).

Housing benefit

HB is a tax free, means-tested weekly benefit paid to people who are liable to pay rent. It can be claimed by people who are working or unemployed. HB is paid and administered by local authorities (councils).

Who can claim

You qualify for HB if:[183]

- you or your partner (see p182) are liable to pay rent on the dwelling you occupy as your home (see below); *and*
- you do not fall within any of the categories of excluded people listed on p182; *and*
- your (and your partner's) income is low enough to qualify (see p183); *and*
- you and your partner do not have savings and other capital worth more than £16,000 (see Chapter 8 for details of how your capital is calculated), unless you or your partner are getting the guarantee credit of PC from 6 October 2003 (see p177), in which case your capital is not taken into account.

Liability to pay rent for your home

Rent includes any payments you make for the use and occupation of premises, including certain service charges and payments for hostel, bed and breakfast and other types of accommodation.[184] Some payments, however, including some types of service charges, are not eligible for HB (see p184).

To qualify for HB, you or your partner must be liable to pay rent under a legally enforceable agreement, although the agreement does not have to be in writing.[185] If you are not legally liable to pay rent but have to do so to keep your home because the liable person has stopped paying, you can be treated as liable.[186] Some people are excluded from HB, however, even though they are liable to pay rent (see p184). If you live with a partner (see p182) only one of you can claim HB.[187] If you are jointly liable to pay rent with other people who are not members of your family (see p182) you can claim HB for your proportion of the rent.[188]

HB is only usually payable in respect of your normal home. If you are temporarily absent from your home, you can get HB for up to 13 weeks or 52 weeks. The rules are the same as for IS housing costs (see p172).[189]

You may be entitled to get HB for two homes if:

- you have temporarily left your home because of fear of violence (HB can be paid for up to 52 weeks on your old and new homes);[190] *or*
- you have moved into a new home and cannot reasonably avoid having to continue to pay rent on your old home. (HB can be paid for up to four weeks on your old and new homes.)[191] DWP guidance[192] suggests that this only applies if you have moved permanently but the regulations do not specify this, so you could argue you are entitled to HB for two homes for up to four weeks, if you have moved into temporary accommodation (eg, supported housing for rehabilitation purposes following a community care assessment).

People excluded from housing benefit

You are excluded from HB if you fall into any of the following categories.

- You are not habitually resident in the UK or you are subject to immigration control (see p139).[193]
- You are a full-time student.[194] Some full-time students are eligible for HB, however, including those who qualify for IS or, income-based JSA, anyone aged 60 or over, lone parents, people who have been incapable of work for 28 weeks and those who qualify for the disability or severe disability premiums (see p169).[195]
- You move permanently into a care home.[196] See Chapter 9 for details of how you can get help with your home fees.
- You own your home, or have a lease of more than 21 years, or are receiving IS housing costs for your accommodation.[197]
- Your rental agreement is not commercial taking into account, in particular, whether the terms are legally enforceable.[198] Note that the fact that you are paying less than the market rent, or that you are renting from a friend or relative, does not necessarily mean that your agreement is not commercial.
- You pay rent to a 'close relative' of yours or your partner's who shares your accommodation.[199] **'Close relative'** means parent, parent-in-law, son, son-in-law, daughter, daughter-in-law, step-parent, step-son, step-daughter, brother, sister or partner of any of the above.[200] You do not count as sharing accommodation if you only share a bathroom, toilet or common access area, or communal rooms in sheltered accommodation, and the rule may not apply if you have exclusive occupation of one or more rooms.[201]
- You are renting a home from your ex-partner, or partner's ex-partner, which you formerly shared with them.[202]
- A child of the person you are renting from is living as part of your family.[203]
- Within the last five years, you or your partner previously owned the accommodation you are renting, unless you can show that you had to relinquish ownership to keep your home – eg, because of mortgage arrears.[204]
- You were previously a non-dependant (see p186) of someone living in your accommodation, or you pay rent to a company or trust with which you have some connection, unless in either case you can show that your rental agreement was not created to enable you to claim HB.[205]
- None of the above apply, but the local authority decides that your agreement to pay rent was created to enable you to claim HB.[206] You should seek advice if this rule is applied to you.

Claiming for others

As with IS, you claim HB for yourself and your family, including your partner and dependent children (see p168). The amount you receive depends on the circumstances of your family.[207]

Amount

HB is a means-tested benefit and the amount you are entitled to depends on your 'applicable amount', your 'income' and your 'eligible rent' (see below for details).

If you are receiving IS, income-based JSA, or the guarantee credit of PC (from 6 October 2003), you are entitled to maximum HB, which is your weekly eligible rent less any non-dependant deductions (see p186).[208] If you have been receiving IS or income-based JSA for 26 continuous weeks, you can continue to get maximum HB for the first four weeks you or your partner take up full-time employment, as long as you notify the local authority within that period.[209]

If you are not receiving IS, income-based JSA, or the guarantee credit of PC, you are entitled to maximum HB (see above) less 65 per cent of the difference between your income and applicable amount (see below). If your income is less than your applicable amount, you are entitled to maximum HB.[210]

Examples of HB calculations are given on p187.

Applicable amount

Your applicable amount is worked out as for IS[211] (see p169) except that:

- from 6 October 2003, if you or your partner are aged 60 or over, your personal allowance is £102.10 (or £116.90 if you are aged 65 or over) if you are a single claimant, and £155.80 (or £175 if you or your partner are aged 65 or over) if you have a partner, and in such cases you will not qualify for a pensioner or higher pensioner premium;
- the family premium is increased by £10.45 if you have a child under the age of one;
- the personal allowance for a single person aged 16-24 and a lone parent under 18 is £43.25 and the lone parent rate of the family premium is £22.20;
- for the purposes of the severe disability premium, any joint tenant or owner, or a landlord or tenant of yours who lives with you, counts as a non-dependant if s/he falls into one of the categories of people who are excluded from HB (see p182);[212]
- to get the bereavement premium (see p171), you must claim HB within eight weeks of ceasing to get a bereavement allowance;
- IS or PC housing costs are not included in your applicable amount (you are not entitled to HB if you are receiving them – see p182).

Income

Details of how to calculate your income are set out in Chapter 8. Note that not all your income counts when working out your HB and that there are different rules if you or your partner are aged 60 or over. Any AA and DLA (see pp144 and 139) you receive are ignored, but IB and CA (see pp158 and 150) count in full. Some of your earnings are disregarded. If you have capital over fixed amounts, you are treated as having a 'tariff income' (see p233 for details).[213]

Eligible rent

Your eligible rent is the amount of rent which is taken into account when calculating your HB. It can include any service charges you have to pay, apart from those excluded under the rules set out below. Eligible service charges include those for management and maintenance costs, lifts, entry phones, gardens and rubbish removal.

Your eligible rent may be significantly less than the rent you actually pay because of the deductions and restrictions described below. This means that HB may not cover the whole of your rent payments even if you are entitled to maximum HB (see p169). You may be able to claim a discretionary housing payment if you need extra help to pay your rent (see p187).

Service charges for which housing benefit is not paid

The following charges are not eligible for HB and are deducted from the rent you pay, when calculating your HB.

- **Fuel charges.**[214] If your rent includes a specified amount for fuel, that amount is deducted when calculating your eligible rent. If your rent includes an unspecified amount for fuel, the following fixed weekly amounts are deducted:
  - £9.65 for heating;
  - £1.20 for hot water;
  - £0.80 for lighting;
  - £1.20 for cooking.

  If you (and your family) occupy only one room, only £5.82 is deducted for heating, or heating plus hot water and/or lighting. Fuel charges for common access areas and for communal rooms in sheltered accommodation are eligible for HB, as are specified charges for the maintenance of a heating system.[215]
- **Water charges.**[216] Any water charges which are included in your rent are not covered by HB.
- **Charges for meals.**[217] If you pay for meals, the following fixed weekly deductions are made when calculating your eligible rent, regardless of the charge you actually pay:
  - £19.50 for each member of your family aged 16 or over and £9.85 for each child who receives at least three meals a day;
  - £2.40 for each member of your family who receives breakfast only;
  - £12.95 for each member of your family aged 16 or over and £6.55 for each child in other cases – ie, half board.
- **Certain other service charges.**[218] Charges for the following items are also ineligible for HB:
  - personal laundry (but charges for the provision of a laundry room or machines are eligible);
  - cleaning rooms and windows other than those in communal areas, or the exterior of any windows that you and other members of your household are unable to clean yourselves;

- leisure items such as sports facilities or TV costs (other than relay for terrestrial channels);
- emergency alarm systems;
- medical expenses and personal and nursing care;
- counselling and support services;
- any other services not connected with the provision of adequate accommodation.

If you are jointly liable for rent which includes ineligible service charges, proportionate deductions are made from your share of the rent.[219] If you live in supported accommodation (see Chapter 3), HB no longer covers service charges for counselling and support, cleaning and emergency alarms. Local authorities will instead fund providers of supported accommodation to arrange for the provision of support and care services to their residents (see p19).

Rent restrictions

If you are a private tenant, your eligible rent may be restricted to an amount determined by the local rent officer. This will not apply to you if:[220]

- you live in local authority or registered housing association accommodation; *or*
- you live in accommodation provided by a housing association, registered charity or voluntary organisation where care, support or supervision is provided, or in accommodation funded by the Resettlement Agency; *or*
- you have been receiving HB for the same accommodation since 1 January 1996.

If you fall into one of the above categories, the local authority can still restrict your eligible rent if it decides your home is unreasonably large or expensive.[221] If this happens, you should seek further information and advice .

If you do not fall into one of the above categories, the local authority will refer your HB claim to an independent local rent officer who will use set criteria to determine whether your eligible rent should be restricted because your home is too large or expensive, or because you are under 25 (see below).[222] See CPAG's *Welfare Benefits and Tax Credits Handbook* for further details about the procedure.

The local authority is bound by the rent officer's determinations.[223] In practice, this means that in most cases, your eligible rent cannot exceed the average local rent for the size of accommodation you need. If you are under 25, your eligible rent will be restricted to the average local rent for one room only plus the shared use of a living room, kitchen, bathroom and toilet, unless you are entitled to the severe disability premium (see p169), or you are under 22 and were formerly in care, or you have a non-dependant (see p186) living with you. You should seek advice if you wish to challenge a rent restriction. If you are considering renting private accommodation, you can ask the local authority for a 'pre-tenancy determination' to find out whether HB will cover your full rent.[224]

Non-dependant deductions

If you have a non-dependant living with you, a deduction is made from your HB on the assumption that s/he is making a contribution towards your rent (whether s/he is or not).

A non-dependant is anyone who normally resides with you, does not have a normal home elsewhere, and shares accommodation with you apart from a bathroom, toilet, or common access area, or a communal room in sheltered accommodation.[225] The following people, however, do not count as non-dependants:[226]

- anyone who is separately liable to pay rent or other housing costs;
- a member of your family for benefit purposes (see p182);
- a person employed by a charitable or voluntary organisation as a resident carer for you or your partner;
- anyone who pays you or your partner, or to whom you pay, rent on a commercial basis;
- anyone who jointly occupies your home and is either a co-owner or joint tenant.

Anyone falling into the last two categories, however, will count as a non-dependant if they are excluded from HB under the rules set out on p182 (apart from students and persons subject to immigration control or who are not habitually resident in the UK).

No non-dependant deductions are made if:

- you or your partner receive AA (see p144) or DLA care component (see p140), or are registered blind; *or*
- a non-dependant is aged under 18, or is aged under 25 and receiving IS or income-based JSA or has been in hospital for more than six weeks (13 weeks after 6 October 2003), or is a full-time student.

The amount deducted depends on the income of the non-dependant.[227] If the non-dependant is not working more than 16 hours a week, there is a standard deduction of £7.40 a week. If the non-dependant is working for more than 16 hours a week the deductions are as follows:

Weekly gross income	*Weekly deduction*
£293 or more	£47.75
£235-£292.99	£43.50
£177-£234.99	£38.20
£137-£176.99	£23.35
£92-£136.99	£17.00
Less than £92	£7.40

From 6 October 2003, the deduction for a non-dependant who is getting PC and who is working more than 16 hours a week is £7.40, regardless of his or her income.[228] Also, from 6 October 2003, if you are aged 65 or over and claiming HB and a non-dependant comes to live with you, any increase in his or her income will not affect your HB for up to a year.[229]

A deduction is made for each non-dependant but only one deduction is made for a non-dependant couple.

Discretionary housing payments[230]

You can be paid a discretionary housing payment (DHP) by the local authority in addition to your HB if you need further help to pay your rent.

The amount and period of payment is up to the local authority but you cannot get a DHP:

- if you are not entitled to HB, or your HB has been suspended;
- which exceeds your rent (less service charges which are not eligible for HB – see p184);
- for any such ineligible service charges (see p184).

You must make a separate claim for a DHP to the local authority. There is no legal right to a payment and no right of appeal to an independent tribunal. You can, however, request a review of any decision relating to a DHP.

Examples of HB calculations

Mr and Mrs Khan are both aged 53 and get IS. They live with their son, aged 28, who has learning difficulties and receives IS and DLA. Their rent is £100 a week, including all their fuel costs. No restrictions are imposed by the rent officer.

They are entitled to maximum HB because they are receiving IS.

1. Their eligible rent = £100 *less* £12.85 deduction for fuel charges (see p184) = £87.15
2. HB = £87.15 eligible rent *less* £7.40 non-dependant deduction (see p186) = £79.75

If Mr Khan starts working and is no longer entitled to IS, and his earnings are assessed for HB purposes as £150 a week, the maximum HB of £79.75 would be reduced by 65 per cent of the difference between their income and their applicable amount.

1.Their applicable amount is £85.75 (personal allowance for a couple).

2.Their income (£150) less their applicable amount (£85.75) = £64.25 x 65% = £41.76
3.HB = £79.75 *less* £41.76 = £37.99

How to claim

Claim forms are available from your local authority or the DWP and should be returned to the HB section of the authority. If you are claiming IS, PC, or income-based JSA, you should claim HB on the standard claim form HCTB1, which should be included in the claim packs for these benefits.

You claim HB for yourself and your family (see p182). Either you or your partner can be the claimant and, as with IS, you can sometimes be better off if one of you claims rather the other (see p174).

HB is paid for a period of up to 60 weeks, after which you have to reclaim.[231] From 6 October 2003, however, HB will be paid for longer periods (up to five years) if you or your partner are aged 60 or over. If you are a local authority tenant, your HB will be paid by reducing your rent (rent rebate). If you are a private tenant, your HB will usually be paid to you (rent allowance) but in specified circumstances, it can be paid directly to your landlord.[232]

Council tax benefit

Council tax benefit (CTB) is a tax free, means-tested weekly benefit paid to people who are liable to pay council tax. It can be claimed by people who are working or unemployed. CTB is paid and administered by local authorities (councils).

Who can claim

You qualify for CTB if:[233]

- you are liable to pay council tax (see p189); *and*
- your income is low enough (see p190); *and*
- you and your partner do not have savings and other capital worth more than £16,000 (see Chapter 8 for details of how your capital is calculated), unless you or your partner are getting the guarantee credit of PC from 6 October 2003 (see p177), in which case your capital is not taken into account; *and*
- you are not a full-time student (there are exceptions, however, as for HB, see p182); *and*
- you are habitually resident in the UK and you are not subject to immigration control (see p139).

As with IS, you claim CTB for yourself and your family, including your partner and dependent children, and the amount you receive depends on your financial and other circumstances.[234]

In certain circumstances, you can qualify for CTB in the form of a 'second adult rebate' regardless of your income or capital, if you have a non-dependant living with you who has a low income and who is not disregarded for council tax discount purposes (see p190).[235] For more details, see CPAG's *Welfare Benefits and Tax Credits Handbook*.

Liability to pay council tax

Council tax is payable on most residential dwellings, unless they are exempt (see below). There are eight different 'bands' (or levels) of council tax, depending on the valuation of the dwelling. You are liable to pay council tax in respect of your 'sole or main residence'[236] even if you are temporarily absent from it. You should remain eligible for CTB as long as you remain liable to pay council tax, including while you are away from home in the circumstances during which IS housing costs remain payable (see p172).[237] Only one council tax bill is payable in respect of each dwelling. A 'hierarchy of liability' determines which resident is liable to pay the bill. In general, owner-occupiers are primarily liable, then tenants, then licensees, then other residents. Partners, joint owners and joint tenants are normally jointly liable. Owners of care homes (and some hostels) and houses in multiple occupation are usually liable rather than the residents.

For more details about liability and appeal rights, see CPAG's *Council Tax Handbook*.

Exemptions from liability

Some dwellings are exempt from council tax, including:[238]

- dwellings which are unoccupied because the former resident is permanently in hospital, a care home, a hostel where care is provided, or anywhere else (including someone else's home) where s/he is receiving *or providing* personal care relating to old age, disablement, illness, mental disorder, or drug/alcohol dependence;
- dwellings wholly occupied by people who are severely mentally impaired;
- dwellings with a self-contained unit occupied by a dependent relative of the occupier of the main part of the dwelling, where that dependent relative is aged over 65 (eg, a 'granny flat'), or substantially and permanently disabled, or severely mentally impaired. This exemption only applies in England and Wales and only the self-contained unit is exempt from the tax.

The disability reduction scheme

The disability reduction scheme[239] applies if your dwelling has an additional kitchen or bathroom for the use of a 'substantially and permanently disabled' person, or another room used predominantly for her/his needs, or enough space for the use of her/his wheelchair. If this applies, your council tax bill is reduced to the valuation band below that for your dwelling (eg, your bill may be reduced from band D to band C). If it is already in the lowest band (band A), your bill is reduced by one-sixth.[240]

The discount scheme

The discount scheme[241] reduces your bill by 25 per cent if there is only one adult resident in the dwelling, or 50 per cent if there are no adult residents. Some people are disregarded as residents, including anyone who is:

- under the age of 18 or a student; *or*
- solely or mainly resident in a care home, hospital, or hostels providing personal care; *or*
- 'severely mentally impaired' (ie, has a permanent severe impairment of intelligence and social functioning, whatever the cause); *or*
- a carer who:
  - provides at least 35 hours care a week for a person who is not their partner or child aged under 18 and who receives the higher rates of the DLA care component or AA; *or*
  - provides care and/or support for at least 24 hours a week, and is employed by the person being looked after and was introduced to that person by, or provides the care or support on behalf of, a local authority, government department or charity and in either case is paid no more than £30 a week for the work.

Amount

CTB is a means-tested benefit and the amount you are entitled to depends on your circumstances. CTB is paid in the form of a rebate – ie, a reduction in your bill.

If you are receiving IS (see p210), income-based JSA (see p175), or the guarantee credit of PC (from 6 October 2003), your council tax is fully rebated (unless your home is in band F or above), apart from any non-dependant deductions which you will have to pay (see below). If you have been receiving IS or income-based JSA for at least 26 continuous weeks, your council tax remains fully rebated for the first four weeks you or your partner take up full-time employment, as long as you notify the local authority within that period.[242]

If you are not receiving IS, income-based JSA, or the guarantee credit of PC, your weekly council tax liability is reduced to 20 per cent of the difference between your income and your applicable amount (see below), plus any non-dependant deductions which you have to pay (see p191). If this figure exceeds your council tax liability you are not entitled to any CTB. If your income is less than your applicable amount your council tax is fully rebated.[243]

Your income is calculated in the same way as for HB. Your applicable amount is also worked out in the same way as for HB (see p183), except that the categories of people who do not count as non-dependants for the purposes of the severe disability premium (see p169) are slightly different.[244] To get the bereavement premium (see p171), you must claim CTB within eight weeks of ceasing to get a bereavement allowance.

Examples of CTB calculations are given on p192.

You should also note the following points.

- If you are jointly liable for council tax with someone other than your partner, your CTB will be calculated on your proportionate share of the bill.[245]
- If your home is in council tax valuation bands F, G or H, you can only get CTB on 11/13, 11/15 and 11/18 respectively of your total council tax liability.[246]
- If you qualify for a second adult rebate (see p188) your council tax is rebated by up to 25 per cent, depending on the income of your non-dependant.[247]
- You can request a discretionary housing payment in addition to CTB to help meet your liability for council tax (see below).

Non-dependant deductions

If you have a non-dependant living with you, a deduction is made from your CTB and will not form part of your rebate, on the assumption that s/he is making a contribution towards your council tax (whether s/he is or not).

The rules about non-dependant deductions are the same as for HB (see p186), apart from the following differences.

- The last two categories of people on p186 who do not count as non-dependants for HB do not apply to CTB. For CTB, a joint occupier who is jointly liable for council tax, or a person other than a close relative (see p413) who is liable to pay you rent on a commercial basis, does not count as a non-dependant unless her/his liability was created to take advantage of the CTB scheme.[248]
- No non-dependant deduction is made for anyone who is receiving IS or income-based JSA (not just those under 25 as for HB), or anyone who is disregarded for council tax discount purposes, apart from students (see p188).[249]
- The standard deduction for a non-dependant who is not working more than 16 hours a week is £2.30.[250]
- If the non-dependant is working more than 16 hours a week, the amount of deduction is as follows:[251]

Weekly gross income	Weekly deduction
£293 or over	£6.95
£235-£292.99	£5.80
£137-£234.99	£4.60
Less than £137 or below	£2.30

- From 6 October 2003, the deduction for a non-dependant who is getting PC and who is working more than 16 hours a week is £2.30, regardless of his or her income.[252]

Discretionary housing payments[253]

You can be paid a discretionary housing payment (DHP) by the local authority in addition to your CTB if you need further help to pay your council tax.

The amount and period of payment is up to the local authority but you cannot get a DHP:

- if you are not entitled to CTB, or your CTB has been suspended, or you are only entitled to a 'second adult rebate' (see p188);
- which exceeds your weekly council tax liability.

You must make a separate claim for a DHP to the local authority. There is no legal right to a payment and no right of appeal to an independent tribunal. You can, however, request a review of any decision relating to a DHP.

Examples of CTB calculations

Mr and Mrs Khan, whose circumstances are set out on p187, live in a band C property. While they are getting IS, they would be entitled to a full rebate of their council tax (there would be no non-dependant deduction for their son because he is in receipt of IS).

When Mr Khan starts work, their weekly council tax liability would be reduced to their income (£150) less their applicable amount (£88.75) = £61.25 x 20% = £12.25. If this is more than their weekly liability, they would not qualify for CTB.

How to claim

The procedure is the same as for HB (see p188). Application forms are available from your local authority, or you can claim on form HCTB1 if you also claiming IS, PC or income-based JSA. CTB is paid by reducing your council tax liability.

Tax credits

Tax credits are tax-free means-tested benefits paid to people who are responsible for children or in low paid work. Although they are called tax credits and are paid and administered by the Inland Revenue, they are similar in character to other social security benefits and should not be confused with income tax allowances. There are two tax credits:

- **child tax credit** (CTC) is paid to families with children (in addition to child benefit);
- **working tax credit** (WTC) is paid to people in low paid work.

You can qualify for either or both tax credits. CTC will replace the child elements of IS and income-based JSA from April 2004 (see p174). WTC replaced working families' tax credit and disabled person's tax credit from 6 April 2003.

Who can claim

To qualify for either tax credit you must be:[254]

- aged 16 or over; *and*

- present and ordinarily resident in the UK (you are treated as present during a temporary absence of up to eight weeks, or up to 12 weeks if you are abroad to get medical treatment for yourself, your partner or your child); *and*
- not subject to immigration control (see p139). The rules are complex and there are exceptions. See CPAG's *Welfare Benefits and Tax Credits Handbook* for details. Note that if you have a partner (see below) and only one of you is subject to immigration control, your entitlement to tax credits is not affected; *and*
- assessed as having a low enough income (see below).

If you have a partner (ie, a spouse, or a person of the opposite sex with whom you are living as a couple), you must make a joint claim for tax credits unless you are permanently separated and your income and entitlement is jointly assessed.

To qualify for child tax credit you or your partner must be responsible for:[255]

- a child under 16; *or*
- a young person under 19 in full-time non-advanced education.

You can claim CTC whether or not you are working. You are responsible for a child or young person if s/he is 'normally living with' you. Only one person can get CTC for a child (the 'main carer'). You cannot get CTC for a child being maintained or accommodated by a local authority (unless the child has been accommodated under the Children Act because of a disability).

You can continue to get CTC:

- for eight weeks after a child or young person dies;
- until the September after the 16th birthday of a child who leaves school at 16;
- for 20 weeks after a young person under 18 leaves education, if s/he registers with the careers services.

To qualify for working tax credit you or your partner must be:[256]

- working at least 16 hours a week and responsible for a child or young person (the rules about when you are responsible are the same as for CTC – see p191); *or*
- aged 25 or over and working at least 30 hours a week; *or*
- aged 50 or over, working at least 16 hours a week and getting CA or bereavement benefits when you claim WTC, or getting IS, JSA, IB or SDA for six months before you claim WTC; *or*
- working at least 16 hours a week, have one of the disabilities listed in the claims pack which puts you at a disadvantage of getting a job (these include specified mobility and sensory and mental difficulties) and satisfy the benefit condition (see p194).

You satisfy the benefit condition if:[257]

- you are getting AA or DLA when you claim WTC; *or*
- you were getting long-term or higher rate short-term IB (see p158), SDA, or a disability or higher pensioner premium of IS, JSA, HB or CTB (see p169), for at least one day in the 182 days before you claim WTC; *or*
- you were incapable of work and as a result you were getting SSP or sick pay (see p158), lower rate short-term IB (see p158), IS, or national insurance contributions (see p153) for at least 20 weeks ending in the eight weeks before you claim WTC, and you have a disability which is likely to last for at least six months and your earnings are at least 20 per cent less than they were before your disability began.

To get WTC, you must be working, or due to start work within seven days, when you claim. The work must be for payment (other than expenses) and be expected to last for at least four weeks. When calculating whether you work for at least 16 or 30 hours a week, the hours you 'normally work' are assessed, ignoring unpaid meal breaks and paid holidays. You are treated as working for at least 16 or 30 hours a week in certain circumstances, if you were doing so immediately before you were sick, or on maternity, paternity or adoption leave.

Amount

Tax credits are means-tested benefits and the amounts you are entitled to depends on your income and other circumstances. Note that there is no capital limit for claiming tax credits but your income from capital is taken into account. Examples of calculations are given on p196.

There are three steps involved in calculating your entitlement to tax credits:[258]

Step one: Calculate your maximum entitlement (see p195). This is the total of all the elements of CTC and WTC to which you are entitled.

Step two: Compare your income (see p196) with the relevant threshold (see p196). If your income is below the threshold, you are entitled to maximum tax credits, as calculated in step one. You are automatically entitled to the maximum if you are getting IS or income-based JSA. If your income is above the threshold, proceed to step three.

Step three: Reduce maximum entitlement by 37 per cent of the amount by which your income exceeds the relevant threshold. The elements of WTC (other than the childcare element) are reduced first, followed by the childcare element and then the child elements of CTC. Entitlement to the family element of CTC is retained unless your income exceeds £50,000 a year, in which case it is reduced by 6.67 per cent of the amount by which your income exceeds that figure.

Note that:

- if you have a partner (see p226), the calculation is based on your joint income;

- entitlement to both tax credits is calculated together;
- entitlement is calculated using annual figures for your income and maximum entitlement for the tax year (April to April) in which you claim (but you are actually paid CTC weekly or four weekly and WTC with your normal wages);
- if you claim part-way through the tax year, or your maximum entitlement changes during the tax year (eg, because you have another child, or start or stop working), the calculation must be repeated for each relevant period by prorating the figures for maximum entitlement, income and thresholds according to the number of days in the period.

Maximum entitlement[259]

Add up the following amounts which are applicable to you:

If you qualify for CTC:	
Family element (one per family)	£545, or £1,090 if you have a baby under one
Child element (per child)	£1,445
Disabled child element (for each child who gets DLA or is registered blind)	£2,115
Severely disabled child element (for each child who gets the highest rate care component of DLA)	£865
If you qualify for WTC:	
Basic element	£1,525
Second adult or lone parent element (If you have a partner or are a lone parent)	£1,500
30-hour element (if you or your partner work at least 30 hours a week – couples with a child can add their hours together)	£620
Disability element (if you or your partner work at least 16 hours a week and satisfy the disability and benefit conditions set out on p194)	£2,040
Severe disability element (if you or your partner get the highest rate care component of DLA)	£865
50 plus element (if you qualify for WTC on the basis of being aged 50 or over – see p193) if you are working at least 30 hours	£1,045 or £1,565
Childcare element (if you are a lone parent, or you and your partner are both working, or one of you is working and the other is incapacitated)	70% of eligible childcare costs (see p196)

Eligible childcare costs are those paid to a registered childminder, or other approved provider (eg, a nursery or after school club). The maximum payable for one child is £94.50 a week and for two or more children £140 a week.[260]

Income

Your income for tax credit purposes is explained in Chapter 8. It is calculated on an annual basis. If you claim tax credits in 2003/04, your entitlement will be initially calculated using your income during the tax year 2001/02.[261] If you claim in 2004/05, your income during 2003/04 will be used. If your income goes down after you claim, or increases by more than £2,500, you can inform the Inland Revenue and your award will be re-assessed.[262] Alternatively, you can wait until you receive a final decision at the end of the tax year (see p197) and your award will be re-adjusted. Any underpayment will be refunded to you. Any overpayment will be recoverable from you (usually by reducing your following year's award).

Thresholds

The relevant threshold if you are eligible for CTC only is £13,230. The relevant threshold if you are entitled to WTC (with or without CTC) is £5,060.[263]

Examples of tax credit calculations

Mr and Mrs Jones have one child, aged 9, who is severely disabled and gets the highest rate care component of DLA. If they are claiming IS or income-based JSA, their entitlement to CTC would be calculated as follows:

Step one: Their maximum entitlement is:

£545	CTC family element
£1,455	CTC child element
£2,155	CTC disabled child element
£865	CTC severely disabled child element
£5,020	maximum CTC

Step two: They are entitled to maximum CTC because they are getting IS.

If Mr Jones was working and earning £15,000 a year, their tax credit entitlement would be calculated as follows:

Step one: Their maximum entitlement is:

£5,020	CTC (see above)
£1,525	WTC basic element
£1,500	WTC second adult element
£8,045	maximum tax credit entitlement

Step two: Their income of £15,000 exceeds the relevant threshold of £5,060 by £9,940

Step three: Their maximum entitlement of £8,045 is reduced by £3,677 (37% of £9,940) to give actual entitlement of £4,368. This would all be paid as CTC.

How to claim

You can make a claim on form TC600, which you can get from Inland Revenue or DWP offices or by telephoning 0845 300 3900 (textphone 0845 300 3909). You can also claim online at www.inlandrevenue.gov.uk. Both tax credits are claimed together on one form.

CTC and the childcare element of WTC are paid directly to the main carer. You can choose to be paid weekly or four weekly. The other elements of WTC are normally paid by your employer with your wages.[264]

Change of circumstances

When you first make your claim, you will receive an 'initial award' for the rest of the tax year, based on your circumstances when you claim and your previous income. If your circumstances change during the year, your award can be re-assessed if you notify the Inland Revenue. Otherwise, you will receive a notice at the end of the tax year asking you to confirm whether the information used to assess your award was correct and to notify any changes there have been during the year. You will then receive a final decision, which may include an under- or overpayment. The end of year notice is treated as an automatic claim for the following year if you are still entitled to tax credits.[265]

You must notify the Inland Revenue if you start or stop living with a partner, or if your childcare costs stop or reduce by more than £10 a week for four weeks.[266] If you fail to notify these changes within three months, you can be fined up to £300.[267] If your maximum entitlement increases during the year, you should also notify the Inland Revenue within three months, as only three months of arrears can be paid as a result of such changes.[268] If your income changes, you can inform the Inland Revenue straightaway or wait until the end of the tax year.

Social fund payments

The social fund is a government fund which makes payments to people on low incomes to meet specified needs. The fund is administered by the DWP. There are two types of payments available from the social fund:

- **funeral grants, maternity grants and winter payments** – you are legally entitled to these payments if you satisfy the rules;
- **community care grants, budgeting loans and crisis loans** – you are eligible for these payments if you satisfy the rules but awards are discretionary and budget limited.

You are not entitled to a social fund payment (apart from a crisis loan following a disaster) if you are subject to immigration control (see p139).

Funeral grants

Funeral grants are paid to people to help with the cost of a funeral of a close relative or friend.

Who can claim

You qualify for a funeral grant if:[269]

- you or your partner have been awarded IS, income-based JSA, PC (from 6 October 2003 – see p176), HB, CTB, CTC at a rate which exceeds the family element (see p195) or WTC which includes the disability or severe disability element (see p195) when you claim a funeral grant, or you receive a backdated award of one of these benefits which covers the date of your claim; *and*
- you or your partner are in one of the categories of people who are eligible to claim (see below); *and*
- you or your partner have accepted responsibility for paying the cost of a funeral (ie, you are liable to pay the cost because, for example, the funeral director's bill is in your name); *and*
- the deceased was ordinarily resident in the UK when s/he died and the funeral takes place in the UK (or, in certain circumstances, in an EEA country – see p168).

You are eligible to claim a funeral grant if you, or your partner, fall into one of the following categories.[270]

- You were the partner of the deceased when s/he died. Partner means spouse, or someone you were living with as husband and wife.[271]
- The deceased was a child for whom you were responsible (you may be excluded if the child had an absent parent who was not getting one of the qualifying benefits listed above).
- You were a 'close relative' (see p150) or close friend of the deceased and it is reasonable for you to accept responsibility for the funeral costs, given the nature and extent of your contact with the deceased.[272] You are excluded from getting a grant as a close relative or close friend, however, if the deceased has a partner, parent or adult son or daughter (unless the parent, son or daughter is receiving one of the qualifying benefits listed above, or was estranged from the deceased when s/he died, or is a student, prisoner or asylum seeker receiving asylum support).[273] You are also excluded if there is a close relative of the deceased who was in closer contact with her/him than you were, or equally close contact if the close relative (or partner) is not getting a qualifying benefit.[274]

Amount

The following amounts can be paid, subject to the deductions below:[275]

- the costs of burial or cremation (including documentation); *plus*
- specified transport costs; *plus*
- up to £700 for other costs – eg, funeral directors' fees, flowers, religious costs.

The following amounts are deducted from an award of a funeral grant:

- any of the deceased's assets available to you without probate or letters of administration[276] (note that the DWP can recover a funeral grant from the deceased's estate);[277]
- any payment made on the death of the deceased from an insurance policy, occupational pension scheme, pre-paid funeral plan, burial club, charity or relative of yours.[278]

How to claim

You should claim a funeral grant on form SF200 which you can get from your local DWP office. You must claim within three months of the date of the funeral.[279]

Sure Start maternity grants

Maternity grants are one-off payments to help with the cost of maternity expenses.

Who can claim

You qualify for a maternity grant if:[280]

- you or your partner have been awarded IS, income-based JSA, PC (from 6 October 2003 – see p176), CTC at a rate which exceeds the family element (see p195) or WTC which includes the disability or severe disability element (see p195) when you claim a maternity grant, or you receive a backdated award of one of these benefits which covers the date of your claim; *and*
- you or a member of your family (as defined for IS – see p182) are pregnant, or have given birth in the last three months (including stillbirth after 24 weeks of pregnancy), or have adopted a baby under 12 months old, or have a parental order for a surrogate child.

Amount

The maternity grant is £500 for each qualifying child.[281]

How to claim

You should claim on form SF100 available from your local DWP office. You must claim in the 11 weeks before the expected week of birth or in the three months after the birth, adoption or parental order. Your claim form must be signed by a health professional to confirm that you have received health and welfare advice.

Winter payments

Winter payments are made to help with the cost of fuel bills.

Who can claim

There are two types of winter payments.

- **Cold weather payments** are paid if the average temperature in your area falls below zero degrees Celsius for at least a week. You qualify for a payment if you

are receiving IS or income-based JSA and either you have a child under five, or you are receiving a pensioner, higher pensioner, disability, enhanced disability, severe disability or disabled child premium (see p169), or you are receiving PC (from 6 October 2003 – see p176) and you are not resident in a care home.[282]
- **Winter fuel payments** are paid to people who are aged 60 or over in the week beginning on the third Monday in September. You cannot get a payment, however, if at that time, you have been in hospital for more than 52 weeks, or you are receiving IS or income-based JSA and are in a care home and have been throughout the previous 12 weeks.[283] If you are in a care home and are not getting IS or JSA, you can get 50 per cent of the payment.

Amount

Cold weather payments are £8.50 for each qualifying week. Winter fuel payments are one-off grants of £200 a household, or £300 if you or your partner are aged 80 or over.

How to claim

There is no need to make a claim for a cold weather payment. You should be paid automatically if you qualify. Anyone who received a winter fuel payment last year or who is getting a retirement pension or other benefit (apart from HB and CTB) in the qualifying week should automatically receive a winter fuel payment. Others should make a claim. You can get a claim form by ringing a special local rate helpline on 08459 15 15 15 (textphone 01325 745136).

Community care grants

Community care grants (CCGs) are paid to help people on IS, income-based JSA, or PC (from 6 October 2003 – see p176) to live independently in the community.

Who can claim

You are eligible for a CCG if:
- you are receiving IS, income-based JSA or PC (from 6 October 2003 – see p176) when you claim a CCG, or you are due to leave institutional or residential care within six weeks of claiming a CCG and are likely to get one of those benefits when you leave;[284] *and*
- you do not have too much capital (see p202); *and*
- the CCG is not for an 'excluded item' (see p201); *and*
- you need the CCG:
  - to help you or a member of your family, or someone for whom you or a member of your family will be providing care, to become established in the community following a stay in institutional or residential care, or to remain in the community rather than enter such care; *or*
  - to ease exceptional pressures on you and your family; *or*
  - to help you set up home as part of a planned resettlement programme; *or*

- to help you care for a prisoner or young offender on temporary release; *or*
- to help you with travel expenses to visit someone who is ill, attend a relative's funeral, ease a domestic crisis, or move to more suitable accommodation.[285]

There is no legal entitlement to a CCG. Payments are discretionary and each DWP district office is given a fixed annual budget for CCGs. Guidance is issued by the DWP (the *Social Fund Guide)* and by each district on the circumstances in which a CCG should be awarded. The guidance is not legally binding, however, and decisions must take into account all the circumstances of each application, including the nature, extent and urgency of the need.[286] The guidance suggests that priority should be given where there is mental or physical disability, illness, general frailty, abuse or neglect, unstable family circumstances, an unsettled way of life and drug or alcohol misuse.

The following points should be noted.

- You must specify the items for which you need the CCG. You can ask for a CCG for any items which are not excluded (see below). If, however, you have been awarded or refused a CCG for a particular item, you cannot get a CCG for the same item for 26 weeks from the date of your application.[287]
- CCGs are most often awarded to help people move out of, or stay out of, institutional or residential care (see p200). This could include hospital, care homes, group homes, supported lodgings, sheltered housing, hostels and any other accommodation which provides residents with substantial care or supervision. If you are moving out of care you need to show that a CCG will help you establish yourself in the community (eg, by helping you set up home). If you live in your own home, you need to show that a CCG will lessen the risk of you going into hospital or residential care – eg, by improving your ability to cope at home and to stay healthy. The type of items you could claim for include furniture and household equipment, moving expenses, clothing and footwear and non-medical items needed because of sickness and disability, including wheelchairs and special beds, mattresses, chairs and equipment to help with everyday living.
- You can also claim a CCG to ease exceptional pressures on you and your family. 'Family' is not defined in the law and could encompass couples (married or not, of any sex[288]), children and adult sons and daughters and other relatives living together. People living on their own, however, are excluded under this provision.[289] 'Exceptional pressures' are not defined in the law and could include disability, sickness, depression, bereavement, family breakdown, poor living conditions and child behavioural problems.

Excluded items

You cannot get a CCG for any of the following items:[290]

- the cost of domestic assistance (including home care) or respite care;

- a medical, surgical, optical, aural or dental item. A medical item, however, should not include an everyday item needed because of a medical condition – eg, non-allergic bedding, a special bed or mattress, special shoes, equipment for everyday living and a wheelchair;
- most housing costs including repairs and improvements (other than minor ones), rent, deposits, mortgage payments, residential accommodation charges and council tax and water charges;
- telephone and fuel charges, educational or training needs, work-related expenses, debts to government departments, court fines and fees, needs which a local authority has a statutory duty to meet and most daily living expenses;
- a need which occurs outside the UK.

There are other exclusions. For a full list, see CPAG's *Welfare Benefits and Tax Credits Handbook*.

Amount

You must specify the amount of CCG you need on your application form (see below). There is no legal maximum but the minimum you can be awarded is £30 (unless the CCG is for travel expenses).[291] You should state the actual or estimated cost of each item you need on your application form. The amount you request should be allowed unless it is unreasonable. The DWP often refers to catalogue prices as a guide to what is reasonable.

Any CCG you are awarded is reduced by the amount of capital you and your partner have in excess of £500 (£1,000 if either of you is aged 60 or over).[292]

How to claim

You should apply for a CCG on form SF300 obtainable from your local DWP office. You should list all the items you need and the actual or estimated cost of each item. You should explain why you need the items, with reference to the purposes for which a CCG can be awarded (see p204), and why your application should be given high priority. A supporting letter from your doctor, social worker or other professional involved in your care may help your case.

Budgeting loans

Budgeting loans (BLs) are interest-free loans paid to help people on IS, income-based JSA, or PC (from 6 October 2003 – see p176) with intermittent expenses.

Who can claim

You are eligible for a BL if:[293]

- you are in receipt of IS, income-based JSA, or PC (from 6 October 2003 – see p176) when you claim a BL and you and/or your partner have been receiving one of those benefits throughout the 26 weeks before your claim is determined, apart from any breaks of up to 28 days; *and*

- you must not have too much capital; *and*
- the BL must be for one or more of the following items:
  - furniture or household equipment;
  - clothing and footwear;
  - rent in advance and/or removal expenses on moving;
  - improvement, maintenance and security of the home;
  - travelling expenses;
  - expenses related to seeking or re-entering work;
- hire purchase and other debts for any of the above.

As with CCGs (see p200), there is no legal entitlement to a payment and each DWP district office is given a fixed annual budget for loans. Unlike CCGs, however, applications are decided in accordance with set criteria, rather than on a discretionary basis.

Repayment of BLs can cause hardship and you should always apply for a CCG rather than a BL if you are eligible (see p200).

Amount

You can request a BL of between £30 and £1,000.[294] Whether you are actually offered a BL and the amount you are offered depends on a number of factors including:[295]

- the length of time you have been receiving benefit;
- the size of your family;
- the amount of any outstanding BLs you have;
- your ability to repay a BL within 78 weeks.

If you are offered a loan, you will be given details of the weekly repayment rate, which can vary from five per cent to 25 per cent of your IS applicable amount (excluding housing costs). You will sometimes be given more than one offer of different amounts with different terms.

Any award, however, is reduced by the amount of any capital you or your partner have in excess of £500 (£1,000 if either of you is aged 60 or over).[296]

BLs are normally recovered by direct deductions from your weekly benefit.

How to claim

You should apply for a BL on form SF500 available from your local DWP office. If you are offered a loan, you are given 14 days to return your acceptance.

Crisis loans

Crisis loans (CLs) are paid to people who have no money because of a crisis. Unlike budgeting loans, they are not restricted to people on benefit.

Who can claim

You are eligible for a CL if:[297]

- you are aged 16 or over; *and*
- you have insufficient resources to meet the immediate needs of yourself and/or your family; *and*
- you need a CL to prevent serious damage or serious risk to your (or a member of your family's) health and safety following an emergency or disaster; *or*
- you need a CL for rent in advance to secure private accommodation following a stay in care (you must also have been awarded a community care grant – see p200); *and*
- you are not in hospital or a care home (unless your discharge is planned within the next two weeks) and the CL is not for an excluded item. Items excluded are the same as for community care grants see (p201) except that living expenses and fuel costs are not excluded but holidays, TVs and cars are; *and*
- you are likely to be able to repay the loan.

As with community care grants (see p200), there is no legal entitlement to a CL. Payments are discretionary and must take into account the circumstances of each case (including the urgency of the need) and guidance is set out in the *Social Fund Guide*. The *Guide* gives examples of when a CL may be appropriate, including where you have lost money, you are waiting for a benefit claim to be processed, or you have suffered an emergency or disaster such as a fire or flood. You can, however, claim in any situation where you have no money.

Amount

You can request a lump sum CL of up to £1,000, or a weekly sum of up to 75 per cent of your IS personal allowance (see p169) plus £38.50 for each child, for living expenses.[298] You will not usually be offered more than you can repay in 78 weeks. You will be given details of the weekly repayment rate which is normally between 5 per cent and 15 per cent of your IS applicable amount excluding housing costs (see p172).

How to claim

You should claim a CL on form SF400 or SF401 from your local DWP office. It is common for DWP staff to advise potential applicants that they do not qualify. You should always insist on completing an application form and being given a written decision. You will normally be interviewed and you should always fully explain your circumstances and why you need a CL.

5. People in hospital

Your benefit may be affected after you or your dependants have been receiving free NHS funded treatment as an inpatient in a hospital or similar institution for the periods specified below.[299] A 'similar institution' to a hospital could include some care homes, hospices and rehabilitation units which provide medical or nursing care, but only if your maintenance and treatment are being directly funded by a health authority and your placement was not arranged by a local authority (even if the NHS is contributing to the cost of your nursing care – see p259).[300]

Separate spells as an inpatient which are separated by 28 days or less are linked together when calculating the periods specified below.[301] For most benefits, you do not count as an inpatient on the day you enter hospital, but you do on the day you are discharged.[302] For attendance allowance (AA) and disability living allowance (DLA), however, you do not count as an inpatient on both the days you enter and leave hospital.[303]

You should inform the benefit authorities promptly if you think that your benefit may be affected by the rules set out below, to avoid being overpaid or underpaid benefit. If you need to claim benefit on the basis of incapacity for work, the hospital can issue medical certificates. You can arrange for someone to collect your benefit while you are in hospital and if you are unable to manage your affairs, another person can act as your appointee (see p111).

See p97 if you need help with fares if you have to attend a hospital for treatment. You may be eligible for a community care grant to cover fares to visit someone in hospital (see p200).

After four weeks

- Any **AA or DLA** you are getting stops after you have been an inpatient for 28 days (but note the special rule below about the mobility component of DLA and that any DLA you are getting for a child continues to be paid until s/he has been an inpatient for 12 weeks).[304] If you are re-admitted as an inpatient within 28 days of a previous stay, your AA or DLA will stop sooner or immediately, because of the linking rule (see above). Also, if you are not entitled to AA or DLA care component because you are living in a care home (see p370), you will not be entitled to them when you become an inpatient, because periods spent in both types of accommodation link, unless they are separated by more than 28 days (this rule does not apply to DLA mobility component).[305] Your AA and DLA should be paid as normal when you are discharged as an inpatient (you should not have to make a fresh claim but should inform the DWP as soon as you are discharged). Note that if you first become entitled to AA or DLA while you are an inpatient, you cannot receive any benefit until you are discharged.[306]
- You can continue to receive the **mobility component of DLA** while you are an inpatient if you had a Motability agreement (see p106) when you entered hospital (benefit normally continues until the agreement ends).[307] If you are terminally ill, you can continue to receive AA or DLA while you are in a non-NHS hospice.[308]

- Your entitlement to the **severe disability premium** paid with income support (IS), housing benefit (HB) and council tax benefit (CTB) and the severe disability addition of pension credit (PC – see p176) stops once you are no longer entitled to AA or DLA. If, however, you are a member of a couple and one or both of you are an inpatient, you can qualify for the premium/addition at the single person's rate.[309] Your entitlement to the disability, enhanced disability, higher pensioner, or disabled child premiums (see p169) paid with IS, is not affected by the withdrawal of AA or DLA.[310] If your IS or PC stops because of the loss of the severe disability premium/addition, your HB and CTB will also stop and you will need to submit a new claim.
- Your entitlement to **carer's allowance** (CA) stops when the person you are caring for loses entitlement to AA or DLA care component (see p205). The **carer's premium/addition** paid with IS, HB, CTB and PC can continue to be paid for eight weeks after CA, or AA/DLA care component stops.

After 12 weeks

- **DLA paid for a child** under 16 stops after s/he has been an inpatient for 12 weeks.[311]
- You remain entitled to CA for up to 12 weeks in any period of 26 weeks while you, or the person you are caring for, are an inpatient.[312] If, however, the person you are caring for is no longer entitled to AA or DLA because s/he is an inpatient, your CA will stop at that point (see above). If your CA stops because you are an inpatient, the person you usually care for may become entitled to the severe disability premium/addition with her/his IS or PC.
- The personal allowance for a child or young person paid with **IS** and **income-based JSA** is reduced to £15.50 after s/he has been an inpatient for 12 weeks.[313] Child-related premiums remain payable, including the disabled child premium (even after the cessation of DLA).[314] **Child benefit and an increase for a child paid with non-means-tested benefits** stop after the child has been an inpatient for 12 weeks, unless you continue to regularly incur expenditure in respect of her/him.[315] Child tax credit is not affected.

After 52 weeks

- After you have been an inpatient for 52 weeks, the basic weekly rates of **incapacity benefit, severe disablement allowance, state retirement pension and bereavement/widow's benefits** are reduced to £15.50 a week.[316] You can be paid less than this if you are unable to act for yourself, your benefit is being paid to the hospital (as your appointee or on your appointee's request) and your doctor certifies that some or all of the benefit cannot be used for your personal comfort or enjoyment.[317] If you have a dependant, in addition to the £15.50 you receive for yourself, you can opt for the remainder of your normal weekly entitlement (including any dependant's increase), less a further deduction of £31, to be paid to her/him (you should be sent a form for this purpose shortly before you have been in hospital for a year).[318] Any increase you receive for a spouse is reduced to £15.50 after s/he has been an inpatient for 52 weeks.[319]

- After you have been an inpatient for 52 weeks, your **IS applicable amount** (see p169) is reduced to £15.50 if you are a single claimant.[320] You are not entitled to any premiums or housing costs. You can be paid less than £15.50 if you are unable to act for yourself, your benefit is being paid to the hospital (as your appointee or on your appointee's request) and your doctor certifies that some or all of the benefit cannot be used for you, but the views of your relatives and the hospital staff must be taken into account. You are no longer treated as a member of a couple for IS purposes once your absence from your partner is likely to substantially exceed 52 weeks (this may happen before you or your partner have been an inpatient for 52 weeks) and you and your partner will need to claim IS separately.[321] If one of you has been an inpatient for 52 weeks but is likely to be discharged in the near future, you can still be treated as a couple and your applicable amount is reduced *by* £15.50.[322] If you are a lone parent and have been an inpatient for 52 weeks, your applicable amount is reduced to £19.35 plus allowances and premiums for your children, but you can be treated as a single claimant (see above) as soon as your absence is likely to substantially exceed 52 weeks.[323]
- After you have been an inpatient for 52 weeks, the standard minimum guarantee of **PC** is reduced to £15.50 when calculating the amount of guarantee credit you are entitled to (see p177).[324] You are no longer entitled to housing costs.[325] Your entitlement to the savings credit is not affected.[326] You are no longer treated as a member of a couple for PC purposes once your absence from your partner is likely to substantially exceed 52 weeks (this may happen before you or your partner have been an inpatient for 52 weeks) and you and your partner will need to claim PC or IS separately.[327] If one of you has been an inpatient for 52 weeks but is likely to be discharged in the near future, you can still be treated as a couple and your applicable amount is reduced *by* £15.50.[328]
- You are no longer entitled to **HB/CTB** once you are likely to be absent from your home for substantially more than 52 weeks, or have been continuously absent from your home for 52 weeks.[329] If you have been an inpatient for 52 weeks before this happens (because of the 28-week linking rule – see p373) and you are not entitled to IS or the guarantee credit of PC, your HB/CTB applicable amount is reduced to £19.35 if you are aged under 60, or £15.50 if you are aged 60 or over (if you are still treated as a member of a couple, your applicable amount is reduced *by* £15.50).[330]
- **Non-dependant deductions** from HB, CTB and housing costs paid with IS and PC are no longer made in respect of a non-dependant who has been an inpatient for more than 52 weeks.[331]

6. Increasing your entitlement to benefit – examples

Many people do not claim all the benefits to which they are entitled. The following examples illustrate how claimants in different circumstances can significantly enhance their income by claiming extra benefits. They particularly show how claming one benefit can increase entitlement to other benefits.

Examples

The abbreviations used in the examples refer to the following benefits. For more details about each benefit, go to the relevant page indicated below:

State retirement pension (see p152)
Incapacity benefit (IB – see p158)
Carer's allowance (CA – see p148)
Attendance allowance (AA – see p144)
Disability living allowance (DLA – see p139)
Income support (IS – see p210)
Pension credit (PC – see p176)
Housing benefit (HB – see p180)
Council tax benefit (CTB – see p188)
Social fund (see p197)

Example 1 – single pensioner living alone

Monica is aged 66 and owns her own home (without a mortgage). She receives a state retirement pension of £85 a week, from which she pays £10 a week council tax. She has no savings.

As her income of £85 is less than her IS applicable amount of £102.10 (£54.65 personal allowance plus £47.45 pensioner premium), she should be advised to claim IS prior to 6 October 2003, which will be worth £17.10 (£102.10 less £85) a week. She will also be entitled to maximum CTB so that she will not have to pay any of her £10 a week council tax. By claiming both IS and CTB she will be able to increase her income by £27.10 a week. For details of how she may also be able to backdate her claims to get arrears of IS and CTB, see Chapter 6.

From 6 October 2003, she will able to claim PC instead of IS (see p176). The guarantee credit of PC will be worth the same amount as IS (£17.10 a week) but she will also be able to claim savings credit of £4.53 (see p178). She will also be entitled to maximum CTB.

By claiming IS or PC, she is also eligible for SF payments (see also Chapter 5 for other sources of financial assistance which may now be available to her).

Example 2 – pensioner couple with disabilities

Margaret and Steve are a married couple who live together in their own home (without a mortgage). They are both aged 79. Their combined income from their state retirement pension and occupational pensions is £175 a week, out of which they pay £20 a week council tax. They have no savings. Both Margaret's and Steve's health has been deteriorating recently and they are now being provided with community care services for several hours a day to assist them with their personal care needs.

As their income of £175 is higher than their IS applicable amount of £155.80 (£85.75 personal allowance plus £70.05 pensioner premium) and higher than their appropriate minimum guarantee of PC (also £155.80), they are not entitled to IS (before 6 October 2003), or PC (after 6 October 2003). They are, however, entitled to CTB which would reduce their council tax to £3.84 a week. See Chapter 6 for details of how their claim for CTB could be backdated.

In view of their deteriorating health and the extent of their personal care needs, however, they should also each be advised to claim AA. If they are each awarded AA for their care needs during the day, this will be worth £38.30 a week each. This would also increase their IS applicable amount and appropriate minimum guarantee of PC to £241.70 (because they will each be entitled to a severe disability premium/addition of £42.95). They should therefore be advised to claim IS (prior to 6 October 2003) or PC (after 6 October 2003) which will be worth an extra £66.70 a week (£241.70 less £175). They will then also be entitled to maximum CTB so that they will no longer have to pay any council tax. They would also be entitled to savings credit of PC of £19.20 a week. By claiming AA, they will increase their income by £147.14 a week prior to 6 October 2003 (£76.60 AA, £66.70 IS and £3.84 council tax). After 6 October 2003, they will increase their income by a further £19.20 a week by claiming savings credit. By claiming IS or PC, they are also eligible for SF payments (see also Chapter 5 for other sources of financial assistance which may now be available to them).

Note that it is important that Margaret and Steve claim IS or PC at the same time as claiming AA, rather than waiting until their AA is awarded, to ensure full arrears are paid when their AA is awarded.

Note also that if Margaret and Steve are spending more than 35 hours a week looking after each other, they could both claim CA, which would also give them entitlement to two carer's premiums/additions.

Example 3 – couple (disabled person and carer)

Brian and Sheila are a married couple aged 58 and 55 who live together in rented accommodation. Brian has physical disabilities and depends on Sheila to help with his personal care needs throughout the day and night. Sheila has also been incapable of work for some time. They have £5,000 savings. They each receive an award of long-term IB of £72.15 a week (totalling £144.30). They also get HB and CTB which means they only have to pay £28.30 a week towards their rent and council tax. Their income of £152.30 (£144.30 IB plus £8 tariff income from savings) is higher than their IS applicable amount of £119 (£85.75 personal allowance plus £33.25 disability premium) so they are not currently entitled to IS.

Because of his extensive personal care needs, Brian should be advised to claim DLA. He can expect to be paid the higher rate care component of £57.20 a week. Sheila should be advised to claim CA. Although she will not actually receive any payment of CA because she is receiving a higher 'earnings replacement benefit' (IB), claiming CA will make her eligible for a carer's premium, paid with IS (see below).

The award of DLA and CA will make them eligible to claim IS, as their applicable amount will now be £160.55 (£119 as p209, plus the enhanced disability premium worth £16.45 a week and the carer's premium worth £25.10 a week). They will be entitled to IS of £8.25 a week (£160.55 less £152.30). They would also then be entitled to maximum HB and CTB, worth another £28.30 a week.

By claiming DLA, CA and IS, their weekly income will increase by £93.75 a week (£57.20 DLA, £8.25 IS and £28.30 HB and CTB). By claiming IS, they will now be eligible for social fund payments (see also Chapter 5, for other sources of financial assistance which may now be available to them).

Note that it is important that Brian and Sheila claim DLA, CA and IS at the same time. Although the claims for CA and IS will be refused if the claim for DLA has not been decided, if they re-claim CA and IS within three months of Brian being awarded DLA, the claims for CA and IS can be backdated to the date of the original claims.

Example 4 – single disabled person and carer

Liz is aged 56 and severely disabled. She lives alone in rented accommodation. She receives IS of £77.95 a week (£54.65 personal allowance plus £23.30 disability premium). She also gets maximum HB and CTB and the mobility and middle rate care components of DLA. Her son Ernie, who lives on his own nearby, is aged 26. He spends a lot of time caring for his mother and gets CA of £43.15 a week. He was working part time for a few hours a week but recently gave up his job because of illness and stress.

Ernie should be advised to claim IS, which will include a carer's premium of £25.10 a week. He should also claim IB. Although his CA will no longer be paid if he is entitled to IB (because IB is an 'earnings replacement benefit' that is paid at a higher rate than CA), he is still entitled to the carer's premium (see p171). As he is no longer actually receiving CA, however, his mother will become entitled to the severe disability premium with her IS (see p102), worth £42.95 a week.

Notes

1. **Types and combinations of benefits and tax credits**
   1 Reg 4 SS(OB) Regs

2. **Disability benefits**
   2 ss71-73 and 75 SSCBA 1992; reg 2 SS(DLA) Regs
   3 s71(3) SSCBA 1992
   4 s72 SSCBA 1992
   5 s72(6) SSCBA 1992

6 *R v NI Commissioner ex parte Secretary of State for Social Services* [1981] reported as an appendix to R(A) 2/80; *Mallinson v Secretary of State for Social Security* [1994] reported as an appendix to R(A) 3/94
7 Reg 8BA SS(AA) Regs; reg 10C SS(DLA) Regs
8 *R v NI Commissioner ex parte Secretary of State for Social Services* (see above); CA/281/1989
9 CDLA/58/1993
10 *R v NI Commissioner ex parte Secretary of State for Social Services* (see above)
11 *ibid; Woodling (HL) (1984)* reported as an appendix to R(A)2/80
12 *Moran v Secretary of State for Social Services*, reported as an appendix to R(A) 1/88
13 R(A) 2/75
14 R(A) 3/86; *Mallinson v Secretary of State for Social Services*
15 *Secretary of State for Social Security v Fairey (aka Halliday)* (HL), 21 May 1997
16 CDLA/85/1994
17 s73(8) SSCBA 1992
18 s73(1) and (2) SSCBA 1992; reg 12 SS(DLA) Regs
19 Reg 12(1)(a) SS(DLA) Regs
20 CM/98/1989
21 Reg 12(4) SS(DLA) Regs
22 CM/208/1989
23 R(M) 1/81
24 R(M) 1/83
25 CDLA/42/1994; CDLA/14307/1996
26 Reg 12(7) and (8) SS(DLA) Regs
27 s73(1) SSCBA 1992
28 s73(4) SSCBA 1992
29 s66(2)(a) SSCBA 1992
30 ss72(5) and 73(12) SSCBA 1992
31 Reg 2(4) SS(DLA) Regs
32 s1(3) SSAA 1992
33 Reg 4 SS(DLA) Regs
34 Reg 6(8) SS(C&P) Regs
35 s19 SSA 1998
36 ss64-66 SSCBA 1992; reg 2 SS(AA) Regs
37 s64 SSCBA 1992
38 s66 SSCBA 1992
39 Reg 2(3) SS(AA) Regs
40 s65(3) and Sch 4 SSCBA 1992
41 Reg 6(8) SS(C&P) Regs
42 s19 SSA 1998
43 ss94, 108 and 109 SSCBA 1992
44 ss103 and 108 SSCBA 1992
45 Sch 7 paras 11 and 12 SSCBA 1992
46 Sch 7 para 13 SSCBA 1992
47 R(I) 22/59; CI/257/1949; CI/159/1950
48 *Fenton v Thorley* [1903] AC 443 (HC)
49 *Moore v Manchester Liners Ltd* [1910] AC 498 (HL)
50 *R v Industrial injuries Commissioner ex parte AEU* [1966] reported as an appendix to R(I) 4/66
51 s99 SSCBA 1992; R(I) 1/88; R(I) 12/75; R(I) 4/70; R(I) 7/85
52 s2(1) SSCBA 1992
53 ss108 and 109 SSCBA 1992; Sch 1 SS(IIPD) Regs
54 *Jones v Secretary of State for Social Services* [1972] reported as an appendix to R(I) 3/69
55 Reg 11(8) and Sch 2 SS(GB) Regs
56 Reg 11 SS(GB) Regs
57 Sch 6 SSCBA 1992
58 Sch 4 SSCBA 1992
59 s104 and Sch 4 SSCBA 1992; reg 19 SS(GB) Regs
60 s105 SSCBA 1992
61 Sch 7 para 11(10) SSCBA 1992
62 Sch 7 para 13 SSCBA 1992

3. **Other non-means-tested benefits**

63 s70 SSCBA 1992; regs 5, 8 and 9 SS(CA) Regs; regs 10 and 13 SS(CE) Regs
64 *Flemming v SoS for Work and Pensions* [2002] EWCA Civ 641, May 10 2002
65 Reg 4 SS(CA) Regs
66 Reg 4(2) SS(CA) Regs
67 RR(CA)O
68 R(G) 3/91
69 Reg 4(1A) SS(CA) Regs
70 s70(7) SSCBA 1992
71 s70(3) and (5) SSCBA 1992
72 s70(6) SSCBA 1992; reg 11 SS(CA) Regs; RR(CA)O
73 Regs 9, 10 and 13 and Sch 3 SS(CE) Regs
74 s90 and Sch 4 SSCBA 1992; SSB(Dep) Regs
75 Regs 6(21) and (22) and 19 SS(C&P) Regs
76 s122(1) SSCBA 1992
77 s44(1) SSCBA 1992
78 s48A SSCBA 1992
79 ss48B and 48BB SSCBA 1992
80 ss48B and 51 SSCBA 1992
81 s78(3) SSCBA 1992; reg 10 SS(WB&RP) Regs
82 ss45, 46, 48A-C 48B SSCBA 1992
83 Sch 4A para 2 SSCBA 1992
84 Sch 3 para 5 SSCBA 1992
85 s44 and Sch 4 SSCBA 1992
86 ss82-85, 86A and 90 SSCBA 1992; SSB(Dep) Regs; SSB(PRT) Regs
87 SS(CE) Regs
88 Sch 5 paras 1 and 2 SSCBA 1992

89 ss36(2), 39A(4), 39A(5)(b), 39B(4) and 39B(5)(b) SSCBA 1992
90 s36 SSCBA 1992
91 s39A SSCBA 1992
92 ss39B and 60(2) and (3) SSCBA 1992
93 ss39C, 44-45A, 46 and 80(5), Schs 4 and 4A SSCBA 1992
94 s39C(5) SSCBA 1992
95 Reg 19(2) SS(C&P) Regs
96 s3 SSAA 1992
97 ss36A-39 SSCBA 1992
98 ss36A-39 SSCBA 1992
99 ss36A-39 SSCBA 1992
100 ss36A-39 SSCBA 1992
101 s30A SSCBA 1992
102 Sch 12 para 1 SSCBA 1992
103 s30C(1) and (5) SSCBA 1992; Reg 5A SS(IB) Regs; Reg 13A SS(IFW) Regs
104 ss30A(3) and 30C SSCBA 1992
105 s21 and Sch 3 SSCBA 1992
106 s30(2A) SSCBA 1992; regs 15-18 SS(IB) Regs
107 s171B SSCBA 1992; reg 2 SS(ME) Regs
108 s171C SSCBA 1992
109 s171C SSCBA 1992; Sch to SS(IFW) Regs
110 Reg 25 SS (IFW) Regs
111 Regs 6 and 8 SS(IFW) Regs
112 Reg 6 (2)(g) SS&CS(DA) Regs
113 Reg 28 SS(IFW) Regs
114 Reg 10 SS(IFW) Regs
115 Regs 10 and 11 SS (IFW) Regs
116 Reg 27 SS(IFW) Regs
117 Regs 12 and 13 SS(IFW) Regs
118 Reg 31 SS(IB)T Regs
119 Reg 13A SS(IFW) Regs
120 Regs 16 and 17 SS (IFW) Regs
121 SS(CE) Regs
122 Reg 10 SS&CS(DA) Regs
123 ss30A and 30B and Sch 4 SSCBA 1992
124 s30B(4) SSCBA 1992
125 ss30A and 30B SSCBA 1992
126 s30B(7) SSCBA 1992; reg 10 SS(IB) Regs
127 s86A and Sch 4 SSCBA 1992; SS(IB-ID) Regs
128 ss80-81 and Sch 4 SSCBA 1992; SS(IB-ID) Regs
129 SS(IB)T Regs
130 s30DD SSCBA 1992
131 Reg 26 SS(IB) Regs
132 s65 WRPA 1999; WRPA(No.9)O Regs
133 s164 SSCBA 1992; SMP Regs
134 s35A SSCBA 1992; SS(MA) Regs
135 s171ZA, B and L SSCBA 1992; SPP&SAP Regs

4. **Means-tested benefits and tax credits**
136 s124 SSCBA 1992
137 Reg 13 IS Regs; C(LC)SSB Regs
138 Reg 4ZA and Sch 1B IS Regs
139 Reg 5 IS Regs
140 Reg 6 IS Regs
141 Reg 6(2) IS Regs
142 Regs 4ZA(3), 13(2)(b) and Sch 1B paras 10 and 12 IS Regs
143 Reg 4 IS Regs; reg 3 SPC Regs
144 s137(1) SSCBA 1992; reg 14 IS Regs
145 Regs 14-16 and Sch 7 para 9 IS Regs
146 s124(4) SSCBA 1992
147 Part 1, Sch 2 IS Regs
148 Para 5, Sch 2 IS Regs
149 Part II, Sch 2 IS Regs
150 Sch 2 paras 9, 9A and 15 IS Regs
151 Sch 2 paras 10, 12 and 15 IS Regs
152 Sch 2 paras 9, 9A and 15 IS Regs
153 Sch 2 paras 11, 12 and 15 IS Regs
154 Sch 2 para 13A IS Regs
155 Sch 2 paras 13 and 15 and regs 2(1) and 3 IS Regs
156 Reg 3(1), (4) and (5) IS Regs
157 Sch 2 paras 14 and 15 IS Regs
158 Sch 2 paras 14ZA and 15 IS Regs
159 Sch 2 para 8A IS Regs
160 Sch 3 IS Regs
161 Sch 3 para 16(2)(k) IS Regs
162 Sch 3 para 3(1) IS Regs
163 Sch 3 para 3(10) IS Regs
164 Sch 3 para 3(8) and (9) IS Regs
165 Sch 3 para 3(11) IS Regs
166 Sch 3 para 3(5) IS Regs; CIS/719/1994
167 *R v Penwith DC ex parte Burt* [1988] 22 HLR 292, QBD
168 Sch 3 para 3(6) IS Regs
169 Sch 3 para 3(7) IS Regs
170 Reg 6(5)-(8) IS Regs
171 ss78(6) –(9) and 105(3) SSAA 1992
172 s106(4)(a) SSAA 1992
173 s106 SSAA 1992
174 s105 SSA 1992
175 Jobseekers Act 1995; Jobseeker's Allowance Regulations 1996 No. 207
176 ss1-4 SPCA 2002; Regs 2-4 CPC Regs
177 Reg 5 SPC Regs
178 s2(2) SPCA 2002
179 s2(3) SPCA 2002; reg 6 and Schs 1 and 2 SPC Regs
180 s3 SPCA 2002; regs 7 and 9 SPC Regs
181 s6-10 SPCA 2002; regs 10-12 SPC Regs
182 Regs 4D-4F SS(C&P) Regs
183 s130 SSCBA 1992; HB Regs; HB&CTB(SPC) Regs
184 Reg 10 HB Regs
185 *R v Rugby BC HBRB ex parte Harrison* [1994] 28 HLR; *R v Poole BC ex parte Ross* [1995] 28 HLR; *R v Warrington BC ex parte Williams* [1997]
186 Reg 6(1)(c) HB Regs

187 s134(2) SSCBA 1992; reg 7(1) HB Regs
188 Reg 10(5) HB Regs
189 s130(1) SSCBA 1992; reg 5 HB Regs
190 Reg 5(5)(a) HB Regs
191 Reg 5(5)(d) HB Regs
192 HB GM para 3.55.4
193 Reg 7A HB Regs
194 Reg 48A HB Regs
195 Reg 48A(2) HB Regs; Reg 9 HB&CTB (SPC) Regs
196 Regs 7(1)(k) and 8 HB Regs
197 Regs 8(2) and 10(2) HB Regs
198 Regs 7(1)(a) and (1A) HB Regs
199 Reg 7(1)(b) HB Regs
200 Reg 2(1) HB Regs
201 Regs 3(4) and 7(1)(b) HB Regs
202 Reg 7(1)(c) HB Regs
203 Reg 7(1)(d) HB Regs
204 Reg 7(1)(h) HB Regs
205 Reg 7(1) (e)-(g) HB Regs
206 Reg 7(1)(l) HB Regs
207 s137 SSCBA 1992; regs 13-15 HB Regs
208 s130(3)(a) SSCBA 1992; reg 61 and Sch 4 para 4 HB Regs; reg 22 HB&CTB (SPC) Regs
209 Sch 5A HB Regs
210 s130(3)(b) SSCBA 1992; reg 61 HB Regs
211 Reg 16 and Sch 2 HB Regs; reg 6 HB&CTB (SPC) Regs
212 Reg 3(3) HB Regs
213 Regs 19-45 HB Regs
214 Sch 1 Part II HB Regs
215 Sch 1 paras 4 and 7 HB Regs
216 Reg 10(3)(a) and (6) HB Regs
217 Sch 1 para 1A HB Regs
218 Sch 1 para 1(a)-(e) HB Regs
219 Reg 10(3) HB Regs
220 Reg 12A and Sch 1A HB Regs; reg 10 HB(Amd) Regs
221 Regs 10(6B) and 11 HB Regs
222 Reg 12A HB Regs
223 Reg 11 HB Regs
224 Reg 12A(1)(c) HB Regs
225 Reg 3 HB Regs
226 Regs 3 and 63 HB Regs
227 Reg 63 HB Regs
228 Reg 11 HB&CTB (SPC) Regs
229 Reg 22 HB&CTB (SPC) Regs
230 s69 CSPSSA 2000; DFA Regs
231 Reg 66 HB Regs
232 Regs 93 and 94 HB Regs
233 s131 SSCBA 1992; CTB Regs; HB&CTB (SPC) Regs
234 s137 SSCBA 1992; regs 5-7 CTB Regs
235 s131(6) SSCBA 1992
236 ss6(5) and 99(1) LGFA 1992
237 s131(3) SSCBA 1992; reg 4C CTB regs
238 CT(ED)O
239 ss13 and 80 LGFA 1992; CT(RD)O
240 CT(RD)(amdt) Regs
241 ss11 and 79 LGFA 1992
242 Sch 5A CTB Regs
243 s131 SSCBA 1992; regs 51-53 CTB Regs
244 Regs 8-37 and Sch 1 CTB Regs
245 Reg 51(3) CTB Regs
246 Reg 51(2A) CTB Regs
247 Reg 54 and Sch 2 CTB Regs
248 Reg 3 CTB Regs
249 Reg 52(6)-(8) CTB Regs
250 Reg 52 CTB Regs
251 Reg 52 CTB Regs
252 Reg 19 HB&CTB (SPC) Regs
253 s69 CSPSSA 2000; DFA Regs
254 ss3 and 42 TCA 2002; TC(R) Regs; TC(I) Regs
255 Regs 3-5 CTC Regs
256 Regs 4 and 9 WTC(EMR) Regs
257 Reg 9 WTC(EMR) Regs
258 TC(ITDR) Regs
259 Regs 7-8 CTC Regs; WTC(EMR) Regs;
260 Regs 13-16 WTC(EMR) Regs
261 TC(C)(TP)(A) Regs
262 s7(3) TCA 2002; reg 5 TC(ITDR) Regs
263 Reg 3 TC(ITDR) Regs
264 ss224(6) and 25 TCA 2002; TC(PB) Regs; TC(PE) Regs
265 ss 14-17 TCA 2002
266 Reg 21 TC(CN) Regs
267 s32 TCA 2002
268 Reg 25 TC(CN) Regs
269 Reg 7 SFM&FE Regs
270 Reg 7(1)(e) SFM&FE Regs
271 Reg 3(1) SFM&FE Regs
272 Reg 7(5) SFM&FE Regs
273 Reg 7(1), (3) and (4) SFM&FE Regs
274 Reg 7(6) SFM&FE Regs
275 Reg 7A SFM&FE Regs
276 Reg 8(1)(a) SFM&FE Regs
277 s78(4) SSAA 1992
278 Reg 8(1) SFM&FE Regs
279 Sch 4 para 9 SS(C&P) Regs
280 Reg 5(1) SFM&FE Regs
281 Reg 5(2) SFM&FE Regs
282 Regs 1A and 2 SFCWP Regs
283 SFWFP Regs
284 SF Dir 25
285 SF Dir 4
286 s140 SSCBA 1992
287 s140(4)(a) SSCBA 1992: SF Dir 7
288 This now appears to have been confirmed in *Fitzpatrick (AP) v Sterling Housing Association Ltd*, (HL) 28 October 1999
289 *R v Secretary of State ex parte Healey*, *The Times*, 22 April 1991
290 SF Dirs 23 and 29

291 SF Dir 28
292 SF Dir 27
293 SF Dirs 2, 8 and 9
294 SF Dir 10
295 SF Dirs 50-53
296 SF Dir 9
297 SF Dirs 3, 14-16, 22 and 23
298 SF Dirs 18, 20 and 21

5. **People in hospital**
299 Reg 2(2) SS(HIP) Regs
300 *White v CAO,* The Times, 2 August 1993; *Botchett v CAO,* The Times, 8 May 1996; *R v North & East Devon HA ex parte Coughlan,* (CCLR), September 1999; paras 18059, 24321 and 24363 DMG; CIS/3325/2000
301 Reg 21(2) IS Regs; reg 18(3) HB Regs; reg 10(3) CTB Regs; reg 17(4) SS(HIP) Regs; reg 8(2) SS(AA) Regs; regs 10(5)(a) and 12B(3) SS(DLA) Regs; Sch 3 para 2(6) SPC Regs
302 Reg 2(2A) SS(HIP) Regs
303 Reg 6(2A) SS(AA) Regs; regs 8(2A) and 12A(2A) SS(DLA) Regs
304 Regs 6 and 8(1) SS(AA) Regs; regs 8, 10(1), 12A and 12B(1) SS(DLA) Regs
305 Reg 8(2) SS(AA) Regs; reg 10(5) SS(DLA) Regs
306 Reg 8(3) SS(AA) Regs; regs 10(3) and 12B(2) SS(DLA) Regs
307 Regs 12B(7) and (8) SS(DLA) Regs
308 Reg 8(4) SS(AA) Regs; regs 10(6) and 12B(9A) SS(DLA) Regs
309 Sch 2 paras 13(3A) and 15(5) IS Regs; Sch 2 para 13(3A) HB Regs; Sch 1 para 14(3A) CTB Regs; reg 6(5) and sch 1 para 1(2)(b) SPC Regs;
310 Sch 2 paras 12(1)(c)(ii), 13A(1) and 14(3) IS Regs
311 Regs 10(2) and 12B(b) SS(DLA) Regs
312 Reg 4(2) SS(ICA) Regs
313 Sch 7 para 3 IS Regs; Sch 5 para 2(a) JSA Regs
314 Sch 2 para 14(6) IS Regs
315 Reg 13 SS(HIP) Regs; reg 4 CB regs
316 Regs 4 and 6 SS(HIP) Regs
317 Reg 16 SS(HIP) Regs
318 Regs 6, 9, 10, and 12 SS(HIP) Regs
319 Reg 11 SS(HIP) Regs
320 Sch 7 para 2 IS Regs
321 Reg 16(2) IS Regs
322 Sch 7 para 1(c) IS Regs
323 Reg 16(2) and sch 7 para 1(b) IS Regs
324 Sch 3 para 2(2)(a) SPC Regs
325 Sch 2 para 4(11) SPC Regs
326 Sch 3 para 2(5) SPC Regs
327 Reg 5(1)(a) SPC Regs
328 Sch 3 para 2(2)(b) SPC Regs
329 Reg 5(8B) and (8C) HB Regs; regs 4C(4) and (5) CTB Regs
330 Regs 16 and 18 HB Regs; regs 8 and 10 CTB Regs
331 Sch 3 para 18(7)(g) IS Regs; Sch 2 para 14(7)(e) SPC Regs; Sch 2 para 17(7)(g) JSA Regs; Reg 63(7)(e) HB Regs; reg 52(7)(d) CTB Regs

Chapter 8

Capital and income for means-tested benefits and tax credits

This chapter covers:

Your entitlement to means-tested benefits and tax credits depends on the amount of capital and income you have. This chapter explains how your capital and income are assessed. The rules are complex and only an outline can be given here, focussing on the main rules most likely to affect you if you or a member of your family have a disability or are a carer. More details about the capital and income rules can be found in CPAG's *Welfare Benefits and Tax Credits Handbook* (see Appendix 5). If you are unsure whether, or how, a particular type of capital or income affects your entitlement, you should seek advice (see Appendix 4)

The rules in this chapter do not apply to non-means-tested benefits (see p137), which are not affected by capital and most forms of income. Some non-means-tested benefits are, however, affected by earnings and occupational pensions, which are assessed under different rules. Chapter 7 indicates when and how this applies.

For details of the special rules that apply if you are living in a care home, see Chapter 17. Note that many of the rules used to assess your capital and income when calculating your care home charges if your placement is being funded by social services, are similar to those outlined in this chapter. There are also significant differences, however, which are highlighted in Chapters 11 and 12.

1. The capital limits

Most means-tested benefits are not payable if you have capital over an upper limit. There is also generally a lower limit, at and below which capital is ignored. Capital between the lower and upper limits is deemed to produce a 'tariff income' (see p233). The amount of the upper and lower limits depends on your age, which benefit you are claiming, and whether you are permanently living in a care home.

There is no upper capital limit for pension credit (PC) (see p176) but capital above the lower limit is deemed to produce a tariff income (see p233). In rare cases, actual income from some types of capital are taken into account for PC and housing benefit (HB)/council tax benefit (CTB) from 6 October 2003 if you or your partner are aged 60 or over (see p233).

There are no capital limits at all for tax credits but actual income from capital is taken into account (see p232).

If you are receiving income support (IS), income-based jobseeker's allowance (JSA) or the guarantee credit of PC, you are automatically entitled to maximum HB and CTB and there is no need to calculate your capital again.

If you (and your partner if you have one) are aged under 60[1]

The upper limit above which benefit is not payable is:

- £8,000 for IS and income-based JSA;
- £16,000 for HB and CTB.

The lower limit at and below which capital is ignored is:

- £3,000 for IS, income-based JSA, HB and CTB.

See p217, however, if you are permanently living in a care home.

If you or your partner are aged 60 or over[2]

The upper limit above which benefit is not payable is:

- £12,000 for IS and income-based JSA;
- £16,000 for HB and CTB, unless you are getting the guarantee credit of PC from 6 October 2003 (see p177), in which case there is no upper limit and all your capital is ignored.

Note: There is no upper limit for PC.

The lower limit at and below which capital is ignored is:

- £6,000 for IS, income-based JSA and PC;
- £6,000 for HB and CTB, unless you are getting the guarantee credit of PC from 6 October 2003 (see p177), in which case there is no lower limit and all your capital is ignored.

See p217, however, if you are permanently living in a care home.

If you are living in a care home[3]

The capital limits are higher if you are permanently living in a care home (see p362 for details).

- The upper limit for IS, income-based JSA and HB is £16,000.
- The lower limit for IS, income-based JSA, PC and HB is £10,000.

2. What capital counts

The term 'capital' is not defined in social security legislation. In general, it means lump sum or one-off payments rather than a series of payments.[4] It includes savings, property and redundancy payments. Capital payments can normally be distinguished from income because they are not payable in respect of any specified period or periods, and they do not form nor are intended to form part of a regular series of payments[5] (although capital can be paid by instalments). However, some capital is treated as income (see p233), and some income is treated as capital (see p220).

Any unspent income becomes capital as soon as the period for which the income can be said to have been paid has lapsed[6] (eg, a weekly retirement pension payment becomes capital a week after it is paid and a monthly occupational pension becomes capital after a month).

Some of your capital is partially or wholly disregarded (see p223). In certain circumstances, however, you can be treated as possessing capital that you no longer have (see p220).

If you are getting IS, income-based JSA or the guarantee credit of PC, you are automatically entitled to maximum HB and CTB and there is no need to calculate your capital again. For tax credits, none of your capital counts but actual income from some capital is taken into account (see p232).

Whose capital counts

Capital belonging to you and your partner (see p226) is taken into account when calculating your entitlement to means-tested benefits and tax credits.[7] It does not matter whether the capital is held jointly or separately. Once you no longer count as a couple, however (eg, because one of you is permanently in a care home), your capital is no longer jointly assessed.

Capital belonging to a dependent child does not count, but if it exceeds £3,000, you may not get IS, income-based JSA, HB or CTB for her/him.[8]

Savings

Your savings (eg, cash you have at home or in a bank or building society, premium bonds, stocks and shares and unit trusts) generally count as capital.

Your savings from past earnings can only be treated as capital when all relevant debts, including tax liabilities, have been deducted.[9] Savings from other past income (including social security benefits) will also be treated as capital after the period for which the income was paid has passed (although payments of arrears of certain benefits may be disregarded for certain periods). There is no provision for disregarding money put aside to pay bills.[10] If you have savings close to the capital limit it may be best to pay bills (eg, gas, electricity, telephone) as soon as possible or by standing order or direct debit, to prevent your capital going over the limit.

Fixed term investments

Capital held in fixed term investments counts. However, if it is presently unobtainable it may have little or no value (but see p228 for jointly held capital). If you can sell your interest, or raise a loan through a reputable bank using the asset as security, or otherwise convert the investment into a realisable form, its value counts. If it takes time to produce evidence about the nature and value of the investment, you may be able to get an interim payment of benefit (see p120) or a social fund crisis loan (see p197).

Property and land

Any property or land which you own counts as capital, although many types of property are disregarded (see p223), including your normal home.

Loans

A loan usually counts as money you possess. You should not, however, be treated as having any capital from:

- a loan granted on condition that you only use the interest but do not touch the capital because the capital element has never been at your disposal;[11]
- money paid to you to be used for a particular purpose on condition that the money must be returned if not used in that way;[12]
- a property you have bought on behalf of someone else who is paying the mortgage;[13]
- money you are holding in a bank account on behalf of someone else and which has to be returned to them at a future date.[14]

Trusts

A trust is a way of owning an asset. In theory, the asset is split into two notional parts: the legal title owned by the trustee, and the beneficial interest owned by the beneficiary. A trustee can never have use of the asset, only the responsibility of looking after it. An adult beneficiary, on the other hand, can ask for the asset at any time. Anything can be held on trust – eg, money, houses or shares. The rules on trusts for social security and other purposes are extremely complex and you should always seek legal advice before setting up a trust and if you think that the benefit authorities are wrongly valuing a trust.

Beneficiaries of trusts

If you are the adult beneficiary of:

- a **non-discretionary trust**, you can obtain the asset from the trustee at any time and therefore effectively own it, so it counts as your capital;
- a **discretionary trust**, the asset itself does not normally count as your capital because you cannot demand payments (of either income or capital) which are only made at the discretion of the trustee within the terms of the trust;
- a trust which gives you the **right to receive payments in the future** (eg, on reaching the age of 25), this right has a present capital value, unless it is disregarded (see p223);
- a **life interest** only (or, in Scotland, a **liferent**) in an asset (ie, you have the right to enjoy the asset in your lifetime but the asset will pass on to someone else when you die), the value of your interest is disregarded,[15] but not the income itself if you get any.

If a beneficiary is under 18, even with a non-discretionary trust s/he has no right to payment until s/he is 18 (or later if that is what the trust stipulates). Her/his interest may nevertheless have a present value.[16]

Trustees

If you hold an asset as a trustee, it is not part of your capital. You are only a trustee if someone gives you an asset on the expressed condition that you hold it for someone else (or use it for their benefit), or if you have expressed the clearest intention that your own asset is for someone else's benefit, and you have renounced its use for yourself[17] (assets other than money may need to be transferred in a particular way to the trust). If money or another asset is given to you to be used for a special purpose, it may be possible to argue that it should not count as your capital. This is called a purpose trust.[18]

Trust funds from personal injury compensation

The value of any trust fund is ignored if it has been set up out of money paid because of a personal injury to you (or to your partner from 6 October 2003 for PC, HB and CTB only, if you or your partner are aged 60 or over and not claiming IS or income-based JSA).[19] Personal injuries compensation held by the Court of Protection (because the injured person is incapable of managing her/his own affairs) and administered by that Court is treated in the same way (as are 'infant funds in court' in respect of injuries to minors or the death of a parent).[20] It is not necessary for the trust to be set up by a formal deed so long as the beneficiary has no direct access to the funds.

'Personal injury' includes not only accidental and criminal injuries, but also any disease and injury resulting from a disease.

Note that the notional income and capital rules (see pp240 and 220) cannot apply to personal injury compensation paid into trusts (or court funds) even if some time has passed before they are paid in. However, if there is no trust, or until one can be set up, the whole of a compensation payment counts as capital, even if the money is held by your solicitor.[21] This does not apply, however, to PC and HB/CTB from 6 October 2003, if you or your partner are aged 60 or over and not claming IS or income-based JSA (the payment is ignored completely as capital).[22]

Trust funds administered by the courts

The value of any trust fund administered by the courts (eg, the Court of Protection) which derives from compensation for personal injury (or, in most cases for minors under the age of 18, from the death of one or both parents) is also disregarded.[23]

Payments from trust funds

Any payments made to you from trust funds or court funds (see above) may count in full as income or capital, depending on the nature of the payment.[24] They are ignored completely, however, for PC and HB/CTB from 6 October 2003 if you or your partner are aged 60 or over and are not claiming IS or income-based JSA.[25] Also, trustees may have a discretion to use the funds to purchase items that would normally be disregarded as capital (eg, personal possessions such as a wheelchair, car or new furniture), or to make payments that would normally be disregarded as income (eg, ineligible housing costs), or to clear debts or pay for holidays, leisure items or educational or medical needs.

Income treated as capital

In certain circumstances, some payments which appear to be income are nevertheless treated as capital. These include income from capital (eg, interest from a bank account), rental income (but rent from disregarded property – see p223 – counts as income), irregular, one-off charitable payments, most payments from trust funds administered by a court and PAYE income tax refunds.[26] This rule does not apply, however, to tax credits, PC or HB/CTB from 6 October 2003 if you or your partner are aged 60 or over and not claiming IS or income-based JSA.

Notional capital

In certain circumstances you are treated as having capital which you do not in fact possess. This is called notional capital.[27] There is a similar rule for notional income (see p240).

You can be treated as having notional capital if:

- you deliberately deprive yourself of capital in order to claim or increase benefit (see p221); *or*

- you fail to apply for capital which is available to you (see p222); *or*
- someone else makes a payment of capital to a third party on your behalf (see p222); *or*
- you receive a payment of capital on behalf of a third party and, instead of handing it on, you use or keep it (see p223).

Note: Only the first and last situations above apply to PC and HB/CTB from 6 October 2003, if you or your partner are aged 60 or over and not claiming IS or income-based JSA. The rules do not apply to tax credits.

Notional capital counts in the same way as capital you actually possess (and is normally subject to the same disregards – see p223), except that in cases of deprivation of capital, a diminishing notional capital rule may be applied so that the value of the notional capital you are treated as having will be considered to reduce over time (see p222).

Deprivation of capital in order to claim or increase benefit

If you deliberately dispose of capital in order to qualify for benefit or more benefit, you are treated as still possessing it. You should always seek advice if you think this rule may be, or is, applied to you but the following points may be of some guidance.

- The rule can only apply if one of your motives (not necessarily the only or predominant motive) for disposing of capital was to retain, gain, or increase your entitlement to benefit (eg, you buy an expensive item because you want it and because using some of your savings will qualify you for benefit).[28]
- What you know about the capital rules, or could reasonably be expected to know from your dealings with the benefit system, is an important factor.[29]
- The longer the period that has elapsed since the disposal of the capital, the less likely it is that it was for the purpose of obtaining benefit,[30] but there is no set 'safe period' after which benefit can be claimed.[31]
- If you pay off a debt which you are required by law to repay immediately, the deprivation rule should not apply.[32] Even if you pay off a debt which you do not have to repay immediately, it must still be shown that you did so with the intention of gaining benefit.[33] Note that from 6 October 2003, for PC and HB/CTB if you or your partner are aged 60 or over and are not claiming IS or income-based JSA, the deprivation rule cannot apply if you are paying off or reducing any debt which you owe, or you are paying for goods and services which you reasonably need.[34]
- For IS and income-based JSA, the rule does not apply if you have placed compensation derived from a personal injury in a trust fund.
- In practice, arguing successfully that you have not deprived yourself of capital to gain benefit may boil down to whether you can show that you would have spent the money in the way you did regardless of the effect on your benefit

entitlement. Where this is unclear, the burden of proof lies with the decision maker.

- For IS and income-based JSA, you can only be affected by this rule if the capital in question is actual capital.[35] So if you are counted as owning half a bank account under the rule about jointly held capital (see p228), but your real share is only a quarter, you cannot be affected by any deprivation of the other quarter. It is even arguable that the deprivation rule should not apply to the quarter which you actually own.[36] There is no equivalent rule for HB/CTB, but you should argue that the same principle applies.
- If a person acting on your behalf as your attorney has misspent your money for her/his own benefit, the amount spent cannot be notional capital (because the disposal will have been unlawful) or actual capital (because you no longer have it), but your right to recover the money may still have an actual capital value.[37]
- Deprivation for the purposes of claiming one benefit (eg, IS) cannot be held to be deprivation for the purposes of claiming another (eg, HB) and each decision maker must reach her/his own decision on each benefit. Even deprivation decisions for HB must be made independently of decisions for CTB.[38] This may result in different conclusions being drawn on any disposal for each benefit, and even where intent is found in two different benefits, there may be different views about the amount of capital that has been deliberately disposed of.[39] Similarly, social services must apply their deprivation rule (see p240), independently of any benefit decision.

The diminishing notional capital rule

There are complicated rules for working out how notional capital under the above deprivation rule should be treated as spent, so that its value is deemed to diminish over time.[40] Broadly, the rules aim to provide for your notional capital to be gradually reduced by the weekly amount of any means-tested benefit you would have been entitled to but for the notional capital rule. For details, see CPAG's *Welfare Benefits and Tax Credits Handbook*.

Failing to apply for capital[41]

Under this rule you are treated as having capital you could get if you applied for it. This does not apply if you fail to apply for capital from:

- a discretionary trust; *or*
- a trust (or court fund) from money paid as a result of a personal injury; *or*
- a personal pension scheme or retirement annuity contract; *or*
- a loan which you could only get if you gave your home or other disregarded capital as security.

Capital payments made to a third party on your behalf

If someone else pays an amount to a third party (eg, an electricity or gas company, or a building society) for you or a member of your family, this may count as your capital if the payment is for food, household fuel, council tax, ordinary clothing or footwear, rent for which HB is payable (less non-dependant deductions), water charges or housing costs met by IS or income-based JSA.[42]

Payments for other kinds of expenses (eg, care home charges, or mortgage capital repayments) are disregarded as are any payments from the Independent Living Funds, the Macfarlane Trusts, the Fund and the Eileen Trust.

Payments from an occupational or personal pension and certain benefits to a third party for IS and income-based JSA and payments derived from certain social security benefits (eg, war disablement pensions and war widows' pensions) which are paid to a third party count as belonging to you.[43]

Capital payments paid to you for a third party

If you (or a member of your family) get a payment for someone not in your family (eg, a relative who does not have a bank account) it only counts as yours if it is kept or used by you.

3. **Disregarded capital**

Some or all of your capital can be disregarded under the rules below. For most benefits, this means that it will not count for the purposes of deciding whether you are over the upper limit (for eligibility) or lower limit (for the calculation of tariff income – see p233). There are no capital limits for tax credits, so none of the rules below apply to them. There is no upper capital limit for pension credit (PC), which means that the rules below are only relevant for deciding how much of your capital counts for the purpose of the tariff income rules (see p233).

Your home

If you own the home you normally live in, its value is ignored. This also applies if you are living away from your home temporarily (see p362) – eg, because you are in a care home. Note that for PC and housing benefit (HB)/council tax benefit (CTB) from 6 October 2003 if you or your partner are aged 60 or over and are not claiming income support (IS)/income-based jobseeker's allowance (JSA), the value of your home is only disregarded for the purposes of the tariff income rule (see p233).

Your home includes any garage, garden, outbuildings and land, together with any premises that you do not occupy as your home but which it is impractical or unreasonable to sell separately – eg, croft land. If you own more than one property only the value of the one normally occupied is disregarded under this rule.[44]

Even if you do not live in it, the value of property can be disregarded during temporary absences and in the following circumstances.[45]

- **If you have left your former home following a marriage or relationship breakdown**, the value of the property is ignored for six months from the date you left, or longer if any of the steps below are taken. If the property is occupied by your former partner who is a lone parent, its value is ignored as long as s/he lives there.

- **If you have sought legal advice or have started legal proceedings in order to occupy property as your home**, the value of the property is ignored for six months from the date you first took either of these steps, or longer if it is reasonable.
- **If you are taking reasonable steps to dispose of any property**, the value of the property is ignored for six months from the date you *first* took such steps, or longer if it is reasonable. This may include a period before you claimed benefit.[46] 'Property' here may include land on its own, even if there are no buildings on it.[47] The test for what constitutes 'reasonable steps' is an objective one. Putting the property in the hands of an estate agent or getting in touch with a prospective purchaser should count,[48] but any period when the house is advertised at an unrealistic sale price should not.[49]
- **If you are carrying out essential repairs or alterations** which are needed so that you can occupy a property as your home, the value of the property is ignored for six months from the date you first take steps to carry out the repairs. 'Steps' may include applying for planning permission or a grant or a loan to make the property habitable, employing an architect or finding someone to do the work.[50] If you cannot move into the property within that period because the work is not finished, its value can be disregarded for as long as is necessary to allow the work to be carried out.
- **If you sell your home** and intend to use the money from the sale to buy another home, the capital is ignored for six months from the date of sale, or longer if it is reasonable. This also applies even if you do not actually own the home but, for a price, you surrender your tenancy rights to a landlord.[51] You do not need to have decided within the six months to buy a *particular* property. It is sufficient if you intend to use the proceeds to buy *some* other home, although your intention must involve more than a mere hope or aspiration. There must be an element of certainty which may be shown by evidence of a practical commitment to another purchase, although this need not involve any binding obligation.[52] If you intend to use only part of the proceeds of the sale to buy another home, only that part is disregarded even if, for example, you have put the rest of the money aside to renovate your new home.[53]
- **If you have acquired a house or flat for occupation** as your home but have not yet moved in, the value of the property is ignored if you intend to live there within six months. The value can be ignored for longer if it is reasonable.
- **If your home is damaged or you lose it altogether**, any payment, including compensation, which you intend to use for its repair, or for acquiring another home, is ignored for six months or longer if it is reasonable.
- **If you have taken out a loan or been given money for the express purpose of essential repairs and improvements** to your home, the value of the loan is

ignored for six months, or longer if it is reasonable. If it is a condition of the loan that it must be returned if the improvements are not carried out, you should argue that it should be ignored altogether.

- **If you have deposited money with a housing association as a condition of occupying your home**, the value of the money is ignored indefinitely. If money deposited for this purpose is to be used to buy another home, this is ignored for six months, or longer if reasonable, in order to allow you to complete the purchase.
- **Grants made to local authority tenants to buy a home or carry out repairs/alterations to it** can also be ignored for six months, or longer if reasonable, to allow completion of the purchase or the repairs/alterations.

Note: The last four disregards do not apply to PC or HB/CTB from 6 October 2003 if you or your partner are aged 60 or over and are not claiming IS or income-based JSA. The following disregards apply instead.

- Any amounts paid to you for the sole purpose of buying a home for you to live in, or carrying out essential repairs to your actual or intended home, is ignored for upto a year.
- Any compensation paid under an insurance policy because of loss or damage to your home, is ignored for up to a year.

When considering whether to increase the period of any disregard, all the circumstances should be considered, especially your (and your family's) personal circumstances, any efforts made by you to use or dispose of the home[54] (if relevant) and the general state of the market (if relevant). In practice, periods of around 18 months are not considered unusual.

It is possible for property to be ignored under more than one of the above disregards in succession.[55]

Some income generated from property which is disregarded is ignored (see p234).

For the treatment of jointly owned property, see p228. For the different rules on the treatment of unoccupied property (which may not be disregarded in financial assessments) by social services, see Chapter 12.

The home of a partner or relative

The value of a home is also ignored if it is occupied wholly or partly by:[56]

- your partner, or a relative of yours, or any member of your family, provided that (in either case) s/he is aged 60 or over or is incapacitated; *or*
- your former partner from whom you are not estranged or divorced; *or*
- for HB/CTB only, your former partner from whom you are estranged or divorced if s/he is a lone parent (this rule does not apply to HB/CTB from 6 October 2003 if you or your partner are aged 60 or over and are not claiming IS or income-based JSA).

Although the rules themselves do not say so, it has been held that this disregard only applies to a property which you previously occupied yourself.[57]

Meaning of terms

'Partner' means your husband or wife or person with whom you are (or, in the case of a former partner, have been) living together as husband and wife.[58]

'Incapacitated' is not defined. Guidance suggests that it refers to someone who is getting or would get an incapacity or disability benefit,[59] but you should argue for a broader interpretation, if necessary.

'Relative' includes a parent; son; daughter; step-parent/son/daughter or parent/son/daughter-in-law; brother or sister; or a partner of any of these people; or a grandparent or grandchild, uncle, aunt, nephew or niece.[60] It also includes half-brothers and sisters and adopted children.[61] If you are claiming PC or HB/CTB from 6 October 2003 and you or your partner are aged 60 or over and are not claiming IS or income-based JSA, 'relative' does not include adopted children, or a grandparent, grandchild, uncle, aunt, nephew or niece.[62]

For the treatment of jointly owned property, see p228. For the similar (but sometimes more generous) rules on the treatment of occupied properties in financial assessments by social services, see Chapter 12.

Other disregards[63]

- **Future interests** in most types of property (but not in a property let by you to tenants)[64] and the right to receive future payments from a variety of sources are ignored.
- **Arrears of certain social security benefits** are ignored for up to 52 weeks (or in certain circumstances until the end of your benefit award) after they have been paid. These include IS, income-based JSA, HB, CTB, attendance allowance, disability living allowance and (for PC and HB/CTB after 6 October 2003 if you or your partner are aged 60 or over and not claiming IS or income-based JSA) carer's allowance, constant attendance allowance and exceptionally severe disablement allowance. Social fund payments are ignored indefinitely unless you are claiming PC or HB/CTB after 6 October 2003 and you or your partner are aged 60 or over and are not claiming IS or income-based JSA. For full details of which benefit arrears are disregarded as capital for which benefits, see CPAG's *Welfare Benefits and Tax Credits Handbook*.
- All **personal possessions**, including items such as jewellery, furniture or a car, are ignored, unless you have bought them in order to be able to claim or get more IS, income-based JSA, and HB/CTB (unless you are claiming HB/CTB after 6 October 2003 and you or your partner are aged 60 or over and are not claiming IS or income-based JSA).

- If you are self-employed, your **business assets** are ignored for as long as you continue to work in that business. If you stop working in the business, you are allowed a reasonable time to sell the assets without their value affecting your benefit.
- **Tax rebates** for the tax relief on interest on a mortgage or loan obtained for buying your home or carrying out repairs or improvements are ignored (unless you are claiming PC or HB/CTB after 6 October 2003 and you or your partner are aged 60 or over and are not claiming IS or income-based JSA).
- The value of a fund held under a **personal pension scheme or retirement annuity contract** is ignored (unless you are claiming PC or HB/CTB after 6 October 2003 and you or your partner are aged 60 or over and are not claiming IS or income-based JSA).
- The surrender value of any **life assurance** or **endowment policy or annuity** is ignored. This applies even if the life assurance aspect of a policy is not the sole or even the main aspect (although the other features of any policy may still be considered under the actual or notional income and capital rules – see pp240 and 220). Any payments under the annuity count as income (but see p239 for when these are ignored).
- Any qualifying **payments under the Supporting People programme** (see p67) made to you or on your behalf are ignored.
- **Payments by social services for children in need and young people who were previously in care** are ignored.
- **Charitable payments** in kind are ignored (unless you are claiming PC or HB/CTB after 6 October 2003 and you or your partner are aged 60 or over and are not claiming IS or income-based JSA), as are all payments from the Macfarlane Trust, the Fund, the Eileen Trust and either of the Independent Living Funds[65] (see p91) and certain payments from money which originally came from them (the rules are the same as for income – see p235).
- Payments of capital from certain **DWP schemes to assist people with disabilities** (such as the 'business on own account' or 'personal reader service') and start-up capital payments from local authorities under the **Blind Homeworkers' Scheme** are also disregarded indefinitely.[66] Special rules apply to the treatment of payments under the New Deal and other employment programmes (see CPAG's *Welfare Benefits and Tax Credits Handbook* for details).
- **Some second world war compensation payments** are disregarded.
- Payments from trusts to people who have contracted variant **Creutzfeld-Jakob disease** and to their families are ignored for varying periods.
- **Funeral plan payments** are ignored for PC and HB/CTB if you or your partner are aged 60 or over and are not claiming IS or income-based JSA.
- **Capital treated as income** (see p233) does not count as capital.

For further details of the above disregards and a full list of other disregards, see CPAG's *Welfare Benefits and Tax Credits Handbook*.

4. How capital is valued

Capital is generally valued at its current market or surrender value (ie, the price that would be paid by a willing buyer), less the value of any debts secured on it, and a deduction of 10 per cent of its value if there would be expenses involved in selling it.[67] If an asset is difficult or impossible to sell, its market value should be heavily discounted, or even nil.[68]

It is not uncommon for an unrealistic assessment to be made of the value of your capital. If you disagree with any decision you can request a revision or appeal (see Chapter 6).

For the valuation of jointly owned property, see below.

Detailed rules apply for the valuation of national savings certificates, shares, unit trusts and overseas assets.[69] See CPAG's *Welfare Benefits and Tax Credit Handbook* for details.

Jointly owned capital

If you jointly own any capital asset in the UK or abroad under a 'joint tenancy' you are treated as owning an equal share of the asset with all other owners (eg, if there are two co-owners, you are each deemed to have a 50 per cent share).[70] This rule does not apply, however, if you jointly own the asset as 'tenants in common'.[71] The key difference between a joint tenancy and a tenancy in common is that with the former each person owns the whole asset (and his/her interest would automatically pass to the other owner(s) if s/he died), whereas with the latter, each person owns a discrete share in the asset (which would be passed on death to whoever is willed to receive it).

In the case of a tenancy in common, your actual share of the asset has to be valued.

In the case of a joint tenancy, only the value of your deemed share counts. This will usually be considerably less than the same proportion of the value of the whole asset. If the asset is a house worth £100,000, for example, the value of a deemed 50 per cent share is likely to be worth considerably less than £50,000 and may be very small or even worthless, particularly if the house is occupied and the other owner is unwilling to sell their share. Whether a sale can be forced[72] will depend on individual circumstances,[73] and valuations should take into account legal costs and the length of time it could take to gain possession. Valuations often fail to take into account official guidance on a range of factors relevant to the assessment of jointly owned properties,[74] and have been criticised for this,[75] and you may need to challenge any decision based on an inadequate valuation. If you are unsure whether the DWP has correctly valued your share of a jointly owned property, you should seek independent advice (see Appendix 4) and if necessary appeal (see Chapter 6).

Treatment of assets when partners separate

When partners separate, assets such as their former home or a bank account may be in joint names and the above rules about jointly owned capital will apply. For example, if a bank account is in joint names, both partners are treated as having a 50 per cent share each. If there is clear evidence, however, that part or all of the money belongs to one party alone, and the joint account has merely been used for convenience, that money should count as if it is in her/his sole ownership.[76] Many couples use joint accounts only for convenience, and it is often only on separation (eg, because one partner needs care in a care home) that they will take steps to separate how much belongs to each. If your former partner is claiming sole ownership of the account (and, for example, puts a stop on the account), you could argue that your interest in the account should be disregarded until the issue of ownership is resolved.

A former partner may also have a right to some or all of an asset that is in your sole name – eg, s/he may have deposited most of the money in a building society account in your name. If this is established, then you may be able to argue that some or all of the asset should not be treated as yours because you are only holding it on trust for your former partner.[77] In that event, the rule about jointly owned capital may have the effect of treating you as owning half of the amount in the account.

5. General rules about income

What counts as income

The term 'income' is not defined in social security legislation. Payments of income are normally made in respect of a specified period or periods and form, or are intended to form, part of a regular series of payments.[78] In this way, payments of income can usually be distinguished from payments of capital (see p217). However, some income is treated as capital (see p220), and some capital is treated as income (see p227). In addition, income will only count if it is paid to you for your own use, and may not count if you cannot prevent it being paid to a third party instead (eg, under an attachment of earnings order[79]).

Not all your income counts. Some of your income is partially or wholly disregarded. In certain circumstances, however, you can be treated as possessing income that you no longer have (see p240).

If you are getting income support (IS), income-based jobseeker's allowance (JSA) or the guarantee credit of pension credit (PC), you are automatically entitled to maximum housing benefit (HB) and council tax benefit (CTB) and there is no need to calculate your income again.

Whose income counts

If you are a member of a couple (see p168) your partner's income is added to yours and calculated in the same way as if it were yours.[80] It does not matter whether the income is received jointly or separately. Once you no longer count as a couple, however (eg, because one of you is permanently in a care home), your income is no longer jointly assessed.

Complex rules determine the circumstances in which the income of a dependent child counts as yours.[81] See CPAG's *Welfare Benefits and Tax Credits Handbook* for details.

Converting income into a weekly amount

IS, income-based JSA, PC, HB and CTB are all calculated on a weekly basis, so your income has to be converted into a weekly amount to determine your entitlement to benefit. Complex rules determine how this is done for each benefit and different types of income and earnings.[82] For HB and CTB, your average weekly income is estimated with reference to an appropriate past period. For IS and income-based JSA, there are detailed rules for converting your income into a weekly amount, including special rules if your income fluctuates (eg, because you do not work every week), or if it is paid for a part week. For full details of all the rules, see CPAG's *Welfare Benefits and Tax Credits Handbook.*

The period covered by income

For HB/CTB, your average weekly income (see above) is used to calculate your weekly entitlement.

For IS/income-based JSA there are special rules for deciding from when, and for how long, payments of income count.[83] Income is usually taken into account from the day it is due to be paid, for a period equal to that in respect of which it was paid (eg, a month's wages is taken into account for a month from the date it is paid). For further details, see CPAG's *Welfare Benefits and Tax Credits Handbook.*

In the case of tax credits, your income is assessed on an annual basis and attributed to each relevant period of the tax year of your claim.

6. Income other than earnings

Most forms of income are taken into account when assessing your entitlement to means-tested benefits and tax credits but some income is partly or wholly disregarded and there are different rules for different benefits.

In the case of tax credits, your gross income (before the deduction of tax) is taken into account. For other benefits, income is taken into account after the deduction of any tax due on it.[84]

Income from other benefits and tax credits[85]

When calculating your entitlement to means-tested benefits, other benefits and tax credits paid to you (or your partner) are either counted in full, or fully or partially ignored. The main categories are listed below. For a complete list, see CPAG's *Welfare Benefits and Tax Credits Handbook.*

Benefits and tax credits which count in full

- contribution-based jobseeker's allowance (JSA);
- incapacity benefit (but the short-term lower rate is ignored for tax credits);
- severe disablement allowance (but this is ignored for tax credits);
- carer's allowance;
- retirement pensions (note that for tax credits, up to £300 a year is disregarded from your income from pensions and investments – see p232);
- bereavement and widow's allowances (bereavement payments are ignored);
- industrial injuries benefits (but these are ignored for tax credits);
- child benefit (but this is ignored for tax credits and pension credit (PC) and there is a disregard of £10.45 a week for income support (IS) and income-based JSA if you have a child under one);
- tax credits (but child tax credit is ignored for PC and the 30-hour element of working tax credit is ignored for housing benefit (HB) and council tax benefit (CTB));
- statutory sick pay and statutory maternity/paternity/adoption pay, less any tax, Class 1 national insurance contributions and half of any pension contributions (but they are ignored for PC and HB/CTB from 6 October 2003 if you or your partner are aged 60 or over and are not getting IS or income-based JSA and they are treated as earnings in other circumstances for HB/CTB and tax credits and subject to a disregard).

Note that the above benefits should only be taken into account if you are actually receiving them. If you are entitled to a benefit but it is not being paid because of the overlapping benefit rules (see p137) or because of delays in payment (or where payment has been suspended), it should not be taken into account as income.

Benefits which are ignored completely

- attendance allowance (AA), disability living allowance (DLA), constant attendance allowance, exceptionally severe disablement allowance and mobility supplement;
- HB and CTB (including discretionary housing payments);
- IS and income-based JSA are ignored for HB, CTB and tax credits;
- guardian's allowance;
- Christmas bonus;
- social fund payments;
- certain special war widows' or widowers' payments;

- bereavement payments;
- for PC and tax credits only, child benefit is ignored;
- for tax credits only, maternity allowance, severe disablement allowance, industrial injuries benefit and short-term lower rate of incapacity benefit are ignored.

Benefits which are partially ignored

- the first £15 (for HB/CTB), or £10 (for IS, income-based JSA or PC), of any award of widowed mother's allowance and widowed parent's allowance;
- the first £10 of most war pensions (only one disregard of £10 is generally allowed, even if you are receiving more than one pension, but local authorities have some discretion to increase the disregard for HB/CTB purposes).
  Note: This disregard does not apply to tax credits.

Income from capital

Actual income from capital

Tax credits

For tax credits, your actual investment income from capital counts (eg, interest and dividends from investments). Certain types of investment income are ignored, however, including:

- interest from a PEP, ISA or TESSA;
- income from savings certificates and the first £70 of interest from National Savings deposits;
- winnings from lotteries, pools and betting;
- interest on personal injury damages;
- annuity payments under a Criminal Injuries Compensation Scheme award and interest on payments of life annuities.

Also, up to £300 a year is disregarded from your total income from investments, property, pensions (including state retirement pension), and any notional income (see p240).[86]

Other benefits

For most benefits, actual income generated from capital (eg, interest on savings) is ignored as income[87] but counts as capital[88] from the date you are due to receive it.

Income derived from certain categories of disregarded capital, however, (including your home, your former home, property you intend to occupy, property occupied by a partner or relative, property up for sale and personal injury trusts not administered by a court – see p223) is treated as income.[89] In most cases, the income is ignored up to the amount of the total mortgage repayments,[90] council tax and water rates paid in respect of the property for the same period over which the income is received.[91] This might apply, for example, to any rent you receive from letting your home while you are in a care home (but see p234 for the treatment of rent from other properties).

The above rules do not apply to PC or HB/CTB from 6 October 2003 if you or your partner are aged 60 or over and are not claiming IS or income-based JSA. Actual income from disregarded capital (see p223) is ignored for these benefits. In rare cases, actual income from certain types of other capital can be taken into account, if it is not disregarded under other rules.[92]

Tariff income from capital[93]

For benefits other than tax credits, any capital (other than disregarded capital) you have between the 'lower' and 'upper' capital limits (see p216) is treated as producing an assumed income called a 'tariff income'. There are two rates of tariff income.

- For PC and HB/CTB from 6 October 2003 if you or your partner are aged 60 or over and are not claiming IS or income-based JSA, the tariff income is £1 for every £500 capital (or part of £500) you have in excess of £6,000 (£10,000 if you are permanently resident in a care home). There is no upper limit for PC. The upper limit for HB/CTB is £16,000. Note, however, that if you are getting the guarantee element of PC, all your capital is disregarded for HB/CTB purposes.
- For all other benefits, the tariff income is £1 for every £250 (or part of £250) you have in excess of £3,000, or £6,000 if you or your partner are aged 60 or over, or £10,000 if you are permanently resident in a care home. The upper limit for IS and income-based JSA is £8,000, or £12,000 if you or your partner are aged 60 or over, or £16,000 if you are permanently resident in a care home. The upper limit for HB/CTB is £16,000.

You should report any increases or decreases in any capital over the lower capital limit as soon as possible to avoid any overpayments or underpayments of benefit.

Note that different capital limits apply to financial assessments undertaken by social services (see Chapter 12).

Capital which counts as income

In certain circumstances, payments of capital count as income (this rule does not apply, however, to PC or HB/CTB from 6 October 2003 if you or your partner are aged 60 or over and are not claiming IS or income-based JSA). They include:

- instalments of capital outstanding either when you first claim benefit, or when your benefit is reviewed,[94] if they would bring you over the relevant capital limit (any balance over the capital limit counts as income and is spread over the number of weeks between each instalment);[95]

- any payment from an annuity[96] (but see p239 for when this is disregarded), including 'structured income settlements' from personal injury compensation awards;[97]
- most arrears of maintenance payments from liable relatives (see p235).

Capital which is counted as income cannot also be treated as producing a tariff income.[98]

For HB/CTB, withdrawals from a capital sum (eg, loans to cover extra expenses for respite care) are sometimes treated as income.[99] You should, however, argue that unless it is paid in instalments it should be treated as capital.[100] Any payments of capital, or any irregular withdrawals from a capital sum which are clearly for one-off items and not regular living expenses, should be treated as capital.

Income from tenants and lodgers

Lettings in your own home

- For most benefits, £4 of your weekly income from tenants or licensees under a formal contractual arrangement is ignored, plus an additional £9.25 if the charge covers heating costs.[101] The balance counts as income. If someone shares your home under an informal arrangement, any payment made by them to you for their living and accommodation costs is ignored,[102] but a non-dependant deduction may be made from HB/CTB or housing costs paid with IS/income-based JSA.
- For PC and HB/CTB from 6 October 2003 if you or your partner are aged 60 or over and are not claiming IS or income-based JSA, £20 of the weekly rent you receive is ignored as income.[103]
- If you have boarders to whom you provide a room and meals on a commercial basis and who are not your close relatives, the first £20 of the weekly charge for each boarder is ignored and half of any balance remaining is then taken into account as your income.[104]

  Note: If income left after applying any of the above disregards is intended to be used to meet any housing costs of your own which are not met by IS, income-based JSA or HB, it can also be disregarded.[105]
- For tax credits, all the income you receive from lettings counts as income (but up to £300 a year is disregarded from your income from property, investments and pensions).[106]

Lettings in other properties

If you let property other than your own home, the rent is normally treated as capital.[107] In the case of tax credits, PC and HB/CTB from 6 October 2003 if you or your partner are aged 60 or over and are not claiming IS or income-based JSA, however, the rent counts in full as income.[108]

Charitable, voluntary and personal injury payments

Payments from the Macfarlane and similar trusts

Any payments, including payments in kind, from the Macfarlane Trust, the Fund, the Eileen Trust, the variant CJD Fund, or either of the Independent Living Funds (see p91) are disregarded in full.[109]

Other payments

For most benefits, charitable, voluntary or personal injury payments (see below) which are made *irregularly* and are intended to be made irregularly are treated as capital and are unlikely to affect your claim unless they take your capital above the lower or upper capital limits (see p216).

Charitable, voluntary or personal injury payments made, or due to be made, *regularly* are completely ignored if they are intended, and used, for anything *except* food, ordinary clothing or footwear, household fuel, council tax, water rates and rent (less any non-dependant deductions) for which HB is payable. For IS/income-based JSA only, they are also ignored if they are for housing costs not met by IS/income-based JSA.

For the treatment of payments for care home costs, see p237.

If not ignored altogether, charitable, voluntary or personal injury payments have a £20 a week disregard (although that may overlap with other disregards for certain war pensions – see p232).[110]

'Charitable' and 'voluntary' payments are not defined in the regulations but a charitable payment is likely to be one made under a charitable trust while a voluntary payment is one where the giver receives nothing in return. Any voluntary payments from a former partner or the parent of your child are treated as maintenance payments (see below). 'Personal injury payments' are payments from a trust or annuity set up from money paid because of a personal injury to you, or payments received under an agreement or court order because of a personal injury to you.[111]

For PC and HB/CTB from 6 October 2003 if you or your partner are aged 60 or over and are not claiming IS or income-based JSA, any payments from a discretionary trust are ignored, unless they are used for food, ordinary clothing and footwear, household fuel, rent, council tax, water charges, housing costs for which PC is payable, or fees payable by you or your partner to a care home, in which case there is a disregard of £20 a week. Payments received under an agreement or court order because of a personal injury to you or your partner (or your child for HB/CTB) are also ignored.[112]

Note that the above rules do not apply to tax credits.

Maintenance payments

If you have separated from your partner, you may be entitled to maintenance payments for yourself and your children. Payments can be made voluntarily, under a court order, or in the case of child maintenance, via the child support scheme (administered by the Child Support Agency). In some cases, your husband or wife is legally liable to maintain you if you are claiming IS or income-based JSA and this liability can be enforced by the DWP.

In most cases, any maintenance you receive counts as income and will affect your means-tested benefits but not tax credits (see below for details). The rules are complex, however, and you should always seek advice (see Appendix 4) before negotiating maintenance agreements and if the application of the rules causes you hardship. If you are paying maintenance to a former partner, the payments are not disregarded when calculating your income for means-tested benefits.[113]

Pension credit

Any maintenance you receive from your spouse or former spouse is taken into account in full as income but does not count as 'qualifying income' when calculating savings credit (see p177). Any maintenance you receive from her/him for a child, however, is ignored.[114]

Tax credits

Any maintenance payments you receive from your former partner, or the parent of your child is ignored.[115]

Income support and income-based JSA

If you are getting maintenance for yourself from your spouse (eg, because you are separated following your admission into a care home) or former spouse (eg, because you are divorced), most regular payments count in full as income. Arrears of maintenance payments also normally count as income and special rules apply for attributing the payment to a past or future period. The rules are complex, however, and you should always seek advice if you receive a lump sum payment of maintenance. Certain types of payments are not treated as maintenance and count as income or capital (and may be disregarded) under the rules set out in the rest of this chapter. These include payments arising from a property settlement on separation or divorce, payments made after the death of your spouse or former spouse and payments made to someone else for your benefit (eg, mortgage capital payments) which it is unreasonable to take account of, and payments you have already used before the DWP makes a decision about it.[116]

If you are getting child support maintenance, up to £10 a week is disregarded as income, if you are subject to the new child support rules, which were introduced on 3 March 2003. If you are subject to the old rules under the previous child support scheme, all your child support maintenance is taken into account as income.[117] For further details (including who is subject to the old and new rules), see CPAG's *Welfare Benefits and Tax Credits Handbook* and CPAG's *Child Support Handbook*.

Housing benefit and council tax benefit

If you have a child, up to £15 a week is disregarded from any maintenance you receive from your former partner or parent of your child (from 6 October 2003, if you or your partner are aged 60 or over and are not claiming IS or income-based JSA, the disregard only applies to maintenance from our spouse or ex-spouse).[118] Irregular payments of maintenance should be taken into account as capital rather than income.

Payments for care home costs

The following rules apply to IS and income-based JSA only.

- Payments made by social services to a care home for a placement they have arranged for you do not count as your income.[119]
- If your placement in a care home has been arranged by social services and you have chosen to enter a home which is more expensive than the local authority would normally fund for a person with your needs, any charitable or voluntary payment (see Chapter 14) to meet the shortfall in fees is ignored as income.[120]
- If your placement in a care home was not arranged by social services, any payment towards your costs in the home is ignored as your income, up to the amount of the difference between your applicable amount (see p169) and the weekly charge for the accommodation.[121]

Community care payments

Note that the disregards listed below do not apply to PC or HB/CTB from 6 October 2003 if you or your partner are aged 60 or over and are not claiming IS or income-based JSA.

- Any payments made under the Community Care (Direct Payments) Act 1996 (or under s12B of the Social Work (Scotland) Act 1968) (see p88 for details) are ignored.[122]
- Any qualifying payment under the Supporting People programme (see p67) made to you or on your behalf is ignored.[123]
- Any payment you receive for looking after a person temporarily in your care is ignored if it is paid under community care arrangements by a local authority, health authority, voluntary organisation, or the person being care for.[124]

Payments for certain housing costs

- For IS and income-based JSA only, payments you receive under a mortgage protection policy which you use to pay housing costs which are not included in your applicable amount (see p169) are ignored. If, however, the amount you receive exceeds the interest and capital payments on a qualifying loan and the premiums on the mortgage protection policy and any buildings insurance policy, the excess counts as your income.[125]

- For IS and income-based JSA only, as long as you have not already used insurance payments for the same purpose, any money you receive which is used to make:
  - capital and interest payments which are not included in your applicable amount;
  - payments of premiums on a building insurance policy or on an insurance policy which you took out against the risk of not being able to make the payments on a loan secured on your home;
  - any rent that is not covered by HB,

  are ignored.[126]
- For HB, CTB and tax credits, payments you receive under an insurance policy to insure against the risk of being unable to maintain payments on a loan secured on your home are ignored (if you actually use them to maintain your payments). If, however, the amount you receive exceeds the premiums on the policy and any policy to insure against loss or damage to your home, the excess counts as your income.[127] This disregard does not apply, however, to HB/CTB from 6 October 2003 if you or your partner are aged 60 or over and are not claiming IS or income-based JSA.

Payments from annuities

The rules are complex and you should seek advice if you are unsure how particular schemes and payments may affect your means-tested benefits and tax credits. You should, however, note the following points.

- Payments from a retirement annuity contract count in full as income.
- Payments from other annuities generally count as income but payments from 'home income schemes' equal to the net interest (after tax) payable on the loan with which the annuity was bought, are ignored for IS, income-based JSA, HB and CTB (but see below), as long as at least 90 per cent of the loan was used to buy the annuity, the loan is secured on your home and was taken out when you (and your partner) were aged 65 or over, and the annuity will end when you and your partner die.[128]
- In the case of PC and HB/CTB from 6 October 2003 if you or your partner are aged 60 or over and are not claiming IS or income-based JSA, the above disregard applies to any annuity, if the conditions set out above are satisfied.[129]

Student grants and loans

The rules are complex and are set out in full in CPAG's *Welfare Benefits and Tax Credits Handbook*. You should, however, note the following points.

- Most student loans and grants are ignored as income for PC and tax credits.[130]
- For other benefits, most grants and loans are taken into account and you can be treated as receiving a student loan, even if you have not applied for one.[131]

- Education maintenance allowances (paid to some young people staying on at school or college after the age of 16) are ignored as income.[132]
- For HB and CTB, some or all of any parental contributions you make to a student's grant or living expenses can be disregarded from your income.[133]

Other income

The treatment of some other common types of income is given below. For further details and a complete list, see CPAG's *Welfare Benefits and Tax Credits Handbook.* If you are unsure about how a particular type of income you have affects your means-tested benefits, you should seek further advice (see Appendix 4).

Income which counts in full

- Any occupational pension, personal pension or retirement annuity (apart from any discretionary payment from a hardship fund).[134]
- For tax credits, most income which is taxable.[135]

Income which is ignored

Note: The disregards listed below do not apply to PC or HB/CTB from 6 October 2003 if you or your partner are aged 60 or over and are not claiming IS or income-based JSA, unless otherwise stated.

- Certain payments from social services to assist children in need and young people who have left care are ignored.[136]
- Adoption, fostering, and residence order payments (custody payments in Scotland) are ignored for PC and HB/CTB from 6 October 2003 if you or your partner are aged 60 or over and are not claiming IS or income-based JSA.[137] For other benefits, the rules depend on the circumstances (see CPAG's *Welfare Benefits and Tax Credits Handbook* for details).[138]
- Certain payments under the New Deal and other government training and employment programmes are disregarded as income (other than training allowances).[139]
- Any payments to cover expenses if you are working as a volunteer are ignored.[140]
- Payments in kind[141] which may include food, fuel, cigarettes,[142] clothing, holidays, gifts, accommodation, or transport are ignored.[143]
- Fares to hospital are ignored.[144]
- Payments by the Home Office to assist prison visits are ignored.[145]
- Payments from discretionary trusts are wholly or partially ignored for PC and HB/CTB from 6 October 2003 if you or your partner are aged 60 or over and are not claiming IS or income-based JSA.
- Any payments you receive under an insurance policy to insure against the risk of being unable to maintain hire purchase or similar payments or other loan payments (eg, credit card debts) are ignored. However, anything you get above

the amount you use to make your payments and the premium for the policy counts as your income.[146]

- Up to £300 a year of your income from pensions, investments, property and notional income is ignored for tax credits.[147]

Notional income

In the circumstances set out below, you can be treated as having income you do not have. This is called notional income.[148] There is a similar rule for notional capital (see p220).

Deprivation of income in order to claim or increase benefit[149]

If you deliberately dispose of income in order to claim or increase your benefit or tax credits, you are treated as though you are still in receipt of the income. The issues involved are the same as those that apply to the deliberate deprivation of capital (see p221).

Note that the rule can only apply if the purpose of the deprivation is to gain benefit for yourself (or your family). It should not, therefore, apply if you stop claiming carer's allowance so that another person (who is not a member of your family) can become or remain entitled to the severe disability premium/addition (see p169).[150] However, if you do not claim a benefit which would clearly be paid if you did, it may be argued that you have failed to apply for income (see below).

A deliberate decision to 'de-retire' and give up your retirement pension (in the expectation of achieving an overall increase in benefit in the future) can come within this deprivation rule.[151]

Failing to apply for income[152]

If you fail to apply for income to which you are entitled without having to fulfil further conditions, you are deemed to have received it from the date you could have obtained it.

This rule does not apply, however, to:

- PC and HB/CTB from 6 October 2003 if you or your partner are aged 60 or over and are not claiming IS or income-based JSA (see p241);
- income from a discretionary trust, a trust set up from money paid as a result of a personal injury, or funds administered by a court as a result of a personal injury or the death of a parent of someone under 18;
- income from a personal pension scheme or retirement annuity if you are under 60 (it does apply in certain circumstances if you are aged 60 or over);
- income from a rehabilitation allowance made under the Employment and Training Act 1973;
- income from tax credits.

The rule can only apply if is certain that the relevant income would be paid to you upon application. It may be difficult for the benefit authorities to show that this applies in a case where you do not claim carer's allowance because of the effect it would have on another person's severe disability premium/addition (see p169).

In the case of PC and HB/CTB from 6 October 2003 if you or your partner are aged 60 or over and are not claiming IS or income-based JSA, you can only be treated as receiving the following income for which you fail to apply:

- the amount of any retirement pension to which you are entitled;
- income from an occupational pension you elect to defer;
- income from a retirement annuity in certain circumstances.[153]

Income due to you which has not been paid[154]

For IS and income-based JSA only, you may be treated as possessing any income owing to you (provided that the income is due to you, or your family, and would be for your own benefit). Examples of when the rule could apply are where you are owed wages (unless you have been made redundant) or an occupational pension (unless there are insufficient funds in the pension scheme to pay you) which are legally due to you. The rule does not apply to payments from a discretionary trust or a trust set up with funds from personal injury money. It should also not apply if any social security benefit, training allowance or similar payment is delayed.

Income paid to a third party on your behalf[155]

If money is paid to a third party on your behalf (eg, the landlord for your rent, or the fuel boards) this can count as notional income. For most benefits, the rule applies in the same way as it does for notional capital (see p222) with the same exceptions. It does not apply, however, to tax credits and in the case of PC and HB/CTB from 6 October 2003 if you or your partner are aged 60 or over and are not claiming IS or income-based JSA, any money paid to a third party on your behalf counts as your income.

Income payments paid to you for a third party[156]

If you or a member of your family get a payment for somebody not in your family (eg, for a relative living with you), it counts as your income if you keep any of it yourself or spend it on yourself or your family. This does not apply if it is a payment from the Macfarlane Trust, the Fund, the Eileen Trust or either of the Independent Living Funds, or a grant for participating in a government training or employment scheme. This rule does not apply to tax credits or PC and HB/CTB from 6 October 2003 if you or your partner are aged 60 or over and are not claiming IS or income-based JSA.

Cheap or unpaid labour[157]

If you are helping another person or an organisation by doing work of a kind which would normally command a wage, or a higher wage, you are deemed to receive a wage similar to that normally paid for that kind of job in that area. This rule does not apply if:

- you can show that the person cannot, in fact, afford to pay, or pay more; *or*
- you work for a charitable or voluntary organisation, or as a volunteer and it is reasonable for you to give your services free of charge; *or*
- you are on most types of government work or training schemes and are not getting a training allowance.

The rule also does not apply in the case of PC and HB/CTB from 6 October 2003 if you or your partner are aged 60 or over and are not claiming IS or income-based JSA.

Even if you are caring for a sick or disabled relative or another person, it may be considered reasonable for her/him to pay you from her/his benefits, unless you can bring yourself within the above exceptions.[158] You may be able to argue, however, that it is reasonable for you to provide services without charge to a close relative out of a sense of family duty, particularly if charging would compromise the relationship. Whether it is reasonable to provide care free of charge depends on the basis on which the arrangement is made, the expectations of the family members concerned, the housing arrangements and the reasons (if appropriate) why a carer gave up any paid work. The risk of a carer losing entitlement to carer's allowance if a charge were made should also be considered as should the likelihood that a relative being looked after would no longer be able to contribute to the household expenses. If there is no realistic alternative to the carer providing services free to a relative who simply will not pay, this would also make it reasonable not to charge.[159] It may also be worth arguing that carers should not charge because they will otherwise lose their statutory right to an assessment of their needs by social services.

Sometimes it may be reasonable to do a job for free out of a sense of community duty, particularly if the job would otherwise have remained undone, and there would be no financial profit to an employer.[160]

7. Earnings from employment and self-employment

This section gives a brief outline of the main rules for assessing how your earnings are taken into account for means-tested benefits. The rules are complex and you should seek advice if you are unsure how your earnings affect your benefits. Further details of the rules can be found in CPAG's *Welfare Benefits and Tax Credits Handbook*.

Note that:

- earnings from employment and self-employment are assessed differently (see p243);

- some of your earnings are ignored (see p244);
- earnings for tax credits are assessed differently to other benefits (see p246).

Earnings from employment

Note: The following rules do not apply to tax credits (see p246).

Calculating your earnings

If you are working for an employer, your gross and net earnings need to be calculated. **'Gross earnings'** means the amount received from your employer less deductions for expenses 'wholly, necessarily and exclusively' incurred by you in order to carry out the duties of your employment (eg, for tools, work equipment, special clothing or uniforms, or the costs of running a car).[161] **'Net earnings'** means your gross earnings less deductions for income tax, Class 1 national insurance contributions and half of contributions made to a personal or occupational pension scheme.[162]

What counts as earnings

Earnings means 'any remuneration or profit derived from . . . employment'. As well as wages, this includes:[163]

- bonus or commission (including tips);
- holiday pay;
- payments made by your employer for expenses which are *not* 'wholly, exclusively and necessarily' incurred in carrying out your job (including travel expenses to and from work and payments to you for looking after members of your family);
- a retainer fee or a guarantee payment;
- for pension credit (PC), housing benefit (HB) and council tax benefit (CTB), any sick pay or maternity/paternity/adoption pay (for income support (IS) and income-based jobseeker's allowance (JSA) this is treated as income other than earnings);
- non-cash vouchers (except to the extent that they are exempt from liability for national insurance contributions);
- certain compensation payments in respect of your employment (eg, pay in lieu of notice and certain employment tribunal awards – for further details see CPAG's *Welfare Benefits and Tax Credits Handbook*).

The following are examples of payments *not* counted as earnings:[164]

- payments in kind (other than non-cash vouchers – see above) – but see p240 for the rules on notional income;
- the value of any accommodation provided as part of your job is ignored for IS and income-based JSA;
- an advance of earnings or a loan from your employer (which counts instead as capital);

- payments towards expenses which are 'wholly, exclusively and necessarily' incurred – eg, travelling expenses in the course of your work;
- occupational pensions (which count in full as income other than earnings).

Amount of and period covered by earnings

Complex rules apply to determine the average weekly amount of your earnings and the period which earnings cover (see p243). There are also special rules on how payments you receive at the end of a job (eg, pay in lieu of notice, holiday pay and compensation payments) are treated. See CPAG's *Welfare Benefits and Tax Credits Handbook* for full details.

Earnings from self-employment

Note: The following rules do not apply to tax credits (see p246).

Your net profit over the period before you claim must be worked out. Net profit consists of all your earnings from self-employment minus:[165]

- any reasonable expenses (see below); *and*
- income tax and national insurance contributions; *and*
- half of any premium paid in respect of a personal pension scheme or a retirement annuity contract which is eligible for tax relief.

Payments for fostering a child or providing temporary respite care under community care arrangements do not count as earnings but as other income which may be ignored (see p239).

Expenses which may be offset from earnings from self-employment must be reasonable and 'wholly, necessarily and exclusively' incurred for the purposes of your business. They include repayments of capital on loans for replacing equipment and machinery or repairing business assets and interest on loans taken out for the business, but do not include any money for setting up or expanding a business, capital expenditure and capital repayments on business loans, most depreciation costs and entertainment expenses.[166]

Childminders are treated as self-employed but their net profit is deemed to be one-third of their earnings less income tax, national insurance contributions and half of certain pension contributions; the rest of their earnings are completely ignored.[167]

Your weekly earnings from self-employment are determined by looking at an 'appropriate period' (normally your last year's trading accounts).

Disregarded earnings[168]

Note: The following rules do not apply to tax credits (see p246).

Some of your net earnings from employment or self-employment are disregarded and do not affect your benefit. The amount of the disregard depends on your circumstances. There are three levels of earnings disregard and the highest one which applies to your circumstances will be allowed. Certain childcare costs may also be offset from earnings (see p246).

£25 disregard

Lone parents claiming HB or CTB have £25 of their earnings ignored. This does not apply to anyone claiming IS, income-based JSA or PC.

£20 disregard

£20 of your earnings is disregarded if:

- for IS, income-based JSA and PC, you are a lone parent; *or*
- you, or your partner, qualify for a carer's premium/addition (see pp169 and 177); *or*
- you or your partner qualify for the disability premium (see p169) (or, for IS/ income-based JSA only, you would do if you were not in hospital or a care home); *or*
- you have a partner, one of you is under 60, and your benefit would include a disability premium but for the fact that one of you qualifies for the higher pensioner premium (see p169) (or, for IS/income-based JSA only, you would do if you were not in hospital or a care home); *or*
- you or your partner are aged 60 or over and qualify for the higher pensioner premium (or, for IS/income-based JSA only, you would if you were not in hospital or a care home) and immediately before you became 60;
  - you were entitled to the £20 disregard because you qualified for the disability premium (see above) (or, for HB and CTB, would have done but for the fact that the higher pensioner premium was payable instead); *and*
  - you were in employment (part-time for IS and income-based JSA) and have remained in employment (ignoring breaks of up to eight weeks).

Note: The last three bullet points do not apply to PC and HB/CTB from 6 October 2003 if you or your partner are aged 60 or over and are not claiming IS or income-based JSA. Instead, you qualify for the £20 disregard if:

- you or your partner are getting long-term incapacity benefit, severe disablement allowance, attendance allowance, disability living allowance, mobility supplement, or, for PC only, the disability or severe disability element of working tax credit; *or*
- you or your partner are registered blind; *or*
- for HB and CTB only, you or your partner have been assessed as incapable of work (see p159) for a continuous period of 364 days (196 days if you are terminally ill); *or*
- you or your partner previously qualified for a £20 disregard in a previous award of IS, income-based JSA, HB or CTB not more than eight weeks before (for PC) you first became entitled to PC, or (for HB or CTB) you reached the age of 60

and the employment you were in is continuing (ignoring breaks of up to eight weeks for HB/CTB); *or*

- for PC only, you or your partner qualified for a £20 disregard immediately before you reached pensionable age because you were getting long-term incapacity benefit or severe disablement allowance and you remain in employment (ignoring breaks of up to eight weeks).

If you qualify under more than one of the above categories, only £20 of your earnings is ignored.

Basic £10 or £5 disregard

If you do not qualify for a £25 or £20 disregard, £5 of your earnings is disregarded if you are single, or £10 if you have a partner (whether or not you are both working).

Additional full-time work disregard

For HB and CTB, there is an additional disregard of £11.90 if:

- you or your partner receive the 30-hour element of working tax credit, or are working at least 30 hours a week and qualify for the disability or higher pensioner premium (see p169); *or*
- you or your partner or are aged 25 or over and are working at least 30 hours a week; *or*
- you are a lone parent and are working at least 30 hours a week; *or*
- you have a child and you and your partner work at least 30 hours a week between you and one of you works at least 16 hours a week.

Childcare costs disregard

For HB and CTB, certain childcare costs of up to £94.50 a week in respect of one child or £140 in respect of two or more children can be deducted from your earnings if you are a lone parent, or a couple and both of you are working at least 16 hours a week, or one of you is working at least 16 hours a week and the other is incapacitated.[169] For further details, see CPAG's *Welfare Benefits and Tax Credits Handbook*.

Calculating your earnings for tax credits

Earnings from employment

Your gross earnings from employment (before tax and other deductions) are taken into account, including expenses, non-cash vouchers subject to tax, statutory sick pay, and any payment of statutory maternity, paternity or adoption pay which exceeds £100 a week.[170]

Deductions allowed include payments of expenses 'wholly, exclusively and necessarily incurred in the performance of the duties of the claimant's employment' plus certain travelling and car parking expenses.[171]

Earnings are assessed along with your other income, on an annual basis.

Earnings from self-employment

Your taxable profits from self-employment, including any trade, profession or vocation (or your share in a partnership's profits) are taken into account and assessed on an annual basis.[172] Expenses 'wholly, necessarily and exclusively' incurred for the purposes of your business can be deducted when calculating taxable profits.

Notes

1. **The capital limits**

1 Regs 45 and 53(1) IS Regs; regs 107(a) and 116(1) JSA Regs; regs 37 and 45(1) HB Regs; regs 28 and 37(1) CTB Regs
2 Regs 45(aa) and 53(1ZA) IS Regs; regs 107(aa) and 116(1ZA) JSA Regs; regs 45(1ZA) HB Regs; reg 37(1ZA) CTB Regs; reg 15(6) SPC Regs; regs 8 and 17 HB&CTB(SPC) Regs
3 Regs 45 and 53 IS Regs; regs 107(b) and 116(1A) JSA Regs; regs 7 and 45 HB Regs; reg 15(6) SPC Regs

2. **What capital counts**

4 para C2.09 GM; para 29020 DMG
5 *R v SBC ex parte Singer* [1973] 1 WLR 713
6 R(IS) 3/93, para 22
7 s136 SSCBA 1992; s13(2) JSA 1995; s5 SPCA 2002; s7 TCA 2002
8 Regs 17(1)(b) and 47 IS Regs; regs 83(b) and 109 JSA Regs; regs 16(b), 19(4) and 39 HB Regs; regs 8(b), 11(4) and 30 CTB Regs
9 R(SB) 2/83; R(SB) 35/83; R(IS) 3/93
10 CIS/654/1991
11 R(SB) 12/86
12 R(SB) 53/83; R(SB) 1/85
13 R(SB) 49/83
14 R(SB) 23/85
15 Sch 10 para 13 IS Regs; Sch 8 para 18 JSA Regs; Sch 5 para 14 HB Regs; Sch 5 para 14 CTB Regs
16 *Peters v CAO* reported as an appendix to R(SB) 3/89
17 R(IS) 1/90
18 *Barclays Bank v Quistclose Investments Ltd* [1970] AC 567; R(SB) 49/83; CFC/21/1989
19 Sch 10 para 12 IS Regs; Sch 8 para 18 JSA Regs; Sch 5 para 13 and Sch 5ZA para 17 HB Regs; Sch 5 para 13 and Sch 5ZA para 17 para 13 CTB Regs;
20 Sch 10 paras 44 and 45 IS Regs; Sch 8 paras 42 and 43 JSA Regs; Sch 5 paras 46 and 47 HB Regs; Sch 5 paras 46 and 47 CTB Regs
21 *Thomas v CAO* (appendix to R(SB) 17/87)
22 Sch 5 para 16(1) SPC Regs; Sch 5ZA para 17(1) HB Regs; Sch 5ZA para 17(1) CTB Regs
23 Sch 10 para 44 IS Regs; Sch 8 para 42 JSA Regs; Sch 5 para 47 HB Regs; Sch 5 para 46 CTB Regs
24 Regs 40 and 46 IS; regs 103 and 108 JSA Regs; regs 33 and 38 HB; regs 24 and 29 CTB Regs; CIS/559/1991
25 Sch 5 para 16 SPC Regs
26 Reg 48 IS Regs; reg 110 JSA Regs; reg 40 HB Regs; reg 31 CTB Regs
27 Reg 51 IS Regs; reg 113 JSA Regs; reg 43 HB Regs; reg 34 CTB Regs; reg 21 SPC Regs
28 R(SB)38/85
29 CIS/124/1990; CSB/1198/1989; R(SB)9/91; CIS/124/1990
30 CIS/264/1989
31 CIS/7330/1995
32 R(SB) 12/91
33 CIS/2627/1995
34 Reg 21(2)(b) SPC Regs

35 Reg 51(7) IS Regs; reg 113(7) JSA Regs
36 CIS/240/1992
37 CIS/12403/1996
38 para C2.69 GM
39 para C2.97 GM
40 Reg 51A IS Regs; reg 114 JSA Regs; reg 43A HB Regs; reg 35 CTB Regs; reg 22 SPC Regs
41 Reg 51(2) IS Regs; reg 113(2) JSA Regs; reg 43(2) HB Regs; reg 34(2) CTB Regs; CIS/368/1994
42 Reg 51(3)(a)(ii) and (8) IS Regs; reg 113(3)(a)(ii) JSA Regs; reg 43(3)(a) and (7) HB Regs; reg 34(3)(a) and (7) CTB Regs
43 Reg 51(3)(a) IS Regs; reg 113(a) JSA Regs; reg 43(3) HB Regs; reg 34(3) CTB Regs

3. **Disregarded capital**
44 Reg 2(1) and Sch 10 para 1 IS Regs; reg 1(3) and Sch 8 para 1 JSA Regs; Sch 5 para 1 HB Regs; Sch 5 para 1 and sch 5ZA para 29CTB Regs; Sch 5 para 27 SPC Regs; R(SB) 3/84; R(IS) 3/96; CIS/427/1991
45 Sch 10 paras 2, 3, 8, 9, 25-28 and 37 IS Regs; Sch 8 paras 2, 3, 5-9, 13 and 14 JSA Regs; Sch 5 paras 2, 3, 9, 10, 24-27 and 37 and Sch 5ZA HB Regs; Sch 5 paras 2, 3, 9, 10, 24-27 and 37 and Sch 5ZA CTB Regs; Sch 5 paras 1-7 and 17-19 SPC Regs
46 CIS/562/1992
47 CIS/7319/1995
48 R(SB) 32/83
49 CIS/7319/1995, para 22
50 *R v London Borough of Tower Hamlets Housing Benefit Review Board ex parte Kapur*, 12 June 2000
51 R(IS) 6/95
52 CIS/685/1992; CIS/8475/1995; CIS/15984/1996
53 R(SB) 14/85
54 para 29578 DMG
55 CIS/6908/1995
56 Sch 10 para 4 IS Regs; Sch 8 para 4 JSA Regs; Sch 5 paras 4 and 24 HB Regs; Sch 5 paras 4 and 24 CTB Regs
57 R(IS) 3/96
58 Reg 2(1) IS Regs; reg 1(3) JSA Regs; reg 2(1) HB; reg 2(1) CTB Regs
59 para 29429 DMG; para C2.12.ii.a and b GM
60 Reg 2(1) IS Regs; reg 2(1) JSA Regs; reg 2(1) HB Regs; not defined for CTB, but the same would be expected to apply
61 CSB/209/1986; CSB/1149/1986; R(SB) 22/87
62 Reg 1(2) SPC Regs; reg 1(2) HB Regs; reg 1(2) CTB Regs
63 Sch 10 IS Regs; Sch 8 JSA Regs; Sch 5 and 5ZA HB Regs; Sch 5 and 5ZA CTB Regs; Sch 5 PC Regs
64 Sch 10 para 5 IS Regs; Sch 8 para 10 JSA Regs; Sch 5 para 6 and Sch 5ZA HB Regs; Sch 5 para 6 and Sch 5ZA CTB Regs
65 Sch 10 para 22 IS Regs; Sch 8 para 27 JSA Regs; Sch 5 para 23 HB Regs; Sch 5 para 23 CTB Regs
66 Sch 10 paras 42-43 IS Regs; Sch 8 paras 40-41 JSA Regs; Sch 5 paras 43-44 HB Regs; Sch 5 paras 42-43 CTB Regs

4. **How capital is valued**
67 Reg 49(a) IS Regs; reg 111(a) JSA Regs; regs 40 and 41(a) HB Regs; reg 32(a) CTB Regs; reg 19(a) SPC Regs; R(SB) 57/83; R(SB) 6/84
68 R(SB) 18/83
69 Regs 49-50 and Sch 10 para 21 IS Regs; regs 111-112 and Sch 8 para 26 JSA Regs; regs 41-42 and Sch 5 para 22 HB Regs; regs 32-33 and Sch 5 para 22 CTB Regs; regs 19 and 20(a) SPC Regs
70 Reg 52 IS Regs; reg 115 JSA Regs; reg 44 HB Regs; reg 36 CTB Regs; reg 23 SPC Regs
71 *Secretary of State for Work and Pensions v Hourigan* [2000] EWCA Civ. 1890, 19 December 2002
72 Under s30 Law of Property Act 1925 or, since 1 January 1997, ss14-15 Trusts of Land and Appointment of Trustees Act 1996
73 Contrast R(IS) 3/96 and *Wilkinson v CAO*, CA, 24 March 2000
74 Memo AOG JSA/IS 35, October 1998
75 CJSA/1114/2000
76 CIS/7097/1995; CIS/15936/1996; CIS/263/1997; CIS/3283/1997 (joint decision – common appendix para 17)
77 R(IS) 2/93

5. **General rules about income**
78 *R v SBC ex parte Singer* [1973] 1 WLR 713
79 R(IS)4/01
80 s136(1) SSCBA 1992; s13(2) JSA 1995; s5 SPCA 2002; s7 TCA 2002
81 Regs 17, 25, 44 and Sch 8 paras 14 and 15 IS Regs; regs 83, 89, 106 and Sch 6 paras 17-18 JSA Regs; regs 16, 19, 36 and Sch 3 paras 13-14 HB Regs; reg 8, 11, 27 and sch 3 paras 13-14 CTB Regs

82 Regs 30 and 32 IS Regs; regs 95 and 97 JSA Regs; regs 21-25 HB Regs; regs 13-17 and 20 CTB regs; reg 17 SPC Regs
83 Reg 29 IS Regs; reg 94 JSA Regs

6. **Income other than earnings**
84 TC(DCI) Regs; reg 40 and Sch 9 para 1 IS Regs; reg 103(1) and (2) and Sch 7 para 1 JSA Regs; regs 28(11) and 33 and Sch 4 para 1 HB Regs; regs 20(11) and 24 and Sch 4 para 1 CTB Regs; reg 17(10) SPC Regs
85 Reg 40 and sch 9 IS Regs; reg 103 and Sch 7 JSA Regs; regs 27(1)(h) and 33 and Schs 4 and 4A HB regs; regs 17(1)(h) and 24 and Schs 4 and 4A CTB Regs; reg 15 SPC Regs; regs 5 and 7 TC(DCI) Regs
86 Reg 10 TC(DCI) Regs
87 Sch 9 para 22(1) IS Regs; Sch 7 para 23(2) JSA Regs; Sch 4 para 15(1) HB Regs; Sch 4 para 15(1) CTB Regs
88 Reg 48(4) IS Regs; reg 110(4) JSA Regs; reg 40(4) HB Regs; reg 31(4) CTB Regs
89 Sch 9 para 22(1) IS Regs; Sch 7 para 23(2) JSA Regs; Sch 4 para 15(1) HB Regs; Sch 4 para 15(1) CTB Regs; *Beattie v Secretary of State for Social Security*, CA, 9 April 2001
90 CFC/13/1993
91 Sch 9 para 22(2) IS Regs; Sch 7 para 23(2) and (3) JSA Regs; Sch 4 para 15(2) HB Regs; Sch 4 para 15(2) CTB Regs
92 S51(1)(i) SPCA 2002; reg 17(6) and Sch 5 Part II SPC Regs; reg 25(1)(g) and Sch 5ZA Part II HB Regs; reg 17(1)(g) and Sch 5ZA Part II CTB Regs
93 Reg 53 IS Regs; reg 116 JSA Regs; regs 25(2) and 45 HB Regs; regs 17(2) and 37 CTB Regs; reg 15(6) SPC Regs
94 Reg 41(1) IS Regs; reg 104(1) JSA Regs; reg 34(1) HB Regs; reg 25(1) CTB Regs
95 Reg 29(2)(a) IS Regs; reg 94(2)(a) JSA Regs; reg 25 HB Regs; reg 17 CTB Regs
96 Reg 41(2) IS Regs; reg 104(2) JSA Regs; reg 34(2) HB Regs; reg 25(2) CTB Regs
97 *Beattie v Secretary of State for Social Security*, [2001]EWCA Civ.498, 9 April 2001 (following CIS/114/1999 to be reported as R(IS) 10/01)
98 Sch 10 para 20 IS Regs; Sch 8 para 25 JSA Regs; Sch 5 para 21 HB Regs; Sch 5 para 21 CTB Regs
99 *R v SBC ex parte Singer* [1973] 1 All ER 931; *R v Oxford County Council ex parte Jack* [1984] 17 HLR 419; *R v West Dorset DC ex parte Poupard* [1988] 20 HLR 295; para C3.118 GM
100 paras C2.09(xix) and 3.118 GM
101 Sch 9 para 19 IS Regs; Sch 7 para 20 JSA Regs; Sch 4 para 20 HB Regs; Sch 4 para 20 CTB Regs
102 Sch 9 para 18 IS Regs; Sch 7 para 19 JSA Regs; Sch 4 para 19 HB Regs; Sch 4 para 19 CTB Regs
103 Sch 4 para 9 SPC Regs; Sch 4A Para 10 HB Regs; Sch 4A para 10 CTB Regs
104 Regs 2(1) and Sch 9 para 20 IS Regs; reg 1(3) and Sch 7 para 21 JSA Regs; Sch 4 para 42 and Sch 4A para 9 HB Regs; Sch 4 para 21and sch 4A para 9 CTB Regs; Sch 4 para 8 SPC Regs
105 CIS/13059/1996
106 Regs 10 and 11 TC(DCI) Regs
107 *CAO v Palfrey and Others, The Times*, 17 February 1995; reg 48(4) IS Regs; reg 110(4) JSA Regs; reg 40(4) HB Regs; reg 31(4) CTB Regs
108 Regs 10 and 11 TC(DCI) Regs; s15(1)(i) SPCA 2002; reg 27(1)(g) HB Regs; reg 17(1)(g) SPC Regs
109 Reg 48(10)(c) and Sch 10 para 22 IS Regs; Sch 7 para 41(1) JSA Regs; Sch 4 para 34 HB Regs; Sch 4 para 35 CTB Regs; Sch 4 para 11 and Sch 5 paras 13 and 15 SPC Regs; reg 10 TC(DCI) Regs
110 Reg 48(9) and Sch 9 para 15 and 15A IS Regs; reg 110(9) and Sch 7 para 15 and 16 JSA Regs; Sch 4 para 13 HB Regs; Sch 4 para 13 CTB Regs
111 *R v Doncaster Borough Council, ex parte Boulton, The Times* December 31 1992
112 Sch 4 paras 11, 13 and 14 SPC Regs; Sch 4A paras 12,14 and 15 HB Regs; Sch 4A paras 12, 14 and 15 CTB egs
113 CIS/683/1993
114 Regs 9 and 15(5)(d) SPC Regs
115 Reg 19, para 10, Table 6 TC(DCI) Regs
116 Regs 54-60 IS Regs; regs 117-124 JSA Regs; CSB/1160/1986; R(SB)1/89
117 Regs 60A–60E IS Regs; regs 125-129 JSA Regs; Sch 9 para 73 IS Regs; paras 7 and 70 JSA Regs
118 Sch 4 para 47 and Sch 4A para 20 B regs; Sch 4 para 46 and sch 4A para 20 CTB Regs
119 Sch 9 para 66 IS Regs; Sch 7 para 64 JSA Regs
120 Sch 9 paras 15A and 30 IS regs; Sch 7 para 16 JSA Regs
121 Sch 9 para 30A IS Regs; Sch 7 para 32 JSA Regs
122 Sch 9 para 58 IS Regs; Sch 7 para 56 JSA Regs; Sch 4 para 67 HB Regs; Sch 4 para 62 CTB Regs; reg 19 Table 6 para 14 TC(DCI) Regs

123 Sch 9 para 76 IS Regs; Sch 7 para 72 JSA Regs; Sch 4 para 75 IS Regs; Sch 4 para 64 CTB Regs; Reg 19 Table 6 para 14A
124 Sch 9 para 27 IS Regs; Sch 7 para 28 JSA Regs; Sch 4 para 25 HB Regs; Sch 4 para 26 CTB Regs; reg 19, Table 8 para 3 TC(DCI) Regs
125 Sch 9 para 29 IS Regs; para 28240 DMG; Sch 7 para 30 JSA Regs
126 Sch 9 para 30 IS Regs; Sch 7 para 31 JSA Regs
127 Sch 4 para 28 HB Regs; Sch 4 para 29 CTB Regs; reg 19 Table 8 para 5 TC(DCI) Regs
128 Reg 41(2) and sch 9 para 17 IS regs; reg 104(2) and Sch 7 para 18 JSA Regs; reg 34(2) and Sch 4 para 16 HB Regs; reg 25(2) and Sch 4 para 16 CTB Regs
129 Sch 4 para 10 SPC Regs; Sch 4A para 11 HB Regs; Sch 4A para 11 CTB Regs
130 s15(1) SPCA 2002; reg 15(5) SPC Regs; reg 8 TC(DCI) Regs
131 Regs 61-69 IS Regs; regs 130-139 JSA Regs; reg 53-69 HB Regs; regs 42-50 CTB Regs
132 Sch 9 para 11 IS Regs; Sch 7 para 12 JSA Regs; Sch 4 para 10 HB Regs; Sch 4 para 10 CTB Regs; reg 19, Table 6 para 5 TC(DCI) Regs
133 Sch 4 para 17 and sch 4A para 18 HB Regs; Sch 4 para 17 and Sch 4A para 18 CTB Regs
134 Reg 40 IS Regs; reg 103 JSA Regs; s15(1)(c) SPC Regs; reg 5 TC(DCI) Regs
135 TC(DCI) Regs
136 Sch 9 para 28 IS Regs; Sch 7 para 29 JSA Regs; Sch 4 para 26 HB Regs; Sch 4 para 27 CTB Regs; reg 19 Table 6 para 9 TC (DCI) Regs
137 Reg 15(1) SPC Regs; reg 27(1) HB Regs; reg 17(1) CTB Regs
138 Sch 9 paras 25 and 26 IS Regs; Sch 7 paras 26 and 27 JSA Regs; Sch 4 paras 23 and 24 HB Regs; Sch 4 paras 24 and 25 CTB Regs; reg 19 Table 6 para 9 TC(DCI) Regs
139 Sch 9 para 13 IS Regs; Sch 7 para 14 CTB Regs; Sch 4 para 11 HB Regs; Sch 4 para 11 CTB Regs; reg 19, Table 6 paras 1-4 TC(DCI) Regs
140 Sch 9 para 2 IS Regs; Sch 7 para 2 JSA Regs; Memo DMG JSA/IS 1; Sch 4 para 2 HB Regs; Sch 4 para 2 CTB Regs; HB/CTB circular A36/2001; reg 19 Table 7 para 1 TC(DCI) Regs
141 Sch 9 para 21 IS Regs; Sch 7 para 22 JSA Regs; Sch 4 para 21 HB Regs; Sch 4 para 22 CTB Regs
142 para C3.73(xiii) GM
143 See para 16491 DMG on related provisions for child benefits
144 Sch 9 para 48 IS Regs; Sch 7 para 47 JSA Regs; Sch 4 para 44 HB Regs; Sch 4 para 43 CTB Regs; reg 19 Table 6 para 12 TC(DCI) Regs
145 Sch 9 para 50 IS Regs; Sch 7 para 49 JSA Regs; Sch 4 para 46 HB Regs; Sch 4 para 45 CTB Regs; reg 19 Table 6 para 13 TC(DCI) Regs
146 Sch 9 para 30ZA IS Regs; Sch 7 para 31A JSA Regs; Sch 4 para 28 HB Regs; Sch 4 para 29 CTB Regs; reg 19 Table 8 para 5 TC(DCI) Regs
147 Reg 3 TC(DCI) Regs
148 Reg 42 IS Regs; reg 105 JSA Regs; regs 35-36 HB Regs; regs 26 and 28 CTB Regs; reg18 SPC Regs; reg 13-17 TC(DCI) Regs
149 Reg 42(1) IS Regs; reg 105(1) JSA Regs; regs 35(1) and 36(6) HB Regs; regs 26(1) and 28(6) CTB Regs; reg 18(6) SPC Regs; reg 15 TC(DCI) Regs
150 paras 28608-616 DMG; CIS/15052/1996
151 CSIS/57/1992
152 Reg 42(2) IS Regs; reg 105(2) JSA Regs; reg 35(2) HB Regs; reg 26(2) CTB Regs; reg 16 TC(DCI) Regs
153 Reg 18(1)-(5) SPC Regs; reg 36(1)-(5) HB Regs; reg 28(1)-(5) CTB Regs
154 Reg 42(3) and (5) IS Regs; reg 105(6) and (10)JSA Regs
155 Reg 42(4)(a)(ii), (4A) and (9) IS Regs; reg 105(10)(a)(ii) JSA Regs; regs 35(3)(a) and (8) and 37 HB Regs; reg 26(3)(a) and (8) and 29 CTB Regs; reg 24 SPC Regs
156 Reg 42(4)(b) IS Regs; reg 105(10)(b) JSA Regs; reg 35(3)(b) HB Regs; reg 26(3)(b) CTB Regs
157 CIS/191/1991; reg 42(6) IS Regs; reg 105(13) JSA Regs; reg 35(5) HB Regs; reg 26(5) CTB Regs; reg 17 TC(DCI) Regs
158 *Sharrock v CAO* (CA), 26 March 1991; CIS/93/1991
159 CIS/93/1991; CIS/422/1992; CIS/701/1994
160 CIS/147/1993

7. **Earnings from employment and self-employment**

161 *Parsons v Hogg* [1985] 2 All ER 897, CA, appendix to R(FIS) 4/85; R(FC) 1/90
162 Reg 36(3) IS Regs; reg 99(1) and (4) JSA Regs; reg 29(3) and 31 HB Regs; regs 20(3) and 23 CTB Regs; regs 17 and 17A SPC Regs
163 Regs 35, 40(4) and 48(3) IS Regs; regs 98, 103 and 110 JSA Regs; regs 28(1), 30(1) and 40(3) HB Regs; regs 19(1), 22(1) and 31(3) CTB Regs; reg 17A SPC Regs
164 Regs 35(2) and 48(5) and Sch 9 para 21 IS Regs; regs 98(2) and 110(5) and Sch 7 para 22 JSA Regs; regs 28(2) and 40(5) and Sch 4 para 21 HB Regs; regs 19(2) and 31(5) and Sch 4 para 22 CTB Regs; reg 17A SPC Regs
165 Reg 38(3) IS Regs; reg 101(4) JSA Regs; regs 31(3) and 34 HB Regs; regs 22(3) and 26 CTB Regs; reg 17B SPC Regs
166 Reg 38 IS Regs; reg 101 JSA Regs; regs 31 and 34 HB Regs; regs 22and 26 CTB Regs; reg 17B SPC Regs
167 Reg 38(9) IS Regs; reg 101(10) JSA Regs; regs 31(9) and 34(8) HB Regs; regs 22(9) and 26(8) CTB Regs; reg 17B SPC Regs
168 Sch 8 paras 4-9 IS Regs; Sch 6 paras 5-12 JSA Regs; Sch 3 paras 3-8 and 16 and Sch 3A paras 2, 4, 5, 7 and 9 HB Regs; Sch 3 paras 3-8 and 16 and Sch 3A paras 2, 4, 5, 7 and 9 CTB Regs; Sch 6 paras 1, 4 and 5 SPC Regs
169 Regs 21, 21A, 26, 27 HB Regs; regs 13, 13A, 18, 19 CTB Regs
170 Reg 4 TC (DCI) Regs
171 Reg 4, Table 1 TC(DCI) Regs
172 Reg 6 TC(DCI) Regs

Part 3

People living in a care home

Chapter 9

Accommodation in a care home

This chapter covers:

1. Deciding to move into a care home

The decision to move into a care home is one of the most important decisions that you can have to make. It may mean giving up your home and sometimes moving to a different area, and is often seen as giving up your independence. But it can be an opportunity to make new, or renew old friendships and be free of the worries of looking after yourself and doing day-to-day chores. It is, however, expensive so it is very important to be sure that you actually need this type of care, *and* to establish whether you can get any help with the fees.

This chapter explains who can get their fees fully covered by the state (see p259), who can get some help from social services (see p266), who gets help from the NHS for nursing costs (see p277), and who has to pay their fees in full (see p280). It is possible to move from one category to another, so you could start by paying for all of the fees yourself but at a later stage ask for help from social services when your capital reduces to a certain level, or at any stage become eligible for NHS funded care if your health needs meet the criteria.

Chapter 17 explains the way your benefits are affected by the type of home, and by whether you are being funded by social services or the NHS.

In this chapter we use the term **'care home'** to cover all types of home which are registered as care homes. Some homes provide nursing care as well as personal care, and where necessary we will make it clear when we are referring only to such homes. The term care home reflects the new terminology used in the registration of homes as they are no longer referred to as residential care homes or nursing homes.

Getting an assessment

Even if you know you can afford to pay the fees of the care home, it is very useful to get an assessment of your needs by social services. Assessments are explained in detail in Chapter 2. The assessment should look at all the options, such as help at home, sheltered accommodation, extra care housing aids and equipment that could help you. You may decide after the assessment, or a period of intermediate care in a care home, that there are ways for you to manage at home.

Equally the assessment may show that your condition is such that you would be eligible for fully funded care by the NHS (see p260) in a home providing nursing care, and so save you a great deal of money.

The assessment should look at which type of home would be suitable for your needs. Social services has been told that they cannot refuse to assess the needs of anyone on the grounds that s/he has financial resources over the capital limit (see p315), and that they should give the person advice about the type of care they require and what services are available.[1] In Scotland following a recent House of Lords ruling on *Robertson v Fife Council*,[2] the Scottish Executive has endorsed the guidance issued by the Confederation of Scottish Local Authorities that states that local authorities must make the arrangements for anyone assessed as needing residential care 'regardless of their ability to pay'.[3] See p327 for more details about this judgment.

It is useful to get an assessment if you are likely to need help with funding in the near future, as it is important to be sure that social services has agreed that you need the type of care you are going into. An Ombudsman found maladministration where a local authority had not properly assessed a person's needs, and as a result the person moved into a nursing home, when only residential care was needed. The local authority had to repay £23,542.[4]

If you require help with funding from social services you will have to be assessed by them first in order to establish that you need this type of care (see p268).

2. Choosing a home

Although there are many different types of homes, the registration standards mean that all homes should be fit for their purpose, and provide the required standard of care set down by the national regulatory bodies. Some charities provide factsheets or booklets giving information about what you should look for when choosing a home. In England, the Department of Health has supported the production of booklet called *The Care Home Guide* by Counsel and Care which is due to be published in the autumn of 2003.

Each home should have a statement of purpose and a services users' guide. Copies of the most recent inspection reports should also be available. This should give you an idea of the way the home is run and what it will and will not allow. Some homes allow you to take pets or your own furniture for your room, or they have a kitchen area where you can make yourself a light meal. Make sure the home will take notice of your likes and dislikes.

Try to go to several homes before you make a decision. What may sound ideal in a brochure might not be so. A visit will help you get a feel for whether you would be comfortable there and get on with the staff and other residents. If you cannot go yourself, make sure someone goes who knows your tastes. Many homes will send staff to visit prospective residents if they cannot go themselves. You should be offered the chance to visit or to have a trial period in the home before making up your mind.

Try to resist being hurried into making a decision and going into the first home you see. This may be difficult if you are in hospital and your bed is needed, but remember it is vital that you are comfortable in the home you live in.

If you are making your own arrangements with the home it is also important to establish exactly what is covered by the fees quoted and whether there are any extra costs that you might have to meet (see p258). You should be given a written contract which states what room you will be occupying, the overall care and services covered in the fee, what the fee is, additional services to be paid for over and above the fee, rights and obligations of the service user and the provider, and the terms and conditions of occupancy.[5] If the home is receiving funding from the NHS for the cost of your registered nursing care (see p279) you should be told how much that is. Regulations will, in England, from September 2003,[6] oblige home owners in homes providing nursing care to provide a breakdown as to which aspect of the fees relate to nursing care and which to personal care and accommodation.[7] If you are being funded by social services or the NHS they should arrange what is covered in their contract, but you should still get a statement of terms and conditions.

When you move in you should have a detailed assessment of your needs and a care plan should be drawn up to provide a basis for the care to be delivered. It should be reviewed by the home at least once a month. It should be drawn up with you and recorded in a way you can understand, and signed by you or your representative.

If your care is being arranged by social services you are allowed your choice of accommodation provided it is suitable for your needs. Your right to choose your accommodation is described in detail on p271. If the NHS is fully funding your care you do not have the same right to choose the home you are in, but you should complain if you think the NHS body arranging your care is being unreasonably restrictive (see p51).

If you are unhappy with the home you are in

Even if you choose a home where you think you could be happy, you may find that you have some concerns. The home might change hands and the new management have different ideas. Or there may be some aspect which you did not consider when you moved in. It is usually best to sort out problems informally as far as possible. If you cannot, then use the home's complaints procedure. All care homes must have a complaints procedure which is clear and accessible. Complaints must be responded to within a maximum of 28 days. If this does not resolve the problem, then:

- you should be informed about how you can take your complaint to the National Care Standards Commission (England), the Care Standards Inspectorate for Wales or the Scottish Commission for the Regulation of Care (which is known as the Care Commission);
- if you are in a local authority home or social services has arranged your care, then you can also use their complaints procedure if you have a complaint against the home they have provided or arranged (see p55). In Wales and Scotland if your complaint is about the standard of nursing in a home providing nursing and social services has arranged your care, they have the responsibility of ensuring that the care they have bought is delivered properly.[8] From April 2003 nursing care in England is arranged by the NHS so if you have a complaint about the standard of nursing you should complain to the NHS, although you can still complain to social services if other aspects of your care are unsatisfactory. If the NHS has arranged your care in a home providing nursing care then you can use the NHS complaints procedures (see p51).

The different types of accommodation

English court cases have established that social services can arrange your accommodation in ordinary housing,[9] but in the vast majority of cases care is provided in either local authority homes or independent care homes which are registered and regulated by the appropriate national body. Some of the independent homes provide nursing care in addition to personal care. Independent homes can be provided by private individuals, private companies, or voluntary or not-for-profit organisations. Some social services departments are either closing their homes or transferring them to the independent sector. As long as there are sufficient independent homes in the area, local authorities do not have to provide them directly.[10] You should compare the costs of local authority homes with those of independent sector homes, as local authority homes can be more expensive.

Under the previous system of regulation in England and Wales, homes which provided both board and personal care had to be registered. Now homes must be registered even if they only provide personal care. This means that some homes which have not provided board and not had to be registered may now need to do so. This could affect the level of benefits you receive as once a home is registered you cannot receive housing benefit. It will mean that you come under the national charging regulations and may find that you are left with only £17.50 (£17.80 in Wales) for personal expenses. You can ask the local authority to either treat you as a less dependent resident or to increase your personal expenses allowance (see p331) if you would be worse off because the home has had to register. Equally some homes have been able to de-register, and make use of the Supporting People provisions by getting transitional housing benefit (see p70). It was not though the intention to alter the type of care that has to be registered as a care home.[11]

Homes which provide nursing care can be run by NHS bodies, or privately by individuals or organisations. Some homes providing nursing are run by not-for-profit organisations. NHS bodies can arrange your accommodation in homes which provide nursing care or hospices. It is a registration requirement that there must be a suitably qualified registered nurse on the premises at all times.

Some homes will continue to provide some accommodation which just offers personal care, and some accommodation which offers nursing care as well. These used to be known as dual registered homes. They now come under a single registration but will need to show that they are able to provide the level of care they are offering.

3. Fees which are fully paid by the state

The amount of public funding you can receive is based on a number of variables and some people receive different amounts of help at different times. The main forms of state help are when your fees are paid by the NHS (which is free and not based on your income or capital); when you get help towards paying your fees through the local authority (which is based on your income and capital); and when a part of your fees in a home providing registered nurse care are met by the NHS. The system in Scotland is different in that although your accommodation and living costs will still be means-tested, there are set levels of payment towards your personal and nursing care costs if you are 65 or over, and for your nursing care alone if you are under 65. Although you may still qualify for fully funded care paid for by the NHS if your condition means you remain the responsibility of the NHS.

There has been much debate about who should pay for the cost of long-term care, particularly for those who need care in care homes. The Royal Commission on Long Term Care recommended that the state should take a larger role[12] and pay for personal care and nursing care. These proposals are reflected to a larger extent in Scotland than they are in the rest of the UK where residents in care homes are still expected to meet all of their personal care costs if they have capital above certain levels, unless they meet the health criteria for fully funded care.

This section looks at who can get full help with their fees in a care home from the state. Although not many people are able to get their fees paid in full by the state, for the individuals concerned this is very important. There are four groups who can get their accommodation and care free of charge in a care home:

- people in a home providing nursing arranged and funded in full by the NHS;
- people receiving intermediate care in a care home (see p75);
- people receiving aftercare in a care home who have previously been detained for treatment in hospital for their psychiatric condition (see p35);
- war pensioners who need skilled nursing care because of disability (see p148).

The responsibility of the NHS to fully fund care in a home providing nursing care

If you want the NHS to fund in full your place in a home providing nursing care you will need to show that you come within the local eligibility criteria for continuing NHS health care, rehabilitation or palliative care. The guidance suggests that such options should always be considered[13] but only about 11 per cent of places in homes providing nursing are arranged and funded by the NHS.

If your assessment (see p45) shows that you need continuing NHS health care (called continuing inpatient care in Scotland and Wales) which can either be in hospital or in a home providing nursing, then your local NHS body should arrange it.[14] It will be free like any stay in hospital. You will still be considered to be a hospital inpatient and so will have limited choice about which home you can go to. Likewise you will be treated as a hospital inpatient for social security purposes, so your benefits will be reduced (see p204).

Guidance was issued in England in 2001 which states a number of key issues when determining whether your care in a care home providing nursing should be fully funded by the NHS. These are that:

- the setting is not the main determinant of such care;
- it is based on the nature of or complexity or intensity or unpredictability of health care needs;
- patients who require palliative care and whose prognosis is that they are likely to die in the near future should be able to choose to remain in NHS funded accommodation including a care home providing nursing; the application of time limits in these cases is not appropriate;
- the eligibility criteria should not require local authorities to provide services beyond those that they can provide under section 21 National Assistance Act 1948 as a package of social care.

Even if you do not come under the criteria for fully funded care the NHS still has the responsibility for providing care that you need over and above what the care home can provide (eg, physiotherapy, occupational therapy, chiropody and specialist equipment) in the same way as if you were in any other setting.[15]

The current guidance in Wales and Scotland sets out four national eligibility criteria for fully funded care in a home providing nursing care:

- you have a complex medical, nursing or other clinical need, or need frequent but not easily predictable interventions under the supervision of a consultant or specialist nurse or other NHS team member; *or*
- you need routine specialist health care equipment or treatments which need specialist staff; *or*
- you have a rapidly degenerating or unstable condition; *or*
- you have a prognosis which suggests you are likely to die in the very near future.[16]

Guidance also makes it clear that the NHS should be prepared to fund rehabilitative and palliative care. There has been concern that some NHS bodies were being unduly restrictive in setting tight time limits on how long they will fund rehabilitative or palliative care.[17]

Within national guidance NHS bodies draw up local eligibility criteria to decide who it will provide health care for and whether it will be in a hospital or home providing nursing care. In one area you might be considered to be the responsibility of the NHS, but in another area you might not. In England, the Strategic Health Authority is responsible for drawing up the criteria for the whole of the area it covers. This means that in England there are 28 different criteria. In Wales local health boards are still using the criteria of the old Health Authorities that covered their areas, but there are plans to work out a Wales wide framework of criteria over the next few months. In Scotland NHS Boards, in conjunction with NHS Trusts in their area, are responsible for drawing up eligibility criteria for continuing inpatient health care.

If you think the NHS should be responsible for your care in a care home, a useful start is to have a copy of the local eligibility criteria. You should be able to get a copy from your local NHS body, social services department or hospital. Your Community Health Council (Health Council in Scotland) or Patient Advice and Liaison Service (PALS) should be able to help if you have problems getting a copy of the criteria. Community Health Councils are to be abolished in England in December 2003 and will be replaced by Patient Forums and the Independent Complaints Advocacy Service.

The 'Coughlan' case

An important test case in the Court of Appeal (referred to in this chapter as the *Coughlan* case) ruled that although the national guidance used in England at the time was lawful, a particular health authority's eligibility criteria were not lawful because they placed rigorous limits on what were considered to be NHS services – ie, the criteria used locally were not consistent with the national guidance. This meant that social services were left providing health care beyond the scope of a department whose primary responsibility is to provide social services.[18]

The national guidance was ruled lawful, but it was criticised by the Court of Appeal as not being clear. As stated above it has been reviewed in England, and Wales is planning to issue new guidance. Scotland currently has no plans to change its guidance. However, the new guidance produced in England in 2001 has come under criticism from the Health Service Ombudsman. She has recently issued a special report on four cases where residents had been refused full funding of their care home fees. She has indicated that the problem may be widespread, and in June 2003 a further three cases were reported. Although the cases in the reports were mainly relating to the way the local NHS bodies have interpreted the old guidance too restrictively, she commented that the new guidance (HSC 2001/015) 'gives no clearer definition than previously of when continuing NHS health care should be provided: if anything it is weaker . . . I have criticised some authorities for having criteria which were out of line with previous guidance: except in extreme cases I fear I would find it even harder now to judge whether criteria were out of line with current guidance. Such an opaque system cannot be fair.'

The Health Ombudsman made a number of important recommendations coming from the four cases where her investigations are complete (there are another thirteen in the pipeline). These include that:

- all strategic health authorities review the criteria used by their predecessor bodies, and the way those criteria were applied from 1996 taking into account the *Coughlan* judgment, Department of Health guidance and her findings; and make efforts to remedy any financial injustice where the criteria, or the way they were applied, were not clearly appropriate or fair, including attempting to identify any patients who were wrongly made to pay for their care in a home, and making appropriate recompense to them or their estates;
- the Department of Health consider how it supports the performance of authorities in this work; review the national guidance, making it much clearer when the NHS must provide funding and when it is left to local NHS body's discretion; consider being more proactive in checking that the criteria used in future follows that guidance.[19]

In England the Department of Health has responded by issuing instructions[20] that all Strategic Health Authorities should have by 28 March 2003, finalised guidance across its area; reviewed previous criteria to ensure that it was in line with the *Coughlan* judgment and if it was not, give estimates of the numbers affected. Although the Ombudsman report was on the situation in England, it could be said to apply equally across Wales and Scotland. Although the Scottish Executive states in a letter to the Chief Executives, that while the report only applied to England, it does recognise that there 'may be a potential for similar situations to arise in Scotland', and goes on to give information about how to handle complaints.[21]

If you are in a home providing nursing care, or have been told you need care in such a home, you should ask whether you should get full funding from the NHS. If the NHS takes responsibility for arranging your care you will not have to pay. You should seek advice if you consider that you should be receiving fully funded NHS care in a home providing nursing care. You can complain to the NHS body using the NHS complaints and review procedures (see p51). If your care is arranged by social services you could also use the social services complaints procedure (see p55) if you think social services has arranged for the type of health care which is beyond their powers. You may wish to seek advice from one of the national information lines (see Appendix 3) or complain to the Ombudsman if you do not get a satisfactory response from the NHS or get legal advice.

As can be seen from the above it is still a very confused picture as to who will get their care fully funded, and it is always worth making enquiries about whether there has been proper consideration of whether you should remain the responsibility of the NHS even though you do not need to be in hospital. There has been a commitment in England to issue directions later in 2003 for when the Community Care (Delayed Discharges etc) Act comes into effect. These will include the requirement that before the NHS body notifies social services that a patient might need community care services, there is a record on the file that an assessment of whether the patient requires NHS continuing care has been undertaken, and that the patient has been informed of her/his right to request a review.[22]

If you are about to be discharged from hospital

A stay in hospital often precedes the need to go into a care home. Unless the NHS agrees to arrange your place in a home providing nursing care, the cost of care in a care home will fall on you either completely if you can afford it (excluding the registered nurse cost – see p278), or with some help from social services (although see p268 for Scotland). It is, therefore, important that you are aware of your rights and understand the process of what should happen, before you are discharged. Chapter 2 describes hospital discharge in general (see p40).

Hospitals in Wales work to the *Hospital Discharge Workbook* which emphasises the multi-disciplinary nature of decisions about discharge and the need for a keyworker, and that planning for discharge should come at an early stage and not at the point you are ready to leave hospital. Current guidance[23] in Wales and Scotland also makes the following points:

- you and your family should be kept informed of the discharge process;
- you should receive information in writing to enable you to take key decisions about continuing care;
- you should be given written details of the likely costs of any of the options being considered, including the availability of social security benefits;
- you should get a written statement of which aspects of your care will be arranged and funded by the NHS.

In England the same guidance was cancelled in 2001. In the meantime, the Department's view is that NHS bodies should continue to use the cancelled guidance in relation to hospital discharge. *Discharge from hospital: pathway, process and practice* a new workbook in England makes the same points as those above. It is planned to issue directions in relation to the legislation that comes into force in October 2003, and which will impose fines from January 2004 on local authorities if you are fit for discharge but you cannot leave hospital because of delay by social services in providing the services you need. There will be very tight time limits, once social service has been notified about you by the NHS, to undertake an assessment and put services into place.[24]

Although you do not have the right to stay in hospital indefinitely if it has been decided that you no longer need hospital care, you do have the right to refuse to be discharged into a care home. A small number of people under mental health legislation do not have this right. Other options should be explored but if you reject these, it may be necessary to implement your discharge home with a package of health and social care. You will probably be charged for your social care in England and Wales, and in Scotland if you are under 65 (see p95). You might also have to pay for some of your care (such as for shopping or housework) in Scotland which does not come under the definition of personal care (see p268).

See p53 for details of your rights for a review or appeal if you disagree with the decision to discharge you. In addition you can use the NHS complaints procedures (p51).

Part funding by the NHS

A number of NHS bodies offer other arrangements, often via social services departments, whereby the health body will meet some of the costs of a home providing nursing care. This is frequently referred to as 50/50 funding.[25] This is different from the NHS payments made for nursing care described on p259.

If the NHS is prepared to pay some of your care home fees, then it is worth checking whether you should in fact have all of your fees met, as it may be that you are borderline for fitting into the eligibility criteria for continuing NHS health care.

If your benefits are affected by such an arrangement it is important to appeal.

Ordinary residence

If you are taken ill and are in hospital, away from home or in a specialist unit in a different health area, the health body in which you are registered with your GP will normally be responsible for your care. In Wales, the Local Health Board where the care home is will pay any NHS costs. The Department of Health is about to issue new guidance that should cover what happens if your care in a care home is fully funded by the NHS and it is in a different area from where you previously lived.[26] This is currently under review by the Scottish Executive.

Fully funded intermediate care: England and Wales

In England and Wales, if you need intermediate care (see p75) provided in a care home, you should not have to pay for it. The guidance states that all intermediate care should be free at the point of use. In order to achieve this, local authorities should agree with their health service partners that the NHS should have underlying responsibility for intermediate care in care homes. Such care would typically last no longer than six weeks.[27] Regulations in England came into effect on 9 June 2003 making it clear that intermediate care is free for up to and including six weeks.[28]

The responsibility to fund aftercare: England and Wales

If you have been compulsorily detained in hospital for treatment under certain sections of the Mental Health Act 1983[29] and have left hospital, there is a duty under s117 of that Act, for both health and social services departments to provide aftercare services until such time as it is agreed by both that such services are no longer needed.[30] There is no power to charge for such services, so if you are placed in a care home, it will be free. This has been upheld in the House of Lords.[31]Aftercare services are not defined but can include residential services.[32] If you need care in a care home because of your mental condition, then unless that condition improves, it is likely you will continue to need residential aftercare services. Just because you have settled in the home does not necessarily mean that you no longer need residential aftercare services; the relevant question of whether you continue to need aftercare services should be addressed.[33]

The High Court[34] has addressed the question of how long aftercare services continue, especially if you still need care in a care home. It found that there may be cases where, in due course, there will be no need for aftercare services for the person's mental condition, but services are still needed for other needs such as physical disability. Each case will have to be examined on the facts. Where the resident has dementia, the Court found it difficult to see how the mental condition could improve to the point where aftercare services would no longer be needed. Seek advice if your condition has not improved and you still need to remain in a care home, but the authorities have decided that you no longer need aftercare and start charging you. An Ombudsman found maladministration where a local authority retrospectively decided aftercare had ended (in this case after the resident had died) from a certain date.[35]

It is estimated that about half the authorities in England and Wales have charged for residential care provided under s117. In some cases this has meant that you have been wrongly charged for your care, in others that you were wrongly told to make your own arrangements and pay the home. Seek urgent advice if you have been detained in hospital under any of the sections listed in note 29 and you are still paying, or have been, paying for care in a care home. It may be possible to get a refund of the payments you have made with interest. In one case the Ombudsman has required a local authority to pay back over £60,000 that had been wrongly paid by a resident.[36] Now that the issue about whether s117 aftercare is free has finally been settled in the House of Lords, local authorities should be trawling to find cases where residents have wrongly paid for their care. The Local Government Ombudsman has issued a special report making recommendations about what local authorities should do regarding reimbursement and payment of interest.[37]

Effects on benefits

In spite of the fact that you do not currently have to pay anything towards your fees in a care home, you can still receive the full rate of income support and other benefits, although it is likely that your attendance allowance (or disability living allowance care component) will not be paid (see p370).

The responsibility to fund aftercare: Scotland

In Scotland, if you are or have been suffering from a mental disorder it is the duty of the social work department to provide aftercare.[38] Accommodation provided as part of aftercare under section 7 of the Mental Health (Scotland) Act 1984 comes under the same charging procedures as are described in Chapter 10, and you will normally be charged. From July 2002 this should only be for your accommodation and living costs, not your personal or nursing care. There may be changes when the Mental Health (Care and Treatment) (Scotland) Bill is implemented in late 2004.

Specialist nursing care through the War Pensions Scheme

A very small number of people can receive funding under the War Pensions Scheme which should, in most cases, meet the full fees of the home providing nursing care. See p148 for further details.

4. Help with fees from social services

If you are not able to get your care home fees fully funded in any of the ways described above, you may still be eligible for some help towards your fees. Since 1993 social services departments have acted as gatekeepers to funding for care in care homes. Each social services department has its own eligibility criteria for deciding who needs care in a care home. These criteria should link with the local criteria for what is provided by the NHS (see p39).

Social services responsibilities: England and Wales

When social services provide or arrange accommodation in a care home for either a temporary or permanent stay, it is nearly always under the National Assistance

Act 1948 but see p361 for services arranged under s117 Mental Health Act 1983. Social services departments have a *duty*[39] to provide or arrange accommodation if:

- you are 18 or over;[40] *and*
- you need care and attention due to:
  - age;
  - illness;
  - disability; *or*
  - any other circumstance (which specifically includes mental disorder, and drug and alcohol dependency). This no longer includes destitute asylum seekers unless any of the other categories apply to them;[41] *and*
- it is not otherwise available to you; *and*
- you normally live in that local authority area; *or*
- you do not but your need is urgent.

Social services departments have a *power* to provide or arrange care in a care home if you:

- are an expectant or nursing mother (it does not matter if you are under 18); *or*
- ordinarily live in another authority's area, provided that authority agrees.[42]

They also have the power to provide hostel accommodation for disabled people who work in workshops provided by the department.[43]

Social services have national rules for working out the amount you will have to contribute towards the cost of accommodation and social care that is provided. From April 2003 although social services can still arrange for your care in a home providing nursing, it no longer is able to arrange for the care you need by a registered nurse.[44] This is now paid for by the NHS (see p277). In Wales, social services can continue to arrange the whole of your care in a home providing nursing although this will change in April 2004, when the responsibility for paying for nursing care passes to the NHS.

Social work responsibilities: Scotland

Social work departments have a *duty* to provide or arrange this kind of accommodation if you are:

- 18 or over;
- a person in need[45] of community care services due to needing care and attention because of infirmity or age;
- suffering from illness or mental disorder or are substantially handicapped by disability; *or*
- in need of care and attention because of drug or alcohol dependency or release from prison or other detention.

'Free' personal and nursing care in Scotland

The Community Care and Health (Scotland) Act 2002 prohibits local authorities from charging for social and personal care provided by them. See Appendix 1 for the definition of the personal and social care for which charges should not be made. This means that social work departments are responsible for certain costs of your care regardless of whether you have over £18,500 (the capital limit in Scotland) or an income large enough to meet your care home fees as long as you need such care. For people aged 65 and over, it is responsible for paying £145 a week if you need personal care and £210 a week if you need both personal and nursing care. If you are under 65 then the social work department is just responsible for paying £65. This amount is paid direct to the home. All residents who moved into a care home after 31 March 2002 and who wish the local authority to contribute to their funding need to request a comprehensive needs assessment. If you were already in a care home prior to 1 April 2002 and apply to the social work department before 1 July 2003 you do not have to have an assessment of your needs.[46]

If you have over £18,500 you should be able to choose the way the care is contracted. You can choose to contract for the accommodation and living costs yourself with the local authority contracting for the personal and/or nursing care, or the local authority can contract for the whole of the placement on the on your behalf and then charge you the full cost of the accommodation and living charges.

If you have less than £18,500 the national charging rules apply, but where after a financial assessment, a local authority's contribution is less than £145 a week (or £210 if you require care in a home providing nursing), it should be increased to that amount.

If you are admitted to hospital, the local authority is responsible for making personal and nursing care payments to the home at full rate for two weeks and at 80 per cent for a subsequent one month or until future placement arrangements have been confirmed.[47] However, subsequent guidance[48] has stated that the Scottish Executive cannot justify the provision of payments beyond 14 days to anyone not receiving services due to a temporary absence from the home.

Deciding if you need help from social services

Before you can get any help with your fees, social services will first assess whether you need care in a care home based on their eligibility criteria for such care. See Chapter 2 for details about assessment and eligibility criteria.

If social services decide you need care in a home providing nursing care they must obtain the consent of the appropriate local NHS body before they can arrange your accommodation. In an emergency, social services can place you in a home without the consent of the NHS but this must be obtained as soon as possible.[49] In Scotland, guidance states that a joint assessment of health and social care needs should be carried out within at least five working days of admission.[50]

If your situation is very urgent social services can place you in a care home without an assessment[51] and do one as soon as possible afterwards.

If you want help from social services with funding your stay in a care home but are told you do not need such care, or that you only need a care home that does not provide nursing when you think you need nursing care, you can complain and ask for a reassessment (see p51). It is important to get a copy of your needs assessment to show why you need the particular care you think you do. Any medical evidence you can get to support you will be helpful.

Capital limits

Social services departments should not count capital under £19,500 (£18,500 in Scotland, £20,000 in Wales) when deciding whether they must provide you with accommodation.[52] The value of your property is not taken into account in relation to the decision whether to provide you with accommodation if you are entering into a deferred payment arrangement with the local authority (see p299). So even if the value of your property is included in the means test it should not affect the decision whether to provide you with residential accommodation.

There has been a recent Scottish case in the House of Lords where it was made clear that the decision whether to provide accommodation should come before any consideration about the capital you have. In Scotland this means that local authorities cannot refuse to arrange your care for you just because you have over the capital limits.[53] The latest Scottish guidance endorses recent COSLA guidance which says that the effect of the judgment is to require local authorities to make the arrangements for you if your care assessment indicates it is required, regardless of your ability to pay.[54]

It is not clear whether this would have the same effect in England because of the different wording of the law. However, if you do not feel able to arrange your own accommodation and there is no one else who is will and able to make the arrangements for you then the local authority has a duty to arrange your accommodation if it assessed that you need to move into a care home.[55] The practical advantages of having the local authority make the arrangements on your behalf is that often because of its purchasing power, the local authority can negotiate a lower price for your care, and also your care would continue to be monitored by social services to make sure that it is adequate and meeting your needs.

Accommodation arranged by social services

If social services has agreed that you need care in a care home arranged by them, the following points should be considered.

How quickly should accommodation be arranged?

Once social services decides that you need care in a care home arranged for you, then it should be done as soon as you have found a suitable place and you are able to move in. There may be delays if there are no vacancies in the home of your choice and you might need to move into another home while you are waiting. Wherever possible you should try to avoid several moves. Much will depend on your circumstances and whether you can arrange suitable care at home while you are waiting for a vacancy, or whether you can stay in hospital during this time.

Delays sometimes occur because social services do not have the resources to fund you and they have placed you on a waiting list. But social services cannot use their lack of resources as a reason for not making the arrangements once a decision has been made that you need the care.[56] They have a duty to provide the accommodation from the date the decision is made.[57] Guidance states that social services should make arrangements without 'undue delay' and if there is going to be a delay they should ensure that suitable arrangements are in place to meet your needs and those of your carer.[58] The latest guidance states that where individuals need to wait, their access to the most appropriate service should be prioritised according to their eligible needs solely, and councils should ensure that in the interim adequate alternative services are provided. Individuals who are waiting should not be asked to pay more than their assessed financial contribution to meet the costs of alternative residential care services arranged or suggested by the council.[59] An Ombudsman found maladministration where a local authority placed a person on a waiting list although there was a place available.[60]

There has also been a court judgment from the Scottish Outer House of Session. In July 2000 a care plan was approved which identified that nursing care would best meet the needs of a 90-year-old man. In August the family were told that his name had been placed on a waiting list and it might be seven to eight months before funding became available. The family had arranged the care themselves even though the resident had less than £16,000 (the then capital limit). In this particular authority at the time of the hearing there were 199 people on a waiting list, of whom about 106 were in hospital. Although the legislation is slightly different in Scotland the court relied on English caselaw which made it clear that once a local authority was satisfied that a person needed services then a duty arose, and shortage of resources will not excuse a failure in the performance of that duty. 'In the present case, in view of the results of the assessment of the needs of the petitioner for community care services and having regard to his inability to make the necessary provision from his own financial resources, the respondents were under an obligation to make some provision for him in the short term as well as promising the most satisfactory solution in the longer term several months hence.' However, the court did not consider that the local authority is obliged to provide the optimum solution immediately, for instance if there are no places available, if there are under-utilised resources within the Health Board, or some other agency which would allow the individual to be cared for in the short to medium term: 'However in my opinion, doing nothing is not an option available to a local authority ... The decision to do nothing and place him on a waiting list is in my opinion *ultra vires*.'[61] As a result of this judgment, the Scottish Executive has advised authorities that date-order queuing without ongoing needs reassessment should no longer be considered an acceptable practice. All local authorities should review their existing practices and put in place protocols to ensure that when resources become available they are provided to those assessed as having highest priority need. Individuals should be systematically reviewed, and when resources become available, these must be used for those in greatest need.[62]

In England, the Community Care (Delayed Discharges etc) Act is likely to mean that long waits to go to a care home from hospital due to lack of funding should get rarer, as the local authority will get fined £100 or £120 a day for each day you have to remain in hospital because you have not been supplied with a place in a care home. However, there are concerns that given the shortage of care home places you might have less choice about the care home you go into direct from hospital, and may have to move later to the home of your choice.

If you are waiting for funding from social services and have been told that the delay is because of lack of resources you should seek advice.

The right to choose accommodation

Directions issued by government[63] give you the right to choose which home you live in as long as:

- it is suitable to your assessed needs;
- a bed is available;
- the person in charge is willing to provide the accommodation subject to the usual terms and conditions laid down by social services;
- it would not cost social services more than it would normally cost for your assessed needs.

You also have the right to go into accommodation that is more expensive than social services would be prepared to pay for provided you have a third party to meet the difference in cost. In some cases you can use your own money to meet the difference.[64] See Chapter 14 for how top-ups work.

If you are already in a home and want to move, you can do so on the same basis as anyone moving into a home for the first time.

Social services has been told there must be a clear, justifiable reason which relates to the criteria of the direction, if they decide not to arrange accommodation in the home of your choice.[65] There have been reports that some authorities, because of lack of financial resources, will only place you in one of their own homes, or one where they have a block contract – ie, where they have contracted for a number of beds. Lack of resources is not part of the criteria in the *Choice of Accommodation Direction*, so you should argue that you should be given your choice. The Local Government Ombudsman found maladministration where a local authority had not explained the provisions in the *Choice of Accommodation Direction*.[66]

Note that in England there are plans to change the *Choice of Accommodation Direction* and consultation is due to begin sometime during summer 2003, so the details in this section may change.

Having a number of homes to choose from

Social services must not set arbitrary ceilings on the amount they are willing to pay for care homes, and must not routinely expect third parties to make up the difference. They must be able to show that there are homes which could provide you with the services you need within the usual cost.[67] If you think that your choice has been limited because only a few homes are within the cost social services will normally pay, then you should seek advice.

Reasons for going to a particular home

You may have reasons for going to a home which is more expensive than social services will normally consider. If your needs can only be adequately met in a home which is more expensive, then social services should meet the full cost of that home, as it is not a question of choice but one of 'paying what the law required' to meet your assessed needs.[68] The Local Government Ombudsman, in the case above, reminded local authorities that they have the discretion to exceed the normal amount they would pay, and that they should not fetter this discretion.[69] Something which is very important to you should be considered as part of your assessed needs – eg, it may be important to be in a home which respects your religious beliefs, or where there are staff who speak your language, or where you can remain in close contact with your friends. Social services has to take into account your psychological and social needs when making their assessment. In some cases a very strongly held preference could be considered to be a psychological or social need.

What if the home you are in increases its fees by more than social services will pay?

Sometimes homes which have been within the social services level of fees, increase them to above the amount social services will pay for your level of need. In such circumstances you could:

- ask for a reassessment to see if social services agree that it is an integral part of your needs to remain in that home; *and/or*
- find a third party to meet the difference; *or*
- ask social services to negotiate on your behalf for the home to only charge what social services will pay; *or*
- move to another home with fees which social services will pay.

It is important to establish whether social services will meet the full cost of the fees if the home you are living in increases them above the normal fee level. If the home is meeting your needs and you are settled there, you should ask for an assessment about the level of risk involved in your having to move. This, along with your social and psychological needs, should be taken into account in your assessment. If social services agrees that it is part of your assessed need to stay in that particular home then it should meet the full cost.

If they disagree then you will need a third party to top up the fee. This could be a relative or a charity (see Chapter 14). You should ask social services to help you find a third party. Social services will remain responsible for the full fees and will arrange with the third party for their contribution to be paid.

The home should not make its own arrangements with either yourself or a relative outside of the social services contract in order to have the increase in fees met. Social services must be involved as they are responsible for the fees (see p275).

If you do not want to move it is important to seek help so that every avenue can be explored, including seeing if the home will only charge you what social services will pay and complaining to local councillors and MPs/MSPs/National Assembly Members in Wales, if you think that social services should pay the full cost. You can also use the social services complaints procedure (see p55). You may wish to seek advice about whether Articles 2 or 8 of the Convention on Human Rights may help you (see p61).

Moving into a home in another area

If you want to move into a home in another area you should be allowed to exercise your choice to do so. However, because of the differences in the cost of homes around the country, you could find difficulties if the area you are moving to only has homes which are much more expensive than your social services will normally pay. The direction tells social services departments that there might be circumstances where the need to be in another area is an integral part of the person's assessed needs – eg, being near relatives.[70] Some authorities will only pay to their own area's levels. If this is a blanket policy it could be challenged as it implies they are not prepared to look at an individual's assessed needs.

Cross-border placements

Although the *Choice of Accommodation Direction* says you can move anywhere in the UK, in practice this is not the case. There is currently no provision for social services in England, Wales and Scotland to pay for care in Northern Ireland or for Northern Ireland health and social services boards to pay for accommodation arranged in England, Wales or Scotland. However, this might change in the future when provisions in the Health and Social Care Act 2001 and the Community Care and Health (Scotland) Act 2002 come into effect which will allow for placements to be made in Northern Ireland, the Isle of Man and the Channel Isles.

Guidance was issued in 1993[71] to clarify what should be done if someone wants to move from England or Wales to Scotland. If you want to move to Scotland you can ask your social services department to arrange for a Scottish authority to arrange a place for you. The two authorities should ensure that the Scottish authority is reimbursed by the English or Welsh authority.

New protocols are being developed to deal with placements between England, Wales and Scotland to take into account the different arrangements for free registered nursing care in England and Wales and free personal and nursing care in Scotland and the new regulatory provisions in all three countries. These are likely to be covered in the consultation on the *Choice Direction* in England. There is a protocol between England and Wales regarding people moving between England and Wales when they need nursing care.[72]

Seeing if you like the home (trial periods)

Normally you are given a little time to see if you like the home you have moved into and there is a trial period before any permanent decision is made. You need to be clear whether social services regard this trial period as a:

- temporary stay (ie, you might go home); *or*
- temporary stay in that particular home to see if you like it, but as there is no possibility of your going home, you are a permanent resident.

This is important as it will affect the way you are charged (see p293) and it could also affect your benefits (see p362). You also need to be sure that social services and the DWP are treating you in the same way and that you agree with the basis of your trial period. The decision whether you are temporary or permanent should be with your agreement, and should be considered to be temporary where there is uncertainty that permanent admission is required.[73]

Guidance also states that a stay which is expected to be permanent might turn out to be temporary and equally a stay which is temporary might turn out to be permanent. In the former case it suggests that it would be unreasonable to continue to apply the rules as if you were permanent, especially those about the way your own home is treated. If your stay is temporary but later becomes permanent, then you should only be charged as a permanent resident from the date that decision is made.[74]

Moving to a different social services area

Sometimes moving into a care home means moving to a different area of the country. In order to avoid disputes between different local authorities about which should be responsible for helping towards the cost of your care, there is guidance about 'ordinary residence'.[75] It is not defined and so does not follow the rules for habitual residence used by the DWP. If you have freely chosen to move into an area with the intention of settling there, you are 'ordinarily resident' in that area. However, if your care in a care home is provided by social services, you will be deemed as continuing to be ordinarily resident in that authority's area even if the home is in another area. But if you move to another authority and make your own arrangements with a care home, you will be ordinarily resident in the area where that home is. If you later need any help with the funding you should apply to the social services department where the home is.

If you are told by the social services department that you are the responsibility of another authority, you should not be left without help during the time it takes to sort out which authority should be responsible for you. Seek advice if this happens. If you have no settled residence, have come from another local authority or from abroad, the social services department where you are now should provisionally accept responsibility and provide you with the services you need.[76] Some people from abroad, come under provisions within the Nationality and Immigration Act 2002 which debars certain individuals from being able to access care services including residential care. If you are refused care because of this Act you should seek advice from a specialist agency dealing with nationality and immigration issues.

Paying your share of the fees

Once social services has made the arrangements for your care, they will work out how much you need to pay according to the rules which are described in the following chapters. Social services are liable for the full fees (or in the case of their own homes, the cost of running them). The cost to social services is known as the standard charge. If you have over the capital limit (see p269) you will have to pay the standard charge. If you cannot afford the standard charge then you will be assessed to decide how much you should pay.[77]

If social services makes the arrangements for you they are liable for the full costs of your care (see p272 if you are in a home more expensive than social services would normally pay). Any contribution towards that cost from you, is the responsibility of social services to collect. Social services makes a contract with the home which should specify what will be provided. You should receive a statement of the terms and conditions that have been specified. It is always useful for you to know what services have been contracted for you, in order that there is no misunderstanding about what should be provided.

NHS services to care homes

If you are getting help with fees from social services and are in a care home, you should still receive NHS services free of charge. You should still be able to receive community health services such as district nursing, incontinence supplies, chiropody and specialist equipment even if your care is purchased by the local authority. You should receive this on the same basis as if you were in your own home, and this can vary from area to area. Some residents find they have to pay out of their personal expenses allowance (see Chapter 13) for adequate supplies of incontinence pads or chiropody services. Guidance stresses that the personal expenses allowance should not be spent on services that have been assessed as necessary to meet your needs by the council or the NHS, and further that any need for incontinence supplies (and in England the latest guidance also includes chiropody services) should be fully reflected in the care plan.[78]

In Wales, until April 2004, the local authority remains responsible for paying for registered nursing care and any incontinence products you need, such as pads, if you are in a home providing nursing care.[79]

If you receive help with fees from social services you should qualify for full help for those NHS services which incur a charge via health benefits (see p95).

Paying for extras

You may wish to pay for extra services supplied by the home which are not part of the basic care package contracted for by social services. In England, the Department of Health's view is that as long as you have the legal capacity to do so, and you are not facing any pressure from either the home or social services, then there is no reason why you cannot enter into a contract with the home owner to provide extra services outside the package to meet your assessed needs.[80] Before you enter into such a contract you should be clear that you know what will be provided. Some local authority contracts specifically exclude owners of care homes entering into any contract in relation to you outside of the local authority's own contract. This is to avoid the possibility of owners of care homes entering into private contracts with residents or relatives to boost the amount of money they receive for looking after you.

Sometimes social services departments arrange non-residential services even if you live in a care home – eg, daytime activities. If they have been negotiated as part of the care home package, they should be included in the standard charge. If it is a separate package, then social services can decide whether or not to charge you under its discretionary charging powers (see p95). However, as residents only have personal expenses allowance and any disregarded income available, the charge, if any, should be minimal.[81]

How you pay your assessed contribution

Once social services has decided how much you have to pay, they should inform you of the amount. Normally social services will pay the home the full cost and you pay your contribution direct to social services.

You can pay your contribution direct to the home with social services paying the remainder. This can only be done if there is agreement to do so from all three parties – ie, yourself, the home and social services.[82] If you would prefer to pay direct to social services then you cannot be made to pay your contribution direct to the home.

Social services remains liable for the whole amount of the fees, so if you do not pay your share they will need to pay the full amount, but will take steps to recover your contribution from you (see Chapter 16).

Other help with the fees

As well as help from social services there are other sources of help with funding. These are:

- using the benefits that are available if social services does not make the contract with the home (England and Wales) although this is not as attractive now that the residential allowance is not paid for residents who move in from 8 April 2002 and even this protection will be abolished from October 2003);
- friends, relatives and charities.

There is nothing to stop you getting help from friends, relatives or charities. In some cases, if you have not been assessed as needing care in a care home you may need to turn to them. Relatives may feel they should help with your fees if there is a waiting list for social services funding, but you should be careful of allowing social services to avoid their duties if they have assessed you as needing care in a care home (see p270).

Charities are normally precluded from paying for services that are the responsibility of the local authority. They may consider topping up your fees if you are in accommodation that is more expensive than social services considers necessary for your needs, or they may help if you have been assessed as not needing care in a care home.

5. NHS payments for registered nursing care (England and Wales)

In England and Wales, from October and December 2001 respectively, the NHS has been responsible for funding the registered nursing element of the fees that you pay if you are in a home providing nursing care. In Scotland from 1 July 2002 it is the local authority which is responsible for paying a contribution towards nursing and/or social care provided in care homes even if you have assets over the capital limits (see p165).

The systems are slightly different in England and Wales – mainly affecting the amount paid (in England there is a banded system and in Wales just one set amount – see p278), which the NHS body pays the care home and whether the NHS has responsibility for all residents in homes providing nursing.

In Wales the NHS is still only responsible for paying for your nursing if you pay for your own care. However in Wales, as has been the case since December 2001, some residents who have their care arranged by the local authority do have their registered nurse care paid by the NHS. This includes residents:

- who have their accommodation arranged by the local authority, but who are paying the full cost because they have over £20,000 – this includes residents who are receiving interim funding pending the sale of their property or who are using the deferred payment arrangements (see p299); *or*
- whose income is such that the local authority pays the home less than £100 a week after the resident's contribution has been made; *or*

- who at some point before April 2003 start to come under the local authority for the first time because their capital has decreased to £20,000 and the NHS has been funding their registered nursing care as they had been funding themselves in full.[83]

All other residents in Wales funded by the local authority still have their nursing care paid for by the local authority rather than the NHS.

In England from April 2003, the NHS took responsibility for paying for the registered nursing you need regardless of whether you are funding yourself or helped with your funding by the local authority. It should not make any difference to the residents who are funded by the local authority, it will just mean that the NHS will also be helping with the fees as well as social services. Your charge by the local authority is unlikely to be altered.

The registered nurse assessment

The definition of what nursing care the NHS pays for is laid down in legislation,[84] and covers the care provided by a registered nurse and the planning, supervision or delegation of care by the registered nurse. It does not cover the time spent by other care staff undertaking the care that has been delegated to them by a registered nurse.

In order to establish whether registered nursing care is required by the resident, there is an assessment by a registered nurse employed by the NHS.

If you require care in a home which provides nursing care then in Wales this is paid at the rate of £100 a week. In England the NHS nurse uses the information from the assessment, and based on his/her knowledge of your needs will place you in one of three bands:

- £40 a week for those whose needs can be met with minimal nursing input (eg, care which could be provided with support from a district nurse) but who have chosen to place themselves in a home providing nursing;
- £75 a week for those who may have multiple care needs and who require the intervention of a registered nurse on, at least, a daily basis, and who may need access to a nurse at any time, but whose condition is stable and predictable, and likely to remain so if treatment and care continues;
- £120 a week for those whose needs for registered nursing care is complex and requires frequent mechanical, technical and/or therapeutic interventions. They need frequent intervention and reassessment by a registered nurse throughout a 24-hour period and their condition is unstable and/or unpredictable.[85]

It is possible on a case-by-case basis to receive more than £120 for registered nursing from the NHS if it is assessed as being needed. However, if you are placed in either of the two higher bands you should always question whether you come under the eligibility criteria for fully funded NHS health care (see p260), before agreeing to just receiving help towards your nursing costs. In all cases an assessment for continuing NHS health care should be carried out before the assessment of the nursing contribution, but as a recent Health Service Ombudsman report has shown this may not have happened or the initial decision may not have been correct.[86]

The guidance that nurses use when deciding which band you should be placed in has some case examples. In one of the cases reported in the Health Services Ombudsman's special report (see p49), she found that 'if the Health Authority had had a reasonable policy, and applied it properly, they would have provided NHS care.' This particular person has needs listed which are remarkably similar to an example in the nurses workbook which tells nurses that they should place that person in the highest band for nursing care.[87] This must bring the guidance the nurses are using into question.

Your need for registered nursing care should be reviewed three months after the first assessment and following this every 12 months. You can ask for a review at any time if your condition has worsened. To ask for a review you need to contact the nursing home co-ordinator – the manager of your care home will be able to tell you where s/he is based.

If you have a complaint about the level of care you have been assessed as needing you can ask for a review via the nursing home co-ordinator and a reassessment will be undertaken. If you are still dissatisfied you can ask for the matter to be referred to the 'continuing care panel' (see p55).

Payments

Once you have been assessed then the appropriate NHS body will make the payment to the care home. In England this is the area in which your GP is based. In Wales it is based on the area in which the home is situated, even if you have a GP in different health area. In England if you are funded by the local authority, it is likely that the local authority will still pay the fees but they are doing so on behalf of the NHS.

Therefore, the care home (or in England, social services if your care is arranged by them) should only charge you for the accommodation and personal care and the fees should be adjusted accordingly. Guidance states that NHS bodies might wish to stipulate that the full financial benefit of any NHS payment should be discounted in any fee payable by the resident. In practice it has been found that not all residents see the benefit of the payment as some homes increased their fees. From April 2002 all residents should have a written contract which should make it clear what is included in the fees.[88] In England from September 2003 care homes fees should be broken down to show the fees payable for accommodation and food, nursing, and personal care. If you fund your own care, you should check carefully what the fee includes and make sure that the amount you get from the NHS is deducted from the fee you have to pay.

Short stays or breaks away from the home

If you are only staying in a home for a short period of care which is not likely to last more than six weeks then, in England, you will be allocated a band but will not necessarily have to have an assessment for this by the NHS registered nurse. The band you are placed in will be based on available records. Similarly in Wales, you will not need to have a full assessment.

NHS bodies should agree with the homes the terms for when you are away from the home. The NHS bodies have been told that they can follow the terms that have been set by social services (typically paying the full fees for up to six weeks). They should also make sure that there is consistency between the way retainers are paid for both local authority funded residents and people who pay for their own care.[89] You should be told what will happen if you leave the home temporarily for any reason.

Incontinence supplies and other equipment

The introduction of free nursing care has been accompanied by the introduction of the NHS taking the responsibility of providing incontinence products (such as pads) to homes providing nursing care for those residents who qualify for NHS nursing care. Up until the introduction of free nursing care, residents in homes providing nursing care had to pay for their own incontinence pads, whereas in all other settings the NHS provides them. In England the provision of incontinence supplies is in addition to the amount that you get through the banding system for registered nursing. In Wales it is included in the £100 if you pay for your own care, and should be part of the social services care plan if the local authority has arranged your care in the home. In Scotland you already get your incontinence supplies on prescription.

You should be able to receive the full range of equipment you are assessed as needing which is not supplied by the home as part of its regulatory requirements. The equipment you need should be specified in your care plan.

Effects on benefits

There should be no effect on any benefit you are paid if you are funding your own care. Regulations have been introduced to ensure that your attendance allowance and disability living allowance (care) will not be affected just because the NHS is paying your registered nursing care costs.[90] If you are funded by the local authority then your benefits will be affected in the ways described in Chapter 17.

6. Paying the full fees yourself

If you are not entitled to help from social services or free care from the NHS, you will have to pay the full fees. This will either mean that you make your own contract with the home, or that in some circumstances social services will make the contract for you but charge you the full cost. Section 5 explains the help you get towards your registered nurse costs if you are in a home providing nursing.

When social services charge you the full cost

If you have capital over the capital limit you could choose to make your own arrangements. You are still entitled to a needs assessment even if you can afford the fees yourself. However, social services departments must satisfy themselves that you are *able* to make your own arrangements with a care home, or have others who are *willing and able* to do so for you.[91] If you are not able and there is no one else who is willing and able, then social services must arrange your care in a care home. In Scotland following from a recent Scottish case in the House of Lords (see p327), authorities are required to make the arrangements for your care in a care home if you are assessed as needing such care, regardless of whether you have above the upper capital limit.[92]

If social services arranges your care they will then charge you the full cost until your capital is reduced to the capital limit for your country (see p294) – although the full cost does not include personal and/or nursing care if you are 65 or over.

If social services has decided that you have deliberately deprived yourself of income or capital to get help with your fees, they may decide to charge you the full cost.

Temporary or interim help from social services

If you have a property or capital which is not immediately available, you may be able to get help with your fees on a temporary or interim basis. You will normally be charged during this period based on your income, but once the capital is realised you will be billed so that you end up paying the full costs incurred by social services. See p299 for details about the deferred payments schemes that are available if you have a property. Remember though that for the first 12 weeks of a permanent stay in a care home the local authority has to disregard the value of your property (see p316). This means that if you own a property and have less than the upper capital limit in other savings, you should always have the choice of having the local authority making the arrangements for you, either just for the first 12 weeks or longer if you decide to use the deferred payments scheme. Seek advice if you are not told about the 12 weeks disregard on your property, or told that as you own a property you must make your own arrangements. It is often to your financial advantage to have the arrangements made by the local authority.

Making your own arrangements with a care home

If you make your own arrangements with a care home, you will need to make your own contract with them. In addition to all the points everybody needs to consider when choosing a home (see p256), it is very important to be clear about, and have written information on, all the financial implications. These include:

- exactly what is included in the fees (eg, laundry, hairdressing, newspapers and chiropody (but ask if you can get chiropody from the local NHS body before you agree to pay for private chiropody in the fees) are sometimes included in the fees but sometimes the cost of services are not included). The costs of continence supplies should not be included in the fees (other than in Wales for local authority funded residents) as these are now supplied by the NHS;
- whether a deposit is required, what it is for and when is it returnable;
- how often the fees are reviewed and what notice is given;
- the minimum period of notice you have to give to leave the home;
- whether you can have a trial period;
- what effect a period in hospital or away on holiday would have on your fees. In the case of a care home providing nursing care, you also need to know the extent of the NHS payment for registered nursing care while you are away.[93]

Although it is not always easy to ask, it is also important to be sure what payment the home would continue to expect if you die, and how soon your room would need to be cleared. It is important that relatives are aware of this to avoid the distress of finding that fees still need to be paid for a short while. The Care Standards Act requires homes to provide contracts and also much of the type of information suggested above.

Remember a contract is an agreement and to some extent you can negotiate the terms and conditions. You may want to seek legal advice.

You should still be able to get any NHS services which are supplied in the community, if they are not provided as part of the registration requirements of the home.

The level of the fees

Research has backed up anecdotal evidence that people making their own arrangements may be charged more for exactly the same facilities as those residents who are funded by social services.[94] Homes will sometimes negotiate their fees, so it can be useful to know what social services would normally pay for someone with your needs. You can then use this to compare the fees of the homes you visit.

It is also important to establish (especially if you are likely to need help from social services in the future) whether the home will drop its fees to the social services level if they take over the arrangements. Some homes are prepared to do this, but others will keep to the fees they set and so you would need to find someone to make up the difference (see p271).

Getting help if you have been funding yourself

Even if you make your own arrangements with a care home you may later need to approach social services to get help with funding once your capital approaches the capital limit. You will normally need to approach the local authority where you now live. The social services department will assess you to see if you need the type of care you are getting. This can sometimes take a few weeks so it is worth approaching them several months before your capital reaches the capital limit so they have time to assess your needs and undertake a financial assessment. Social services have been told that when residents whose capital is approaching the capital limit, they should undertake the assessment as soon as reasonably practicable and if necessary take over the arrangements to ensure that the resident is not forced to use capital below the limit.[95] More recent guidance in England has strengthened this and reminded local authorities that once they are aware of a resident's circumstances any undue delay in assessment or funding would be in breach of their statutory duties, therefore the local authority could be liable to reimburse the resident.[96] You should also apply for income support when your capital reaches the capital limit. Note that, from October 2003 you may qualify for pension credit even if you cannot get help from social services because your capital is above the capital limit for your country (see p294) as there are no capital limits for pension credit (PC – see p176). See pxix for the proposals for changes to charges due to PC.

Occasionally social services will decide you do not need care in a care home and will neither make the arrangements nor help to fund you. If they do not think you need nursing care you may need to move to a care home which does not provide nursing. This does not happen very often. If it does, you can ask for a review of the assessment to make sure social services has taken all your needs into account. You should also seek advice.

Couples

If you are one of a couple with a joint account of over £39,000 and you are funding yourself in a care home, it may be worth considering splitting your account. This is because you will not get help from social services until your joint capital is down to £39,000 (when you are counted as each having £19,500). For example if you have a joint account of £49,000 you will need to spend £10,000 on fees before you can get help. If you split your account so you each have £24,500, you will only need to spend £5,000 before you can get help. The figures are different in Scotland and Wales because of the different capital limits.

Getting funding from the NHS

If your condition worsens while you are in a care home you may meet the eligibility criteria for NHS funded care (see p260) or you might qualify for registered nurse care funded by the NHS (see p278). If you are in a care home and become a hospital inpatient you should then be assessed under the normal hospital discharge rules (see p263). If you are in a home which provides nursing you might continue to be nursed through your worsening condition without going to hospital. You should ask your GP for an assessment to see whether you now come under the local eligibility criteria for continuing NHS health care. If you do, then the NHS should take over the funding of your care, although it may not agree to do so at the home you are in.

Following the *Coughlan* decision (see p261) and the new guidance in England (see p39) some NHS bodies have changed their eligibility criteria. You might find that although your condition has not worsened you are now eligible for continuing NHS health care. It is worth checking if the eligibility criteria have been changed as a result of the judgment and the guidance and to ask for a reassessment of whether you fall within NHS funded care. You may now want to challenge why the NHS has not funded you given that the Ombudsman has suggested that significant numbers of people may have wrongly been paying for their care (see p39).

7. Dealing with your money in a care home

Unless you are unable to manage you should remain in control of your financial affairs and pay the charges yourself, or you may have decided to appoint an attorney to do this for you. In this way, you can be sure the correct charge is paid and that you keep your personal expenses allowance.

Some homes take residents' pension books and collect their benefits on their behalf as an agent. Although this might make it easier for you because you do not need to go to the post office, you might wish to consider other ways of having your benefits paid, so that you keep full control over all your money. For instance having your benefits paid into a bank account and setting up a standing order or direct debit to pay your fees. Methods of paying benefits will change over the next couple of years and so this will affect how your benefits are collected if you cannot collect them yourself. See p119 for details of the changes.

If you cannot manage your financial affairs

If you are unable to give social services the information they need to assess your charge because you lack the mental capacity, then they have been told to find out if anyone has power of attorney, receivership or appointeeship (a financial power of attorney, a financial intervenor, someone appointed under an intervention order, a withdrawer or appointeeship in Scotland) or appointeeship. If no one has taken on any of these roles, social services cannot properly financially assess you until someone has been duly authorised to act for you. In practice, many authorities will make the arrangements for your care and give an estimate of the likely costs to you. They are unlikely to refuse to make the arrangements just because you have no one to give them financial details.

If there is no one suitable to act for you, social services may become your appointee or receiver (guardian in Scotland), depending on your financial circumstances but this would only be as a last resort.

There are some very significant legal differences in Scotland regarding the management of another person's affairs, with a wide variety of different legal appointments possible under the Adults with Incapacity (Scotland) Act 2000. The court system is also very different from England and Wales and legal advice should be sought about these matters.

In England and Wales changes are also proposed in a draft *Mental Incapacity Bill*. This section only outlines the different methods of currently dealing with your finances if you can no longer manage them yourself. See Appendix 5 for further reading.

Appointeeship

The Secretary of State can authorise someone to act on your behalf in relation to benefits if you cannot claim for yourself or if you can no longer deal with your financial affairs.[97] Your appointee would take on all the rights and responsibilities as a claimant – eg, notifying the DWP of any change of circumstances. Your appointee is responsible for making sure the benefits received are spent on your behalf. If you are in a care home this would include ensuring that the benefits are used to pay your assessed charge.

Appointeeship only gives authority to deal with your benefits and any small amount of capital which has accumulated from those benefits. It *does not* give any authority to deal with your other income or capital. In England and Wales, if you have other income or capital, there would need to be an application to the Court of Protection through the Public Guardianship Office (see p286). The Public Guardianship Office suggested that if you have savings from benefits of no more than one month's accommodation costs and about £500 as a cash float, no other authority would normally be needed. In Scotland, a financial guardian should be appointed to deal with all financial affairs if there is no power of attorney (see p289). In practice, many relatives assist people on an informal basis. However, since April 2001 new rules came into effect in Scotland[98] to enable the access of funds in certain circumstances (see below).

Authorisation to access funds (Scotland)

Carers and other individuals (but not social work staff) can obtain authority to access the funds of an adult to meet living expenses. In order to make use of the Access to Funds scheme, an application has to be made to the Public Guardian, the authority responsible for managing and supervising access to accounts. The Public Guardian will authorise how much money may be transferred from the adult's account to a designated account, and will give a certificate to the person who is allowed to open the designated account and access the funds transferred into that account. It can be used for day-to-day living expenses and for paying the regular bills of people living at home or for payments for care in a care home. The Public Guardian will be able to request records. Authority to access funds in this way will be given for a period of up to three years at the first application, although this may become indefinite when it is renewed.[99]

Enduring power of attorney (England and Wales)

If you have already appointed an attorney under an enduring power[100] then the power for them to act for you will continue if you lose the mental capacity to manage your financial affairs. However, the enduring power of attorney will only remain valid if the person or persons you have named register it with the Public Guardianship Office (see below) once they have reason to believe that you have become or are becoming incapable of managing your affairs.

As the power extends beyond the time you are capable of managing your affairs, it is very important that you choose someone that you completely trust. The person must be over 18, and in most cases will be a relative or friend. If your financial affairs are complex you may wish to appoint a professional – eg, a solicitor or accountant. The appointment of a single attorney may offer less security for your assets than a joint or joint and several attorneyship.

Normally you will have made an enduring power of attorney long before you need care in a care home, although it can be done at any time as long as at the time of signing the forms, you are capable of understanding what the enduring power of attorney is and what it is intended to do.

The attorney(s) can take over your affairs at once while you are still capable of managing your affairs, or you can specify that you only want the attorney(s) to take over when you are no longer mentally capable of acting for yourself.

An attorney can only do the things you have authorised them to do. If you have given your attorney(s) a general power, they have complete authority to act on your behalf in relation to financial matters. You can give limited powers, by defining precisely what the attorney can and cannot do, although you will need to consider other arrangements for dealing with those affairs outside the limited power of attorney.

If you are no longer capable of managing your financial affairs, and have been assessed for your charges by social services, then they will deal with your attorney(s). They should seek proof that the power has been registered in order to establish that they are dealing with a duly authorised person. If it is not yet registered then your attorney should be advised by social services about the need to register it.

Registering the enduring power of attorney

The enduring power of attorney is registered by applying to the Public Guardianship Office which is the administrative arm of the Court of Protection. No medical evidence is required. As soon as the application is made, the powers of the attorney are suspended until registration has taken place. This can take a while as there are rules about who has to be notified (you and at least three of your nearest relatives in priority). Once these people have been notified the application should be sent to the Public Guardianship Office with the registration fee. This fee can be waived or reduced, and you should be given details of when the Public Guardianship will normally remit the fee when you apply to register. The papers are held for 35 days after the last notification. If there are no objections it will be registered.

During this time it may be difficult to pay the homes fees or the social services charges because the attorneyship is suspended. However, the rules allow for your money to be used for your immediate needs. The Public Guardianship Office will be able to advise your attorney on this.

After registration

Your attorney will be responsible for your income and capital, and for paying your charges. Responsibilities may include selling your former home if you are required to pay the full cost of the home. If there is any question about your charge it will be for your attorney to take this up with social services (see p297).

Revoking an enduring power of attorney

Neither the Public Guardianship Office nor the Court of Protection normally supervise the actions of an attorney once registration has taken place. This may change in the future. You can revoke an enduring power of attorney at any time while you are still mentally capable, but once it is registered it cannot be revoked by you.

If your attorney fails to pay your charges to social services or there are other concerns that the attorney may be abusing her/his power, then social services may ask the Court of Protection to investigate the suitability of the attorney. If necessary the Court will supervise the exercise of the powers and as a last resort could impose a receivership order.

Power of attorney (Scotland)

Since April 2001, there is a new system of 'continuing attorneys' (sometimes referred to as the 'financial attorney') and 'welfare attorneys'. A person who wishes to have someone to look after her/his financial affairs if s/he loses capacity, can stipulate this when granting a power of attorney. A welfare attorney can be granted to someone you want to make welfare decisions once you no longer have the capacity to do so yourself. This can include consent to medical treatment (but not in relation to certain types of treatment carried out under the Mental Health (Scotland) Act 1984), and decisions about care or accommodation. The power of attorney must be written, and signed by the person granting it, stating clearly what powers are granted. It must also include a certificate signed by a solicitor, advocate or medical practitioner that they are satisfied that you understand what you are signing and are not acting under undue influence. The powers of a welfare attorney cannot be exercised until the person granting the attorney loses capacity in relation to these areas. The power of attorney must be registered with the Public Guardian and any changes must be notified to the Public Guardian.[101]

The Adults with Incapacity (Scotland) Act 2000 is being implemented in stages. The new Office of the Public Guardian came into operation on 1 April 2001. Continuing powers of attorney have to state that they are to be ongoing after the granter becomes incapacitated and at that point the power has to be registered with the Office. *Curator bonis* and *tutors dative* were replaced by a new financial guardianship provision which came into operation on 1 April 2002. There are transitional arrangements for those already authorised by that date. There are no more appointments of curators, but existing curators will continue but be subject to the same controls as financial guardians. Both in enactments and documents, references to curators shall be construed as references to guardians with similar powers appointed under the Adults with Incapacity (Scotland) Act 2000.

Receivership and short orders (England and Wales)

If you have lost the capacity to deal with your financial affairs and appointeeship is not appropriate because you have income and capital that is not related to benefits, and you have not made an enduring power of attorney, then the Court of Protection will need to be involved in authorising the management of your financial affairs.

The Court of Protection can make orders for people who are incapable, by reason of mental disorder, of managing their own affairs. If this is the case you will become a 'patient' of the court.

There are two types of order:

- receivership;
- a short order, if your affairs are simple and can be covered by a few directions authorising the way your money or property should be used for your benefit. This may include paying fees to the home or local authority charges.

Normally the receiver will be a relative, friend, or solicitor. Social services can cause an application to be made when this is needed and there is no one else to make that application. You must be notified of the application (although in rare cases it might be waived if it would cause harm or distress).

The court only has jurisdiction if medical evidence has established that you are suffering from a mental disorder, and it must be satisfied that you are also incapable of managing your financial affairs.

The responsibilities of the receiver

Your receiver should do everything in relation to your property and financial affairs that the court has ordered or authorised. For some actions, the receiver must obtain specific authority from the Public Guardianship Office. These include:

- using your savings or capital;

- buying or selling property;
- varying your investments;
- taking or defending legal proceedings.

Patients are encouraged to deal with as much of their financial affairs as they can. So although your receiver may be paying your fees on your behalf, you may be able to manage your personal expenses allowance or your pension book.

Your receiver will have to submit accounts of all receipts and payments made on your behalf, when requested to, usually annually.

Social services will arrange for your receiver to pay any charges due and if your receiver fails to pay may ask the court to intervene and if necessary to change the receiver or take on the receivership themselves.

Social services as receiver

Most social services departments are reluctant to take on the role of receiver, but will do so if necessary. Who has the role varies from local authority to local authority. In some areas it will be the director, or a person with specific responsibilities for receivership or appointeeship, or a person in the finance section. Many recognise the conflict of interest when they are the receiver or appointee and yet also collect charges. Until recently the Public Guardianship Office did not visit patients where the local authority is the receiver. Some visits are now carried out. Some local authorities when they are the receiver, use advocacy services to oversee your interests, or the receiver is a person who is separate from the finance section, in order to keep the conflict of interest to a minimum. Social services, like any other receiver, may have to account for its actions in the way it handles your money.

Financial guardians in Scotland

In Scotland a person known as a financial guardian can be appointed to manage a person's financial affairs. This replaced the previous system of appointing a *curator bonis*. Those who have already been appointed as a *curator bonis* will be subject to the same controls as guardians. An application may be made to the sheriff's court. Financial guardians are supervised by the Office of the Public Guardian. Applications from lay people are encouraged. However where the management of finances is likely to be complex then they may wish to employ an accountant to help. Solicitors may also be appointed as financial guardians. In some circumstances the local authority may petition the court to appoint a financial guardian. Local authorities are not allowed to petition to become financial guardians themselves. Individuals or local authorities can apply to the court for an intervention order. This is an application to make a 'one-off' decision which may be of a financial nature – eg, the sale of the house.

For further information and application forms contact The Office of the Public Guardian (see Appendix 3) or visit the website www.scotscourts.gov.uk.

Part 4 of the Adults with Incapacity (Scotland) Act 2000 provides for the management, by care homes and independent hospitals, of the funds and property of residents who are unable to carry out this function themselves. Authorisation, control and regulation of these arrangements are the responsibility of the Scottish Commission for the Regulation of Care (The Care Commission).[102]

Notes

1. **Deciding to move into a care home**
   1 LAC (98)19; WOC 27/98; Scottish CRAG Annex G
   2 5 CCLR 543
   3 Annex D HLD (2003)7
   4 LGOR 00/C/3176

2. **Choosing a home**
   5 Reg 5 Care Homes Regulations 2001 SI No 3965
   6 The Care Home (Amendment No.2) Regs 2003 SI No.1703
   7 DoH Press Release 2002/0124
   8 LGOR 97/A/4002 Bexley
   9 *R v Bristol City Council ex parte Penfold* (CCLR), June 1998 and *R v Wigan MBC ex parte Tammadge* (CCLR), December 1998
   10 *R v Wandsworth LBC ex parte Beckwith*

3. **Fees which are fully paid by the state**
   11 *Supported Housing and Care Homes-Guidance on Regulation.* DH August 2002
   12 *With Respect to Old Age,* Royal Commission 1999
   13 HSC 2001/015; LAC (2001)18; WHC (95)7; WOC 16/95: MEL (1996)22 but note new guidance only applies in England. In Scotland and Wales earlier guidance still applies. Draft guidance similar to that in England has been produced in Wales but has not yet been finalised.
   14 ss3(1) and 23 NHSA 1977; NHS(S)A 1978
   15 HSC 2001/015; LAC (2001)18
   16 WHC (95)7; WOC 16/95: NHS MEL (1996)22
   17 EL (96)8
   18 *R v N and E Devon ex parte Coughlan* (CCLR), September 1999
   19 *NHS Funding for Long-term Care,* Health Service Ombudsman, 20 February 2002
   20 www.doh.gov.uk/jointunit/ccc.htm
   21 *Handling Complaints about the Funding of Continuing Care,* Scottish Executive, 13 June 2003
   22 *Hansard,* House of Lords, 17 March 2003 col 15
   23 WHC (95)7; WOC 16/95; MEL (1996)22
   24 Community Care (Delayed Discharges etc) Act
   25 The legal basis of such payments is uncertain. NHS bodies can make payments to various statutory and voluntary bodies under s28A NHSA 1977, which cannot be used for any health function, only in connection with the functions of the organisation receiving the payment. From April 2000 there were changes to this in England caused by the HA 1999 and some functions of the NHS will be able to be delegated, and it will be easier for money to be passed from the NHS to local authorities and *vice versa.* Under s64 HSPHA 1968 grants can be made to voluntary organisations (only) which provide services similar to services provided by the NHS.
   26 For up to date information see www.doh.gov.uk/pricare/responsiblecommissioner/
   27 LAC (2001)1 and NAFWC 43/02
   28 Community Care (Delayed Discharges etc) Act (Qualifying Services) (England) Regs 2003 SI No.1196
   29 ss3, 37, 47 or 48 MHA 1983
   30 s117 MHA 1983

31 *R v Manchester CC ex p Stennet (HoL)* 5 CCLR, December 2002
32 *Clunis v Camden and Islington Health Authority* (CCLR), March 1998
33 LGOR 97/0177 and 97/0755 Clywd and Conwy
34 *R v LB Richmond ex parte Watson; R v Redcar and Cleveland ex parte Armstrong; R v Manchester ex parte Stennett; R v Harrow ex parte Cobham* (CCLR), December 1999
35 LGOR 00/B/8307 Leicestershire CC
36 LGOR 98/B/0341 Wiltshire CC
37 *The Funding of After-care under section 117 of the Mental Health Act 1983*, LGO, July 2003
38 s8(1) MH(S)A 1984

4. **Help with fees from social services**

39 ss21 and 24 NAA 1948 and LAC (93)10; WOC 35/93
40 Those under 18 come under the CA 1989
41 s116 Immigration and Asylum Act 1999. Also *O v LB Wandswort* and *Bhikha and Leicester City Council*, 22 June 2000, 3 (CCLR), September 2000
42 LAC (93)10; WOC 35/93
43 s29 NAA 1948 and LAC (93)10; WOC 35/93 Appendix 2
44 s49 HSCA 2001
45 s12 SW(S)A 1968
46 Community Care (Assessment of Needs) Scotland Regs 2002
47 CCD 04/2002
48 CCC 05/2002
49 s26 NAA 1948
50 SWSG 10/98
51 s47(5) NHSCCA 1990; s12A(5) SW(S)A 1968
52 NA(RADR)(E) Regs and LAC (2001)25; WOC 27/98; SWSG 2/99
53 *Fife v Robertson,* House of Lords, CCLR, December 2002
54 HDL (2003)7
55 LAC (98)19
56 *R v Sefton MBC ex parte Help the Aged and Blanchard* (CA) (CCLR), December 1997
57 *R v Wigan MBC ex parte Tammadge* (CCLR), December 1998
58 LAC (98)19; WOC 27/98; SWSG 2/99
59 LAC (2002)11; NAfW 14/02; CCD 3/2002
60 LGOR 00/B/599
61 *MacGregor v South Lanarkshire Council* Outer House of Session, CCLR, June 2001
62 The Scottish Executive, Health Department (Directorate of Service Policy and Planning) advised local authorities in a letter (17 January 2003) ref FW/COSLA/MacGregor 2
63 LAC (92)27: WOC 12/93; SWSG 5/93 *Choice of Accommodation Directions*
64 Regulations have replaced parts of the *Choice of Accommodation Directions* directions; LAC(2002) 25; LAC (2002)29; CCD 6/2002; NAfWC 21/2003
65 LAC (92)27; WOC 12/93; SWSG 5/93 para 7
66 LGOR 97/A/3218 Merton
67 LAC (2001)29; WOC 12/93; SWSG 5/93 para 10
68 *R v Avon County Council ex parte M* (CCLR), June 1999
69 LGOR 97/A/3218 Merton
70 LAC (92)27; WOC 12/93; SWSG 5/93 para 7.6
71 LAC (93)18; SWSG 6/94
72 and NAfWC 12/2003
73 LAC (2002)11; NAfWC 14/02; CCD 3/2002
74 paras 3.004 and 3.004A CRAG; paras 3.004 and 3.004A Scottish CRAG
75 LAC (93)7; WOC 41/93; SWSG 1/96
76 LAC (93)10; WOC 35/93; SWSG 1/96
77 s22 NAA 1948; NA(AR) Regs
78 LAC (2002)11; LAC (2003)8; NAfW 14/02; CCD 3/2002; HLD (2003)7
79 HSC 2001/015; LAC (2001)18; HSC 2001/017; LAC (2001)26; NAfWC 34/01
80 Letter from the DoH to the Association of County Councils, November 1996
81 para 1.024A CRAG; para 1.017A Scottish CRAG
82 s26(3A) NAA 1948 and para 1.023 CRAG; para 1.015 Scottish CRAG

5. **NHS payments for registered nursing care (England and Wales)**

83 NAfWC 34/01
84 s49 HSCS 2001
85 NHS Funded Nursing Care Practice Guide and Workbook and HSC 2001/017; LAC (2001)26; NAfWC 34/01
86 *NHS Funding for Long-term Care*, HSO, 20 February 2002
87 Annex C case no E 420/00-01 *NHS funding for long term care.* Health Services Ombudsman 2003 and compare with Example 4 in the *NHS funded nursing care Practice Guide and Workbook* DH 2001

88 CSA 2000
89 LAC (2003)7 HSC 2003/6
90 SS(AA/DLA) Regs

6. **Paying the full fees yourself**

91 LAC (98)19; WOC 27/98; SWSG 2/99
92 HLD (2003)7 Annex D
93 LAC (2003)7;HSC 2003/6
94 *Disparities between market rates and state funding and residential care*, JRF Finding 678, June 1998
95 LAC 98/19 and LAC (2001)25; WOC 27/98; SWSG 2/99
96 LAC (2001)25

7. **Dealing with your money in a care home**

97 Reg 33 SS(C&P) Regs
98 Part III Adults with Incapacity (Scotland) Act 2000
99 *Code of Practice for Persons under Part 3 to Access Funds of an Adult*, Scottish Executive
100 Enduring Power of Attorney Act 1985
101 Part 2 Adults with Incapacity (Scotland) Act 2000 and *Code of Practice for Continuing and Welfare Attorneys*, Scottish Executive, September 2000
102 Adults with Incapacity (Scotland) Act 2000 and (Comm. No. 4) Order 2003

Chapter 10

Financial assessments and charges in care homes

This chapter covers:

1. The financial assessment

There are no set rules about the way the financial assessment is carried out. Guidance makes it clear that the financial assessment should be carried out after the decision on what sort of care you need (the needs assessment).[1] This means that you should not be asked questions about your finances until you have had a needs assessment and it has been agreed that care in a care home is appropriate. If you are asked about your capital early on in your needs assessment or told you will have to make your own arrangements, before a proper calculation of your income or capital is done, or if you are not told about when your property is disregarded you should complain (see p55).

If it is determined that you need care in a care home, legislation allows social services to calculate your resources (see Chapters 11 and 12) to establish whether you need to be provided with residential accommodation by them or you can afford to make your own arrangements (see p256).[2] If you have capital of above the capital limit for your country (see p315) then in some circumstances social services will decide they do not need to make the arrangements for you (see p297).

If this happens you will still be able to receive payments from the NHS towards any nursing care in a care home which provides nursing (note, in Wales payments towards nursing care costs will only be available for self-funding residents until 2004 when they will be extended to all residents as in England). In Scotland you can still receive payments towards both your nursing and personal care if you have above the capital limit and you are 65 or over. If you are under 65 you can receive payments towards your nursing care (see p268).

It is important to note that following the *Robertson v Fife* case (27 July 2002) it has been made clear that the provision of services to a person who is assessed as being in need of them is not related to the ability of the person to meet the costs (see p327).

If you are placed in a care home by social services, legislation requires that you repay them the cost of the accommodation if you are capable of doing so.[3] A 'standard rate' is fixed for the accommodation and if you have sufficient income or capital you will be required to pay the full cost – ie, the 'standard rate'.[4]

The 'standard rate' for local authority care homes is the full cost to social services of your placement.[5] The 'standard rate' for independent care homes is the gross cost to social services of providing or paying for your placement under the contract with the home.[6]

If you cannot meet the cost in full, and you provide the necessary financial information for an assessment to be carried out, social services will only charge the amount determined by the assessment.[7]

If you help in the running of your care home and it is managed by the local authority, part of your charges may be waived in recognition of this.[8]

Legislation provides for the assessment of resources required by social services to establish your contribution to the cost of your placement in a care home – ie, the charge (see Chapters 11 and 12).[9] After you have paid the assessed charge you should not be left with less than £17.50 (£17.80 in Wales) for your personal expenses (see Chapter 13).

For the first eight weeks of any placement, social services do not have to carry out a financial assessment (although some do). Instead they can charge what they consider to be reasonable.[10] If you consider that the charge is unreasonable you can ask social services for a full financial assessment.

Calculation used by social services in the financial assessment to determine your contribution to the cost

Total assessable income (including any tariff income from your capital, see Chapters 11 and 12)

minus

Outgoings (for a temporary resident who has outgoings for her/his home in the community, see Chapter 13)

minus

Personal expenses allowance (see Chapter 13)

equals

Contribution to accommodation and care costs (charge)

See Chapter 18 for example calculations.

Collecting financial information

The way local authorities collect financial information varies. In some areas a financial assessment officer will go through the assessment with you. In other authorities your care assessor/social worker/manager will help you fill in the form. In others you will be sent a form to complete yourself.

However, once the form is completed, it will normally go to the section in the local authority that deals with calculating how much you will have to pay. This is normally the finance section in social services.

Unlike for social security benefits, there is no standard form used throughout the country for the financial assessment. Each local authority has devised its own form. In some cases the same form will cover both domiciliary and residential charges. As these charges are based on different legislation, the form should make it clear which parts you need to fill in if you are going into a care home. The forms should not require information about your partner's income and capital as it is only your resources which can be taken into account, and financial assessment forms for ascertaining a resident's resources should not be used for collecting the financial details of the partner.[11] If the form asks questions that are irrelevant you should complain.

Verifying the details you have given

Social services has been told it is good practice to verify information – eg, to look at bank statements. They should also make use of information available to them from other departments within the authority (eg, housing benefit and council tax records) to verify details. They have been advised to check, with your permission, with other agencies such as the DWP, banks and pension firms. It is for authorities themselves to determine the extent to which, and circumstances in which, they will verify information.[12]

Claiming social security benefits

As some benefits are used to pay social services charges, it is in the interests of social services to ensure that you claim all the benefits to which you are entitled (see Chapter 17). Social services has been advised to maintain good links with the DWP.[13] It should be made as smooth as possible for you to claim benefits and for details to be transferred from one department to another.

How much help you get from social services in claiming benefits varies around the country. In some areas the person filling in the financial assessment form will also help you to complete the income support (IS) (minimum income guarantee (MIG) for people aged 60 or over) claim form at the same time, if this is appropriate, and send it to the DWP. In other areas you will be advised to make a claim and told how to get the claim form.

Information about how much you have to pay

Social services should give you clear information about how much you should be expected to pay, and how this has been calculated. They should explain the normal weekly assessed charge and any reasons why the charge may change.[14] Changes in charges are most likely to occur during the first few weeks in a care home when your attendance allowance (AA) or disability living allowance care component (DLA care) is usually withdrawn or extra IS becomes payable (see Chapter 17). Changes may also occur if there is any other increase or decrease in the amount of your income and/or capital (see below).

Social services should also explain how you should pay. If you have agreed to pay your part of the charge directly to the home, you will need to arrange with the home how frequently you will pay (see p276). If you are going to be billed by social services, you should be given some choice about the method of payment. Most social services prefer direct debit, but if you want to choose to pay in another way you should explore the possibility with them. If you think that social services has limited the range of payment methods, you should complain (see p55).

2. Reviews of your assessment

It has been left to each local authority to make its own arrangements about how frequently and when your charge will be reviewed and the policy to adopt if undercharging or overcharging occurs.[15]

Nearly all social services departments review their charges annually at the time when your benefits are uprated. This is also the time when the home you are in is most likely to alter its fees.

However, your income or capital could change at any time – eg, you could inherit money, your occupational or private pension could go up or your savings could go down because you have been using some of the money to supplement the low personal expenses allowance (see p331). You should inform social services when you have a change of circumstances, in the same way as you should inform the DWP.

If you have capital between the lower and upper capital limit you should inform social services every time it goes up or down a £250 band (see p308). Unless you do this, when your capital has gone down you are likely to continue to be charged at a higher rate until the annual review of charges. Some social services have computer systems to track the tariff income and will alter it automatically. Others do not and so it is safer to regularly inform them of changes. If they refuse to reassess you when you tell them about a change of circumstances, you should complain as you may be charged too much.

3. If you have a complaint about your charge

If you have a concern about your charge, you have a right to complain about it using the complaints procedure[16] (see p55). As the rules for charging are national, a complaint will normally be to resolve an error in the calculation or in the interpretation of the rules. These are often dealt with in the initial stage by discussing it with the finance officer dealing with your case.

It is important to check the calculation very carefully to make sure that your income and capital used in the calculation are correct. You also need to check that any bills presented on the sale of your former home accurately reflect whether you were a temporary or permanent resident at the start of your stay. You should be clear about exactly what period is covered and that increases in fees are correctly recorded, along with what you may have already paid from your income.

Social services has some discretion, which includes:

- the way jointly owned property is valued (see p317);
- whether your former home can be disregarded (see p319);
- whether you have deprived yourself of capital (see p324);
- whether your personal expenses allowance will be varied (see p331);
- whether a liable relative payment is expected (see p340);
- whether you are required to have a third party to top up (see p334);
- whether you count as a temporary or permanent resident (see p301);
- how frequently reviews are carried out (see p296).

In these cases it is more likely that you will need to take your complaint through to the formal stage and maybe to a complaints panel. Some social services have a separate procedure for appeals against charges. This should not debar you, however, from using the complaints procedure, and you should not have to go through that appeal procedure before you are allowed to make a formal complaint. If you have concerns about your charges you can also use the other remedies outlined in Chapter 2. It is always wise to seek advice.

4. Paying the full cost of your care home (including deferred payment agreements)

You may be able to meet the full cost of your accommodation and care without financial help from social services.

If social services has not contracted with the care home for your accommodation and care and you continue to receive income support (IS) (note, all references to IS also apply to income-based jobseeker's allowance) then you are described as a self-funding **'loophole'** case as you will also be entitled to continue to receive any attendance allowance (AA) or disability living allowance care component (DLA care) (see p376). The loophole option has become less viable as a way of meeting care home fees due to the abolition of the residential allowance part of IS in April 2002. From October 2003 transitional protection for claims made before April 2002 will also be abolished (see p368).

If you are not receiving financial help from social services (whether or not social services has contracted with the care home), or you are only receiving it on a temporary repayable basis (see below for when this may apply) and you are not in receipt of IS, then you are described as **self-funding** or **retrospectively self-funding**.

With the introduction of pension credit for people aged 60 or over from October 2003 the circumstances in which you will be treated as self-funding may change (see pp368 and 376).

If you have capital in excess of the capital limit for your country (see p315) you will be required to pay the full cost of your accommodation and care – ie, you will be self-funding. However, this does not mean that you cannot receive help from social services in terms of an assessment of your needs to establish what services you require, and help to find a suitable care home.[17] Contacting social services for this type of help will benefit you if or when your capital reduces to the capital limit for your country (see p315), because at that point social services will help fund your placement (as long as your assessable income is less than the care home fee), as they have previously agreed that it meets your assessed needs.

Even if you are self-funding you could still benefit from social services arranging your placement and contracting with the care home as fees are often higher for self-funding residents without a social services contract. However, some social services authorities will not contract with a care home if you are self-funding (sometimes called full cost) unless you or your representative are unable to arrange the placement (see p269). A social services contract will not affect your entitlement to DLA care or AA if you are self-funding, unlike if you are taking advantage of the loophole option where a social services contract will mean that DLA care or AA is not payable (see p376).

If you are required to meet the full cost of your accommodation and care because you are a permanent resident and your home in the community (after the 12-week disregard – see p316) is valued at more than the capital limit for your country (see p315), you may not actually be able to pay the full cost until your house is sold (but see p376 to find out if you could take advantage of the 'loophole' option). In this situation, social services can help meet the cost of your accommodation and care and claim the amount back from you when your property is sold (see p376). The deferred payment scheme provides for these circumstances (see p299). For DLA care or AA purposes you are considered to be retrospectively self-funding (see p380).

Deferred payment agreements

The Health and Social Care Act 2001 or, in Scotland, the Community Care and Health (Scotland) Act 2002 provides for deferred payment agreements.[18]

A deferred payment agreement allows social services to take a legal charge in their favour on your main or only home or, in Scotland, a grant to the local authority of a standard security over the home, instead of the full contribution towards the cost of your accommodation and care in a care home. This arrangement allows you to keep your home while you are in a care home for the duration of the deferred payment agreement.

The provision of social services being able to take a legal charge on your property is not a new power. A power already existed and continues to exist under another enactment if you fail to pay the assessed charge in circumstances where an outstanding debt is being pursued.[19]

Deferred payments are only a way of putting off making payment of the full cost to social services for your accommodation and care in a care home. The full cost payment will have to be made at some point from the proceeds of the sale of your property whether it is sold in your lifetime or not. It is not a way of preserving the asset to pass on to your family or friends after your death.

Eligibility

Deferred payment agreements are available to you if you:

- do not have a current mandatory or discretionary property disregard applied to your property (although you may enter a deferred payment agreement following the 12-week property disregard);
- do not have capital (apart from the value of your home) above the upper capital limit in England (£19,500) and Wales (£20,000) or the lower capital limit in Scotland (£11,500);
- cannot meet the full cost of the care home from your income;
- do not wish to sell your home or you are unable to sell your home quickly enough to pay for your fees. In Scotland, you must also be able to grant the authority a standard security against your home to secure a reasonable estimate of the total amount which will be covered.

Social services has discretion over whether they agree to a deferred payment agreement with individual residents. However, in Wales directions place a duty on local authorities to draw attention to and offer deferred payment arrangements to all eligible or prospective residents.[20] The guidance advises that discretion (or in Wales, *some* discretion) should be exercised in cases such as where there is an outstanding mortgage on the property or the deferred payment is very high, as these circumstances may limit the ability to offer deferred payments to other residents.[21] When your home is eventually sold, it should be possible for you or your estate to pay back the deferred contribution including any top-up (see Chapter 14).[22] Any refusal by social services to agree to a deferred payment agreement should be put in writing giving reasons. You should use the complaints procedure if you wish to challenge the decision (see p55).

Further guidance on deferred payment agreements was issued in October 2002 (England only) as there had only been limited use of the power to allow deferred payments by a number of local authorities.[23] A model draft legal agreement for creating a legal charge for deferred payment agreements was referred to in the guidance as being available on the CRAG website.[24] In Scotland further guidance was issued in March 2003 but there is no model draft legal agreement.[25] In Wales the original guidance, which introduced deferred payment agreements from April 2003, also contains a model deferred payment agreement.[26]

Operating the deferred payment scheme

Social services should carry out a financial assessment in the normal way to determine the amount that you should contribute towards the cost of your accommodation and care. The amount that is then deferred and ultimately recovered from the value of the property is the difference between the contribution and the full cost of the care home. In addition, you may be able to defer the amount of any top-up required for more expensive accommodation, if appropriate (see Chapter 14).[27]

Deferred payment agreements:

- must be made in writing and social services should ensure that you understand what you are committing yourself to;
- last from the day you enter into the agreement until 56 days after your death or the date you (or your representative) terminates the agreement – eg, because a property is sold;
- cannot be terminated by social services although they can advise you to terminate it;
- can include a reasonable rate of interest but only from 56 days after your death or the day after the agreement is terminated;
- cannot include any legal expenses such as the cost of land registry searches although social services may ask you to pay these expenses up front.

Social services should advise a resident wishing to enter a deferred payment agreement to seek independent financial advice and be aware of how it will affect their social security benefits (see below).[28] Guidance states that social services should be prepared to put you in touch with persons who can offer independent advice on requesting and agreeing to a deferred payment agreement.[29]

Social security benefits and social services charging issues

- If you choose not to sell your property, you will not be able to claim IS if the property is worth more than £16,000 (net value after allowable deductions). Your weekly contribution to the fees will therefore be less. This means that the amount that social services will eventually recover will be higher.

- If your property is for sale and only a small amount of IS is payable (ie, less than the amount of AA/DLA care) due to the level of your other income, then you would usually be better off not claiming IS in order to receive AA/DLA care (see below). This is likely not to apply from October 2003 (see p375).
- If you are **not** claiming IS and you have a deferred payment arrangement, you are entitled to continue to receive your AA/DLA care as you will be repaying social services the full amount of the cost of your accommodation and care and therefore you are a 'retrospective self-funder'. From October 2003 it is likely that claiming IS or PC will not affect the payability of AA/DLA care in these situations (see p375).
  Social services will include AA/DLA care in your assessed contribution thus lowering the amount left to recover from the value of the property when it is eventually sold. However, in Scotland if the local authority is paying your care costs, you will not get AA/DLA care even if you have to repay your accommodation costs.
- If you have ongoing expenses to maintain your property, social services has discretion to allow a variation of your personal expenses allowance (see p331) to enable you to maintain your property. However, this will increase the amount recoverable by social services from the value of the property when it is eventually sold.
- You may need to check the net value of your capital (including the property against which your payment is deferred) every so often as when it reduces to the capital limit for your country (see p315) you may be able to get non-repayable funding from social services.

There are various considerations that need to be taken into account if you are a home owner going into a care home. The flow chart *The home-owner self-funding maze* (see p378) looks at the choices available and the benefits and charging implications.

5. Types of stay in a care home

There are three basic types of stay in a care home.

- **Permanent stay:** for financial assessment purposes a permanent resident is defined as a 'resident who is not a temporary resident'.[30] Guidance states that 'an admission is permanent if the agreed intention is for the resident to remain in residential care.'[31]
- **Temporary stay:** a temporary resident is defined as one whose stay is unlikely to exceed 52 weeks or, in exceptional circumstances, unlikely substantially to exceed that period.[32] (This is a similar definition to that for social security benefit purposes except that for benefit purposes it is a temporary absence

from your normal home with additional conditions that have to be satisfied – see p362.) Guidance states that 'an admission is temporary either if it is intended to last for a limited time period, such as respite, or there is uncertainty that permanent admission is required.'[33]
A series or planned programme of *temporary* stays is often referred to as **respite stays** (as for social security benefit purposes). Social services may apply a flat-rate charge without assessment if the stay is for less than eight weeks (see p294).
- **Trial period stay:** this is not defined in the charging legislation. However, it is defined in social security legislation (see p363), and the 13-week rule for trial period stays is referred to in the charging guidance as 'applying to people who enter residential accommodation initially on a temporary basis during which it is decided whether they need to stay in residential accommodation or can return home. Their stay in residential accommodation is generally a conditional one with a number of factors influencing whether or not they will return home or eventually stay permanently in residential accommodation'.[34] This indicates that a trial period stay should be treated as a temporary stay until a decision is made as to whether it is to become permanent.
More recent guidance introduces the scenario of where there is uncertainty that permanent admission is required and states that in these circumstances the stay is temporary.[35]
However, some social services treat a trial period (sometimes called temporary with a view to permanent) as a permanent stay. This is likely to be due to the fact that social services is advised that their statistical returns for the Department of Health should treat trial periods as permanent stays.[36] This can be challenged using the complaints procedure (see p297) if you are disadvantaged in the financial assessment by having your stay treated as permanent – eg, if the value of your home in the community is taken into account as capital from the 13th week after the beginning of your trial period instead of the 13th week after the beginning of when it is agreed that your stay is now permanent.

Some social services departments only use the 'permanent' or 'temporary' definitions of types of stay, which can cause problems for social security benefits in terms of whether the 52-week temporary rule or the 13-week trial period rule should be applied. In these circumstances you will need to provide further information to housing authorities and/or the DWP.

It is recognised that a stay which was initially expected to be permanent may turn out to be temporary and *vice versa*. In these circumstances, social services is advised to assess you according to your actual circumstances at the time (see p319).[37] Similarly, in the case of a trial period, if it is decided that you will either definitely return home at a future date (ie, you become temporary) or that you will not be returning home (ie, you become permanent) then the financial assessment should be revised accordingly.

6. Temporary absences from care homes

Payment of care home fees

There are no rules governing the payment of care home fees during a temporary absence (including going into hospital). If your placement is funded wholly or partly by social services the arrangements will usually be covered in their contract or service agreement with the care home (including temporary absence due to admission to hospital).

Many social services departments have adopted or adapted the pre-1993 temporary absence rules for preserved rights which no longer exist. This means that often social services makes an 80 per cent payment to the care home if you are absent (eg, in hospital). However, this will usually only be for a limited number of weeks until a review of your circumstances is undertaken.

Variation of your contribution to the local authority

If you are away from the care home and, as a result the amount of your social security benefits has changed, you should tell social services. They should then review your financial assessment to establish a level of contribution to care costs which reflects your new level of benefit. However, if you receive attendance allowance (AA) or disability living allowance care component (DLA care) for any period that you are in the community, social services may vary the personal expenses allowance (PEA) (see below) by at least the same amount so that in effect the AA or DLA care is ignored in the calculation of your contribution during your absence.

Variation of personal expenses allowance

If you are away from the care home because you are on holiday or visiting family or friends, social services can use their discretion to vary your PEA to enable you to have more money (see p331).[38]

Notes

1. **The financial assessment**

1 *Community Care in the Next Decade and Beyond*, Policy Guidance 1990; para 3.31 *Assessment and Care Management* SW11/91
2 HSCA 2001; LAC (2001)25; para 1.007A CRAG
3 s22(1) NAA 1948 as amended by NHSCCA 1990; s87 SW(S)A 1968
4 s22(3) NAA 1948
5 s22(2) NAA 1948
6 s26(2) NAA 1948
7 s22(2) NAA 1948
8 s23(3) NAA 1948
9 NA(AR) Regs as amended
10 s22(5A) NAA 1948
11 para 11.005 CRAG and LAC (2002)11; NAfWC 14/02; CCD 3/2002
12 LAC (98)8; WOC 12/98 para 10; SWSG 6/98 para 9
13 para 1.026 CRAG; para 1.024 Scottish CRAG; Joint IS/JSA Bulletin 10/00
14 para 1.015 CRAG; para 1.013 Scottish CRAG

2. **Reviews of your assessment**

15 LAC (94)1; WOC 4/94; SWSG 5/94 para 16

3. **If you have a complaint about your charge**

16 para 1.027 CRAG; para 1.025 Scottish CRAG

4. **Paying the full cost of your care home**

17 LAC (98)19; WOC 27/98; SWSG 2/99
18 s55 HSCA 2001; s6 CCH(S)A 2002
19 s22 HASSASSAA 1983 and para 16 of Annex to LAC (2001)25
20 National Assistance Services, Wales; NAfWC 21/2003 Appendix 3
21 para 9 LAC(2001)25; para 5 NAfWC 21/2003
22 para 7 Appendix 1 LAC (2001)29
23 LAC (2002)15; para 24 NAfWC 21/2003
24 www.doh.gov.uk/scg/crag
25 HDL (2003)7
26 NAfWC 21/2003 Appendix 2
27 NA(RA)(RC)(E) Regs 2001; NA(RA)(APRCAS)(W) Regs
28 para 13 LAC (2001)25; para 9 NAfWC 21/2003
29 para 15 Annex to LAC (2002)11
30 Reg 2 NA(AR)(amdt2) Regs, 9 April 2001
31 para 25 Annex to LAC(2002) 11; para 3.001A CRAG
32 Reg 2(1) NA(AR) Regs
33 para 25 Annex to LAC(2002) 11; para 3.001A CRAG
34 paras 3.002 and 8 CRAG; para 3.002 SWSG 8/96; LAC (95)7; WOC 22/95; para 9 SWSG 13/95(9)
35 para 25 Annex to LAC(2002) 11; para 3.001A CRAG
36 Form SRI Local Authority Supported Residents 2001/02 Guidance Notes 3-4
37 paras 3.004 and 3.004A CRAG

6. **Temporary absences from care homes**

38 para 8 LAC (97)5; para 15 SWSG 7/97

Chapter 11

Income – financial assessments

This chapter covers:

Legislation provides for the assessment by social services of a resident's or prospective resident's income to establish her/his contribution to the cost of placement in a care home.[1] Income is treated in a similar way to that for income support purposes (see Chapter 8). This chapter concentrates on the key differences.

1. General

Whatever your income, you will be left with no less than £17.50 (£17.80 in Wales) a week personal expenses allowance[2] in addition to any income disregarded in the assessment[3] (see Chapter 12). The rest of your income will go towards meeting the standard rate (see p294) for your accommodation.

All your income will be included as assessable income in the social services financial assessment unless it is partially or fully disregarded.[4] Your income is calculated on a weekly basis and includes capital treated as income (see p308), tariff income (see p308) and notional income[5] (see p309). The most common forms of income for people going into a care home are:

- state retirement pension and other social security benefits such as income support (or pension credit for people aged 60 or over from October 2003), housing benefit, council tax benefit, incapacity benefit, severe disablement allowance, disability living allowance and attendance allowance;

- occupational or personal pensions;
- trust income;
- assumed tariff income from capital (see p308).

If you have a partner, her/his income will not be included in the assessment even if you are only a temporary resident. Unlike the DWP, social services does not have any powers to assess couples jointly.

2. Treatment of income

The treatment of income for financial assessment purposes is very similar to the treatment of income for the calculation of income support (see Chapter 8).[6]

Temporary residents' (including respite and trial period residents – see p301) and permanent residents' income is treated the same except that for temporary residents a disregard can be allowed to meet financial commitments for your usual home in the community. These are often called outgoings (see p332).[7] There are also differences in the way disability living allowance care component and attendance allowance are treated for temporary and permanent residents (see p307).

3. Income fully taken into account

Most income that is fully taken into account for income support (IS) purposes (see Chapter 8) is also fully taken into account for social services financial assessment purposes, with the important additions of:

- third party payments (see Chapter 14). This type of payment is considered to be notional income (see p309);[8]
- IS and income-based jobseeker's allowance minus any amount for housing costs (see p172);[9]
- from October 2003 pension credit (PC) replaces IS for people aged 60 or over. It is likely that the guarantee credit component of PC will be treated in the same way that IS is treated. However, it is not yet known how the savings credit component will be treated (see pxix for more information);
- attendance allowance(AA)/disability living allowance care component (DLA care) (including constant attendance allowance and exceptionally severe disablement allowance payable with industrial injury disablement benefit or war disablement benefit – see pp145 and 148) where it is paid to **permanent** residents[10] (for temporary residents it is fully disregarded – see p307).
  Note: AA/DLA care is not usually payable after 28 days (or less) of being in a care home (see p373);

- housing benefit (HB) if you are living permanently in an unregistered establishment or a local authority care home not providing board so HB is being paid to meet the accommodation charge[11] (see less dependent resident section, p311). Note that this may only apply until the care home is required to register under the Care Standards Act 2000 which may mean that HB is no longer payable (see p67).

Where a social security benefit is subject to a reduction (other than a reduction because of voluntary unemployment) – eg, because of an earlier overpayment – the amount taken into account is the gross amount of benefit before reduction.[12]

4. Income partially disregarded

Most income which is partially disregarded for income support purposes (see Chapter 8) is also partially disregarded for social services financial assessment purposes, with the important addition of:

- 50 per cent of an occupational pension, personal pension or payment from a retirement annuity if you pass at least this amount to your spouse as long as s/he is not living with you in the care home. (If you pass nothing or less than 50 per cent then there is no disregard.[13]) If you are an unmarried partner rather than a spouse, social services can use their discretionary powers to vary the personal expenses allowance to achieve a similar effect (see p331).[14]

If you are one of a married couple, you should be given advice by social services about the 50 per cent disregard, including the fact that you can decide whether to pass 50 per cent of your pension to your spouse or not, and whether your spouse would be better off after taking account of the effect of the pension on benefits.[15]

5. Income fully disregarded

Most income that is fully disregarded for income support (IS) purposes (see Chapter 8) is also fully disregarded for social services financial assessment purposes with the *important exception of:*

- attendance allowance/disability living allowance care component (DLA care), including constant attendance allowance and exceptionally severe disablement allowance payable with industrial injury disablement benefit or war disablement benefit (see pp145 and 148), where it is paid to **permanent** residents.[16] It is only fully disregarded for **temporary** residents (see p306);

and with the important additions of:

- housing costs (eg, mortgage interest) paid as part of IS/income-based jobseeker's allowance (see p172) for your home in the community;[17]

- child benefit (see p164) and child support maintenance payments unless the child is living with you;[18]
- child tax credit.

As for IS, DLA mobility component, war widow's special pension, the new Supporting People payments (see p67),[19] guardian's allowance, housing benefit and council tax benefit paid for your home in the community, are also disregarded.[20] In April 2003, contributory benefits dependants' additions were abolished although existing claims will be protected and payments will continue to be disregarded if they are paid to the people for whom they are intended.

6. Capital treated as income

Most capital treated as income for income support purposes (see p233) is also treated as income for social services financial assessment purposes. In addition any capital payments from a third party will be treated as income where social services agrees to place you in a higher cost care home if there is a third party willing to contribute towards the higher costs (see Chapter 14).

A lump-sum payment made by the third party will be divided by the number of weeks for which the payment is made and taken fully into account as part of your income.[21] However, any third party payments made to you to help clear arrears of charges for your care home will be treated as capital not income.[22]

If such payments are made directly to social services they are not treated as belonging to you.[23]

7. Tariff income

As for income support (IS) (see p233), a tariff income amount of £1 for every £250 or part thereof is added to your weekly assessable income for financial assessment purposes where your capital is between the lower and upper capital limits for your country (see p315).[24] For example, in England for £15,000 capital you would be assessed as having a tariff income of £12 a week. For financial assessment purposes these capital limits apply to both temporary and permanent residents.

Many social services departments only review financial assessments annually and therefore if your capital of more than the lower capital limit for your country (see p315) has reduced before the annual review, and as a result your tariff income reduces, you should make sure you inform social services so that the correct tariff income can be applied from the correct date. If you are in receipt of IS you will also need to inform the DWP.

8. Trust income

As for income support (IS) (see p219), where you are the beneficiary of income only, produced by a life interest trust but you are not absolutely entitled to the trust fund as a whole, the income will normally be taken fully into account for financial assessment purposes.[25] The value of the right to receive income is a capital asset but it is fully disregarded for financial assessment purposes (see p323).[26]

If you are the beneficiary of a discretionary trust fund where payments are made wholly at the discretion of the trustees and there is no absolute entitlement to either income or capital, the trust fund itself will not be treated as a capital asset.[27]

Income or payments from a discretionary trust (and some payments from fixed trusts where the trustees have a discretion within the terms of the trust) are treated as voluntary payments (as the trustees are under no obligation to make them)[28] and they are treated in the same way as for IS (see p235). If the payments are regular in nature they are treated as income (see below) and if the payments are irregular in nature they are treated as capital.[29]

Under new rules implemented in October 2002, all payments from a personal injury trust fund (or a payment from an annuity purchased from funds derived from a payment made in consequence of any personal injury or any payment received by virtue of any agreement or court order to make payments to you in consequence of any personal injury) are disregarded in the same way as charitable or voluntary payments.[30]

Charitable, voluntary and personal compensation payments (as described above) of up to £20 a week are disregarded as income provided that the total income to be disregarded does not exceed £20.[31] Regular payments which are intended and used for any item which was not taken into account when the standard rate (see p294) was fixed for the accommodation provided, are also disregarded – eg, a payment to enable you to have your own telephone or television.[32]

Official guidance explains in some detail the different types of trust funds and how they should be treated for financial assessment purposes.[33]

9. Notional income

As for income support (IS) in certain circumstances you are treated as having income which you do not actually have.[34] There are five types of income which are treated as notional income for financial assessment purposes. They are:

- income paid to social services by a third party to contribute towards the fees of a home where they are higher than the normal amounts that social services

will pay (see Chapter 14).[35] However, payments made by a third person directly to social services in respect of a resident's arrears of charges for accommodation and care in a care home should not be treated as the resident's notional income;[36]
- income paid to a third party in respect of you or a member of your family for any item which was taken into account when the standard rate (see p294) was fixed for accommodation provided;[37]
- income which would be available on application[38] (see below);
- income which is due but has not yet been paid;[39]
- income you have deprived yourself of in order to avoid a charge or to reduce the charge payable (see below).[40]

Income available on application

For income which you have not yet acquired to be taken into account, social services must be satisfied that it would in fact be available to you if you made an application. As for IS, some types of income cannot be taken into account as notional income. These include income which may be paid under a discretionary trust, working tax credit, severe disablement allowance and employment service rehabilitation allowance. In addition, any income which would be fully disregarded (eg, housing benefit) will not be included as notional income.[41]

If an income that would be available if you applied is taken into account as notional income (eg, occupational pension not claimed) social services will assume that the application was made on the date that they first became aware of the possible income.[42]

Some social services departments assume an amount of IS as part of your income in the financial assessment, even if you are not receiving it nor have been advised to make a claim. If you are not aware that a source of income would be available to you upon application, it will be difficult for social services to argue that it can be treated as notional income. If this has happened to you, seek further advice (see Appendix 4).

10. Deprivation

The rules on deprivation of income for financial assessment purposes are similar to the rules for income support (IS) (see p240). Any income which you have disposed of or deprived yourself of in order to avoid a charge or to reduce the charge payable, will be considered by social services to be notional income and will be treated as actual income taken into account in the financial assessment in addition to any other assessable income.[43] The avoidance test is subjective, therefore your evidence on the reasons for any deprivation is very important (see p240).[44]

You will be considered to have deprived yourself of a resource if social services is aware that, as a result of your own act, you cease to possess that resource[45] and you would have continued to receive it had you not relinquished or transferred it.[46] The onus is on you to prove that you no longer have an income, otherwise social services will treat you as still possessing the actual income.[47]

Social services should only consider the question of deprivation where the income concerned would have been taken into account in the financial assessment. Therefore, income such as a charitable payment of less than £20 a week, which is ignored in the financial assessment, would not lead to deprivation being considered.

Guidance to social services on questions for consideration in deciding whether the deprivation was *in order to avoid or reduce the charge*, makes it clear that the purpose of the deprivation should be examined.[48] If there is more than one reason why you deprived yourself of an income and one of the reasons was to avoid or reduce the charge, it does not matter whether it was the main reason or not, as long as it was a significant reason.[49] The guidance also states that the timing of the deprivation should be considered,[50] although under the regulations[51] deprivation can be considered for resources disposed of at any time as it is only in some circumstances[52] that the six-month restriction applies (see p351).

If you have sold the right to receive an income resource for the purposes of avoiding or reducing the charge, then your income has been converted into a capital asset and social services can take account of either the former income resource or, where applicable, the difference between the former income resource and the tariff income or the increase in tariff income.[53]

It is important to note that following the Scottish *Robertson v Fife* case (see p327) it has been made clear that the provision of services to a person who is assessed as being in need of them is not related to the ability of the person to meet the costs. Despite the differences in Scottish and English legislation it is arguable that this ruling applies equally in England (see p327).

See p324 for more information on issues of deprivation.

11. Less dependent residents

You are a less dependent resident if you are a prospective resident or a resident in:

- an independent care home which is not required to be registered; *or*
- a local authority care home that does *not* provide board. ('Board' is defined as at least some cooked or prepared meals, cooked or prepared by someone other than the residents and eaten in the care home and the cost of which is included in the standard rate fixed for the care home.[54])

In these circumstances social services has complete discretion to ignore the whole of the charging assessment if it is 'reasonable in the circumstances'. This is because it has been recognised that to live as independently as possible, you will need to be left with more than the personal expenses allowance (PEA).[55]

This may be subject to change as, since April 2002 under the Care Standards Act 2000 (or in Scotland, the Regulation of Care (Scotland) Act 2001), all care homes, even those not providing board, are required to register and therefore the specific category of less dependent resident, defined for charging purposes (and for housing benefit entitlement – see p369) may no longer exist. In fact, the same effect – allowing more than the normal amount of PEA in order to live as independently as possible – can be achieved by a variation of the PEA (see p331).

Notes

1 Part II NA(AR) Regs

1. **General**
2 NA(SPR)(E) Regs
3 s22(4) NAA 1948
4 Sch 2 (earnings) and Sch 3 (income other than earnings) NA(AR) Regs
5 Reg 9 NA(AR) Regs

2. **Treatment of income**
6 IS Regs
7 Sch 3 para 27 NA(AR) Regs

3. **Income fully taken into account**
8 Reg 17(4) NA(AR) Regs
9 Reg l5(1) and Sch 3 para 26 NA(AR) Regs and para 8.006 CRAG; para 8.006 Scottish CRAG
10 Reg l5(1) NA(AR) Regs and para 8.006 CRAG; para 8.006 Scottish CRAG
11 Reg l5(1) NA(AR) Regs and para 8.006 CRAG; para 8.006 SWSG 8/96
12 Reg l5(3) NA(AR) Regs and para 8.007 CRAG; WOC 29/27; para 4 Scottish CRAG

4. **Income partially disregarded**
13 Reg 10A NA(AR) Regs
14 para 5.005 CRAG; para 5.005 Scottish CRAG
15 para 4 LAC (97)5; para 4 SWSG 7/97

5. **Income fully disregarded**
16 Sch 3 para 6 NA(AR) Regs
17 Sch 3 para 26 NA(AR) Regs
18 Sch 3 para 28A NA(AR) Regs
19 Sch 3 para 28D NA(AR) Regs; para 3.010A CRAG
20 Sch 3 paras 3, 4 and 28 NA(AR) Regs

6. **Capital treated as income**
21 Reg 16(4) NA(AR) Regs
22 Reg 22(8) NA(AR) Regs; para 6.045A CRAG; para 6.044A Scottish CRAG
23 para 8.062A CRAG; para 8.062A Scottish CRAG

7. **Tariff income**
24 Reg 28 NA(AR) Regs

8. **Trust income**
25 Para 10.017 CRAG; para 10.017 Scottish CRAG
26 Sch 4 para 11 NA(AR) Regs; para 10.015 CRAG; para 10.015 Scottish CRAG
27 Para 10.020 CRAG; para 10.020 Scottish CRAG
28 Para 10.021 CRAG; para 10.021 Scottish CRAG
29 Reg 22(7) NA(AR) Regs; para 8.052 CRAG
30 Sch 3 para 10 as amended NA(AR) Regs; para 10.026 CRAG
31 Sch 3 para 10(1) NA(AR) Regs
32 Sch 3 para 10(2) NA(AR) Regs
33 s10 CRAG; s10 Scottish CRAG

9. **Notional income**
34 Reg 17 NA(AR) Regs
35 Reg 17(4) NA(AR) Regs
36 Reg 17(5) NA(AR) Regs

37 Reg 17(3) NA(AR) Regs
38 Reg 17(2) NA(AR) Regs
39 Reg 17(2) NA(AR) Regs
40 Reg 17(1) NA(AR) Regs
41 Para 8.065 CRAG; para 8.065 Scottish CRAG
42 Para 8.069 CRAG; para 8.069 Scottish CRAG

10. **Deprivation**
43 Reg 17(1) NA(AR) Regs
44 *The Queen (on the application of the Personal Representatives of Christopher Beeson) and Dorset County Council and the Secretary of State for Health,* [2001] EWHC Admin 986, 30 November 2001, [2002] EWCA Civ 1812, 18 December 2002)
45 para 8.072 CRAG; para 8.072 Scottish CRAG
46 para 8.075 CRAG; para 8.075 Scottish CRAG
47 para 8.076 CRAG; para 8.076 Scottish CRAG
48 paras 8.073-8.080 CRAG; paras 8.073-8.080 Scottish CRAG
49 para 8.077 CRAG; para 8.077 Scottish CRAG
50 para 8.078 CRAG; para 8.072 Scottish CRAG
51 Reg 17(1) NA(AR) Regs
52 s21 HASSASSAA 1983
53 para 8.080 CRAG; para 8.080 Scottish CRAG

11. **Less dependent residents**
54 Reg 2(1) NA(AR) Regs and para 2.009 CRAG; para 2.004 Scottish CRAG
55 Reg 5 NA(AR) Regs and para 2.007 CRAG; para 2.005 Scottish CRAG

Chapter 12

Capital and property – financial assessments

This chapter covers:

Legislation provides for the assessment of a resident's or prospective resident's capital (including property) by social services to establish the contribution to the cost of the placement in a care home.[1]

Capital and property are treated in a similar way to that for income support purposes (see Chapter 8). This chapter concentrates on the key differences.

1. General

Capital includes all assets, in or outside the UK, unless disregarded.[2] It also includes income treated as capital (see p322) and notional capital[3] (see p323). Some of the most common forms of capital are:

- property (buildings and land);
- savings;
- National Savings Certificates;
- Premium Bonds;
- stocks and shares or any other type of investment;
- trust funds.

If you have a partner, her/his capital will not be included in the assessment even if you are only a temporary resident. Unlike the DWP, social services does not have any powers to assess couples jointly.

2. Treatment of capital

The value of your capital, after the appropriate disregards (p319) have been applied, will be assessed by social services and may affect the amount of your contribution to the cost of your placement.

Since April 2001 the capital limits are reviewed every year.[4] The capital limits from April 2003 are:

	Lower	*Upper*
England	£12,000	£19,500
Wales	£12,250	£20,000
Scotland	£11,500	£18,500

Social services will not assume any tariff income (see p308) on capital up to the lower limit for your country (see above).[5] If you have between the lower and upper capital limits for your country, social services will assume a tariff income of £1 a week for every £250 or part thereof above the lower capital limit, thus increasing your assessable income (see p308).[6]

Unlike the capital limits for IS, the capital limits for financial assessments apply to both temporary (including respite and trial period – see p301 for definitions) and permanent residents.

If you have capital of more than the upper capital limit for your country (see above), you will be expected to meet the whole cost of your accommodation yourself until your capital drops to the upper capital limit or less.[7] This means that you will be 'self-funding' and it could affect some social security benefits payable to you.

Social services must provide care in a care home for you if you are assessed as needing it unless it is 'otherwise available' to you.[8] The Health and Social Care Act 2001 and its subsequent regulations reaffirm that social services cannot say that accommodation is 'otherwise available' because of your capital if you have less than the upper capital limit (see above). Comparable provision for Scotland is in the Community Care and Health (Scotland) Act 2002 (see Appendix 1).

It is also important to note that following the Scottish *Robertson v Fife* House of Lords case (25 July 2002) it has been made clear that the provision of services to a person who is assessed as being in need of them is not related to the ability of the person to meet the costs (see p327). Despite the differences in Scottish and English legislation it is arguable that this ruling applies equally in England (see p327).

The treatment of capital for financial assessment purposes is very similar to the treatment of capital for the calculation of IS (see Chapter 8).[9] Temporary residents' (including respite and trial period residents – see p301 for definitions) and permanent residents' capital is treated in the same way except that for temporary residents the value of your home in the community is disregarded indefinitely (see below).

The value of your home in the community

Temporary resident

If you are a temporary resident (including respite and trial period residents – see p301 for definitions), the value of your home in the community is disregarded as long as:

- you intend to return to your home and it is still available to you; *or*
- you are selling your home in order to buy another more suitable home to return to.[10]

Permanent resident

First 12 weeks

If you are a permanent resident and the value of your home in the community is not disregarded indefinitely (see p319) then the 12-week property disregard will be applied.[11]

If you are a temporary resident and you subsequently become permanent, the 12-week property disregard will apply from the date on which you become permanent.

If you are a permanent resident but you leave the care home before the end of the 12 weeks and then re-enter a care home again on a permanent basis within 52 weeks you will be entitled to the balance of the 12-week disregard. If you re-enter a care home again on a permanent basis more than 52 weeks later you will qualify for the 12-week disregard again.[12]

After 12 weeks

The value of your home in the community will be taken into account as capital unless it is disregarded (see p319). As for IS, its value will be based on the current selling price, less any debts secured on it (eg, a mortgage),[13] and less 10 per cent in recognition of the expenses incurred in selling it. Once your home is sold and the capital realised it is the actual amount of the expenses incurred that are deducted from the proceeds.[14]

If you decide to sell your home in the community, see p318 for what happens while it is for sale.

Social services does not have the power to enforce the sale of your property and they may not withdraw services if your charge is not met as the duty to make residential provision where there is an assessed need is not conditional upon the payment of the assessed contribution.[15]

If you choose not to sell your property you may consider entering into a deferred payment agreement with social services (see p299). If you do not have a deferred payment agreement and your charge is not paid you will be accruing a debt to social services which may be pursued.

Other property

Any other property you own (or jointly own – see below) will also be taken into account as capital and will be valued in the same way as your home in the community.

Ownership

In some cases there may be a difference between the legal and the beneficial ownership of capital such as a property. If another person has been contributing towards the mortgage and/or running costs of your property (including your own home) s/he may be able to establish a beneficial interest in your property, even if it is legally owned by you. If a beneficial ownership is established, then the property will be valued as if it is jointly owned (see CPAG's *Welfare Benefits and Tax Credits Handbook*).

Jointly owned land or property

Where you jointly own land or property (including your home in the community), social services must assess the value of your actual interest/share in the property[16] unless the value is disregarded (see p319).

The size of any beneficial interest in the property may be a complex question and you may need to seek legal advice. How that interest is to be valued will depend on whether the co-owner(s) are in occupation or not (see CPAG's *Welfare Benefits and Tax Credits Handbook*).

Official guidance deals with joint beneficial ownership of property.[17] It states that the value of the interest is governed by your 'ability to re-assign the beneficial interest to somebody else' and 'there being a market, ie, the interest being such as to attract a willing buyer for the interest'.

The guidance further states that the value would be heavily influenced by whether the other joint owner(s) would be able to buy your share. If the joint owner(s) cannot or does not want to do this, in many cases, it would be unlikely that an outsider would be willing to buy into the property. Even if someone was willing to buy into the property, the value of this interest could be very low or effectively nil.

Social services is advised to get a professional valuation if they are unsure of your share or if you dispute the valuation. The cost of any valuation should be borne by social services as they do not have any power to charge for costs incurred in connection with the financial assessment process.

In practice, valuing your share in a jointly owned property is very difficult. It is important to seek advice if you think your share has been overvalued. It is often useful to investigate whether a local estate agent would put your share on the market. This is unlikely as it is extremely difficult to find a buyer for a part share of a property, unless the property is let and the 'capital' interest is in the nature of an investment.

Jointly owned capital (other than property)

If you jointly own capital with another person (except any interest in property or land – see p317) it will be divided in equal shares for financial assessment purposes in order to determine the assessable capital, regardless of what your actual share is.[18] Unlike for IS, this also applies if you are a temporary or permanent resident and you jointly own capital with your partner as social services has no power to assess a couple according to their joint resources.

This means that if you have, for example, a joint bank account with your sister containing £25,000 and £10,000 belongs to you and £15,000 belongs to your sister, social services will assess £12,500 as your share. An adviser, anticipating this decision, may advise that the joint account be closed and two separate accounts opened for each person so that you would have the £10,000 in an account in your sole name. The notional capital rules (see p323) should not be applied in these circumstances as this would not constitute a deprivation of capital because you are still in possession of your actual beneficial entitlement.[19]

Property owned but rented to tenants

If you let your property to tenants and the value of your property is not disregarded, social services will include its capital value in your financial assessment. If the value takes your capital level to above the capital limit for your country (see p315), then you will be charged the full standard rate for your accommodation and care. Guidance states that it will then be for you to agree to pay the rental income (along with any other income) to social services in order to reduce any accruing debt.[20]

3. If your home is for sale

If you are a permanent resident and the value of your home in the community is not subject to a mandatory or discretionary disregard (see p321) then it will be taken into account after the 12-week disregard period (see p316). Unlike for income support (IS) purposes, this applies even if it is for sale.

If you cannot pay your accommodation and care costs (which will usually be the full standard rate charge (see p294) if your property plus any other capital to be taken into account is valued at above the capital limit for your country (see p315), until your property is sold and you receive the proceeds of the sale, social services can help meet your accommodation and care costs. You will, however, have to pay back the full amount once your property is sold. This arrangement could be an informal bridging loan or a formalised deferred payment agreement (see p299).

In these circumstances, social services has powers to put a 'legal charge' ('charging order' in Scotland) on your property in order to recover the amount that they have paid towards your costs once your property is sold. The capital limits that are applied when a 'charge' is placed on your property are the capital limits that are in force at the time (ie, before April 1996 – £8,000; from April 1996 – £16,000; from April 2001 – £18,500; from April 2002 – £19,000 (£18,500 in Scotland); from April 2003 – £19,500 (England) or £20,000 (Wales) or £18,500 (Scotland)).

There may be an alternative way forward in this situation if you are going into an independent care home. This is often referred to as the 'loophole option' (England and Wales only – see p297) and it means you may be able to get extra social security benefits to help meet your accommodation and care costs as long as social services does not contract with the care home for your placement. In this situation, social services would not be helping with the payment of your care costs for the time until your home was sold, therefore there would be no money owed to social services from the proceeds of the sale. However, this option has become less viable since April 2002 when the residential allowance part of IS was abolished for new claimants. This means that there is a larger shortfall when relying on benefits to meet the cost of the care home (see p368). In October 2003 the transitional protection for residents in receipt of the residential allowance part of IS since before April 2002 will also be abolished. Therefore residents who have been taking advantage of the 'loophole' option may need to seek funding from social services (see p376).

4. Capital disregarded indefinitely

Most capital that is disregarded indefinitely for income support (IS) purposes (see p223) is also disregarded indefinitely for social services financial assessment purposes, with the important exception that:

- the 52-week limit on the disregard of arrears and non-payment compensation of certain benefits that has been lifted for IS purposes in specified circumstances (see p226) remains in force for financial assessment purposes;[21]

and with the addition that:

- social services has discretionary powers to allow a disregard of the value of your former home where you are a **permanent** resident and it is occupied, wholly or in part, if they think it is reasonable to do so (see p321).[22] This is in addition to the mandatory 'defined circumstances', most of which also apply to IS.[23]

The 'defined circumstances' for a disregard of the value of a former home in the community to apply where you are a permanent resident are where it is occupied wholly or in part by:

- your spouse/partner or former partner (except where you are estranged or divorced from your partner/former partner); *or*
- your estranged or divorced partner where they are a lone parent with a dependent child; *or*
- a relative of yours or a relative of a member of your family who is:
  - aged 60 or over; *or*
  - incapacitated; *or*
  - aged under 16 and is a child for whom you are responsible.[24]

The property disregard applies only to premises which were occupied as your home.[25] A social security commissioner[26] held that 'premises' was to be interpreted in accordance with the definition of 'dwelling occupied as the home'.[27]

If your partner, children or relatives continue to live in your home, the help they can receive for their housing costs depends on their circumstances. If they are paying the housing costs, even though you are the person liable for them, they can claim housing benefit or IS housing costs instead of you (see pp172 and 180).

Meaning of terms

'Relative' means parent, parent-in-law, brother, sister, son, son-in-law, daughter, daughter-in-law, step-parent, step-son, step-daughter (or the partner of any of these), a grandchild, grandparent, uncle, aunt, niece or nephew.[28]

'Family' includes:

- a married or unmarried couple and any person who is a member of the same household and the responsibility of either or both members of the couple; *or*
- a person who is not a member of a married or unmarried couple and who is a member of the same household and your responsibility.[29]

'Incapacitated' is not defined in the regulations, but guidance states that it is reasonable to conclude that a relative is incapacitated if s/he is receiving one of the following benefits: incapacity benefit, severe disablement allowance, disability living allowance, attendance allowance or constant attendance allowance, or s/he would satisfy the incapacity conditions for any of these.[30]

Discretion to disregard

Guidance is provided to social services on their discretionary powers to disregard the value of your former home, in which another person continues to live, in circumstances other than those specified in the legislation. This could be where your home is the sole residence of someone who has given up their own home in order to care for you.[31] Social services' discretion could also be applied where you were permanently living with a lesbian or gay partner or an adult son or daughter in your home and they are remaining there. Where social services has used their discretion in these types of circumstances, they can review their decision at any time. Guidance suggests that it would be reasonable to begin taking account of the value of a property when the carer dies or moves out.[32]

If you intend to return home

As for IS (see p223), the value of a dwelling normally occupied as your home will be disregarded if your stay is *temporary* (including respite and trial period stays – see p301 for definitions) and you intend to return to your home which is still available to you, or you are taking reasonable steps to dispose of your home in order to acquire another property to return to.[33]

The value of any other property that you own (or jointly own) besides your own home will be taken into account as capital.

If your stay is initially thought to be permanent but turns out to be temporary, your home should be treated in the same way as if you had been temporary from the outset.[34] This provision arguably means that the financial assessment undertaken by social services would have to be retrospectively reviewed and any excess payments made refunded or any charges placed on your property lifted. However, this is at variance with other parts of the guidance dealing with temporary residents where it is stated that if a stay turns out to be temporary, then social services should not *continue* to treat you as permanent.[35] If this affects you, you should seek further advice.

5. Capital disregarded for 26 weeks or longer

Most capital that is disregarded for 26 weeks or longer for income support purposes (see p223) is also disregarded for 26 weeks or longer for social services financial assessment purposes, with the important exception that:

- social services does not have the power to disregard property that is for sale (see p318).

6. Capital disregarded for 52 weeks

Most capital that is disregarded for 52 weeks for income support (IS) purposes (see p223) is also disregarded for 52 weeks for social services financial assessment purposes, with the important addition of:

- arrears and non-payment compensation of certain benefits even if the amount is £5,000 or over;[36]
- IS is included in the list of benefits for which the balance of any arrears paid or any compensation paid due to non-payment is disregarded as capital for a period of 52 weeks.[37] Any payment of this type should be treated as income over the period for which it is payable and any amount left over after the period for which it is treated as income has elapsed should be treated as capital.[38]

Example

You are assessed as being able to pay £75 a week towards the cost of your placement on the basis of your current income pending receipt of IS.

It is explained to you that the charge will be reassessed or retrospectively reviewed once IS is received and that back payments will be required.

Although not required to do so, you can choose to make payments of £90 a week.

After six weeks, arrears of IS at £35 a week (£210) are received.

The charges are reassessed/retrospectively reviewed, and you are required to pay £110 a week, from the start of your placement.

As you have been paying £15 a week more than originally required, the arrears payable to the local authority are £120 rather than the full £210 IS arrears.

The remaining £90 becomes capital and is disregarded for 52 weeks.

7. Income treated as capital

As for income support purposes (see p223), any income derived from capital (eg, rental income) is normally treated as capital rather than income, from the date on which it is normally due to be paid[39] unless it is income derived from capital disregarded – eg, any capital held in trust which is as a result of a personal injury.[40]

Interest paid on capital will be treated as capital from the date on which it is paid. However, there is an assumed income from any capital over the capital limit for your country (see p315)[41] (see also tariff income, p308).

8. Trust funds

The rules about capital placed in a trust fund for social services financial assessment purposes are the same as for income support purposes (see p218). If you are a beneficiary of a non-discretionary or absolute entitlement trust, the value of the capital asset and any income derived from the capital, is normally taken into account as capital in the calculation of your contribution.[42]

The important exception to this is where the capital held in trust is derived from a personal injury compensation payment, in which case both the capital and the capital value of any right to receive income are fully disregarded.[43] For the treatment of any payments made to you from the capital, see below.

If you are a beneficiary of a trust where the deed directs that you are to receive income produced by the trust capital only, then you only have an absolute entitlement to the income. These trusts are known as life interest or fixed interest trusts. The right to receive the income from a life interest trust has a capital value but it is disregarded for financial assessment purposes.[44] For the treatment of the income from these types of trusts, see p309.

A discretionary trust fund where payments are made wholly at the discretion of the trustees and there is no absolute entitlement to either capital or income will not be treated as a capital asset.[45] For the treatment of payments made from a discretionary trust fund, see p309.

Official guidance explains the different types of trust funds and how they should be treated for financial assessment purposes.[46]

9. Notional capital

The notional capital rules are similar to the notional income rules (see p309) and the notional capital rules for income support (see p220). In certain circumstances you may be treated as possessing a capital asset even where you do not in fact possess it.[47] The important difference is that the notional income rules are mandatory but the notional capital rules for financial assessment purposes are discretionary. You *will* be treated as possessing income of which you have deprived yourself for the purpose of decreasing the amount that you may be liable to pay for your accommodation; but you *may* be treated as possessing capital of which you have deprived yourself for the purpose of decreasing the amount that you may be liable to pay for your accommodation. This means that social services has discretion on whether to apply the rules.

There are three main circumstances in which you *may* be treated as having notional capital:

- where you deliberately deprive yourself of capital in order to reduce the amount of charge you have to pay (see p324);

- where you fail to apply for capital which is available to you (capital payable under a trust derived from a payment made in consequence of a personal injury cannot be taken into account as notional capital);
- where someone else makes a payment of capital to a third party on your behalf, unless it is for an item which was not taken into account when the standard rate was fixed for your accommodation.[48]

10. Deprivation

The rules on deprivation for financial assessments are similar to the rules for income support (IS) (see p221). Any capital which you have disposed of, or deprived yourself of, in order to avoid a charge or to reduce the charge payable towards the cost of your care home, may be considered by social services to be notional capital and as such may be treated as actual capital and taken into account in the financial assessment.[49]

Social services should only consider questions of deprivation of capital when you cease to possess capital which would otherwise be taken into account.[50] As with deprivation of income, it is up to you to prove that you no longer have the resource, otherwise it will be treated as actual capital.

If you have used capital to acquire personal possessions to avoid or reduce the charge, then the market value of those personal possessions would not be disregarded.[51]

Guidance to social services sets out the questions for consideration when deciding whether the deprivation was *in order to avoid or reduce the charge*.[52]

It is important to note that you, as the resident, should not be treated as depriving yourself of capital in order to reduce your charge if you enable your spouse to purchase a smaller property by making available to her/him part of your share of the proceeds from the sale of the property you shared as your home.

As with the rules regarding the deprivation of income, the purpose and timing of the deprivation should be considered. The guidance suggests it would be unreasonable to decide that a resident had disposed of an asset in order to reduce her/his charge for accommodation when the disposal took place at a time when s/he was fit and healthy and could not have foreseen the need for a move to residential accommodation.

However, a Scottish Court case (*Yule*)[53] cast some doubt on the use of this argument (see p325), although a more recent case (*Beeson*)[54] in England makes it clear that (at least in England and Wales) the resident's intentions need to be examined using a subjective test not an objective one (see p326).

Another Scottish case (*Robertson*),[55] in which the Outer and Inner House of Sessions adopted the same hard-line approach as in *Yule*, was overturned by the House of Lords[56] and while the correct application of the deprivation test was not examined, an important principle regarding notional capital and the provision of accommodation was established (see p327).

See p327 for what happens when deprivation has been decided and notional capital has been taken into account in your financial assessment.

Yule v South Lanarkshire Council

In this case, Mrs Yule transferred the ownership of her home to her granddaughter more than a year before there was any significant deterioration in her health. However, the Council decided that it was done in order to avoid or reduce the charge. The Council dismissed information to the contrary, supplied by the client's granddaughter and solicitor, concluding that the same result could have been achieved had the client left the property to her granddaughter in a will.

The Scottish Outer House of Session did not accept the submission that 'the respondents [ie, the Council] could only make the decision which they did if there was evidence that the claimant knew of the existence of a capital limit (an issue considered to be significant by social security commissioners) and that she had foreseen the making of an application for the relevant benefit'. The Court held that 'the respondents were entitled to draw inferences from the information received by them ... The decision on matters of fact is left to the respondents and there is no appeal. Accordingly the weight given by the respondents to particular pieces of evidence is entirely a matter for them and not open to challenge'.

The case was appealed to the Inner House of Session but the decision was upheld.[57] The Court considered that it was not necessary that the applicant should know of the capital limit and that no specific finding is required as to the exact state of knowledge or intention of the applicant if it is a reasonable inference that it must have been a purpose of the transaction to avoid having to pay charges. This is contrary to the judgment in the *Beeson* case (see p326).

In the *Yule* case the judgment sought to differentiate between the financial assessment/charging regulations and the social security legislation by stating that they have to be looked at differently, 'not least because the purpose of the individual may have been formed possibly some time ahead of the prospect that he or she might require to enter such residential accommodation'.[58]

They also stated that 'we agree with the Lord Ordinary that it is open to a local authority to reach a view as to the purpose of a transaction such as the present, without any specific finding as to the exact state of knowledge or intention of the applicant, so long as the primary facts are such as reasonably to lead to the inference that the purpose was at least in part that specified in regulation 25(1)'.[59]

The approach of the Courts in this case is arguably, in the light of the *Beeson* case (see p326), an objective one as there was no evidence of the subjective intention of Mrs Yule when she made the gift of her house. Guidance makes it clear that it is the subjective intention and purpose at the time of transfer that needs to be examined[60] and that avoiding the charge must be a **significant** purpose of any transfer.[61]

Beeson v Dorset County Council

The resident in this case had transferred the ownership of his house to his son by deed of gift after he had suffered a stroke but two and a half years before entering a care home. The council decided that he had deprived himself of the capital asset for the purpose of decreasing the amount that he was liable to pay for his accommodation. This decision was upheld following an appeal through the complaints procedure.

In the judgment this case was distinguished from *Yule* due to the existence of evidence from the resident's family about his and their state of mind at the relevant time. Commenting on the *Yule* judgment, the Judge in *Beeson* states: 'Although the court held that it is not necessary for the claimant to know of 'the' capital limit and that no specific finding is required as to the exact state of knowledge or intention of the applicant, I do not see how an applicant could be found to have the relevant purpose unless he was aware of the possibility that he might be provided with accommodation and that he might be liable to pay for it.'

The resident's son gave evidence to the council that the funding of residential care did not come into his father's thoughts and that the transfer took place at a time when his father intended to live and ultimately die in his home. Although there was evidence to the contrary, this evidence was considered by the Court to be of central importance. It was stated that if this evidence was accepted, then on the correct subjective test required by regulation 25,[62] it could not be considered that the transfer was for the purpose of decreasing the amount that the resident was liable to pay for his accommodation.[63]

The Court found that the panel that heard the resident's case under the council's complaints procedure had either failed to apply the correct subjective test or if it had applied the subjective test, it failed to give adequate reasons as to why the evidence was rejected. It was concluded that the panel did not direct itself correctly.[64]

This case also considered whether the relevant statutory procedure is incompatible with Article 6(1) of the European Convention on Human Rights. The judgment was that the system used by the council in determining the question of deprivation did not comply with Article 6(1) because the panel established under the social services complaints procedure did not amount to an independent review of the facts and, because there was no such review, judicial review was not an adequate means of appeal.

However, this part of the Judgment was overturned on appeal to the Court of Appeal.[65]

The *Beeson* case provides a more helpful examination of the issues involved in deprivation and notional capital cases. It goes into detail on the statutory requirements that councils have to apply themselves to the correct test using the correct procedure and ultimately to provide an adequately reasoned decision which demonstrates the correct application.

Robertson v Fife Council

In this case the council had decided that Mrs Robertson had deliberately deprived herself of capital by transferring the ownership of her property to her sons and therefore, as she notionally possessed capital of over the upper capital limit, it did not have any duty to provide her with accommodation.

Although the Scottish Outer and Inner House of Session judgments took the same approach as in *Yule* on the interpretation of the application of the rules regarding the deprivation of capital, the House of Lords[66] overturned the judgments stating that 'the assessment of need and decisions as to whether they call for the provision of any of the community services comes first. The assessment of means and the requirement to pay what the person can afford, comes afterwards. Notional capital can be taken into account at the stage when charges are being made for the services. But it must be left out of account at the earlier stage when decisions are being taken to provide these services.'[67]

Although this is a Scottish case, the system in England and Wales is similar, especially with regard to the assessment of need and the ability to make payments. Therefore it can be argued that the principle applies and should be followed in all cases.

There may also be an argument that this case would not have been brought in England or Wales because the provision of accommodation was not 'otherwise available' (see p315) to Mrs Robertson. Therefore social services' duty to provide accommodation still existed.

11. Diminishing notional capital

Where you have been assessed as having notional capital, social services should reduce the amount of that notional capital each week by the difference between the rate which you are paying for the accommodation and the rate you would have paid if you were not treated as possessing the notional capital.[68]

Notes

1 Part III NA(AR) Regs

1. **General**
2 Sch 4 (Capital to be disregarded) NA(AR) Regs
3 Regs 21, 22 and 25 NA(AR) Regs

2. **Treatment of capital**
4 DoH press release 2001/0015, 5 January 2001
5 Reg 21 NA(AR) Regs
6 Reg 28 NA(AR) Regs
7 Reg 20 NA(AR) Regs
8 s21 NAA 1948 and *R v Sefton MBC ex parte Help the Aged and Others* [1997] I CCLR 57 CA; para 11 LAC (98)8; WOC 12/98; s12 SW(S)A 1968 and SWSG 6/98
9 IS Regs
10 Sch 4 para 1 NA(AR) Regs and para 7.002 CRAG; para 7.002 Scottish CRAG
11 Sch 4 para 1A and para 7.002A CRAG; para 7.002A Scottish CRAG
12 para 7.002B CRAG; para 7.002B Scottish CRAG
13 Reg 23(1)(b) NA(AR) Regs and para 6.011b CRAG; para 6.010B Scottish CRAG
14 Reg 23(1)(a) NA(AR) Regs; para 6.011a and 6.015 CRAG; para 6.010a Scottish CRAG and para 6.014 Scottish CRAG
15 ss22(1) and 25(2) NAA 1948
16 Reg 27(2) NA(AR) Regs
17 paras 7.012-7.014A CRAG; paras 7.012-7.014a Scottish CRAG
18 Reg 27(1) NA(AR) Regs
19 para 6.010 CRAG; para 6.009 Scottish CRAG
20 para 7.017 CRAG; para 7.017 Scottish CRAG
21 Sch 4 para 6 NA(AR) Regs as amended by NA(AR)(A)(No.2)(E) Regs 2002 or in Scotland by NA(AR)(A)(S) Regs 2003. For Scotland, between the rule change for IS on 14.10.02 and the amendment on 28.02.03 such payments should be treated in accordance with the IS Regulations.

4. **Capital disregarded indefinitely**
22 Sch 4 para 18 NA(AR) Regs
23 Sch 4 paras 2 and 2A NA(AR) Regs
24 para 7.003 CRAG
25 para 7.003 CRAG and Sch 4 para 2 NA(AR) Regs
26 CIS/767/1993
27 Reg 2(1) IS Regs
28 para 7.004 CRAG; para 7.004 Scottish CRAG
29 para 7.004A CRAG; para 7.004 Scottish CRAG
30 para 7.005 CRAG; para 7.005 Scottish CRAG
31 para 7.007 CRAG; para 7.007 Scottish CRAG
32 para 7.008 CRAG; para 7.008 Scottish CRAG
33 Sch 4 para 1 NA(AR) Regs
34 Note to para 7.002 CRAG; para 7.002 Scottish CRAG
35 para 3.004 CRAG; para 3.004 Scottish CRAG

6. **Capital disregarded for 52 weeks**
36 Sch 4 para 6 NA(AR) Regs as amended by NA(AR)(A)(No.2)(E) Regs 2002 or in Scotland by NA(AR)(A)(S) Regs 2003. For Scotland, between the rule change for IS on 14.10.02 and the amendment on 28.02.03 such payments should be treated in accordance with the IS Regulations.
37 Sch 4 para 6 NA(AR) Regs
38 para 6.030 CRAG; para 6.029 Scottish CRAG

7. **Income treated as capital**
39 Reg 22(4) NA(AR) Regs
40 Sch 3 para 14 NA(AR) Regs
41 Regs 9 and 28 NA(AR) Regs

8. **Trust funds**
42 Reg 22(4) NA(AR) Regs
43 Sch 4 para 10 NA(AR) Regs and para 10.025 CRAG; para 10.025 Scottish CRAG
44 Sch 4 para 11 NA(AR) Regs and para 10.015 CRAG; para 10.015 Scottish CRAG
45 para 10.020 CRAG; para 10.020 Scottish CRAG
46 Chapter 10 CRAG; Chapter 10 Scottish CRAG

9. **Notional capital**
47 Reg 25 NA(AR) Regs
48 Reg 25(3) NA(AR) Regs

10. **Deprivation**
49 Reg 25(1) NA(AR) Regs
50 para 6.058 CRAG; para 6.057 Scottish CRAG
51 para 6.065 CRAG; para 6.064 Scottish CRAG
52 paras 6.057-6.066 CRAG; para 6.056-6.065 Scottish CRAG
53 *Yule v South Lanarkshire Council*, 12 May 1999
54 *The Queen (on the application of the Personal Representative of Christopher Beeson) and Dorset County Council and the Secretary of State for Health*, Case no. CO/25/2001, 30 November 2001 (Court of Appeal case No. C/2001/2839 18 December 2002)
55 *Robertson v Fife Council*, 12 May 1999
56 *Robertson v Fife Council*, 25 July 2002 HL [2002]UKHL35
57 Court of Session (Inner House) Reclaiming motion in petition of *David Yule v South Lanarkshire Council*, 15 August 2000
58 Para 29 of Yule Court of Appeal decision
59 Reg 25(1) NA(AR) Regs; quote from para 33 of *Yule* Court of Appeal decision
60 para 6064 CRAG
61 para 6062 CRAG
62 Reg 25 NA(AR) Regs
63 para 38 of the *Beeson* Judgment
64 para 39 of the *Beeson* Judgment
65 The Secretary of State for Health – Appellant and the Personal Representative of Christopher Beeson – Respondent
66 *Robertson v Fife Council* 25 July 2002 [2002]UKHL35
67 para 53 *Robertson v Fife Council*

11. **Diminishing notional capital**
68 Reg 26 NA(AR) Regs

Chapter 13

Personal expenses allowance and outgoings

This chapter covers:

1. Personal expenses allowance (below)
2. Outgoings (p332)

1. Personal expenses allowance

Legislation requires social services to allow you to keep a minimum amount of your income after the payment of your care home fees.[1] This personal expenses allowance (PEA) is set by regulations made each year.[2] For 2003/04 the minimum amount is £17.50 a week in England and Scotland or £17.80 in Wales.

You will get the same amount whether you are a temporary or permanent resident in a local authority or an independent care home. Current guidance states that the resident will normally supply her/his own clothes, but in cases of special need or emergency (eg, if all your clothes are lost in a fire), the local authority may supply replacement clothing.[3]

It is intended that your PEA should be spent as you wish on personal items – eg, toiletries, stationery, gifts. Guidance states that neither the care home provider nor social services have any authority to require you to spend your PEA in any particular way and pressure of any kind to the contrary is extremely poor practice.[4] If you are not able to manage your PEA because of ill health, social services may (subject to your agreement or that of your attorney or appointee) deposit it in a bank account on your behalf and use it to provide for your smaller needs. Many social services departments have set up a savings account system that is administered by them. Any money that is unspent on your death will form part of your estate.

Social services cannot allow you to use your PEA to help pay for more expensive accommodation even if you wish to do this.[5] In addition, care homes should not expect you to use your PEA for aspects of board, lodgings and care that have been contracted for, or assessed as necessary to meet your needs, by social services or the NHS.[6] In new guidance councils are reminded again that the PEA should not be spent in this way. The guidance also states that councils should ensure that individual residents' needs for continence supplies or chiropody are fully reflected in their care plan.[7] The guidance states that you are not precluded from buying extra services from the care home where these are genuinely additional to those services that have been contracted for or assessed as necessary by social services or the NHS.[8]

If you are a permanent resident the PEA is the amount that you will normally be left with out of your income when you have made your contribution to the cost of your accommodation and care. However, if you are in receipt of attendance allowance or disability living allowance care component, which is normally payable for the first four weeks of your stay (see p370), and you are a temporary resident, you will have this income in addition to your PEA.

If you are in receipt of, or claim disability living allowance mobility component or any other disregarded income (eg, war widow's special pension),[9] this will continue in payment and will be additional income on top of your PEA, whether you are a temporary or permanent resident.

Increasing the personal expenses allowance

An increase in the PEA is usually called a 'variation'. Social services has discretion to allow more than the minimum amount in 'special circumstances'.[10] Guidance gives examples of where a local authority might consider allowing a different amount:

- where you need to keep more of your income to help you lead a more independent life. This may be appropriate if you do not qualify as a 'less dependent' resident (see p311) solely because you live in an independent care home or in local authority accommodation where board is provided;
- where you have a dependent child, the needs of the child (whether or not they are placed with you) should be considered in the PEA;
- where you are temporarily in residential accommodation and you receive income support (IS) which includes an amount for a partner, social services should consider the needs of your partner in the PEA. Social services should not request a charge that would leave your partner without enough money to live on. However, social services could consider the appropriate applicable amount of IS for your partner as being enough to live on;
- where you are one of an unmarried couple, social services is not required to disregard 50 per cent of any private pension that you pay to your partner. However, where you are the main recipient of your overall income they can use their discretion to increase your PEA to enable you to pass some of your income to your partner. Social services is advised to bear in mind that increasing your partner's income could lead to a reduction in her/his benefits – eg, IS.[11]

Social services is reminded that they have the power to increase your PEA, particularly where certain activities or services can contribute significantly to your independence and wellbeing.[12]

Further guidance states that if you are temporarily absent from your care home, social services has the discretion to vary the PEA upwards to enable you to have more money while staying with family or friends.[13]

2. Outgoings

If you are a temporary resident, social services can disregard a reasonable amount of your income to meet outgoings that you may have for your home in the community. This also includes outgoings on a home you are taking steps to sell in order to acquire another more suitable home to which you will return.[14]

If you are a permanent resident, you are normally not considered to have outgoings as you would no longer have a home in the community. However, it may be that you still have outgoings – eg, while your home is up for sale. If this is the case, social services can consider a variation of your PEA (see p331) to allow you to meet these commitments. It is only temporary residents who are eligible for a disregard on their income to meet outgoings in respect of their home in the community.

Guidance sets out a list of examples of outgoings.

Where income support (IS) and/or housing benefit (HB) are in payment, extra costs not met by benefit might be:

- fixed heating charges;
- water rates;
- mortgage payments or rent not met by IS/HB;
- service charges not met by IS/HB;
- insurance premiums;
- housing support charges not met by the local authority.[15]

Where neither IS nor HB are being paid, your outgoings might include:

- interest charges on a hire purchase agreement to buy the dwelling you occupy as your home;
- interest charges on loans for repairs or improvements to the dwelling;
- ground rent or other rental relating to a long tenancy;
- service charges;
- housing support charges (made under Supporting People);
- standard charges for fuel;
- payments under a co-ownership scheme or tenancy agreement or licence of a Crown tenant.[16]

If you share your home in the community with a partner or other adults, any outgoings allowed will normally be divided equally and only your share will be included in the extra amount allowed for outgoings in the financial assessment.

Notes

1. **Personal expenses allowance**
   1 s22(4) NAA 1948
   2 NA(SPR)(E) Regs
   3 para 5.001 CRAG; para 5.001 Scottish CRAG
   4 para 5 Annex to LAC(2002)11; para 4 Annex to LAC(2003)8
   5 para 8.018 CRAG; para 8.018 Scottish CRAG
   6 para 5 Annex to LAC(2002)11; para 5.001 CRAG and Scottish CRAG
   7 para 4 Annex to LAC(2003)8
   8 para 6 Annex to LAC(2002)11
   9 Sch 3 para 25 NA(AR) Regs; para 8.046 CRAG; para 8.046 Scottish CRAG
   10 s22(4) NAA 1948
   11 para 5.005 CRAG; para 5.005 SWSG 8/96
   12 para 6 Annex to LAC(2002)11
   13 para 8 LAC (97)5; WOC 29/27; para 15 SWSG 7/97

2. **Outgoings**
   14 Sch 3 para 27 NA(AR) Regs
   15 para 3.011 CRAG; para 3.011 Scottish CRAG
   16 para 3.012 CRAG; para 3.012 Scottish CRAG

Chapter 14

Resident and third party top-ups

This chapter covers:

1. Who can top-up

If you are planning to move into, or are already in, a care home which is more expensive than social services would normally pay for someone with your level of needs, you or someone else (ie, a third party) will need to pay the difference. However, you, as the resident, can only pay the difference if you are subject to a 12-week property disregard (see p316) or you have a deferred payment agreement (see p299) and you have certain disregarded income or capital from which to make the payment.[1] For your right to choose your accommodation, see p271.

A third party may be any person, relative, friend or organisation (eg, a charity or your employer) willing to make up the difference. Since October 2001 (or July 2002 in Scotland) if your spouse makes maintenance payments to your care costs as a liable relative, s/he cannot make third party top-ups. In Wales this limitation does not apply. In England it does to top-up agreements made prior to 1 October 2001 and does not apply to liable relatives who are not making contributions (see p339).[2]

Note: England, Wales and Scotland are consulting on the possibility of removing the liable relatives rule for residential care.

In addition, you or a third party must reasonably be expected to continue to make top-up payments for the duration of your care arrangements. Social services must be assured that there is every chance that the third party will continue to have the resources to make the payments.[3]

Social services should not seek top-ups in cases where they decide to offer you a place in more expensive accommodation – eg, where, at the time, there is no suitable accommodation available within social services 'usual cost'.[4]

Care home providers should not seek top-ups from you or a third party where your placement is provided under contract with social services. If the care home provider approaches you in this manner you should report it to social services.

The question of resident or third party top-ups only arises if you need social services help with funding your care in a care home. It is not an issue if you are able to pay for your own care and do not need to ask social services for help with the fees.

Yourself as a third party

Except in the specific circumstances of where you are subject to the 12-week property disregard or where you have a deferred payment agreement (see p299), you cannot act as your own third party.[5]

In 1994, guidance made it clear that you cannot use your personal expenses allowance to pay for more expensive accommodation.[6] However, it was not until 1998 that misleading information was corrected to make it clear that neither can you use your own resources to pay for more expensive accommodation.[7] There has been a High Court decision which held that the revised guidance is correct.[8]

Resident/self top-ups

Since October 2001 you can make your own top-up payment (called 'additional payments' in the legislation) for more expensive accommodation if you are a 'relevant resident'.[9] You are a **'relevant resident'** if you either:

- have a 12-week property disregard on the property that used to be your home in the community (for the duration of the 12-week disregard only) (see p316); *or*
- have a deferred payment agreement (see p299).

If you have had a 12-week property disregard it is likely that after 12 weeks you will go on to a deferred payment arrangement if your property is for sale but not sold yet or you have decided not to sell your property. In these circumstances you will be able to continue to top-up yourself as a relevant resident.

As a relevant resident you must also have a **relevant income or capital disregard** applied to you, or other capital resources, before you are allowed to top-up yourself.[10]

If you are subject to a 12-week property disregard you may top-up from:

- disregarded earnings which include:
  - £5 (if you do not qualify for the higher disregard) (see p246);
  - £20 (if you qualify – eg, are entitled to attendance allowance/disability living allowance (DLA) or getting the disability premium or higher pensioner premium in your income support applicable amount) (see p245);
- disregarded income which includes:
  - DLA mobility component (see p231);

  - certain regular charitable or voluntary payments (see p235);
  - up to £10 of war disablement pension (see p232);
- disregarded capital which includes:
  - any payment made under the Macfarlane Trust or the Eileen Trust;
  - arrears payments of certain benefits;

  but *excluding* the value of the property that is disregarded for the first 12 weeks;
- other capital resources, *excluding* your home, but only up to the value of the lower capital limit for your country (see p315).

  Note that where these resources are used to top-up and you have resources above the lower capital limit, the level of tariff income that applies during the 12 weeks of topping-up is the same as it would be if you were not using the capital to top up – ie, there is no reduction in the tariff income figure applied.[11]

If you have a deferred payment agreement, you may top-up from similar disregarded resources:

- disregarded earnings (see p244);
- disregarded income (see p307);
- disregarded capital (see p223 but without the exclusion of the value of the property);
- other capital resources, *including* the value of your property that is subject to the deferred payment agreement but you must be left with total capital resources under the means test to the value of the lower capital limit.

  Note that when the value of property is used as collateral for top-ups, the amount of the top-up is added to your deferred contribution and is eventually repaid when the home is sold – see p299.

Social services should assure that when residents top-up against the value of their home when it is subject to a deferred payment agreement, that they can pay back the deferred contribution and the top-up.[12]

2. Resident and third party responsibilities

Social services contract to pay the full fees of the care home and you or the third party agrees to pay social services (or defer against the value of your property) the difference between what they would normally pay and the cost of the accommodation. This can be done by:

- you or the third party paying social services; *or*
- you or the third party paying the home direct, if the third party, and/or you and the homeowner agree.[13]

Social services should tell you and your third party that as the fees and the amounts that social services is prepared to pay do not necessarily increase at the same rate, increases may not be evenly split. If the home's fees rise faster than the level social services will pay, then that increase will fall on you or the third party. Resident and third party contributions should be regularly reviewed.[14]

Any failure by your third party to pay the level of contribution may mean you have to leave the home of your choice. It is suggested that social services should make legally binding contracts with residents or third parties (although charities have restrictions on such contracts) specifying:

- failure to keep up payments will normally result in the resident having to move to other accommodation. However, where resident's top-ups are being made against the value of property subject to a deferred payment agreement, social services will have assured itself from the outset that top-up payments are viable and recoverable when the home is sold;
- an increase in a resident's income will not necessarily lessen the need for a top-up contribution, as the resident's own income is subject to charging in the normal way;
- that a rise in the accommodation fees will not automatically be shared equally between social services, resident (if making a top-up) and third party; *and*
- if the care home fails to honour its contractual conditions, social services must reserve the right to terminate the contract.[15]

3. Assessing your charge

When you or a third party make a top-up *payment* (rather than a top-up added to any deferred contribution – see p299) to meet the difference between the amount social services will pay and the actual cost of your care home, that payment is treated as your income (if you are making the payment)[16] or notional income (if a third party is making the payment)[17] and is fully taken into account. Social services retains the liability to pay the full costs of the home, but can recoup more money from you because of the top-up payment.

Example

The home you have chosen costs £380 and social services will normally only pay £340. Your son has agreed to pay the extra £40. Your own assessed income is £250 a week, but you are counted as having £290 because the amount your son pays is notionally treated as your income. Social services charges you £272.50 (leaving you with £17.50 personal expenses allowance). Social services only has to pay the home the difference of £107.50.

Notes

1. **Who can top-up**
   1 s54 HSCA 2001; LAC (2001)29; NA(RAAPAR)(E) Regs
   2 para 16 LAC (2001)29; para 8.018A CRAG
   3 paras 6 and 7 LAC (2001)29
   4 para 4 LAC (2001)29
   5 paras 8.018 and 8.019A CRAG; para 8.018 Scottish CRAG
   6 LAC (94)1 (para 13); WOC 4/94; SWSG 5/94
   7 para 6 LAC (98)8
   8 *R v E Sussex ex parte Ward,* CCLR, June 2000
   9 Reg 2 NA(RAAPAR)(E) Regs
   10 Reg 4 NA(RAAAR)(E) Regs; para 6 LAC (2001)29
   11 Reg 28(4) NA(AR) Regs
   12 para 7 LAC (2001)29

2. **Resident and third party responsibilities**
   13 para 8 LAC (2001)29
   14 para 8 LAC (2001)29
   15 para 13 LAC (2001)29

3. **Assessing your charge**
   16 Reg 16A NA(AR) Regs; para 8.019C CRAG
   17 Reg 17(4) NA(AR) Regs; para 8.062 CRAG; para 8.062 Scottish CRAG

Chapter 15

Liable relatives – social services

This chapter covers:

1. Who is a liable relative (below)
2. Assessment forms (p340)
3. Pursuing liable relative payments (p340)
4. The treatment of liable relative payments (p341)
5. Maintenance you pay (p342)

There are similar rules for people who claim income support or income-based jobseeker's allowance (see Chapter 7). However, there are no equivalent rules for pension credit. See pxx for proposals to end the rules regarding liable relatives.

1. Who is a liable relative

Legislation currently states that spouses are liable to maintain one another (and their children).[1] Such 'liable relatives' may be asked to contribute to the costs of care if you require funding from social services when you enter a care home.[2] Guidance sets out how and when social services should seek 'liable relative contributions' from married partners when one of them enters a care home either on a temporary or permanent basis.[3] If social services has a policy on its approach to liable relative contributions, it should be put in writing and discussed with your spouse if s/he is asked for a contribution towards the cost of your accommodation and care.[4] No one else, including an unmarried partner or a sponsor, if you are a person from abroad, is liable to maintain you.

A liable relative who is making a maintenance payment cannot also act as a third party for any top-up payment required for more expensive accommodation (see p334).[5] This does not apply in Scotland as long as the local authority is satisfied that the spouse can sustain both the top-up payment and the maintenance. Scottish authorities have been advised to exercise particular caution both about sustainability and the effects on the finances of the liable relative.[6]

2. Assessment forms

Social services has no power to assess couples jointly under the National Assistance Act 1948. This means that even if you have a spouse who is a liable relative, the social services financial assessment form should not ask for information about her/his resources.[7]

Social services should first assess your ability to pay solely on your own resources to establish the contribution you are able to pay without assistance from your spouse.[8] Only if you are unable to pay the full charge should social services consider whether it is worth pursuing your spouse for maintenance towards the shortfall.[9]

Some social services departments have a separate form which your spouse may be asked to complete. Social services cannot insist on the completion of the form or on your spouse disclosing information about her/his resources.[10] Your spouse should not feel pressured into giving this information. If s/he has been asked to provide this information and is worried about it, s/he should seek advice.

However, even if your spouse does not wish to supply details of her/his resources, social services can still negotiate a liable relative contribution from her/him, and they should not charge your spouse in the absence of details unless negotiation has taken place.[11]

3. Pursuing liable relative payments

If you get income support (IS) and social services pursue maintenance for you from a liable relative, the DWP will merely reduce your IS by the amount of any liable relative payments you receive. This would reduce what social services can charge to the original amount, so it may not be worth them pursuing maintenance if you receive IS.[12] Guidance states that the liable relative should not experience hardship as a result of making a contribution and that they should be left with income above means-tested benefits with reasonable expenses allowed.[13]

The guidance refers to both permanent and temporary residents.[14] However, this presents a problem for social services if you are a *temporary* resident and your spouse is receiving IS in respect of both of you as a couple. Your spouse may be asked for a liable relatives contribution equal to the amount of IS that is paid to her/him for you. However, while this would leave her/him with an amount of IS for her/himself only, it would obviously not be *above* the level of means-tested benefits. Local authorities might wish to exercise their discretion if your spouse at home would have a reduced income during your temporary stay. This will become more important when pension credit comes into effect as, unlike IS, there will be no provisions for calculating benefit as if you and your spouse were a single person during a temporary stay (see p368).

Social services cannot force your spouse either to give information about her/his resources or to make a payment. Even if your spouse has already given information about her/his resources social services still cannot insist that s/he makes a liable relative payment. Neither can social services refuse to provide a service or delay arranging a service for you because your spouse refuses to disclose financial information or make a payment.[15]

Ultimately only the courts can enforce an appropriate payment and legislation provides for social services to refer a case to the magistrates' court or sheriff's court in Scotland.[16] However, as with all enforcement measures, social services will have to decide whether in terms of the cost and the potential for adverse publicity, the recoupment of expenditure is worth pursuing to this stage. Guidance states that court action should only be considered as a last resort.[17]

If social services approaches your spouse and s/he is happy to disclose her/his resources and/or make a liable relative payment, then the question that arises is the amount. There are no national rules governing the amount of liable relative payments although some social services departments operate their own means test.

Any amount that is arrived at by a social services means test is not enforceable by them. You may wish to offer a different amount. The guidance states that social services should consider what would be 'appropriate' and that this will involve discussion and negotiation with your spouse, and will be determined to a large extent by her/his financial circumstances in relation to her/his expenditure and normal standard of living.[18] You should seek advice and complain (see p55) if you think the local authority is being unreasonable in the way they are treating you in requesting a payment or the amount they expect you to pay.

4. The treatment of liable relative payments

A liable relative payment is the payment made by your spouse who is liable to maintain you.[19] Certain payments are not treated as liable relative payments even though they are made by a liable relative. These are the same as for income support (IS).[20]

A liable relative payment can be considered as a periodical or non-periodical payment by social services. Periodical payments and arrears of periodical payments are made for an identifiable period and a weekly income figure is calculated accordingly. The rules for the treatment of non-periodical payments, which are payments that are not made for identifiable periods, are slightly different from the rules which apply for IS. The rules are as follows.

- If you are on IS the DWP calculates the number of weeks for which IS will be withdrawn. Social services should work out the same number of weeks by dividing the payment by the amount of IS normally paid (plus any disregards which would be applicable if the payment was a regular payment of earnings).

Any remaining amount should be taken into account in the assessment of the final week.[21]

- If you are not on IS the payment is divided by the difference between the standard charge (ie, the full charge) and the contribution you have been assessed to make from your own resources. Any remaining amount should be taken into account as income for the final week.[22]

Example

Mrs Webster is paying a charge (A) of £120.

The standard charge (B) is £250.

She receives a lump sum maintenance payment (C) of £750.

The number of weeks over which the payment should be taken into account is calculated as follows:

C (B – A) = 5.77 weeks

Mrs Webster therefore pays the standard charge at £250 for five weeks.

In week six Mrs Webster will have £100 left from the payment (having used £130 (B – A) a week for the five weeks to meet the extra charge). This should be used to calculate the charge for week six.[23]

Periodical and non-periodical payments may be made at the same time. If the periodical payment is less than the difference between the standard charge and the amount you would be liable to pay if you did not receive any liable relative payment, the non-periodical payment should be taken into account over a number of weeks, calculated by dividing the payment by the difference between the standard charge and the amount you had previously been contributing.[24] Where the weekly liable relative payment is equal to, or more than, the difference between the standard charge and the contribution you would be assessed as paying if you did not receive a liable relative payment, then the non-periodical payment should be treated as capital.[25]

5. Maintenance you pay

If you are in a care home and you are contributing to the maintenance of someone, there is no specific provision to allow a disregard of the amount that you pay from the assessment of your income unless it is a payment of at least 50 per cent of an occupational pension, personal pension or retirement annuity made to your spouse who is not living with you. In these circumstances 50 per cent of your occupational pension, personal pension or retirement annuity will be disregarded as income in your financial assessment (see p307).[26] These rules only apply to the social services assessment, there are no similar rules for income support (IS), for which all your occupational pension counts as income when working out your IS amount.

There is also a provision not to treat any part of an occupational pension, personal pension or retirement annuity that your spouse is legally entitled to receive (eg, by means of a court order) as income belonging to you, and therefore it would not form part of your income for financial assessment purposes.[27] If, in addition, you pass at least 50 per cent of the part of the occupational pension, personal pension or retirement annuity belonging to you, to your spouse, the 50 per cent disregard will still apply.[28]

If you pay maintenance as a liable relative from income other than an occupational pension, personal pension or retirement annuity then you may need to seek advice about whether the change in your circumstances (ie, becoming a resident in a care home) will affect your liability.

If you remain liable to make maintenance payments, social services may, in special circumstances, be able to use their discretion to increase your personal expenses allowance in order to enable you to continue to meet the commitment.[29]

Notes

1. **Who is a liable relative**
   1 s42 NAA 1948; s97(3) SW(S)A 1968
   2 paras 11.001 and 11.002 CRAG (England, Scotland and Wales)
   3 para 11 CRAG (England, Scotland and Wales)
   4 para 11.004B CRAG (England and Wales); para 11.004A Scottish CRAG
   5 para 16 Appendix 1 LAC (2001)29; para 8.018A English CRAG; para 11.004A Welsh CRAG; regs 2 and 4 NA(RAAPAR)(E) Regs
   6 para 19 CCD 6/2002 and para 18.018B Scottish CRAG

2. **Assessment forms**
   7 para 11.005 CRAG (England, Scotland and Wales)
   8 para 11.006i CRAG (England, Scotland and Wales)
   9 para 11.006ii CRAG (England, Scotland and Wales)
   10 para 11.005 CRAG (England, Scotland and Wales)
   11 para 11.005A CRAG (England, Scotland and Wales)

3. **Pursuing liable relative payments**
   12 para 11.003 CRAG (England, Scotland and Wales)
   13 paras 11.004 and 11.006iii CRAG (England, Scotland and Wales);
   14 para 18 LAC (2002)11
   15 paras 11.005A and 11.006A CRAG (England, Scotland and Wales)
   16 s43 NAA 1948; para 18(c)
   17 para 11.006iv CRAG (England, Scotland and Wales)
   18 paras 11.004 and 11.006iii CRAG (England, Scotland and Wales)

4. **The treatment of liable relative payments**
   19 s42 NAA 1948
   20 para 11.008 CRAG (England, Scotland and Wales)
   21 Reg 18(2) NA(AR) Regs and para 11.021 CRAG (England, Scotland and Wales)
   22 para 11.022 CRAG (England, Scotland and Wales)
   23 Reg 32(1) NA(AR) Regs and para 11.022 CRAG (England, Scotland and Wales)

24 Reg 32(2) NA(AR) Regs and para 11.023 CRAG (England, Scotland and Wales)
25 Reg 34(1) NA(AR) Regs and para 11.024 CRAG (England, Scotland and Wales)

5. **Maintenance you pay**

26 Sch 3 para 10A NA(AR) Regs and para 8.024A CRAG (England, Scotland and Wales)
27 para 8.024C CRAG (England, Scotland and Wales);
28 para 8.024C CRAG (England, Scotland and Wales)
29 s22(4) NAA 1948 and para 5.005 CRAG (England, Scotland and Wales)

Chapter 16

Collection of charges and enforcement

This chapter covers:

1. How charges are collected

When social services departments arrange for your care, either in one of their own homes or in an independent care home, they must establish how much you should pay using the rules described in the previous chapters. They must ensure you are given a clear explanation, usually in writing, of how your charge has been calculated and how much it will be each week. They should also inform you of why your charge may fluctuate. This is especially important in the first few weeks, when changes to your benefits will affect how much you have to pay[1] (see Chapter 17). You should also be told how you will be billed for your charge.

There are two ways to pay if you are in an independent care home:

- social services pay the home the full cost and you pay social services your assessed contribution;[2]
- you can pay your assessed contribution direct to the home and social services will pay the difference if you, the home owner, and social services all agree.[3]

The latter method was introduced for administrative efficiency only and *has* to be with the agreement of all parties. If any of you disagree then social services has to pay the full cost and bill you for your contribution.

Social services has the contractual obligation with the home, and is responsible for paying the full fees. If you do not pay your contribution, it is social services' responsibility to recover the charge from you,[4] not the home. In practice, some social services departments use this method of collection without making it clear that it must be with your agreement and do not explain the alternative.

2. If you cannot or will not pay your charge

Social services departments cannot stop providing you with care in a care home purely because you are unable or unwilling to pay the assessed charge.[5] There are a variety of methods they can use for pursuing money owed to them. It is up to each authority to decide what enforcement actions to take.

Each social services department has its own procedures for tracking debts and following them up. Some have early warning signals built into their systems so that as soon as you have missed a few payments you are visited to establish the reason. If you pay the home direct it is likely there will be an arrangement for any non-payment to be reported. Some authorities have panels to monitor debts when they reach a certain level and to decide on any enforcement action.

You do not normally have a contractual relationship with social services when they arrange your accommodation, but the legislation provides that any sum due under the National Assistance Act is recoverable as a civil debt.[6] This allows social services to take the same steps as any creditor to enforce payment of your assessed contributions.

You should normally have enough money to pay your assessed contribution, but there may be times when this is not the case. The most common reasons are:

- you have been assessed to pay the full cost because of your capital, but it is not possible to access it because an application for receivership is with the Court of Protection (or in Scotland an application for a financial guardian is with the Public Guardian's Office) (see p288) or an application has been made to register an Enduring Power of Attorney in England and Wales (see p286). Social services should be prepared to wait in these circumstances. The person taking over your affairs may be able to get permission from the Public Guardianship Office (or the Public Guardian's Office in Scotland) to enable the fees to be paid in the interim. S/he should ring the customer services section of the Public Guardianship/Guardian's Office for advice. See Chapter 9 for details about the provisions if you cannot manage your financial affairs;
- you have been assessed as paying the full cost because you have a property, the value of which is correctly included in the assessment but which has not yet been sold and you have not entered into a deferred payment agreement (see p348);
- you have been assessed as paying a charge based on the assumption that you receive income support (IS). Because social services finance officers are aware of the amount which is usually paid if you are in a care home, the calculation often assumes you receive this amount. You should always check your calculation very carefully and see if it tallies with your income, which includes any IS you get. It may be that you have not applied for IS, or there has been a decision that you are not entitled, but social services is not aware of this. Or the amount that the DWP has paid may be different to what the finance officer

thinks should be paid. There can be a number of reasons for this. You should ask social services for a reassessment. You should not be charged as if you have IS if you have not applied for it, unless you have deliberately decided not to apply. In this case it could be considered to be notional income (see p309). If it is necessary to appeal about the level of IS you get, you should ask social services to assess your charge based on what you currently receive and reassess you if you win the appeal.

If you do not wish to pay your assessed charge (eg, because you disagree with the amount calculated or you are in dispute about the value of a jointly owned property) you should seek advice about the subject under dispute and whether you should make any payments and if so how much, while the dispute is resolved. If there is any other reason you are not willing to pay the charges you have been assessed to pay, it is likely that social services will be prepared to consider remedies to enforce payment of the money due.

Actions to avoid debts building up

- If you are becoming forgetful and have difficulty in managing your financial affairs, social services may help you to get a friend or relative to become an appointee (if you do not have much capital and your main income is benefits). If you have already granted an enduring power of attorney (continuing power of attorney in Scotland, see p287) and can no longer manage your affairs, it will need to be registered, so that your attorney can take over your affairs. Or social services may suggest that someone approaches the Court of Protection to become your receiver (or, in Scotland, a financial guardian to manage your financial affairs). For more details on appointees, attorneys and receivers, see Chapter 9.
- If your appointee, attorney or receiver/financial guardian does not pay the charges, social services will negotiate with her/him and may inform the relevant authority in order to get her/him removed from dealing with your affairs. If necessary social services may take over this role.
- Some local authorities have money advisers who could offer you budgeting advice and ways of making it easier to pay your charge, if this happens to be the problem. If you have other debts, a money adviser may be able to help with negotiating with your creditors. In exceptional circumstances, social services may allow you an extra personal expenses allowance (see Chapter 13). In some cases social services may be prepared to write off your debt to them.
- If you are getting IS or income-based jobseeker's allowance and are not using it to pay your charges, the DWP can pay your benefit direct to social services if it is in your interests and if social services has arranged your accommodation. If you have arranged your own accommodation, the deduction can be paid to the home. In the case of a home run by a voluntary organisation for people

dependent on alcohol or drugs, direct payments can be made even if you are not in debt.[7] Your consent is not needed.[8]

3. Legal charges on your property

Social services departments cannot force you to sell your property in order to pay the assessed charge (which in most cases will be the full cost) without a court order. Instead, if you fail to pay your assessed charge they may create a legal charge on your interest in any land that is in England and Wales[9] (called a charging order in Scotland).[10] A legal charge means that when you sell your property the local authority will have a call on the proceeds to cover the amount owed, rather like when you have a mortgage which is paid off when the sale goes through. Note that a legal charge can only be created under these rules if you have failed to pay your charge, so unless you have a debt to social services there is no power for them to create a legal charge on your land. See p299 for details of the deferred payment agreements, which is where you can enter into a voluntary agreement which ensures your charges are eventually paid.

The charge may be registered against your property so that social services will know when it is sold. If the title to your property is registered, the charge will be put on the central Land Register. If your property does not yet have a registered title a Class B land charge will be put on the Land Register.[11] If the land is in Scotland then the charging order is recorded in the Register of Sasines or registered in the Land Register as appropriate.[12]

The charge is created by a declaration in writing[13] and guidance in England and Wales says that social services should advise or assist you to consult a solicitor if they are considering creating a legal charge.[14]

Jointly owned property

In England and Wales local authorities have been advised to register a 'caution' in the cases of jointly owned property.[15] A caution affords local authorities less protection than a legal charge, but would alert them if a sale is going through, so that they could take action.

Social services are referred to the guidance about valuing jointly owned property.[16] Before any caution is registered it is important that the value of your interest in the property has been established, as it may have a low or nil value if there is no willing buyer.

You should complain if you disagree with the valuation of jointly owned property and if your complaint goes to a complaints panel you could ask for all the panel members to be independent of the local authority. See p56 for more details about complaints panels.

Charging interest

Interest on the legal charge or charging order cannot be charged during your lifetime, but will be added from the date you die.[17] The interest has to be at a 'reasonable rate'. How local authorities set the rate varies around the country, but most use formulas which are within average market rates.

When social services has used debt enforcement legislation to place a legal charge,[18] interest can be charged from the date of the resident's death.[19] If you have entered in to a deferred payment agreement, interest will only be charged from 56 days after your death (see p300).

Costs of creating the charge

The law is silent on whether social services or you should bear the cost of creating the legal charge or charging order. Some authorities will pass the cost on to you. If this happens you should establish under what legislation this is done, as the law only relates to the failure to pay the assessed charge. You should complain (see p297) if you consider that you should not be charged for the costs, or if you think they are too high.

Calculating the debt accrued

You continue to be charged for the full cost of your care home fees, until such time as your debt means that the value of your property and any other capital you have has reduced to the upper capital limit. From that point charges should be based on your income and tariff income, until the value of your property and other capital is down to the lower capital limit and from then, only based on your income (see pp308 and 315).

In the case of property it can be difficult to calculate the debt, as it is based on a valuation which may or may not reflect the final price you receive. It only becomes a problem if the value of your property after your debt has been taken into account, falls to the upper capital limit.

In practice it appears that most social services departments readjust the amount you owe when the property is sold, as they can base the calculation of your debt on the actual sale price of your property. In some cases this will mean that you are asked to pay more if your property is sold for more than expected, or you might be charged less or refunded some money if your property sells for less than the amount at which it has been valued.

A rule of thumb is that you should not be left with total capital (other capital and the proceeds of the sale of your property) of less than the lower capital limit for your country (see p294) unless:

- your debt accrued before 1996 when the capital limits changed from £8,000 to £16,000. If by 1 April 1996 your debt had already taken you below £10,000 then it should have stopped accruing any further at that point and remained at the point it had reached under the old capital limits. There have been further

increases to the capital limits since then which might mean that if your debt had taken you below the lower capital limit by the time of the change, you could be left with less than the current lower capital limit;
- interest has been charged under the rules explained on p348. As interest is added to the debt, this interest could take capital below the lower capital limit.

4. Deprivation of assets

If social services decides that you have given away your assets or not applied for them, in order to avoid or lessen your liability for charges for your care (see p324), then it *will* in the case of income and *may* in the case of capital treat you as if you still possess those assets.[20] This means that your charge will be assessed as if you still have that income or capital (see below and pp309 and 323). Unless you are able to pay the assessed charge you will accrue a debt which can be enforced as a civil debt, or if you still own any land, a legal charge (or charging order in Scotland) on it can be created by the local authority. If you have given away your property then there is no power for a legal charge to be created on it as you no longer have an interest in land.

The House of Lords has recently ruled on a Scottish case, where the local authority was arguing that it did not have to make the arrangements to accommodate someone who had deprived herself of capital, because it could take the 'notional capital' (see p323) into account. This took her above the upper capital limits. The House of Lords overturned the previous rulings in the Scottish courts and found that the first test is the needs assessment and the assessment of means is second. Notional capital can be taken into account at the stage when charges are being made for the services, but it must be left out of account at the earlier stage, when decisions are being made whether to provide accommodation.[21] The rules are different in England and Wales and it has yet to be tested whether this ruling has effect outside Scotland.

Diminishing notional capital

In the case of capital, if social services decides to treat you as having capital you have given away, you will be assessed as notionally having that amount, but it will be reduced each week.[22] The amount of the reduction will be the difference between what you actually pay and the amount you would have paid if you had not been treated as having capital which you have given away.

Example

You have been assessed as having £9,000 actual capital and £20,500 notional capital which you have given away. Your weekly income means you are assessed as having to pay £150 and the home you are in costs £350. The level of your notional capital will be reduced by £200 a week which is what social services has to pay because you gave away your capital. This means that after 50 weeks you will be reassessed as having only £ £19,500 and your assessed charge will be reduced to the level of your income plus tariff income from capital above £12,000. You will still owe a debt to the local authority which it may try to recoup. (Please not the figures will be different in Scotland and Wales.)

Transferring the liability to the person who has received your assets

In addition to deciding whether to treat you as if you still have the assets, social services has the legal power to take enforcement proceedings against the person (or persons) who now owns the assets if you have knowingly and with the intention of avoiding charges, transferred them, either for nothing or at less than their value.[23] Even if the person to whom you transferred those assets was unaware that you did this to avoid paying charges, s/he will still have the liability for your fees transferred to her/him. The question is whether *you* knowingly transferred your assets to avoid charges.

This rule can only be used if you transferred your assets within the six months immediately before you went into residential accommodation. Guidance makes it clear that in this context 'residential accommodation' is where social services has assessed you as needing care in a care home *and* has arranged it for you in an independent or local authority home. Even if you are already in an independent home when you transfer your assets, if you have not been assessed and not had your placement arranged by social services within six months of the transfer, this rule does not apply. The guidance gives an example of a resident who paid for his own accommodation in full for two years, then the following March gave his daughter £20,000 and continued to self-fund until December, when he approached the local authority for support.[24] In this case the six-month rule does not apply, but social services could treat the resident as still possessing the capital (see p350). Time limits only apply to the transfer of liability to pay onto the person who has received the asset. There appear to be no time limits for social services to treat you as still possessing your assets.

Calculating the cost for which the owner is liable

Once social services decides that you have transferred your assets to another person within the six months prior to going into care, knowingly to avoid or lessen the charges, then the owner is liable to pay the difference between what you actually pay social services and what you have been assessed as having to pay.[25]

The amount for which the person who has received the asset is liable should be restricted to the current value of the amount transferred. If the asset has been transferred to more than one person, each person can only be held liable up to the value of her/his share of the asset.[26]

The asset is valued at the amount that would have been realised on the open market at the time it was transferred, and secured debts and reasonable costs of sale will be taken into account.[27]

5. Court action that can be used

It is beyond the scope of this book to give advice about dealing with any debts you have to social services caused by charges for care (see CPAG's *Debt Advice Handbook*). As with any debt it is important to negotiate at an early stage and check carefully that you are actually liable for the debt (this is particularly so if someone else is managing your affairs and they receive the bills) and that you agree with the calculation of the amount owing. As your debt may have built up over several years, and you will probably have been paying some of the cost out of your income, which will have altered over time, mistakes can be made. You should also establish whether the debt can still be collected as there are time limits. These are normally six years, but in the case of money owed for your care home charges, proceedings for its recovery can only be brought within three years of the sum becoming due.[28] Seek advice if your debt accrued more than three years ago.

Although debt advisers (or money advisers) may have had little experience of dealing with debts for care home charges, they should be very experienced in negotiating and checking whether the debt can be enforced. Your local Citizens Advice Bureau may have a debt adviser, or sometimes local authorities offer money advice, although they may be limited in the amount of advice they can offer if you are in dispute with their employing authority.

This section lists possible action through the courts that social services has at its disposal. Although court action has to date rarely been used and there may be concern about taking frail residents to court, the provisions are there. Where there are debts, local authorities have to justify inaction to their auditors. Often the threat of legal action resolves the problem for local authorities because the debt is settled before going to court. A recent much publicised case was where a trust had been set up relating to the property and the council issued a writ against both the resident and her son. It was finally settled out of court, but only just before the hearing was due.[29] It is important to seek advice before agreeing to settle the debt if you have doubts or queries.

Civil debt

Where the assessed charges have not been paid, local authorities can seek to recover the sum as a civil debt.[30] Proceedings under this legislation may be brought at any time within three years of the sum becoming due.[31] If the debt being recovered is older than three years, seek advice.

If the local authority intends to issue proceedings, it will normally be its legal department that writes giving you notice and a final chance of settling the debt.

In England and Wales your case will be dealt with in the magistrates' court, although there is no rule which would stop a local authority from using county court or bankruptcy proceedings. In Scotland it would be normally the sheriff's court and may be the Court of Session.

It is more likely that social services will be prepared to pursue the person who now owns your assets if you gave them away or sold them for less than their value within six months of needing social services help with paying for care in a care home. If that person who is now liable to pay part of your fees (see p351) does not do so, the local authority could pursue the debt through the courts.

If you have given false information

It is an offence to give information which you know to be false. In England and Wales if you do so, you could be fined up to £100 or up to three months in prison or both.[32] Proceedings may be started at any time within three months from the date on which, in the opinion of the local authority, sufficient evidence comes to light to justify a prosecution, or within 12 months of the offence, whichever is longer.

Although this provision has existed since 1948 there is no evidence that it has ever been used. It is more likely that social services would use their other enforcement procedures to recover the money owed.

Recovery from a liable relative

If your spouse fails to make maintenance payments, s/he can be forced to do so through the family court[33] (see p340). Only the courts can decide what is an appropriate amount of maintenance to pay.[34]

Using insolvency procedures

The Insolvency Act 1986 (England and Wales)

There are two provisions in this Act which social services could consider if you owe more than £750, have transferred your assets and are unable to pay your charge.

- If you have given away your assets at an undervalue and can be declared bankrupt, the local authority can apply to the court for an order to set the 'gift' aside. The time limits are five years before the presentation of the petition, if you were bankrupt at the time of the transaction, or became insolvent because of the transaction, and two years in all other cases.[35] The court may make such orders as it thinks fit for restoring the position to what it would have been before the transaction.
- If the local authority can prove that the purpose of giving away your assets at an undervalue was to place them beyond the reach of a possible creditor.[36]

There are no time limits on these powers and you do not need to be declared bankrupt.

It may be difficult for the local authority to prove, although if you have used a business which specialises in avoiding assets being taken into account, this could be considered to be useful to the local authority in establishing your motive. Normally solicitors' files are confidential but a case has established that in some cases the court could require disclosure, it has not yet been tested in a case relating to care charges.[37]

Bankruptcy (Scotland) Act 1985

There is provision in the Bankruptcy (Scotland) Act 1985 which might be considered if you owe more than £1,500, whereby you can be declared bankrupt and have your assets transferred when you are unable to pay your charge.

It is possible that proceedings could be taken by the local authority to set aside a transfer which is known under the legislation as a gratuitous alienation. This is where an asset has been transferred, either for no payment or for payment of less than the value of the asset. The time limit for challenging such a transfer is five years before the date of bankruptcy where the person to whom the asset is transferred is an associate and two years, for any other person.[38]

Notes

1. **How charges are collected**
   1 para 1.015 CRAG (England and Wales); para 1.013 CRAG (Scotland)
   2 s22(3) NAA 1948
   3 s23(3A) NAA 1948; paras 1.023-1.024 CRAG (England and Wales); paras 1.015-1.016 CRAG (Scotland)
   4 para 1.024 CRAG; para 1.016 CRAG (Scotland)

2. **If you cannot or will not pay your charge**
   5 This is because of the mandatory nature of s21 NAA 1948 and LAC (93)10 and WOC/35/93. In Scotland it is because of the mandatory nature of s59 SW(S)A 1968 and ss7 and 8 MH(S)A 1984
   6 s56 NAA 1948; s87 SW(S)A 1968
   7 Sch 9 para 4 SS(C&P) Regs
   8 Sch 9 para 8 SS(C&P) Regs

3. **Legal charges on your property**
   9 s22(1) HASSASSAA 1983
   10 CO(RA)(S)O 1993; SWSG 15/93
   11 s22(8) HASSASSAA 1983
   12 s23(3) HASSASSAA 1983
   13 s22(7) HASSASSAA 1983
   14 Annex D3.4 CRAG
   15 Annex D3.5 CRAG
   16 paras 7.012 and 7.014 CRAG (England, Scotland and Wales)
   17 s24 HASSASSAA 1983
   18 s22 HASSASSAA 1983
   19 Annex D3A CRAG (England and Wales)

4. **Deprivation of assets**
   20 Regs 17(1) and 25(1) NA(AR) Regs; paras 8.071 and 6.057 CRAG (England and Wales); paras 8.071 and 6.056 Scottish CRAG
   21 *Robertson v Fife Council*, House of Lords 5 CCLR 543

22 Reg 26 NA(AR) Regs; para 6.068 CRAG (England and Wales); para 6.067CRAG (Scotland)
23 s21 HASSASSAA 1983
24 Annex D2.1 CRAG (England and Wales)
25 s21(1) HASSASSAA 1983 and Annex D2.6 CRAG(England and Wales); para 9 SWSG 7/97
26 s21(4) and (5) HASSASSAA 1983 and Annexes D2.4 and D2.5 CRAG (England and Wales); SWSG 15/93 para 2.4
27 s21(7) HASSASSAA 1983 and Annex D2.3 CRAG (England and Wales); SWSG 15/93 para 2.3

5. **Court action that can be used**
28 s56(2) NAA 1948
29 *East Anglian Daily Times*, 4 March 2003
30 s56 NAA 1948
31 s56(2) NAA 1948
32 s52 NAA 1948
33 s43(6) NAA 1948 (applies in Scotland by virtue of s87(3) SW(S)A 1968)
34 para 11.006 CRAG (England, Scotland and Wales)
35 ss339 and 341 IA 1986
36 s423 IA 1986
37 *Barclays Bank v Eustice* (1995)
38 s34 B(S)A 1985

Chapter 17

Social security benefits in care homes

This chapter covers:
1. Types of care home (below)
2. Types of stay (p362)
3. Social security benefits affected (p363)
4. Self-funding (including 'loophole' cases and retrospective self-funding) (p375)
5. Temporary absences from care homes (including going into hospital) (p380)
6. Other sources of financial assistance in care homes (p381)
7. Effects on carers (p382)

All references to income support also apply to income-based jobseeker's allowance.

1. Types of care home

Accommodation and care is usually provided in either:
- local authority care homes (sometimes known as Part III homes or Part IV homes in Scotland); *or*
- independent care homes; *or*
- independent care homes which provide nursing.

Under the Care Standards Act 2000 or in Scotland, the Regulation of Care (Scotland) Act 2001, the term 'care home' is used to describe all the above types of accommodation which are required to register under this new scheme with the National Care Standards Commission (England) or the National Assembly for Wales or the Scottish Commission for the Regulation of Care.

On 1 April 2002 the Care Standards Act 2000 (or in Scotland, the Regulation of Care (Scotland) Act 2001) repealed the Registered Homes Act 1984[1] (or in Scotland, section 61 Social Work (Scotland) Act 1968 or section 10 Nursing Homes Registration (Scotland) Act 1938) under which 'residential care homes' and 'nursing homes' were obliged to register with local authorities.

There have been no amending social security regulations to replace references to the 1984 Act (or the Scottish equivalents) and the terms 'residential care home', nursing home' and 'residential accommodation'.[2]

However, for benefit purposes, since April 2002, all these types of accommodation are treated in the same way unless a care home which provides nursing (a nursing home) is considered to be a 'hospital or similar institution' (see p358).

From October 2003, when pension credit is introduced, the definition of 'care home' in the legislation is being amended to reflect the definition used in the Care Standards Act 2000 (or in Scotland, the Regulation of Care (Scotland) Act 2001).

In England and Wales, an establishment is a care home if it provides accommodation, together with nursing or personal care, for people who:

- are, or have been, ill; *or*
- have, or have had, a mental disroder; *or*
- are disabled or infirm; *or*
- are, or have been, dependent on alcohol or drugs.

An establishment is not a care home if it is:

- a hospital; *or*
- an independent clinic.[3]

In Scotland, an establishment is a care home if it is accommodation in which a care home service is provided – ie, a service providing accommodation with nursing, personal care or personal support for people by reason of their vulnerability or need.

An establishment is not a care home if it is:

- a hospital; *or*
- a public, independent or grant-aided school; *or*
- a private psychiatric hospital; *or*
- an independent clinic; *or*
- an independent medical agency.[4]

There are special rules if you receive care in the following types of accommodation:

- hospitals or similar institutions;
- hospices;
- joint funded accommodation;
- s28A funded accommodation;[5]
- aftercare accommodation provided under s117 Mental Health Act 1983 (England and Wales).

If you receive care in a **care home which does not provide board** (ie, you were a 'less dependent resident' prior to April 2002), the benefits payable to you may change as a result of these types of care home now being required to register (see p67).[6] You will usually receive the ordinary rates of income support (IS) (subject to the conditions of entitlement – see p166) but you may no longer be eligible to claim housing benefit (HB) because registration usually prevents entitlement to HB.[7]

If you receive care in a registered **Abbeyfield Home** you will be treated in the same way as a resident in any other type of registered care home (see p72). If your Abbeyfield Home is not registered then you will be treated in the same way as a person in supported accommodation and therefore be eligible to claim HB (see p181).

Hospitals or similar institutions

Special rules apply if you are considered to be an inpatient in a hospital or similar institution. Your accommodation and care will then be provided free of charge by the NHS (see p259), DLA care and mobility components or AA will not be payable to you after four weeks (or sooner if you have been in hospital or a care home within the previous 28 days) and other benefits will only be payable at a reduced rate after 52 weeks.[8]

It will usually be clear when you are an inpatient in a hospital. However, if you are not actually in a hospital it will sometimes be unclear whether these special rules apply, as even if you are in a care home, or what may appear to be supported accommodation, you may still be treated as if you were a hospital inpatient.

The term **'hospital or similar institution'** is not defined in social security legislation,[9] but the test of whether the special rules apply has been considered in a number of social security commissioners' decisions[10] and by the courts.[11] Essentially, the test is whether on the particular facts you should be considered to be:

- maintained free of charge;
- undergoing medical or other treatment as an inpatient;[12]
- under the relevant NHS Act;[13]
- in a hospital or similar institution.

If you cannot be considered to be living in a hospital or similar institution, you will not be treated as if you were in hospital (and it will not then matter whether you are being maintained free of charge or undergoing medical treatment as an inpatient).[14]

Social security commissioners have held that the term **'hospital'** means:

- any institution for the reception and treatment of persons suffering from illness;
- any maternity home; *and*
- any institution for the reception of and treatment of persons during convalescence or persons requiring medical rehabilitation.[15]

It also includes clinics, dispensaries and outpatient departments maintained in connection with any such home or institution.

It has also been held that a **'similar institution'** connotes 'some sort of formal body or structure which controls all aspects of the treatment or care that is provided including the premises in which the treatment is carried out'.[16] In that case a claimant was undergoing medical or other treatment provided by NHS staff at public expense, but because it was provided in a privately rented house where rent was paid and the claimant was responsible for expenditure on food and other outgoings, the claimant could not be considered to be living in an 'institution' at all, let alone a 'similar' one.

It has been further held that a crucial test to determine whether an establishment is a 'similar institution' is 'the treatment and care given by the establishment and the similarity between those and the treatment and care which are provided in a hospital,' which will be 'a question of fact and degree in each case'.[17] Another social security commissioner held that what the staff in an establishment do is more important than whether they are employed by the NHS, so that if NHS staff provide social rather than medical care, or supervise residents in a lifestyle which is more typical of a home than a hospital, then it is likely that the establishment cannot be considered to be an institution similar to a hospital.[18]

In other cases, care homes which provide nursing have been held to be similar institutions, where claimants have been discharged from hospital into the homes.[19] This included one person who suffered from a mental disorder, and the hospital rules were considered to apply because this was considered to be an 'illness' for which the treatment was provided.[20] In these cases it was considered relevant that the claimants were undergoing medical or other treatment (which included nursing care) and were 'inpatients' as they received treatment on the premises of an institution and they were maintained free of charge as they were not private fee-paying patients in a NHS or Trust hospital.

Social services and the NHS may have negotiated between themselves who should be responsible for the arrangements and cost of your care. However, social security rules apply independently of any arrangements they may have agreed, and just because the health authorities do not consider that they have any 'continuing care' responsibilities for you (eg, on moving from a hospital to a care home which provides nursing), this does not mean that you may not still be treated as if you are living in a hospital or similar institution.

You can only be treated as a hospital inpatient if you are maintained free of charge while undergoing treatment in a NHS hospital or similar institution. You are regarded as being maintained free of charge unless the accommodation and services are provided under legislation which relates to fee-paying patients in NHS hospitals.[21] Caselaw suggests that even where considerable contributions to your maintenance are made you will still be treated as an inpatient.[22] There are conflicting commissioners' decisions on whether you actually need to be in the hospital for 24 hours a day to be treated as being maintained free of charge as an inpatient, or whether absences for a period within the 24 hours still bring you within the meaning.[23] The 'full-out' words in the amendment to the legislation deem the condition of being maintained free of charge to be satisfied if you are undergoing treatment as an inpatient unless you are a private patient in a NHS hospital.[24]

A recent commissioner's decision[25] held that a person was not maintained free of charge just because the NHS was making a contribution to a part of the services provided. In this case the residents were previously in long-stay NHS mental hospitals and they were suffering severe mental impairment. It was stated that the conditions were developmental disorders not clinically treatable conditions or 'illnesses' but they needed continuous care and supervision in a care home which provides nursing. It was held that the care home was a hospital or similar institution and the residents were receiving treatment. However, the issue was whether they were maintained free of charge while undergoing the treatment as inpatients in the care home under the defined NHS legislation.[26] The NHS was purchasing some extra day care services for some of the residents but this never extended to the cost of the accommodation or daily maintenance (which was purchased by the local authority). It was held that 'maintained free of charge' refers not only to medical treatment but also to basic maintenance and subsistence needs (accommodation and food) and that arrangements made under the defined NHS legislation must not only be for treatment, but also for maintenance for the hospital inpatient regulations to apply.

Hospices

You may receive care in a '**hospice**' which is defined as 'a hospital or other institution whose primary function is to provide palliative care for persons resident there who are suffering from a progressive disease in its final stages' (but not an NHS hospital).[27] This is usually arranged via your GP through the NHS. For benefit purposes a hospice is a 'hospital or similar institution', and therefore the same rules as for being in a hospital apply (see p204). The only difference is that DLA mobility component will continue in payment beyond 28 days[28] and the DLA care component or AA will also continue in payment beyond 28 days.[29]

Joint funded accommodation

You may receive care in a care home which is purchased out of a local NHS body and social services budget (this arrangement is sometimes called 50/50 funding) (see p264). In these circumstances, the benefit situation is far from clear. There can be confusion over whether you should be considered as having your accommodation provided by the NHS under the 'similar institution' part of the definition of a 'hospital or similar institution' (see p358), in which case you should receive your care free of charge and the hospital rate of benefits will apply (see p204); or whether you should be considered as having your accommodation provided by social services, in which case the rules for social security benefits in care homes will apply. It is important to find out what the terms of the contract with the home are in respect of your placement. Often the NHS funding for your placement is received by social services rather than by the care home and therefore it is social services who has assessed your need, arranged and contracted with a home for the provision of your accommodation and care[30] and they are required[31] to charge you subject to the means tests.[32]

If your benefits have been reduced to hospital inpatient rates, but you are still responsible for paying towards the cost of your accommodation and care, seek advice (see Appendix 4).

Section 28A funded accommodation

You may receive care in a care home that receives a s28A[33] grant from the NHS to help towards the running costs of the home. If you are able to meet the fees of the care home (charged at a reduced rate due to the NHS grant payable) from your benefits (including DLA care component or AA) and/or other income and capital then you may not need, or in fact be able, to be placed in the care home by social services.[34] This is because you are able to organise and pay for your own accommodation and care (ie, it is 'otherwise available'[35] than being provided for by social services).

This does not mean that social services cannot help you with finding a suitable care home to meet your needs. However, you rather than social services would contract with the care home to provide your accommodation and care.

This type of arrangement means that for the purposes of DLA care component or AA you should not be considered to be in 'certain accommodation' (see p370). Therefore, (subject to the normal conditions of entitlement – see p139) DLA care component or AA should be payable. If your DLA care component or AA is suspended when you enter a care home under these arrangements you should seek advice (see Appendix 4).

Aftercare accommodation provided under section 117 Mental Health Act 1983 (England and Wales)

You may receive care in a care home as part of aftercare services provided under s117 of the Mental Health Act 1983 (MHA) if you have been previously detained in hospital under a compulsory order (see p387).[36] Currently, in these circumstances this chapter will apply to you as you will normally be entitled to IS and other benefits (subject to the other conditions of entitlement) in the same way as if you had been placed in a care home under the National Assistance Act 1948 (NAA) (but see p362 for DLA care and AA) even though social services cannot charge for accommodation provided under s117.[37]

This means that you would be receiving the normal rates of IS applicable to you without having to make any contribution to the costs of your accommodation and care whereas other people, perhaps placed in the same care home, under the provisions of the NAA would be required to make a contribution to the costs which would normally leave them with only the personal expenses allowance (see Chapter 13).

It is recognised that this is inconsistent with the intention that IS is payable in these circumstances for the purpose of helping you meet the costs of your accommodation and care, however there have been no changes to IS legislation yet.

It is not clear whether DLA care component is payable when you are placed in a care home under s117. Arguably, accommodation provided under this legislation is not treated as 'certain accommodation' as defined for the purposes of the prevention of payment of DLA care component or AA.[38] The MHA is not specifically referred to in the DLA or AA legislation,[39] unlike Part III of the NAA. However, it may be considered to fall within the provisions of 'any other enactment relating to persons under disability'[40] even though official guidance[41] does not include the MHA as an Act relating to people with disabilities.

Aftercare accommodation provided under section 7 Mental Health (Scotland) Act 1984

This Act places a similar legal duty on social work departments in Scotland to provide aftercare services (see p266). The benefit position is also the same, however social work departments in Scotland can charge for aftercare services, therefore this chapter and Chapter 10 are likely to apply in respect of residential aftercare services.

2. Types of stay

There are three basic types of stay in a care home.

- **Permanent stay**: there is no definition of a permanent stay although a working definition that is consistent with the definitions of temporary and trial period is a stay which is permanent from the day you enter the care home, or if you enter on a temporary or trial period basis, from any subsequent day on which you make the decision that you do not intend to return to the community to live.
- **Temporary stay**: social security legislation defines a temporary stay in terms of a temporary absence from your normal home in the community. The conditions are that:
  - you intend to return to your home in the community; *and*
  - the part of your home normally occupied by you has not been let or sub-let in the meantime; *and*
  - the period of your absence is unlikely to exceed 52 weeks, or, in exceptional circumstances, is unlikely to substantially exceed that period.[42]

A series, or planned programme of temporary stays are often referred to as respite stays.

- **Trial period stay**: is a stay in a care home which is treated as a temporary stay but 'for the purpose of ascertaining whether the accommodation suits [your] needs' and 'with the intention of returning to the dwelling which [you] normally occupy as [your] home should, in the event, the residential accommodation prove not to suit [your] needs'. In these circumstances IS housing costs, HB and CTB can continue to be paid for up to 13 weeks in respect of your home in the community, where:
  - you intend to return to your home (if the care home does not suit your needs); *and*
  - the part of your home normally occupied by you has not been let or sub-let in the meantime; *and*
  - the period of absence is unlikely to exceed 13 weeks.[43]

  You will also be entitled to those benefits for 13 weeks even if your absence extends beyond 13 weeks as long as your total absence does not exceed 52 weeks.[44] If the type of your stay changes (ie, in social security terms the reason for your absence changes once the absence has begun) it is the latest reason for absence which determines whether the temporary or trial period rules apply. Whether benefit is still payable for any period remaining will depend on whether you still satisfy the general qualifying rules for that period and on how long the absence has already lasted, as the period of absence is always measured from the date that you ceased to occupy your home in the community and not the date that the reason for your absence changed.

  Unlike for many other aspects of the social security benefits system, there are no linking rules for periods of absence. Therefore, if you are in a care home for a trial period or temporary stay and you genuinely return home for at least 24 hours, you can subsequently receive benefit for a fresh period of absence of either 13 weeks (trial period) or 52 weeks (temporary).

  There is no definition of 'trial period' for financial assessment and charging purposes (see p301) consequently, this can cause problems for the correct payment. For more information, see p405.

3. Social security benefits affected

If you go into a care home (see p356) either temporarily (including for a trial period) or permanently (see p362 for definitions) the following benefits may be affected:

- income support (IS)('minimum income guarantee' (MIG) for people aged 60 or over)/income-based jobseeker's allowance (JSA);
- pension credit (PC) (from October 2003);

- housing benefit (HB);
- council tax benefit (CTB);
- disability living allowance (DLA) care component and attendance allowance (AA) (including constant attendance allowance and exceptionally severe disablement allowance payable with industrial injury disablement benefit or war disablement benefit);
- social fund payments

The way these benefits are affected depends on whether the resident is:
- a temporary or permanent resident; *and*
- a single person or one of a couple.

See Chapter 18 for example calculations.

All other social security benefits (eg, DLA mobility component (but if your care home is considered to be a hospital or similar institution – see p358), state retirement pension or incapacity benefit) can be claimed and paid in the normal way when you are in a care home subject to the standard rules (see Chapter 7).

Income support/income-based jobseeker's allowance

In April 2002 the rules for the payment of IS in care homes changed.

If you have moved into a care home since April 2003 or if you moved into a care home since April 2002 but you were not in receipt of IS, any payment of, or claim for IS will be determined in the same way whether you are in a Part III local authority care home or an independent sector care home. For all new and repeat claims the old Part III local authority residential accommodation flat rate equivalent to the basic state pension (£77.45) and the independent care home residential allowance (£65.50) have been abolished.[45]

This means that if you are a resident claiming IS since 8 April 2002 you will have your IS calculated in the normal way, with a personal allowance and premiums (see Chapter 18 for example calculations).

If you were a resident in a care home in receipt of IS prior to April 2002, see the transitional protection rules on p368. These rules will apply to you until October 2003 when the Part III rate and residential allowance will be abolished for all residents and funding transferred to social services.

If you were in receipt of IS at the preserved rights rates[46] then you should have been transferred onto the standard rate of IS and social services funding from 8 April 2002 when preserved rights rates were abolished. There is no transitional protection.

If you enter, or are expected to enter, a care home for a period of no more than eight weeks, your IS can be altered or paid from the day of admission. If your stay is expected to be more than eight weeks, your IS can only be altered or paid from the start of your benefit week.[47]

If you are aged under 60 years, any claim for IS should be made on an A1 claim form. If you are aged 60 or over, IS is called the **'minimum income guarantee'** (MIG) and if you are going into a care home on a permanent basis you should use claim form MIG1R. If you are aged 60 or over and you are going into a care home for a temporary or trial period stay (see p362 for definitions) you should complete claim form MIG1. All claim forms are available from your local DWP office.

From October 2003 PC replaces IS/MIG for people aged 60 or over (see p176).

Capital limits in care homes

- **Temporary stay:** the IS capital limits that apply during a temporary stay are the same as those that apply in the community:
  - under 60 years; £3,000 lower limit, £8,000 upper limit;
  - 60 years or over; £6,000 lower limit, £12,000 upper limit.

  Capital at the lower limit or below is disregarded. A tariff income is applied to capital between the lower and upper limits of £1 for every £250 or part thereof. There is no entitlement to IS if you have capital above the upper capital limit.
- **Permanent stay:** the IS capital limits that apply during a permanent stay are £10,000 lower limit and £16,000 upper limit. These limits apply to all age groups. Capital at or below £10,000 is disregarded. A tariff income is applied to capital between £10,000 and £16,000 of £1 for every £250 or part thereof. There is no entitlement to IS if you have capital above £16,000.

Single person in a care home

- **Temporary stay:** the amount of any IS you receive will usually be the same as the amount you received in the community. However, where the severe disability premium and the enhanced disability premium (if applicable), are included in your IS, they will no longer be included where DLA care component or AA has ceased (see p367).
- **Permanently stay:** the amount of any IS you receive will usually be the same as the amount you received in the community. However, the amount of any IS you receive will change in the following circumstances:
  - If you have capital between £3,000 and £8,000 (under 60) or £6,000 and £12,000 (60 or over) then there will be a reduction in the amount of tariff income (and therefore an increase in IS) applied due to the different capital limits in a care home.
  - If you have capital between £8,000 and £16,000 (under 60) or £12,000 and £16,000 (60 or over) then you may become entitled to IS due to the upper capital limit applied in a care home.
  - If you are a single person living with a non-dependant in the community or you had a carer in receipt of carer's allowance in the community you may become entitled to, or there may be a change in, the amount of any IS payable due to the severe disability premium being included in your

applicable amount for the time that any DLA care component or AA remains in payment (see below).

Couple where both are in the same room in the same care home

- **Temporary stay**: there will usually be no change from the amount of any IS you receive as a couple in the community. You will still both be treated as a couple. However, where the severe disability premium and the enhanced disability premium (if applicable), are included in your IS, they will no longer be paid where DLA care component or AA has ceased (see p367).
- **Permanent stay**: caselaw suggests that if one or both of you are permanent residents you should not be treated as a couple.[48] This means that you should both be treated as single people with the appropriate single person's applicable amount – personal allowance and premiums. You and your partner's IS entitlement will be calculated using your individual resources and it will be paid to each of you separately. Housing costs will no longer be included in your applicable amount.

Couple where one member is in a care home or where both are in different care homes or both are in different rooms in the same care home

- **Temporary stay** (ie, temporarily separated): the applicable amount is either:
  - the normal personal allowance for a couple, plus any appropriate premiums at the couple rate, plus housing costs for your home in the community where appropriate; *or*
  - the aggregate of the normal personal allowance for each of you as if you were single people, plus any appropriate premiums for each of you at the single person rate, plus any housing costs for your home in the community where appropriate,

  whichever is the greater.[49]

  Usually, the greater amount will be two single person's applicable amounts. An exception is where one member of the couple is in a care home and the other is in hospital for more than 52 weeks.

  Note that if your stay in care is temporary, even if the single person applicable amounts are used, you and your partner will still be assessed as a couple in terms of your resources (capital and income), which will be aggregated and IS will be paid to the person who claims in respect of both of you.
- **Permanent stay:** you will no longer be treated as a couple. You will be treated as single people with the appropriate single person's applicable amount – personal allowance and premiums. Your IS entitlement will be calculated using your individual resources (capital and income) and it will be paid to each of you separately. Any jointly held capital will be assessed as split equally

between the two of you (see p228). Housing costs will no longer be included in the applicable amount of the person(s) in care.

The severe disability premium

Where you are entering a care home on a **permanent** basis and you are still in receipt of AA or DLA care component (middle or higher rate), the severe disability premium (SDP) should be included in your applicable amount as a single person or as one of a couple being treated as a single person.[50]

If you are entering a care home for a **temporary stay** (including respite and trial period stays), there is often confusion about whether or not the SDP should be included in your applicable amount.

If you are a **single person** in receipt of DLA care component (middle or higher rate) or AA and the SDP is not included in your applicable amount when you are in your home in the community because there is a 'non-dependant' living with you, or CA is in payment to your carer, then you will not be entitled to the SDP when you go temporarily into a care home.[51] If you do receive the SDP in your applicable amount when you are at home in the community then you will continue to receive it in the care home for a s long as you are in receipt of DLA care component (middle or higher rate) or AA.

If you are **one member of a couple** and you are temporarily separated from your partner, the SDP can be included in the applicable amount for each person in receipt of DLA care component (middle or higher rate) or AA even where it was not included in the applicable amount when you were at home (as long as CA is not paid to a person who cares for you). Until June 2002, guidance stated that this applies when you are a joint tenant or joint home owner with your partner.[52] However, a recent commissioner's decision held that this guidance was misconceived and that it was unlikely that it was intended that entitlement to the SDP should depend on the claimants property rights.[53] The commissioner further held that where a couple are assessed as single claimants (see p366) it implies that they are being treated as normally living apart for the purposes of calculating the applicable amount, therefore they cannot each be treated as a non-dependant of the other.[54] The commissioner concludes that in this case, where the temporary resident's wife was getting AA but the resident's AA had been suspended (as he had been in hospital for more than 28 days prior to his move into a care home), a single SDP should be included in their applicable amount.[55] It would be consistent with the approach in this decision for a single SDP to be included in the applicable amount of a temporary resident who was still in receipt of AA or DLA care component (middle or higher rate) where their partner in the community (or in hospital) would normally (when they were living together in the community) have prevented its inclusion.

As a result of the decision, guidance issued in June 2002 summarises the 'whichever is the greater' special assessment (see p366) and the commissioner's decision.[56] This guidance, with examples added, has been incorporated in the *Decision Makers Guide*.[57]

Transitional protection to the residential allowance and the Part III residential accommodation rate from April 2002 to October 2003

In April 2002 the residential allowance part of IS and the Part III residential accommodation rate were abolished for new claimants. However, if you were resident in a care home on 7 April 2002 and you were in receipt of the residential allowance or Part III rate, you are transitionally protected[58] and you will continue to be eligible for these amounts while you remain in, or you are only temporarily absent (see below) from the care home, until 5 October 2003 when the transitional protection ends.[59]

A temporary absence for the purpose of the residential allowance where you are not in hospital is up to three weeks.[60] If you are in hospital then under the new hospital downrating rules (see p380)[61] (which do not apply to AA and DLA) there is no reduction in social security benefits until you have been in hospital for a period of 52 weeks therefore the residential allowance will continue in payment during this temporary absence from the care home as long as your IS entitlement continues. Similarly, the Part III residential accommodation rate will continue to apply during a temporary absence of up to 52 weeks as long as your IS entitlement continues.

From 6 October 2003 resources for the payment of the residential allowance will be transferred to social services. In most cases this will increase the amount of the contribution from social services to the cost of your accommodation and care and will reduce the amount of the contribution that you are required to make. However, the amount you are left with after you have paid your contribution should not be affected – you will still be left with at least £17.50 (£17.80 in Wales) personal expenses allowance (see p330).

Any move from one independent care home to another or one local authority care home to another will not affect transitional protection as there would not be a break in entitlement.

Pension credit (from October 2003)

From October 2003, pension credit (PC – see p176) replaces IS/MIG for people aged 60 or over. PC has two components – the guarantee credit and, for pensioners aged 65 or over, the savings credit. Although PC rules are similar to IS rules, especially for the guarantee credit, there are some important differences which may affect entitlement when a person goes into a care home.

- For both components, capital under £6,000 for temporary residents or £10,000 for permanent residents is still ignored but there is no capital limit.
- For both components, tariff income on capital above £6,000 or £10,000 is £1 a week for every £500 or part thereof, instead of £1 for every £250.[62]

- For both components there will normally be a specified 'assessed income period' of five years or less.[63] During a typical five year award period certain elements of your income are treated as constant with deemed annual increases built in. It is not a fixed award as the deemed increases will alter the amount of the award from year to year.
  This will mean that usually, if you are in receipt of AA or DLA care component you will still need to inform the Disability Benefits Unit if you go into a care home permanently or if your temporary stay will be for more than 28 days (or less if you have been in hospital or a care home within the previous 29 days, as this period will be linked – see p373).
- Unlike for IS, there is no provision for the treatment of couples as two single people in terms of their applicable amount where one is going into a care home on a temporary basis. This means that you will continue to be treated as a couple which raises issues about the amount that social services include in your financial assessment as the amount left for your partner in the community should be sufficient to meet her/his needs.[64] If you are in a care home on a temporary basis at the point of transition from IS to PC, there will be a transitional additional amount payable within the appropriate amount of PC. This amount will be reduced by any future increases in the appropriate minimum guarantee.[65]
  Permanent residents will continue to be treated as single people for PC purposes.[66]
- From October 2003 you will be considered to be self-funding and therefore your AA or DLA care component will not cease after 28 days (or less if you have had a previous stay in hospital or a care home within the previous 29 days) where you are in receipt of PC (or IS) and have a social services contract at full cost (ie, there is no funding provided by social services) or funding is only being provided on a temporary repayable basis (see p380). See p376 for more information.

Housing benefit

You will not usually be able to get HB (see p180) towards the cost of a registered care home.[67] The exceptions are where:

- You were entitled to HB in respect of a independent sector care home on 29 October 1990. You remain eligible for HB in any independent sector care home without time limit.[68]
- You were entitled to HB on 31 March 1993 and you were either:
  - in remunerative work; *or*
  - paying a commercial rent to a non-resident close relative;[69] *or*
  - living in an unregistered home with less than four residents.

  You remain eligible for HB as long as you do not break your claim and you continue to live in the same home, disregarding temporary absences[70] of up to 13 or 52 weeks.[71]

As care homes (including local authority care homes) which provide personal care are now required to be registered, even if they do not also provide board (see p67)[72] it means that HB may no longer be payable to you as a 'less dependent resident'[73] once your care home becomes registered under the Care Standards Act 2000 (or in Scotland, the Regulation of Care (Scotland) Act 2001). Instead you may receive funding or additional funding for your accommodation from social services subject to the charging assessment (see p293).

If you go into a care home for a **temporary** stay (including respite stays – see p362) you can continue to receive HB in respect of your home in the community for up to 52 weeks. If you have entered a care home on a **trial period** basis (see p362), HB will be paid for up to 13 weeks in respect of your home in the community. You cannot usually get HB for your home in the community if you are in a care home and you decide to become a **permanent** resident, as you no longer 'normally occupy'[74] a home in the community (however, see p402).

If you become entitled to IS for the period of your stay in a care home, you will need to reclaim HB upon your return to your home in the community.

If you are **one of a couple** and you are going into care permanently while your partner is remaining at home in the community, you will need to make sure that your partner claims HB if it was previously claimed under your name.

Council tax benefit

You will only be able to get CTB if you are liable to pay council tax in respect of your home in the community (see p188). The rules for getting CTB during a **temporary** stay are the same as for HB (see p369).

If you are a **permanent** resident, and therefore the care home has become your 'sole or main' home, *and* your home in the community is left unoccupied, you will be exempt from council tax.[75]

If you are one of a couple and your partner is now living alone in your home in the community, s/he will be able to get a 25 per cent status discount on her/his council tax as a single person[76] and may qualify for CTB (see p188).

Disability living allowance care component and attendance allowance

The DLA care component and AA (including constant attendance allowance and exceptionally severe disablement allowance payable with industrial injury disablement or war disablement benefit) are affected by a stay, whether **temporary or permanent**, in 'certain accommodation' (also called 'special accommodation') other than hospitals (for the effect on DLA/AA of a stay in hospital or similar institution, see p204).

Certain accommodation

AA/DLA care component is not payable after a period of 28 days (see p205) in 'certain accommodation' unless you are considered to be self-funding (see p380).

The DLA mobility component is not affected by a stay in certain accommodation (but is affected by stays in hospitals or similar institutions – see p204). For the rules on whether your accommodation may be treated as a hospital or similar institution, see p356.

If your accommodation has been arranged as part of a programme of aftercare under s117 of the Mental Health Act 1983, see p361.

'Certain accommodation' is defined as where your accommodation is provided:

- in pursuance of Part III of the National Assistance Act 1948, or Part IV of the Social Work (Scotland) Act 1968 or s7 of the Mental Health (Scotland) Act 1984; *or*[77]
- in circumstances where the cost of the accommodation (see below) is borne wholly or partly out of public or local funds in pursuance of those enactments or any other enactment relating to persons under disability (or, for DLA care component only, to young persons or to education or training);[78] *or*
- in circumstances where the cost of the accommodation *may be borne* wholly or partly out of public or local funds in pursuance of those enactments or any other enactment relating to persons under disability (or, for DLA care component only, to young persons or to education or training).[79] This is sometimes called the 'may be borne' provision.

  It has been authoritatively confirmed that the 'may be borne' provision no longer has any significant effect in England and Wales[80] (although it may still apply in Scotland). This is because it was held that if you have made your own arrangements, there is no power for a local authority to intervene or make payments towards the cost unless the care home is not suitable for your needs.[81]

It will usually be clear when you are in 'certain accommodation'. Sometimes, however, it will be less clear as the rules can be complicated by many inter-related provisions and exceptions. If the DWP decides you are not entitled to AA or DLA care component because it is considered that you live in 'certain accommodation' and you have any doubts you should seek advice (see Appendix 4).

The 'cost of accommodation' referred to in the definition of 'certain accommodation' (see above) does not include:[82]

- domiciliary services provided for a person in a private dwelling; *or*
- improvements made to, or furniture and equipment provided for, a person in a private dwelling; *or*
- one-off irregular improvements made to, or furniture and equipment provided for, care homes for which a grant has been made out of public or local funds; *or*
- social and recreational activities provided outside the accommodation for which a grant has been made out of public or local funds; *or*

- the purchase or running of a motor vehicle to be used in connection with the accommodation for which a grant has been made out of public or local funds; *or*
- services provided pursuant to the National Health Service Act 1977 or the National Health Service (Scotland) Act 1978 – eg, free nursing care in care homes which provide nursing.

It should not always be assumed that arrangements made by social services for providing accommodation and care have necessarily been made under Part III of the National Assistance Act 1948 (NAA). Sometimes, social services may be using other powers to make payments towards the costs of your care or they may be contributing towards the running costs of the home, but are not actually contributing towards the costs of your own placement under Part III of NAA. In such circumstances, there is no reason why AA/DLA care component may not continue to be paid to you.[83] You should seek advice if your AA/DLA care has been suspended in these circumstances (see Appendix 4).

There have been a number of social security commissioners' decisions and court judgments on the issue of what constitutes 'certain accommodation'.

A social security commissioner held that a group home for people with learning disabilities should be treated as 'certain accommodation' even though the costs of the home were not borne out of public funds, there were no resident care staff (only visiting carers), and the residents were paying rent, were responsible for their own meals and paying for their other outgoings. This decision was based on the conclusion that the accommodation must have been provided under Part III of NAA because it was not accepted that there could be any other statutory basis for providing the accommodation. In that case the authority was a county council, and as any responsibility for providing housing was instead a district council responsibility, social services must, it was decided, have provided the accommodation under Part III.[84]

However, this decision appears to have been discredited, as another social security commissioner has taken a more reasoned view, finding that a county council may well have other powers to provide accommodation[85] and that it is not necessary to decide what they are. In this case, there was a lease in the form of a tenancy agreement, this was sufficient to show that the accommodation was not provided under Part III. Even though the accommodation was owned and managed by the county council, this was a fact which would only disentitle someone to AA/DLA care component if the cost of the accommodation is, or may be, borne out of public funds.[86] The commissioner also took the view that it would be unsatisfactory if entitlement to AA/DLA care component depended on whether a claimant lived within the boundaries of a county council (which are not housing authorities) or a metropolitan or unitary authority (which are both social services and housing authorities).[87]

A recent social security commissioner's decision has taken a similar approach stating that 'a home which is mainly used where arrangements have been made under Part III, or which was built for that purpose, could be used to accommodate a person to whom the local authority had no duty under Part III'.[88] In this case the claimant had moved from the respite unit in the local authority care home to a transition unit for the purpose of rehabilitation. During his stay in the transitional unit social services made contributions to the cost of his accommodation and care but it was held that these payments could not be payments under Part III of the NAA as there had been:

- no assessment of need under section 47 of the National Health Service and Community Care Act 1990 which was an essential gateway for the provision of services under Part III; *and*
- no standard charge identified for the accommodation; *and consequently*
- no assessment of individual ability to pay as required by NAA section 22.

The social security commissioner in this case went on to decide that accommodation could have been provided under section 137 of the Local Government Act 1972. This is a general power that gives local authorities the power to incur expenditure not authorised by any other enactment.[89]

Since October 2000 social services also has the power to provide accommodation under section 2 of the Local Government Act which promotes well-being. Section 2 was introduced in part as a response to what was seen as a restrictive view by the courts of the activities that can be pursued using section 137 of the Local Government Act 1972 which led to uncertainty amongst local authorities and their potential partners about the extent to which authorities can rely on their general powers to undertake certain activities.[90] Section 2 extends local authorities' general powers to enable them to have 'the freedom to work with other local public, private and voluntary organisations to develop solutions to local problems.[91]

The linking rule

There is an exception in the legislation that means that DLA care component or AA is usually payable for the first 28 days of a stay in 'certain accommodation'[92] even if you are not self-funding. However, if you have had a stay in certain accommodation or in a hospital or similar institution within the previous 28 days, that period of stay will be linked to your present stay so that benefit will only be paid for a total of 28 days including the period of your previous stay. The day you enter a care home and the day you leave do not count as days in certain accommodation.[93] If you first claim DLA care component or AA when you are already in certain accommodation it is not payable until you leave (unless you are self-funding). If you go into certain accommodation again (even within 28 days), your 28 day concession will start from the first day of that stay.

If you are receiving respite care (ie, a planned programme of temporary stays) you may be able to arrange a pattern of stays that allows you to keep your DLA care component or AA. The example illustrates how the 'linking rule' works.

Example

Mr Hammond is in receipt of AA and he has respite care every weekend. He goes into a care home on a Friday and leaves on the following Monday. This is counted as two days of respite care (Saturday and Sunday) because the day of entering (Friday) and the day of leaving (Monday) are not counted.

Mr Hammond continues with this pattern of respite care but he is mindful that each of his weekend stays after his first stay are being linked together because they are within 28 days of the previous stay. This means that after 14 weekend stays of two days each he has reached the end of his 28 days' payment of AA while in care. If Mr Hammond spent a 15th weekend in respite care, his AA would stop for the two days in care and only start in payment again when he went home until his next respite care stay, when it would stop again.

However, in order to avoid any break in the payment of his AA, Mr Hammond breaks the 'link' by having shorter respite care stays. For four weekends following the 14th weekend stay he doesn't go into the care home until the Saturday and he leaves on Sunday. As there are no days counted as days in care, he has effectively spent 29 days without a stay in care, thus breaking the link. On the 19th weekend, Mr Hammond goes back to going into the care home on a Friday and leaving on a Monday. If he continues to repeat this pattern his AA will be paid without any break for his stays in the care home.

For reasons demonstrated in the above example, it is important to inform the Disability Benefits Unit (see Appendix 3), as well as your local DWP office, of any stay in a care home and, if you have a pattern of respite care planned, to advise them of this in advance. If you cannot arrange your respite care to break the link, you will at some point have to send your order book back. In this situation, it may be better to receive your benefit by way of automatic credit transfer payments, as the Unit can adjust each credit transfer payment as necessary. You should contact the Disability Benefits Unit about this.

Social fund payments

If you are a permanent resident in a residential care or nursing home (see p362 for definitions) you are excluded from receiving a **crisis loan** from the discretionary social fund unless you are planning to move out within the next two weeks.[94]

For **community care grants** and **budgeting loans** the same rules apply as if you were living in the community (see p200) except that it is unlikely that you would satisfy the criteria for the purpose of a community care grant[95] unless it is to help with travel expenses in certain specified situations[96] or you are moving out of the care home into the community.[97]

The same rules as for people living in the community also apply for the regulated social fund payments for **funeral expenses** (see p197) and **Sure Start maternity grants** (see p199). However, as a permanent resident in a care home you cannot receive regulated **cold weather payments.**[98]

You are eligible to receive regulated **winter fuel payment**, subject to the same rules as if you were living in the community (see p199), if you are a resident in a care home as long as you are *not* in receipt of IS or income-based JSA (or PC from October 2003).[99] The amount of the payment will be 50 per cent of the annual lump sum which is currently £200.[100]

4. Self-funding (including 'loophole' cases and retrospective self-funding)

You are described as '**self-funding**' if you can meet the whole cost of your accommodation and care in a care home from your own resources (or with help from relatives, friends or a charity), without any financial help from social services, *and* without claiming income support (IS)/income-based jobseeker's allowance (JSA) and/or housing benefit (HB).[101] Until 19 June 2000 you could only count as self-funding for benefit purposes if you were in an independent sector care home. Since then the definition also includes those residents in a local authority care home.[102] You will also be treated as a self-funder if you receive help from the NHS with the nursing care element of your care in a care home which provides nursing.

You may be required to meet the whole cost of your accommodation and care because of the level of your income or capital (see Chapters 11 and 12). In most cases it is the level of a person's capital that determines whether they will be required to fund themselves.

If you are making your own arrangements to go into a care home but it is likely that your capital will eventually fall to the upper capital limits for your country (see p315) or less, it would be sensible to talk to social services first and perhaps have an assessment of your needs carried out so that there will not be a problem in the future if you ask for financial help from social services.

Disability living allowance care component/attendance allowance

If you are self-funding you will be able to continue receiving any DLA care/AA to which you are entitled beyond the first 28 days in a care home. Even if social services has helped you find the placement and contracted with the home to provide your accommodation and care, you will still be able to get DLA care/AA *as long as you are meeting the whole cost yourself* (or with help from relatives, friends or a charity) without IS or funding from social services.[103]

Note: From October 2003 the Government intends to break the link between the payability of DLA care/AA and income related benefits. If you are not receiving help with the cost of your accommodation and care (on a non-refundable basis) from social services, you will be able to continue to receive DLA care/AA even if you are in receipt of IS/PC. If you are receiving help with the cost of your accommodation and care from social services on a temporary refundable basis (ie, you are a retrospective self-funder), see p380.

'Loophole' cases

Note: With the intended changes to the payability rules of DLA care/AA in a care home from October 2003 (see above) there will no longer be 'loophole' cases where the payment of DLA care/AA and IS/PC at the same time is dependent on there not being a contract (at full cost) between social services and the care home for your accommodation and care. Until the implementation of these changes in October 2003 the following applies.

In **England** and **Wales** only, under the 'may be borne' provision (see p370), it was intended that the DLA care/AA should not be payable where your 'accommodation may be funded wholly or partly out of public funds which includes local authority funding'.[104] However, it has been shown that this provision has no real function because if you have made your own arrangements, social services do not have the power to intervene (as accommodation and care are 'otherwise available'[105]) unless the home is not suitable for your needs.[106]

Therefore as long as social services does not have a current contract with the care home for the provision and funding of your accommodation and care, you can continue to receive DLA care/AA after the first 28 days, *even if you receive IS*. You will therefore also be eligible for the severe disability premium to be included in your IS. This is called the **'loophole'** option as it allows for both IS and DLA care/AA to be in payment at the same time.

However, depending on the level of the fee for the care home, there is still likely to be a shortfall between the fee and the total amount of IS you receive (either on its own or as a top-up of other income such as state retirement pension) and DLA care/AA. The amount of the shortfall is greater since April 2002 when the residential allowance part of IS was abolished for new claims and from October 2003 the residential allowance part of IS will be abolished on all claims (see p368). This means that this option is no longer viable for the majority of residents.

If you can still meet the shortfall, this option may be particularly preferable if you have a property to sell and can meet the shortfall on a short-term basis until it is sold because, once your house is sold, any IS and DLA care/AA paid to you is not repayable to the DWP. If you are funded by social services you would lose your DLA care/AA (and the severe disability premium and enhanced disability premium where applicable) and, when your home is sold, you will have to repay social services all the money they had paid on your behalf.

Social services departments are advised by guidance that, as part of the whole assessment process, they should provide full information about the financial consequences of different options.[107] An Ombudsman case reported that a council had met the full costs of a placement in a care home in the period before the financial assessment was complete, on the assumption that the family could not do so until the resident's home was sold. It was accepted by the council that it should have put the option of paying the full cost to the family, given its knowledge of the rules governing the payment of AA. In this case the DWP decided that because social services had made payments wrongly, it could backdate AA for that period (albeit on an extra statutory basis).[108]

Also in a recent social security commissioner's case,[109] social services had become involved in a person's placement by contracting with the care home but the person was able to, and did, make the payments for their accommodation and care to the home out of their own resources, albeit that a claim for IS had been made (also the subject of an appeal). The case was remitted to a tribunal for rehearing with the direction that the question for determination by the new tribunal was not whether social services *did act* under the National Assistance Act 1948,[110] but whether it had *the power to act* – ie, whether the care and attention was 'otherwise available' and if it was there was no power to act, and therefore the 'loophole' provision could become effective and AA would be payable.

If you took advantage of the 'loophole' option before 8 April 2002 you may find that from October 2003 you can no longer manage to pay your own fees without the residential allowance in your IS. The Pension Service has written to everyone who took the 'loophole' option (and has offered to visit all residents) to explain the changes and advise them to contact their local social services office if they will need help paying care home fees from October 2003. However, some social services departments may not be aware of all the issues and better-off options needing to be explored, or they may turn people away until nearer October 2003. If you do not have a property to sell and your current benefit income with the residential allowance does not meet the cost of your care home you might want social services to start helping you with funding straightaway and not wait until October 2003. Seek advice if this applies to you.

In **Scotland**, the DWP has interpreted the same regulations as meaning that DLA care/AA cannot be paid to people who make their own arrangements. This is because the Scottish legislation gives social work departments wider powers to provide accommodation. Since July 2002, if you are 65 or over, you can get help from the local authority under the 'free personal care' arrangements and so most people will be funded by the local authority and not able to get DLA care/AA because of this.

The home owner self-funding maze

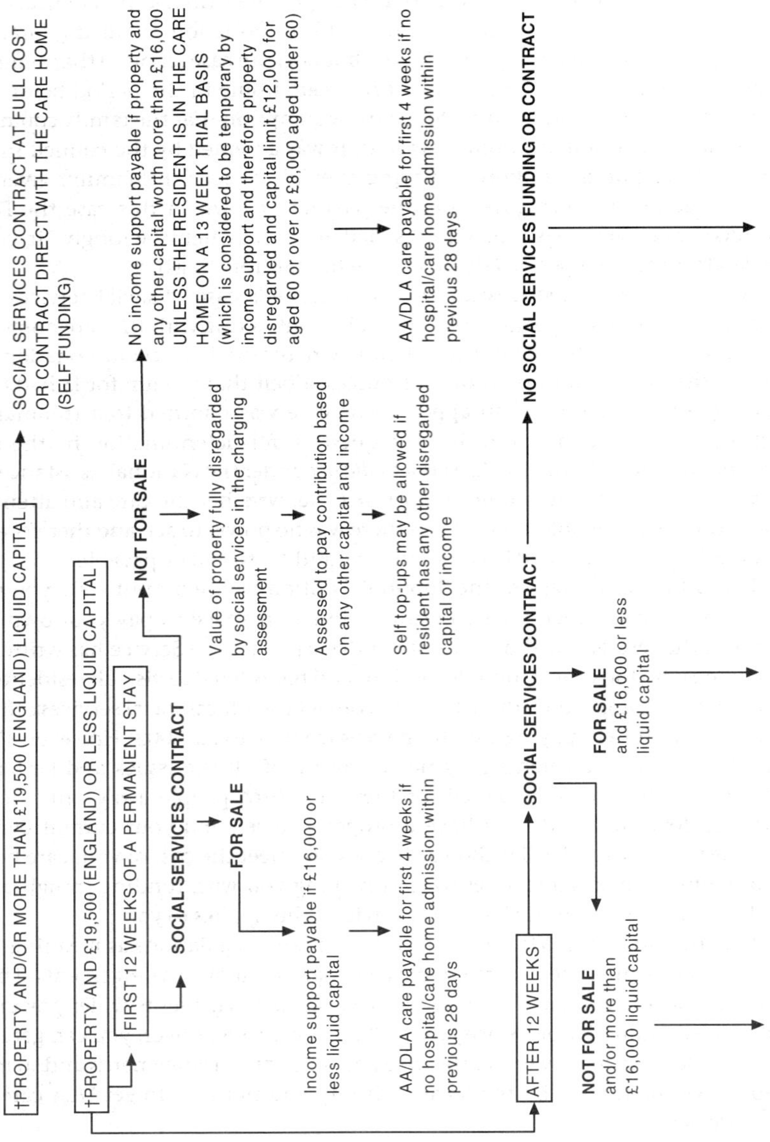

DEFERRED PAYMENT AGREEMENT
(Retrospective self-funding)

SOCIAL SECURITY BENEFITS
- AA/DLA care payable
- Income support not payable

DEFERRED PAYMENT AGREEMENT
(Retrospective self-funding)

SOCIAL SECURITY BENEFITS
- AA/DLA care payable as long as no income support in payment*
- Income support payable subject to normal conditions of entitlement*

LOOPHOLE PROVISION
(England and Wales only)

- AA/DLA care payable
- Income support payable
- Other benefits such as retirement pension, incapacity benefit remain in payment
- No recovery of charges as no social services funding
- Resident or relative/friend etc. will need to be able to meet the shortfall between care home fees and income**

- Other benefits such as Retirement pension, Incapacity benefit remain in payment

SOCIAL SERVICES CHARGES
- Assessed to pay contribution based on income (including AA/DLA care and income support) and any liquid capital
- Social services will recover the difference between the contribution and the full cost from the value of the property when it is eventually sold
- The resident can defer the amount of any self top-up if appropriate

Note: If the resident has a property but has not got enough other capital or income to pay the full cost and they do not wish to enter into a deferred payment agreement then social services can take a legal charge on the value of the property to recover the debt when the property is sold.

† Property normally occupied as the residents home and not disregarded under any of the defined (e.g. partner or disabled relative or relative over 60 still living there) or discretionary (where appropriate) circumstances. For Scotland liquid capital must be £11,500 or less to be eligible for a deferred payment agreement.

* If income support payable is less than AA/DLA payable the resident would usually be better off not claiming income support in order to receive AA/DLA care until October 2003 when the legislation is due to change (see p376).

** Typical income (April 2003 rates) for disabled pensioner is £145.05 income support (including any pension or other benefits) and either £57.20 or £38.30 AA/DLA care. Total Income £205.25 or £183.35. If the cost of the care home is £300 a shortfall of £97.75 or £116.65 plus any personal expenses will be required.

THIS DOCUMENT IS FOR INFORMATION PURPOSES ONLY AND IS NOT INTENDED AS AN AUTHORITATIVE STATEMENT OF LAW. SOCIAL SERVICES RECOMMEND THAT YOU SHOULD SEEK INDEPENDANT LEGAL/FINANCIAL ADVICE IF YOU ARE A HOME-OWNER GOING INTO A CARE HOME.

Retrospective self-funding

If you are required to meet the whole cost of your accommodation and care because you have a property worth more than the upper capital limit for your country (see p315), but you have not sold the property yet or you are awaiting the release of other funds and you do not have additional resources with which to pay the full cost, social services can make payments to the care home for your placement until your property is sold or your funds are released and you then refund social services. If you are awaiting the sale of your property or you have chosen not to sell your property social services has powers to create a legal charge on your property.[111]

Deferred payment agreements can be arranged where social services defer the difference between the full cost and the assessed contribution against the value of your property. The deferred payment is then recouped upon the eventual sale of the property (see p299). There was conflicting caselaw about whether DLA care/AA was payable for the period you were retrospectively self-funding in 'certain accommodation' (see p370). Essentially, this was finally settled by two social security commissioners' decisions[112] confirming the approach taken by the Court of Appeal in Northern Ireland[113] that claimants were not prevented from receiving DLA care/AA if social services is only making payments toward the cost of the accommodation and care on a refundable basis – ie, they were retrospectively self-funding. The current rules mean that you are only considered to be retrospectively self-funding and entitled to DLA care/AA if you are not getting IS (or income-based JSA or HB); however, from October 2003 it is intended that getting these benefits or PC will not prevent the payment of DLA care/AA as a retrospective self-funder.

Guidance followed in August 2001 stating that 'benefits should be paid unless and until the point is reached where there is a real risk that the proceeds are inadequate to make full repayment'.[114] Written evidence of an agreement to repay social services from the sale proceeds or release of funds will need to exist.[115]

The flow chart *The home owners self-funding maze* (see p378) looks at the choices available and the benefits and charging implications if you are self-funding because you are a homeowner.

5. Temporary absences from care homes (including going into hospital)

Until the Budget statement on 9 April 2003, the rules for the rates of benefits payable when a person went into hospital from a care home were different to those applied when a person went into hospital from the community. With the announcement which had immediate effect, the planned extension of the period before the downrating of benefits from 6 to 13 weeks was superseded.[116] The downrating of benefits does not occur now until after a period of 52 weeks as an inpatient.[117] These rules (which do not apply to DLA or AA) also apply to you if you are temporarily absent from a care home because you have gone into hospital.[118]

This means that where you have transitional protection to the residential allowance part of IS until it is abolished in October 2003, it will continue in payment for any temporary absence due to hospital admission of up to 52 weeks instead of the six weeks previously allowed (see p368).

If you are temporarily absent from a care home for any other reason (eg, you are visiting friends or relatives) any residential allowance included in your IS until its abolition in October 2003 will continue for three weeks.

During these types of temporary absence the DLA care component or AA may become payable. Consequently, you may also become entitled to the severe disability premium in your IS applicable amount.

6. Other sources of financial assistance in care homes

Health benefits

If you are a permanent resident in a care home and your placement is being wholly or partly funded by social services you can obtain an HC2 certificate from the Health Benefits Division of the Prescription Pricing Authority for full exemption from NHS charges (eg, prescriptions, dental treatment) and fares to hospital by completing a special short application form HC1(RC).[119] This exemption does not, however, apply to charges for sight tests and glasses, but you may be exempt on other grounds (see p95). The capital limit is £19,500 with tariff income rules applied for capital in excess of £12,000. Your certificate will last for 12 months and you should make a repeat claim about four weeks before your certificate expires.

If you do not receive any funding for your placement from social services you may still be able to get a full or partial exemption for the same charges under the normal rules that apply for health benefits in the community (see p95).

Special help for war pensioners

If you get a war disablement pension or you have had a gratuity for your disability, you can apply to the Veterans Agency (previously called the War Pensions Agency) for free medical treatment and services that you need wholly or mainly because of that disability. You are not means-tested for these services (ie, it does not matter how much income or capital you have), but you must apply before arranging for them.

You may be able to get help for the fees of care homes which provide nursing where you are provided with skilled nursing care if you need permanent care in a care home, or if you need a short break for convalescence, or if you need a respite break in order to give your carer a break.

For a permanent stay in a care home which provides nursing you must need 24-hour nursing care because of your pensioned disability. The Veterans Agency can pay up to a maximum of £437 (£497 in London) a week for fees provided that social services has not been involved in assessing your nursing needs or arranging a placement. A higher rate can be paid if there is no other care home which provides nursing which is suitable for your needs. In this situation your basic war disablement pension will continue to be paid in full while you are in the nursing home but any constant attendance allowance payable will stop after four weeks. Some other extra allowances such as unemployability supplement are reduced or withdrawn after eight weeks.

For a short-term break for convalescence you can claim nursing home fees for a maximum of four weeks a year. However, if you have recently been discharged from hospital or are recovering from an operation, the Veterans Agency is unlikely to pay as it considers this is an NHS responsibility.

For a respite break you may be able to claim nursing home fees if your carer needs a break from caring for you for medical reasons (medical evidence is required).

Other expenses for medical treatment and services may also be available. You can ask your local war pensioners' welfare officer to visit you to discuss your needs and help you apply for any services.

Help from charities

A charity may be able to help you with some of the costs of a stay in a care home if your benefits and/or social services funding cannot meet the full charges of the home. This may happen where the charge for a care home is more expensive than the amount usually allowed by social services and you cannot meet the shortfall.

Your social services department may know of appropriate charities that you could contact. There are also publications (eg, *Guide to Grants for Individuals in Need* or the *Charities Digest*) available from your local library.

The organisations Counsel and Care for the Elderly,[120] the Elderly Accommodation Council[121] or the Royal United Kingdom Beneficent Association[122] may be able to help you find an appropriate charity.

7. Effects on carers

If you are the carer of a person who goes into a care home for a temporary (including respite or trial periods) or permanent stay, the following benefits you receive will be affected:

- carer's allowance (CA) (previously called invalid care allowance)(see p150);
- income support (IS)/income-based jobseeker's allowance (JSA) or pension credit (PC) from October 2003 (see p210).

If the person you are caring for receives disability living allowance (DLA) care component (middle or higher rates) or attendance allowance (AA), you may be claiming CA for caring for them. The CA rules allow breaks in care of up to 12 weeks within a 26-week period. Up to four weeks of the 12-week period are allowed for any temporary breaks in care – eg, holidays or if the person you care for goes into a care home for a temporary or respite stay. The remaining eight weeks of the 12-week period allow for either you, as the carer, or the person you care for, to undergo medical or other treatment as an inpatient in hospital. However, if the person you care for goes into hospital or into a care home and they are not self-funding, their DLA care component or AA will stop after four weeks, or sooner if they have had a previous stay in hospital or a care home within the previous 28 days (see p375). This means your CA will also stop.

The person you care for may be able to arrange a pattern of respite care that allows them to keep their DLA care component or AA (see example on p374) thus allowing you to keep your CA. All changes of circumstances (yours or the person you care for) must be reported to the CA Unit. The main rule to remember is that you can be paid CA for any week (Sunday through to Saturday) in which you are caring for the disabled person for at least 35 hours, so odd days or weekends away are unlikely to affect your entitlement.

If the person you care for goes into a care home permanently, and your CA stops, you continue to be eligible for IS with the carer's premium (£25.10) included in your IS applicable amount or from October 2003 the carer's rate of PC for a further eight weeks. After this you may need to claim income-based JSA instead if you are under 60. The carer's premium is also included in any calculation for housing benefit, council tax benefit, income-based JSA and health benefits for eight weeks after your CA stops (see p171).

If, as a carer, you are also responsible for the disabled person's benefits because they cannot manage their financial affairs (ie, you are their appointee/attorney/receiver – see p111) you may wish to continue in this role when the disabled person is living in a care home. In this capacity you may also have the added responsibility of forwarding the contribution to social services for their accommodation and care costs and of providing information for the social services financial assessment. If you do not wish to have this responsibility you could choose to relinquish the appointeeship in favour of social services. The social services office responsible for organising the disabled person's placement should be able to give you further information about this.

Notes

1. Types of care home

1 s117 and Sch 6 CSA 2000
2 The definitions of 'nursing home' and 'residential care home' were moved from reg 19 to reg 2(1) ISG Regs on 8.4.02 when reg 19 was repealed. The definition of 'residential accommodation' can still be found in reg 21(3) ISG Regs to which reg 2(1) refers.
3 paras 77005 and 77006 DMG; reg 1(2) SPC Regs
4 paras 77007 and 77008 DMG; reg 1(2) SPC Regs
5 s28 NHSA 1977
6 CSA 2000
7 Reg 7(1)(k) HB Regs
8 SS(HIP&MA) Regs 2003 SI 2003 No.1195
9 Reg 2(2) SS(HIP) Regs; reg 8(1) SS(DLA) Regs; reg 6(1) SS(AA) Regs; reg 21 IS Regs
10 CP/63/1988; CIS/371/1990; CDLA/7980/95; CDLA/2496/97
11 *White and Others v CAO, The Times,* 2 August 1993; R(IS) 18/94; *Botchett v CAO, The Times, 8 May 1996* (R(IS) 10/96)
12 Reg 2(2) SS(HIP) Regs; reg 8(1) SS(DLA) Regs; reg 6(1) SS(AA) Regs 1991
13 NHSA 1997, NHS(S)A 1978, NHSCCA 1990
14 CIS/371/1990; CDLA/2496/1997; CDLA/7980/1995
15 CP/63/1988 – CIS/371/1990; *White and Others v CAO, The Times*, 2 August 1993 (R(IS) 18/1994); CDLA/7980/1995; CDLA/2496/1997
16 CDLA/7980/1995
17 CIS/371/1990
18 CDLA/2496/1997
19 *Botchett v CAO, The Times, 8 May 1996;* CIS/371/1990; R(IS) 10/1996; *White and Others v CAO, The Times*, 2 August 1993; R(IS) 18/1994
20 *White and Others v CAO, The Times*, 2 August 1993; R(IS) 18/1994
21 s65 NHSA 1977; s58 NHS(S)A 1978 or Sch 2 para 14 NHSCCA 1990; Sch 7A NHS(S)A 1978
22 CS/249/1989 and R(IS) 7/92
23 CS/249/1989 held that a person needs to be in hospital 24 hours a day to be treated as maintained free of charge as an inpatient. CIS/192/1991 and CS/94/1992 held that absences during the 24-hour period do not affect inpatient status nor that of being maintained free of charge.
24 Reg 2(2) SS(HIP) Regs as amended by reg11 SS(MP)(No.2) Regs (16 November 1992)
25 CIS/3325/2000 and others
26 Reg 2(2) SS(HIP) Regs as amended by reg 11 SS(MP)(No.2) Regs (16 November 1992)
27 Reg 10(7) SS(DLA) Regs; reg 8(5) SS(AA) Regs
28 Reg 12B(9A) SS(DLA) Regs
29 Reg 10(6) SS(DLA) Regs; reg 8(4) SS(AA) Regs
30 s26 NAA 1948
31 s22 NAA 1948
32 Under NA(AR) Regs
33 s28A NHSA 1977 payable to housing associations and charitable or voluntary organisations as well as social services
34 Under Part III NAA 1948
35 s21 Part III NAA 1948
36 ss3, 37, 47 or 48 MHA 1983
37 *R v Redcar & Cleveland BC ex parte Armstrong; R v Manchester City Council ex parte Stennett; R v Harrow London BC ex parte Cobham* HL 25.7.02
38 Reg 7(1) SS(AA) Regs; reg 9(1) SS(DLA) Regs
39 Reg 9(1)(a) SS(DLA) Regs; reg 7(1)(a) SS(AA) Regs
40 Reg 9(1)(b) and (c) SS(DLA) Regs; reg 7(1)(b) and (c) SS(AA) Regs
41 para 61715 and Appendix 1 (Chapter 61) DMG

2. Types of stay

42 Sch 3 para 3(11) IS Regs; reg 5(8B) HB Regs; reg 4C(4) CTB Regs
43 Sch 3 paras 3(8)-(10) IS Regs; regs 5(7B)-(8) HB Regs; regs 4(1)-(3) CTB Regs
44 CIS/613/1997

3. **Social security benefits affected**

45 SSA(RCNH) Regs
46 *See* Chapter 20, 3rd edn *Paying for Care Handbook*
47 Reg 26 and Sch 7 para 7(2)(c) SS(C&P) Regs
48 CIS/4934/1997; CIS/4935/1997; CIS/5232/1997; CIS/5237/1997 and CIS/3767/1997 and common appendix to these decisions.
49 Sch 7 para 9 IS regs
50 para 23230 DMG and Reg 3(4) IS regs
51 para 23229 DMG and Reg 3(1) IS regs
52 para 23230 DMG and Reg 3(4) IS regs
53 para 13 CIS/1544/2001
54 para 12 CIS/1544/2001
55 para 13 CIS/1544/2001
56 DMG letter 05/02, 14 June 2002
57 DMG vol 4 para 23231-33 amended November 2002
58 DWP News Release *New simplicity for care home customers,* 21 May 2002
59 Reg 21(1B) and Sch 2 para 2A(6) IS Regs and Memo DMG vol JSA/IS 09 (January 2002)
60 Reg 2(1A) IS Regs and para 13 Memo DMG vol JSA/IS 09 (January 2002)
61 SS(HIP&MA) Regs 2003 SI 2003 No.1195
62 s15(2) SPCA 2002; reg 15(6) SPC Regs
63 para 24267 vol 4 Amendment 7 August 2002 DMG
64 Reg 5(1)(a) and Sch 2 paras 4(8), (11)(c)(ix) and (12) SPC Regs
65 Sch 1 part III para 6 SPC Regs 2002
66 Reg 5(1)(b) SPC Regs
67 Reg 7(1)(k) HB Regs
68 Reg 7(2)(c) & (d) HB Regs
69 Reg 2(1) HB Regs
70 Reg 5(8) & (8B) HB Regs
71 Reg 7(4)-(12) HB Regs
72 CSA 2000; RC(S) Act 2001
73 Reg 8(2) HB Regs
74 Reg 5(1) HB Regs
75 CT(ED)0 amended from 1 April 1994
76 s11 (England and Wales) and s79 LGFA (Scotland)1992
77 Reg 9(1)(a) SS(DLA) Regs; reg 7(1)(a) SS(AA) Regs
78 Reg 9(1)(b) SS(DLA) Regs; reg 7(1)(b) SS(AA) Regs
79 Reg 9(1)(c) SS(DLA) Regs; reg 7(1)(c) SS(AA) Regs
80 *Steane v CAO and Another* HL 24 July 1996; CA/2985/1997
81 The power under Part III of NAA 1948 applies only to accommodation which is not 'otherwise available' to the claimant.
82 Reg 7(5) SS(AA) Regs; reg 9(6) SS(DLA) Regs as amended by the SS(AA/DLA) Regs
83 *Steane v CAO and Another* HL 24 July 1996
84 CDLA/13479/1996
85 CDLA/1465/1998
86 s28 HA 1985 (reserve powers to provide housing accommodation) or s31 (powers of bodies corporate to sell or let land for housing purposes).
87 Reg 9(1)(b) and (c) SS(DLA) Regs; reg 7(1)(b) and (c) SS(AA) Regs
88 CDLA/2127/2000 para 21
89 CDLA/2127/2000 para 50
90 *Explanatory Notes* to Local Government Act 2000 para 8
91 *Explanatory Notes* to Local Government Act 2000 para 11
92 Reg 10(1) SS(DLA) Regs; reg 8(1) SS(AA) Regs
93 Reg 10(2) SS(DLA) Regs; reg 8(2) SS(AA) Regs
94 SF Dir 15
95 SF Dir 4
96 SF Dir 4(b)
97 SF Dir 4(a)(i)
98 Reg 1A(3) SFCWP Regs
99 Reg 1(2)(3) & (3A) SFWFP Regs
100 Reg 2(b)(ii) SFWFP Regs

4. **Self-funding (including 'loophole' cases and retrospective self-funding)**

101 Reg 10(8) SS(DLA) Regs; reg 8(6) SS(AA) Regs
102 Reg 10(9) SS(DLA) Regs; reg 8(7) SS(AA) Regs
103 para 61715 and 61735 DMG
104 Reg 9(1)(c) SS(DLA) Regs; reg 7(1)(c) SS(AA) Regs
105 s21(1)(a) NAA 1948
106 *Steane v CAO* 1996; para 61723 DMG
107 Part 1D of letter to Directors of Social Services dated 12 September 1994 from ACC and AMA
108 Complaint No.98/C/1842 against Stockport MBC, 30 March 1999
109 CA/2985/1997
110 s21(1)(a) NAA 1948
111 s22 HASSASSAA 1983 and s55 HSCA 2001
112 CA/2604/98 and CA/2937/1997
113 CARC 3117 NI Court of Appeal, *CAO and Creighton et al*, 15 December 1999

114 para 61775 vol 10 DMG Amendment 2, 2 August 2001
115 para 61777 vol 10 DMG Amendment 2, 2 August 2001

5. Temporary absences from care homes

116 DWP Press Release 9.4.03 PENS0904 – Budget
117 SS(HIP&MA) Regs
118 Reg 2(9) SS(HIP&MA) Regs

6. Other sources of financial assistance in care homes

119 Reg 4(m) NHS(TERC) Regs
120 Twyman House, 16 Bonny Street, London NW1 9PG; tel: 0845 300 7585
121 46A Chiswick High Road, London W4 1SZ; tel: 020 8742 1182
122 Tel: 020 7602 6274

Chapter 18

Calculations – benefits and charges

This chapter covers:

1. Basic example income support and contribution calculations (below)
2. Complex example income support and contribution calculations (p394)

All examples assume that social services undertakes a financial assessment for any length of stay in a care home (although this is not always the case – see p294). The examples also assume a lower capital limit of £12,000 and an upper capital limit of £19,500 which apply in England. For Scotland the capital limits are £11,500 and £18,500 and for Wales the capital limits are £12,500 and £20,000.

From October 2003, pension credit (PC) replaces income support (IS) and minimum income guarantee (MIG) for people aged 60 or over. Although PC rules are similar to IS rules, there are some important differences which may affect entitlement when a person goes into a care home (see p368).

This means that the IS calculation part of each example where PC is claimed instead of IS/MIG will not apply and a similar calculation for PC entitlement will need to be undertaken.

An award of PC instead of IS/MIG for one of a couple going into a care home for a temporary stay will also have an effect on the contribution calculation in terms of how the amount of PC awarded to one member of the couple in respect of both members will be split to allow an appropriate amount each. This is because, under PC rules, a couple's appropriate amount will no longer be the total of the two single people's appropriate amounts added together (see p368).

1. Basic example income support and contribution calculations

This section includes examples for:

- single person, local authority or independent care home, temporary stay (Example 1 – p388);

- single person, local authority or independent care home, permanent stay (Example 2 – p389);
- couple – one entering a local authority or independent care home, temporary stay (Example 3 – p391)
- couple – one entering a local authority or independent care home, permanent stay (Example 4 – p392).

Example 1: Single person, local authority or independent care home, temporary stay

Mr Thomas (86) is a single person living in a rented council house.
His income before entering the care home is made up of state retirement pension, income support (IS) and attendance allowance (AA).
Mr Thomas also receives maximum housing benefit and council tax benefit (CTB).
He has savings of £7,000.
He goes into the care home for a temporary stay of two weeks.

Income support calculation

Mr Thomas's IS was, and continues to be calculated in the following way:

Income	State retirement pension	£91.65
	Tariff income from savings	£4.00
	Total	**£95.65**

(AA of £57.20 disregarded)

Applicable amount	£54.65	(Personal allowance)
	£47.45	(Higher pensioner premium)
	£42.95	(Severe disability premium)
Total	**£145.05**	

Applicable amount (£145.05) *minus* **Income** (£95.65) = **IS** (£49.40)

Mr Thomas is entitled to IS of £49.40 a week paid on top of his state retirement pension and AA.

Contribution calculation

Social services calculates his contribution to the charge based on his financial assessment.
There are different capital rules that apply for financial assessment purposes. Any capital/savings of £12,000 or less is disregarded so Mr Thomas's savings of £7,000 are completely disregarded in the financial assessment.
His contribution to the cost of his accommodation and care will be calculated in the following way:

Income	State retirement pension	£91.65
	Income support	£49.40
	Total	**£141.05**

(AA of £57.20 disregarded)

Outgoings	Water rates	£4.00
	Standard charges for fuel	£2.50
	Total	**£6.50**
Personal expenses allowance (PEA)		**£17.50**

Income (£141.05) *minus* **Outgoings** (£6.50) *minus* **PEA** (£17.50) = **Contribution** (£117.05)

Mr Thomas's contribution to the cost is £117.05 a week.
Mr Thomas will be left with £81.20 a week (AA, outgoings and PEA).
The full cost of social services residential accommodation is £291 a week.
Social services contribution to the cost is £173.95 a week.

Example 2: Single person, local authority or independent care home, permanent stay

Mr Smith (58) is a single person. He is a home owner (without a mortgage) and he lives with his sister (70). His income before entering the care home is made up of long-term incapacity benefit (IB), work pension and disability living allowance (DLA) care and mobility components. He also receives some CTB. Mr Smith is not entitled to in IS while he is living in the community.

Usually, for a single person the amount of IS payable in the care home would be the same as that paid in the community. However, an exception is where a person is living with a non-dependant in the community as this has an effect on eligibility for the severe disability premium.

He goes into a care home which provides nursing, on a permanent basis. As he is a permanent resident in the care home, he is no longer liable for council tax.

Mr Smith makes a claim for IS. His home in the community is not taken into account as his elderly sister is still living there.

Income support calculation

Mr Smith's claim for IS is calculated in the following way:

Income	IB (long-term)	£87.30
	Work pension	£6.00
	Total	**£93.30**

(DLA mobility component £39.95 disregarded as income)
(DLA care component £57.20 payable for first 4 weeks but disregarded as income)

Applicable amount 1	£54.65	(Personal allowance)
(first 4 weeks)	£23.30	(Disability premium)
	£11.40	(Enhanced disability premium)
	£42.95	(Severe disability premium)
Total	**£132.30**	

Applicable amount (£132.30) *minus* **Income** (£93.30) = **IS** (£39.00)

Mr Smith is entitled IS of £39.00 a week for the first 4 weeks of his stay (paid on top of his long-term IB, work pension and DLA).

Applicable amount 2	£54.65	(Personal allowance)
(after 4 weeks)	£23.30	(Disability premium)
Total	***£77.95***	

The severe disability premium and enhanced disability premium are only applicable while Mr Smith continues to receive the qualifying benefit of DLA care component, but this is stopped after 28 days in the care home.

Applicable amount (£77.95) *minus* **Income** (£93.30) = **IS** (nil)

Mr Smith is not entitled to IS after 4 weeks of his stay as he has excess income of £15.35 a week (his only income will be his long-term IB, work pension and DLA mobility component).

Contribution calculation

Mr Smith's IS claim has been decided by the DWP, he informs social services and they amend his financial assessment. His home in the community is not taken into account as capital because his elderly sister is still living there. There are no disregards on Mr Smith's income for 'outgoings' as he is permanently away from his home in the community.

Mr Smith's contribution to the cost of his accommodation and care will be calculated in the following way:

Income 1	IB (long-term)	£87.30
(first 4 weeks)	Work pension	£6.00
	IS	£39.00
	DLA care component	£57.20
	Total	**£189.50**

(DLA mobility component £39.95 disregarded as income)

Personal expenses allowances (PEA) **£17.50**

Income (£189.50) *minus* **PEA** (£17.50) = **Contribution** (£172.00)

Mr Smith's contribution to the cost for the first 4 weeks is £172.00 a week.
Mr Smith will be left with £57.45 a week (DLA mobility component and PEA).
The full cost of the nursing home is £420 a week.
Social services' contribution to the cost for the first 4 weeks is £248 a week.

Income 2	IB (long-term)	£87.30
(after 4 weeks)	Work pension	£6.00
	Total	**£93.30**

(DLA mobility component £39.95 disregarded as income)

Personal expenses allowances (PEA) **£17.50**

Income (£93.30) *minus* **PEA** (£17.50) = **Contribution** (£75.80)

Mr Smith's contribution to the cost after 4 weeks is £75.80 a week.
Mr Smith will be left with £57.45 a week (DLA mobility component and PEA).

The full cost of the care home is £420 a week.
Social services' contribution to the cost after the first 4 weeks is £344.20 a week.

Example 3: Couple – one entering a local authority or independent care home, temporary stay

Mr and Mrs Gill, aged 65 and 63 years respectively, are joint home owners (without a mortgage). Mr Gill's weekly income before entering the care home is made up of state retirement pension, IS and DLA care and mobility components. Mrs Gill receives state retirement pension and she has an underlying entitlement to carer's allowance. Maximum CTB is in payment. Mr Gill goes into a care home for a temporary stay of three weeks.

Income support calculation

The IS in payment to Mr Gill for Mrs Gill and himself as a couple is recalculated in the following way:

Income	State retirement pension (Mr Gill)	£86.35
	State retirement pension (Mrs Gill)	£46.35
	Work pension (Mr Gill)	£5.75
	Total	**£138.45**

(DLA mobility component (Mr Gill) £39.95 disregarded as income)
(DLA care component (Mr Gill) £38.30 disregarded as income)

Applicable amount

Mr Gill	£54.65	(Personal allowance)
	£47.45	(Single higher pensioner premium)
	£42.95	(Severe disability premium)
Mrs Gill	£54.65	(Single personal allowance)
	£47.45	(Single pensioner premium)
	£25.10	(Carer's premium)
Total	**£272.25**	

Applicable amount (£272.25) *minus* **Income** (£138.45) = **IS** (£133.80)

Mr and Mrs Gill are entitled to IS of £133.80 a week payable to Mr Gill as the claimant (on top of Mr Gill's state retirement pension, work pension and DLA, and Mrs Gill's state retirement pension).

IS is payable at a higher rate while Mr Gill is staying in a care home than it was when they were both in the community. This is because their applicable amount is calculated as if they were single people. Their income is still added together because Mr Gill is only a temporary resident in the care home. During Mr Gill's temporary stay, they will continue to receive maximum council tax benefit as they remain entitled to IS.

Contribution calculation

After Mr and Mrs Gill's IS has been reconsidered by the DWP, they inform social services and Mr Gill's financial assessment is amended. Although Mr and Mrs Gill are a couple, for financial assessment purposes Mr Gill, as the person going into care, will be assessed on his income *only*.

However, as Mr Gill receives IS for himself and Mrs Gill based on a calculation of their joint income, social services will consider increasing his PEA in order to allow enough for Mrs Gill to meet her personal expenses.

If the PEA is increased so that Mr Gill can give Mrs Gill an appropriate amount to meet her living expenses then the 'outgoings' can be shared equally and only half of the total amount disregarded from Mr Gill's income. (Note, if there were any other adults living with Mr and Mrs Gill, the 'outgoings' would be shared between the total number of people sharing the home and only Mr Gill's appropriate share allowed as a disregard on his income.)

Mr Gill's contribution to the cost of his accommodation and care will be calculated in the following way:

Income	State retirement pension	£86.35
	Work pension	£5.75
	IS	£133.80
	Total	**£225.90**

(DLA mobility component £39.95 disregarded as income)
(DLA care component £38.30 disregarded as income)

Outgoings	Water rates (£4.50 ÷ 2)	£2.25
	Standard charge for fuel (£2.50 ÷ 2)	£1.25
	Building and contents insurance (£10 ÷ 2)	£5.00
	Total	**£8.50**
Personal expenses allowance (PEA)		
(normal rate for Mr Gill)		£17.50
(amount for Mrs Gill)*		£80.85
Total		**£98.35**

*The amount for Mrs Gill is calculated on the basis of her IS applicable amount of £127.20 minus her income of £46.35 state retirement pension.

Income (£225.90) *minus* **Outgoings** (£8.50) *minus* **PEA** (£98.35) = **Contribution** (£119.05)

Mr Gill's contribution to the cost is £119.05 a week.
Mr Gill will be left with £185.10 a week (£80.85 of which he will give to Mrs Gill).
The full cost of the care home is £252 a week.
Social services' contribution to the cost is £132.95 a week.

Example 4: Couple – one entering a local authority or independent care home, permanent stay

Mr and Mrs Cooper aged 65 and 55 years respectively are council tenants. Mr Cooper's weekly income is made up of state retirement pension and a work pension. Mrs Cooper's weekly income before entering the care home is made up of short-term IB and DLA care and mobility components. They have joint savings of £22,000. They are not entitled to IS as a couple in the community. Mrs Cooper goes into a care home on a permanent basis.

As Mr and Mrs Cooper are now permanently separated they will be treated as single people for IS purposes. Mr Cooper's income (£82.35 state retirement pension, £28 work pension, £20 tariff income) is higher than his applicable amount (£54.65 personal allowance, £47.45 pensioner premium); therefore he is not entitled to IS. Mrs Cooper claims IS as a single person. It is calculated in the following way:

Income support calculation

Income	IB (short-term)	£64.35
	Tariff income from savings	£4.00
	Total	**£68.35**

(DLA care component: £57.20 payable for first 4 weeks but disregarded as income)
(DLA mobility component: £15.15 disregarded as income)

Applicable amount 1	£54.65	(Single personal allowance)
(first 4 weeks)	£23.30	(Disability premium)
	£11.40	(Enhanced disability premium)
	£42.95	(Severe disability premium)
Total	**£132.30**	

Applicable amount (£132.30) *minus* **Income** (£68.35) = **IS** (£63.95)

Mrs Cooper is entitled to IS of £63.95 a week for the first 4 weeks of her stay (paid on top of her IB and DLA).

Applicable amount 2	£54.65	(Single personal allowance)
(after 4 weeks)	£23.30	(Disability premium)
Total	**£77.95**	

Applicable amount (£77.95) *minus* **Income** (£68.35) = **IS** (£9.60)

Mrs Cooper is entitled to IS of £9.60 a week after 4 weeks of her stay (paid on top of her IB and DLA).

After 4 weeks Mrs Cooper's DLA care component would stop and therefore the severe disability and enhanced disability premiums would not be included in her applicable amount.

Contribution calculation

After Mrs Cooper's IS claim has been decided by the DWP she informs social services and her financial assessment is amended. Mr and Mrs Cooper's joint savings are divided equally.

There are different capital rules that apply for financial assessment purposes. Any capital/savings of £12,000 or less is disregarded; therefore Mrs Cooper's share of the £11,000 savings is completely disregarded in the financial assessment.

There are no disregards on Mrs Cooper's income for 'outgoings' as she is permanently away from her home in the community.

Mrs Cooper's contribution to the cost of her accommodation and care will be calculated in the following way:

Income 1	IB (short-term)	£64.35
(first 4 weeks)	IS	£63.95
	DLA care component	£57.20
	Total	**£185.50**

(DLA mobility component: £15.15 disregarded)

Personal expenses allowances (PEA) **£17.50**

Income (£185.50) *minus* **PEA** (£17.50) = **Contribution** (£168.00)

Mrs Cooper's contribution to the cost for the first 4 weeks is £168.00 a week.
Mrs Cooper will be left with £32.65 a week (DLA mobility component and PEA).
The full cost of the care home is £291.00 a week.
Social services contribution to the cost for the first 4 weeks is £123.00 a week.

Income 2	IB (short-term)	£64.35
(after 4 weeks)	IS	£9.60
	Total	**£73.95**

(DLA mobility component – £15.15 disregarded)
Personal expenses allowances (PEA) **£17.50**
Income (£73.95) *minus* **PEA** (£17.50) = **Contribution** (£56.45)
Mrs Cooper's contribution to the cost after 4 weeks is £56.45 a week.
Mrs Cooper will be left with £32.65 a week (DLA mobility component and PEA).
The full cost of the care home is £291.00 a week.
Social services' contribution to the cost after 4 weeks is £234.55 a week.

2. Complex example income support and contribution calculations

This section includes examples of calculations with:

- occupational pension (Example 1 – below);
- liable relative payment (Example 2 – p396);
- income support claimed by partner in the community (Example 3 – p397);
- third party contribution (Example 4 – p399).

Example 1: Occupational pension

Mr and Mrs Lucas, both aged 76 years, are home owners (without a mortgage). Mr Lucas's weekly income is made up of state retirement pension, an occupational pension and attendance allowance (AA). Mrs Lucas's weekly income is made up of state retirement pension and industrial injury disablement benefit. They do not receive any council tax benefit (CTB) and they are not entitled to income support (IS) as a couple in the community. **Mr Lucas goes into a care home which provides nursing on a permanent basis.**

Mr Lucas is advised by social services that 50 per cent of his occupational pension can be disregarded by social services if he passes at least 50 per cent to his wife (see p307). He decides to do this, as social services has told him that Mrs Lucas would not be entitled to IS in her own right with the level of her existing income and, although no amount of CTB would be payable if Mrs Lucas received half of Mr Lucas's occupational pension, they decide that, as she would have a 25 per cent status discount as the only occupant of their home anyway (see p189), it would be more advantageous for her to have the extra income.

Income support calculation

As Mr and Mrs Lucas are now considered to be permanently separated, they will be treated as single people for IS purposes. Therefore, Mr Lucas claims IS in his own right. His claim will be calculated in the following way:

Income	State retirement pension	£77.45
	Occupational pension	£63.50
	Total	**£140.95**

(AA of £57.20 is payable for first 4 weeks but disregarded as income)

Applicable amount 1	£54.65	(Single personal allowance)
(first 4 weeks)	£47.45	(Single higher pensioner premium)
	£42.95	(Severe disability premium)
Total	**£145.05**	

Applicable amount (£145.05) *minus* **income** (£140.95) = **IS** (£4.10)

Mr Lucas is entitled to IS of £4.10 a week for the first 4 weeks of his stay (paid on top of his state retirement pension, occupational pension and AA).

After 4 weeks, Mr Lucas's AA stops and his IS is recalculated in the following way:

Applicable amount 2	£54.65	(Single personal allowance)
(after 4 weeks)	£47.45	(Single enhanced pensioner premium)
Total	**£102.10**	

The severe disability premium is no longer applicable as Mr Lucas is no longer getting AA.

Applicable amount (£102.10) *minus* **Income** (£140.95) = **IS** (nil)

Mr Lucas is not entitled to IS after 4 weeks of his stay as he has excess income of £38.85 (he will only receive his state retirement pension and occupational pension).

Contribution calculation

After Mr Lucas's IS claim has been decided by the DWP, he informs social services and his financial assessment is amended. There are no disregards on his income for outgoings as he is permanently away from his home in the community.

Mr Lucas's contribution to the cost of his accommodation and care costs will be calculated in the following way:

Income 1	State retirement pension	£77.45
(first 4 weeks)	Occupational pension (total amount £63.50 but 50 per cent disregarded as passed to his wife)	£31.75
	IS	£4.10
	AA	£57.20
	Total	**£170.50**

(AA is taken into account as Mr Lucas is a permanent resident)

Personal expenses allowance (PEA) £17.50

Income (£170.50) *minus* **PEA** (£17.50) = **Contribution** (£153)

Mr Lucas's contribution to the cost for the first 4 weeks is £153.00 a week.
Mr Lucas will be left with £17.50 a week (PEA).
The full cost of the care home which provides nursing is £372 a week.
Social services' contribution to the cost for the first 4 weeks is £219 a week.

Income 2	State retirement pension	£77.45
(after 4 weeks)	Occupational pension (total amount £63.50 but 50 per cent disregarded as passed to his wife)	£31.75
	Total	**£109.20**

Personal expenses allowance (PEA) **£17.50**
Income (£109.20) *minus* **PEA** (£17.50) = **Contribution** (£91.70)

Mr Lucas's contribution to the cost after 4 weeks is £91.70 a week.
Mr Lucas will be left with £17.50 a week (PEA).
The full cost of the care home which provides nursing is £372 a week.
Social services' contribution after 4 weeks is £280.30 a week.

Example 2: Liable relative payment

Mr and Mrs Lawlor, aged 62 and 58 respectively, are joint home owners (without a mortgage). Mr Lawlor is in full-time employment. Mrs Lawlor is in receipt of long-term incapacity benefit (IB), disability living allowance (DLA) care and mobility components. They do not receive any means-tested benefits. **Mrs Lawlor goes into a care home for a 4-week temporary stay while adaptations are made to their home.**

Income support calculation
As Mrs Lawlor's stay is only temporary, they will continue to be treated as a couple by the DWP and they will not be entitled to IS because Mr Lawlor is in full-time employment. Mrs Lawlor will continue to receive her long-term IB, DLA care and mobility components.

Contribution calculation
Although the DWP will still treat Mr and Mrs Lawlor as a couple, social services can only undertake a financial assessment of Mrs Lawlor's resources. Mrs Lawlor's contribution to her accommodation and care costs will be calculated in the following way:

Income	Long-term IB	£72.15
	Total	**£72.15**

(DLA care component £38.30 disregarded as income as temporary stay)
(DLA mobility component £39.95 disregarded as income)

Outgoings	Water rates (£4.00 ÷ 2)	£2.00
	Standard charge for fuel (£1.90 ÷ 2)	£0.95
	Building and contents insurance (£8.80 ÷ 2)	£4.40
	Council tax (£14.50 ÷ 2)	£7.25
Total		**£14.60**

Personal expenses allowance (PEA) £17.50

Income (£72.15) *minus* **Outgoings** (£14.60) *minus* **PEA** (£17.50) = **Contribution** (£40.05)

Mrs Lawlor's contribution to the cost is £40.05 a week.
Mrs Lawlor will be left with £110.35 a week (PEA, outgoings, DLA care and mobility components).
The full cost of the care home is £291 a week.
As Mrs Lawlor's contribution does not cover the full cost and she has a liable relative (her husband) living in the community who is in full-time employment, social services considers that it is appropriate to ask him for a contribution to Mrs Lawlor's care costs.
If Mrs Lawlor had been able to claim IS as a single person, social services would have had a contribution of £88.80 a week from Mrs Lawlor (income of £72.15 IB *plus* £48.75 IS *minus* outgoings of £14.60 and PEA of £17.50). They ask Mr Lawlor for a contribution of £48.75 a week (the difference between £88.80 and £40.05, Mrs Lawlor's actual contribution). Mr Lawlor says he cannot afford this amount due to his financial commitments and he offers to pay £30 a week. Social services accepts this amount. However, if they had considered it was not a reasonable amount they could ask Mr Lawlor to provide financial details in order to consider what would be an appropriate amount.

Example 3: Income support claimed by partner in the community

Mr and Mrs Lloyd, aged 75 and 70 years respectively, are council tenants. Mr Lloyd's weekly income is made up of state retirement pension, work pension, IS and AA. Mrs Lloyd's weekly income is made up of state retirement pension and AA. They each have an underlying entitlement to carer's allowance and they also receive maximum housing benefit (HB) and council tax benefit (CTB). **Mrs Lloyd enters a care home for a 2-week temporary stay while Mr Lloyd is in hospital.**

Income support calculation

As Mr and Mrs Lloyd are only temporarily separated, the DWP will continue to treat them as a couple for the purposes of calculating their resources, although the single person's applicable amounts will be used (as the sum total is greater than the applicable amount for a couple). Mr Lloyd applies for a reconsideration of the IS paid to him in respect of both of them. It will be calculated in the following way:

Income	State retirement pension (Mr Lloyd)	£90.17
	Work pension (Mr Lloyd)	£17.40
	State retirement pension (Mrs Lloyd)	£47.45
	Total	**£155.02**

(AA (Mrs Lloyd) £57.20 disregarded as income)
(AA (Mr Lloyd) £38.30 disregarded as income)

Applicable amount	Mr Lloyd	£54.65	(Single personal allowance)
		£47.45	(Single higher pensioner premium)
		£42.95	(Severe disability premium)
		£25.10	(Carer's premium)
	Mrs Lloyd	£54.65	(Single personal allowance)
		£47.45	(Single higher pensioner premium)
		£42.95	(Severe disability premium)
		£25.10	(Carer's premium)
Total		**£340.30**	

Applicable amount (£340.30) *minus* **Income** (£155.02) = **IS** (£185.28)

Mr and Mrs Lloyd are entitled to IS of £185.28 a week, payable to Mr Lloyd as the claimant (paid on top of Mr Lloyd's state retirement pension, work pension and AA).

Contribution calculation
Although the DWP will still treat Mr and Mrs Lloyd as a couple for the purposes of calculating their resources, social services can only undertake a financial assessment of Mrs Lloyd's resources.
However, social services is aware that IS is paid to Mr Lloyd in respect of both of them as they drafted the letter for Mr Lloyd asking for a reconsideration.
Mrs Lloyd's contribution to her accommodation and care costs will be calculated in the following way:

Income	State retirement pension	£47.45
	Total	**£47.45**

(AA £57.20 disregarded as income as temporary stay)

Outgoings:	Water rates (£5.00 ÷ 2)	£2.50
	Standard charge for fuel (£1.90 ÷ 2)	£0.95
	Total	**£3.45**
Personal expenses allowance (PEA)		£17.50

Income (£47.45) *minus* **Outgoings** (£3.45) *minus* **PEA** (£17.50) = **Contribution** (£26.50)

Mrs Lloyd's contribution to the cost is £26.50 a week.
Social services asks Mr Lloyd for an amount that they consider would be being paid by way of IS to him in respect of Mrs Lloyd. They calculate this in the following way:

Applicable amount in respect of Mrs Lloyd	£54.65	(Personal allowance)
	£47.45	(Higher pensioner premium)
	£42.95	(Severe disability premium)
	£25.10	(Carer's premium)
Total	**£170.15**	
Mrs Lloyd's income	£47.45	(State retirement pension)

Applicable amount (£170.15) *minus* **Income** (£47.45) = **IS** in respect of Mrs Lloyd (£122.70)

Social services asks Mr Lloyd for £122.70 a week of the IS payment towards the cost of Mrs Lloyd's accommodation and care.

The total contribution to the cost from Mr and Mrs Lloyd is £149.20 a week.

Mrs Lloyd will be left with £20.95 a week (PEA and outgoings).

The full cost of the care home is £291 a week.

Social services' contribution to the cost is £141.80 a week.

Mr Lloyd would be left with IS for himself calculated by the DWP in the following way:

Applicable amount in respect of Mr Lloyd	£54.65	(Personal allowance)
	£47.45	(Higher pensioner premium)
	£42.95	(Severe disability premium)
	£25.10	(Carer's premium)
Total	**£170.15**	

Mr Lloyd's income	State retirement pension	£90.17
	Work pension	£17.40
	Total	**£107.57**

Applicable amount (£170.15) *minus* **Income** (£107.57) = **IS** in respect of Mr Lloyd (£62.58)

Mr Lloyd will be left with £62.58 IS for himself (paid on top of his AA, state retirement pension and work pension).

Mr Lloyd may not be willing or able to make the contribution asked of him by social services. In these circumstances social services may ask for a lower amount or refer the case to the courts for a decision.

If Mr Lloyd does not receive the amount of IS that is assumed by social services then he may need to appeal against the decision and advise social services accordingly.

Example 4: Third party contribution

Mr Chand (64) is a single person living in a housing association property. His weekly income before entering care is made up of long-term IB, IS and DLA care and mobility components. He also receives maximum HB and CTB and his son claims carer's allowance (CA) for caring for him. **Mr Chand goes into a care home for a 3-week temporary stay**. He has chosen a care home which costs £15 a week more than social services will pay for a person with his needs. There are other homes available within the usual cost that are suitable but Mr Chand wishes to go to the higher-cost home. Mr Chand's son agrees to pay the extra £15 and he enters into a contract with social services to make this payment.

Income support calculation

Mr Chand's IS entitlement remains the same as he is a single person living on his own in the community and he has no savings. It is calculated in the following way:

Income	Long-term IB	£87.30
	Total	**£87.30**

(DLA care component £57.20, DLA mobility component £39.95 and the third party contribution £15 disregarded as income)

Applicable amount	£54.65	(Personal allowance)
	£47.45	(Higher pensioner premium)
Total	**£102.10**	

(The severe disability premium is not included in Mr Chand's applicable amount as his son is in receipt of CA)

Applicable amount (£102.10) *minus* **income** (£87.30) = **IS** (£14.80)

Mr Chand is entitled to IS of £14.80 a week (paid on top of his long-term IB and DLA care and mobility components).

Contribution calculation

Social services undertakes a financial assessment. Mr Chand's contribution is calculated in the following way:

Income	Long-term IB	£87.30
	IS	£14.80
	Third party contribution	£15.00
	Total	**£117.10**

(DLA care component £57.20 and DLA mobility component £39.95 disregarded as income)

Outgoings	Water rates	£4.00
	Standard charge for fuel	£1.90
	Service charge (not met by HB)	£2.50
	Total	**£8.40**
Personal expenses allowance (PEA)		£17.50

Income (£117.10) *minus* **Outgoings** (£8.40) *minus* **PEA** (£17.50) = **Contribution** (£91.20)

Mr Chand's contribution to the cost is £76.20 a week.
His son's contribution to the cost is £15 a week.
Mr Chand will be left with £123.05 (PEA, outgoings, DLA care and mobility components).
The full cost of the care home is £306 a week.
Social services' contribution to the cost is £214.80 a week (no more than it would have been if the full cost of the care home was £291 a week – ie, the usual cost).

Chapter 19

Common problems – benefits and charges

This chapter covers:

1. Housing benefit and income support

Housing benefit and notice of termination of tenancy

If your home in the community is rented and you receive housing benefit (HB) you may experience a problem if you go into a care home for a trial period or on a permanent basis (see p362 for definitions of these types of stay).

The problem arises because HB can usually only be paid on your normal home (see p181).[1] Therefore, if you have decided to leave it permanently (ie, become a permanent resident in a care home) there is usually no further entitlement to benefit. Of course, in order to give the notice of termination of tenancy required by housing authorities (usually four weeks) you must have decided you are not going to return to your home in the community. The period of that notice is not then covered by HB. The only time this would not happen is where you were able to plan that on a certain date, which was also the date of the end of the notice of termination period, you would enter the care home on a permanent basis. Often, however, going into a care home cannot be planned in this way.

This issue was raised with the HB policy section at the then DSS in October 1995 following the introduction of the 'trial period' in April 1995, in an attempt to change the HB regulations to allow payment to the end of the contractual liability in these circumstances. The response was that perhaps local authorities might wish to consider a much shorter notice of termination period when people are in residential accommodation on a trial basis and they then decide to stay permanently.[2]

In practice, a number of solutions have been adopted by housing and social services authorities. The most notable of these are:

- some housing authorities have written off the rent for the notice period on a case-by-case basis;
- some social services departments have increased the personal expenses allowance (PEA) (ie, charged less) during the notice period while full rent is being paid.

Another approach is that HB legislation[3] allows you to be treated as occupying a home from which you have moved if you are liable to make payments in respect of two dwellings (in this case your previous home, where there is still a rent liability during the notice period, and your new accommodation in the care home) and the liability could not reasonably be avoided. This allows an HB payment for up to four weeks. The DWP considers that this only applies where both homes are eligible for HB but this is not stated in the legislation and few such claims have been successful.

Different DWP local offices

If you are moving permanently to a care home outside the area covered by your current DWP local office, your claims will be transferred to the relevant office in your new area. For temporary stays there should be no change from the DWP local office for your normal home address.

Claims for income support

From October 1997 regulations have meant that most people claiming income support (IS) need to supply all the evidence requested on the claim form in order for the claim to be valid. One month to supply all the evidence requested is allowed from the date of any notification of the intention to make a claim, or the date on which an incomplete claim form is received by the DWP and the missing information is requested.[4]

A standard form for the notification of the intention to make a claim has been suggested as good practice by the Local Government Association.[5] If the required information is not submitted within the one-month period it is likely that IS will only be paid from any later date on which the information or evidence is provided unless certain specified conditions apply.[6]

The encouragement of prompt and complete claims is important to social services finances as they can only make an assessment for your contribution to accommodation and care costs on the basis of the capital you have and the income (including IS) you receive (but see notional income, p309). However, since the abolition of the residential allowance in the IS applicable amount in April 2002 (see p368), the number of residents becoming entitled to IS upon entering a care home has significantly decreased.

There will usually be no reward for you in making a valid IS claim as your PEA will remain the same whatever happens to your benefits (see p330). However, if you do not claim any IS to which you are entitled, social services could treat you as having notional income and you may find that all your other income has to be used to pay for your care home costs and you have none left for your own personal expenses.

It is in social services' interest to provide help and advice in the claiming of social security benefits. If a claim for IS is made late it can be backdated for up to three months but only if there is a specified special reason.[7] If you were misled by incorrect advice from social services this is only considered to be a special reason if the advice was in writing. Claims can also be backdated for up to one month for specified administrative reasons (also see p362).[8]

Couples

For IS purposes, the treatment of couples or one member of a couple in care homes has always been more problematic and complex than the treatment of a single person. Upon a claim, revision or supersession (see Chapter 6), the DWP needs to establish whether the stay is temporary, trial period or permanent. Different rules apply for couples depending on the type of stay (see p405). Often the DWP fails to apply two single person rates when they calculate the applicable amount for a couple, one of whom is in a care home (see p366).

A common problem is where both members of a couple are permanent residents in a shared room in the same care home. It used to be the case that if a couple were in separate rooms in the same care home or one was in a residential wing and the other in a nursing wing of a dual registered care home, they could be treated as single people, but where a couple were sharing a room they would be treated as a couple as they were maintaining a common household. However, commissioners' decisions have held the view that 'an essential attribute of a household is a domestic establishment' and that 'if the degree of independence and self-sufficiency falls below a certain level, there is no longer a domestic establishment and therefore no longer a household'.[9]

This means that IS may become payable to one or both members of the couple treated as a single people when it would not have been payable to them as a couple – eg, when one member of the couple has significantly less individual resources or when the couple have joint savings of more than £16,000 but when it is divided their individual shares are less than this amount.

2. Disability living allowance care component and attendance allowance

Completing enquiry forms

There are two common enquiry forms that are sent out by the DWP's Disability Benefits Unit to collect information to enable them to make a decision on whether disability living allowance care component (DLA care)/attendance allowance (AA) (and in some situations of stays in hospital or similar institutions, disability living allowance mobility component (DLA mobility)) is payable while you are in the care home.

Form DBD26 is sent to the manager or owner of the care home. This form asks about the type of accommodation you are in, when you moved in, where you lived before, who pays for your care, and whether you have spent any time away from the home.

Form DBD46LA or DBD46HA is sent to social services or the local NHS body, depending on which authority is helping with the cost of your placement. This form asks whether the authority owns or manages the care home, whether any money has been paid towards the cost of your stay, whether there is an agreement to recover money from the sale of a house or other release of funds (see p299), and under which legislation monies have been paid.

Both of these forms need to be completed accurately and carefully, especially if you are trying to establish that DLA care/AA should continue in payment. Often forms are incorrectly completed for various reasons, not least because authorities are less than sure about what legislation they are making payments under. This can lead to benefits being withdrawn incorrectly (see p370). There can also be delays caused because of the late return of these forms.

Overpayments

Overpayments of DLA care/AA commonly occur because the DWP has not been informed about your stay in a care home. This is especially the case in a respite care situation where your stays might only be for weekends but are on a regular basis, so there may come a time when the 28-day entitlement period is exceeded (see p370).

Overpayments of benefits may be recoverable from you if you have failed to disclose, or misrepresented, a material fact.

All the circumstances of your arrangements for care in a care home and any change in those circumstances should be notified to the DWP in writing.

3. Financial assessments and charging

Types of stay

Problems can occur with social services definitions of the types of stay in care homes. A permanent stay is straightforward but trial periods and temporary stays can be more problematic (see p301 for definitions).

A trial period stay is considered to be of a temporary nature by the DWP but often social services regards trial periods as permanent stays because a permanent resource is being committed from the budget. This means that the value of your home in the community may be taken into account as capital from the 13th week of your stay under the rules that apply to permanent stays rather than from the 13th week after the beginning of when your stay becomes permanent – ie, being disregarded under the rules that apply to temporary stays during the trial period.

There is no definition of 'trial period' in financial assessment regulations, but guidance indicates that this type of stay should be treated as temporary (see p301).[10]

Problems can occur for couples if a stay which is actually permanent from the first day is automatically described as a trial period. This is because if one of a couple (or both) is in a care home on a trial period basis they will be assessed as a couple for IS purposes and their resources aggregated, whereas if the stay is a permanent stay they will be treated as single people for IS purposes and their resources will not be aggregated. This could mean the difference between IS being payable or not.

There can also be problems with temporary stays where social services insist on a definite date when the stay will end for it to be considered as a temporary stay. This is not correct. The definition of temporary stay in the legislation is a stay unlikely to exceed 52 weeks, or in exceptional circumstances, unlikely substantially to exceed that period.[11]

Any decision made by social services can be challenged using the complaints procedure (see p297).

Couples (married or unmarried)

Financial assessments for one member of a couple going into a care home on a temporary basis are more complex and therefore problems can occur. The problems involve the need to ensure that, if the person going into care is the main benefit recipient for both of them as a couple, there will be a variation of the resident's personal expenses allowance so that the resident can continue to support her/his partner (see p331).

If the person staying in the community is the main benefit recipient for both of them as a couple then social services may ask her/him to make a contribution to the costs of the placement (see p339).

Financial assessments before entering a care home

Social services can undertake a financial assessment *before* you enter a care home if you are a prospective resident.[12] This means that the income they assess includes benefits that are only applicable to you in the community. As explained in Chapter 17, in some situations some benefits will change when you enter the care home so the initial contribution calculated will not be the amount that you will actually be required to pay when you enter the care home. This can be confusing, although some social services departments attempt to explain the situation in the letter they send you about your financial assessment.

If your benefits change as a result of entering the care home, social services will need to be advised of the new amounts so they can complete a retrospective reassessment and advise you of the actual amount that you will be required to contribute.

Assuming income support

If social services undertakes a financial assessment *before* you enter a care home (see above) they may make an assumption about your entitlement to, and the amount of, IS that will become payable when you enter the care home. This can cause problems because it involves treating IS as notional income (see p309), and also because social services financial assessors are not usually benefits specialists and may make an incorrect assumption. This is a problem particularly with regard to the severe disability premium element of IS which is subject to complex rules.

If your IS entitlement has been assumed you should check that what you actually receive when your entitlement has been decided is the same amount as social services assumed. If it is not, you should challenge the social services decision using their complaints procedure (see p297). Alternatively, the amount of your IS may be incorrect. In this situation social services may be able to help you challenge the DWP decision. In any event, social services cannot assess you on an amount of IS that is not in payment. They will have to re-assess you on the basis of your actual income.

50 per cent pension disregard

If you pass at least 50 per cent of your occupational or personal pension or payment from a retirement annuity to your spouse with whom you are not residing, 50 per cent will be disregarded from your income. Social services should give you advice about this disregard and the fact that you have a choice of whether to pass 50 per cent to your spouse or not. They should also advise you about whether your spouse would be better off after taking account of the effect of the pension on social security benefits.[13]

In practice, many social services departments do not give this advice. You should seek independent advice if you have been disadvantaged by the lack of social services advice.

Loophole cases (England and Wales only)

Loophole cases are discussed on p376. Often social services does not appreciate the benefits implications of the actions it takes or the advice it gives. This means you could lose benefits to which you might otherwise have been entitled if a different choice or course of action was taken. Social services is advised that as part of the whole assessment process it should provide *full* information about the financial consequences of the different options.[14] This was confirmed by an Ombudsman investigation where it was accepted by the social services concerned that it should have put the option of paying the full cost of the placement in a care home to the family, given its knowledge of the rules governing the payment of attendance allowance.[15]

Deprivation of income or capital

If social services has decided that, or is considering whether, you have deprived yourself of income or capital in order to avoid a charge or reduce the charge payable (see pp310 and 324), there are various courses of action that it may be able to take in order to attempt to secure the assessed contribution payable, taking into account the notional income or capital. However, it is important to remember that the placement you have been assessed as needing should not be delayed or withheld, even if you have deprived yourself of income or capital or you have not made the payment of the assessed contribution. Social services has a duty to provide residential care where it is needed and not otherwise available to you. In Scotland the same principle applies, although the wording of the legislation varies.[16] This principle has been confirmed by the House of Lords in the *Robertson v Fife* case (see p327).

4. Social security benefits and social services charges

Benefits and charging pay days

If you are expected to go into a care home for a period of up to eight weeks, your income support (IS) can be paid from the day of admission. However, if your stay is expected to be more than eight weeks, your IS can only be altered from the start of your benefit week. Social services charges should be based on what you actually receive, so if there are days when you receive less money, you should be charged less.

Treatment of jointly owned property

Social services and the DWP may treat property that is jointly owned differently. If you own property with one or more people, the DWP usually treat, you as owning an equal share, even if your actual share may be more or less than this.[17] The deemed equal share is then valued. However, a recent Court of Appeal decision[18] makes it clear that this should only apply where the joint owners are joint tenants and therefore each owner has an equal share of the whole beneficial interest in the property. It does not apply where the joint owners are tenants-in-common and each have a separate share of the property which can be identified separately and may be a 10 per cent or 25 per cent share even where there are only two owners, rather than a 50 per cent share. The DWP has detailed guidance[19] and a special agency, the Valuation Office Agency, which deals with more complex valuations.

Social services values your *actual* share in the jointly owned property.[20] Therefore, if you have more or less than an equal share, the valuation amount may differ from that assessed by the DWP. Unlike the DWP, social services has little guidance on how to proceed in these cases. However, if you dispute a social services valuation, guidance states that a professional valuation should be obtained (see p317).[21] This should not be an expense passed on to you as there is no provision to charge for such an item.

Both the DWP and social services value the share that they each determine belongs to you in the same way, by establishing the current market or surrender value – ie, the price a willing buyer would pay to a willing seller for the share, less 10 per cent if there would be costs involved in selling, and less any mortgage or debt secured on the property (see p317).

Capital limits for temporary stays

If you enter a care home for a temporary stay and you have capital over £8,000 (£12,000 if you or your partner are aged 60 or over), you will not be able to claim IS because for temporary residents the capital limit is £8,000 (£12,000 if you or your partner are aged 60 or over), the same as for people living in the community.

However, the social services capital limit for temporary residents is £19,500 in England, £20,000 in Wales and £18,500 in Scotland – the same as for permanent residents. This will not be a problem for you but for social services who will be required to fund your placement without any IS to include in the financial assessment to offset some of the costs.

Capital limit for permanent stays

From April 2001, the upper capital limit for financial assessment purposes became different to the upper capital limit for IS purposes. Consequently, social services will be required to help fund your placement if you have between £16,000 and

£19,500 in England, £20,000 in Wales and £18,500 in Scotland, without any IS to include in the financial assessment to offset some of the costs.

Disregard of home in the community for financial assessments

Where there is no mandatory or discretionary disregard applied to your home in the community, its value is disregarded in the financial assessment for the first 12 weeks of any permanent stay in a care home (see Chapter 12). There is no similar disregard for IS purposes. Therefore, unless the property can be disregarded by the DWP because there is a mandatory disregard that applies or it is for sale, its value will be taken into account and there will be no IS payments for social services to include in the financial assessment to offset some of the costs of your placement.

This situation can also arise when social services has applied a discretionary disregard (see p321) on your property as social security legislation does not allow for discretionary disregards.

Notes

1. **Housing benefit and income support**
1 Reg 5 HB Regs
2 AMA social services circular 104/1995, 23 October 1995
3 Reg 5(5)(d) HB Regs
4 Reg 4(1A)–4(1C); reg 6(1A) SS(C&P) Regs
5 Attached to LGA circular 126/98, dated 26 February 1998
6 Reg 4(1B) SS(C&P) Regs
7 Reg 19(4) and (5) SS(C&P) Regs
8 Reg 19(6) SS(C&P) Regs
9 CIS/4934/1997; CIS/4935/1997; CIS/5232/1997; CIS/5237/1997 and CIS/3767/1997 and common appendix to these decisions

3. **Financial assessments and charging**
10 para 8 LAC (95)7; WOC 22/95; para 13 SWSG 13/95
11 Reg 2(1) NA(AR) Regs
12 LAC (98)19; WOC 27/98; SWSG 2/99; NA(AR)(Amdt2) Regs
13 para 4 LAC (97)5; WOC 29/97; para 2 SWSG 7/97
14 Part 1D of letter to Directors of Social Services dated 12 September 1994 from ACC and AMA
15 Ombudsman investigation against Stockport MBC, Complaint No.98/C.1842, 30 March 1999
16 s21(1)(a) NAA 1948; ss12 and 13 SW(S)A 1968

4. **Social security benefits and social services charges**
17 Reg 52 IS Regs
18 *James Hourigan on behalf of his mother Mary Hourigan (deceased) v Secretary of State for Work and Pensions,* [2002] EWCA Civ 1890, 19 December 2002 (appeal by Secretary of State against CIS 5906/99)
19 Memo AOG JSA/IS (98)35
20 Reg 27(2) NA(AR) Regs
21 para 7 LAC (97)5; WOC 29/97; para 8 SWSG 7/97

Appendices

Appendix 1

Key legislation

Reproduced in this appendix is some of the key legislation governing some of the powers and duties of social services departments (and health authorities) relevant to this *Handbook*. It contains the following legislation which applies in **England and Wales**:

1. ss21, 22, 26, 26A and s29 National Assistance Act 1948 (below)
2. ss45 and 65 Health Services and Public Health Act 1968 (p419)
3. ss7–7D Local Authority Social Services Act 1970 (p420)
4. ss1 and 2 Chronically Sick and Disabled Persons Act 1970 (p421)
5. ss1–3, 21 and Schedule 8 paras 1–3 National Health Service Act 1977 (p422)
6. ss17, 21, 22 and 24 Health and Social Services and Social Security Adjudications Act 1983 (p424)
7. s117 Mental Health Act 1983 (p427)
8. ss4, 8 and 16 Disabled Persons (Services, Consultation and Representation) Act 1986 (p427)
9. ss46 and 47 National Health Service and Community Care Act 1990 (p428)
10. s1 Carers (Recognition and Services) Act 1995 (p430)
11. ss1, 2 and 3 Carers and Disabled Children Act 2000 (p430)
12. s 2 Local Government Act 2000 (p431)
13. ss49,54,55, 56, 57and 58 Health and Social Care Act 2001 (p432)

It also reproduces the following legislation which applies in **Scotland**:

14. ss4–5B, 12–12B, 13-14 and 86A–87 Social Work (Scotland) Act 1968 (p433)
15. ss1, 36 and 37 NHS (Scotland) Act 1978 (p439)
16. ss7–8 Mental Health (Scotland) Act 1984 (p440)
17. s117 Scotland Act 1998 (p440)
18. s2 Regulation of Care (Scotland) Act 2001 (p440)
19. s1 and Sch 1 Community Care and Health (Scotland) Act 2002 (p441)

1. **National Assistance Act 1948**

Duty of local authorities to provide accommodation

21.–(1) Subject to and in accordance with the provisions of this Part of this Act, a local authority may with the approval of the Secretary of State, and to such extent as he may direct shall, make arrangements for providing–

(a) residential accommodation for persons aged 18 or over who by reason of age, illness, disability or any other circumstances are in need of care and attention which is not otherwise available to them; and

(aa) residential accommodation for expectant and nursing mothers who are in need of care and attention which is not otherwise available to them.

[(1A) and (1B) omitted]

(2) In making any such arrangements a local authority shall have regard to the welfare of all persons for whom accommodation is provided, and in particular to the need for providing accommodation of different descriptions suited to different descriptions of such persons as are mentioned in the last foregoing subsection.

"(2A) In determining for the purposes of paragraph (a) or (aa) of subsection (1) of this section whether care and attention are otherwise available to a person, a local authority shall disregard so much of the person's resources as may be specified in, or determined in accordance with, regulations made by the Secretary of State for the purposes of this subsection

(2B) In subsection (2A) of this section the reference to a person's resources is a reference to his resources within the meaning of regulations made for the purposes of that subsection."

(3) [*repealed*]

(4) Subject to section 26 of this Act, accommodation provided by a local authority in the exercise of their functions under this section shall be provided in premises managed by the authority or, to such extent as may be determined in accordance with the arrangements under this section, in such premises managed by another local authority as may be agreed between the two authorities and on such terms as to the reimbursement of expenditure incurred by the said other authority, as may be so agreed.

(5) References in this Act to accommodation provided under this Part thereof shall be construed as references to accommodation provided in accordance with this and the five next following sections, and as including references to board and other services, amenities and requisites provided in connection with the accommodation except where in the opinion of the authority managing the premises their provision is unnecessary.

(6) References in this Act to a local authority providing accommodation shall be construed, in any case where a local authority agree with another local authority for the provision of accommodation in premises managed by the said authority, as references to the first–mentioned local authority.

(7) Without prejudice to the generality of the foregoing provisions of this section, a local authority may–

(a) provide, in such cases as they may consider appropriate, for the conveyance of persons to and from premises in which accommodation is provided for them under this Part of the Act;

(b) make arrangements for the provision on the premises in which accommodation is being provided of such other services as appear to the authority to be required.

(8) Nothing in this section shall authorise or require a local authority to make any provision authorised or required to be made (whether by that or by any other authority) by or under any enactment not contained in this Part of this Act, or authorised or required to be provided under the National Health Service Act 1977.

Charges to be made for accommodation

22.—(1) Subject to section 26 of this Act, where a person is provided with accommodation under this Part of this Act the local authority providing the accommodation shall recover from him the amount of the payment which he is liable to make.

(2) Subject to the following provisions of this section, the payment which a person is liable to make for any such accommodation shall be in accordance with a standard rate fixed for that accommodation by the authority managing the premises in which it is provided and that standard rate shall represent the full cost to the authority of providing that accommodation.

(3) Where a person for whom accommodation in premises managed by any local authority is provided, or proposed to be provided, under this Part of this Act satisfies the local authority that he is unable to pay therefore at the standard rate, the authority shall assess his ability to pay, and accordingly determine at what lower rate he shall be liable to pay for the accommodation.

(4) In assessing for the purposes of the last foregoing subsection a person's ability to pay, a local authority shall assume that he will need for his personal requirements such sum per week as may be prescribed by the Minister, or such other sum as in special circumstances the authority may consider appropriate.

(4A) Regulations made for the purposes of subsection (4) of this section may prescribe different sums for different circumstances.

(5) In assessing as aforesaid a person's ability to pay, a local authority shall give effect to regulations made by the Secretary of State for the purposes of this subsection except that, until the first such regulations come into force, a local authority shall give effect to Part III of Schedule 1 to the Supplementary Benefits Act 1976, as it had effect immediately before the amendments made by Schedule 2 to the Social Security Act 1980.

(5A) If they think fit, an authority managing premises in which accommodation is provided for a person shall have power on each occasion when they provide accommodation for him, irrespective of his means, to limit to such amount as appears to them reasonable for him to pay the payments required from him for his accommodation during a period commencing when they begin to provide the accommodation for him and ending not more than eight weeks after that.

(6) [*repealed*]

(7) [*repealed*]

(8) Where accommodation is provided by a local authority in premises managed by another local authority, the payment therefore under this section shall be made to the authority managing the premises and not to the authority providing the accommodation, but the authority managing the premises shall account for the payment to the authority providing the accommodation.

(9) [*repealed*]

Provision of accommodation in premises maintained by voluntary organisations

26.—(1) Subject to subsections (1A) and (1B) below, arrangements under section 21 of this Act may include arrangements made with a voluntary organisation or with any other person who is not a local authority where—

(a) that organisation or person manages premises which provide for reward accommodation falling within subsection (1)(a) or (aa) of that section, and

(b) the arrangements are for the provision of such accommodation in those premises.

(1A) Subject to subsection (1B) below, arrangements made with any voluntary organisation or other person by virtue of this section must, if they are for the provision of residential accommodation with both board and personal care for such persons as are mentioned in section 1(1) of the Registered Homes Act 1984 (requirement for registration), be arrangements for the provision of such accommodation in a residential care home which is managed by the organisation or person in question, being such a home in respect of which that organisation or persons—

(a) is registered under Part 1 of that Act, or

(b) is not required to be so registered by virtue of section 1(4)(a) or (b) of that Act (certain small homes) or by virtue of the home being managed or provided by an exempt body;

and for this purpose 'personal care' and 'residential care home' have the same meaning as in that Part of that Act.

(1B) Arrangements made with any voluntary organisation or other person by virtue of this section must, if they are for the provision of residential accommodation where nursing care is provided, be arrangements for the provision of such accommodation in premises which are managed by the organisation or persons in question, being premises—

(a) in respect of which that organisation or person is registered under Part 11 of the Registered Homes Act 1984, or

(b) which, by reason only of being maintained or controlled by an exempt body, do not fall within the definition of a nursing home in section 21 of that Act.

(1C) Subject to subsection (1D) below, no such arrangements as are mentioned in subsection (1B) above may be made by an authority for the accommodation of any person without the consent of such Health Authority as may be determined in accordance with regulations.

(1D) Subsection (1C) above does not apply to the making by an authority of temporary arrangements for the accommodation of any person as a matter of urgency; but, as soon as practicable after any such temporary arrangements have been made, the authority shall seek the consent required by subsection (1C) above to the making of appropriate arrangements for the accommodation of the person concerned.

(1E) No arrangements may be made by virtue of this section with a person who has been convicted of an offence under any provision of—

(a) the Registered Homes Act 1948 (or any enactment replaced by that Act); or

(b) regulations made under section 16 or section 26 of that Act (or under any corresponding provisions of any such enactment).

(2) Any arrangements made by virtue of this section shall provide for the making by the local authority to the other party thereto of payments in respect of the accommodation provided at such rates as may be determined by or under the arrangements and subject to subsection (3A) below the local authority shall recover from each person for whom accommodation is provided under the arrangements the amount of the refund which he is liable to make in accordance with the following provisions of this section.

(3) Subject to subsection (3A) below, a person for whom accommodation is provided under any such arrangements shall, in lieu of being liable to make payment therefore in accordance with section twenty–two of this Act, refund to the local authority any payments made in respect of him under the last foregoing subsection:

Provided that where a person for whom accommodation is provided, or proposed to be provided, under any such arrangements satisfies the local authority that he is unable to make refund at the full rate determined under that subsection, subsections (3) to (5) of section twenty–two of this Act shall, with the necessary modifications, apply as they apply where a person satisfies the local authority of his inability to pay at the standard rate as mentioned in the said subsection (3).

(3A) Where accommodation in any premises is provided for any person under any arrangements made by virtue of this section and the local authority, the person concerned and the voluntary organisation or the other person managing the premises (in this subsection referred to as 'the provider') agree that this section shall apply—

(a) so long as the person concerned makes the payments for which he is liable under paragraph (b) below, he shall not be liable to make any refund under subsection (3) above and the local authority shall not be liable to make any payment under subsection (2) above in respect of the accommodation provided for him;
(b) the person concerned shall be liable to pay to the provider such sums as he would otherwise (under subsection (3) above) be liable to pay by way of refund to the local authority; and
(c) the local authority shall be liable to pay to the provider the difference between the sums paid by virtue of paragraph (b) above and the payments which, but for paragraph (a) above, the authority would be liable to pay under subsection (2) above.

(4) Subsections (5A), (7) and (9) of the said section 22 shall, with the necessary modifications, apply for the purposes of the last foregoing subsection as they apply for the purposes of the said section 22.

(4A) Section 21(5) of this Act shall have effect as respects accommodation provided under arrangements made by virtue of this section with the substitution for the references to the authority managing the premises of a reference to the authority making the arrangements.

(5) Where in any premises accommodation is being provided under this section in accordance with arrangements made by any local authority, any person authorised in that behalf by the authority may at all reasonable times enter and inspect the premises

(6) [*repealed*]

(7) In this section the expression 'voluntary organisation' includes any association which is a housing association for the purposes of the Housing Act 1936, 'small home' means an establishment falling within section 1(4) of the Registered Homes Act 1984 and 'exempt body' means an authority or body constituted by an Act of Parliament or incorporated by Royal Charter.

Exclusion of powers to provide accommodation under this Part in certain cases

26A.—(1) Subject to subsection (3) of this section, no accommodation may be provided under section 21 or 26 of this Act for any person who immediately before the date on which this section comes into force was ordinarily resident in relevant premises.

(2) In subsection (1) 'relevant premises' means—
(a) premises in respect of which any person is registered under the Registered Homes Act 1984;
(b) premises in respect of which such registration is not required by virtue of their being managed or provided by an exempt body;
(c) premises which do not fall within the definition of a nursing home in section 21 of that Act by reason only of their being maintained or controlled by an exempt body; and
(d) such other premises as the Secretary of State may by regulations prescribe;

and in this subsection 'exempt body' has the same meaning as in section 26 of this Act.

(3) The Secretary of State may by regulations provide that, in such cases and subject to such conditions as may be prescribed, subsection (1) of this section shall not apply in relation to such classes of persons as may be prescribed in the regulations.

(4) The Secretary of State shall by regulations prescribe the circumstances in which persons are to be treated as being ordinarily resident in any premises for the purposes of subsection (1) of this section.

(5) This section does not affect the validity of any contract made before the date on which this section comes into force for the provision of accommodation on or after that date or anything done in pursuance of such a contract.

Welfare arrangements for blind, deaf, dumb and crippled persons, etc

29.—(1) A local authority may, with the approval of the Secretary of State, and to such extent as he may direct in relation to persons ordinarily resident in the area of the local authority shall make arrangements for promoting the welfare of persons to whom this section applies, that is to say persons aged eighteen or over who are blind, deaf or dumb or who suffer from mental disorder of any description, and other persons aged eighteen or over who are substantially and permanently handicapped by illness, injury, or congenital deformity or such other disabilities as may be prescribed by the Minister.

(2) [*repealed*]

(3) [*repealed*]

(4) Without prejudice to the generality of the provisions of subsection (1) of this section, arrangements may be made thereunder–

(a) for informing persons to whom arrangements under that subsection relate of the services available for them thereunder;

(b) for giving such persons instruction in their own homes or elsewhere in methods of overcoming the effects of their disabilities;

(c) for providing workshops where such persons may be engaged (whether under a contract of service or otherwise) in suitable work, and hostels where persons engaged in the workshops, and other persons to whom arrangements under subsection (1) of this section relate and for whom work or training is being provided in pursuance of the Disabled Persons (Employment) Act 1944 or the Employment and Training Act 1973 may live;

(d) for providing persons to whom arrangements under subsection (1) of this section relate with suitable work (whether under a contract of service or otherwise) in their own homes or elsewhere;

(e) for helping such persons in disposing of the produce of their work; for providing such persons with recreational facilities in their own homes or elsewhere;

(f) for providing such persons with recreational facilities in their own homes or elsewhere;

(g) for compiling and maintaining classified registers of the persons to whom arrangements under subsection (1) of this section relate.

(4A) Where accommodation in a hostel is provided under paragraph (c) of subsection (4) of this section—

(a) if the hostel is managed by a local authority, section 22 of this Act shall apply as it applies where accommodation is provided under s21;

(b) if the accommodation is provided in a hostel managed by a person other than a local authority under arrangements made with that person, subsections (2) to (4A) of section 26 of this Act shall apply as they apply where accommodation is provided under arrangements made by virtue of that section; and

(c) sections 32 and 43 of this Act shall apply as they apply where accommodation is provided under sections 21 to 26;

and in this subsection references to 'accommodation' include references to board and other services, amenities and requisites provided in connection with the accommodation, except where in the opinion of the authority managing the premises or, in the case mentioned in paragraph (b) above, the authority making the arrangements their provision is unnecessary.

(5) [*repealed*]

(6) Nothing in the foregoing provisions of this section shall authorise or require—

(a) the payment of money to persons to whom this section applies, other than persons for whom work is provided under arrangements made by virtue of paragraph (c) or paragraph (d) of subsection (4) of this section or who are engaged in work which they are enabled to perform in consequence of anything done in pursuance of arrangements made under this section; or

(b) the provision of any accommodation or services required to be provided under the National Health Service Act 1977.

(7) A person engaged in work in a workshop provided under paragraph (c) of subsection (4) of this section, or a person in receipt of a superannuation allowance granted on his retirement from engagement in any such workshop, shall be deemed for the purposes of this Act to continue to be ordinarily resident in the area in which he was ordinarily resident immediately before he was accepted for work in that workshop; and for the purposes of this subsection a course of training in such workshop shall be deemed to be work in that workshop.

2. Health Services and Public Health Act 1968

Promotion, by local authorities, of the welfare of old people

45.—(1) A local authority may with the approval of the Secretary of State, and to such extent as he may direct shall, make arrangements for promoting the welfare of old people.

(2) [*repealed*]

(3) A local authority may employ as their agent for the purposes of this section any voluntary organisation or any person carrying on, professionally or by way of trade or business, activities which consist of or include the provision of services for old people, being an organisation or person appearing to the authority to be capable of promoting the welfare of old people.

(4) No arrangements under this section shall provide—

(a) for the payment of money to old people except in so far as the arrangements may provide for the remuneration of old people engaged in suitable work in accordance with the arrangements;

(b) for making available any accommodation or services required to be provided under the National Health Service Act 1977.

Financial and other assistance by local authorities to certain voluntary organisations

65.—(1) A local authority may give assistance by way of grant or by way of loan, or partly in the one way and partly in the other, to a voluntary organisation whose activities consist in, or include, the provision of a service similar to a relevant service, the promotion of the provision of a relevant service or a similar one, the publicising of a relevant service or a similar one or the giving of advice with respect to the manner in which a relevant service or a similar one can best be provided, and so may the Greater London Council.

(2) A local authority may also assist any such voluntary organisation as aforesaid by permitting them to use premises belonging to the authority on such terms as may be agreed, and by making available furniture, vehicles or equipment (whether by way of gift, or loan or otherwise) and the services of any staff whoa re employed by the authority in connection with the premises or other things which they permit the organisation to use.

(3) In this section – . . .

(c)'relevant service' means a service the provision of which must or may, by virtue of the relevant enactments, be secured by the local authority. . .

3. **Local Authority Social Services Act 1970**

Local authorities to exercise social services functions under guidance of Secretary of State

7.—(1) Local authorities shall, in the exercise of their social services functions, including the exercise of any discretion conferred by any relevant enactment, act under the general guidance of the Secretary of State.

Directions by the Secretary of State as to exercise of social services functions

7A—(1) Without prejudice to section 7 of this Act, every local authority shall exercise their social services functions in accordance with such directions as may be given to them under this section by the Secretary of State.

(2) Directions under this section—

(a) shall be given in writing; and

(b) may be given to a particular authority, or to authorities of a particular class, or to authorities generally.

Complaints procedure

7B—(1) The Secretary of State may by order require local authorities to establish a procedure for considering any representations (including any complaints) which are made to them by a qualifying individual, or anyone acting on his behalf, in relation to the discharge of, or any failure to discharge, any of their social services functions in respect of that individual.

(2) In relation to a particular local authority, an individual is a qualifying individual for the purposes of subsection (1) above if—

(a) the authority have a power or a duty to provide, or to secure the provision of, a service for him; and

(b) his need or possible need for such a service has (by whatever means) come to the attention of the authority.

(3) A local authority shall comply with any directions given by the Secretary of State as to the procedure to be adopted in considering representations made as mentioned in subsection (1) above and as to the taking of such action as may be necessary in consequence of such representations.

(4) Local authorities shall give such publicity to any procedure established pursuant to this section as they consider appropriate.

Inquiries

7C—(1) The Secretary of State may cause an inquiry to be held in any case where, whether on representations made to him or otherwise, he considers it advisable to do so in connection with the exercise by any local authority of any of their social services functions (except in so far as those functions relate to persons under the age of eighteen).

(2) Subsections (2) to (5) of section 250 of the Local Government Act 1972 (powers in relation to local inquiries) shall apply in relation to an inquiry under this section as they apply in relation to an inquiry under that section.

Default powers of Secretary of State as respects social services functions of local authorities

7D—(1) If the Secretary of State is satisfied that any local authority have failed, without reasonable excuse, to comply with any of their duties which are social services functions (other than a duty imposed by or under the Children Act 1989), he may make an order declaring that authority to be in default with respect to the duty in question.

(2) An order under subsection (1) may contain such directions for the purpose of ensuring that the duty is complied with within such period as may be specified in the order as appear to the Secretary of State to be necessary.

(3) Any such direction shall, on the application of the Secretary of State, be enforceable by mandamus.

4. **Chronically Sick and Disabled Persons Act 1970**

Information as to need for and existence of welfare services

1(1) It shall be the duty of every local authority having functions under section 29 of the National Assistance Act 1948 to inform themselves of the number of persons to whom that section applies within their area and of the need for the making by the authority of arrangements under that section for such persons.

(2) Every such local authority—

(a) shall cause to be published from time to time at such times and in such manner as they consider appropriate general information as to the services provided under arrangements made by the authority under the said section 29 which are for the time being available in the area; and

(b) shall ensure that any such person as aforesaid who uses any of those services is informed of any other service provided by the authority (whether under any such arrangements or not) which in the opinion of the authority is relevant to his needs and of any service provided by any other authority or organisation which in the opinion of the authority is so relevant and of which particulars are in the authorities' possession.

Provision of welfare services

2.—(1) Where a local authority having functions under s29 National Assistance Act 1948 are satisfied in the case of any person to whom that section applies who is ordinarily resident in their area that it is necessary in order to meet the needs of that person for that authority to make arrangements for all or any of the following matters, namely:–

(a) the provision of practical assistance for that person in his home;

(b) the provision for that person of, or assistance to that person in obtaining, wireless, television, library or similar recreational facilities;

(c) the provision for that person of lectures, games, outings or other recreational facilities outside his home or assistance to that person in taking advantage of educational facilities available to him;

(d) the provision for that person of facilities for, or assistance in, travelling to and from his home for the purpose of participating in any services provided under arrangements made by the authority under the said section 29 or, with the approval of the authority, in any services provided otherwise than as aforesaid which are similar to services which could be provided under such arrangements;

(e) the provision of assistance for that person in arranging for the carrying out of any works of adaptation in his home or the provision of any additional facilities designed to secure his greater safety, comfort or convenience;

(f) facilitating the taking of holidays by that person, whether at holiday homes or otherwise and whether provided under arrangements made by the authority or otherwise;

(g) the provision of meals for that person whether in his home or elsewhere;

(h) the provision for that person of, or assistance to that person in obtaining, a telephone and any special equipment necessary to enable him to use a telephone,

then, subject to the provisions of section 7(1) of the Local Authority Social Services Act 1970 (which requires local authorities in the exercise of certain functions, including functions under the said section 29, to act under the general guidance of the Secretary of State) and to the provisions of section 7A of that Act (which requires local authorities to exercise their social services functions in accordance with directions given by the Secretary of State) it shall be the duty of that Authority to make those arrangements in exercise of their functions under the said section 29.

5. National Health Service Act 1977

Secretary of State's duty as to health service

1.—(1) It is the Secretary of State's duty to continue the promotion in England and Wales of a comprehensive health service designed to secure improvement—

(a) in the physical and mental health of the people of those countries; and

(b) in the prevention, diagnosis and treatment of illness, and for that purpose to provide or secure the effective provision of services in accordance with this Act.

(2)The services so provided shall be free of charge except in so far as the making and recovery of charges is expressly provided for by or under any enactment, whenever passed.

Secretary of State's general power as to services

2. Without prejudice to the Secretary of State's powers apart from this section, he has power—

(a) to provide such services as he considers appropriate for the purpose of discharging any duty imposed on him by this Act; and

(b) to do any other thing whatsoever which is calculated to facilitate, or is conducive or incidental to, the discharge of such a duty.

This section is subject to section 3(3) below.

Services generally

3.—(1) It is the Secretary of State's duty to provide throughout England and Wales, to such extent as he considers necessary to meet all reasonable requirements—

(a) hospital accommodation;

(b) other accommodation for the purpose of any service provided under this Act;

(c) medical, dental, nursing and ambulance services;

(d) such other facilities for the care of expectant mothers and young children as he considers are appropriate as part of the health service;
(e) such facilities for the prevention of illness, the care of persons suffering from illness and the after care of persons who have suffered from illness as he considers are appropriate as part of the health service;
(f) such other services as are required for the diagnosis and treatment of illness.

(2) . . .

(3) Nothing in section 2 above or in this section affects the provisions of Part II of this Act (which relates to arrangements with practitioners for the provision of medical, dental, ophthalmic and pharmaceutical services).

Co–operation and assistance

Local social services authorities

21.—(1) Subject to paragraphs (d) and (e) of section 3(1) above, the services described in Schedule 8 to this Act in relation to—
(a) care of mothers,
(b) prevention, care and after care,
(b) home help and laundry facilities,
(c) are functions exercisable by local social services authorities, and that Schedule has effect accordingly.

(2) A local social services authority who provide premises, furniture or equipment for any of the purposes of this Act may permit the use of the premises, furniture or equipment–
(a) by any other social services authority, or
(b) by any of the bodies constituted under this act, or (c)
(c) by a local education authority,

This permission may be on such terms (including terms with respect to the services of any staff employed by the authority giving permission) as may be agreed.

Schedule 8: Local Social Services Authorities

Care of mothers and young children

1.—(1) A local social services authority may, with the Secretary of State's approval, and to such extent as he may direct shall, make arrangements for the care of expectant and nursing mothers (other than for the provision of residential accommodation for them).

Prevention, care and after–care

2.—(1) A local social services authority may, with the Secretary of State's approval, and to such extent as he may direct shall, make arrangements for the purpose of the prevention of illness and for the care of persons suffering, from illness and for the after–care of persons who have been suffering and in particular for–
(a) [*repealed*]
(b) the provision for persons whose care is undertaken with a view to preventing them from becoming ill, persons suffering from illness and persons who have been so suffering, of centres or other facilities for training them or keeping them suitably occupied and the equipment and maintenance of such centres;
(c) the provision, for the benefit of such persons as are mentioned in paragraph (b) above, of ancillary or supplemental services; and
(d) for the exercise of the functions of the Authority in respect of persons suffering from mental disorder who are received into the guardianship under Part II or III of the

Mental Health Act 1983(whether the guardianship of the local social services authority or of other persons).

Such an authority shall neither have the power nor be subject to a duty to make under this paragraph arrangements to provide facilities for any of mentioned in section 15(1) of the Disabled Persons (Employment) Act 1944.

(2) No arrangements under this paragraph shall provide for the payment of money to persons for whose benefit they are made except–

(a) in so far as they may provide for the remuneration of such persons engaged in suitable work in accordance with the arrangements, of such amounts as the local social services authority think fit in respect of their occasional personal expenses where it appears to that authority that no such payment would otherwise be made.

[2(A) and 2(B) omitted]

(3) The Secretary of State may make regulations as to the conduct of premises in which, in pursuance of arrangements made under this paragraph, are provided for persons whose care is undertaken with a view to preventing them from becoming sufferers from mental disorder within the meaning of that Act of 1983 or who are, or have been, so suffering, facilities for training them or keeping them suitably occupied.

(4) [*repealed*]

(4A) This paragraph does not apply in relation to persons under the age of 18.

(4AA) No authority is authorised or may be required under this paragraph to provide residential accommodation for any person.

Home help and laundry facilities

3.—(1) It is the duty of every local social services authority to provide on such a scale as is adequate for the needs of their area, or to arrange for the provision on such a scale as is so adequate, of home help for households where such help is required owing to the presence of—

a person who is suffering from illness, lying–in, an expectant mother, aged, handicapped as a result of having suffered from illness or by congenital deformity,

and every such Authority has power to provide or arrange for the provision of laundry facilities for households for which home help is being, or can be, provided under this sub–paragraph.

(2) [repealed]

6. Health and Social Services and Social Security Adjudications Act 1983

Charges for local authority services in England and Wales

17.–(1) Subject to subsection (3) below, an authority providing a service to which this section applies may recover such charge (if any) for it as they consider reasonable.

(2) This section applies to services provided under the following enactments–

(a) section 29 if the National Assistance Act 1948 (welfare arrangements for blind, deaf, dumb, and crippled persons etc.);

(b) section 45(1) of the Health Services and Public Health Act 1968 (welfare of old people);

(c) Schedule 8 to the National Health Service Act 1977 (care of mothers and young children, prevention of illness and care and after–care and home help and laundry facilities);

(d) section 8 of the Residential Homes Act 1980 (meals and recreation for old people); and

(e) paragraph 1 of Part II of Schedule 9 to this Act other than the provision of services for which payment may be required under section 22 or 26 of the National Assistance Act 1948.

(3) If a person—

(a) avails himself of a service to which this section applies, and

(b) satisfies the authority providing the service that his means are insufficient for it to be reasonably practicable for him to pay for the service the amount which he would otherwise be obliged to pay for it,

the authority shall not require him to pay more for it than it appears to them that it is reasonable practicable for him to pay.

(4) Any charge under this section may, without prejudice to any other method of recovery, be recovered summarily as a civil debt.

Recovery of sums due to local authority where persons in residential accommodation have disposed of assets

21.–(1) Subject to the following provisions of this section, where—

(a) a person avails himself of Part III accommodation; and

(b) that person knowingly and with the intention of avoiding charges for the accommodation—

(i) has transferred any asset to which this section applies to some other person or person not more than six months before the date on which he begins to reside in such accommodation; or

(ii) transfers any such asset to some other person or persons while residing in the accommodation; and

(c) either—

(i) the consideration for the transfer is less than the value of the asset; or

(ii) there is no consideration for the transfer,

the person or persons to whom the asset is transferred by the person availing himself of the accommodation shall be liable to pay to the local authority providing the accommodation or arranging for its provision the difference between the amount assessed as due to be paid for the accommodation by the person availing himself of it and the amount which the local authority receive from him for it.

(2) This section applies to cash and any other asset which falls to be taken into account for the purpose of assessing under section 22 of the National Assistance Act 1948 the ability to pay for the accommodation of the person availing himself of it.

(3) Subsection 1(1) above shall have effect in relation to a transfer by a person who leaves Part Ill accommodation and subsequently resumes residence in such accommodation as if the period of six months mentioned in paragraph (b)(i) were a period of six months before the date on which he resumed residence in such accommodation.

(3A) If the Secretary of State so directs, subsection (1) above shall not apply in such cases as may be specified in the direction.

(4) Where a person has transferred an asset to which this section applies to more than one person, the liability of each of the persons to whom it was transferred shall be in proportion to the benefit accruing to him from the transfer.

(5) A person's liability under this section shall not exceed the benefit accruing to him from the transfer.

(6) Subject to subsection (7) below, the value of any asset to which this section applies, other than cash, which has been transferred shall be taken to be the amount of the consideration which would have been realised for it if it had been sold on the open market by a willing seller at the time of the transfer.

(7) For the purpose of calculating the value of an asset under subsection (6) above there shall be deducted from the amount of the consideration—

(a) the amount of any incumbrance on the asset; and

(b) a reasonable amount in respect of the expenses of the sale.

(8) In this Part of this Act 'Part 111 accommodation' means accommodation provided under sections 21 to 26 of the National Assistance Act 1948, and, in the application of this Part of this Act to Scotland, means accommodation provided under the Social Work (Scotland) Act 1968 or section 7 (functions of local authorities) of the Mental Health (Scotland) Act 1984.

Arrears of contributions charged on interest in land in England and Wales

22.—(1) Subject to subsection (2) below, where a person who avails himself of Part 111 accommodation provided by a local authority in England, Wales or Scotland—

(a) fails to pay any sum assessed as due to be paid by him for the accommodation; and

(d) has a beneficial interest in land in England and Wales;

the local authority may create a charge in their favour on his interest in the land.

(2) In the case of a person who has interests in more than one parcel of land the charge under this section shall be upon his interest in such one of the parcels as the local authority may determine.

(2A) In determining whether to exercise their power under subsection (1) above and in making any determination under subsection (2) above, the local authority shall comply with any directions given to them by the Secretary of State as to the exercise of those functions.

(3)[repealed]

(4) Subject to subsection (5) below, a charge under this section shall be in respect of any amount assessed as due to be paid which is outstanding from time to time.

(5) The charge on the interest of an equitable joint tenant in land shall be in respect of an amount not exceeding the value of the interest that he would enjoy in the land if the joint tenancy were severed but the creation of such a charge shall not sever the joint tenancy.

(6) On the death of a joint tenant in the proceeds of sale of land held upon trust for sale whose interest in the proceeds is subject to a charge under this section—

(a) if there are surviving joint tenants, their interests in the proceeds; and

(b) if the land vests in one person, or one person is entitled to have it vested in him, his interest in it,

shall become subject to a charge for an amount not exceeding the amount of the charge to which the interest of the deceased joint tenant was subject by virtue of subsection (5) above.

(7) A charge under this section shall be created by a declaration in writing made by the local authority.

(8) Any such charge, other than a charge on the interest of an equitable joint tenant in land, shall in the case of unregistered land be a land charge of Class B within the meaning of section 2 of the Land Charges Act 1972 and in the case of registered land be a registrable charge taking effect as a charge by way of legal mortgage.

Interest on sums charged on or secured over interest in land

24.—(1) Any sum charged on or secured over an interest in land under this Part of this Act shall bear interest from the day after that on which the person for whom the local authority provided the accommodation dies.

(2) The rate of interest shall be such reasonable rate as the Secretary of State may direct or, if no such direction is given, as the local authority may determine.

7. Mental Health Act 1983

Aftercare

117.—(1) This section applies to persons who are detained under section 3 above, or admitted to a hospital in pursuance of a hospital order made under section 37 above, or transferred to a hospital in pursuance of a transfer direction made under section 47 or 48 above, and then cease to be detained and (whether or not immediately after so ceasing) leave hospital.

(2) It shall be the duty of the Health Authority and of the local social services authority to provide, in co-operation with relevant voluntary agencies, aftercare services for any person to whom this section applies until such time as the Health Authority and the local social services authority are satisfied that the person concerned is no longer in need of such services but they shall not be so satisfied in the case of a patient who is subject to aftercare under supervision at any time while he so remains subject.

(2A) It shall be the duty of the Health Authority to secure that at all times while a patient is subject to aftercare under supervision–

(a) a person who is a registered medical practitioner approved for the purposes of section 12 above by the Secretary of State as having special experience in the diagnosis or treatment of mental disorder is in charge of the medical treatment provided for the patient as part of the aftercare services provided for him under this section; and

(b) a person professionally concerned with any of the aftercare services so provided is supervising him with a view to securing that he receives the aftercare services so provided.

(2B) Section 32 above shall apply for the purposes of this section as it applies for the purposes of Part II of this Act.

(3) In this section 'the Health Authority' means the Health Authority and 'the local social services authority' means the local social services authority for the area in which the person concerned is resident or to which he is sent on discharge by the hospital in which he was detained.

8. Disabled Persons (Services, Consultation and Representation) Act 1986

4. When requested to do so by—

(a) a disabled person ...

(c) any person who provides care for him in the circumstances mentioned in section 8, a local authority shall decide whether the needs of the disabled person call for the provision by the authority of any services in accordance with section 2(1) of the 1970 Act (provision for welfare services).

8.—(1) Where—

(a) a disabled person is living at home and receiving a substantial amount of care on a regular basis from another person (who is not a person employed to provide such care by any body in the exercise of its functions under any enactment), and

(b) it falls to a local authority to decide whether the disabled person's needs call for the provision by them of any services for him under any of the welfare enactments,

the local authority shall, in deciding that question, have regard to the ability of that other person to continue to provide such care on a regular basis.

16.In this Act—

. . .

'disabled person'—

(a) in relation to England and Wales, means

(i) in the case of a person aged 18 or over, a person to whom s29 of the National Assistance Act 1948 applies. . .

9. National Health Service and Community Care Act 1990

Local authority plans for community care services

46.—(1) Each local authority–

(a) shall, within such period after the day appointed for the coming into force of this section as the Secretary of State may direct, prepare and publish a plan for the provision of community care services in their area;

(b) shall keep the plan prepared by them under paragraph (a) above and any further plans prepared by them under this section under review; and

(c) shall, at such intervals as the Secretary of State may direct, prepare and publish modifications to the current plan, or if the case requires, a new plan.

(2) In carrying out any of their functions under paragraphs (a) to (c) of subsection (1) above, a local authority shall consult—

(a) any Health Authority the whole or any part of whose district lies within the area of the local authority;

(b) [*repealed*]

(c) in so far as any proposed plan, review or modifications of a plan may affect or be affected by the provision or availability of housing and the local authority is not itself a local housing authority, within the meaning of the Housing Act 1985, every such local housing authority whose area is within the area of the local authority;

(d) such voluntary organisations as appear to the authority to represent the interests of persons who use or are likely to use any community care services within the area of the authority or the interests of private carers who, within that area, provide care to persons for whom, in the exercise of their social services functions, the local authority have a power or a duty to provide a service;

(e) such voluntary housing agencies and other bodies as appear to the local authority to provide housing or community care services in their area; and

(f) such other persons as the Secretary of State may direct.

(3) In this section—

'local authority' means the council of a county, a county borough, a metropolitan district or a London borough or the Common Council of the City of London;

'community care services' means services which a local authority may provide or arrange to be provided under any of the following provisions—

(a) Part III of the National Assistance Act 1948;

(b) section 45 of the Health Services and Public Health Act 1968;

(c) section 21 of and Schedule 8 to the National Health Service Act 1977; and

(d) section 117 of the Mental Health Act 1983; and

'private carer' means a person who is not employed to provide the care in question by any body in the exercise of its function under any enactment.

Assessment of needs for community care services

47.—(1) Subject to subsections (5) and (6) below, where it appears to a local authority that any person for whom they may provide or arrange for the provision of community care services may be in need of any such services, the authority—

(a) shall carry out an assessment of his needs for those services; and

(b) having regard to the results of that assessment, shall then decide whether his needs call for the provision by them of any such services.

(2) If at any time during the assessment of the needs of any person under subsection (1)(a) above it appears to a local authority that he is a disabled person, the authority—

(a) shall proceed to make such a decision as to the services he requires as is mentioned in section 4 of the Disabled Persons (Services, Consultation and Representation) Act 1986 without his requesting them to do so under that section; and

(b) shall inform him that they will be doing so and of his rights under that Act.

(3) If at any time during the assessment of the needs of any person under subsection (1)(a) above, it appears to a local authority—

(a) that there may be a need for the provision to that person by such Health Authority as may be determined in accordance with regulations of any services under the National Health Service Act 1977, or

(b) that there may be the need for the provision to him of any services which fall within the functions of a local housing authority (within the meaning of the Housing Act 1985) which is not the local authority carrying out the assessment,

the local authority shall notify that Health Authority or local housing authority and invite them to assist, to such extent as is reasonable in the circumstances, in the making of the assessment; and, in making their decision as to the provision of services needed for the person in question, the local authority shall take into account any services which are likely to be made available for him by that Health Authority or local housing authority.

(4) The Secretary of State may give directions as to the manner in which an assessment under this section is to be carried out or the form it is to take but, subject to any such directions and to subsection (7) below, it shall be carried out in such manner and take such form as the local authority consider appropriate.

(5) Nothing in this section shall prevent a local authority from temporarily providing or arranging for the provision of community care services for any person without carrying out a prior assessment of his needs in accordance with the preceding provisions of this section if, in the opinion of the authority, the condition of that person is such that he requires those services as a matter of urgency.

(6) If, by virtue of subsection (5) above, community care services have been provided temporarily for any person as a matter of urgency, then, as soon as practicable thereafter, an assessment of his needs shall be made in accordance with the preceding provisions of this section.

. . .

10. Carers (Recognition and Services) Act 1995

Assessment of ability of carers to prow de care: England and Wales

1.– (1) Subject to subsection (3) below, in any case where—

(a) a local authority carry out an assessment under section 47(1)(a) of the National Health Service and Community Care Act 1990 of the needs of a person ('the relevant person') for community care services, and

(b) an individual ('the carer') provides or intends to provide a substantial amount of care on a regular basis for the relevant person,

the carer may request the local authority, before they make their decision as to whether the needs of the relevant person call for the provision of any services, to carry out an assessment of his ability to provide and continue to provide care for the relevant person; and if he makes such a request, the local authority shall carry out such an assessment and shall take into account the results of that assessment in making that decision.

(2) Subject to subsection (3) below, in any case where—

(a) a local authority assess the needs of a disabled child for the purpose of Part III of the Children Act 1989 or section 2 of the Chronically Sick and Disabled Persons Act 1970, and

(b) an individual ('the carer') provides or intends to provide a substantial amount of care on a regular basis for the disabled child,

the carer may request the local authority, before they make their decision as to whether the needs of the disabled child call for the provision of any services, to carry out an assessment of his ability to provide and continue to provide care for the disabled child; and if he makes such a request, the local authority shall carry out such an assessment and shall take into account the results of that assessment in making that decision.

(3) No request may be made under subsection (1) or (2) above by an individual who provides or will provide the care in question—

(a) by virtue of a contract of employment or other contract with any person; or

(b) as a volunteer for a voluntary organisation. . .

11. Carers and Disabled Children Act 2000

1.— (1) If an individual aged 16 or over ('the carer')—

(a) provides or intends to provide a substantial amount of care on a regular basis for another individual aged 18 or over ('the person cared for'); and

(b) asks a local authority to carry out an assessment of his ability to provide and to continue to provide care for the person cared for,

the local authority must carry out such an assessment if it is satisfied that the person cared for is someone for whom it may provide or arrange for the provision of community care services.

(2) For the purposes of such an assessment, the local authority may take into account, so far as it considers it to be material, an assessment under section 1(1) of the Carers (Recognition and Services) Act 1995.

(3) Subsection (1) does not apply if the individual provides or will provide the care in question—

(a) by virtue of a contract of employment or other contract with any person; or

(b) as a volunteer for a voluntary organisation.

(4) The Secretary of State (or, in relation to Wales, the National Assembly for Wales) may give directions as to the manner in which an assessment under subsection (1) is to be carried out or the form it is to take.

(5) Subject to any such directions, it is to be carried out in such manner, and is to take such form, as the local authority considers appropriate.

(6) In this section, 'voluntary organisation' has the same meaning as in the National Assistance Act 1948.

2.—(1) The local authority must consider the assessment and decide—

(a) whether the carer has needs in relation to the care which he provides or intends to provide;

(b) if so, whether they could be satisfied (wholly or partly) by services which the local authority may provide; and

(c) if they could be so satisfied, whether or not to provide services to the carer.

(2) The services referred to are any services which—

(a) the local authority sees fit to provide; and

(b) will in the local authority's view help the carer care for the person cared for,

and may take the form of physical help or other forms of support.

(3) A service, although provided to the carer—

(a) may take the form of a service delivered to the person cared for if it is one which, if provided to him instead of to the carer, could fall within community care services and they both agree it is to be so delivered; but

(b) if a service is delivered to the person cared for it may not, except in prescribed circumstances, include anything of an intimate nature.

(4) Regulations may make provision about what is, or is not, of an intimate nature for the purposes of subsection (3).

3.—(1) Regulations may make provision for the issue of vouchers by local authorities.

12. **Local Government Act 2000**

2.—(1) Every local authority are to have power to do anything which they consider is likely to achieve any one or more of the following objects—

(a) the promotion or improvement of the economic well-being of their area,

(b) the promotion or improvement of the social well-being of their area, and

(c) the promotion or improvement of the environmental well-being of their area.

(2) The power under subsection (1) may be exercised in relation to or for the benefit of—

(a) the whole or any part of a local authority's area, or

(b) all or any persons resident or present in a local authority's area.

(3) In determining whether or how to exercise the power under subsection (1), a local authority must have regard to their strategy under section 4.

(4) The power under subsection (1) includes power for a local authority to—

(a) incur expenditure,

(b) give financial assistance to any person,
(c) enter into arrangements or agreements with any person,
(d) co-operate with, or facilitate or co-ordinate the activities of, any person,
(e) exercise on behalf of any person any functions of that person, and
(f) provide staff, goods, services or accommodation to any person.

(5) The power under subsection (1) includes power for a local authority to do anything in relation to, or for the benefit of, any person or area situated outside their area if they consider that it is likely to achieve any one or more of the objects in that subsection.

(6) Nothing in subsection (4) or (5) affects the generality of the power under subsection (1).

Limits on power to promote well-being.

3.—(1) The power under section 2(1) does not enable a local authority to do anything which they are unable to do by virtue of any prohibition, restriction or limitation on their powers which is contained in any enactment (whenever passed or made).

(2) The power under section 2(1) does not enable a local authority to raise money (whether by precepts, borrowing or otherwise)

(3) The Secretary of State may by order make provision preventing local authorities from doing, by virtue of section 2(1), anything which is specified, or is of a description specified, in the order.

(4) Before making an order under subsection (3), the Secretary of State must consult such representatives of local government and such other persons (if any) as he considers appropriate.

(5) Before exercising the power under section 2(1), a local authority must have regard to any guidance for the time being issued by the Secretary of State about the exercise of that power.

(6) Before issuing any guidance under subsection (5), the Secretary of State must consult such representatives of local government and such other persons (if any) as he considers appropriate.

(7) In its application to Wales, this section has effect as if for any reference to the Secretary of State there were substituted a reference to the National Assembly for Wales.

(8) In this section "enactment" includes an enactment comprised in subordinate legislation (within the meaning of the Interpretation Act 1978).

13. **Health and Social Care Act 2001**

Exclusion of nursing care from community care services

49—(1) Nothing in the enactments relating to the provision of community care services shall authorise or require a local authority, in or in connection with the provision of any such services, to—
(a) provide for any person, or
(b) arrange for any person to be provided with,
nursing care by a registered nurse.

(2) In this section 'nursing care by a registered nurse' means any services provided by a registered nurse and involving—
(a) the provision of care, or
(b) the planning, supervision or delegation of the provision of care,

other than any services which, having regard to their nature and the circumstances in which they are provided, do not need to be provided by a registered nurse.

Please note that this currently only applies in England. In Wales it is in force for residents who fund their own care and is planned come into force in full (ie for all local authority funded residents) from April 2004.

Please note that Wales has not yet made regulations under section 56, and so Direct Payments made in Wales are still made under the Community Care (Direct Payments) Act 1996 (See CPAG's *Paying For Care Handbook* 3rd edition for relevant text of that Act).

14. Social Work (Scotland) Act 1968

Provisions relating to performance of functions by local authorities

4. Where a function is assigned to a local authority under this Act or section 7 (functions of local authorities) or 8 (provision of after–care services) of the Mental Health (Scotland) Act 1984 or Part II of the Children (Scotland) Act 1995 and a voluntary organisation or other person, including another local authority is able to assist in the performance of that function, the local authority may make arrangements with such an organisation or other person for the provision of such assistance as aforesaid.

Powers of Secretary of State

5.—(1) Local authorities shall perform their functions under this Act. . . under the general guidance of the Secretary of State.

(1A) Without prejudice to subsection (1) above, the Secretary of State may issue directions to local authorities, either individually or collectively, as to the manner in which they are to exercise any of their functions. . .and a local authority shall comply with any direction made under this subsection.

Local authority plans for community care services

5A.—(1) Within such period after the day appointed for the coming into force of this section as the Secretary of State may direct, and in accordance with the provisions of this section, each local authority shall prepare and publish a plan for the provision of community care services in their area.

(2) Each local authority shall from time to time review any plan prepared by them under subsection (1) above, and shall, in the light of any such review, prepare and publish—

(a) any modifications to the plan under review; or

(b) if the case requires, a new plan.

(3) In preparing any plan or carrying out any review under subsection (1) or, as the case may be, subsection (2) above the authority shall consult—

(a) any Health Board providing services under the National Health Service (Scotland) Act 1978 in the area of the authority;

(b) [*repealed*]

(c) such voluntary organisations as appear to the authority to represent the interests of persons who use or are likely to use any community care services within the area of the authority or the interests of private carers who, within that area, provide care to persons for whom, in the exercise of their functions under this Act or any of the enactments mentioned in section 5(1B) of this Act, the local authority have a power or a duty to provide, or to secure the provision of, a service;

(d) such voluntary housing agencies and other bodies as appear to the authority to provide housing or community care services in their area; and

(e) such other persons as the Secretary of State may direct.

(4) In this section—

'community care services' means services, other than services for children, which a local authority are under a duty or have a power to provide, or to secure the provision of, under Part II of this Act or section 7 (functions of local authorities), 8 (provision of after-care services) or 11 (training and occupation of the mentally handicapped) of the Mental Health (Scotland) Act 1984; and

'private carer' means a person who is not employed to provide the care in question by any body in the exercise of its functions under any enactment.

Complaints procedure

5B.—(1) Subject to the provisions of this section, the Secretary of State may by order require local authorities to establish a procedure whereby a person, or anyone acting on his behalf, may make representations (including complaints) in relation to the authority's discharge of, or failure to discharge, any of their functions. . .in respect of that person.

(2) For the purposes of subsection (1) of this section, 'person' means any person for whom the local authority have a power or a duty to provide, or to secure the provision of, a service, and whose need or possible need for such a service has (by whatever means) come to the attention of the authority.

(3) An order under subsection (1) of this section may be commenced at different times in respect of such different classes of person as may be specified in the order.

(6) A local authority shall comply with any directions given by the Secretary of State as to the procedure to be adopted in considering representations made as mentioned in subsection (1) of this section and as to the taking of such action as may be necessary in consequence of such representations.

(7) Every local authority shall give such publicity to the procedure established under this section as they consider appropriate.

General social welfare services of local authorities

12.–(1) It shall be the duty of every local authority to promote social welfare by making available advice, guidance and assistance on such a scale as may be appropriate for their area, and in that behalf to make arrangements and to provide or secure the provision of such facilities (including the provision or arranging for the provision of residential and other establishments) as they may consider suitable and adequate, and such assistance may, subject to subsections (3) to (5) of this section, be given in kind or in cash to, or in respect of, any relevant person.

(2) A person is a relevant person for the purposes of this section if, not being less than eighteen years of age, he is in need requiring assistance in kind or, in exceptional circumstances constituting an emergency, in cash, where the giving of assistance in either form would avoid the local authority being caused greater expense in the giving of assistance in another form, or where probable aggravation of the person's need would cause greater expense to the local authority on a later occasion.

(3) Before giving assistance to, or in respect of, a person in cash under subsection (1) of this section a local authority shall have regard to his eligibility for receiving assistance from

any other statutory body and, if he is eligible, to the availability to him of that assistance in his time of need.

(4) Assistance given in kind or in cash to, or in respect of, persons under this section may be given unconditionally or subject to such conditions as to the repayment of the assistance, or of its real value, whether in whole or in part, as the local authority may consider reasonable having regard to the means of the person receiving the assistance and to the eligibility of the person for assistance from any other statutory body.

(5) Nothing in the provisions of this section shall affect the performance by a local authority of their functions under any other enactment

(6) For the purposes of subsection (2) of this section 'person in need' includes a person who is in need of care and attention arising out of drug or alcohol dependency or release from prison or other form of detention.

Duty of local authority to assess needs

12A.–(1) Subject to the provisions of this section, where it appears to a local authority that any person for whom they are under a duty or have a power to provide, or to secure the provision of, community care services may be in need of any such services, the authority–

(a) shall make an assessment of the needs of that person for those services; and

(b) having regard to the results of that assessment, shall then decide whether the needs of that person call for the provision of any such services.

(2) Before deciding, under subsection (1)(b) of this section, that the needs of any person call for the provision of nursing care, a local authority shall consult a medical practitioner.

(3) If, while they are carrying out their duty under subsection (1) of this section, it appears to a local authority that there may be a need for the provision to any person to whom that subsection applies–

(a) of any services under the National Health Service (Scotland) Act 1978 by the Health Board–

(i) in whose area he is ordinarily resident; or

(ii) in whose area the services to be supplied by the local authority are, or are likely, to be provided; or

(b) of any services which fall within the functions of a housing authority (within the meaning of section 130 (housing) of the Local Government (Scotland) Act 1973) which is not the local authority carrying out the assessment,

the local authority shall so notify that Health Board or housing authority, and shall request information from them as to what services are likely to be made available to that person by that Health Board or housing authority; and, thereafter, in carrying out their said duty, the local authority shall take unto account any information received by them in response to that request.

(3A) Subject to subsection (3B) below, in any case where–

(a) a local authority make an assessment of the needs of any person ('the relevant person') under subsection (1) (a) above, and

(b) a person ('the carer') provides or intends to provide a substantial amount of care on a regular basis for the relevant person,

the carer may request the local authority, before they make their decision under subsection (1)(b) above, to make an assessment of his ability to provide and to continue to provide care for the relevant person; and if he makes such a request, the local authority shall make such an assessment and shall have regard to the results of that assessment in making that decision.

(3B) No request may be made under subsection (3A) above by a person who provides or will provide the care in question–

(a) by virtue of a contract of employment or other contract; or

(b) as a volunteer for a voluntary organisation.

(3C) Section 8 of the Disabled Persons (Services, Consultation and Representation) Act 1986 (duty of local authority to take into account ability of carers) shall not apply in any case where an assessment is made under subsection (3A) above in respect of a person who provides the care in question for a disabled person.

(4) Where a local authority are making an assessment under this section and it appears to them that the person concerned is a disabled person, they shall–

(a) proceed to make such a decision as to the services he requires as is mentioned in section 4 of the Disabled Persons (Services, Consultation and Representation) Act 1986 without his requesting them to do so under that section; and

(b) inform him that they will be doing so and of his rights under that Act.

(5) Nothing in this section shall prevent a local authority from providing or arranging for the provision of community care services for any person without carrying out a prior assessment of his needs in accordance with the preceding provisions of this section if, in the opinion of the authority, the condition of that person is such that he requires those services as a matter of urgency.

(6) If, by virtue of subsection (5) of this section, community care services have been provided for any person as a matter of urgency, then, as soon as practicable thereafter, an assessment of his needs shall be made in accordance with the preceding provisions of this section.

(7) This section is without prejudice to section 3 of the said Act of 1986.

(8) In this section—

'community care services' has the same meaning as in section 5A of this Act;

'disabled person' has the same meaning as in the said Act of 1986;

'medical practitioner' means a fully registered person within the meaning of section 55 (interpretation) of the Medical Act 1983; and

'person' means a natural person.

Direct payments in respect of community care services

12B.—(1) Where, as respects a person in need—

(a) a local authority have decided under section 12A of this Act that his needs call for the provision of any service which is a community care service within the meaning of section 5A of this act, and

(b) the person is of a description which is specified for the purposes of this subsection by regulations,

the authority may, if the person consents, make to him, in respect of his securing the provision of the service, a payment of such amount as, subject to subsection (2) below, they think fit.

(2) If—

(a) an authority pay under subsection (1) above at a rate below their estimate of the reasonable cost of securing the provision of the service concerned, and

(b) the person to whom the payment is made satisfies the authority that his means are insufficient for it to be reasonably practicable for him to make up the difference,

the authority shall so adjust the payment to him under that subsection as to avoid there being a greater difference than that which appears to them to be reasonable practicable for him to make up.

Power of local authorities to assist persons in need in disposal of produce of their work

13. Where, by virtue of section 12 of this Act, a local authority make arrangements or provide or secure the provision of facilities for the engagement of persons in need (whether under a contract of service or otherwise) in suitable work, that local authority may assist such persons in disposing of the produce of their work.

Residential accommodation with nursing

13A.—(1) Without prejudice to section 12 of this Act, a local authority shall make such arrangements as they consider appropriate and adequate for the provision of suitable residential accommodation where nursing is provided for persons who appear to them to be in need of such accommodation by reason of infirmity, age, illness or mental disorder, dependency on drugs or alcohol or being substantially handicapped by any deformity or disability.

(2) The arrangements made by virtue of subsection (1) above shall be made with a voluntary or other organisation or other person, being an organisation or person managing premises which are—

(a) a nursing home within the meaning of section 10(2)(a) of the Nursing Homes Registration (Scotland) Act 1938 in respect of which that organisation or person is registered or exempt from registration under that Act; or

(b) a private hospital registered under section 12 of the Mental Health (Scotland) Act 1984,

for the provision of accommodation in those premises.

(3) The provisions of section 6 of this Act apply in relation to premises where accommodation is provided for the purposes of this section as they apply in relation to establishments provided for the purposes of this Act.

Provision of care and aftercare

13B.—(1) Subject to subsection (2) below, a local authority may with the approval of the Secretary of State, and shall, if and to the extent that the Secretary of State so directs, make arrangements for the purpose of the prevention of illness, the care of persons suffering from illness, and the after–care of such persons.

(2) The arrangements which may be made under subsection (1) above do not include arrangements in respect of medical, dental or nursing care, or health visiting.

Home help and laundry facilities

14.—(1) It shall be the duty of every local authority to provide on such scale as is adequate for the needs of their area, or to arrange for the provision on such a scale as is so adequate of, domiciliary services for households where such services are required owing to the presence, or the proposed presence, of a person in need or a person who is an expectant mother or lying–in, and every such authority shall have power to provide or arrange for the provision of laundry facilities for households for which domiciliary services are being, or can be, provided under this subsection.

(2) [*repealed*]

(3) [*repealed*]

(4) On the coming into operation of the provisions of this and the last two foregoing sections, the provisions of sections 13, 44 and 45 of the Health Services and Public Health Act 1968 shall cease to have effect.

Exclusion of powers to provide accommodation in certain cases

86A.—(1) Subject to subsection (3) below, no accommodation may be provided under this Act for any person who, immediately before the date on which this section comes into force, was ordinarily resident in relevant premises.

(2) In subsection (1) above 'relevant premises' means—

(a) any establishment in respect of which a person is registered under section 62 of this Act;

(b) any nursing home within the meaning of the Nursing Homes Registration (Scotland) Act 1938 in respect of which a person is registered or exempt from registration under that Act;

(c) any private hospital registered under section 12 of the Mental Health (Scotland) Act 1984; and

(d) such other premises as the Secretary of State may by regulations prescribe.

(3) The Secretary of State may by regulations provided that in such cases and subject to such conditions as my be prescribed subsection (1) above shall not apply in relation to such classes of persons as may be prescribed in the regulations.

(4) The Secretary of State shall by regulations prescribe the circumstances in which persons are to be treated as being ordinarily resident in any premises for the purposes of subsection (1) above.

(5) This section does not affect the validity of any contract made before the date on which this section comes into force for the provision of accommodation on or after that date or anything done in pursuance of such as contract.

Charges that may be made for services and accommodation

87.—(1) Subject to. . . the following provisions of this section, a local authority providing a service under this Act or section 7 (functions of local authorities) or 8 (provision of after-care services) of the Mental Health (Scotland) Act 1984. . . may recover such charge (if any) for it as they consider reasonable.

(1A) If a person—

(a) avails himself of a service provided under this Act or section 7 or 8 of the said Act of 1984. . . ; and

(b) satisfies the authority providing the service that his means are insufficient for it to be reasonably practicable for him to pay for the service the amount which he would otherwise be obliged to pay for it,

the authority shall not require him to pay more for it than it appears to them that it is reasonably practicable for him to pay.

(2) Persons. . ., for whom accommodation is provided under this Act or section 7 of the said Act of 1984, shall be required to pay for that accommodation in accordance with the subsequent provisions of this section.

(3) Subject to the following provisions of this section, accommodation provided under this Act or section 7 of the said Act of 1984 shall be regarded as accommodation provided under Part III of the National Assistance Act 1948, and sections 22(2) to (8) and 26(2) to (4). . . and sections 42. . . and 43 of the said Act of 1948 (which make provision for the mutual maintenance of wives and husbands and the maintenance of their children by recovery of

assistance from persons liable for maintenance and for affiliation orders, etc.) shall apply accordingly.

(4) In the application of the said section 22, for any reference to the Minister there shall be substituted a reference to the Secretary of State, and in the application of the said section 26, any references to arrangements under a scheme for the provision of accommodation shall be construed as references to arrangements made by a local authority with a voluntary organisation or any other person or body for the provision of accommodation under this Act or section 7 of the said Act of 1984.

(5) The Secretary of State may, with the consent of the Treasury, make regulations for modifying or adjusting the rates at which payments under this section are made, where such a course appears to him to be justified, and any such regulations may provide for the waiving of any such payment in whole or in part in such circumstances as may be specified in the regulations.

15. NHS (Scotland) Act 1978

Secretary of State

1.—(1) It shall continue to be the duty of the Secretary of State to promote in Scotland a comprehensive and integrated health service designed to secure–

(a) improvement in the physical and mental health of the people of Scotland, and

(b) the prevention, diagnosis and treatment of illness,

and for that purpose to provide or secure the effective provision of services in accordance with the provisions of this Act.

(2) The services so provided shall be free of charge, except in so far as the making and recovery of charges is expressly provided for by or under any enactment, whenever passed.

Other Services and Facilities

36.—(1) It shall be the duty of the Secretary of State to provide throughout Scotland, to such extent as he considers necessary to meet all reasonable requirements, accommodation and services of the following descriptions–

(a) hospital accommodation, including accommodation at state hospitals;

(b) premises other than hospitals at which facilities are available for any of the services provide under this Act;

(c) medical, nursing and other services, whether in such accommodation or premises, in the home of the patient or elsewhere.

(2) Where accommodation or premises provided under this section afford facilities for the provision of general medical, general dental or general ophthalmic services, or of pharmaceutical services, they shall be made available for those services on such terms and conditions as the Secretary of State may determine.

37. The Secretary of State shall make arrangements, to such extent as he considers necessary to meet all reasonable requirements, for the purposes of the prevention if illness, the care of persons suffering from illness or the after–care of such persons.

16. Mental Health (Scotland) Act 1984

Local Authority Services

7.—(1) In relation to persons who are or have been suffering from mental disorder a local authority may, with the approval of the Secretary of State and shall, to such extent as he may direct, make arrangements for any of the following purposes–

(a) the provision, equipment and maintenance of residential accommodation, and the care of persons for the time being resident in accommodation so provided;

(b) the exercise by the local authority of their functions under the following provisions of this Act in respect of persons under guardianship (whether under the guardianship of a local authority or of any other person);

(c) the provision of any ancillary or supplementary services;

(d) the supervision of persons suffering from mental handicap who are neither liable to detention in a hospital nor subject to guardianship.

(2) The reference in subsection (1)(a) of this section to the care of persons for the time being resident in accommodation provided by a local authority includes, in the case of persons so resident who are under the age of 16 years, the payment to those persons of such amounts as he local authority think fit in respect of their personal expenses where it appears to that authority that no such payment would otherwise be made.

8.—(1) A local authority shall provide after–care services for any persons who are or have been suffering from mental disorder.

(2) In providing after–care services under subsection (1) of this section a local authority shall co–operate with such health board or boards and such voluntary organisations as appear to the local authority to be concerned.

(3) The duty imposed by this section is without prejudice to any other power or duty which a local authority may have in relation to the provision of after–care services.

17. Scotland Act 1998

Ministers of the Crown

117.—So far as may be necessary for the purpose or in consequence of the exercise of a function by a member of the Scottish Executive within devolved competence, any pre–commencement enactment or prerogative instrument, and any other instrument or document, shall be read as if references to a Minster of the Crown (however described) were or included references to the Scottish Ministers.

18. s2 Regulation of Care (Scotland) Act 2001

(28) In this Act, unless the context otherwise requires-

'someone who cares for' (or 'a person who cares for') a person, means someone who, being an individual, provides on a regular basis a substantial amount of care for that person, not having contracted to do so and not doing so for payment or in the course of providing a care service;

'vulnerability or need', in relation to a person, means vulnerability or need arising by reason of that person-

(a) being affected by infirmity or ageing;
(b) being, or having been, affected by disability, illness or mental disorder;
(c) being, or having been, dependent on alcohol or drugs; *or*
(d) being of a young age;

'personal care' means care which relates to the day to day physical tasks and needs of the person cared for (as for example, but without prejudice to that generality, to eating and washing) and to mental processes related to those tasks and needs (as for example, but without prejudice to that generality, to remembering to eat and wash); *and*

'personal support' means counselling, or other help, provided as part of a planned programme of care.

19. Community Care and Health (Scotland) Act 2002

Regulations as respects charging and not charging for social care

1(1) Subject to subsection (2)(a) below, a local authority are not to charge for social care provided by them (or the provision of which is secured by them) if that social care is-

(a) personal care as defined in section 2(28) of the Regulation of Care (Scotland) Act 2001 (asp 8);
(b) personal support as so defined;
(c) whether or not such personal care or personal support, care of a kind for the time being mentioned in schedule 1 to this Act; or
(d) whether or not from a registered nurse, nursing care.

(2) The Scottish Ministers may (either or both)-

(a) by regulations qualify the requirements of subsection (1) above in such way as they think fit;
(b) by order amend schedule 1 to this Act.

(3) In paragraph (d) of subsection (1) above, 'nursing care' does not include such social care as falls within any of paragraphs (a) to (c) of that subsection.

(4) Subject to subsection (1) above, the Scottish Ministers may by regulations-

(a) require a local authority-
    (i) to charge; or
    (ii) not to charge,

for such social care provided by (or the provision of which is secured by) the authority as may be specified in the regulations;

(b) where a requirement is made under paragraph (a)(i) above, specify the amount to be charged or factors which the authority must (either or both)-
    (i) take into account;
    (ii) not take into account,

in determining any such amount; and

(c) where a requirement is made under paragraph (a)(ii) above, qualify that requirement in such way as they think fit.

(5) Regulations under subsection (4) above may-

(a) specify, as a factor which the authority must take into account by virtue of paragraph (b) of that subsection, the maximum amount which may be charged for the social care in question or for that and such other social care (being social care provided to the same person by the authority) as may be specified in the regulations; *or*

(b) provide that a person who, in such manner and by reference to such factors as may be specified in the regulations, is assessed by the authority as unable to pay the amount falling to be charged by virtue of that paragraph is required to pay only so much as appears from the assessment to be reasonably practicable for that person.

(6) In section 87 of the 1968 Act (charges that may be made for services and accommodation), after subsection (1A) there is inserted the following subsection-

'(1B) Subsections (1) and (1A) above do not apply as respects any amount required not to be charged by subsection (1) of section 1 of the Community Care and Health (Scotland) Act 2002 (asp 5) (charging and not charging for social care) or required to be charged or not to be charged by virtue of subsection (4) of that section.'

(7) Regulations under this section may make such transitional provision as the Scottish Ministers consider necessary or expedient, modifying either or both of subsections (1) and (2) of section 12A of the 1968 Act (duty of local authority to assess needs of certain persons for community care services) in their application to persons who, immediately before the date of coming into force of this section, were receiving such services in residential accommodation and for whom the local authority were not, at that time, providing or securing the provision either of the services or the accommodation.

SCHEDULE 1

Social care not ordinarily charged for

1. As regards the personal hygiene of the person cared for-
   - (a) shaving;
   - (b) cleaning teeth (whether or not they are artificial) by means of a brush or dental floss and (in the case of artificial teeth) by means of soaking;
   - (c) providing assistance in rinsing the mouth;
   - (d) keeping finger nails and toe nails trimmed;
   - (e) assisting the person with going to the toilet or with using a bedpan or other receptacle;
   - (f) where the person is fitted with a catheter or stoma, providing such assistance as is requisite to ensure cleanliness and that the skin is kept in a favourable hygienic condition;
   - (g) where the person is incontinent-
     - (i) the consequential making of the person's bed and consequential changing and laundering of the person's bedding and clothing; and
     - (ii) caring for the person's skin to ensure that it is not adversely affected.

2. As regards the person's eating requirements-
   - (a) assisting with the preparation of food;
   - (b) assisting in the fulfilment of special dietary needs.

3. If the person is immobile or substantially immobile, dealing with the problems of that immobility.

4. If the person requires medical treatment, assisting with medication, as for example by-
   - (a) applying creams or lotions;
   - (b) administering eye drops;
   - (c) applying dressings in cases where this can be done without the physical involvement of a registered nurse or of a medical practitioner;
   - (d) assisting with the administration of oxygen as part of a course of therapy.

5. With regard to the person's general well-being-
   (a) assisting with getting dressed;
   (b) assisting with surgical appliances, prosthesis and mechanical and manual equipment;
   (c) assisting with getting up and with going to bed;
   (d) the provision of devices to help memory and of safety devices;
   (e) behaviour management and psychological support.

Appendix 2

Key guidance

The following are some of the key circulars issued to social services departments which are useful for establishing whether or how much you pay for your care. These and other circulars mentioned in the text can be obtained from:

- **England**: Department of Health, PO Box 777, London SE1 6XH (also circulars from 1995 at www.doh.gov.uk/coin.htm).
- **Wales**: Welsh Assembly, Crown Buildings, Cathays Park CF10 3NQ (also circulars from 1999 at www.assembly.wales.gov.uk). Note from 1999 the names of Welsh circulars have changed. WOCs are now issued as NAfWCs.
- **Scotland**: Scottish Executive, Community Care Division, James Craig Walk, Edinburgh EH1 3BA (also from www.show.scot.nhs.uk/sehd). Note from 1999 names of Scottish circulars have changed. SWSGs are now issued as CCDs and MELs are now issued as HDLs.

	England	*Wales*	*Scotland*
Charges			
Includes the full guidance for charges with previous circulars annexed	LAC (2003)8 CRAG consolidates the previous versions of CRAG	NAfWC 19/2003 and 21/2003 consolidate the previous versions of CRAG	HDL 7/2003 consolidates most of the previous SWSGs/CCDs relating to CRAG, See also HDL 6/2003 and CCD3/2003

	England	*Wales*	*Scotland*
Covers discretionary charges for adult services	LAC (01)32 *Fairer charging policies for home care and other non-residential social services*	NAfWC 17/2003 interim guidance and NAfWC 28/2002	SWSG1/97 and guidance on charging policies for non-residential services that enable older people to remain in their own home issued by COSLA 2002. Free personal care guidance CCD 4/2002

Other Important Circulars

Choice of Accommodation	LAC (92)27 LAC (93)18 LAC (01) 29	WOC12/93 WOC47/93 NAfWC 21/2003	SWSG5/93 SWSG6/94
Ordinary residence	LAC(93)7	WOC35/93	SWSG1/96
NHS responsibilities for meeting continuing health care needs please note there may be changes to the Welsh guidance.	LAC (01)18 HSC 2001/015	WOC 16/95 WHC (95)7	MEL (1996)22
Discharge from NHS inpatient care-arrangements for receiving decisions on eligibility for NHS continuing care	LAC (95)17 HSG 95/39 This has been cancelled in England and so far not replaced.	WHC(95)7	MEL (1996)22
Guidance on the Community Care (Residential Accommodation) Act 1998	LAC (98)	WOC 27/98	SWSG2/99 CCD 3/2002

Guidance on free nursing care (and personal care in Scotland)	LAC (2001)26 HSC 2001/1 And LAC 2003 (7)	NAfWc 34/2001 and NAfWC 12/ 2003	CCD4/2002
Guidance on intermediate care (England) 6 week free care (Wales) 4 weeks free care (Scotland)	LAC) (2001)01 LAC (2003)14	NAfWC 05/2002 NAfWC 43/2002	CCD2/2001

Appendix 3

Useful addresses

Government departments/agencies UK wide

Appeals Service
4th floor
Whittington House
19-30 Alfred Place
London WC1E 7LW
Tel 020 7712 2600
www.appeals-service.gov.uk

Department for Work and Pensions (benefits)
Quarry House
Quarry Hill
Leeds LS2 7UA
Tel: 0113 232 4000
www.dwp.gov.uk

Department for Work and Pensions (policy)
The Adelphi
1-11 John Adam Street
London WC2N 6HT
Tel: 020 7962 8000
www.dwp.gov.uk

Disability Benefit Unit
Warbreck House
Warbreck Hill Road
Blackpool
Lancashire FY2 0YE
Tel: 0845 712 3456
Textphone: 0845 722 4433

Independent Living Fund
PO Box 7525
Nottingham NG2 4ZT
Tel: 0845 601 8815
email: funds@ilf.org.uk
www.ilf.org.uk

Independent Review Service for the Social Fund
Centre City Podium
5 Hill Street
Birmingham B5 4UB
Tel: 0121 606 2100
www.irssf.gov.uk

Inland Revenue (tax credits)
Tax Credits Office
Preston
PR1 0SB
Tel: 0845 300 3909
www.inlandrevenue.gov.uk

Inland Revenue (child benefit and guardian's allowance)
Child Benefit Office
Washington
PO Box 1
Newcastle upon Tyne
NE88 1AA
Tel: 0845 302 1444

The Parliamentary Ombudsman
Millbank Tower
Millbank
London SW1P 4QP
Tel: 0845 015 4033
www.ombudsman.org.uk

Pensions and Overseas Benefits Directorate
Tyneview Park
Whitley Road
Newcastle-upon-Tyne
NE98 1BA
Tel: 0191 218 7878
Textphone: 0191 218 2160
www.dwp.gov.uk

Regional Disability Benefits Centres

Birmingham DBC
Five Ways Complex
Edgbaston
Birmingham B15 1SL
Tel: 0121 626 2000
Covers: West Midlands, Shropshire, Hereford and Worcester, Staffordshire, Leicestershire, Warwickshire, Northamptonshire, Derbyshire, Nottinghamshire, Lincolnshire

Bootle DBC
St Martin's House
Stanley Precinct
Bootle L69 9BN
Tel: 0151 934 6000
Covers: Merseyside, Central and North West Lancashire, Cumbria, North, South and West Cheshire

Bristol DBC
Government Buildings
Flowers Hill
Bristol BS4 5LA
Tel: 0117 971 8311
Covers: Cornwall, Devon, Wiltshire, Gloucestershire, Bristol, Somerset, Dorset

Leeds DBC
Government Buildings
Otley Road
Leeds LS16 5PU
Tel: 0113 230 9000
Covers: Derbyshire (High Peak), East Cheshire, Yorkshire, East Lancashire, part of Tyne and Wear

Manchester DBC
Albert Bridge House
Bridge Street
Manchester
M60 9DA
Tel 0161 831 2000
Covers: Greater Manchester and surrounding areas

Newcastle DBC
Regent Centre
Arden House
Regent Centre
Regent Farm Road
Newcastle-upon-Tyne
NE3 3JN
Tel: 0191 223 3000
Covers: Tyne and Wear, Durham, Northumberland, Cleveland

Sutton DBC
Sutherland House
29-37 Brighton Road
Sutton
Surrey SM2 5AN
Tel: 020 8652 6000
Covers: London postal districts WC1 and WC2, SE1-SE28, SW1-SW20, W1, W6, W8 and W14, Kent, Berkshire, Hampshire, Surrey, East Sussex, West Sussex, Isle of Wight, Kingston, Woking, Hounslow, Twickenham

Wembley DBC
Olympic House
Wembley
Middlesex HA9 0DL
Tel: 020 8795 8400
Covers: London postal districts EC1-EC4, E1-E18, N1-N27, NW1-NW11, W2-W5, W7, W9-W13, Buckinghamshire, Bedfordshire, Essex, Cambridgeshire, Hertfordshire, Middlesex (except Hounslow and Twickenham), Oxfordshire, Suffolk, Norfolk

Edinburgh DBC
Argyle House
3 Lady Lawson Street
Edinburgh EH3 9SH
Tel: 0131 222 5467
Minicom: 0131 222 5494
Covers: the eastern part of Scotland, including Edinburgh, Perth, Dundee and Aberdeen

Glasgow DBC
29 Cadogan Street
Glasgow G2 7BN
Tel: 0141 249 3500
Covers: West of Scotland including Glasgow, Strathclyde, Ayrshire, Oban, part of the Western Isles and Outer Hebrides

Cardiff DBC
Government Buildings
St Agnes Road
Cardiff CF14 4YJ
Tel: 029 2058 6002
Covers: Wales

Government departments/agencies nationally based

England	Scotland	Wales
Department of Health Wellington House 133-155 Waterloo Road London SE1 8UG Tel: 020 7972 2000 www.doh.gov.uk	**Scottish Executive** Community Care Division James Craig Walk Edinburgh EH1 3BA Tel: 0131 244 3635 www.scotland.gov.uk	**National Assembly for Wales** Public Information Cardiff Bay Cardiff CF99 1NA Tel: 029 2089 8200 www.wales.gov.uk
Office of the Social Security and Child Support Commisioners Harp House 83 Farringdon Street London EC4A 4DH Tel: 020 7353 5145	**Office of the Social Security and Child Support Commissioners** 23 Melville Street Edinburgh EH3 7PW Tel: 0131 225 2201	As England
Health Service Ombudsman Millbank Tower London SW1P 4QP Helpline: 0845 015 4033 www.ombudsman.org.uk.	**Health Service Ombudsman** 28 Thistle Street Edinburgh EH2 1EN Tel: 0845 601 0456 www.ombudsman.org.uk.	**Health Service Ombudsman** 5th floor Capital Tower Grey Friars Road Cardiff CF10 3AG Tel: 0845 601 0987 www.ombudsman.org.uk
Local Government Ombudsman Call 0845 602 1983 for details of the Ombudsman covering your area. www.lgo.org.uk	**Local Government Ombudsman** 23 Walker Street Edinburgh EH3 7HX Tel: 0131 225 5300 www.ombudslgscot.org.uk	**Local Government Ombudsman** Derwen House Court Road Bridgend CF31 1BN Tel: 01656 661325 www.ombudsman-wales.org
Mental Health Act Commission Maid Marian House 56 Houndsgate Nottingham NG1 6BG Tel: 0115 943 7100 www.mhac.trent.nhs.uk	**Mental Welfare Commission for Scotland** K floor, Argyle House 3 Lady Lawson Street Edinburgh EH3 9SH Tel: 0131 222 6111	As England

National Social Care Commission
St Nicholas Building
St Nicholas Street
Newcastle-upon-Tyne
NE1 1NB
Tel: 0191 233 3556
email: enquiries@ncsc
www.carestandards.org.uk

Scottish Commission for the Regulation of Care (Care Commission)
Compass House
11 Riverside Drive
Dundee DD1 2NY
Tel: 01382 207100
www.carecommission.com

Care Standards Inspectorate for Wales
Heol Billingley
Parc Nantgarw
Nanatgarw CF15 7 QZ
Tel: 01443 848450
www.wales.go.uk/subisocial policycarestandards/

Public Guardianship Office
Archway Tower
2 Junction Road
London
N19 5SZ
Tel: 0845 330 2900
www.guardianship.gov.uk

The Office of the Public Guardian
Hadrian House
Callendar Business Park
Callendar Road
FK1 1XR
Tel: 01324 678 300
E-mail: opg@scotcourts.gov.uk
Website: www.publicguardian-scotland.gov.uk

As England

Government-based phonelines

Benefit Enquiry Line
0800 882 200
Textphone: 0800 243 355
Specialises in benefit advice for disabled people, their carers and representatives.

Disability Benefits Customer Care Helpline
0845 712 3456
Textphone: 0845 722 4433
For enquiries on DLA or AA claims and general enquiries on disability benefits.

NHS Direct
(England & Wales)
Tel: 0845 4647

Major voluntary organisations nationally based

Space precludes listing all but the major organisations which offer information and advice about paying for care and other aspects of community care.

England

Age Concern England
Astral House
1268 London Road
London SW16 4ER
Information Line: 0800 00 99 66.
www.ageconcern.org.uk

Alzheimer's Society
Gordon House
10 Greencoat Place
London SW1P 1PH
Tel: 020 7306 0606
Helpline: 0845 300 0336
www.alzheimers.org.uk

CarersUK
20-25 Glasshouse Yard
London EC1A 4JT
Tel: 020 7490 8818
Advice Line: 0808 808 7777
www.carersonline.org.uk

Counsel and Care for the Elderly
Twyman House
16 Bonny Street
London NW1 9PG
Tel: 0845 300 7585
Advice on care at home, care homes, community care and financial help.

Scotland

Age Concern Scotland
113 Rose Street
Edinburgh
EH2 3DT
Tel: 0131 220 3345

Alzheimer Scotland – Action on Dementia
22 Drumsheugh Gardens
Edinburgh EH3 7RN
Tel: 0131 243 1453
24 Hour Freephone: 0808 808 3000.
www.alscot.org

Carers Scotland
91 Mitchell Street
Glasgow G1 3LN
Tel: 0141 221 9141
email: info@carerscotland.demon.co.uk
www.carersonline.org.uk

Wales

Age Concern Cymru
4th floor
1 Cathedral Road
Cardiff CF11 9SD
Tel: 029 2037 1566
Welsh language line: 0800 371 131

Alzheimer's Society
Baltic House
Mount Stuart Square
Cardiff CF10 5FH
Tel: 029 2043 1990
www.alzheimers.org.uk

Carers Wales
River House
Ynys Bridge Court
Gwaelod-y-Garth
Cardiff CF15 9SS
Tel: 029 2081 1370
www.carersonline.org.uk

Disability Wales
Wenddu Court
Caerphilly Business Park
Caerphilly CF83 1XL
Tel: 029 2088 7325
Promotes recognition of, and support for, all disabled people in Wales.

Help the Aged 207-221 Pentonville Road London N1 9UZ Senior Line: 0808 800 6565 www.helptheaged.org.uk	**Help the Aged** 11 Granton Square Edinburgh EH5 1HX Tel: 0131 556 4666 www.helptheaged.org.uk	**Help the Aged** CSV House Williams Way Cardiff CF10 5DY Tel: 029 2041 5711 www.helptheaged.org.uk
Law Society 113 Chancery Lane London WC2A 1PL Tel: 020 7242 1222 www.lawsociety.org.uk	**Law Society of Scotland** 26 Drumsheugh Gardens Edinburgh EH3 7YR Tel: 0131 226 7411 www.lawscot.org.uk	As England
MENCAP 123 Golden Lane London EC1Y 0RT Tel: 020 7454 0454 www.mencap.org.uk	**ENABLE** 6th Floor 7 Buchanan Street Glasgow G1 3HL Tel: 0141 226 4541	**MENCAP** 31 Lambourne Crescent Cardiff CF14 5GF Tel: 029 2074 7588
Mind (The National Association of Mental Health) Granta House 15-19 The Broadway London E15 4BQ Tel: 020 8519 2122 London Info Line: 020 8522 1728 Outside London: 0845 766 0163 www.mind.org.uk		**Mind Cymru** 3rd Floor, Quebec House Castlebridge Cowbridge Road East Cardiff CF11 9AB Tel: 029 2039 5123 Information Line: 0845 766 0163 www.mind.org.uk
Royal National Institute for the Blind 105 Judd Street London WC1H 9NE Helpline: 08457 669 999 www.rnib.org.uk	**Royal National Institute for the Blind (Scotland)** Dunedin House 25 Ravelston Terrace Edinburgh EH4 3TP Tel: 0131 311 8500 www.rnib.org.uk	**Royal National Institute for the Blind (Cymru)** Trident House East Moors Road Cardiff CF24 5TD Tel: 029 2045 0440 www.rnib.org.uk

Royal National Institute for Deaf People
19-23 Featherstone Street
London EC1Y 8SL
Helpline: 0808 808 0123
Text: 0808 808 9000
Tinnitus Helpline: 0808 808 6666
Tinnitus Text Helpline: 0808 808 0007
www.rnid.org.uk

RNID Scotland
Floor 3
Crowngate Business Centre
Brook Street
Glasgow G40 3AP
Tel: 0141 554 0053
Text: 0141 550 5750
www.rnid.org.uk

Royal National Institute for the Deaf (Cymru)
33-35 Cathedral Road
Cardiff CF11 9HB
Tel: 029 2033 3034
Text 029 2033 3036
www.rnid.org.uk

Major voluntary organisations – UK wide

Space precludes listing all but the major organisations which offer information and advice about paying for care and other aspects of community care.

Child Poverty Action Group
94 White Lion Street
London N1 9PF
Tel: 020 7837 7979
www.cpag.org.uk

Dial UK
St Catherine's
Tickhill Road
Doncaster DN4 8QN
Tel: 01302 310 123
www.dialuk.org.uk
(Disability information)

Disabled Living Centres Council
Red Bank House
4 St Chads Street
Manchester M8 8QA
Tel: 0161 834 1044

Law Centres Federation
Duchess House
18-19 Warren Street
London W1P 5LR
Tel: 020 7387 8570
www.lawcentres.org.uk

Citizens Advice
Myddelton House
115-123 Pentonville Road
London N1 9LZ
Tel: 020 7833 2181
www.citizensadvice.org.uk

National Centre for Independent Living
250 Kennington Lane
London SE11 5RD
Tel: 020 7587 1663
ncil@ncil.org.uk
www.ncil.org.uk

The Patient's Association
PO Box 935
Harrow
Middlesex HA1 3YJ
Tel: 020 8423 9111
Helpline: 0845 608 4455
Text: 020 8423 0623
www.patients-association.com

Public Law Project
14 Bloomsbury Square
London WC1A 2LP
Tel: 020 7269 0570
www.publiclawproject.org.uk

RADAR (Royal Association for Disability and Rehabilitation)
12 City Forum
250 City Road
London EC1V 8AF
Tel: 020 7250 3222
Minicom: 020 7250 4119
www.radar.org.uk

Appendix 4

Information and advice

Independent advice and representation

It is sometimes difficult for unsupported individuals to get a positive response from the DWP. You may be taken more seriously if it is clear you have taken advice about your entitlement or have an adviser assisting you.

If you want advice or help with a benefit problem, the following agencies may be able to assist.

- Citizens advice bureaux (CAB) and other local advice centres provide information and advice about benefits and may be able to represent you.
- Law centres can often help in a similar way to a CAB or advice centre.
- Local authority welfare rights workers provide a service in many areas and some arrange advice sessions and take-up campaigns locally.
- Local organisations for particular groups of claimants may offer help. For instance, there are unemployed centres, pensioners groups and centres for people with disabilities.
- Solicitors can give free legal advice to people on low incomes under the 'Legal help' or 'Claim 10' scheme. This does not cover the cost of representation at an appeal hearing but can cover the cost of preparing written submissions and obtaining evidence such as medical reports. However, solicitors do not always have a good working knowledge of the benefit rules and you may need to shop around until you find one who does.

You can find details of advice centres and lawyers in the phone book either under 'advice' or in the 'community' section at the front of the book. Your library or community centre may have details of where to get advice in your area. The Legal Services Commission has a list of many organisations who provide advice in different areas of law including welfare benefits and community care. You can phone them on 0845 608 1122 or access this information over the internet at www.justask.org.uk and search the 'directory' for advisers and lawyers within 5, 10 or 40 miles of your home.

Advice from CPAG

Unfortunately, CPAG is unable to deal with enquiries directly from members of the public, but if you are an adviser you can phone the advice line from 2 pm to 4 pm, Monday to Friday on 020 7833 4627. This is a special phone line; do not ring the main CPAG number. Alternatively, you can write to us at the Citizens' Rights Office, CPAG, 94 White Lion Street, London N1 9PF. Organisations based in Scotland can contact CPAG in Scotland at Suite 9, Ladywell Centre, 94 Duke Street, Glasgow, G4 0UW. A phone line is open for Scottish advisers on Tuesday and Wednesday mornings between 10 am and 12 noon on 0141 552 0552.

Advice from the DWP

You can find an address and phone numbers for your local DWP office in the phone book. They should be able to give you contact details for any office dealing with particular benefits. If you are disabled, you can obtain free telephone advice on benefits on 0800 882 200 (in Northern Ireland 0800 220 674), minicom: 0800 243 355. This is for general advice and not specific queries on individual claims.

If English is not your first language, ask your local DWP office to arrange for advice in your own language.

Finding help on the internet

Some information about benefits and a selection of leaflets and forms is available on the DWP website at: www.dwp.gov.uk. The Department of Health website (www.doh.gov.uk) also contains a large amount of information including all the circulars, and often information to local authorities and NHS bodies in the form of advice or frequently asked questions.

CPAG has a website which carries some articles about upcoming legislation and information about our publications, training and campaigning activity at www.cpag.org.uk.

The RightsNet website at www.rightsnet.org.uk carries details of new legislation and policies affecting social security benefits. It also has links to other useful sites.

Most Acts and Regulations can be found on the government information website at www.hmso.gov.uk and for information regarding tax credits see www.inlandrevenue.gov.uk.

You can find recent decisions of the social security commissioners at www.osscsc.gov.uk. You can also find many decisions from 1995 to the end of 2001 at www.hywels.demon.co.uk.

Appendix 5

Books, leaflets and periodicals

Many of the books listed here will be in your local library. Stationery Office books are available from Stationery Office bookshops and also from many others. They may be ordered by post, telephone or fax from The Publications Centre, PO Box 276, London SW8 5DT (tel: 020 7873 9090, fax: 020 7873 8200; general enquiries tel: 020 7873 0011, fax: 020 7873 8247; www.hmso.gov.uk). Many of the publications listed are available from CPAG; see below for order details, or order from www.cpag.org.uk. For social security information in electronic format see details of the *Welfare Benefits and Tax Credits CD-ROM* given below.

1. Textbooks

From poor law to community care, Means and Smith, 1998 (second edition). Policy Press. A history of the development of welfare services for older people.
Community Care and the Law, Luke Clements, 2000 (second edition). Legal Action Group. An overview and analysis of the legislation.
Community Care Practice and the Law, Michael Mandelstam, 1999 (second edition). Jessica Kingsley Publishers. A guide to law and practice, containing digests of over three hundred legal judgements and ombudsman investigations.
Managing Other People's Money, Penny Letts, 1998 (second edition). Age Concern. A guide to the power available to take over arrangements.
Home from Home: your guide to choosing a care home, 1998. Kings Fund. Suggests questions to ask when choosing a home.
Long Term Care for Older People, Margaret Richards, 2001. Jordans. A comprehensive explanation of the responsibilities of local authorities and the NHS for providing publicly funded long term care, with a detailed and practical analysis of the funding arrangements.
Moving on from Community Care, Lorna Easterbrook, 2003. Age Concern. An up-to-date analysis of community care and the current legislation.

2. Caselaw and legislation

Welfare Benefits and Tax Credits Handbook, CPAG. Comprehensive interpretation of all social security law. £30.00 (£7.50 for claimants) (April 2003)

Welfare Benefits CD-ROM, CPAG. Includes: all social security legislation consolidated; over 1,000 commissioners' decisions, most with commentary; guidance; the *Welfare Benefits and Tax Credits Handbook* with links to the relevant legislation, decisions and guidance; CPAG's *Housing Benefit and Council Tax Benefit Legislation* (with commentary); significant housing benefit and council tax benefit circulars; the *Child Support Handbook* and child support regulations. Updated three times a year. Free trial disks are available from CPAG. Phone Liz Dawson on 020 7837 7979 ext 212 for prices.

The Law Relating to Social Security, Stationery Office, looseleaf, 11 vols. All the legislation but without any comment. Known as the 'Blue Book'. Vols 6, 7, 8 and 11 deal with means-tested benefits.

Social Security Legislation, Volume I: Non-Means-Tested Benefits, D Bonner, I Hooker and R White (Sweet & Maxwell). Legislation with commentary. Available from CPAG (£68).

Social Security Legislation, Volume II: Income Support, Jobseeker's Allowance, Tax Credits and the Social Fund, J Mesher, P Wood, R Poynter, N Wikeley and D Bonner (Sweet & Maxwell). Legislation with commentary. Available from CPAG (£68).

Social Security Legislation, Volume III: Administration, Adjudication and the European Dimension, M Rowland and R White (Sweet & Maxwell). Available from CPAG (October 2003, £68).

Social Security Legislation, Volume IV: Tax Credits, Wikeley/Williams (Sweet & Maxwell). Available from CPAG (October 2003, £68)

Social Security Legislation – updating supplement to Volumes I, II, III and IV (Sweet & Maxwell). Available from CPAG (March 2004, £42).

CPAG's Housing Benefit and Council Tax Benefit Legislation, L Findlay, R Poynter, P Stagg and M Ward (CPAG). Contains legislation with a detailed commentary. 2003/04 edition available from CPAG, (£79 including Supplement). This publication is also on the Welfare Benefits and Tax Credits CD-ROM (see p458).

The Social Fund: Law and Practice, T Buck (Sweet & Maxwell). Includes legislation, guidance and commentary. The 2nd edition (July 2000) is available from CPAG for £49 if you are a CPAG member.

Encyclopaedia of Social Services and Child Care Law (Sweet & Maxwell). The legislation affecting social services with some commentary. Loose leaf with regular updates.

Community Care Law Reports, LAG. Quarterly update of legal cases and guidance.

Social Fund Directions, are available on the IRS website at www.irssf.demon.co.uk/ssdir.htm.

3. Official guidance

Charging for Residential Accommodation Guide, (Department of Health, one vol).

Fair Charging Policies for Home Care and other Non-residential Services, (Department of Health)

Housing Benefit and Council Tax Benefit Guidance Manual, (Stationary Office, looseleaf).
The Social Fund Guide, (Stationary Office, looseleaf 2 vols.)

4. Leaflets and booklets

The DWP publishes many leaflets which cover particular benefits or particular groups of claimants or contributors. They are free from your local DWP office, or on Freephone 0800 666 555. If you want to order large numbers of leaflets, you can join the Publicity Register by contacting the DWP, 3rd Floor South, 1 Trevelyan Square, Leeds LS1 6EB, tel. 0645 540 000 (local rate). The DWP also has a leaflets Unit at Block 4, Government Buildings, Honeypot Lane, Stanmore, Middlesex HA7 1AY. Free leaflets on HB/CTB are available from the relevant department of your local council.

A selection of leaflets is available on www.dwp.gov.uk. The Department of Health also produces some leaflets including: *A Guide to receiving Direct Payments; A Practical Guide for Disabled People; Helping you to stay independent.*

Most local authorities also produce a range of leaflets on the services they provide.

5. Periodicals

CPAG's *Welfare Rights Bulletin* is published every two months by CPAG. It covers developments in social security law and updates the *Welfare Benefits and Tax Credits Handbook* between editions. The annual subscription is £28 but is sent automatically to CPAG Rights and Comprehensive Members. For subscription and membership details contact CPAG.

Articles on social security and social welfare can also be found in *Legal Action* (Legal Action Group, monthly magazine), the *Journal of Social Security Law* (Sweet & Maxwell, quarterly), and the *Adviser* (NACAB, every two months).
Journal of Social Welfare and Family Law, quarterly, Routledge.
Community Care Magazine, weekly.
Elderly Client Adviser, bi-monthly, Ark Publishing.
Elderly Law and Finance, quarterly, Jordan Press.
Disability Rights Bulletin, 3 times a year, Disability Alliance.

6. Other publications – general

Please note that some non-CPAG publications (Sweet & Maxwell, Disability Alliance, etc) are available to order from CPAG if you are a CPAG member/ subscriber.

Child Support Handbook (CPAG), £18.50 (11th edition, autumn 2003) (£5.00 for claimants). Also available on the *Welfare Benefits and Tax Credits CD-ROM.*
Council Tax Handbook (CPAG), £13.95 (5th edition, December 2002)
Debt Advice Handbook (CPAG), £14.95 (5th edition, November 2002)
Fuel Rights Handbook (CPAG), £13.95 (12th edition, February 2002)
Migration and Social Security Handbook (CPAG), £17.95 (3rd edition, October 2002)
A Guide to Housing Benefit and Council Tax Benefit (Shelter/CIOH), £20.95 (July 2003) available from CPAG
Disability Rights Handbook (Disability Alliance), £14.00 (May 2003) available from CPAG
The Young Person's Handbook, £10.95 (6th edition, November 2002) available from CPAG
Welfare-to-Work Handbook (CESI), £18.95 (1st edition, August 2003, available from CPAG)

For CPAG publications and most of those in Sections 2 and 6 contact:

CPAG, 94 White Lion Street, London N1 9PF, tel: 020 7837 7979, fax: 020 7837 6414. Order forms are also available at: www.cpag.org.uk. For postage and packing add a flat rate charge: for orders up to £9.99 in value, add £1.30; order value £10-199.99 add £3.30; for £200+ add £5.30.

Appendix 6

Abbreviations used in the notes

References are to statutes and regulations as amended up to 20 May 2002.

AC	Appeal Cases
All ER	All England Reports
CA	Court of Appeal
CAO	Chief Adjudication Officer
CCLR	Community Care Law Reports
DC	Divisional Court
ECHR	European Convention on Human Rights
ECtHR	European Court of Human Rights
EWHC	England and Wales High Court
HC	High Court
HL	House of Lords
HLR	Housing Law Reports
NAB	National Assistance Board
para(s)	paragraph(s)
QBD	Queen's Bench Division
reg(s)	regulation(s)
s(s)	section(s)
SBC	Supplementary Benefits Commission
Sch(s)	Schedule(s)
TLR	Times Law Reports
WLR	Weekly Law Reports

Acts of Parliament

B(S)A 1985	Bankruptcy (Scotland) Act 1985
CA 1989	Children Act 1989
CC(DD)A 2003	Community Care (Delayed Discharges etc) Act 2003
CCDPA 1996	Community Care (Direct Payments) Act 1996
CCH(S)A	Community Care and Health (Scotland) Act 2002
CDCA 2000	Carers and Disabled Children Act 2000
CRSA 1995	Carers (Recognition and Services) Act 1995
CSA 2000	Care Standards Act 2000

CSDPA 1970	Chronically Sick and Disabled Persons Act 1970
CSPSSA 2000	Child Support, Pensions and Social Security Act 2000
DPSCRA 1986	Disabled Persons (Services, Consultation and Representation) Act 1986
H(S)A 1987	Housing (Scotland) Act 1987
HA 1985	Housing Act 1985
HA 1996	Housing Act 1996
HA 1999	Health Act 1999
HASSASSAA 1983	The Health and Social Services and Social Security Adjudication Act 1983
HCPA 1995	Hospital Complaints Procedure Act 1995
HGCRA 1996	Housing Grants, Construction and Regeneration Act 1996
HSCA 2001	Health Service Commissioners Act 2001
HSCA 1993	Health Service Commissioners Act 1993
HSPHA 1948	Health Services and Public Health Act 1948
IA 1986	Insolvency Act 1986
JSA 1995	Jobseekers Act 1995
LASSA 1970	Local Authority Social Services Act 1970
LG(S)A 1975	Local Government (Scotland) Act 1975
LGA 1974	Local Government Act 1974
LGFA 1992	Local Government Finance Act 1992
LGHA 1989	Local Government and Housing Act 1989
MHA 1983	Mental Health Act 1983
MH(S)A 1984	Mental Health (Scotland) Act 1984
NAA 1948	National Assistance Act 1948
NHSA 1977	National Health Service Act 1977
NHS(S)A 1978	National Health Service (Scotland) Act 1978
NHSCCA 1990	National Health Services Act and Community Care Act 1990
RHA 1984	Registered Homes Act 1984
SPCA 2002	State Pension Credit Act 2002
SSA 1998	Social Security Act 1998
SSAA 1992	Social Security Administration Act 1992
SSCBA 1992	Social Security Contributions and Benefits Act 1992
SW(S)A 1968	Social Work (Scotland) Act 1968
TCA 2002	Tax Credits Act 2002
WRPA 1999	Welfare Reform and Pensions Act 1999

Regulations

C(LC)SSB Regs	The Child (Leaving Care) Social Security Benefits Regulations 2001 No.3074

CC(DD)(QS)(E) Regs	The Community Care (Delayed Discharge etc) Act (Qualifying Services) (England) Regulations 2003 No. 1196
CCDP Regs	Community Care (Direct Payments) Regulations 1997 No.734
CCSCCSDP(E) Regs	The Community Care, Services for Carers and Children's Services (Direct Payment) (England) Regulations 2003 No.762
CO(RA)(S)O 1993	The Charging Order (Residential Accommodation) (Scotland) Order 1993
CT(ED)O	The Council Tax (Exempt Dwellings) Order 1992 No.558 as amended: 1994 No.539
CT(RD) Regs	The Council Tax (Regulations for Disabilities) Regulations 1992 No.554
CT(RD)(Amdt) Regs	The Council Tax (Reductions for Disabilities) (Amendment) Regulations 1999
CT(RD) Regs	The Council Tax (Reductions for Disability) Regulations 1992 No. 554
CTB Regs	The Council Tax Benefit (General) Regulations 1992 No.1814
DFA Regs	The Discretionary Financial Assistance Regulations 2001 No.1167
DP(BMV) Regs	The Disabled Persons (Badges for Motor Vehicles) Regulations 1982
DWA Regs	The Disability Working Allowance (General) Regulations 1991 No.2887
HB Regs	The Housing Benefit (General) Regulations 1987 No.1971
HB&CTB(DA) Regs	The Housing Benefit and Council Tax Benefit (Decisions and Appeals) Regulations 2001 No.1002
HEES(E)	The Home Energy Efficiency Scheme (England) Regulations
HEES(W)	The Home Energy Efficiency Scheme (Wales) Regulations
HRA Regs	The Home Repair Assistance Regulations 1996
HRG Regs	The Housing Renewal Grants Regulations 1996
IRBS(Amdt2) Regs	The Income-related Benefits Schemes (Miscellaneous Amendments) (No.2) Regulations 1995 No.1339
IS Regs	The Income Support (General) Regulations 1987 No.1967
JSA Regs	The Jobseeker's Allowance Regulations 1996 No.207

N(RA)(RC)(E) Regs	The National Assistance (Residential Accommodation) (Relevant Contributions) (England) Regulations 2001 No.3069
NA(AR) Regs	The National Assistance (Assessment of Resources) Regulations 1992 No.2977
NA(AR)(A)(E) Regs	The National Assistance (Assessment of Resources) (Amendment) (England) Regulations 2002 No.410
NA(AR)(Amdt2) Regs	The National Assistance (Assessment of Resources) (Amendment) (No.2) Regulations 1998 No.1730
NA(AR)(Amdt2) Regs	The National Assistance (Assessment of Resources) (Amendment) (No.2) Regulations 2001 No.1066
NA(RAAPAR)(E) Regs	The National Assistance (Residential Accommodation) (Additional Payments and Assessment of Resources) (Amendment) (England) Regulations 2001 No.3441
NA(RADR)(E) Regs	The National Assistance (Residential Accommodation) (Disregarding of Resources) (England) Regulations 2001 No.3067
NA(SPR)(E) Regs	The National Assistance (Sums for Personal Requirements) (England) Regulations 2001 No.411
NHS(CDA) Regs	The National Health Service (Charges for Drugs and Appliances) Regulations 2000 No.620
NHS(CDA)(S) Regs	The National Health Service (Charges for Drugs and Appliances) (Scotland) Regulations 2001 No.430
NHS(CDA)(W) Regs	The Nationla Health Service (Charges for Drugs and Appliances) (Wales) Regulations 2001 No.1358(W86)
NHS(DC) Regs	The National Health Service (Dental Charges) Regulations 1989 No.394
NHS(DC)(S) Regs	The National Health Service (Dental Charges) (Scotland) Regulations 1989 No.363
NHS(GOS) Regs	The National Health Service (General Ophthalmic Services) Regulations 1986 No.975
NHS(OCP) Regs	The National Health Service (Optical Charges and Payments) Regulations 1997 No.818
NHS(OCP)(S) Regs	The National Health Service (Optical Charges and Payments) (Scotland) Regulations 1998 No.642
NHS(TERC) Regs	The National Health Service (Travelling Expenses and Remission of Charges) Regulations 1988 No.551
NHS(TERC)(S) Regs	The National Health Service (Travelling Expenses and Remission of Charges) (Scotland) Regulations 1988 No.546
RR(CA)O	The Regulatory Reform (Carer's Allowance) Order 2002
SFCWP Regs	The Social Fund Cold Weather Payments (General) Regulations 1988 No.1724

SFM&FE Regs	The Social Fund Maternity and Funeral Expenses (General) Regulations 1987 No.481
SFWFP Regs	The Social Fund Winter Fuel Payment Regulations 2000 No.729
SMP Regs	The Statutory Maternity Pay (General) Regulations 1986 No.1960
SPC Regs	The State Pension Credit Regulations 2002 No. 1792
SS(AA) Regs	The Social Security (Attendance Allowance) Regulations 1991 No.2740
SS(AA/DLA) Regs	The Social Security (Attendance Allowance and Disability Living Allowance) (Amendment) Regulations 2002 No.208
SS(C&P) Regs	The Social Security (Claims and Payments) Regulations 1987 No.1968
SS(CE) Regs	The Social Security (Computation of Earnings) Regulations 1996 No.2745
SS(DLA) Regs	The Social Security (Disability Living Allowance) Regulations 1991 No.2890
SS(GB) Regs	The Social Security (General Benefits) Regulations 1982 No.1408
SS(HIP) Regs	The Social Security (Hospital In-Patients) Regulations 1975 No.555
SS(IB) Regs	The Social Security (Incapacity Benefit) Regulations 1994 No.2946
SS(IB-ID) Regs	The Social Security (Incapacity Benefit – Increases for Dependants) Regulations 1994 No.2945
SS(IB)T Regs	The Social Security (Incapacity Benefit) (Transitional) Regulations 1995 No.310
SS(ICA) Regs	The Social Security (Invalid Care Allowance) Regulations 1976 No.409
SS(IFW) Regs	The Social Security (Incapacity for Work) (General) Regulations 1995 No.311
SS(IIPD) Regs	The Social Security (Industrial Injuries) (Prescribed Diseases) Regulations 1985 No.967
SS(MA) Regs	The Social Security (Miscellaneous Amendments) Regulations 1998 No.563
SS(ME) Regs	The Social Security (Medical Evidence) Regulations 1976 No.615
SS(MP)(No.2) Regs	The Social Security (Miscellaneous Provisions) Amendment (No.2) Regulations 1992 No.2595
SS(OB) Regs	The Social Security (Overlapping Benefits) Regulations 1979 No.597

SS(PAOR) Regs	The Social Security (Payments on account, Overpayments and Recovery) Regulations 1988 No.664
SS(WB&RP) Regs	The Social Security (Widow's Benefit and Retirement Pensions) Regulations 1979 No.642
SSA(CLED) Regs	The Social Security Amendment (Capital Limits and Earnings Disregards) Regulations 2000 No.2545
SSA(RCNH) Regs	The Social Security Amendment (Residential Care and Nursing Homes) Regulations 2001 No.3767
SSB(Dep) Regs	The Social Security Benefit (Dependency) Regulations 1977 No.343
SSB(PRT) Regs	The Social Security Benefit (Persons Residing Together) Regulations 1977 No.956
SS&CS(DA) Regs	The Social Security and Child Support (Decisions and Appeals) Regulations 1999 No.991
SSCP Regs	The Social Security Commissioners Procedure Regulations 1987 No.214
TC(A)(No 2) Regs	The Tax Credits (Claims and Notifications) Regulations 2002 No.2014
TC(CN) Regs	The Tax Credits (Claims and Notifications) Regulations 2002 No.2014
TC(DCI) Regs	The Tax Credit (Definition and Calculation of Income) Regulations 2002 No.2006
TC(NA) Regs	The Tax Credits (Notice of Appeal) Regulations 2002 No.3119
WRPA(No 9)O	The Welfare Reform & Pensions Act 1999 (Commencement No 9 and Transitional and Savings Provisions) Order 2000 No. 2958

Other information

AOG	The Adjudication Officers' Guide now superseded by the DMG
CRAG	Charging for Residential Accommodation
DMG	The Decision Makers Guide; vols1-7 and 9-12
GM	The Housing Benefit and Council Tax Benefit Guidance Manual
LGOR	Local Government Ombudsman's Report
SFDir	Directions on the Discretionary Social Fund

References like CIS/142/1990 and R(SB) 3/89 are references to commissioners' decisions.

Index

How to use this Index

Entries against the bold headings direct you to the general information on the subject, or where the subject is covered most fully. Sub-entries are listed alphabetically and direct you to specific aspects of the subject.